THE STRUGGLE CONTINUES

THE STRUGGLE CONTINUES

50 Years of Tyranny in Zimbabwe

David Coltart

First published by Jacana Media (Pty) Ltd
First and second impression 2016

10 Orange Street
Sunnyside
Auckland Park 2092
South Africa
+2711 628 3200
www.jacana.co.za

ISBN 978-1-4314-2318-7

Cover design by Shawn Paikin
Author photograph on the back cover flap © V Kaufman
All photographs in this book are from David Coltart's personal collection,
    unless otherwise stated
Set in Stempel Garamond 10.5/14.5pt
Printed and bound by ABC Press, Cape Town
Job no. 002718

Also available as an e-book:
d-PDF 978-1-4314-2319-4
ePUB 978-1-4314-2320-0
mobi file 978-1-4314-2321-7

See a complete list of Jacana titles at www.jacana.co.za

This book is dedicated to Jenny, Jessica, Douglas, Scott Winston, Bethany and my late parents, Bill and Nora

Praise for *The Struggle Continues*

"*David Coltart's* The Struggle Continues ... *is a brilliantly engaging deep dive into Zimbabwe's political history, one that is equal parts damning and altogether optimistic about Zimbabwe's inherent potential. For a people that has suffered so much under the yoke of repression – first under brutal minority rule and later by a homegrown despot – Zimbabweans have the uncanny ability to press forward with grace, dignity, and personal charm. David Coltart embodies all of those qualities, and captures them expertly in this book. A must read for anyone who is intrigued by Zimbabwean politics and history, but also those interested in the power of our common humanity and the strength that is inside us all.*"
– KERRY KENNEDY, PRESIDENT, ROBERT F. KENNEDY HUMAN RIGHTS

"*This magnificent book is far more than just the autobiography of one of the most significant figures in Zimbabwean history; it is also a history of Zimbabwe itself, and a moral testament.*"
– PETER OBORNE, POLITICAL COLUMNIST OF THE *DAILY MAIL*, AND AUTHOR OF *THE RISE OF POLITICAL LYING*, *THE TRIUMPH OF THE POLITICAL CLASS* AND *BASIL D'OLIVEIRA: CRICKET AND CONSPIRACY: THE UNTOLD STORY*

"*A searing, heartfelt, brutally honest account of the turbulent modern history of Zimbabwe, written by a man who through love of country and strength of character put himself at the centre of its most epochal events. But what sets Coltart's book apart from other African political memoirs is a beautiful, crisp, clear-eyed prose that reads at times like a thriller. For anyone who wants to understand the complexities and multiple truths of Zimbabwe and its people – buy this book.*"
– DOUGLAS ROGERS, JOURNALIST, TRAVEL WRITER AND AUTHOR OF *THE LAST RESORT*

"*The high mortality rate among politicians who have had the temerity to oppose Robert Mugabe means that authentic insider books about the workings of Zimbabwean politics are very rare. David Coltart has served as an Opposition MP, a Senator and a Cabinet Minister and has survived several attempts on his life to tell the tale. His book would be invaluable for this alone. But it is much more. It is the story of a courageous and committed man who has dedicated his life to fighting for human rights and democracy in Zimbabwe, a country that he so clearly loves. He provides a compelling account, often in harrowing detail, of the terror and oppression that has scarred that country since its independence. But he is equally unsparing in his depiction of the discrimination and brutality of the colonial era, his own role in that and his personal awakening to the injustice and prejudice that underpinned the Rhodesian dream. My own window on Zimbabwean politics was relatively brief and at a time when, in the Western media, the victims of Mugabe's regime were portrayed largely as white farmers. While many of them did suffer cruelly, David's book shows that this was but one facet of a much longer and deeper malaise in which millions of black Zimbabweans were denied justice and brutalised if they objected. What emerges is a sobering account of man's inhumanity to man. But David's determination to fight for the rights of all Zimbabweans, regardless of skin colour or ethnicity, alongside his colleagues in the human rights movement and later the MDC, is ultimately an uplifting story. If, as the book's title suggests, Zimbabwe may still realise its potential it will be due in no small measure to the efforts of the many unsung heroes who emerge from the pages of this book.*"
– SIR BRIAN DONNELLY, BRITISH HIGH COMMISSIONER,
LATER AMBASSADOR, TO ZIMBABWE, 2001–2004

"*David Coltart tells a story that is part auto-biography and part the dramatic history of his country, Zimbabwe. The telling is all the more compelling because it is told from his own ever-changing vantage point and shifting sensibilities. What emerges from this dramatic journey is a sense of courageous personal conviction and a faith in the inspiring resilience of his countrymen and women.*"
– NICHOLAS "FINK" HAYSOM, SPECIAL REPRESENTATIVE OF THE SECRETARY
GENERAL FOR AFGHANISTAN, AND FORMER LEGAL ADVISOR TO PRESIDENT
NELSON MANDELA, 1994 TO 1999

"David Coltart has written an important book which will enrich literature on Zimbabwean society spanning decades, including most importantly, key areas of political and legal history dating back to the colonial days up to the current era. It is often said people who forget their history are bound to repeat the mistakes of old. Here Coltart offers a rich, honest, diverse account of the story of Zimbabwe, as seen through his eyes and experiences, which will, hopefully, help present and future generations learn from the errors of the past. The book's strength lies in its detail and the honesty and forthrightness of the author, who does not sugar-coat his past but incudes all aspects of his experiences and aspects of his country, the beautiful and the ugly. This is, no doubt, a significant contribution at a time when Zimbabwe is crying out for such accounts from key figures who have played an important role in shaping its history."

– DR ALEX MAGAISA, UNIVERSITY OF KENT. FORMER ADVISER TO PRIME MINISTER MORGAN R TSVANGIRAI, 2012–2013

"This elegantly written book amounts to far more than the memoir of a politician, lawyer and campaigner. In essence, David Coltart has composed an extended love letter to Zimbabwe, to the "people, hills, rivers, plains and trees" of a land that "becomes deeply embedded in one's soul". His own story is entwined with that of his country. Born in southern Zimbabwe to a mother whose ancestors had arrived in Africa in 1820, Coltart served in the Rhodesian security forces as a young man before becoming a lawyer and opposition politician at the height of Robert Mugabe's repression. Those of us who were privileged to meet Coltart during this critical period never guessed at the precautions he was forced to take, nor that on public occasions he would - as he reveals in this book - wear a bullet-proof vest beneath his shirt. Coltart rose to become education minister and almost single-handedly revived a shattered school system. In the process, he helped to transform millions of young lives. He is still waiting for Zimbabwe to break free of the crippling burden of repression. But the pages of this book are devoid of bitterness or recrimination; they are filled, instead, with a sense of hope and of the unfulfilled potential of the country he loves."

– DAVID BLAIR, CHIEF FOREIGN CORRESPONDENT, *DAILY TELEGRAPH*

CONTENTS

INTRODUCTION

This is an autobiographical political history of the last six decades of Zimbabwean history, an era of great turbulence through which I have lived. It has not been easy to write this book for two principal reasons.

Firstly, as the title states, the struggle for democracy continues. There are still powerful forces in control of Zimbabwe, which have used violence to wrest and maintain power. Many people still fear for their lives and livelihoods; this has meant that many names of people mentioned in the book have had to be changed to protect the living. In addition, I have not been able to write about some events because, if I did so, it would compromise innocent people.

Secondly, it has been difficult to write about my own life. My desire is that this be a true record of what I have done and thought over these years. For that reason, I have written about my contemporaneous thought and actions through the different chapters of my life, some of which will be offensive, particularly to people who have suffered under the oppression of white minority rule. Although I experienced a Damascene moment in 1981 regarding my Christian faith, my political outlook has evolved more slowly, and I hope it continues to evolve. I have changed from a teenager who thought that Ian Smith was a hero into an adult who believes his policies were both disastrous and morally wrong. It therefore would be disingenuous of me to suggest that I have always held my current views. But that creates problems for any reader who suffered under Rhodesian rule when they read the first seven chapters of this book. Because of this, rather like TV news channels who warn people of "flash photography", I warn that some of what I write about will be difficult to digest. A close black friend, who had been imprisoned by the Rhodesians, after reading those chapters said he was left angered and wondered whether this was the same person he knew now. I could have massaged the past or left vast chunks of it out but I have felt it necessary to confront it. In doing so, I am not seeking to be an apologist; it stems from a belief that unless we truthfully confront our past as individuals and as a nation, we will never be able to learn from the mistakes we have made. Writing about the past in the manner I have is not intended to justify all that I and others have done – it is more to explain it. I regret some things I have done; if I could have my life over I certainly would not have done some of those things. I cannot enumerate them all here. Suffice it to say that there are many things, especially prior to Independence in 1980, I would have done differently, had I had the benefit of maturity, perspective and hindsight as I have now. While I do reflect a bit through the narrative, this book is largely a chronological history rather than a philosophical treatise. Accordingly, my hope is that readers will persevere through these tough periods, understanding that that was the perspective I had at the time, but not a perspective I necessarily hold to now.

The last 60 years of Zimbabwean history have been tumultuous times which, although utterly exhausting, have left me more enthralled than ever by this great nation. One of my stock phrases is that Zimbabwe has everything save for one ingredient. She is stunningly beautiful; has mountains, rivers, savannah plains, teak forests, rich soils, abundant water; she has some of the world's most amazing tourist attractions, including the Victoria Falls, Mana Pools and the Chimanimani Mountains; has some of the most literate, hardworking, and kindest people on the planet; she is richly endowed with minerals of every description; has one of the best infrastructures in Africa. What she needs is summed up in the vision that Abraham Lincoln espoused – a Nation, under God, which experiences a new birth of freedom in which government of the people, by the people and for the people is cherished.

After 70 years of undemocratic colonial rule, that vision was starting to flicker into life in the 1950s when I was born, but just months later it was subverted and has been suppressed ever since. Almost six decades of arrogant, violent and abusive rule have passed but the inherent strengths and assets of Zimbabwe remain. My prayer is that this perspective of

Zimbabwe, since 1957, will highlight where our nation has gone awry but, more importantly, will remind the world of the great hope which still lies within her.

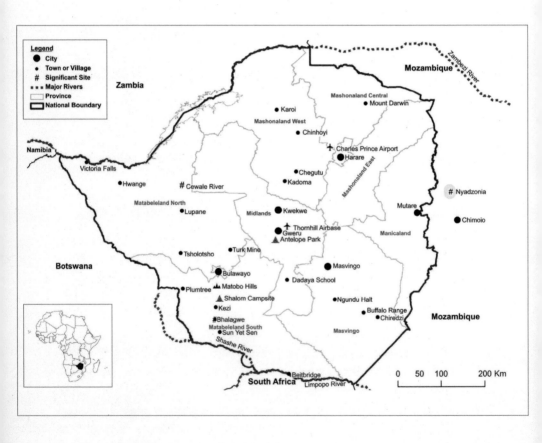

CHAPTER 1

ROOTS

"These (MPs) do not deserve to be in Zimbabwe and we shall take steps to ensure that they are not entitled to our land in Zimbabwe. These, like Coltart ... are not part of our society. They belong to Britain and let them go there. If they want to live here, we will say 'stay', but your place is in prison and nowhere else. Otherwise your home is outside the country."[1]

– ROBERT MUGABE SPEAKING TO SUPPORTERS AT
HARARE AIRPORT ON 5 SEPTEMBER 2002

Twenty miles south of Gweru, close to the heart of Zimbabwe, a grove of msasa trees gives way to open rolling hills that seem to flow to all the horizons. The Somabula Flats look more like an American prairie than an African plain, the soil too acidic for all but the hardiest trees. Unlike elsewhere in the country, which is mostly well treed, sweeping vistas of golden grass undulate uninterrupted across the hilltops. In winter, bitterly cold winds blow up from the south, occasionally even freezing the Vungu River, which snakes across the grasslands.

The bridge over the river on the bumpy road from Gweru south to Bulawayo is flanked by non-indigenous poplar trees, reinforcing the notion that one could be on another continent. But just a few miles on, from the crest of a small hill, you can glimpse the glorious mauve outcrops of the granite hills that mark the northern reaches of the uniquely African Matobo Hills (also referred to as the Matopos), which leaves you in no doubt where you are.

I first caught sight of them in August 1961, but, as beautiful as those hills are, at the time I had other things on my mind. At the age of three,

I was too impatient to get to our new home to notice much about the landscape. Instead of admiring the view, I focused on the only man-made structure we'd passed for what seemed an eternity – a ruin by the side of the road.

"Is that our new home?" I asked my parents, anxious to escape from our wood-panelled Morris Minor. My mother smiled and patiently explained that the ruins belonged to someone else and that we still had a long way to travel before we got to the house that would be our new home in Bulawayo, where my father had been transferred to open a new bank. Disappointed that the journey was not over, I concentrated on the road ahead winding its way through the hills. I think it was then that I first developed, subconsciously, my deep love and passion for Zimbabwe. The people, hills, rivers, plains, trees, grasses of this land are intoxicating – everyone who visits experiences it: an irresistible attraction that becomes deeply embedded in one's soul.

Although, like the poplar trees that we passed that afternoon when we crossed the Vungu River bridge, I am not originally indigenous to Zimbabwe either, my matrilineal African roots run deep, planted by my great-great-great-grandmother who, as a thirteen-year-old girl named Rhoda Trollip, sailed with her parents and eight siblings from Portsmouth, England to the Eastern Cape of South Africa in January 1820 on a ship called the *Weymouth*.

They were part of a wave of emigrants fleeing the massive social upheaval that seized Britain in the aftermath of the Napoleonic and American wars. When the Battle of Waterloo ended the former war in 1815, agriculture fell into severe depression, causing spiralling food prices, unemployment, poverty and industrial unrest. The British government opted to defuse things, in part, by resettling the restless in the Eastern Cape of South Africa. The governor of the Cape Colony, Lord Charles Somerset, was already anxious to settle the Eastern Cape, albeit for different reasons. His strategy was to provide a buffer of settlers to contain Xhosa tribes east of the Fish River. But he did suggest privately that potential immigrants should be warned of the dangers.[2]

In July 1819, the British government offered emigrants a deal similar to the one they'd earlier deployed in Canada: free passage and food for the voyage to "South East Africa", as it was called; 100-acre grants of land on a "quit rent" payable after the first ten years; and free tents, seed, food and implements so that the settlers could make it through the first harvest. Disregarding Somerset's suggestion, no mention was made of the potential dangers of intruding into areas already inhabited by the Xhosa people; indeed the only mention of the Xhosa people was that they could not be hired as labourers.

Many of the settlers joined "proprietary parties" led by men with capital who recruited workers who contracted to serve them for a given number of years. Rhoda's family were neither wealthy enough to lead such a group nor poor enough to need such indenture. Rather, they joined a joint stock party that was granted assets and land as a group. For many in Rhoda's party, the voyage was the end of the journey; measles raged and eighteen children and four adults died before reaching Africa.

The family cleared a plot of land on the Riet River near Bathurst, just south of the present Grahamstown. They called their farm Standerwyck, after Standerwyck Court near Tytherington, a village in Somerset close to the Wiltshire border. Four years after they arrived, on 6 February 1824, Rhoda married James Collett, who'd arrived two years earlier on the *Salisbury*. A trader working out of Grahamstown, James had his heart set on farming and, in 1832, he sold all of his merchandise and bought Elephant Fountain, south west of the town now known as Fort Beaufort.

It was a bold, or perhaps risky move, since Elephant Fountain was located in so-called "neutral territory", in fact territory formerly occupied by Xhosa tribes.[3] Throughout his trading career, James had maintained a good relationship with Xhosa and Hottentot people, but his situation changed dramatically with the move to Elephant Fountain, setting up the first, but certainly not the last, of his battles with Xhosa people over land, a struggle all too familiar wherever colonies have been planted. Suddenly, James was no longer providing the Xhosa the trade they wanted; he was living on the land that had been theirs and grazing cattle they envied. Stock theft became a fact of life. In less than a year, he and his neighbours lost 40 oxen, eight cows and twelve horses. By Christmas 1834, violence had erupted, as James described in an urgent note to the authorities on 26 December:

> *"The feelings of us all on this large establishment this morning can be imagined, but us few can adequately describe them. Nothing but burning homesteads in every direction. Many bodies of ...[4] had passed us in the night and proceeded deeper into the Colony, but fortunately, we were unmolested during the night."*[5]

By the new year herds of livestock in the district were being systematically plundered, and within three months James was at the end of his tether. He wrote in his journal:

> "O Lord in the greatness of Thy mercy save me from infidelity and unbelief, strengthen my staggering faith in the over ruling providence of thee my God, how can I sink with such a prop as my Eternal God? Why these wicked … should be suffered to rob me of my three span of valuable oxen I have with such assiduity been for several years matching and training, and all those choice milch cows which supplied us with butter and my dear children and people with milk in abundance."[6]

On 13 May the house was raided by Xhosa tribesmen and Rhoda's younger brother's wife and baby were stabbed with an assegai. She died the next day, although the infant survived. James and Rhoda hung on as an uneasy peace developed. Still, despite ongoing skirmishes, James managed to increase his holdings – to eleven farms on which he grazed over 3 500 sheep. However, in 1841 he moved his family to greener and safer pastures outside the so-called "neutral" lands on two farms near the town of Cradock in the Great Fish River valley, Groenfontein and Dassenkrantz. He sold up the farms in the Fort Beaufort district in 1842 and moved away permanently from the contentious border area. While Rhoda and James's children subsequently had to do military service, the horrors of May 1835 were never repeated again.

Gradually, the colonists cemented their control and their concerns turned from defending themselves from people they viewed as marauding tribesmen to addressing a shortage of labour. The solution dreamt up by Colonial Secretary Lord Grey was to send a shipload of Irish convicts to the Cape, a move endorsed by the unelected Legislative Council for the Western and Eastern provinces. Furious, James dubbed the plan a "diabolical scheme rejected by all colonists!"[7] He supported an Anti-Convict Association, which was formed, and which forced the resignation of all but one member of the appointed Legislative Council. Alarmed at the reaction, in July 1853 the British government agreed to the creation of an elected government for the Cape. While this was a step towards a more democratic order, only white males could vote.

James was elected to this first Parliament on 19 April 1854, but it was almost an election by default. His only mention of it was a diary entry that day: "*Rode to Craddock [sic] this morning. Felt much discouraged when unexpectedly election over before our arrival. Informed that I had been elected without opposition a member for our new and eventful Parliament.*"[8] But his was not a long career in politics. After one term, he withdrew; the two-week wagon trek to Cape Town was too much for a farmer who understood how little he could achieve in the city for his neighbours in the Eastern Province.

In the space of 20 years, between 1824 and 1844, James and Rhoda had nine children. The seventh, my great-great-grandfather, Joseph Collett, was born before James and Rhoda left Elephant Fountain farm. Joseph and his wife, Emily Simpson, never settled down on one plot of land, but led a somewhat nomadic existence on a variety of farms in the northern and eastern Cape. The second of their eleven children, Alice, however, never budged from the Middelburg district of the Eastern Province, where she married Fred Every, whose family originally hailed from Wiltshire. Their last child, Ada, my grandmother, was born there on Christmas Eve 1900 in Middelburg town, and my mother Nora was born there too, 27 years later.

Unlike her mother and grandmother, Nora moved well beyond the narrow confines of the Cape. First, she moved to London to study nursing. Then, rather than return to South Africa, she accepted a job at Gwelo (now Gweru) Central Hospital in Rhodesia, a country north of South Africa across the Limpopo, which she had never seen.

Although the Eastern Cape had been settled for 80 years by whites by the time my grandmother was born, the territory then known as Rhodesia had only been relatively recently occupied by white settlers at the turn of the century. A year after Joseph was born in 1838 Ndebele king Mzilikazi commenced his trek north from present South Africa to Zimbabwe. Mzilikazi had fallen out with the Zulu king, King Shaka, in 1823 and he fled Zululand, eventually ending up in the Transvaal (present-day Gauteng). Mzilikazi dominated the Transvaal for a decade, through the Mfecane[9] (which means "crushing" or "scattering" in isiNdebele).

It was here, in 1835, that Mzilikazi met and became friends with the Scottish missionary Robert Moffat. This was to become a lifelong friendship and was deep enough to motivate Mzilikazi to go to extraordinary lengths to assist Moffat in getting supplies to his son-in-law David Livingstone in 1859.[10] With British settlers flooding into the Cape,

Dutch-speaking colonists became increasingly irritated by British rule. The vast majority were farmers ("boers") and, seeking greener pastures in southern Africa's hinterland, they trekked north en masse to escape British rule and occupied the Transvaal in 1836, forcing Mzilikazi to flee north two years later. On crossing the Limpopo, Mzilikazi squeezed out disparate weak and smaller tribes and in 1840 established his Mthwakazi kingdom, roughly bounded by the Limpopo to the south, the Kalahari desert to the west, the Zambezi to the north and Portuguese settlers to the east in what is modern-day Mozambique. Under the Royal House of Khumalo and using considerable statesmanship, Mzilikazi was able to meld the many tribes he conquered with his own people into an ethnically diverse but centralised kingdom. He established his capital in Ko-Bulawayo, the present-day Bulawayo. On his death in 1868 he was succeeded by his son Lobengula.

In 1888, Cecil John Rhodes managed to extract an agreement, known as the Rudd Concession, from King Lobengula, which allowed the British to prospect over all the territory under Lobengula's control in exchange for a gunboat on the Zambezi, rifles, ammunition and a payment to Lobengula of £100 per month. Rhodes's emissary, the phlegmatic Charles Dunell Rudd, had given an absolute assurance to Lobengula that the Europeans had no intention of actually settling in the area or seeking land. Rhodes, in a cunning volte-face, used that agreement, the Rudd Concession, and considerable deception to obtain a Royal Charter signed by Queen Victoria in October 1889, enabling his British South Africa Company to occupy Mashonaland, a region well beyond the borders of Lobengula's hegemony. He cobbled together an expeditionary force of 196 farmers, professionals, artisans and soldiers supported by a 500-man police force (the genesis of the British South Africa Police – BSAP) and moved north, despite Lobengula's protestations that the Rudd Concession's agreement was being violated. At first, the troops skirted Lobengula's territory and raised the Union Jack in present-day Harare. But three years later, they invaded the Mthwakazi kingdom, defeated Lobengula and raised the British flag in Bulawayo, on 4 November 1893, 25 years to the day after Mzilikazi had been interred at Entumbane in the Matobo Hills.[11]

From its curious beginnings as a state run by a company, and absurdly named after a living human being, Southern Rhodesia developed rapidly. Unlike so many other colonies, the white people who settled there were settling for life and they invested heavily in constructing solid infrastructure. In 1923 the British government allowed the all-white electorate to choose by referendum whether to become a province of the Union of South Africa or a "Responsible Government". Despite a vigorous campaign by the legendary Boer War general Jan Smuts for the Union cause, the largely English-speaking Rhodesians opted for a more independent course out of fear of being swallowed up by South African Afrikaners.

Shortly after the conclusion of World War II conditions became more favourable for a federation in Central Africa. An association with Northern Rhodesia (present-day Zambia) was mooted in 1915 but the latter's relatively weak economy and the fear of being overwhelmed by black people deterred white Southern Rhodesians. The subsequent discovery of copper in Northern Rhodesia made an economic association more palatable. In addition the extremist political attitudes in South Africa, following the accession to power of the National Party in 1948 and the spread of African nationalism in the north, left English-speaking white Southern Rhodesians feeling isolated. This resulted in the formation of the Central African Federation in 1953, comprising Southern Rhodesia, Northern Rhodesia and Nyasaland.

The new Federal government went on a recruiting drive. Many English-speaking South Africans were attracted north across the Limpopo and my mother, who had just completed her nursing course at St Bartholomew's Hospital in London, was one person who responded. She was posted to Gwelo Central Hospital. My mother had emigrated from South Africa partly for the adventure and partly to escape the strictures imposed on South African society by the overtly racist National Party. At the very time that apartheid was taking root in South Africa, the Federation of Central Africa, of which Southern Rhodesia was the dominant part, was offering hope to whites for a vibrant and more liberal society.

Soon after arriving in Gwelo my mother met my father, William Coltart, a Scot educated at George Watson's College in Edinburgh, who had served as the Royal Scots regiment Adjutant in North Africa and Italy during World War II. Like Rhoda Trollip, whose family had fled the misery of Britain after the Napoleonic Wars, he immigrated to Southern Rhodesia in 1952 with the wave of Britons who, grinding out an existence in post-World War II Britain, were attracted to southern Africa by its enormous beauty and potential. He was posted to Gwelo to open a new branch of Grindlays Bank.

His had begun as a hardscrabble family. My grandfather, James Robert Coltart, relished telling that shortly after his election as a bailiff of Edinburgh, an American cousin had decided that such high office must indicate royal ancestry. She travelled to Scotland and insisted that my grandfather assist her in tracing the family tree. They made good progress until they found a 15th century church entry about a Coltart who had been "hung by the neck until dead for stealing sheep". Not surprisingly, they decided that there was not much point in going any further back.

My more recent ancestors had managed to stay within the confines of the law. My great-great-great-grandfather, Robert Coltart, was a weaver in Rhonehouse, near Castle Douglas in the south west of Scotland. The inscription on the back of a painting of his cottage handed down to me reads that he was the "William Edgar of Samuel Rutherfords Crockett's 'Lochinvar'". His offspring wound up in Leith, then one of the poorest areas of Edinburgh.

I have in my possession an old New Testament which has the inscription "*Miss Hutchinson from a friend Feb 14th 1878*". This was a Valentine's gift to my great-grandmother, Margaret Hutchinson, who was born in 1859 in Dalkeith, five miles south of Edinburgh, from my great-grandfather and her future husband, William Coltart. She was widowed only three years into their marriage and then had to fend for herself and her two young sons by renting a house in Leith and taking in lodgers. The first Sunday after moving to Leith she saw that the Foot of Leith Walk, an open area, was occupied by a group of people in blue uniforms loudly singing hymns, accompanied by a brass band. She stopped to listen and before long was engaged by caring folk; this resulted in her becoming a staunch adherent to the Salvation Army for the remainder of her long life. More so she was a woman with a deep trust in God who was a tower of strength in the family. By all accounts hers was not a nominal, shallow faith but a real one, demonstrated through integrity, hard work and a compassionate and generous spirit. My father records that "she lived in my father's house from the time when I was four years old until her death (in 1953) at the age of 94 and ... was the most important character in my formative years".[12]

From these humble beginnings, my grandfather managed to pull himself up by his bootstraps. He left school at the age of twelve and went on to become a successful amateur footballer, professional photographer and politician. A founder of the Leith Amateurs, for whom he played centre half, he also played for Hibernian, then a Scottish first league side, the only amateur of a team of professionals. Despite the successes of the Leith Amateurs, they never managed to win the coveted Scottish Amateurs Cup, the blue riband of the national game, until the year after James's retirement from their ranks. A year later, however, they got through to the semi-finals and with two games to go to potential victory, their centre half fell sick with pneumonia. A delegation persuaded James to replace him and the Leith Amateurs went on to victory, first against Queens Park and then against Paisley Academicals in the final, giving my grandfather in just two games the Cup that had eluded him for a decade.

His entry into Scottish politics was impelled by the same delegation that had prevailed upon him to play in those Scottish Cup games. Worried about the state of school playing fields, they had again called at his studio with the suggestion that he stand for election to the Leith school board. James wasn't keen on the notion since electioneering was expensive and time consuming. But his friends had gamed out the election, which was based on a peculiar system. Voters cast their ballots not for a single candidate but for the number of vacancies open on the board. James's friends, however, found 100 people willing to "plump", as the saying went, only for him. So with neither an undue amount of work nor expense he was duly elected and began a career in municipal politics which spanned some 30 years, culminating in his election as Deputy Lord Provost of Edinburgh in 1938.

I have no doubt it was the imbuing of that gritty spirit in my father by my great-grandmother and grandfather which influenced him to emigrate to Southern Rhodesia and which played a role in attracting my mother to him when they met in Gwelo. Whatever the case, their relationship flourished and they were married in Grahamstown, in the Eastern Cape, in 1955.

I was born in Birchenough House, in Gwelo, on 4 October 1957.

Although only a first generation African on my paternal side, I am the fifth generation born in Africa on my maternal side. My wife Jenny has even deeper African roots. Her forebears – her great- (times seven) grandparents Charles and Catherine Marais – were Huguenots from Plessis in France, who sailed from Europe on the *Voorschoten* which arrived at Saldanha Bay in the Cape of Good Hope on 13 April 1688. Our children are tenth generation Africans. As such we do not consider ourselves European; I suppose, to use American parlance, we are European Africans, but our allegiance is to Africa and Zimbabwe.

Almost 60 years on, the fervency I first experienced on that drive down to Bulawayo with my parents as a small boy has flowered into a profound love and appreciation of a land which, to put it mildly, has had a very bad press abroad.

CHAPTER 2

STORM CLOUDS GATHER
1957 TO 1965

"The stump that hits the toes of the person walking in front of you will also hit the toe of the person walking behind. When the big finger burns, the small ones also burn."

– CHENJERAI HOVE, *SHADOWS*

When I was born Southern Rhodesia's economy was booming. In 1957 it was bigger than countries such as Singapore and South Korea. This was achieved on the back of four years of unprecedented growth following the formation of the Central African Federation (comprising the present-day Zimbabwe, Zambia and Malawi). Sir Roy Welensky, the second prime minister of the Federation, who took office on 2 November 1956, boasted that the record of "constructive work from 1953 onwards was second to none".[13] His vision of the Federation was of a vibrant state within the British Empire that sought to retain predominant power for the white minority while moving in a progressive political direction, in contrast to apartheid South Africa. There is plenty of evidence to this day of the fantastic growth that took place during this period. The tender for the construction of Lake Kariba, one of the world's largest dams, was floated by the Federal government in August 1955 and construction started soon thereafter. Many of Zimbabwe's iconic buildings, airports, and hospitals were built during this period.

Some of our best schools were built at this time, too, including my own school, Christian Brothers College (1953) and others, like Falcon College (1954), Peterhouse (1955) and Arundel (1956). One stark fact, however, is that most of this construction was for the benefit of the white minority. There was little similar development for black people.

Although most black citizens of Southern Rhodesia (Zimbabwe), Northern Rhodesia (Zambia) and Nyasaland (Malawi) had more rights and better living conditions than those who lived under the increasingly authoritarian and harsh apartheid regime south of the Limpopo, most were deeply suspicious of, and hostile towards, the Federation, believing that the racially discriminatory policies of Southern Rhodesia would be applied to both Northern Rhodesia and Nyasaland. Only a few white leaders enjoyed the trust and respect of black people throughout southern Africa. Black people noted those white leaders who saw them as mere chattels and those who appeared genuinely interested in their advancement. Nothing demonstrated this more than the difference between South Africa and Southern Rhodesia during this period in how education curricula were developed. In South Africa Bantu Education, which was introduced by the National Party, was based on the premise that blacks should only be educated to be labourers. In sharp contrast, the Southern Rhodesian government embraced a curriculum first developed in 1934 by Grace Todd, the wife of Southern Rhodesia's fifth prime minister, Sir Garfield Todd, who took office in September 1953. The Todds both came from strong Scottish roots. His grandparents came from Ayrshire, where his great-grandfather farmed close to Robert Burns. Her grandparents were tenant farmers in Perthshire. Grace Todd's African primary education curriculum, commonly known as the "Dadaya Scheme", formed the bedrock of Zimbabwe's excellent education system.[14] When he became prime minister, Todd introduced reforms aimed at improving the education of the black majority by investing heavily in black schools. His government introduced a plan to give elementary education to every black child of school age. He doubled the number of primary schools and gave grants to missionary-run schools to introduce secondary school and pre-university courses for black children.

Unlike previous white governments, Todd's made progression towards extending political rights to black Rhodesians. During Todd's tenure an investigation was made by Sir Robert Tredgold into voting rights for all. As a result an Electoral Amendment Act was passed in 1957 which, while not as liberal as Tredgold had recommended, did extend the franchise. Todd also introduced the appellation "Mr" for blacks instead of "AM" ("African Male"). Blacks were unable to buy and sell alcohol in the so-called native reserves. Under influence from large alcohol distributors, Todd ended this prohibition and allowed black residents of the reserves to drink European beer and wine, though not spirits. Todd pushed a bill through parliament allowing for multiracial trade unions, thereby undercutting the growing white nationalist influence in the unions. Lastly, in a bid to increase the number of blacks eligible to vote from 2 per cent to 16 per cent of the electorate, he lowered property and education qualifications, but this was rejected. These reforms were seen as dangerously radical by most whites.

These positive developments took a dramatic turn for the worse when, in January 1958, the whole Southern Rhodesian cabinet resigned, claiming they had lost confidence in Garfield Todd's leadership. The loss of confidence was partly because of Todd's "supposedly over-liberal policy towards Africans".[15] Todd lost the premiership on 8 February 1958 and although he was replaced by a relatively liberal person in Sir Edgar Whitehead, the die was cast. Todd was hardly a liberal in the Western sense. In some respects he was conservative, but he was also a visionary and a man way ahead of his time. Todd's farewell statement was remarkably prescient. He said: "We must make it possible for every individual to lead the good life, to win a place in the sun. We are in danger of becoming a race of fear-ridden neurotics – we who live in the finest country on earth." Being much better connected to rising black nationalist leaders such as Robert Mugabe, whom he had employed as a teacher at Dadaya prior to becoming prime minister, Todd understood black frustrations and aspirations better than most whites.

Whitehead's government pursued a policy of "partnership" which was founded on an acceptance that blacks would play an increasing, but gradual, role in national affairs, including politics, in the future. While it was a policy that turned its back on apartheid and racial separation, Whitehead was not able to gain the trust among black leaders that Todd had enjoyed. As a result storm clouds started brewing; neither black nationalists nor an increasing number of whites were happy with Whitehead's policy. While 1958 was otherwise a reasonably peaceful year, as the decade drew to a close tensions heightened. In February 1959 the Southern Rhodesian government, fearing similar violence to that which had broken out in Nyasaland, declared a state of emergency for the first time and arrested nearly 500 leaders of the leading black nationalist party, the African National Congress, which was also banned. That state of emergency was never lifted and remained in place until 1987.

The rising tension did not affect my parents' lives. In fact they described the 1950s as a golden age both in Rhodesia and in their personal lives. In truth most whites were blind to the dangers that were brewing. There was very little industrial unrest and from white peoples' perspectives race relations appeared good. Most white people were in superficial master/servant relationships with black people. Children of different races didn't interact much. Black people lived in dormitories located far from white suburbs. In short, there was little meaningful contact between races. Contact was discouraged by law and white culture, which resulted in most whites being ignorant of what black people's daily struggles and thoughts actually were. While the Todd family was the exception, my family was typical of most moderately wealthy middle-class white Rhodesians. We lived in a magnificent bank house on the Selukwe Road near the Gwelo Kopje, one of the premier suburbs. From photographs and my parents' recollections, our time in Gwelo was idyllic. My father played golf twice a week, my mother tennis. They played bridge regularly. The civil service was efficient and, for whites at least, the country ran like clockwork. We travelled to Scotland on holiday by ship, the *Edinburgh Castle*, and we also began a tradition of an annual holiday in Port Alfred, where we stayed with my grandmother Ada, trekking all the way along strip roads on a journey that would take three days. Weekends were often spent out at farmer clients of my father's and my earliest memories are of the wide open spaces and stunning beauty of Africa.

My first realisation that there was a more serious side to life occurred shortly after my third birthday. The Congo obtained its independence in June 1960 and it rapidly descended into chaos; whites were targeted and by the end of the year thousands of mainly Belgian refugees flooded into Southern Rhodesia. My parents gave accommodation to a family who told harrowing tales of what was happening in the Congo. While little was written about this at the time, Belgian colonialism had sown the seeds of brutality through decades of gross atrocities perpetrated against the Congolese people. When colonialism came to an end a bitter harvest was reaped by whites, who were evicted overnight from their homes.[16] The spectre of thousands of Belgian refugees in their country had a profound effect on the mindset of white Southern Rhodesians.

Although I was largely protected from them, tensions were beginning to rise throughout Southern Africa. The Sharpeville massacre had taken place in South Africa in March 1960. In Southern Rhodesia itself, 1960 saw the worst rioting and bloodshed since the 1890s. A Royal Commission had been appointed, under Lord Monckton, to look into the future of the Federation. When its report was released in October 1960 black Southern Rhodesians opposed it because it did not recommend the immediate dissolution of the Federation and they resented "the fabricated conclusion that the Africans in Southern Rhodesia favour Federation". The release of the commission's report was accompanied by serious riots and strikes in major urban centres, including Gwelo.[17] Two houses belonging to whites and four belonging to coloureds[18] were burnt out; factories and stores were destroyed. Nobody was killed but fourteen blacks were injured. In Gwelo itself angry whites threatened to take matters into their own hands and the army was called in to control the town. My father, as a military veteran of World War II, was drafted into a police reserve force and his blue helmet, gas mask, baton and police fatigues made an impression on me as a three-year-old.

White Rhodesians, right across the political spectrum, were equally dissatisfied with the Monckton Commission. Welensky was disappointed that it opened up the possibility of the Federation breaking up; Ian Smith, in a speech to the Federal Assembly on 25 October 1960, rejected all the proposed concessions to black nationalists and argued that racial discrimination in the Federation had been "much exaggerated". Whitehead started pushing for greater independence for Southern Rhodesia, a sentiment fuelled by independence being granted to other British colonies and by increasingly vociferous calls for independence by right-wing whites.

Instead of seeking dialogue with black nationalist leaders, Whitehead reacted to the explosion of anger and pressure from the right by enacting harsh new legislation. In November 1960 he introduced an egregious new law, the Law and Order (Maintenance) Act, which was to be used for decades to crush democracy in the country. Sir Robert Tredgold, Chief Justice of the Federation (and grandson of Robert Moffat, Mzilikazi's great friend), resigned in protest. He argued that the act "outrages almost every basic human right, and is, in addition, an unwarranted invasion by the executive of the sphere of the courts".[19]

The British responded to the growing crisis by convening a Constitutional conference in February 1961 which was attended by

15

Whitehead's United Federal Party (UFP), the forerunner of the Rhodesian Front, the Dominion Party (DP), Todd's Central Africa Party (CAP) and the effective successor of the banned ANC, the National Democratic Party (NDP), led by veteran nationalist Joshua Nkomo. Much of the conference discussions focused on the franchise qualifications. Up until then Southern Rhodesia had a franchise which was not ostensibly racially based but which in practice excluded the vast majority of black citizens. The debate ranged from a demand for "one man one vote" from the NDP to an attempt by the DP to tighten the qualifications. In essence what was agreed was an extension of the franchise but less than the NDP's aim of universal suffrage. Initially, the NDP and Joshua Nkomo himself agreed publicly to the new constitutional proposals (while also saying that they would continue the campaign for "one man one vote") but within a few weeks, under intense pressure from both inside the party and from other nationalist leaders, such as Kenneth Kaunda and Dr Hastings Banda, it was announced that they did not support them. The DP had made clear its objections from the outset.

The government organised a referendum to enable voters to have their say on 24 July 1961. The NDP organised its own referendum the day before and several hundred thousand black Southern Rhodesians overwhelmingly voted against the constitution. The official referendum, in which whites voted almost exclusively, saw Whitehead's UFP triumph over the opposing DP by 41 949 in favour to 21 846 against. At face value it was a victory for tolerance. Whitehead proclaimed that "extremism (was) dead" and that blacks could now "play their part fully in the political life of the country". The reality was that white opinion had in fact shifted sharply to the right and the result was an illusion.

With the benefit of hindsight it is ironic that majority rule was only achieved through armed struggle, years *after* it might have been achieved in terms of the 1961 franchise proposals. Whitehead and the British government estimated that the franchise proposals would result in majority rule being obtained in between twelve and fifteen years. That debate is academic now; the tragic reality was that while the 1961 constitution offered a peaceful evolution towards majority rule, its effective rejection by both the nationalistic DP and NDP parties steered the country towards the course of violence and armed struggle. Southern Rhodesia lacked a Martin Luther King who, at that time in America, was gaining ground in his quest to use non-violence to obtain justice.

Shortly after the referendum in August 1961 my father was transferred to Bulawayo to open up a new branch of Grindlays Bank there. Despite the political turmoil, Southern Rhodesia was still booming. My earliest memory of Bulawayo was trooping around the new Grindlays Bank building which was being constructed at the corner of 8th Avenue and Main Street (now Joshua Nkomo Street) next to the statue of Cecil John Rhodes which bestrode the intersection (and which has now been replaced by Nkomo's statue). My father was a perfectionist and a stickler for detail and when it came to the construction of the building, which remains an attractive edifice, it bore these marks in many ways. For example, he believed that bank managers needed to be accessible to their clients and so his office was in the foyer rather than tucked away behind batteries of secretaries.

Despite my confusion when driving down to Bulawayo in thinking that our new home was going to be just outside Gweru on the Somabula Flats, we instead moved into a very grand bank house at 47 Cecil Avenue in the suburb of Hillside. While my father was busy getting the new bank running, life for me was blissful. I was fortunate that my mother worked at home, was a wonderful cook and, in my mind at least, seemed to devote all her time to me. Our home, however, was always a hive of activity because my mother took on the task of hosting dinners for bank clients and my father used his study for business meetings. As was typical of Southern Rhodesian middle-class households of the time, my parents had two domestic servants – a full time cook/housekeeper and a gardener.

The Whitehead government continued its policy of attacking nationalists. This was one of the few points of agreement between his government and the right-wing opposition. In November 1961 the government banned the NDP. Nationalist leaders responded by forming a new political party, which for the first time bore what was then for whites an emotive and radical name – Zimbabwe. They called the party the Zimbabwe African People's Union (ZAPU).

At the same time that nationalist views were hardening, so the right wing among whites was getting better organised. Previously, the right wing had been disjointed because many of its leaders had strongly differing views on policy. The resignation in February 1962 of William Harper, the leader of the DP and a man who was distrusted and disliked by many of his right-wing colleagues, paved the way for productive negotiations to establish a united opposition. This resulted in the formation of the Rhodesian Front in March 1962 – the die was now cast for conflict between nationalists and the white right.

In many ways 1962 was a watershed year. Whitehead's government, bolstered by the referendum victory, prepared for a general election that year, confident that it could easily win with the support of moderate whites and black voters. With this in mind they pressed ahead with measures and policies to liberalise Southern Rhodesia. In October 1962 Whitehead predicted to a United Nations committee in New York that blacks would form a majority of voters "within fifteen years".[20] The UFP congress, held in November, one third of which comprised black members, agreed to wide-ranging progressive policies – if the party won the election, all racial discrimination was to be abolished, the Land Apportionment Act repealed and the franchise expanded to include "certain responsible, civilised and educated groups" of all races.

Ironically, ZAPU and the RF, although diametrically opposed to each other, both worked hard in each other's interests through the course of the year. For the first time fear became a major factor in a Southern Rhodesian election campaign. The UFP used it to warn whites of the need to embrace change in Africa to prevent violence; the RF exploited fears of nationalist violence and racial integration; nationalists fomented a pattern of violence in black townships, some of it gruesome, causing unprecedented fear among black and white people.

For example, in October 1962 a black police reservist was burnt alive after petrol was poured over him. Acts of sabotage commenced, including the burning of a massive swathe of forest estate in the Eastern Districts. That September Joshua Nkomo had taken the first step in pursuing armed struggle by acquiring weapons in Egypt, having been authorised to do so by the ZAPU central committee.[21] On his return to Rhodesia Nkomo was restricted to his place of birth, Kezi, and basically subjected to house arrest. From restriction he issued a leaflet advising blacks not to participate in the forthcoming elections.

As white opinion was drifting to the right, the black vote became critical to the UFP. Blacks listened to Nkomo, however, by not registering to vote and by abstaining in the December 1962 poll. The net result was electoral triumph for the right-wing RF, which went against what most pundits had predicted. A majority of both black and white rejected the UFP's policy of partnership – for right-wing whites it was a triumph over what the RF portrayed as appeasement; for nationalists it was a triumph because it defined the battleground more easily. Nkomo made this clear when he wrote about it in his autobiography, *Nkomo – The Story of My Life*:

> "(The RF's) election made our task easier. We no longer had to struggle to make clear to outsiders that the regime in our country really was different from those in other colonies that the British were abandoning. African politics and white politics were now under leaderships with no illusions about the other. The fight was now on."[22]

The tragedy for the nation was that the battle lines were now drawn and both nationalists and the RF were committed to a violent resolution of the power struggle.

* * *

Far too young to be aware of anything of the political tensions that were swirling around in the country, I commenced kindergarten at Hillside School in January 1963. The school was right across the road from our house and nearly all of my friends lived close by. The streets were safe and afternoons were spent playing, walking, swimming and riding bicycles in the neighbourhood.

During this period my parents first employed two domestic workers, Vashiko Time Oliver and Peter Muchakagara. Vashiko, a Mozambican and the cook, was a powerfully built boxer. Peter was a Manica, from the Eastern Highlands. He was our gardener and he had a wonderful sense of humour. I knew only kindness from both men; they looked after my every need and were very protective of me. One morning a friend and I made mud mortars which we attached to flexible sticks from a Kenyan coffee tree in the yard. We hid behind the garden wall under a tree and flicked off the mud bombs, bombarding a man selling ice-creams opposite our home outside the school. One bomb landed close to him and the ice-creams he was selling. Irate with these two impish youngsters, he stormed across the road to confront us. Before he got near us Vashiko intervened and prevented the man from venting his wrath on us. A heated exchange between the two ensued, during which a full report was made of our sins. Vashiko prevailed but afterwards instructed me to stop the fusillade and later reported the incident to my father when he returned home at lunchtime. I had to retreat back up the Kenyan coffee tree for the entire lunch break to avoid the stinging hand of my father. This was the commencement of a lifelong friendship between me, Vashiko and Peter. Ironically, though, the friendship blinded me as a young child to the true nature of race relations at the time. I had little idea then of the humiliation these two men faced daily; it was only years later, as a teenager, that I began to have some notion of their perpetual grind.

* * *

When the new parliament opened, in February 1963, it was in an entirely new atmosphere. What had been a "clubby, intimate place" became "colder and increasingly bitter".[23] The right-wing, all-white RF government benches faced the multiracial UFP benches. Ironically, for the first time black and white MPs sat together but the atmosphere was already poisoned and RF MPs were deaf to the appeals made by moderate black MPs. Surprisingly, the restriction orders imposed on nationalist leaders were lifted soon after the RF took power, but at the same time the RF announced that it would use the courts to deal with breaches of law and order. This announcement was followed by a series of new laws, for example imposing mandatory death sentences for relatively trivial offences, the so-called "Hanging Bill". Another was a permanent ban on Sunday political meetings, which traditionally was the main day for nationalist meetings. The new laws became weapons in the hands of the RF and nationalist leaders were regularly brought before court for alleged infractions of increasingly repressive legislation.

In April 1963 the executive of the banned ZAPU went into exile to Tanganyika. Among them were Joshua Nkomo, Robert Mugabe, and the Reverend Ndabaningi Sithole. Tensions were growing within the nationalists and there were some who accused Nkomo of indecision and weakness. Leaving the executive behind in Dar es Salaam, Nkomo returned to rally his supporters at home, but tensions continued to grow, and in July he openly criticised the members of the executive who were opposed to him, naming them in a public rally in Salisbury, and dismissing them shortly thereafter. This in turn led to the rebels, who were by then back in Southern Rhodesia, announcing the formation of a new political party, the Zimbabwe African National Union (ZANU). The party was formed at Enos Nkala's house in Highfield, Salisbury, on

8 August 1963. Its president was Sithole, and Mugabe, Leopold Takawira, Herbert Chitepo and Nkala were on its executive. Although its policies were similar to those of ZAPU, the new party had stronger socialist leanings.

A further die was cast. ZANU would turn out to be far more militant than ZAPU. Just as white politics was veering to the right under the RF, so nationalist politics was now veering to the left. Both extremes were increasingly resolved to allow violence to prevail. It also marked the beginning of deep and often violent divisions within the nationalist movement. ZANU was unequivocally committed to armed struggle and its first group of five guerrillas, which included a young man named Emmerson Mnangagwa,[24] left for training in China on 22 September 1963.[25] This in turn introduced a further dynamic, with China supporting ZANU and the Soviet Union supporting ZAPU.

The year 1963 also saw the end of the Federation, a factor which no doubt fuelled nationalists' aspirations for immediate majority rule. Within a few days of the RF taking office, the British government announced that Nyasaland would be able to secede from the Federation, which was a further blow to moderates within the UFP. The RF was not disconcerted by this move, however, because although the Federation provided some economic benefits for whites, their main concern was to secure independence for Southern Rhodesia. RF Prime Minister Winston Field believed that Federation had in fact "delayed real independence".[26]

The British pushed ahead with their plans and in June a conference was held in Victoria Falls, which agreed how the assets of the Federation would be shared on its dissolution. The Federation was formally dissolved on 31 December 1963, snuffing out the last hopes of moderates within the UFP. The dissolution of the Federation and concomitant granting of independence to Nyasaland and Northern Rhodesia in 1964 drove the debate for independence in Southern Rhodesia among white and black.

It was in fact Winston Field's perceived failure to secure independence that led to him being forced out by his cabinet on 13 April 1964 and replaced by Ian Smith. The key reason why this happened was that Field was against a Unilateral Declaration of Independence whereas Smith was in favour. Smith was also not prepared to make any concessions – "Thus far and no further" became a favourite phrase of his. The change in leadership also marked the end of rule by the so called "Establishment" – rule by men who were absolutely committed to the Queen and the

British Commonwealth. My parents were "Establishment people"; both of them were monarchists to the core and they were deeply worried about Smith's accession to power.

One of Smith's first acts after taking office was to clamp down on nationalist leaders. In February the RF had abandoned its earlier stated policy of using the courts and resorted to restrictions without trial. Powers of restriction in terms of the Law and Order (Maintenance) Act were extended to 90 days and then to one year. Greater powers were introduced to control gatherings and prison sentences dramatically increased for a variety of "subversive offences". Smith used these new powers on 16 April 1964, restricting Nkomo and other nationalist leaders to Gonakudzingwa, a desolate, uncomfortably hot outpost near the Mozambique border. Mugabe was already in jail, having been arrested on his return to Rhodesia from Dar es Salaam the previous December, and he was to remain in jail for a further eleven years.

Violence broke out almost immediately. A day after Nkomo's restriction riots broke out in Salisbury and Bulawayo; houses were stoned, cars overturned and incidents of arson rocketed. On 4 July 1964 ZANU guerrillas led by William Ndangana set up a roadblock and killed a white man of Afrikaans descent named Petros Oberholtzer in the Chimanimani farming area of eastern Zimbabwe. Ndangana and his men came to be known as the "Crocodile Gang". By August "terror in the African townships (was) no longer strange but the order of the day".[27]

Instead of trying to negotiate, the RF dug its heels in. ZANU, the People's Caretaker Council (PCC) (ZAPU's successor party following its banning in 1963) and *The Daily News* were banned by the RF on 26 August by the new minister of Justice, Law and Order, Desmond Lardner-Burke.

At the same time the RF made some policy decisions which greatly exacerbated tensions. In particular it started to reverse some of the progressive education policies introduced by Garfield Todd. It cut back on spending on African education, and teacher enrolment decreased; then it introduced school fees for the first time, substantial sums for poor black workers, causing a decline in the numbers of black children attending school. There was a sense among black Rhodesians that this was a deliberate policy, similar to the apartheid Bantu Education policies, to emasculate African education. Nationalists exploited public anger and urban schools became the centre of struggle. Schools were boycotted, some were burnt down, teachers were assaulted and their cars set alight. At one stage in the year African school enrolment in Salisbury schools fell "from 20,000 to a few hundred".[28] Nothing, I have learnt in my adulthood, is closer to black Zimbabweans' hearts than the education of their children, then and now. In short, no policy could have had a more deleterious effect on the way the RF was viewed by black people than this one.

* * *

In contrast to most black Rhodesian children I started Standard 1 in January 1965 at a magnificent school, Hillside Primary. Unlike schools for black Rhodesians, it was world class with what were then state of the art teaching and sporting facilities. It was also within easy walking distance of home. The school was reserved for whites only; all the teachers were white and the only black staff were labourers. Despite the outstanding facilities, my elevation to primary school came as a bit of a shock to me because the classes were much bigger and the environment robust; this was a challenge to the protected existence of an only child with an attentive mother. But Hillside Primary was still an island of serenity, totally cut off from the turmoil going on in black schools and the country at large. Every morning we were lined up with military discipline to sing the national anthem as the Rhodesian flag was raised. From this early age we were pumped with propaganda that all was well in the country and that white Rhodesians had a unique standing in the world.

Politically, the year 1965 was dominated by the RF's drive for independence. The government started the year by clamping down even further on all nationalist groups through the banning of more organisations, including trade unions and some churches. In March, Lardner-Burke amended the Law and Order (Maintenance) Act by increasing powers of restriction without trial from one year to five years. Even that was insufficient in his mind; he admitted in parliament that he "would love to have preventative detention".[29]

A general election was held in May, which further consolidated RF power. The RF swept every single white constituency seat, securing 79 per cent of the white vote. The successor of the UFP, the Rhodesia Party, won a smattering of District seats with the support of black voters on what was called the "B" roll. In the run up to the election the RF had made it clear that it would brook no opposition from either black nationalists or even from among whites. An RF MP, JA Newington, speaking in parliament, condemned "subversive elements within (parliament) willingly do(ing) the enemy's work" and was appalled at having to spend time "in debates that only bring about disunity".[30] Smith, delivering a campaign speech in Fort Victoria, when criticised that Rhodesia was becoming a one-party state, responded, "In Rhodesia the opposition, through their policy of vacillation and appeasement, is so bankrupt that they are incapable of providing opposition." To all intents and purposes, though, after the election Southern Rhodesia had become a *de facto* one-party state.

My parents became increasingly concerned about the RF's intentions and the growing intolerance in Rhodesian society. After watching *The Sound of Music*, which premiered in Rhodesia close to the election my father muttered about the sharp irony of the rapturous reception Rhodesians gave the film; in his view Rhodesia was becoming increasingly like the Austria the Von Trapp family had to contend with after Nazi occupation. The curtailment of freedom of thought and speech particularly rankled him. He came home one day complaining bitterly about having received a visit at the bank from members of the Central Intelligence Organisation (CIO). He had been openly advising clients that a unilateral declaration of independence would ultimately damage their businesses and set Rhodesia on a collision course with the rest of the world. In an unprecedented move, he had also approved an overdraft facility to Nkomo while he was under restriction orders. This had not gone down well with the CIO, who came to warn him to curb his subversive behaviour. My father gave them a mouthful in return about how he had not fought in the Royal Scots against fascism in Germany only for it to reappear in a British colony.

Despite the worries of people like my parents and last-minute efforts of the British government to dissuade them, the RF continued with its helter-skelter policy to declare independence. Somewhat disingenuously, at 11 am on 11 November 1965, Armistice Day, during the traditional two minutes' silence to remember the fallen in the two World Wars, the Rhodesian cabinet gathered around Smith as he signed the Declaration of Independence. The declaration itself and the ceremony were modelled on the American declaration but omitted two key phrases, that "all men are created equal" and the "consent of the governed". The timing was made to emphasise the sacrifices that Rhodesians had made for Britain. Attached to the declaration was an amended version of the 1961 constitution, severing all ties to Whitehall and creating a separate Rhodesian monarchy (making Elizabeth II "Queen of Rhodesia", a title which she was never well disposed to take up).

As was his custom, my father came home for lunch that Thursday. The Rhodesian Broadcasting Corporation had announced that the prime minister would be addressing the nation at 1.15 pm. After a quick lunch we moved to my father's study to listen to the radio. I sat on my father's lap with my mother alongside us as Smith announced what he and the cabinet had done in his clipped Rhodesian accent. My father shook his head throughout the broadcast and at the end turned to me and said in his lilting Scottish brogue, "Oh, Davie boy – Mr Smith has done a very silly thing."

CHAPTER 3

PHONEY PRECURSOR TO WAR
1965 TO 1970

"Neither party expected for the war the magnitude or the duration which it ... attained. Neither anticipated that the cause of the conflict might cease with, or even before, the conflict itself should cease. Each looked for an easier triumph, and a result less fundamental and astounding. Both read the same Bible, and pray to the same God; and each invokes his aid against the other. It may seem strange that any men should dare to ask a just God's assistance in wringing their bread from the sweat of other men's faces."

– President Abraham Lincoln's
second inaugural address, 4 March 1865

Ian Smith's first act after proclaiming UDI was to meet with the governor of Southern Rhodesia, Sir Humphrey Gibbs, to advise him what he had done. Gibbs, like Smith, was a farmer and his response to Smith's news was that he would retire to his farm in Nyamandlovu to see if he could get any more milk out of his cows. Although Smith recorded in his memoirs that they had been "friends for many years" and that he gave "instructions that (Gibbs) should be allowed to continue living in his residence with no pressures placed on him",[31] the reality was different. Whitehall told Gibbs he could not retire and on 15 November 1965 he advised the government that he was going to stay on as legal governor, effectively dismissing Smith and his cabinet. The government retaliated by disconnecting Gibbs's telephone lines and withdrawing his official car and salary. For three and half years Gibbs was to live as if he were under house arrest. He seldom left Government House, fearing that the

RF would lock him out. Friends rallied to his aid – a group of Gibbs's Bulawayo-based business and farming colleagues passed the hat around and bought him a new car, which was presented to him as a surprise after a church service at the Bulawayo Anglican cathedral, St John's. However, the treatment of Gibbs by the RF set the tone for the post-UDI era.

In his UDI address, Smith said that it "had struck a blow for the preservation of justice, civilisation and Christianity", and this became the RF's mantra. Rhodesia was fighting for the whole of Western society and the battle was against "forces of evil" which were threatening to eradicate Western civilisation. It increasingly followed that all who opposed UDI logically were part of these forces of evil. Shortly before UDI, on 5 November, a state of emergency had been proclaimed throughout Rhodesia. As Judith Todd wrote at the time, this "stripped the last vestiges of disguise from a police state masquerading as a democracy".[32] Police could now arrest without a warrant and it became an offence to make "statements causing alarm", or writing anything which might cause "despondency". Nationalist leaders were either in detention or in prison. Press censorship and petrol rationing were imposed; the Argus Group, owners of *The Herald* and *Chronicle* newspapers, responded to censorship laws by producing pages with more blank spaces than printed ones. Import licences were cancelled and emigration allowances were cut to £100.

Inside the country news of UDI was generally received calmly apart from some isolated incidents of passing cars being stoned in a few black townships outside Bulawayo. A few dissenters were arrested, most prominently Leo Baron, Nkomo's German-born lawyer, whose links with black nationalists and communists were seen by the RF as "subversive". Baron was arrested just nine minutes after UDI was announced. Garfield Todd had been served with a one-year restriction order shortly before the declaration was made, confining him to his ranch near Shabani, even preventing him from going to church. Smith, without a shred of evidence, publicly claimed that Todd had travelled to Zambia, hinting that he was involved in sabotage and killings.[33] Even Lord Malvern, former Prime Minister Godfrey Huggins, was censored. He had signed a book opened by Gibbs at Government House, earning the wrath of the RF by indicating his opposition to UDI.

The Rhodesian Broadcasting Corporation (RBC), which for many years had generally followed the line of the government of the day, now became a propaganda arm of the RF. Men on the far right, such as Harvey Ward, who was appointed director of News Broadcasts, were given key posts. Ivor Benson, who prior to UDI had mused whether the press could "be left to do as it pleases" and that only criticism which sprang from "(our) values and motives" should be allowed, was appointed government's Chief Censor. The civil service, military and police were progressively purged of people who opposed UDI and replaced with those who supported UDI and the RF. The government increasingly became blended in with, and indistinguishable from, the party. Although the judiciary remained reasonably independent at first, it, too, gradually succumbed and even Chief Justice Hugh Beadle, who at first had sided with Gibbs, eventually ruled in a manner that benefited the RF.

The British responded to UDI by imposing sanctions and an oil embargo on Rhodesia. My father, concerned about the effects of the oil embargo, bought us all bicycles. But he need not have worried – although sanctions did bite initially, for example the Rhodesian Iron and Steel Corporation was forced to close down two of its three blast furnaces in early 1966, their main effect was to boost a spirit of white nationalism and give energy to sometimes ingenious circumvention. The latter started a pattern of subterfuge and breaking of laws "in the national interest" which subsists to this day. Sanctions busters became folk heroes in Rhodesia, in much the same way that those who get around sanctions in Zimbabwe today are lauded.

Most nationalist leaders were in detention or prison when UDI was declared; it was interpreted by them as a stark reminder that there was no prospect of a negotiated settlement. Both ZAPU and ZANU met separately to formulate and expedite military strategies. The ZANU leadership issued the Sikombela Declaration (named after the detention camp where most were held), which authorised Herbert Chitepo to establish a war council to be known as Dare ReChimurenga. They worked quickly and in April 1966 four groups of guerrillas crossed over the Zambezi into Rhodesia. Two of the groups were arrested soon after crossing over but the others avoided detection for a while. On 28 April 1966 the Battle of Sinoia (now called Chinhoyi) was fought. For the first time the Air Force was involved and the entire group was wiped out. Despite this overwhelming white Rhodesian victory, it became a propaganda godsend to the nationalists. The battle marked the beginning of what ZANU called the Liberation Struggle or Second Chimurenga.

Even Rhodesia's Intelligence chief, Ken Flower, acknowledged the bravery of these men, who fought against tremendous odds[34] and in doing so provided the first martyrs in a shooting war. A few weeks later, on 18 May, the final group murdered Johannes Viljoen and his wife at Nevada farm near Sinoia; in the follow up the entire group was either killed or detained. Likewise five separate ZAPU groups crossed the Zambezi during July and August, but once again all the guerrillas were killed or arrested within a few months.

Because of the Rhodesians' overwhelming superiority on the battlefield, a sense of military invincibility crept into the security forces and into the RF itself. Flower pointed out that the start to this war, and during the first stage of the war between the Rhodesians and nationalist forces, which lasted some seven years, there was a deliberate policy to conduct it as a "silent war" and security forces' victories went "unheralded". Between 1964 and 1966 Flower records that some 100 ZANLA and ZIPRA guerrillas[35] were killed without the loss of a single soldier or policeman.[36] Because of the secrecy, the public was oblivious to what was going on and the attendant dangers of a guerrilla war. This was certainly the case in my family.

Another matter hidden from the public was that the RF had completely miscalculated Britain's response to UDI. They were anxious to get negotiations under way. Flower wrote of Smith's anxiety to "re-open negotiations (eight days after UDI – 'the nine-day-wonder!'), rescind UDI and revert to constitutional government".[37] Flower also writes of how flabbergasted he was when the RF minister of Agriculture, Lord Graham, asked him whether he thought tobacco would be subject to sanctions, after he had sent numerous briefs to him warning the cabinet that tobacco would be the "first and most certain to be sanctioned". Accordingly, after Harold Wilson's Labour Party was re-elected in 1966 and had started exploring avenues for talks, the RF were receptive. This culminated in the talks held on the British warship HMS *Tiger* off Gibraltar in December 1966.

Smith records the "pleasant surprise" the RF delegation received in reconciling differences between the RF and the British on the constitution.[38] They in fact agreed on a new constitution which allowed for a gradual evolution towards majority rule. More black seats would be created in parliament, which would lead eventually towards a majority as more blacks became enfranchised through improved educational and income earning opportunities. The sticking point was the process to return the Southern Rhodesian government back to legality. The British wanted Smith to accept the dissolution of his government on the understanding that Gibbs would then ask him to form a new government. Smith countered by suggesting that the British carry out their test of acceptability[39] on the new constitution, and once that had happened the new constitution would be made law by the existing parliament. Unable to resolve this disagreement, Smith agreed to take the proposal back to his cabinet.

Flower records that despite Smith's reservations about the process, which would return the government to legality, he considered the British proposals acceptable.[40] When the RF cabinet met to discuss the proposals on 5 December 1966 a majority were in favour of accepting them, but they were scuppered by three ministers, namely Harper (minister of Internal Affairs), Lord Graham and Clifford Dupont. Smith feared a division in cabinet and he feared being deposed, as Field and Todd had been before him; because of this he insisted on an absolute consensus, which in effect gave all power to an extreme right-wing minority. Flower's belief is that Smith's "inherent strengths and weaknesses decided the issue"; Smith "appeared strongest when saying 'No'" and "feared being wrong by saying 'Yes'".[41] Whatever the case, the decision represented another lost opportunity.

The year ended with another event which undoubtedly further poisoned the political atmosphere, even to this day. Shortly after the collapse of the *Tiger* talks Robert Mugabe received word in prison from his sister Sabina that his only child, Nhamodzenyika, had died of malaria in Ghana.[42] He was devastated by the news and applied to be released temporarily so that he could travel to Ghana to bury his son. Surprisingly, the application received support from one of Mugabe's minders, Detective Inspector Tony Bradshaw of the Special Branch, who felt that Mugabe would honour a pledge to return. In any event, Bradshaw believed that an act of kindness might soften the hardened attitudes of detained nationalists. His advice was not followed, however. Mugabe was not allowed to bury his son and his bitterness deepened.

* * *

Throughout 1966 I had not been especially happy at Hillside School and my parents decided that they needed to get me out of the large and more doctrinaire government school and into Christian Brothers College (CBC) for the first term of 1967. CBC was a private school run by Irish Catholic brothers with a penchant for brandy and strict discipline. It was nominally a multiracial school, although during my entire schooling there were never more than a handful of black and coloured boys who attended. Crucially, however, from my parents' perspective, the brothers would not reinforce the prevailing RF propaganda of the time.

CBC was a relatively small school – there were only about 280 boys starting in Standard 3 (for boys turning ten) and ending in Upper Sixth – with only one small class per grade. Shortly before the term started I was taken by my parents to the school for the first time. We were met by the headmaster, Brother Levins, a huge grey-haired man, with a kindly face. His Irish accent, although different to my father's Scots accent, was familiar and comforting. Levins was dressed in a black habit and his office had Catholic paraphernalia everywhere, including a prominent crucifix. My parents were Protestant, my father a Presbyterian, my mother a "low church" Anglican, and so the sight of Christ on the cross and the hallowed paintings of the Virgin Mary were a novelty to me. "David will be very happy here, but he must listen, otherwise he will frequently feel the strap," said Brother Levins. He was right on both counts.

CBC could not have been more different to Hillside School. For a start CBC was not co-ed and my class was much smaller than the one I had been in before; all the brothers wore habits, either black or white; unlike Hillside, which drew children from the surrounding upper-middle-class suburbs, CBC gave preference to Catholics from throughout the city, and so for the first time there was an eclectic mix; there were sons of surgeons, dentists, and railway engine drivers. My first teacher at CBC was an octogenarian, Brother Carol, who had a deceptively quick and hard palm, which I experienced in my first week. Thinking he was not watching, I had been chattering to the boy with whom I shared a desk when he appeared from nowhere and clapped me right out of my seat with a shout in a broad Irish accent, "Stop wastin' my time, boy!" We all soon learnt that as humorous and kind as the brothers were, their straps were never far away. These were purpose built out of leather, with a rigid handle and a foot-long, one-inch wide whippy shaft. The slightest infraction would lead a call to stick one's hand out, followed by several painful whacks to an outstretched palm.

From the very first week at CBC, I was taught by the brothers to respect all people irrespective of their background, status or race. The brothers themselves shunned the materialistic lifestyles which most white Rhodesians enjoyed. They lived communally in the Brothers' House, a one-storey block on the school campus, and dressed very simply, alternating between their white and black habits. I adjusted to their rhythm and simplicity and my school reports immediately started to reflect the more relaxed atmosphere. Due to a combination of the oil embargo, petrol rationing and the safe roads, I started cycling to school. My route took me along a tree-lined cycle track on Cecil Avenue, and then up the Essexvale Road to CBC. Bulawayo was then, as it is now, a sleepy city and so my rides to and from school were a highlight of the day, meeting up with friends and gradually discovering alternate and exciting routes. But it was still a cocooned environment. Aside from my daily interaction with our cook and gardener, Vashiko and Peter, I did not have much interaction with black people, nor did I have any idea of their concerns and daily battles. There was not a single black boy in my class and the only black adults at school were labourers. Our curriculum, too, was Eurocentric. My first report, dated 28 April 1967, records that we studied English, History (British), Arithmetic, Geography (European) and Nature Study. The only African language I studied was Afrikaans. Within weeks of starting school we were taught a variety of Afrikaans folk songs, such as "Vat jou goed en trek, Ferreira".[43] The teaching of an indigenous African language was never even considered.

The military victories of 1966, added to the healthy state of the Rhodesian economy, made the RF feel more secure and society at large increasingly jingoistic. Imperialistic songs were also part of our diet at CBC, despite Irish disdain for Britain. Another favourite was the Boer War song "We are marching to Pretoria".

Although we were taught Afrikaans, the subliminal message was clear: somehow we white English-speaking Rhodesians were a cut above everyone, even our Afrikaans neighbours to the south.

Midway through 1967 the intensity of the largely hidden war went up a notch. ZAPU had entered into a temporary military alliance with the South African ANC's armed wing Umkhonto we Sizwe (MK).[44] A joint intelligence and reconnaissance structure was established, with Dumiso Dabengwa and Eric Manzi as the respective leaders from ZAPU and MK. In July some 200 guerrillas from both ZIPRA and MK, under the leadership of John Dube and Chris Hani respectively, crossed the

Zambezi at the third gorge below Victoria Falls with the intention of moving through Wankie National Park[45] towards South Africa.[46] They were intercepted and a bloody battle followed in which for the first time Rhodesian security forces did not fare as well as they had in the past. While they killed 30 guerrillas and captured most of the force, it was at the cost of seven dead and thirteen wounded of their men. But the battle was to lead to a significant change in the power balance. The South African government was alarmed that MK had been so bold and so agreement was reached with Smith's government that 2 000 South African police and South African Air Force helicopters be deployed to help guard the Zambezi Valley.

Despite the annihilation of guerrillas in 1967, further joint ZIPRA-MK operations were planned and what Smith himself admitted as the "biggest incursion to date commenced at the beginning of 1968".[47] During March and April a series of running battles were waged in the north east of the country near Sipolilo, resulting in the death of 69 guerrillas and 50 captured.

As these battles were playing out, a significant event concerning guerrilla action occurred involving the Queen. A group of six captured guerrillas had been convicted of acts of terrorism and sentenced to death by the Rhodesian High Court. The Queen, for the first and only time since UDI, had been advised to exercise her constitutional right and she granted a reprieve. The pope also made a plea for clemency. The case attracted world-wide attention, which resulted in an emergency cabinet meeting being called on the eve of the men's execution. Cabinet, despite being advised by Flower to uphold the Queen's reprieve, decided to go ahead with the hangings.

One final joint ZIPRA-MK incursion took place in September 1968 over a wide front of the Zambezi Valley, but within weeks the entire contingent was accounted for. The overwhelming victories on the battlefield, together with the impunity of the Rhodesian cabinet in acting against the wishes of the Queen, created a sense of invincibility. The morale of the guerrilla armies was shattered. Even Herbert Chitepo admitted: "It is useless to engage in conventional warfare with well equipped Rhodesian and South African troops along the Zambezi River."[48] Flower records that the "war virtually stopped for 4 years".[49]

Paradoxically, the well-publicised murders of Oberholtzer and the Viljoens had helped the RF by cementing the fears of white Rhodesians that they faced a violent communist-inspired terrorist threat. These fears were fuelled by an increasingly efficient propaganda machine, which highlighted terrorism and sanctions but still projected a victorious air. Although Smith was concerned about sanctions, the void caused by falling trade with Britain was replaced by trade with France, Japan and Italy. Smith boasted that Rhodesian "sanctions busters were in full stride, thriving on the opportunities which presented themselves".[50] Increasingly, the battle was portrayed as one between "right thinking, honourable" people and the British Labour "socialist government". In his autobiography Smith relates an incident which "warmed his heart" about the Russians buying top quality Rhodesian chrome, through sanctions busters, at half the price at which the Russians were selling their inferior quality chrome to the Americans. "Such was the price the Americans had to pay for allowing the British socialist government to seduce them into joining the sanctions war," wrote Smith.[51] Robert Mugabe was to portray ZANU PF's own battle against sanctions in a similar vein 40 years later. Just as Mugabe held out Tony Blair as Zimbabwe's poster boy of deceit, so Harold Wilson became white Rhodesia's *bête noire*.

While Rhodesian television screens showed very few images of the guerrilla conflict within our own borders, they were plastered with haunting images of the genocide unfolding in Biafra, Nigeria. Genocide was indeed taking place – on 10 September 1968 Richard Nixon said in a campaign speech: "Genocide is what is taking place right now – and starvation is the grim reaper."[52] What helped Rhodesian propaganda all the more was the fact that Harold Wilson was increasingly under attack for his support of the Gowon regime, which was responsible for the Biafran tragedy. In a debate on Biafra he watched in the House of Commons on 12 August 1968, Chinua Achebe describes Wilson as the "villain of the peace", the head of a government which was "largely unmoved by the tragedy".[53] The double standard of the Labour Party – in the way it handled Nigeria and Rhodesia – assisted the RF in portraying Wilson as a disreputable character. At the same time Biafra portended a powerful image in the minds of white Rhodesians regarding the consequences of majority rule. The images of skeletal children my own age fleeing the conflict had a profound impact on me at the time.

Despite my parents' open and the brothers' more subtle criticism of the RF regime, national white hero worship of Ian Smith was rubbing off on me. At about this time I was introduced to Smith. One of my father's closest friends was a Jewish businessman, Ralph Harris, who was a Bulawayo city councillor (later to become mayor) and well connected. We were invited to a party at the Harris home; soon after we arrived, Ian Smith walked in the front door. I happened to be around and was introduced to him. He struck me as a handsome, friendly, tall man with a warm handshake. Although it was just a fleeting meeting and exchange of words, as a ten-year-old boy I was impressed, much to the alarm of my parents.

In early October, Smith and Wilson met again, this time on HMS *Fearless*, to see whether a settlement could be arrived at. Although Smith writes that the British insistence on "a return to legality" remained a stumbling block, most historians believe that the *Fearless* terms offered by the British were softer than the *Tiger* terms. At the time the *New Statesman* parodied the NIBMAR (No independence before majority rule) principles by stating that what was offered was "unimpeded progress towards minority rule". Constitutional expert Claire Palley predicted that according to the constitutional formula, "it was possible to predict 2004 as the earliest date"[54] for majority rule. Despite the British bending over backwards, the RF rejected the proposals again. The precise details of the discussions were hidden from the public and Smith misled the nation when he spoke on radio on 19 November 1968 stating that "this alternative proposal is infinitely worse than the original one".[55]

With hindsight it is clear that the RF was hell bent on severing ties with Britain permanently and entrenching white minority rule, no doubt buoyed by the military successes of the year. As a result Smith had little real interest in reaching any sort of compromise with the British. On the third anniversary of UDI, 11 November 1968, a new white and green Rhodesian flag was raised and the old predominantly blue Southern Rhodesian flag, with the Union Jack in its top left-hand corner, was dispensed with. Without a trace of irony, or acceptance of responsibility, Smith wrote later that had the British "played their cards correctly" Zimbabwe would still have a flag displaying a Union Jack now instead of one with a "Marxist red star".[56]

In 1967 the RF had established a constitutional commission to look into the drafting of a new constitution "to advise on the constitutional framework best suited to the sovereign independent status of Rhodesia". The commission was chaired by a well-known Salisbury (Harare) lawyer, Sam Whaley, and included Bob Cole (a friend of my father's and later to be my senior partner in the law firm I joined in 1983), a white educationalist, HH Cole, Charles Mzingeli, a black trade unionist, and SM Sigola, an Ndebele chief. In April 1968 the commission produced, at least from an RF perspective, a "liberal" report. It did not envisage majority rule but recommended an electoral system that would ultimately produce racial parity in parliament and government. The RF caucus objected and started drafting its own amendments. In a meeting before cabinet in August 1968, Whaley and Cole explained why what they had drafted was necessary and objected to the changes proposed by cabinet. It was pointed out that it was "vital to maintain African support" and if this was ignored it "would mean the end of African co-operation".[57] Despite the fact that the proposed constitution did not allow for any evolution towards majority rule, and dramatically reversed the 1961 constitution, and the constitutional proposals agreed between the British and the RF in the *Tiger* and *Fearless* talks, the RF went ahead and produced a draft constitution early in 1969 that was the "enshrinement of white minority rule".[58]

My father retired from Grindlays at that time to set up a new finance house, Fincor, which resulted in several changes to our lives. We moved out of the bank house to a more modest home in Fortunes Gate; it was a house I was to spend the next eleven years in and one which played a role in deepening my love for the bush – it had a much bigger garden which backed onto a kopje. Climbing to the top of what seemed to be a massive granite boulder gave me wonderful views of the beautiful savannah plains which stretched out to the north. Soon after moving into our new home in April 1969, we took our first family holiday back to Scotland. It was the first time I had experienced real cold, necessitating the purchase of my first pair of long trousers. I remember one aspect of that holiday with acute embarrassment: I was a precocious, opinionated eleven-year-old and very willing to argue, as I proceeded to do at every opportunity, that Mr Smith was fully justified in declaring UDI. My parents were mortified and our friends and relatives in Britain no doubt horrified by how pervasive RF propaganda was.

We returned home to the publication of the proposed new republican constitution, which was followed by a referendum on it in June 1969. By a two-to-one majority the overwhelmingly white electorate voted in favour of a white republic. My parents voted against the new constitution. Unbeknown to anyone outside of a tight circle within the

ZANU leadership, just as white Rhodesia was lurching to the right, so the leadership of ZANU was foreswearing any moderation. Ndabaningi Sithole, the then president of ZANU, had been caught red handed plotting to assassinate Smith and minister of Law and Order Lardner-Burke. He was charged with treason and saved his neck by agreeing to renounce violence. His colleagues in prison were appalled and at a secret central committee meeting held in prison Robert Mugabe was elected to be the new party leader. Mugabe was absolutely committed to armed struggle and with his election evaporated any hope that war might be avoided.

The Republic of Rhodesia was proclaimed on 1 March 1970, just weeks after I started high school by progressing to Form 1 at CBC. An election followed in April for a lower House of Assembly (comprising 66 members, 50 whites, who were voted for by whites, coloureds and Asians, and 16 blacks, 8 of whom were voted in by a minuscule black roll and the balance by chiefs) and a Senate (comprising 13 whites and 10 chiefs). The election campaign provided me with my first insight into the way Rhodesian politics operated. The father of one of my closest friends at CBC, Hilary Norton, stood against the RF for the moderate Centre Party in a local Bulawayo constituency. When this became known in class, Norton's son, Alan, was ridiculed. Alan was too popular a boy to be completely ostracised, but nevertheless the vast majority of boys in our class expressed their disgust that anyone could stand against Smith's RF.

For the second successive time since UDI the RF won every single white seat in the election. The chiefs in parliament owed their allegiance to the government that paid their salaries, so little opposition came from that quarter.

The economy was picking up, with new industries making the country self sustainable, which boosted the morale of whites no end. Virtually the entire nationalist leadership was in detention or prison. Not only were their attempts at armed struggle in tatters, but they were riven with divisions. Very few bookies would have provided good odds that majority rule would come within a decade.

CHAPTER 4

THE CALM BEFORE THE STORM
1970 TO 1975

"The possibility of peaceful change in Rhodesia is remote, but it is there."
— JUDITH TODD, WRITING FROM LONDON, NOVEMBER 1972

The morale of white Rhodesians probably reached its zenith in mid 1970. Just months after the declaration of the Republic of Rhodesia, the Conservatives swept to power in Britain in June. In the minds of RF supporters Smith's sang-froid appeared to have prevailed over Wilson's duplicity. The new British Prime Minister, Edward Heath, was more concerned about Britain's accession to the European Common Market than he was about resolving the Rhodesian question. Moreover he appointed Sir Alec Douglas-Home, an aristocrat and ex-county cricketer, as Foreign Secretary. Douglas-Home was keen to settle the dispute and was known to be far more sympathetic towards white Rhodesians than anyone in Labour had ever been. He immediately initiated contact with the RF and his emissaries struck a quick rapport with Smith. There was little pressure, though, to rush a settlement – the economy was showing growth and white immigration was constant. Talks about talks began towards the end of 1970.

My life as a twelve-year-old at this time could not have been more blissful. After three years at CBC, and having moved up from primary to high school, school was getting better every term. By this time I had a good, close circle of friends (all white) and we lived the life of Riley. Most of our homes were within a few kilometres of each other; we also had tolerant, permissive parents who allowed us to roam freely on our bicycles so long as we got in before dark. Bulawayo has one of the best climates in the world – my father used to boast that one could play golf every day of the year and he was right. I loved the Fortunes Gate home as it was close to the veld – honey brown bush interrupted only by glorious indigenous trees and rocky granite outcrops; ideal terrain for spending endless afternoons exploring, climbing, building forts, pretending we were in the wild west. Another passion was go-karting. Within a two-kilometre radius of our home there were plenty of hilly roads and me and my friends spent hours constructing and racing our karts. We were inspired by Bulawayo's own Formula 1 racing driver, John Love. As unlikely as it may seem now, Bulawayo then had an annual Formula 1 race (as part of the South African Championship) and in 1970 a purpose-built track was being built, the Breedon Everard raceway. The centre of my social life at this time was Napier Avenue in Hillside, a few kilometres away from Fortunes Gate. My best friend Mark Gilmore lived at Number 20, and two houses down from him lived David Bilang, and within a stone's throw of David lived Rob Nixon and Chris Brittlebank; all of us went to CBC and all of us were sports mad. Chris's home had a long, steep driveway, perfect for go-karting. Mark and I were only-children but David, Rob and Chris all had at least one sister each which, as we moved into adolescence, made for an increasing attraction. They were carefree days, afternoons spent in each other's gardens or homes playing all the games that young boys do. Politics and the plight of black people didn't enter our heads.

Although sport had been an integral part of our primary schooling, at high school it was now taught in earnest. Our class master was a new South African brother, Peter Phillips, who was much younger than most of the Irish brothers and a sports fanatic. Virtually every afternoon of term was spent in the cricket nets, on rugby fields or running in the bush which surrounded CBC. Although I was lousy at team sports, attendance at practice was compulsory and I soon developed a deep love for sport. My father, realising that I had little chance of playing on a CBC team (our classes were so small that we only managed a single team per grade), started teaching me golf at the nearby Bulawayo Country Club. Within weeks I was hooked and every spare moment, when I wasn't in the nets, bushwhacking or go-karting, was spent on the golf course.

On the golf course was where I first started to interact with other black people beyond Vashiko and Pete. I got to know the caddies. Most of these were dirt-poor young men who had missed out on an education. They were older than me, but almost all were kind, tolerant and patient. Most could play golf well and supplemented my father's coaching. But of course these were superficial relationships – still very much in the category of master and servant. I was oblivious to the reality of life for most black Rhodesians.

It was on the sports field that our class had its first taste of the effects of racial discrimination. In Form 1, a coloured boy, Phillip Hendricks, joined our class. Being such a small school, our teams were generally weak and we were thrashed by the much larger, all-white government schools such as Milton, Gifford and Hamilton. We were all delighted to discover in the cricket nets that Hendricks was an outstanding opening batsman and naturally he was quickly selected for our under-13 cricket team. All was well until we had to play an away match against Milton. A day before the game Brother Peter Phillips came into class looking sombre and said, "I am sad to tell you that Milton have rung me to say that Hendricks can't play in our team at Milton." We were all shocked and asked why not. Phillips replied, "Because they say that government rules state that only whites can use the facilities at white government schools. I told them that God views all these boys the same and that I was disgusted. The Milton coach said he had no choice. What do you want to do?" Fortunately the response was unanimous – we would not play against Milton unless Hendricks was part of the team. In our naivety we were shocked; how could someone be stopped from playing cricket just because of the colour of his skin? After all, Hendricks was not only a superb player, capable of virtually winning single handed, but he was also our friend. This episode had a profound effect on the whole class which, just months before, had ridiculed Alan Norton's father for having the temerity to oppose Smith's RF in the general election. We had now come face to face with the effects of RF policy which increasingly reflected the apartheid policies just south of the border in South Africa. The policies appeared painless in the abstract and it was only when applied to a friend that we started to see the absurdity of it all. Needless to say, Brother Phillips was delighted with our decision and told the Milton master that we would all rather not play than leave Hendricks out of the team.

Our concern regarding Phillip Hendricks's plight was largely selfish and superficial. He had much further to ride to school than most of us because his family had to live in the coloured suburb, Barham Green. Bulawayo was precisely planned: all black people had to stay in townships which were to the west of the city, separated from white, coloured and Asian suburbs by the Botswana/Victoria Falls railway line. Coloured and Asian people were allocated suburbs in the centre of the city and most whites lived in the south, east and north east of the city. Chinese people were considered "honorary" whites and so one of the boys in our class, Bruce Eeson, who was of Chinese ancestry, lived close by in a white suburb even though he wasn't white. I and the rest of my class had little understanding at the time of the challenges and daily humiliation Hendricks experienced – and he wasn't even a black child; black children faced even tougher challenges. The brothers would on occasion tease out a class discussion on the injustice of it all but there was a limit to what they could do.

Racism ran deep and existed even between different sectors of the white community. Greeks, Italians and Portuguese were looked down on by the Rhodesian equivalent of Wasps[59] and it was considered *infra dig* to associate with them.

Jews were openly discriminated against, much to the fury of my father. At this time I learnt another lesson about how stratified our society was. Ralph Harris was about to become mayor of Bulawayo and my father thought it appropriate that he become a member of the Bulawayo Club. One of Rhodes's first acts after the establishment of Bulawayo was to assist in establishing the club and he became one of its three principal members.[60] In 1934 Prince George, Duke of Kent had laid the foundation stone of this magnificent new building and it remains one of Bulawayo's finest structures today. My father was a member of the club, which was just a block away from his former office at Grindlays and his then office at Fincor. In 1970 he had his fingers burnt when he seconded the nomination of a local headmaster – a Wasp – and the nominee was blackballed, much to my father's chagrin. Having suffered that embarrassment, he took the precaution of canvassing members prior to putting Harris's name forward and was appalled to find out that, simply because Harris was Jewish, the nomination would fail. As my father was wont to do, he expressed his disgust inside the club and at home.

Racial discrimination against blacks was far worse than that experienced by coloureds and Asians. The 1969 constitution had obliterated any prospect of a slow transition to majority rule and an end to discriminatory laws and practices; indeed the RF was steadily moving backwards as its extreme right wing strove to mirror apartheid. It was in this context that British envoys Sir Max Aitken and Lord Goodman commenced formal discussions with the RF in April 1971. Under complete cover of secrecy during the course of the year, as Smith put it, "the decks were sufficiently cleared" to the satisfaction of the British. No attempt was made during these negotiations to seek the opinion of black people, far less their leaders in detention, or even moderate white leaders like Todd and Gibbs.

The quintessential Rhodesian public holiday was the Rhodes and Founders long weekend, celebrated on the first or second Monday of July; it was declared a holiday in 1895 to commemorate Rhodes's birthday (5 July 1853). In 1972 my parents, I and my closest friend Mark Gilmore spent the Rhodes and Founders weekend at the farm of "Skinny" Evans in Lalapanzi, just outside Gwelo. "Skinny", who was anything but, was a barrel-chested farmer with an equally big heart. Although he and my father were poles apart in appearance, background and calling, they had a good friendship. On arrival we were thrown the keys to a 50cc Honda motorcycle and Mark and I explored every nook and cranny of the farm from sunup to sundown. Every evening we came in exhilarated, but soaked and frozen to the bone from the *guti*. I came down with a severe case of pneumonia which almost killed me and kept me out of school for the rest of the winter term. I was nursed back to health at home by my mother and Dr Paul Fehrsen, who also happened to be one of Garfield Todd's closest friends. In those days doctors in Bulawayo made house visits and in my drowsy state I was treated to lengthy discourses at my bedside between my parents and Dr Fehrsen about the current state of Rhodesian politics. Dr Fehrsen was someone I admired and so his utterly disdainful remarks about what the RF was up to intrigued and made an impression on me. He was particularly concerned that the RF would reach agreement with the British without consulting black people.

That is precisely what happened. On 15 November, Douglas-Home flew out to Salisbury and after a series of intense discussions with Smith, agreement was reached and signed within a week. The key term which had caused the RF to reject the *Tiger* and *Fearless* terms, "the restoration of legality", was removed. In general the terms were much softer than those offered by Labour: the 1969 constitution was moderated but the franchise would remain racially segregated; limited majority rule would only happen after decades of black educational and financial advancement. In reality, discrimination in education and commerce would make majority rule elusive. As Smith himself wrote, "there would be no mad rush into one man one vote".[61] In other words, it appeared to be an agreement which perfectly suited the RF, with few compromises having been made.

The only hurdle left was to ensure that the agreement was acceptable to the Rhodesian people as a whole, and in this lies one of the great enigmas of this period. The RF and the British agreed to appoint a commission, headed by Lord Pearce, which would canvas the views of all Rhodesians. Smith wrote that he was frustrated by the delay in the start of the work of the commission, concerned that "dilly-dallying would play into the hands of mischief makers". He had his doubts, he said, about getting an "honest assessment from our black people", most of whom he declared "did not understand the meaning of the word 'constitution'" and were "bemused by all the talking",[62] revealing white supremacist thinking at its worst. In contrast, Flower wrote that despite the favourable terms the RF were "unhappy with (them)" and "had no intention of trying to make it work". At the core of this was the belief that Rhodesia was winning and that making a concession to majority rule, no matter how remote, was starting down the slippery slope. When Smith complained that the British were deliberately delaying the start of the commission, the CIO asked why this time should not be used to mobilise support for the proposals. It was at this point that Flower says they got "the truth of the matter". Secretary for African Affairs Hostes Nicolle, who was an advocate of apartheid-type policies, was hostile towards any agreement that would give any more power to black people.[63] African Affairs fell under the ministry that would have to play a pivotal role in securing black support for the Douglas-Home proposals. Flower points out that Nichole had also played a key role in derailing the *Fearless* talks.

Despite the public stance being taken by the RF, i.e. that they were in favour of the settlement, they in fact did much to scupper its acceptance. While the nationalist parties rallied around the formation of the new African National Council in December 1971 under the leadership of the cleric Bishop Abel Muzorewa to oppose the terms, and mobilised a massive "no" vote, they were helped by the RF. Perversely, just weeks after the commission began its work, on 18 January 1972, Garfield Todd and his daughter Judith were arrested and detained. At a press conference a few weeks later Smith mendaciously said that the Todds were among those responsible for "burning, intimidation, violence, rioting and looting". In fact Todd was one of the few white people black Rhodesians trusted and news of his detention would have spread like wildfire, a detention that even moderate black people would have interpreted as a sign that there was something seriously wrong with the proposals. Any allegation that the Todds were involved in violence rode in the face of their lifelong commitment to non-violence. Flower concluded that the need to settle "took second place to the need to satisfy Smith's objective – 'no majority rule in a thousand years'".[64]

Whatever the case, the Pearce Commission concluded its work on 12 March 1972 and released its report two months later. It concluded that while most whites, coloureds and Asians were in favour of the proposals, an overwhelming number of blacks were not. The reason given was because of the "overriding distrust of the government by African people". This feeling was summed up by Pat Bashford, leader of Rhodesia's moderate Centre Party who, although supportive of the proposals, said of the RF: "We know only too well the political dangers inseparable from conferring legality upon those who have shown such little regard for the rule of law. We realise the dubious value of solemn assurances uttered by men to whom oaths of allegiance are but scraps of paper to be torn up at will." If white moderates felt that way, it is no wonder blacks rejected what turned out to be the last attempt to settle the Anglo-Rhodesian dispute through peaceful negotiation. Most whites were shocked by the finding of the Pearce Commission – that what seemed an obvious way forward to them was rejected by blacks. It was a stark reminder of the massive gulf between the reality of black opinion and RF propaganda, which claimed that Rhodesia had the happiest black people on the continent. While there is no doubt that extremists had threatened and cajoled many black people into opposing the agreement, most contemporaneous neutral commentators understood that blacks were not "content to be (whites') meek acolytes".[65]

There is one final anecdote about this period. Unbeknown to the Todds, their detention order had been reviewed by a tribunal in early February which recommended their continued detention. Neither they nor their lawyers were given any opportunity to be heard. On 22 February, Garfield and Judith were collected from their respective prisons in Gatooma and Marandellas and driven to their Hokonui Ranch near Shabani. On the way they were both served with fresh detention orders, these ones, however, confining them to the house at the ranch and barring them from speaking to anyone other than family members, employees, their doctor and lawyer. Garfield and Grace Todd were anxious that Judith go free. As the family doctor, Dr Paul Fehrsen, on hearing this, took it upon himself to visit. He brought with him a blonde wig, blue-tinted glasses and the suggestion that he and his wife Paddy smuggle Judith across the border into Botswana. Judith declined the offer because she feared imperilling her parents by breaching the detention order with their knowledge. Criminal charges were never brought against Garfield and Judith; Smith's allegation that they were responsible for violence was exposed as groundless.

White business had assumed that a settlement would be reached with the Conservatives and the failure to do so was shocking. This in turn led to a drop in business confidence and the economy gradually began to falter. There was an acute shortage of railways rolling stock, foreign currency became scarcer and, horror of horrors, whisky was in short supply. I became keenly aware of this through the grumblings of my father's bridge group. Every Friday evening my father and a core group of his friends – lawyers Alastair Calderwood, Frank Bryce Hendrie, and David Ross, and businessmen Tommy Thomson and Basil Kaufman – would gather at our home for bridge. They were all of the same mindset. They opposed the RF and its strictures and they did not keep their views secret. Whisky was the Holy Grail and whenever its shortage affected their bridge, UDI was readily, and loudly, accused. It was in fact that triad of lawyers who first captured my interest in doing law; they were all engaging, humorous, articulate men. Without even knowing anything about their profession, I was immediately attracted to it simply because of their characters.

A second event which had a profound impact on my thinking happened that year. My mother's youngest brother, Ev Hensley, had followed her up to Rhodesia in the mid 1960s to go farming north of Salisbury. After being a manager, he managed to scrape together enough money to buy his own farm, Amajuba, in the Sipolilo district in 1971. Sipolilo is on the edge of the Zambezi escarpment, as the crow flies not far from the Zambezi and Zambian and Mozambican borders. It had been the scene of some guerrilla activity in the late 1960s. In August

1972 my mother and I holidayed on the farm. I went out with my uncle every day to inspect the tobacco fields that had been carved out of thick bush and were surrounded by well treed kopjes. The kopjes provided glorious vistas if one was energetic enough to climb them. One day in my ramblings I came across a kopje with a cave that appeared to have been recently occupied; there were the blackened remains of a fire and signs that a few people had slept there, with grass flattened out on the granite floor. The cave provided a particularly good vantage point and I thought what a magnificent fort it would make. When I came down from my reverie I told my uncle what I had seen. He immediately climbed back up with me and conducted a detailed search of the cave but found nothing more than a few cigarette ends. It didn't end there, however. He reported the finding to the local police and it was then that I realised the latent fear that many farmers had of guerrilla activity, even though there had been no clashes for almost four years. It was also the first time that I perceived a direct threat to my family.

In fact, during this period the Portuguese in neighbouring Mozambique were losing their war against Frelimo, the Mozambican black nationalist party and guerrilla army. By the late 1960s, Frelimo effectively occupied all of Mozambique from a line along the Zambezi River to the Tanzanian border; in 1968 they had opened a new sector south of the Zambezi in Tete province, which was a massive blow to the Rhodesians. To counter this, the Rhodesians, with the support of the Portuguese, had deployed troops into Mozambique to try to keep Frelimo north of the Zambezi. But this was not sufficient to stem ZANLA infiltration, who were co-operating closely with Frelimo. Although ZAPU had also had ties with Frelimo, in 1971 it lost this "important and strategic contact".[66] Flower states that in the latter half of 1971 intelligence showed that ZANLA guerrillas were infiltrating the north east of Rhodesia and that they were now living among the population. They had "moved ahead in the spirit world by invoking the national spirit of 'Chaminuka', the greatest Shona prophet from the first Chimurenga in the 1890s".[67] No longer were the guerrillas massing in great numbers – their tactics had changed completely. In July 1972, Flower warned the RF cabinet that this infiltration was but a prelude to a significant conflict between black and white, and indeed by the year end it was clear that ZANLA guerrillas had a significant foothold in the north east. Smith first made the public aware of this on 4 December 1972 in a broadcast, stating: "The security situation is far more serious than it appears on the surface."

Two days before Christmas, a new phase of war started with the attack on Altena farm in the Centenary district by 21 guerrillas led by a young man, Solomon Mujuru (known then by his *nom de guerre* Rex Nhongo), who was to become Zimbabwe's first army commander post independence. Mujuru had initially joined ZAPU but following eruptions within the party had crossed over to ZANLA in early 1971.

The start of a new phase of war shocked white Rhodesians but given past experience and the pitiful lack of information, or debate, it was assumed that the security forces would get to grips with the situation. Black people in the areas known to be at risk immediately found themselves in a terrible dilemma, caught between the guerrillas and security forces. Giving away information about guerrillas to security forces invited torture, at least, and even murder; not doing so invited torture and the application of harsh new laws which allowed the imposition of collective fines, confiscation of cattle and the burning of villages for all those suspected of aiding and abetting guerrillas.

RF propaganda started to feed the Rhodesian public with a steady diet of horrendous photographs and stories of atrocities committed by ZANLA guerrillas. Captured guerrillas and documents provided evidence of training and links to China. It was the time of Mao Zedong's Cultural Revolution and none of the horrors of that revolution were held back by the RBC. The Vietnam War was also nearing its perilous end. The horrors of Vietnam had also been well publicised and Rhodesians had taken much morbid interest in its atrocities. In short, the opening months of 1973 held much, both internationally and locally, to captivate and instil terror in the minds of fifteen-year-olds such as me.

Life in Bulawayo, which was far removed from the north east of the country, was, for me at least, very good. Although 1973 was my O level year, which brought with it increased academic pressures, I was revelling in all the opportunities provided by the wonderful climate and lifestyle I enjoyed. My lack of sporting prowess had kept me out of school teams for my first three years of high school, but my father's encouragement on the golf course was starting to bear fruit. For the first time in my life I was selected to a team – reserve of the Matabeleland Junior team which was to play in the annual inter-provincial tournament at Greta Park, in what was then known as Mashaba, a mining town just west of Fort Victoria. Greta Park was an exquisite golf course, set among towering hills and groves of msasa trees; it was my first taste of the lowveld (the unique south east of Zimbabwe), an area I was to return to four years later in much more challenging circumstances. As things turned out, Manicaland province could not muster a full team and so I ended up being drafted into their team to make up the numbers. I was awestruck by the quality of the players – among them were Nick Price, Dennis Watson and Tony Johnstone, all of whom made their mark in world golf in the years that followed. There were no players of colour; it was an all-white affair, except for the black caddies of course.

There could not have been a more privileged gathering of young boys in Rhodesia. We might not have thought so, but in fact the situation was surreal. The storm into which nearly all of us would be sucked was building but we were oblivious. If we saw dark clouds on the horizon, we knew nothing of their portent and how they would affect our lives.

Just weeks after getting home from Greta Park a relatively young RF MP, Allan Savory, shocked the white community by stating in parliament that if he were black, he would probably be a guerrilla because of black people's justifiable grievances. Controversially, he referred to fighters as "guerrillas" rather than "terrorists" and he also said that the war required a political, not a military, solution. He went on to suggest that nationalist leaders be invited to a constitutional conference, a suggestion which Smith described as "irresponsible and evil".

Indeed, it was relatively easy for the RF to be dismissive of Savory, because in the course of 1973 Rhodesian security forces increasingly gained the ascendancy in the war. Although they had not had any knock-out punches, a combination of factors made the war containable to the north east of the country, at least in the short term. Thousands of rural people were moved into "protected villages" similar to those used in the Malayan emergency in the 1950s; a cordon sanitaire coupled with a no-go area was built along the Mozambique border; and a new fire force technique using concentrated fire from helicopter gunships proved to be an extremely effective tactic against exposed guerrillas. But whereas in Malaya-protected villages were part of a "hearts and minds" programme to win support, all the programme did in Rhodesia was alienate rural dwellers even more, who saw it as collective punishment.

The complacency of the Rhodesian government can be seen in its dealings in the course of 1973 with Bishop Abel Muzorewa and his African National Council. It took an approach from Muzorewa to

Smith in July for talks to be reopened. When they did Smith stuck rigidly to the 1971 proposals and in the course of the talks several ANC members were arrested, adding further pressure to Muzorewa. On 17 August 1973, Smith and Muzorewa reached agreement and issued a joint statement: Muzorewa now accepted the 1971 proposals, falling far short of majority rule, and he would lobby the British government to accept them. Muzorewa was quickly shown to be out of step with his own executive, however, who just days after the meeting rejected them out of hand. Although the detained nationalist leaders also subsequently issued a message rejecting Muzorewa's deal, this would not have worried the RF too much. Not only did the leaders all remain in detention or prison, but also abroad the nationalist movements, embroiled in their own conflicts, were seriously divided.

In the circumstances, I wrote my O level exams at the end of 1973 with the country in a state of relative stability. All of that changed rather dramatically in the new year.

On 25 April 1974, the Carnation Revolution took place in Portugal; it was a peaceful military coup organised by low-ranking officers calling themselves the Armed Forces Movement. The colonial wars fought by the Portuguese in Angola and Mozambique were consuming as much as 40 per cent of the Portuguese budget and the cost was steadily rising. The Portuguese military was overstretched and there was no political solution or end in sight. While human losses were relatively small, the war as a whole had already entered its second decade. The Portuguese ruling Estado Novo regime faced criticism from the international community and was becoming increasingly isolated. Thousands of young men were emigrating to avoid conscription, and the wars were generally becoming increasingly unpopular. One of the first things the new rulers did was sue for peace in Mozambique and to start the process of handing over to Frelimo. In a stroke the security situation in Rhodesia deteriorated dramatically and indeed became completely untenable. The 1 231 km border between Rhodesia and Mozambique was impossible to defend; aside from its length, it was generally rugged country, ideal for guerrillas. It also extended right to the south east of the country, exposing Rhodesia's soft underbelly, with its road and rail lifelines to South Africa.

While Smith entertained ideas of Mozambique splitting in half, with Frelimo taking over the territory north of the Zambezi and everything south forming some alliance with South Africa and Rhodesia,[68] the South

African government and its prime minister, John Vorster, understood the full ramifications of the Carnation Revolution immediately. Vorster was under no illusions. He realised that Mozambique would inevitably be taken over by Frelimo and that if an accommodation with Frelimo was not reached, a variety of key South African interests would be affected: power from the Cahora Bassa hydroelectric dam on the Zambezi, Mozambican migrant labour, and the port facilities of the Mozambican capital Lourenço Marques (present-day Maputo). Furthermore, it was obvious to the South Africans that from a military perspective Rhodesia was no longer defensible. Even if it could not be said publicly, Rhodesia was expendable. South Africa needed to concentrate on its own defence. Sure enough, the Portuguese handed Mozambique over to Frelimo in September and, on 23 October 1974, Vorster spelled out to the South African parliament for the first time his vision of *détente*.

Shortly after Vorster's speech to parliament a meeting was held between Smith and the South African minister of Foreign Affairs, Hilgard Muller, in Salisbury. Muller explained that Vorster had met with a number of black leaders, including Zambia's President Kaunda, and that he believed that if the Rhodesian problem were solved, this would bring peace to the whole of Southern Africa. Kaunda had told Vorster that he was keen to settle and that he would support the South African initiative. What it required was Rhodesian cooperation and, in particular, the release of the nationalist leaders who remained in detention. South Africa and Zambia would be the main brokers of a settlement deal. Although Smith was sceptical, he agreed to their request, no doubt also alarmed by the subtle but clear indication that South Africa would not support Rhodesia wholeheartedly in a military solution. With the collapse of Portuguese support and its Mozambican ports closed to them, Rhodesia could only survive with its South African lifeline. The writing on the wall could not have been clearer to the RF government. Flower recorded in his diary on 1 December 1974: "South Africa, in search of 'detente' with black Africa, is prepared to ditch us."[69]

Pursuant to the deal, all the main nationalist leaders, including Nkomo, Sithole and Mugabe, were released from detention and flown to Lusaka early in December. After days of wrangling, a ceasefire, arranged between Vorster and Kaunda, commenced, but it was honoured more in the breach than in its observance. At the time and indeed throughout the following year the various nationalist parties, but especially ZANU, were riven with dissension and division. Kaunda and Nyerere managed to cobble together an umbrella body, the United African National Council (UANC), under the leadership of Muzorewa; Sithole (ZANU), Nkomo (ZAPU) and James Chikerema (representing a break-away smaller body, the Front for the Liberation of Zimbabwe, or FROLIZI) signed up. Kaunda and Nyerere were still suspicious of Robert Mugabe's claim to have replaced Sithole and so Mugabe took a back seat.

In February 1975, Smith was asked to travel to Cape Town to meet Vorster. Upon arrival he was greeted with the news that the South Africans would be pulling their forces out of Rhodesia. The reason given was ironic: because Rhodesia was not implementing apartheid-like policies, South Africans felt that it was a cause not worth the lives of their young men! Smith viewed the decision as "subtle blackmail" to ensure the Rhodesians stuck to the *détente* agenda; in any event the decision profoundly shocked the Rhodesian cabinet.

Two highly significant things happened shortly after the Rhodesians received this news. On 18 March 1975 the external leader of ZANU, Rhodesia's first black barrister, Herbert Chitepo, was assassinated in a car bomb blast outside his home in Lusaka. Although there was suspicion at the time that he had been murdered by elements within ZANU, Flower subsequently claimed that the Rhodesian CIO was responsible, because they saw Chitepo as a major obstacle to brokering a peace deal.[70] Whoever was responsible, the leadership of ZANU was now opened up for Mugabe, who had spent the first few months of 1975 back in Rhodesia mobilising support and lying low.

At the end of April, Mugabe managed to walk across the border with Edgar Tekere into Mozambique. Mugabe had understood the opportunities provided by his release and by Frelimo's control of Mozambique. He saw no point in negotiating with the RF and was absolutely dedicated to prosecuting the war. Mugabe was initially viewed with much suspicion by President Samora Machel, who banished both him and Tekere for the remainder of 1975 to the coastal town of Quelimane,[71] far removed from both guerrilla and refugee camps. It eventually took the determined and sustained effort of ZANLA leaders such as Solomon Mujuru and Wilfred Mhanda to secure Mugabe's acceptance by guerrillas, which only occurred in 1976.[72]

While the war in the north east appeared to be on the wane by mid 1975, the prospect of military service loomed large as I completed my final year at high school. Whereas in the past young white men could choose to delay their one-year national service and go to university first, with the growing threat, the Rhodesian government had decreed that all white boys had to do service immediately on turning eighteen, straight after school. There was considerable debate in CBC about military service but the overwhelming view among the boys was that in the face of the "communist" threat it was the honourable thing to do. Some of the brothers tried, subtly, to get us to think about the issues but they were never outspoken in encouraging us to avoid the draft. There was no doubt disquiet in many Catholic circles about what was happening in war zones. In April 1975 Father Dieter Scholz, a Jesuit priest and deputy chair of the Catholic Commission for Justice and Peace (CCJP), travelled to London with dossiers containing evidence of atrocities committed by Rhodesian security forces, which resulted in the publication of a human rights report, *The Man in the Middle.* The report graphically detailed brutal methods employed by security forces and brought the Catholic Church into conflict with the RF. At the same time the CCJP's lawyers started legal proceedings against the minister of Law and Order, Lardner-Burke, for the torture of civilians by policemen at Mount Darwin police station in the north east. To counter these legal actions, the RF rushed through notorious new legislation in parliament. One was the Compensation and Indemnity Act, which gave blanket indemnity to members of the security forces who caused injury or loss to civilians. Although it had the effect of stopping the cases dead in their tracks, it also, ironically, confirmed that the Catholic Church reports were true.

Although I had by now a deep respect for the Catholic Church because of the influence of the Irish brothers, I had not read the human rights report the Church had produced and the views of my peers predominated. I was also conscious of my young cousins on the front line in Sipolilo and so, through a combination of these factors, I became convinced of the need to do national service. This led to a series of debates within our home. The first occurred when I came home remonstrating about the number of Jewish boys my age who had left school that year early to avoid the draft. My father took issue with me on two counts. First he was appalled that my comments focused on Jews alone as there were other gentile boys who had done the same thing. In upbraiding me he said that he had not fought Hitler for his own son to make anti-Semitic comments. Secondly, he questioned whether there wasn't some merit to avoiding the draft as in his view the war was being prosecuted by unprincipled men. We had never discussed in detail what I would do, because we had never anticipated this dilemma. Our assumption all along had been that I would go straight to university after school to study law. Although I would have preferred to go on to university, all of my schoolmates at CBC were going to do national service and now I argued I should as well. I knew that if I went to university I would have to evade the draft and leave the country. My parents, especially my mother, were distressed and so began several months of discussion within our home. They did all they could to persuade me to avoid the draft but my mind was set. In my mind I was not fighting to defend UDI, the RF or Smith. Although my childish, blind support for Smith had waned a bit, I remained very naive and influenced by the overwhelmingly predominant view that white Rhodesians held, namely, that it was cowardly not to defend one's country. My friends and I were aware of the talks taking place; in my mind national service was a necessary evil to secure a smooth, gradual transition to majority rule rather than a revolution.

I decided to write my A levels mid year (November was the usual time) and resolved to start service as soon as I could. Because I wanted to do law, my parents and I agreed that I would go into the Police so that I could at the very least learn something about the law. My mother was also somewhat comforted by the thought that I was less likely to see action in the Police. The only snag was that one could not guarantee getting into the Police to do national service; generally the Police selected the cream – in Rhodesian terms that meant boys who had played first team cricket or rugby, which I had not. Accordingly, to guarantee getting into the Police I decided I would sign up for three years. I wrote my last exam at CBC, set by the British Associated Examination Board, on 4 August 1975.

In early August, Smith had agreed with Vorster that he would attend a peace conference to be held on the Victoria Falls bridge with the United African National Council (UANC). We were all hopeful that it would bring peace – it was the first time that Smith would enter direct negotiations with nationalist leaders. As it turned out the conference, which was finally held on 25 August, was a farce. In fact it was doomed from the start. For one thing the principal protagonist, Mugabe, did not even bother to attend as he was too busy mobilising for war and Vorster was hardly an "honest broker", being one of the key architects of apartheid. Smith felt bulldozed into the conference and wrote in his memoirs that the plan was "bizarre" and "impractical" and that he felt the Rhodesians were being "used as a pawn in a South African game".[73]

Several South African railway carriages were brought up and they straddled the Victoria Falls bridge. In one carriage, which had been centred above a white line marking the boundary between Zambia and Rhodesia, a long table was carefully positioned. The nationalist delegation, led by Muzorewa, Sithole, Nkomo and Chikerema, sat on the Zambian side, opposite the Rhodesian delegation, on the Rhodesian side, which was led by Smith. Nkomo felt that Smith had been "shoved to the negotiating table" and was in no mood to compromise.[74] Even Smith's own memoirs reveal this. He writes of nationalist leaders returning to "their parrot-cry of being a suppressed people who had been denied freedom in their own country" and, without a hint of irony, that he told the leaders that there was "nothing preventing them all from returning home and leading normal, peaceful lives".[75] This was being said to leaders such as Nkomo, who had been in detention for a decade and never convicted of any offence. Be that as it may, another opportunity for genuine dialogue with nationalist leaders who were prepared to consider alternatives to war, in a process backed by presidents Kaunda and Nyerere, was squandered. Even with the benefit of hindsight, it still shocks me that the RF, with all the knowledge it had at the time of the growing military threat, showed so little determination to avoid war.

A few days after the collapse of the talks, having passed my A levels, I took a train to Salisbury for interviews and medicals with the British South Africa Police. I was accepted and told to report for training on 1 October, which I duly did. I was seventeen years old.

CHAPTER 5

PEACE IS OVER AND DONE
1975 AND 1976

"For the peace, that I deem'd no peace, is over and done,
And now by the side of the Black and the Baltic deep,
And deathful-grinning mouths of the fortress, flames
The blood-red blossom of war with a heart of fire."
– ALFRED LORD TENNYSON, "MAUD"

Having decided to leave school early to join the BSAP, most of my
friends, who had been with me since Standard 3 at CBC, came to
see me off at Bulawayo railway station on Tuesday evening, 30 September
1975. My father always used the overnight train from Bulawayo to
Salisbury for his business trips and, for whites at least, it was a treat.
Blacks could only travel economy class, which comprised hard, upright
benches, impossible to sleep on. But whites travelled 1st or 2nd class;
both were luxurious with green leather-covered seats, burnished brass
fittings and solid wood finishes. I was allocated my own coupé and the
bed was made up with crisp, well-starched white sheets. As I packed my
gear into the compartment there was a great buzz of excitement from
everyone except my parents; my mother was tearful – her only child was
going off to fight in a war about which she had grave reservations.

Early the next morning on arrival in Salisbury I was collected by
a BSAP bus and driven to Morris Depot, a picturesque training camp
for white recruits situated adjacent to State House where the governors
of Southern Rhodesia and, latterly, the President of Rhodesia, lived.
On the other side of Morris Depot was Tomlinson Depot, the larger

and rather drab camp for black recruits. In the course of the day the members of Squad 7/75 congregated. In one sense we were a disparate bunch; only a few of us had A levels, one or two were Englishmen, some were sons of policemen, others sons of farmers. But in another sense we were uniform: all of us were white, and almost all had British roots. There wasn't a single Afrikaner among us. Most of us had been born in Rhodesia, and all were determined to defeat "the communist threat". The surnames themselves tell a story: Barker, Pascoe, Lovett, Tucker, Dakyns, Terry, Veronneau, Clark, Akehurst, Kenchington, Johnstone, Allman and Cowling. Coltart. We would not have been out of place on an English parade ground. For all Rhodesia's rebellion against the monarchy, the British South Africa Police was an archetypal British colonial institution. The force's name and motto, *Pro Rege, Pro Lege, Pro Patria* (for the King, Law and Country), betrayed this. No one discussed the illegality of the regime we served, nor the fundamental injustices prevailing in Rhodesia. The brothers at CBC, who had constantly challenged us to think, were now replaced by instructors who had no time for politics. Their job was to turn us from an indisciplined rabble into men who would implement orders.

We were allocated a man-mountain, one Inspector Mike Lambourne, as our training instructor and whatever illusions I had about this being a holiday camp were soon shattered. Minutes after we had signed in, he started barking instructions in a booming voice. Although it was a police training camp, it had a strong paramilitary bent. We had most of our hair shorn off, were issued with all manner of uniforms, including camouflage, and were then marched down to Ordnance and issued with brand new South African-made FN rifles. Mine was not a typical Rhodesian huntin', fishin', shootin' family – the only birdies I had ever shot were the few I had managed on the golf course – so just firing my first shot with a high velocity automatic rifle was a petrifying experience.

We were told in the first few days that our squad was to be in training for some nine months; we were to be an equitation squad which would only pass out when parliament was opened midway through the following year with its police escort. Each of us was allocated a horse; in my case two, a beautiful chestnut gelding called Cadet and deep brown mare called Flair. Equitation required an early start to the day. We had to put on puttees and jodhpurs (the former having to be wound equidistant around one's calves), clean out the stables and present the horse we were riding in perfect condition before 5 am. On the first day I attempted this, I thought I had presented myself perfectly before the equitation instructor, Section Officer Hacking. The instructor's calling was always to find something wrong; after failing to find any impediment, such as sawgrass in my horse's tail or a loose thread on my uniform, he finally scowled at my legs and said, "Coltart, where did you get those legs from?!" I am a skinnymalink at the best of times but the puttees had accentuated my pins, so I shouted back (as we always had to): "Lion Match Company, sir!" As quick as a flash he responded, "Well, Coltart, then you had bloody well better not get them wet today or they will fall off!"

A few days later in the training ring I had allowed Cadet to get too far behind the other horses and he took it upon himself to gallop and catch up. In the course of the gallop I, being a novice rider, fell off. Hacking came charging up to me and berated me, while restraining a laugh, for "dismounting without permission".

The instructors' sense of humour shown in those early exchanges blunted the initial shock of not having any of my home comforts and before long it started to become an adventure.

Were it not for the unjust and futile cause, the training was of great benefit to a pampered teenager like me. I learnt to make my own bed, wash my own clothes, polish my boots and keep my room tidy – none of which I had been adept at before. Although physically demanding, it was all new and exciting; I was learning new skills such as drill, shooting, typing, defensive driving, criminal law and first aid. Each squad had to navigate an assault course with terrifying obstacles in the fastest possible time. Most things had to be done on the double and we underwent long training runs and marches. Within weeks I was fitter than I'd ever been. Because I was the only member of my squad who played cricket, I was released to practise and play for the police team. The food was plentiful and good; the beer cheap (subsidised) and drunk in the rowdy but warm company of one's comrades. At the end of each day there was always plenty to laugh about in the mess.

The tone of the training reflected the state of the war during those last few months of 1975. The nationalist armies were in such disarray that there was hardly any action in the north east. We were primarily being trained as policemen to go out and investigate crime, rather than fight a war.

But with the benefit of hindsight the thrust of my training also reflected a shocking gulf between intelligence being provided to the RF cabinet and its response to it. Flower writes of Rhodesia's "no-win" position deteriorating to a "losing" position by the end of 1975. The CIO knew that ZANLA guerrillas were penetrating south along Rhodesia's eastern border and that guerrilla recruitment in the second half of 1975 had soared to unprecedented levels. They knew that whereas guerrilla strength was measured in scores for a decade, "never totalling more than 300", it was now "numbering in thousands". This was all put in a paper submitted to cabinet in September 1975.[76] Flower records his frustration – the government had an "ostrich-like stance", he said, and its continued policies were "utterly illogical".

With full knowledge of these dire warnings, Smith entered into further talks with Nkomo and a declaration of intent to negotiate was signed by the two men on 1 December 1975. A conference began in earnest in Salisbury on 11 December. It had the backing of presidents Kaunda and Nyerere, with the latter sending one of Nkomo's six legal advisers, Roland Brown, to attend.[77] Writing later about the events Smith was vague about what happened in the talks but Nkomo gave a lot of detail: his delegation went to "great lengths", he claimed, to offer acceptable conditions, including seats reserved for white people. But the RF wouldn't budge in its opposition to majority rule and so the talks dragged on.

There was no discernible change to our training routine through December and as far as we knew we were scheduled to be in Morris Depot for several months still. I had heard that a few of my CBC friends were going to be starting their national service in January, including my closest friend Mark Gilmore, and I wrote to my parents rejoicing that we were all going to pass out together in March 1976. Part of Christmas that year was spent guarding the whole of Police General Headquarters (PGHQ) on my own. The blue, multi-storeyed, castle-like building was set in beautiful gardens, next to State House and diagonally opposite the prime minister's residence, which at the time was called Independence. Remarkably, the security of the building was lax and the entire headquarters, containing, as it must have done, highly sensitive information, was left in my care from 5 pm on Christmas Eve to midday on Christmas Day. My parents, who had driven up from Bulawayo to spend Christmas with me, popped in and spent a few hours with me. Had anyone chosen to attack they would have found a very unprepared guard.

The lag between the CIO's warning about the deteriorating security situation and government policy suddenly narrowed at the end of the year. Shortly after Christmas it was announced that our training was to be curtailed and that we were now going to pass out on 15 January instead. The new year also brought our first Counter Insurgency (COIN) training, which was clearly rushed. Although we had done route marches within Salisbury and had had some training in depot, this was the first time we were taken to the bush. The "bush" in fact was Goromonzi Tribal Trust Lands (TTLs), a short distance outside Salisbury. We started with a few days at a camp where we were taught bush-patrol formations, skirmishing, map reading, tracking, rudimentary tracking and how to identify land-mines buried in gravel roads. Then, armed with this 101 course in fighting a guerrilla war, we were divided up into squads and ordered to get from A to B across the TTL in the course of a few days. It was the first time I had ever had to negotiate across the countryside and as most of the squad were also "townies" like me, it was a case of the blind leading the blind. We all eventually managed to get to our rendezvous without much incident, but in retrospect it was hardly adequate training for what we were about to face.

Within a few days of returning to depot from the COIN exercise our passing out ceremony was held, with little of the pomp and ceremony we had expected. A relatively junior officer was our guest of honour; there was no police band and the ceremony only involved our squad and a squad of policewomen. I had been adjudged the best recruit of Squad 7/75 and so in the course of the ceremony marched up to the dais to collect my certificate. A photograph was taken of me which was published in the BSAP magazine *Outpost* and kept in the police archives. A quarter of a century later that photograph would be hauled out by ZANU PF and used on the second page of Mugabe's 2002 presidential election manifesto, alleging that it proved that I had been in the Selous Scouts and was a murderer.

One of the privileges of being best recruit, so I was told, was that I was permitted to choose which province to be posted to. Oblivious to the mounting danger in that province, I applied for Manicaland but, providentially, my request was denied and I found myself posted to Matabeleland. Bulawayo felt deserted because all my schoolmates had started their national service training by then. While the powers that be were deciding where to send me, I was allocated to the riot squad in Bulawayo.

Within days of arriving we were told that Nkomo was flying in to Bulawayo and we would have to monitor his visit. I was astounded by his reception: thousands of people came out to Bulawayo airport to welcome him and we had great difficulty keeping the massive crowd from deluging the apron. We then accompanied the winding procession of tens of cars, buses and trucks back to an area adjacent to Nkomo's home in Pelandaba and the White City football stadium, where a massive crowd awaited him. We were swamped by a sea of people, but what amazed me was that the crowd was good-natured and I never once felt scared. Nkomo called for peace and spoke about the difficulties they were having in the ongoing talks, but he was never inflammatory, and after encouraging the crowd he ended the gathering and the crowd dispersed peacefully. The goodwill of the people that day was palpable.

After spending February in Bulawayo, I finally drove out to war in my lime green 1968 VW Beetle, which I had inherited from my beloved maternal grandmother Ada Hensley who had died in 1974. I had been posted to a sleepy village called Kezi, 100 km south of Bulawayo. I drove out alone on a narrow tar road, the first part of which was well known and loved by me. The road south takes one through the Matobo Hills, where Rhodes is buried at what he termed World's View. It is no wonder he was enchanted by the place – Matobo is the name given to the hills by the Ndebele king Mzilikazi and means "bald heads". It is an exquisite wilderness of granite kopjes, lusciously wooded valleys, wetlands, rivers and dams covering an area of 3 100 km², of which 424 km² is a national park. Maleme Rest Camp, within the national park, was a favourite of ours and many weekends were spent there with my parents during my childhood. Now, for the first time, I drove through and beyond the hills to the flat plains which lie to its south and extend to the Shashe River, which forms the border with Botswana. The Kezi police district, bounded by the hills to the north and the great mile-wide sandy Shashe River to the south, was divided into two very distinct and different portions: white commercial ranch land in the north and a black poverty trap – Tribal Trust Lands, which included Nkomo's home near St Joseph's Mission at Mbembeswana – in the south.

I arrived in Kezi at the very end of an era that had lasted several decades. The village itself was tiny. It was located on the southern bank of the normally dry Mwewe River and boasted a row of spartan stores, a post office, district commissioner's offices, a club (for whites only) and the police camp. Aside from the police charge office and cells, there were two old colonial homes for the member in charge and his deputy, a modern four-bedroomed house for the single white officers and several rows of much smaller houses for the black non-commissioned police officers. A kilometre from the police station was the club, which had tennis courts, a pool and a squash court. Our day started with "Stables" at 6.30 am. Although horse patrols had been phased out, the tradition stood, only now it was the Land Rovers we checked every day. We stood down at 4.30 pm and the evenings were usually pretty raucous affairs down at the club, where many of the local white civil servants and farmers congregated. There was no security threat at that time and the general atmosphere appeared to be relaxed. On 9 March I wrote to my parents:

> "Today I went out with Constable Sibanda (probably my best friend I have made so far!) to two assaults. We did about 120kms, driving all over TTLs and going into villages. One is certainly treated like gold when entering a village and this is the police work that appealed to me when I joined."[78]

Race relations, at least on the surface, appeared good both within the camp and between the police and the general public. After years of indoctrination about white supremacy, the naive assumption that an eighteen-year-old patrol officer, as I was, could easily command experienced black policemen came naturally. This was the first time in my life that I had had any interaction with black people in any circumstance other than a master/servant relationship. But my life was to depend on the support I received from my black "subordinates" so I was relieved by the warmth of their reception. Within weeks I was to find that these men were highly competent and completely reliable. I was also to find within a few months that my assessment about the state of race relations was wrong.

There was still hope that a peaceful settlement might be arrived at. Nkomo, who, not unexpectedly, was deeply revered in his home area, was still in negotiations with Smith, and everyone knew that. But in mid March the talks finally collapsed. The RF would not budge on majority rule. The most they were prepared to offer was the prospect of bringing some black leaders into cabinet. Later Nkomo wrote the following:

"In talking to Smith I took a big personal risk. I am still criticised for trying to negotiate with Smith. I longed for majority rule in Zimbabwe, and justice for my people. I wanted those things with as little killing as possible, and with as little bitterness as possible between the white people and the black people who had an equal right to live in the new nation of Zimbabwe. I knew all too well that fierce fighting would mean grave problems at the end of the war. But now it had to start again, and I was to do my share."[79]

A few days after the talks collapsed, on 20 March 1976, Smith gave a national broadcast on radio in which he said: "Let me say it again. I don't believe in black majority rule ever in Rhodesia, not in a thousand years. I repeat that I believe in blacks and whites working together. If one day it is white and the next day it is black, I believe we have failed and it will be a disaster for Rhodesia."

The collapse of those talks came as a blow, especially in Kezi because there was so much hope that they would work. The talks were the "last chance saloon" for the avoidance of war. Although Mugabe and ZANU were organising flat out for war, Nkomo had the support of Nyerere and Kaunda and, most importantly, was a long-standing, credible nationalist leader. Although the war would probably not have been avoided, it would have been much more difficult for ZANU to prosecute alone. On the eastern border the war was already escalating rapidly. In February there had been attacks at Chipinga[80] tea estates in the south of Manicaland and in the Honde Valley, near the tourist area of Inyanga,[81] indicating the spread of ZANLA infiltration. In early March, Samora Machel had closed the border and announced that Mozambique was now at war with Rhodesia. With the collapse of the Nkomo talks, the possibility of the Zambian front opening became a reality and there were warnings of massive recruitment of youth taking place along areas adjacent to the Botswana border.

In the context of that threat, I was ordered to start my first border patrol along the Shashe River on 12 April. Aside from my brief COIN training at Morris Depot, this was the first time I had gone on patrol, let alone in a curfew area, let alone in command of other men, in this case constables Murima and Kanye-Kanye. The area along the Shashe River is desolate and thinly populated, the river a mile-wide channel of sand for most of the year, flanked by massive acacia trees. There had been good rains upstream and so a third of the expanse of sand was flooded, but even so it was easy to walk across the river to Botswana as there were no fences and, unlike the Limpopo, very few crocodiles. The three of us bailed out of the Land Rover (which was being driven by another policeman) as it moved slowly through a small river bed so that our presence would not be noticed, but we should not have bothered because the imposition of a curfew within a five-kilometre cordon sanitaire was effective. Every day we set up an OP (observation point) in some thicket along the river before moving along in the late afternoon and then, just before dusk, setting up an ambush position for the night. What would have happened if we had come across a well-trained section of guerrillas God only knows. We were lightly armed; each of us had an FN rifle with three magazines. On the second day I tried in vain to radio our base, only to discover that the batteries ran completely flat within a minute. Even if the radio had worked, the nearest base was at Sun Yet Sen police camp, which was hours away by vehicle and a good 40 kilometres as the crow flies. Despite this it was a wonderful time; Murima and Kanye-Kanye were excellent company and both men had a wicked sense of humour. It was the first time that I had ever spent any length of time with black men. These two constables initiated my love of the Zimbabwean staple *sadza/isitshwala*[82] and relish which, as is so often the case with "camp cooking", was heavenly. They were also bush smart and began teaching me practical bushcraft. More than anything, I knew implicitly that I could trust them, which I did. It would have been the easiest thing in the world for them to overpower me and force me across the river to Botswana; on the contrary, I sensed that if we were attacked, these men would watch my back. So five days passed with me soaking up all they had to teach me, enjoying the African bush, the stunning stars at night and the occasional whoop of a hyena. We hardly saw anything – a few tracks of people crossing the river, an old man who had been allowed to stay in the curfew area to harvest his crops, an abandoned irrigation project on the confluence of the Shashe and Mambale rivers. My greatest disappointment getting back to Kezi was to discover that what I thought was a magnificent tan was in fact dark orange Shashe dust which simply washed off in the shower.

A day after getting back, the gravity of the war was brought forcefully home. On the early evening of 18 April four young white South African tourists riding motorcycles came across what appeared to be a robbery on the Fort Victoria/Beitbridge road. It was in fact a group of twelve ZANLA guerrillas who proceeded to gun them down. The effect of that attack was profoundly shocking; those of us who were unaware of the spread of guerrilla activity suddenly woke up to the reality that Rhodesia's lifeline to South Africa was under threat. The attack took place several hundred kilometres from the Mozambique border and worryingly close to South Africa. Unbeknown to us was that thousands of ZANLA guerrillas had been infiltrating for months along the eastern border, deep into the south east of the country and they were only now showing their presence.

The RF responded to this threat ten days later by bringing in some black ministers to give government, in Flower's words, "a multiracial veneer". A few moderate chiefs, including chiefs Jeremiah Chirau and Kayisa Ndiweni (representing Shona and Ndebele people respectively) were brought into cabinet. It was clear even to me as an eighteen-year-old that it wasn't going to work. On 3 May I wrote the following in a letter to my parents:

> "I am not very pleased with Mr Smith's statement of policy. It is clear to the world and even to the most ignorant that these Chiefs are basically just glorified civil servants and are merely puppets. Mr Smith talks of a coalition government, but the trouble is that the Chiefs have not been elected to Parliament and are not members of any political party, so what parties does the coalition consist of? I am still pro-Smith, but I do think that this is one of the biggest mistakes he has made. The trouble with Mr Smith's policy is that he has almost taken the law into his own hands and where does he go from here. At least in the past the RF was elected lawfully into Parliament but now it seems that Mr Smith has got the power to pick and choose the exact people he wants to be in Parliament. As I am still forming my ideas and theories, I have yet to hit the nail on the head – but I am amazed at Mr Smith trying to fool the world with such a feeble move."[83]

Smith, in fact, did not fool the world and the war got under way in earnest. Having believed Smith against the views of my parents for so many years, I was in the uncomfortable position of realising my error and that letter was the first admission I made of it.

Kezi, in the south west of the country, was a long way from the Mozambique border and so there was no obvious security threat and life continued as normal. In another letter to my parents later that month, I wrote presciently: *"Crime wise, Kezi has been amazingly quiet – almost as if the locals are brewing up for something."* On 17 May I did another border patrol, this time with my first friend made at Kezi, Sibanda, who had just passed his exams to become a sergeant, and Murima. Again it was serenely quiet and the greatest excitement came on the final day when a Rhodesian Air Force Hawker Hunter jet came barrelling up the Shashe River just a few hundred metres over us, early in the morning; we were already in an OP and camouflaged so it didn't see us. It evoked mixed emotions in me, however – one was a feeling of terror at the prospect of having that machine coming at me, but with it came the realisation that, firstly, it was travelling too fast to see me and, secondly, it was on our side in any event.

The patrol ended on 20 May. I couldn't wait because I had short leave due to me and, what was more, all my schoolmates had finished their training by then and were going to be back in Bulawayo for the weekend prior to being deployed throughout the country.

Although none of us had then tasted the full horror of war, our times together became escapist; weekends home were drunken affairs and that weekend was no exception. A certain mythology had built up in our minds about white Rhodesian conscripts – we were the best trained, bravest, brightest young men in the world and could drink anyone under the table. That Friday evening, 21 May, was no exception and I woke up late the next morning with a cracker of a hangover. That afternoon I received a call from a very anxious member in charge ordering me to return to base immediately; he couldn't tell me anything save that there had been a "terrorist attack" and I was needed for the follow up. The security situation had been so peaceful that I had not even brought my FN rifle into town with me, and so I faced the prospect of driving back to Kezi in the gathering gloom weaponless and not having any clue where or how this attack had taken place. A friend loaned me a 9mm pistol and a friend of my mother's, a devout Catholic, came by as I was leaving, pinned a St Christopher on my chest and prayed for me as I drove off alone. My mother stood in the driveway and waved me off in floods of tears.

After a nervous, skittish drive back, I arrived to the news that early that morning a local farmer, Jacob van Vuuren, and his fourteen-year-old son had been shot in cold blood by a lone ZIPRA guerrilla, who had waved them down as they drove to their farm. When they stopped to give him a lift he pulled out an AK-47 and gunned them down. Jock Meaklim, a schoolfriend of mine who was doing his national service in the BSAP, and who was also stationed at Kezi, had attended the scene. He was still in shock by what he had witnessed.

It was our first, shocking, taste of war, and the atmosphere in Kezi changed overnight. Security was beefed up, communications with farmers, doctors and teachers in the district improved, and the army moved in. But local attitudes also changed – and for the worse. The somewhat relaxed and carefree interaction between police and the public was replaced by suspicion and growing hostility. My own terminology changed too. For the first time in letters home I referred to "terrs" – terrorists – and wrote of the need to catch and deal with "these murderers".

Unbeknown to us at the time, the murder of the Van Vuurens was a result of seismic changes that were taking place within the nationalist armies. The single body to represent all the nationalist forces that had been formed in Lusaka in late 1975 had been accompanied by an OAU order that all weapons and materiel be channelled through this body, the UANC. This in turn had caused the formation of the Zimbabwe People's Army (ZIPA), including both ZIPRA and ZANLA, and a concomitant integrated command system under Solomon Mujuru aka Rex Nhongo. However, in October 1975 ZANLA guerrillas had issued the Mgagao Declaration, which included a statement that they only trusted Mugabe and would only speak to the UANC through Mugabe.[84] Within months the relationship between ZIPRA and ZANLA combatants in Mozambique had broken down and fighting erupted between the two forces. Totally outnumbered, ZIPRA guerrillas fled Mozambique and many made their way back to Zambia through Rhodesia and Botswana. One of these guerrillas, Rogers Nkala, had made his way from Mozambique and was on the last leg of his journey to Botswana when he had flagged down the Van Vuurens, murdered them, stolen their car and used it to flee to the Botswana border. He would have crossed over a section of the Shashe I had patrolled just the week before. It was not the last we were to hear of Rogers Nkala.

Although the Van Vuuren murders shook up the entire Kezi

community and led to a flurry of activity as everyone prepared for war, in reality it was the only hostile guerrilla incident we experienced in the district for the entire seventeen-month period I was stationed there until July 1977. However, our method of policing changed: for a start our standard grey Land Rover station wagons were replaced with mine-protected, camouflaged Land Rovers and a variety of other purpose-built vehicles – each with animal names such as Puma, Crocodile and Kudu. We were supplied with a Hyena, a troop carrier built on a VW chassis designed to protect its occupants from ambushes and land-mines. It was constructed of thick steel plate and armoured glass, in a V-shape to dissipate the blast of both land-mines and RPG 7 rockets. Arriving in such military-type vehicles destroyed any pretence that we were just policemen arriving at a crime scene. Inevitably, fear and distrust between the public and police grew.

Two incidents which happened in the months that followed illustrate the tension. The first occurred when I was on vehicle patrol with newly promoted Sergeant Sibanda in the northern commercial farming area of the district. This area is particularly beautiful, bounded as it is by the southern reaches of the Matobo Hills and dominated by its highest mountain, Silozwe. Our job was to check every farmhouse in the area, many of which were unoccupied. One afternoon I had inspected a Christian camp, Shalom, located on one of the farms. I had been to it once before as a schoolboy on a Cub camp but now it was hauntingly deserted. In a sense it was a metaphor for the country – my memory of a vibrant, packed camp full of excited little boys replaced by lonely fear as cautiously, rifles at the ready, we went through all the huts to check there was no evidence of a guerrilla presence. From there we drove on to the next farmhouse, Luma, which was marked on our inventory as unoccupied. Luma farmhouse, which sits on a slight rise commanding a magnificent view of Mount Silozwe, is approached by a long driveway flanked by bougainvillaea. As we slowly drove up the driveway we became aware of raucous laughter and music coming from the house. Guerrillas had been known to break into abandoned farmhouses so, fearing the worst, Sibanda and I quickly debussed, radioed for assistance, and then leopard-crawled up to the house expecting a firefight to break out any second. However, as I got closer I recognised white Rhodesian accents so I called out, maintaining my position behind cover. Four white men in Rhodesian camouflage emerged from the house. It turned out that one of them was the owner of the farm, Andy Conolly. He and three of his mates were on call-up and together constituted a Police Anti Terrorist Unit (PATU) which was meant to be patrolling the Shashe River over 100 kilometres to the south of where they were. They had tired of their patrol, somehow got a lift north to Luma and had started a few days of very comfortable rest and recuperation, reporting back to base by radio periodically that all was well on the Shashe! Andy Conolly has since become a good friend and I still unmercifully pull his leg about his conduct helping us lose the war.

The second incident, which occurred in late July, brought the story of Rogers Nkala full circle. After escaping to Botswana, Nkala had rejoined ZIPRA in Zambia and was promptly redeployed back into Rhodesia. He made his way to Luveve township in Bulawayo where his presence was discovered. The house he was in was surrounded and after a fierce firefight with police details he was shot dead. The powers that be decided that an example should be made of him; his bloody, mutilated body was sent out to Kezi and taken for display to all the areas he had passed through before and after the Van Vuuren murder. Finally, the body was taken to his home area in the neighbouring police district of Tuli, where, without notice, it was dumped in the yard of his distraught mother. Needless to say, the intended purpose of this all, to shock and intimidate, had the opposite effect. Attitudes simply hardened.

The treatment of Nkala's body reflected a general hardening of attitudes in Salisbury and a determination to ignore the Geneva Convention. Guerrillas were to be treated as terrorists; they were viewed as criminals, not soldiers. With guerrillas penetrating in massive numbers along the entire Mozambique border, pressure also grew for preventative strikes into Mozambique. In late July, the Selous Scouts were given permission to reconnoitre a suspected ZANLA base at the Nyadzonia River in Mozambique about 50 kilometres from the Rhodesian border. In an audacious raid some 84 Selous Scouts in fourteen vehicles, disguised as Frelimo soldiers, drove into the camp, called the occupants to a gathering point and then mowed them down with rifles and anti-aircraft guns mounted on the backs of trucks. Some 1 028 men, women and children were killed. A further 309 were wounded and 1 000 were listed as missing.[85] Although there is dispute over whether Nyadzonia was a refugee camp or a ZANLA training camp, the truth appears to be somewhere in between. Ken Flower described it as nothing more than "a staging camp in which low level training took place".[86] Edgar Tekere, one-time secretary general of ZANU, the man who had accompanied Mugabe when he crossed into Mozambique in 1975, later told Granada Television that it was a "military installation".[87] Whatever the case, it was a massacre – over two thousand people were killed, there was hardly any fire returned, there were no Selous Scouts fatalities and only one of them was seriously injured. The extraordinarily low Rhodesian casualties give the lie to it being primarily a military training camp, but perhaps the most damning indictment was Flower's statement: "(The Security Force) communiqué was 'terse' because we were not prepared to take responsibility for lying about the nature of the raid and could not devise a formula which would account for the death of such large numbers of unarmed, untrained people."[88]

Although from a narrow military perspective the raid was successful, from every other perspective it was disastrous. Prime Minister Vorster, embarrassed by the raid, punitively withdrew South African helicopter pilots. The massacre also energised Machel and Nyerere; the former called all the nationalist leaders to Maputo and then sent them to Nyadzonia.[89] Both presidents convened a summit in Dar es Salaam in early September and committed themselves to "throw their full weight behind the guerrillas". Nyerere handed the huge Nachingwea camp in southern Tanzania over to ZIPA. He also insisted on agreement being reached regarding a united front – culminating in the formation of the Patriotic Front, an alliance of the militant nationalists.

The attack on Nyadzonia was the first of numerous raids into Mozambique and Zambia in the coming years; while some were against genuine military training camps, many were not. The vastly different, and disproportionate, casualty rate between attackers and defenders remains one of the most serious indictments against Rhodesian forces. The flood of youth streaming out of Rhodesia for training continued to increase. If anything, passions were inflamed even more. The incursions of guerrillas into Rhodesia continued unabated, which should have served as a stark reminder to the Rhodesian government that even missions like this – "successful" in the eyes of some – that killed hundreds, made little impact on the conduct of the war. Perhaps worst of all, Nyadzonia has left a bitter legacy to this day. Hundreds more young black people were killed in a few hours than the total number of whites who died during the entire war. This incident more than any other has left a searing wound, one

69

that still poisons relationships between whites and blacks in Zimbabwe.

In the year I had been in the police, Rhodesia had changed dramatically. In September 1975 only the north east of the country was affected by a low-grade infiltration of a guerrilla army which was split and in chaos. Just a year later thousands of guerrillas had infiltrated more than half the country. Despite the mayhem all around me, I still had a charmed time of it. I had not been shot at and I had not had to fire a shot in combat myself. With benefit of hindsight I can see that providence saw me posted to one of the safest districts in the country. Although it was a border district, Kezi adjoined a relatively neutral country, Botswana, and was almost equidistant from our two hostile neighbours, Mozambique and Zambia.

CHAPTER 6

ALL OUT WAR
SEPTEMBER 1976 TO FEBRUARY 1978

"We make war that we may live in peace."
> – ARISTOTLE, NICOMACHEAN ETHICS

A few days after Machel and Nyerere's summit in Dar es Salaam in early September 1976 with nationalist leaders, Vorster held a meeting in Switzerland with US Secretary of State Henry Kissinger. After South Africa's failed foray into Angola to defeat the Cuban-backed MPLA, Vorster was all the more keen to settle the Rhodesian crisis. South-West Africa, with almost double the number of Afrikaners than Rhodesia, was a greater strategic interest. South African Intelligence had repeatedly told Flower that they wanted to resolve the Rhodesian crisis before they were forced into a settlement over South-West Africa.[90] It was Vorster's belief that if he could use Rhodesia as a foil he would get American support for a more favourable settlement. The international outcry over Nyadzonia brought the deepening crisis in Rhodesia into sharp focus, prompting the meeting in Switzerland, itself a culmination of months of discussions between Vorster and Kissinger. The quid pro quo was that the US would support anti-Marxist groups in Angola and reduce pressure on the South-West African Question in exchange for increased South African pressure on Smith.

Vorster invited Smith to a meeting in Pretoria on 14 September to outline the broad terms of his discussions with Kissinger. Not so subtle pressure was already being exerted by the South Africans to the extent that Smith had to include his minister of Transport in the delegation because South Africa was experiencing "transport bottlenecks"... affecting Rhodesia's "vital supplies".[91] In fact, Rhodesian railway wagons were seriously backed up in South Africa. The game was now up – the RF would have to agree to a new constitution leading to majority rule within two years. There would be an interim Council of State which would share power; and a trust fund of US$2 billion would be set up to stabilise the country. Kissinger was confident he had the backing of Kaunda and Nyerere for the plan. Smith was invited to notify his cabinet and to meet with Kissinger at the end of the week.

On Sunday, 19 September, Kissinger met with Vorster and Smith at Libertas, the South African prime minister's residence in Pretoria. Although he was sympathetic, Kissinger spelt out five terms:

1. The Rhodesian government had to agree to majority rule within two years;
2. Rhodesian representatives would meet black leaders to work out an interim government until majority rule was implemented;
3. The interim government would consist of a Council of State half white and black with a white chairman;
4. All members would have to swear an oath that they would work for rapid progress to majority rule; and
5. The United Kingdom and Rhodesia would enact enabling legislation to bring about majority rule.

Smith haggled about the need for "responsible" majority rule and wondered whether it would not be better to renounce UDI, but at the end of the day Kissinger prevailed. He pointed out that both Machel and Nyerere favoured a military victory and would use any excuse to back out. Also Kissinger was unconfident of success in the forthcoming US elections and felt that the Democrats would be far less sympathetic. The British had essentially wiped their hands of the issue. The Soviets were eager to support the nationalist armies. In short, as Smith later told the Rhodesian public, "The alternative to accepting the proposals was (explained) in the clearest of terms, which left no room for misunderstanding."[92]

The RF had painted itself into a corner. Even its closest allies were unable to get them out of it. On 24 September Smith announced on radio the RF's acceptance of the Kissinger proposals, for the first time accepting majority rule, albeit his own version of it: "It will be a 'majority rule' constitution … we support majority rule, provided it is responsible rule."[93]

* * *

In the same month that all these dramatic events were taking place, my thoughts on everything that was happening in the country were challenged in unusual circumstances. Intelligence had been received that ZIPRA guerrillas were infiltrating the north of the district in the Matobo Hills and I was despatched to conduct a foot patrol through the commercial farms that bordered the hills. My mandate was to sweep through "likely looking hiding places", and to assist me in this I was accompanied by, for the first time, a San tracker named Maplank. Constable Mangwiro, Maplank and I started scouring the hills from the west, going into every nook and cranny. Maplank was highly skilled and gave a non-stop commentary, sharing intricate details of all the animals that had crossed our path. On the evening of the second day we arrived at Gumela, a lush, well-watered farm with numerous dams and, a novelty in dry Matabeleland, two perennial streams. Gumela was owned by former RF MP Allan Savory and we were warmly welcomed by his business partner Tom Orford, his wife Dawn and Savory's daughter, Megan. I was immediately struck by the respect shown towards Maplank and Mangwiro, so unlike the disparaging attitude shown by many white farmers. We based up at Gumela for two nights, spending the intervening day walking deep into the Matopos to investigate, unsuccessfully, a report that ZIPRA were recruiting around the Njelele mountain shrine. On both evenings I ended up in deep political discussions with the Orfords. Tom Orford was an outstanding environmentalist (he had been involved in Operation Noah, which was set up to rescue wildlife trapped by rising water following the construction of the Kariba dam). He was one of the first few in the game department, started Kyle National Park, and brought the first white rhino into Rhodesia. He also shared Alan Savory's political views and so was outspoken against the RF. He was sceptical about the RF's willingness to move towards majority rule and highly critical of the way the war was being conducted. It was difficult to argue against him; his life's work demonstrated a deep love of the country and he had a wealth of knowledge about what was actually happening in the country. In particular he felt the war was unwinnable and was grievously poisoning relationships between black and white. Orford's sentiments matched what I had observed recently, so I left Gumela with much food for thought, if not yet conviction.

My letters home from this point describe a growing sense of disquiet. On 13 October I wrote: *"Kezi, fortunately, is quiet but the feeling out here is that we are all sitting around a time bomb and we know it is going to go off – we are just not sure when."*[94] And on 31 October: *"… today's [security] communiques were rather disheartening … an indication of things to come."*[95] This feeling was compounded when my schoolfriend Mark Gilmore related an incident when we were jointly on leave that month in Bulawayo. Gilmore had been posted to a remote police station, Tuli, in a neighbouring district, in September. Shortly after his arrival there, a territorial army unit was deployed into the area on border patrols. With the growing guerrilla presence, a new operational area, "Tangent", had been proclaimed and with it a curfew from 6 pm until 6 am. On the day the unit left the district, Gilmore came across their trucks and was struck by the soldiers' exuberance about the success of a recent "contact". He thought nothing further of it until a few days later he saw photographs of the people who had been killed in the contact. About ten people had been shot – most of them were children. Nearly all the deceased had gunshot wounds to their heads, something very unusual for a curfew ambush which, according to the soldiers, had taken place within the curfew period at dusk. Then parents of the children came to the police station to report that the incident had taken place well before the curfew. A murder docket was opened by Tuli police but Gilmore was profoundly shocked when the case was closed on the instructions of the district commanding officer.

Gilmore and I had both recently turned nineteen. It was becoming hard to understand how fighting for law and order, Christianity and Western civilisation was compatible with our superiors' actions of turning a blind eye to cold-blooded murder. The Catholic bishop of Manicaland, Donal Lamont, had recently written an open letter to Smith complaining of the "barbarity" of Rhodesian security forces and the "absurdity" of justifying it in the name of Christianity. Although Lamont was viewed by us at the time as a "terrorist sympathiser", for me there was more than a ring of truth in what he said. Superficially my views did not change, but my confidence in the justness of the Rhodesian cause started to be seriously undermined at this juncture.

Amidst this anxiety, I hoped that the Kissinger proposals would yield an end to the war. My father for the first time felt that Smith was at last acting sensibly and we were all encouraged when a conference was convened by the British government in Geneva to implement the Kissinger proposals. With the benefit of hindsight the conference was doomed from the beginning but at the time we held out great hopes for it. The British appointed their ambassador to the UN, Ivor Richard, to chair the summit, but he was unable to overcome the deep antagonism and distrust between the parties. The principal protagonists, Smith and Mugabe, were cut from the same cloth. Neither demonstrated the statesmanship of Mandela and De Klerk when those two men would bring South Africa back from the brink in the 1990s. Although Mandela and De Klerk negotiated in vastly different circumstances, it is difficult to imagine that they would have been so willing, as it seemed Smith and Mugabe were, to let war determine the outcome.

The RF delegation believed that the purpose of the conference was to implement the Kissinger proposals; the proposals were, of course, proposals that had been agreed to by Smith and Kissinger without any discussion with or input from nationalist leaders. The nationalist delegations, therefore, believed that the Kissinger proposals were merely a *basis* for negotiation and that the principal reason for the conference was to arrange the transfer of power to a black government. The opening few weeks dealt with a projected date for independence with the RF wanting the two-year period they had agreed with Kissinger, and Mugabe and Nkomo arguing for this to happen sooner, namely, on 1 December 1977. Mugabe adopted a particularly hardline position early on, advising the conference that "none of the white exploiters will be allowed to keep an acre of their land".[96]

This was the first time that Mugabe had attended an international meeting and had come face to face with Smith. The two men clashed from the very beginning, trading insults. Further haggling moved the date to 1 March 1978, a suggested British compromise. The conference dragged on for weeks, going nowhere. Smith returned to Rhodesia, saying he had a country to run. He went back to Geneva in early December, only for the conference to flounder on a nationalist desire that there be a British presence during the transition, something the RF found unacceptable.

With the conference going nowhere, the British Foreign Secretary Anthony Crosland decided in mid December to adjourn it. Smith and

Mugabe left, both determined to pursue their own agendas. The British tried to resuscitate the conference early in 1977 but failed. There was deep mutual distrust between the nationalists and the RF and both sides had little desire to settle. Mugabe in particular felt that he was gaining the upper hand in the war and there were strong elements within the RF who felt that they could survive without a settlement. The RF would not budge from its position that the Kissinger deal was "all or nothing",[97] even though they knew that the deal had not involved anyone else. The Patriotic Front would not budge from its position of a rapid handover, which they knew would be unacceptable to the RF. In short, both sides were seemingly happy for the war to continue, which it did for another three years at the cost of thousands of lives. Given Smith's majority rule concession, it seems incomprehensible today that statesmen could not have worked out a compromise formula for a peaceful transition.

News of the collapse of the Geneva talks in early 1977 coincided with me being posted to a Kezi police sub-station, Sun Yet Sen. This was a small, lonely and remote outpost much closer to the Botswana border. The prefabricated living quarters were hellishly hot, with cardboard-thin walls that offered no protection to rocket attack. The nearest help was over 50 kilometres away on a rocky dirt road which was easy to land-mine. The station itself sits on a small hill overlooking dry, unattractive scrub. In short, it had little to commend it. My sense of gloom was exacerbated by the knowledge that most of my schoolfriends were ending their year of national service and heading off to university. It was in this pessimistic mood that I was profoundly influenced from another, quite unexpected quarter. Over Christmas of 1976 I had bought Stevie Wonder's new album *Songs in the Key of Life* and in the many long hours alone at the beginning of 1977 I played it interminably. I was struck by the lyrics of many of the songs: "Pastime Paradise", "Love's in Need of Love Today", "Saturn", "Black Man", "I am Singing" and "As" are all anthems against racial discrimination, hate and injustice. Wonder's poetry and views challenged me. Powerful lyrics about justice, love and hate stood in such marked contrast to everything around me. The personal rebuke to humanity about contributing to make earth hell in the song "As" struck a deep chord within me.

Stevie Wonder's music became balm at this bleak outpost. This blind black American singer made me think long and hard about my entire belief system: about racial superiority, about my own patronising attitudes towards black people, about the justice of the war itself and of course about my own role in it. It was merely the beginning of a process. I had not at that point started seriously to question the justice of our cause but as I look back I have no doubt that God used these songs to start me along a new path.

While the war intensified in other parts of the country, for some reason it remained relatively quiet in the Kezi district for the few months I was stationed at Sun Yet Sen. We received sporadic reports of ZIPRA guerrillas recruiting, robbing buses and addressing villagers in the area, but they avoided contact with Rhodesian security forces. My only direct involvement in the war effort was when a Special Branch officer, Keith Holland, arrived from Gwanda with news that they had had a report of an arms cache. We headed off in a Land Rover to a rocky outcrop about 20 kilometres from the police station. The cache was reported to be in a cave and so we scoured the hill, eventually finding evidence of arms placed at the back of a narrow sliver in the rocks. Keith was a well-built fellow, as were the supporting soldiers, and only my skinny frame would fit down the narrow passageway. Knowing that caches were sometimes booby-trapped, I cautiously squeezed down to the end where I found several rusted AK-47 rifles and two grenades. I extracted them and handed them out one at a time to Holland. Once we got them all out into the sunlight we realised that the grenades were seriously corroded and in a bad way. There was no way we could safely take them back bouncing around on the floor of the Land Rover so it was decided that I should hold them in my hands on the journey back. "If only our mothers could see us now," I joked as the vehicle made its tortuous way back to the station along corrugated, bumpy dirt roads.

By this time I was firmly decided on studying law and so I started doing part-time studies through UNISA,[98] but it was hard going. The one benefit of going to Sun Yet Sen was that as second-in-command I now prosecuted the station's criminal cases. This kept me out of doing patrols and put me in good stead for a transfer to CID, which I applied for in March. In April I was able to go on leave for the first time and I spent it doing a tour of South African universities, visiting schoolfriends, and deciding which university I would like to go to. The normality of university contrasted dramatically with the war and for the first time I wondered whether it would be possible to curtail my service. Even though my contract extended until September 1978, I had heard that it was possible to buy oneself out early.

It seems that my feelings were shared by many servicemen at the time. Smith states that at this time there was "a definite indication of declining confidence among our fighting men" and "some were openly making plans to emigrate".[99] Flower wrote that in January 1977 the War Council was advised that the "country was losing ground militarily", to which Smith replied that he understood that there "would be no end of war until a political solution was achieved".[100] Tragically, though, there were powerful elements in the RF who would not brook compromise, and they included Dupont and Lardner-Burke. Tied to this was strong pressure being applied by the military to have more say in the way matters were conducted. Up to this point guerrilla activity had been treated as criminal activity, not a war, and the BSAP was the senior force. Smith resisted change but eventually relented and agreed to Lieutenant-General Walls becoming commander-in-chief under a new Combined Operations (COMOPS). Prior to this decision army commanders had persuaded government to conscript all whites on the basis of one-month-in and two-months-out. Rhodesia was now fully at war and any other pretence evaporated.

Even though the extreme right in cabinet were reluctant to settle, it seems that Smith was now convinced of the need to do so. In February 1977, he met Vorster and reiterated his commitment to majority rule within two years, working with a freely elected government, allowing black nationalist leaders back into the country, permitting them to canvas and being prepared to allow other countries to supervise the elections.[101] This was followed up by a meeting between Smith and the new British Foreign Secretary David Owen in April and a policy of allowing black nationalists back into the country. Sithole returned in July and lines of communication were kept open with Muzorewa and others. As history shows, this was all too little and too late as Mugabe and now Nkomo were pushing ahead with the war, and guerrillas were pushing deeper and deeper into the country.

I eventually got my wish to be transferred to CID in July and to my parents' great delight I was posted to Bulawayo. That joy was short-lived, however, because within a few days I was advised that I would alternate one month in Bulawayo with one month in an operational area. On 10 August 1977 I started my first one-month stint at Buffalo Range airport Joint Operations Command (JOC) centre, located in the centre of the Chiredzi and Triangle sugar cane farming areas in Rhodesia's lowveld. After my languid eighteen months at Kezi, I was thrown into one of the fiercest theatres of the war. Buffalo Range is only 83 kilometres from the Mozambique border and it was the nerve centre of the Rhodesian war effort in what COMOPS had named Operation Repulse and ZANLA described as the Gaza sector. The Fire Force for the region was based there with a heavy Air Force presence, mainly comprising Allouette and Bell helicopter gunships and Lynx aircraft. I had not received any prior briefing about what I would be doing so was surprised on arrival to be told that I was the JOC Special Branch "research officer". My primary task was to gather intelligence arising from all contacts with guerrillas; this involved attending battle scenes after the event to recover rifle cartridges for forensic examination, guerrilla diaries and whatever other paraphernalia they had left behind on the battleground. All killed guerrillas were to be ferried back to the JOC for fingerprinting and photographing. Captured guerrillas were handed over to more senior officers.

On 14 August I wrote home: *"I have attended several meetings with the SB Superintendent, Army and Airforce officers at the JOC – big stuff for a 19 year old who only 3 weeks ago was a Patrol officer at Kezi."*

I had attended to dead bodies in road accidents in Kezi but within days I was having to deal with the more gruesome aftermath of war – bodies ripped apart by 20 mm guns mounted on the gunships or 30 mm canon fire from Hawker Hunter jets. As the helicopters or troop carriers returned from contacts, the dead guerrillas would be delivered to the SB compound. I, with my subordinate sergeants and constables, would then take the dead men's fingerprints, scour their clothing for diaries or other means of identification and finally photograph what was left of them. More often than not their faces were grotesquely disfigured and I am sure most would have been hardly recognisable to their loved ones. Most guerrillas kept detailed diaries of where they had been, action they had been involved in and the *noms de guerre* of their comrades – all of which yielded a wealth of intelligence. All the weapons found with the guerrillas would then be recorded and taken to a nearby rifle range and fired so that the used cartridges could be recovered. Those cartridges were then sealed along with cartridges recovered at the battleground and sent off for forensic examination in Salisbury. The ballistics unit at Morris Depot was able to match cartridges to weapons, and cartridges to guerrilla incidents countrywide. Aside from providing evidence at the trials of captured guerrillas, the trail of cartridges also provided valuable intelligence about the movements of guerrillas, the size of their units and who was doing what. The entire process demonstrated the contradictory approach to the war – on the one hand each incident was treated as a crime, and yet on the other as an act of war. At the end of the evidence-gathering exercise the guerrilla corpses were covered and placed in the back of Land Rovers for subordinates to dispose of.

After two weeks of going through this daily routine I decided that I should see how and where my subordinates were burying the bodies. One afternoon we had to dispose of a dead guerrilla and I joined a black sergeant and constable in loading the body onto the open back of a Land Rover and covering it with a tarpaulin. We then drove through the centre of Chiredzi. There were schoolchildren, mothers pushing prams, farmers getting supplies on the streets we drove along, all of them ignorant of the awful load we had, going about their normal business as if there wasn't a war raging all around them. The sergeant, who was permanently based at Buffalo Range, had done this umpteen times before and knew the complicated route through the bush beyond Chiredzi to a mine shaft. When we arrived we uncovered the mine shaft and hauled the shattered body off the vehicle. As we did so the body's torso caught on a jagged flap and we battled to unhook it; it felt like a final protest from this unknown guerrilla. The body was then thrown down the mine shaft, unceremoniously, without even a prayer. A sack of lime had been brought along and it was cast down the shaft after the body. Then the opening was sealed. As we performed this shocking ritual I had a heavy weight in my stomach; I wondered who this young man's parents were, where he had come from, what his name was. He looked about my age and I couldn't help but think of the anguish my mother would feel if I was dumped in this way, in an unmarked grave, lost with countless other nameless souls. Although I was fortunate only to have to do this once, it had a profound effect on me. Whenever I see a "tomb to an unknown soldier" today I am reminded of the poignancy of that incident. Although what I had to do that day was routine for many more junior policemen, and nothing compared to the horrors of what others experienced in the war, it was the nadir of my war. The incident still haunts me, but that day it provoked in me an abhorrence of war, a view which has continued to strengthen to this day. Sadly, the practice of throwing corpses down mine shafts, without giving deceased people a decent burial, continued after independence. I suspect that two of my close friends who disappeared since 2000 met a similar fate.

During my time at Buffalo Range I was to make another terrible discovery. As mentioned above, captured guerrillas were always interrogated first by experienced senior officers who were permanent members of SB, before being taken back to "scenes of crime" to make indications. In this initial process many guerrillas were "turned" and ended up fighting for the Selous Scouts as pseudo guerrillas; those who could not be "turned" were prosecuted. I learnt that various interrogation methods, such as the use of water-boarding and electric shock treatment, were used to extract information from guerrillas. Bar talk in the mess was full of gory detail of how guerrillas had "sung" after being tortured.

The brutality of war dehumanised men on both sides and the use of torture was mentioned glibly; captured guerrillas were not viewed as soldiers, but terrorists, which justified torture in their minds. War brings out the best and worst in men. Atrocities were committed by both sides, and the atrocities committed by guerrillas during the Rhodesian war against civilians inflamed men, most of whom in normal civilian life were sane, rational people. Although I didn't commit torture myself, its use troubled me from the outset. At the time, however, I was sufficiently hardened not to seriously question its use. Along with the disposal of bodies policy, it initially rankled inside me, then started to sow further seeds of doubt in my mind about whether we were fighting a just war. That sense of disquiet grew in my mind, especially when I thought about what my father, himself a war veteran, would think about the use of torture.

A few days after the body disposal incident, on 23 August I was woken before daybreak to accompany troops reacting to a farmhouse attack. We were transported by an Allouette helicopter flown by a South African pilot. We flew north following the Chiredzi River at tree height on a cold day with leaden skies and arrived with a flourish on the front lawn of the farmhouse. Several hours before our arrival in the middle of the night ZANLA guerrillas had stonked the house with mortars, RPG 7 rockets and small arms. The farmer, with his wife and four children, aged from five to seventeen, were uninjured and stoically greeted us with coffee and scones. It was the second time they had been attacked but this time was less effective than the first, when the house had suffered a direct hit from an RPG 7. I scoured the surrounds and established thirteen firing positions, collecting spent cartridge cases in different plastic bags as I went along, while the troops accompanying me located the guerrillas' exit route and followed spoor. After a few hours the troops returned, having lost the spoor, wiped out by persistent *guti*.[102] While waiting for the troops' return, the farmer told me of his woes. Aside from the psychological toll on his family, he had lost 800 head of cattle to rustlers in the space of a few months; the government compensated 70 per cent of his loss, but in the long run he would lose money; farming was becoming well nigh impossible and he didn't know how much longer he could continue to subject his wife and family to the trauma they had experienced. He, his wife and the two older children had fought back bravely but he shuddered to think what would happen if the guerrillas had killed him and broken through the security fence. Every time he went out to inspect his cattle or crops he was a sitting duck. Having achieved virtually nothing, save for collecting several hundred spent cartridges and a few rocket fragments for forensic examination, we returned to the safety of the JOC that evening, leaving this fragile family to face another night alone. For all the excitement of thinking I was a latter-day Audie Murphy, I was sobered that evening back at base. That farmer and hundreds like him could not be protected by us; guerrillas could attack with impunity, vanish into the bush and return again and again. Ultimately, even if they didn't kill the farmer, they would drive him off, and there was precious little we could do.

A week later I saw some of the anguish suffered by poor black peasant farmers. We received a report from the TTL adjoining the farm which had been attacked that a young girl had been murdered by guerrillas in a village. For protection I was allocated a PATU stick of police reservists, a batch of four white teachers who were spending their school vacation on call-up. Only God knows what they thought about being subjected to the command of a nineteen-year-old but I suppose that, given that I had in theory eighteen months' experience, they may have been conned into thinking that I was an old hand. They included Erith Harris, a more unlikely soldier one could not hope to find. Erith is the epitome of a gentle-man and was to become headmaster of my children's primary school in Bulawayo a decade later. His colleagues were in a similar mould. It was perilous enough going into this particular TTL, which was thoroughly infiltrated by ZANLA combatants, but they were thoroughly unprepared for the horror that was to follow. When we arrived in the village I asked to speak to the parents of the girl who had died. They confirmed that she had died a few days before but denied that she had been murdered; they were adamant she had died of internal haemorrhaging. The loss of their daughter was clearly painful enough, so I was reluctant to press the issue but our source had been as adamant about the murder. I asked where they had buried her and the parents pointed to a copse nestled in a kopje some 300 metres away from their home. Leaving them standing there, I went to inspect the grave with my bunch of teachers. As traumatic as it was I decided the only way to establish the truth was to exhume the body. To the absolute horror of the teachers I started to dig up the grave and ordered them to help me. We eventually got to the body and hauled it out. I examined the body of the teenage girl and it was clear that she had been shot several times. We reburied her and returned to the village where I explained that I had seen the gunshot wounds. Her mother started wailing as her father related that one guerrilla had indeed shot her in a fit of pique. They did not know why he had killed their daughter but were too afraid to report the murder lest the guerrillas return. They begged me not to do anything further as nothing would bring her back. Although the parents had in theory committed an offence, by failing to report the incident, I recommended in my own report that they should not be prosecuted. They had suffered a cruel loss and the discovery of the crime itself would have compromised them in the eyes of guerrillas who might still be in the area, who were not to know they had played no part in exposing their daughter's murder.

As I returned to the safety of Buffalo Range JOC I was struck by the insanity of war: these parents were completely innocent, had suffered immeasurable loss with their daughter's murder and in trying to remain alive had not reported the tragedy. A source had taken it upon himself to report the matter which necessitated an investigation, which in normal circumstances would have brought what the parents desired – justice. However, in the throes of war justice was impossible and all that the exposure of the crime achieved was to endanger the lives of its surviving victims. As with the white commercial farmer and his family, there was nothing we could do to protect this black family grieving the loss of their daughter.

Despite my growing sense of disquiet and my gradual change in outlook, my time at Buffalo Range, combined with the bombing by guerrillas of a Woolworths store in Salisbury on 8 August (killing 11 people and injuring 70), hardened me, something which is recorded in my letters home. Guerrillas were only referred to by me as "terrs", I applauded the RF's landslide victory in the general election held on 31 August and I was appalled by the proposals put forward to Smith by David Owen and the US ambassador to the UN, Andrew Young on 1 September. Included in their proposals was a demand that guerrilla forces be merged with Rhodesian security forces under the command of the UN. I wrote home: " ... *the initial reaction in the JOC was that Dr Owen had to be kidding – but the joke soon wore off and attitudes have hardened completely ... we all know that the only alternative is the continuation of the war.*" But I added the rider: "*our present strategy of only reacting to the actions of the terrs will not win the war*".[103] The solution in the secure confines of the JOC was to take the war to the nationalist forces; it was naively possible in that environment to think Rhodesia had the capacity to be more proactive waging war.

After a month at Buffalo Range I returned to Bulawayo, considerably sobered. Back in the sanity and peacefulness of my parents' home, the stark difference between the principles they had tried to inculcate in me and the harshness of the military base unnerved me and left me increasingly conflicted. Although I was fighting a war, my father had often spoken of the respect the Royal Scots had shown towards Italian civilians in World War II, and how even captured German prisoners of war were treated well. What started as disquiet in my mind grew into a realisation that what I was having to do, or might have to do in future, ran contrary to all my parents stood for. The "normal" of the Buffalo Range JOC was exposed as abnormal when compared to the decency of my parents. But I was placed in a dilemma. I couldn't discuss the issue with anyone because I felt no one would understand. Although at the time I had no religious faith, looking back I see this as a period when God first sowed some other seeds in my mind. It was the beginning of seeing and believing the total depravity of man, something which overwhelmed me because I felt unable to influence or even temper it. The cascading hatred and violence was all around me. Where could I turn when the "good guys" were actually also the bad guys? Where was the plumb line for what was right when everything was bad, evil, awful, wicked and soul-less? Here began a rooting of insight which, four years later, worked towards my understanding of the absolute depravity of man and my coming to faith in Jesus Christ, whose character was the antithesis of evil. War had exposed wholesale depravity on all sides, and I was being sucked into it, relentlessly. It was expressed in the merciless killing of a father and son in Kezi, the dumping of guerrilla bodies down mine shafts as if they had no worth, the callous bullets in the body of an innocent sixteen-year-old girl, the protracted, vicious, repeated torture of captured guerrillas, and the apparent enjoyment of it all, expressed by a drunken officer at the bar trying to impress his friends – "after a good wind up, he squealed and then he sang", followed by laughter.

I have been left with a profound sense that torture is evil. Although I was aged just nineteen at the time, I am ashamed that I did not do more then to prevent its use or speak out against it. However, I believe that it is only through such revelations that we can prevent the use of these antediluvian practices in future. My war experiences formed the foundation for my absolute opposition to the use of violence in any conflict and my hatred of war itself. Tragically, the use of torture has become deeply ingrained in our law enforcement agencies. Torture has been used ever since, and is still used, by the BSAP's successor, the Zimbabwe Republic Police (ZRP), and other state agencies to this day. Aside from it being reprehensible and a crime against humanity, in my later experience as a defence counsel it has been shown time and again to be a poor method of obtaining reliable intelligence. These crimes, along with atrocities committed by all the armies in the war, were never prosecuted as they were covered by an amnesty agreed to by all the parties to the Lancaster House settlement in 1979. The amnesty, combined with the absence of any truth commission, resulted in these horrors never being confronted and dealt with, as they should have been. The use of torture within our security forces remains a plague in our nation.

In September 1977 I made the firm decision to apply to shorten my three-year contract, to get out early and go to university in 1978. My parents were delighted with the news and my father helped me draft what we hoped would be a sufficiently persuasive letter to Police headquarters. I was too ashamed to share with my parents what I had seen and experienced, knowing that they would be horrified, so the letter was couched in terms which focused on my desire to study law. However, at the root of my application was my profound distress and inner turmoil about the demands being made of me by the war. In short, I felt trapped in a cause in which I no longer had confidence, and could not think then, as a nineteen-year-old, of any other way out.

I was not the only one questioning the war. Midway through my break a curious incident happened beyond the view of everyone, including members of the RF cabinet. On 24 September Smith had a private meeting with Tiny Rowland, a mining magnate with close links to Kaunda and Nkomo. Rowland claimed to be an emissary from Kaunda who was upset by the failure of the US, UK and South Africa to broker a settlement and said he was keen to meet one-on-one with Smith. Without advising his cabinet, Smith agreed to meet and flew out the next day to Lusaka in Rowland's private jet, where he met Kaunda and members of his cabinet. Even Kaunda had doubted that Smith would come and only believed it when he stepped out of the plane. In many respects the trip was remarkable. Smith could easily have been arrested or worse but at this stage he was clearly so anxious to reach an agreement that he was prepared to take the risk. It appears that the meeting was cordial and, according to Smith, Kaunda said he was desperate to bring the war to an end and was prepared to use Kissinger's terms as a basis for negotiation. Both were frustrated by Owen's and Young's machinations. Although nothing was agreed, it was a constructive meeting and Smith and his team returned "smiling", "devoid of bitter frustration" (as they had experienced in their dealings with the South Africans), and "more comfortable speaking to our black enemies" because "although we might disagree with them, at least we knew where we stood".[104] Smith described the meeting as a "tragi-comedy", which indeed it was. He clearly had a rapport with both Kaunda and Nkomo, something he had not had with others. The tragedy is that they were not able to build on this to bring the war to an end. As it turned out nothing came of this meeting but it remains an interesting footnote demonstrating that Smith was prepared to work outside the box. The war was too far gone, however, and ZANLA in particular saw no reason to settle when another year or two of war would give them absolute power.

Shortly before I turned 20 in early October 1977, I was advised that I would not be going back to Buffalo Range JOC for my next stint, but would be given my own command of the Special Branch (SB) base at Ngundu Halt. October is described as "suicide" month in Zimbabwe and it lived up to its reputation when I arrived at Ngundu on the tenth. It was stinking hot and dry, and remained so for the four weeks I was there. In one sense Ngundu has not changed in the three decades since I was stationed there. It straddles the main road between then Salisbury and

Beitbridge, on the South African border, a road which hasn't changed at all since the 1970s, nestled in among towering hills swathed in msasa trees which turn the entire landscape to rust-gold in spring as their new leaves come out. However, Ngundu itself was a sleepy, tiny village comprising a few stores and an old thatched farmhouse, which had been converted into the SB base, situated next to the main road. The base itself was responsible for a sliver of land of some 100 square kilometres, bounded by the Runde River to the south and west and the Tokwe River to the north east. The main security concern was the tar road which wound through a succession of densely wooded granite-topped hills, all ideal for guerrilla ambush sites. The main highlight of our day was the civilian convoy. This consisted of a long snake of civilian cars protected by three police pickups mounted with MAG machine guns and a Cessna Lynx aircraft above. My chief responsibility was to ensure we had sufficient intelligence to anticipate any attack on the convoy.

I was somewhat overawed by the responsibility thrust on me. The area was a hive of guerrilla activity; the logbook of the officer from whom I had taken over revealed that there had been numerous contacts in the previous three weeks. Some 29 guerrillas had been killed, for the loss of no Rhodesian security forces. I had under my command 22 men, black and white, and I was the youngest, in some cases by a considerable margin. Anxious to get my bearings, I visited all the neighbouring stations and had just started to explore areas beyond the immediate perimeter of the main road when I had my first, and thankfully last, narrow escape. We were driving down a dirt road when one of our accompanying vehicles used by Internal Affairs[105] struck a land-mine. There was a deafening roar and a dust cloud behind my vehicle, but remarkably, although the vehicle was wrecked, no one was injured. It was the closest I came to serious physical harm during the entire war. Looking back, I can see that I only survived the war by God's grace. One of the men who took over from me as officer in charge of Ngundu Halt in 1978 was killed in action.

The land-mine incident was followed by a spate of sightings of guerrillas and a major contact just north of my boundary in which Hawker Hunter jets had been called in. I visited the scene the day after it had occurred to inspect the aftermath. Phosphorous ammunition had been used, along with rockets, and much of the granite behind which guerrillas had sought refuge was bloodstained, shattered and pockmarked. Having seen for myself the sight of Hawker Hunters coming down the Shashe

River the previous year I could imagine the terror of the guerrillas as the jets came in. For the first time I thought of the courage it must have taken to stand and fight. The scene of the contact was over 200 kilometres from the border with Mozambique; the guerrillas had lugged all their weapons and ammunition through hostile territory without radios, without the ability to call for air support or ambulances. If they were injured, they could not be casevaced out – if they were lucky, they could be carried back out by their comrades 200 kilometres to Mozambique. My letters home still referred to guerrillas as "terrs", but that incident evoked a new flicker of appreciation for the bravery of some of these men.

About a fortnight after this battle, in which several guerrillas had been killed and a few captured, a senior officer arrived at the base with one of the captured guerrillas, who had been slightly wounded. The young guerrilla handed over to me at Ngundu Halt had already been interrogated at the JOC. I was tasked with taking him on indications. This was a throwback to what seemed a lifetime ago of helping prepare a docket for prosecution, only now I had to take him back to where he and his comrades had been based so that we could get a better understanding of the tactics they were employing. He was a slight, wiry young man about my age, hardly the archetypical terrorist I had in my mind; having sustained a gunshot wound to his leg, he was still sore and hobbling around, walking made all the more difficult by his manacles. He didn't show any signs of torture, nor did he complain of having been tortured, but looking back on it I suppose he would have thought I was an unlikely candidate to treat any complaint sympathetically. Being the first guerrilla I had had contact with, I was immediately struck by his intelligence and humanity. Over the course of the next few days as we drove and walked through the district I was able to find out more about his life. He had been educated up to Form 4, passed his O levels, but had then reached a dead end; his dreams of doing further studies were dashed and the only work he could get was menial labour. Treated disparagingly by whites and encouraged by elders to go to war, he had walked across to Mozambique, believing that the only way he could have a future was by ending white rule. It struck me that he had the same aspirations I had. Just a few days before he had been handed over to me I had written a joyous note to my parents: *"I have heard from Superintendent Patterson that my discharge has been provisionally approved pending receipt of my acceptance by the University of Cape Town (UCT)"*,[106] the very thing this young fellow desired. It made me think about what I would have done had I been in his shoes. I drove him back to the Buffalo Range JOC not knowing what fate awaited him, but with a new perspective on "terrs". I do not remember either his name or *nom de guerre* and can but hope that he survived the war.

The remainder of that tour of duty was relatively uneventful. For some unknown reason guerrilla activity tailed off. Whether this was because of the security force successes I do not know but, whatever the reason, contacts and reports of sightings and guerrilla activity dried up, so much so that a coloured army unit radioed in one day to report simply "*bravo, tango, oscar*". The radio operator was confused and asked them to explain. "*Bravo, tango, oscar,*" came the reply. "I still don't get you," said the operator, to which came, "Oh man, you are not listening to tunes enough – bravo, tango, oscar – Bachman-Turner Overdrive – "We ain't seen nothing yet!"[107] My letters home did not display the same sense of humour. I wrote repeatedly and anxiously to my parents, a veritable barrage of letters one after the other, all enquiring whether I had received my letter of acceptance from UCT, on which my discharge depended. In a letter dated 24 October I wrote that I was "*very perturbed about the latest developments in South Africa – Mr Kruger must need his head read; I cannot credit that they are all so blind to the consequences of their actions. Although I do not intend to get embroiled in politics at university my feelings at present are that I must do all I can to help South Africans 'see the light' without getting myself into trouble.*"[108] Steve Biko had been murdered by the South African police on 12 September 1977 and the minister of Police Jimmy Kruger had responded to the news by stating that it "left him cold". I was horrified that the South Africans did not appear to have learnt anything from the mistakes we Rhodesians had made leading to a ghastly war.

With the lull in guerrilla activity, I naively decided to embark on my own "hearts and minds campaign" in an effort to get more local people on side. I instructed that every effort should be made to speak courteously to people; I went to visit key leaders in the area, expressing my desire that there should be a cordial relationship between my base and all the people and that any abusive or unruly behaviour of security forces should be reported to me. Although no doubt the people I spoke to were sceptical, my hope was that this would lead to more intelligence coming in from more sympathetic villagers. In my naivety of course I had not thought through that increased cooperation by villagers with Rhodesian security forces would inevitably lead to conflict between them and guerrillas. They were truly always in a no win situation.

Young people, myself included in 1977, generally think they are immortal and my letters home had conveyed that. News of the land-mine, 29 guerrillas killed and the like had only served to alarm my parents and so they were greatly relieved when, on the evening of 10 November, I came home unscathed. There was even further relief when my acceptance papers from UCT arrived a few days later. Within days my schoolmates returned home after their first year at various South African universities and their regaling us all with stories of how much fun university was only whetted my appetite.

The Anglo-American proposals, touted by Owen and Young, finally floundered that November. One of their key elements was a ceasefire which would be administered by a UN-appointed military supremo and a British Resident Commissioner. Lieutenant-General Prem Chand and Field Marshal Lord Carver were proposed to fill those positions and in November they arrived in Salisbury to work out details of a ceasefire. Aside from the technicalities, they faced enormous political difficulties. Both Nkomo and Mugabe wanted the war to continue and Rhodesian forces were hardly defeated. Some of Carver's orders, such as the disbandment of certain units like the Selous Scouts, were anathema to the Rhodesians. On 19 November 1977, Smith dismissed the visit as a "lamentable failure of Britain's traditional travelling circuses". Within a week, in a speech delivered in Bulawayo, Smith formally accepted the principle of one man one vote; it was key to the start of meaningful talks with internal nationalist leaders such as Sithole, Muzorewa and Chikerema.

My final tour of duty started on 10 December 1977. Shortly before driving down to Ngundu Halt, having received my acceptance to UCT, my early discharge from the BSAP was approved. My parents were overjoyed but all the same they both found my departure difficult; my father bit his lip while my mother implored me, tears welling up, to be sensible as I "only had four weeks of danger left". On the evening before my departure I had a raucous party with my schoolfriends who had also been called up for their Christmas vacation. The deteriorating situation was well known – a few boys from the class below us at school in Bulawayo had died that year – and paradoxically this gave added zest to our parties. Remarkably, within a week most of us were together again: of all the places they could have been posted throughout the length and breadth of Rhodesia they ended up at a base just 12 kilometres south of Ngundu and a few were actually allocated to serve under my command.

On my arrival back I was furious to find that an army unit, tracking down guerrillas into my area from a neighbouring area, had failed to get information they wanted about the whereabouts of the guerrillas and, as a punitive measure, had burnt an entire line of huts. It had completely undermined my "hearts and minds" effort. When I complained to the local army commander he brusquely dismissed me, clearly thinking I was an impertinent junior. Dissatisfied with this, I took the matter up at a sub JOC meeting at Fort Victoria airport and was shocked to be told that no action would be taken. My argument that this would turn the local community against us met a brick wall, disillusioning me even further.

Just days later providence intervened again. We had received a report of guerrilla activity near to Berejena Mission to the west of the district. There was a long history of collaboration between the Catholic-run mission and ZANLA. Before my arrival at Ngundu, in January 1977 the Father Superior of the Mission, Swiss-born Father Paul Egli, had been convicted of failing to report terrorists and sentenced to five years imprisonment.[109] Berejena could only be reached by a single dirt road which traversed a succession of well-wooded valleys and therefore was a great ambush alley. We set off early in two mine-proofed vehicles, a large Puma troop carrier and a smaller Hyena. Everyone was jovial as we trundled up the tarred main Salisbury road but as soon as we turned down the dirt Berejena road the tension rose. There had been a good start to the rains and the bush was thick so the 20-kilometre stretch down to the mission needed unrelenting vigilance. The chatter stopped and everyone took their weapons off safety and trained them into the bush. We had not gone five kilometres when the Hyena started to overheat; we came to a stop, debussed and while the rest of the men fanned out into the bush to guard, we established that a rubber radiator hose had burst and could not be replaced. We would have to turn back and return the next day. This we did and when we finally got to Berejena Mission early the next day, a source explained how lucky we had been. ZANLA had heard of our originally intended visit and some 20 guerrillas had waited in ambush for us all day. As we neared the Beitbridge road that afternoon, having navigated our way back along the Berejena road, we stopped for a break and a photograph – the relief on our faces in that grainy photograph is palpable.

On 17 December rain started falling in a manner never seen before or since. That rainy season of 1977/1978 was the heaviest on record. My father, who religiously recorded daily rainfall, recorded 1 375 mm, almost double Bulawayo's average. Ngundu Halt was no different. It rained every day from 17 December until my last day in the bush, 10 January 1978. By Christmas the roads were impassable and several army Mercedes Benz 45 vehicles sank down to their axles in the mud. Guerrilla activity also tailed off and my last few weeks of the war were spent doing all we could to prevent water from pouring through the base's ageing thatch.

I flew back to Bulawayo from Fort Victoria on an Air Rhodesia Viscount. As we came in to land at Bulawayo, through driving rain, I had an overwhelming sense of relief – I had survived. As beautiful as the clouds and emerald green fields were, however, I knew the weather would work to the benefit of guerrillas flooding into the country, providing more cover, more ambush sites, more danger for those still fighting the war on the Rhodesian side.

I was discharged on 31 January and spent a few weeks frantically getting ready for university. Nature had one remaining surprise for me. On the evening before I left for UCT, Friday, 17 February 1978, I had a celebratory dinner with my parents. My father had recorded 88 mm of rain that day and he was marvelling at how we had already received 900 mm that season. After dinner with my parents, I drove off in my VW Beetle to have a final drink with my police mates at Hillside mess. It had been raining all day and as I came down Cecil Avenue I could see that water was flowing over the bridge across the Matsheumhlope River. Having ridden or driven over that bridge and its dry river for my entire life, I assumed it couldn't be dangerous and so started to drive across. I had forgotten that VW Beetles float and what looked like a benign small flow over the top of the bridge lifted the vehicle and swept me across the road towards the torrent of the main river charging under and around the bridge. I quickly opened the door, allowing water to pour in, which dropped the car and it jammed between a light-pole and the edge of the bridge, saving me from being swept down the roaring flooded river. I clambered out the window and made my way to dry land. Cars, driven by people more cautious than me, were lined up on the other side and

I asked one of them to drive to the police mess with a message to send a Land Rover to haul my VW out. Although my mates did not believe the report at first, it gave us plenty to laugh about later. My trusty lime green VW had seen me to Kezi and back safely.

CHAPTER 7

DEVIL'S MADNESS
1978 TO 1980

"When we ... all demand: What are we fighting for? Then, then we'll
end that stupid crime, that devil's madness – War"
– CANADIAN POET ROBERT W SERVICE, 1921, FROM THE POEM "MICHAEL"

The old Bulawayo airport terminal was one of the quaintest on the
planet. It had a balcony overlooking the apron, the thick savannah
woodlands which surround the airport and, in the distance, the high-rise
buildings of Bulawayo, and beyond them on the horizon, the Matobo
Hills. Although a relatively large city, Bulawayo has always been intimate
and warm and that balcony, generally packed with well wishers, embodied
that spirit. Families could shout out a greeting or a fond farewell from the
balcony, as our parents did when many of my schoolmates and I left for
university on 18 February 1978 on an orange-tailed SAA Boeing 727. The
flight south to Johannesburg flies directly over the Matopos and Kezi
and I peered out of the window, recognising many of the places I had
been tramping around the last few years – the narrow, bumpy roads, the
brown, muddy-watered dams which dotted the countryside, Sun Yet Sen
camp and finally the broad Shashe River, pumping bank to bank because
of the good rains. As we crossed over the Shashe the realisation that the
war was over for me finally sank in. I had become mightily disillusioned
with the war effort and battled to reconcile what I had seen with fighting
for the "preservation of Christianity and Western civilisation". Against
that I still had a leaden weight of guilt at leaving behind so many loved
ones who daily had to run the gauntlet of ambushes, or face the threat

of bombs placed in stores. But I was overwhelmed by a sense of relief. I had survived the war; I was alive and unscathed – or so I thought. Many friends had not been so lucky. Some had died, others had been injured, and many more had deep psychological scars, having been involved in bloody battles with guerrillas. Having never been involved in a battle, having never even shot at a person, never mind killed one, I thought I had escaped the mental trauma of the war.

It didn't take me long though to settle in at UCT. I took up residence in College House, the oldest on campus, established in 1887. Its motto "The unfading spirit of youth" was appropriate both for its *joie de vivre* and for the enormous quantities of beer drunk in its pub, the Pint and Puss. I had a ready-made set of friends as several schoolfriends had already had a year at UCT and knew the ropes. There were many ex-Rhodesian servicemen in College, who set a raucous tone. It was the perfect escape for us all and the first few months were a blur of parties, trips to Cape Town's legendary beaches and wine route, plus a bit of work thrown in between. In many ways we were anachronistic – we prided ourselves in being the only real men who could drink more than anyone else and were instantly recognisable on campus in our shorts, veldskoens and Rhodesian paraphernalia, such as camouflage hats. UCT, described pejoratively by many white South Africans as Little Moscow on the Hill, was a bastion of liberalism and so we stuck out as a large, vocal group of conservatives. The war was never far from our minds and all of us anxiously followed what was going on from a distance. Undoubtedly, as was the case with so many Vietnam War veterans, many of us were in need of counselling, which we didn't get, rather drowning the vivid images of war in beer.

The war in Rhodesia continued to gather momentum, as did the internal talks between Smith and Sithole, Muzorewa and Chirau. On 15 February a major breakthrough was achieved, with agreement being reached on the number of white seats and a related constitutional provision giving whites a blocking mechanism. Sithole tried to persuade the British and Nkomo to recognise and join the process but failed. Eventually, on 1 March final agreement was reached and was signed by the four leaders beneath a picture of Cecil Rhodes. The hope was that this would stop the war, end sanctions and readmit the country to the international community. But the hope was in vain and there were no takers. Josiah Chinamano, vice-president of ZAPU, aptly said: "it is a basic principle of human relations that if you want peace you must speak to your enemies and not your friends".[110] The UN Security Council rejected the agreement on 14 March, describing it as "illegal". Britain and the USA withheld their support too. Undeterred, the four-man executive council was sworn in and the transitional government got working. In early April hundreds of detainees were released, mostly Muzorewa and Sithole supporters, which was followed by an announcement that executions of political prisoners would end. A ministerial council was formed, comprising nine RF members and three apiece from the three black co-signatories. There were some impressive new ministers: James Chikerema had been in nationalist politics for 34 years; he was joined by Ernest Bulle, a respected academic, and outstanding lawyer Byron Hove. For his part Smith dropped some of his most hardline ministers, such as Lardner-Burke. Things got off to a bad start, however, and Hove soon lost his job after pressing for the rapid advancement of blacks in the civil service. It also became clear that the war, far from ending, was intensifying.

Down at UCT, with all the early festivities over, I knuckled down to academia. The first year of my BA, LLB degree was broad in scope and I was cutting my teeth on Sociology, Political Science, African Government and Law, and Latin. Inevitably, the first three subjects challenged many of my existing belief systems and before long I was in conflict with some of my lecturers. It was the beginning of a fundamental change in my outlook; thankfully my professors and tutors argued with me patiently. After a few months at university I was desperately unhappy, so much so that by May I was writing to my parents that I was *"unsettled"*, questioning whether *"law is really suited to me"*.[111] Having not written an exam for three years I was also anxious about whether I would even pass. I questioned South Africa's viability, urging my parents if forced to flee Rhodesia *"not to rush to South Africa because that would be foolish"*. I was confused by the alternative views presented to me daily in lectures which challenged nearly all my assumptions about Rhodesia. Although disillusioned by the end of my tour of duty, I had never seriously questioned the *raison d'être* of Rhodesia, but was now forced to do so.

Two significant things happened in July to settle me. The first was that I was elected to the Rhodesia Society, which represented the interests of nearly 900 Rhodesian students at UCT. Also elected, as chair, was Andrew Ladley, who had also been in the military but had a progressive view of

Rhodesia. I trusted him because of his past and he was a respected senior student in the law faculty. He gently challenged our views and in the course of the next year got the entire committee to think more positively about the country. Soon after my election I attended the society's annual dinner which was addressed by the co-minister of finance Ernest Bulle, who impressed me greatly with his eloquence and positive outlook.

The second positive event that month was that I fell in love for the first time – with a gentle South African student who was quietly critical of racial prejudice and unaffected by the trauma which affected most Rhodesian students. She quickly became balm in my life and got me focused on my studies again. Towards the end of August I was able to write home that I was *"feeling far more settled"* and would *"press ahead with law"*.[112]

These developments in my life happened in the nick of time, because at the beginning of September one of the most shocking incidents, from a white perspective, of the entire war occurred. On the afternoon of 3 September an Air Rhodesia Viscount was shot down near Kariba by ZIPRA guerrillas using a Russian SAM 7 surface-to-air missile. Remarkably, the pilots managed to land the aircraft but it hit a ditch, tumbled and burst into flames. Thirty of the passengers were killed on impact but 18 survived, only for 10 of them, including women and children, to then be murdered by guerrillas who arrived at the scene of the crash. Almost worse than the incident itself was Nkomo's reaction. He was phoned by the BBC for comment and he laughed in the course of the interview. It seemed astonishingly callous and left most of us on campus apoplectic.[113] My own views hardened again, but I also recognised the political consequences. I wrote to my parents, saying, *"I believe this will be a major turning point in the war because it excludes our only hope – Nkomo – from the internal settlement and the only alternative is war to the bitter end."*[114]

My views were sadly prescient, but at the time I did not appreciate just how catastrophic this event was to the peace process. Unbeknown to us, Smith had been speaking secretly to Nkomo just weeks before the incident, which then put the kibosh on future talks. It had become increasingly clear to Smith as the year moved on that the internal settlement had failed. Muzorewa and Sithole were at loggerheads and both had failed dismally in their promise to stop the war. Smith's thoughts had turned again to Nkomo and the CIO had been tasked with setting up a meeting with him. As a result, on the evening of 14 August Smith flew to Lusaka and met overnight with Nkomo, Brigadier Garba from Nigeria and Kaunda, returning to Rhodesia before dawn. They had, in Smith's words, "constructive" talks about bringing both Nkomo and Mugabe into the internal arrangement, although Smith was sceptical that Mugabe would agree. Garba advised that he would speak to Mugabe and Machel, but they did not turn out to be the only obstacle. Nyerere was annoyed by his exclusion. Nkomo and Mugabe met, but the latter could not be persuaded to settle. On 25 August, Smith got a message from Lusaka that Mugabe was obstinate, something that was confirmed when Muzorewa and Sithole met Zambian government officials in Lusaka on 2 September. Be that as it may, the tragic events of 3 September ended all further prospects of peace and the war continued unabated for another sixteen months. The Rhodesians responded with a new determination to raid Zambia and Mozambique and violence spiralled.

For the first time my parents felt there was no future left for them in Rhodesia. All that my father had warned of had come to pass. The absence of any international criticism of the downing of the Viscount deeply shocked my father as it became apparent that there was little sympathy left for white Rhodesians, even those who had opposed Smith. Shortly before my 21st birthday I received a letter from my father suggesting that the family should emigrate to Scotland. Neither he nor my mother wanted me doing military service again during my December university vacation. Although I did not want to serve again either, I was desperate to go home but at the same time I recognised that in doing so I might be called up again. I wrote back, pleading with my parents to delay their decision until the following February so that I could have one final Christmas at home. It was the start of a rift between myself and my parents, something that had never been there before. I disagreed with my father's view that the long-term prospects were worse than the short-term, arguing that *"when the dust has settled Rhodesia/Zimbabwe will and can become a nation greater than the West can offer"*. I concluded: *"I just can't bear deserting all the wonderful people (black and white) in Rhodesia."*[115] In the end the compromise reached was that my parents would remain and I would do everything I could to avoid being called up for service.

Having safely negotiated my end of year exams, I returned home for Christmas. I was shocked by the deterioration of the war; although we all took every opportunity to keep in touch with what was happening at home, the Rhodesian propaganda machine was effective in hiding the full extent of guerrilla infiltration and activity. Particularly gruesome events, such as the massacre of missionaries at Elim the previous June or the shooting down of the Viscount, were well reported on, but the staggering numbers of guerrillas in the country and the fact that large areas of the country had become no go areas were only known to those still serving.

Soon after I got home on 11 December a unit of six guerrillas fired several RPG 7 rockets into bulk fuel storage tanks in Salisbury's industrial sites – there was a massive explosion and a pall of black smoke hung over the city for a week in the ensuing blaze. It was a stark message that the war was being lost, a fact confirmed to me in hushed tones when I met up with friends who were still serving. They told me of security forces completely outnumbered in contacts with literally hundreds of guerrillas, something that was simply unheard of just ten months before when I had last served. Increasingly, Security Force action was focused on raids into neighbouring countries. Some in the know tried to bring the reality of the situation home. Garfield Todd wrote in vain to *The Herald* in December 1978, pointing out that "three-quarters of (the) country (was) under martial law" and spoke about white responsibility for "the tragedy which is engulfing the nation".[116]

With the backdrop of war, much of the discussion at home turned on the new proposed constitution which had been unveiled at the end of November. Although the constitution would usher in black majority rule, it included many provisions to ensure that majority rule would be "responsible" in the newly named State of Zimbabwe-Rhodesia. Inordinate powers were given to the RF: a new black prime minister would have to choose a percentage of his cabinet from all political parties; Law and Order and Defence were to remain in white hands; the Public Service Commission, responsible for civil service appointments, would be dominated by whites. Property rights were strongly protected, ensuring that there would be no change to land holdings. Any change to the constitution would require the support of at least six whites to pass. It was a constitution which may have been accepted by a majority of black Rhodesians and the international community in the 1960s, but it was far too little and too late. In early 1979 whites overwhelmingly voted in favour of the constitution in a referendum, once again following the lead given to them by Smith.

In those days one could not get a law degree without passing Latin, a subject I had not distinguished myself in at school. Because I had failed Latin, I had to do an introductory Latin course in first year at UCT which for some reason was examined in January. This necessitated me going down to Cape Town early in 1979. Surprisingly, I converted an almost unmarkable O level paper into an upper-second and overnight my nemesis had been overcome. Much of my exhilaration dissipated after our first Roman Law 1 lecture. Aside from the realisation that we would have to study an endless series of Latin legal texts, our professor, an austere Austrian named Schiller, sobered us up considerably by inviting each student to note the person sitting on either side of him or her, as only one of the three would go through to Roman Law 2. Assignments were piled upon us and when one of my colleagues asked whether they were all compulsory Schiller replied in his German accent, "No, zey are not compulsory, but zere again neizer is breathing! If you do not breathe, you die; if you do not do my assignments, you fail." I got the message.

On 12 February 1979 came the tragic news that another Air Rhodesia Viscount, the *Umniati*, had been shot down by ZIPRA guerrillas in similar circumstances to the previous year. A Soviet-made SAM 7 downed it, only this time there were no survivors. On this occasion the loss came much closer to home. I had moved out of College House into student digs and the godparents of one of the girls in the house, Dee Aston, were on the flight. As a result Dee delayed her arrival in Cape Town to be with her godparents' three orphaned daughters. The muted response from the British Labour government enraged me and I ranted in letters home that they had *"given the Patriotic Front a free ticket to indulge in whatever takes their fancy"*.[117] Looking back, I am intrigued that most of my anger was directed against Nkomo and the British Labour Party. Mugabe at that time was a largely unknown quantity; the Rhodesian Front propaganda machine ignored him. His only profile had been his performance in the 1976 Geneva talks.

Our opening few weeks in digs were incident packed. My poor housemates were subjected to my culinary "skills" for the first time. Having been a cosseted only child with an indulgent mother, I had a limited repertoire and my first offering was boerewors burnt to a crisp in white wine. Far less amusing was an incident which took place a few weeks after Dee Aston arrived back at UCT. Early one Saturday morning we heard scuffling noises coming from Aston's room. I burst into the room to find Aston on the floor being beaten and kicked by a man. The assailant immediately ran out an external door with me in hot pursuit dressed only in shorts. I chased him through the streets of Newlands for a few kilometres, screaming for assistance as I ran; two other men joined in the chase and we eventually cornered the villain, enabling the police to arrest him. A few months later I was subpoenaed to give evidence against the accused. It turned out that he was an escaped prisoner, one Sulaiman Jack, who had ten previous convictions for violent crime and was wanted for the attempted murder and attempted rape of several women. I was somewhat relieved I had not managed to catch up to him alone.

Between 17 and 21 April 1979 "Zimbabwean-Rhodesians" of all races went to the polls for the first time. Although the Patriotic Front was determined to disrupt the election, only 19 out of 932 polling stations were attacked and none was closed down. Almost 1.9 million people voted out of a possible 2.8 million eligible voters, a 63 per cent turnout, which in all the circumstances was remarkable. Muzorewa's UANC party won convincingly with Sithole's ZANU Party and Chief Kayisa Ndiweni's United Federal Party making up the balance. The RF predictably won all of the 28 reserved white seats. Although many observers felt that, in the context of the war, the election was relatively free and fair, the international community ignored the event save for the UN passing a resolution that it was illegal. Nothing changed on the ground and the war raged on.

The only glimmer of hope came with the election to office on 4 May of Margaret Thatcher's Conservative Party in the UK. Callaghan's Labour Party had failed spectacularly in bringing the war to an end and I heaved a sigh of relief when I heard the election result. Within days of Thatcher's election the US senate passed a resolution advocating that Zimbabwe-Rhodesia be recognised. Any hopes that there would be immediate progress were soon dashed, however. The Commonwealth acted quickly to rein Thatcher in and President Carter announced that the US would not be lifting sanctions.

In my own life a few seeds of hope were planted at this time. The British evangelist David Watson spoke at UCT's Jameson Hall and a few of my law friends, who were professing Christians, invited me to accompany them. Although I routinely read my Bible, it was the King James Version and to that extent I found it remote; to me it was ancient literature which had little to speak into my life. As a teenager I had gone to the Presbyterian church in Bulawayo occasionally with my mother, but my father had always battled to reconcile a loving, sovereign God with all that he had experienced and seen in World War II and so he rarely attended services. With little discussion at home about religion I had never been challenged to think through my beliefs. Although I would always write "Christian" on passport applications and the like, it was more a statement of culture than of faith. So on this occasion, while sceptical about Christianity, I was persuaded to attend primarily because I was told that Watson was an excellent speaker.

Jameson Hall is a neo-classical building, with massive Grecian columns, which dominates the centre of the UCT campus. It commands a stunningly beautiful view across the Cape Flats to the distant Hottentots Holland mountains, which in winter are usually snow capped. All UCT graduation ceremonies are held in the hall which can seat several thousand people. I went along expecting a few hundred students and was astonished to find the hall packed to the rafters. As a speaker Watson was spellbinding and for the first time I heard the Gospel preached with great clarity and simplicity. He spoke about being able to place all our worries before God and said that forgiveness was open to all, irrespective of our past or status – a message which was pleasing for me to hear. I was challenged to consider what my life was all about, but not sufficiently to do anything about it. For the time being Watson's message merely wedged in the recesses of my mind.

Another talk given at UCT at this time also had a profound effect on me. The SRC arranged for Advocate Kennedy Sibanda to address students. Sibanda was the chief counsel for ZAPU, a nationalist leader who had remained in Zimbabwe-Rhodesia and who had represented countless ZAPU activists and captured ZIPRA guerrillas. He eloquently presented a view I had never heard before and graciously answered many hostile questions put to him by Zimbabwe-Rhodesian students who were particularly angered by ZIPRA's downing of the civilian aircraft. His speech included a catalogue of breaches of human rights and the law by the Rhodesian security forces. He argued that the new constitution, although a step forward, did not amount to a meaningful change which black Zimbabweans needed. Although I didn't agree with all he had to say, it challenged my thought process further.

During the mid year winter vacation, I travelled to Sipolilo, near the Zambian border in the north east of the country, to spend time with my uncle and his family on their tobacco farm. It was almost a decade since I had last been there. I had been told they were having a tough time of it and I wanted to assist in whatever way I could. The conditions I found them living under were profoundly shocking. The area was overrun with guerrillas, numerous farmers had been killed and life for them was sheer hell. The homestead was like a fort, surrounded by fences and Claymore mines. Every time my uncle went out to inspect lands, his wife feared he wouldn't come back. The agri-alert system, a network of radios connecting farmers to each other and the security forces, spewed out daily reports of ambushes and other guerrilla activity. My young cousins were in boarding school, which was safer for them, but getting to school itself was nightmarish. The gravel roads were often mined and the convoys they used to escort them subjected to ambushes. In July 1979 there seemed no end to the war and my uncle was given an ultimatum by his wife to choose between his marriage and the farm. He chose the former and a few weeks after I left them they abandoned the farm and emigrated.

Fortunately, although depressed about the situation at home, when I got back to UCT the Rhodesia Society committee provided succour and encouragement. Under Andrew Ladley's leadership we responded constructively to the new Zimbabwe-Rhodesia. We resolved to change our name to the "Zimbabwe Society", feeling that this was what the country would end up being called and wanting to be progressive.

After the announcement of Muzorewa's cabinet we initiated plans to invite members of the new government to speak early in August at a Focus on Zimbabwe-Rhodesia week. Minister of Education Edward Mazaiwana, Ndabaningi Sithole and Lieutenant-General Walls came to speak in a whirlwind of dinners and talks at the university. Walls's attendance caused a stir and shortly before he was due to speak at Jameson Hall huge banners sprang up around campus decrying his visit, one imploring students to "Reject Walls – the enemy of the people of Zimbabwe". Mazaiwana and Walls impressed us, although Sithole didn't. I wrote home to my parents that I had *still not changed my impressions of the man – a very shrewd politician and one I would not trust further than I could throw*.[118] What struck me about both Mazaiwana and Walls was that they wanted the war to end and were doing all in their power to make that happen.

Just weeks after the Focus week ended, a new chapter in my life opened, one which was to become a mainstay. I wrote home about it:

"I have decided to do something far more rewarding [than the UCT Sailing committee, of which I had been a member] and have joined Legal Aid. In Cape Town there is a squatter camp called Crossroads and it has been virtually adopted by the University. Crossroads is the result of the Nationalist government's terrible policy: the government refuses to build houses for these people as it says they are not citizens of South Africa (even though they work here) and will thus not build anything but single men's hostels. All the families, it says, should be sent back to the Transkei as only the men's labour is needed in Cape Town. UCT Legal Aid opened a clinic at Crossroads last week and they appealed to students to come and help (previously only third years and above could help, but they have now 'lowered' the standard to 2nd years). We went out for the first time yesterday and we all found it an exhilarating experience. The way these people have organised themselves is incredible; with no money at all they have set out streets, elected a Mayor, numbered their houses, built a school and clinic. Their attitude to us was very friendly. The clinic is held every Saturday and we have an attorney in attendance to advise us on points of law that we don't know about. The work is interesting … and tremendously satisfying as one feels one is doing a worthwhile service for people who have a worse lot in life than our own."[119]

Most of my Saturday mornings for the rest of my university career were to be taken up in Crossroads.

Crossroads then was a bleak, squalid camp just west of Cape Town airport, a stark contrast to UCT set beneath Devil's Peak in the plush southern suburbs of the city. Although the residents lived in dire circumstances, they had a marvellous sense of humour. Critically, the time there gave me an insight into some of the extreme injustices suffered by black southern Africans and this was to be a turning point in my life.

While this was happening in August there were dramatic developments on the home front. The weekend before the Focus week a meeting of infinitely greater significance had been held in Lusaka. This was the Commonwealth Heads of Government Meeting, which paved the way for an end to the war. Through a deft intervention by the Queen, the gulf which existed between Thatcher and frontline state leaders such as Kaunda was bridged. Thatcher insisted on calling Nkomo and Mugabe "terrorists" and the British government had deep-rooted concerns about ZIPRA anti-aircraft missiles being used to shoot down the Queen's aircraft. From Kaunda's perspective Rhodesian security forces were raiding ZIPRA camps frequently and he naturally saw nationalist leaders as freedom fighters. Kaunda wanted Nkomo to be part of the welcoming party, which would infuriate Thatcher, and proposed referring to "freedom fighters" in his welcoming speech. A British military team was stationed at Lusaka airport with direct contact with Zambian anti-aircraft batteries to ensure that the Queen's plane would not be shot out of the sky. Agreement was reached that Nkomo would not be present at the airport and on arrival the Queen chatted privately to Kaunda, who promptly agreed to amend his speech.[120] That got proceedings off to a good start and by the end of the meeting on 6 August a consensus had been achieved. Thatcher advised the conference that while Britain had every intention of granting independence to Rhodesia, it would not be done under the current constitution, or the internal settlement, both of which were defective. The powers given to the white minority were "disproportionate to their demographic representation".[121]

Having achieved a consensus within the Commonwealth, Thatcher moved quickly; invitations were issued to all parties to attend a constitutional conference in London in September. Unlike the disastrous 1976 Geneva conference where the chair was out of his depth, Thatcher appointed her most senior and trusted colleague Lord Peter Carrington to conduct proceedings. It was clear from the outset that Thatcher was determined to do all in her power to bring about peace.

The Lancaster House conference began on 10 September in the atmosphere of an escalating war. In the days before it started the Rhodesians had launched a massive attack on Mozambique in Operation Ulric and its raids on ZIPRA camps continued. Carrington, however, was equal to the task and skilfully kept the disparate groups on track. The first issue – the constitution – was dealt with remarkably quickly, although with dire consequences for the future. Smith was determined to ensure that "white rights" were protected. Instead of focusing on the entrenchment of fundamental rights and a meaningful separation of powers (something far more problematic for a dictator in the long run), Smith argued for the protection of white land rights and the provision of white seats. Unlike De Klerk and the National Party, who a decade later in South Africa argued for universal rights to be entrenched, the RF focused on short-term representation of whites in parliament, and the retention of racist clauses in the new constitution. It led to a seriously flawed constitution which could be changed at will, as happened, leading to a shocking concentration of power in the executive. No doubt with his eye on the long term, Mugabe conceded to these issues, many of which would only apply for an initial period of seven years. Mugabe provisionally accepted the terms and details of the proposed constitution which were published on 3 October, only to do a volte-face. Carrington let it be known that he would go ahead without the Patriotic Front, which had its intended effect, resulting in agreement being reached on the constitution by mid October.

The conference then moved on to the transitional arrangements, including who would govern the country and the ceasefire terms. Walls flew into London on 27 October and in doing so presented an entirely new perspective; if Smith had little political power, and to that extent was irrelevant, Walls represented the undefeated Rhodesian military which still demonstrated a capacity to keep the war going. Carrington quickly got Walls on side by promising him privately that if Muzorewa stood down and agreed to be replaced by a British governor, Walls would remain in charge of the military and be able to conduct operations during the transitional period. Having won Walls over, Carrington tried to persuade Mugabe that the British governor should use the white-dominated military and civil service to run the transitional government pending the election. Threatening to "pack (his) bags and go back to war", Mugabe demanded that the Rhodesian military be disbanded and replaced by United Nations peacekeepers. Eventually, through the intervention of the Commonwealth and in particular Machel and Kaunda, who forced Mugabe back to the negotiating table, a compromise was agreed to in the form of a Commonwealth Monitoring Force and a clause placing Rhodesian forces under the same restrictions as the two guerrilla armies. After a considerable amount of brinkmanship the Lancaster House agreement was signed on 21 December 1979.

Significantly, there was no discussion whatsoever in the Lancaster House talks about the need for a truth telling. Unlike in South Africa, the issue of a truth, justice and reconciliation commission or process was not even part of the agenda. The assumption of all parties was that the horrors of the past two decades would simply be swept under the carpet. What drove the entire process was the desire to end a ghastly war; no doubt the understanding that all had committed atrocities resulted in this unstated consensus that immunity from prosecution be granted to all. It was to be one of the worst legacies of Lancaster House, and underpinned the decades of human rights abuses that were to follow.

Like most people, I was unaware of all the wrangling going on at Lancaster House, as only snippets of reliable information came out. I was focused on ensuring that I would not be part of Professor Schiller's two-thirds majority who would not get into third year law. In the midst of all of this my parents wrote to me to say they were contemplating leaving Zimbabwe. My father's health was poor and they were thoroughly unnerved by ZANU PF's anti-white rhetoric. They asked what I felt they should do. Remarkably, despite the prevailing doom, I felt confident enough to write: *"I am excited by the thought of a new nation and, though I might be blinded by optimism at the moment, feel that I will be able to get to the top, even as a white man, in the new Zimbabwe."* The letter was tempered with some realism in that while I indicated that I wanted to return I realised that if my parents had to *"leave as refugees"*, or if they felt that they were *"going to be caught in a whirlwind then (they) must get out"*.[122] In the same letter I ruled out moving to South Africa and expressed the view that South Africa was being *"prepared for war"* and that *"the conflict (was) going to spread"*. Having been through one war, I had no desire to get involved in another.

The arrival of the new British governor, Winston Churchill's son-in-law, Lord Christopher Soames, effectively turned the constitutional watch back to 1965. He was followed by the arrival of the 1 200-strong Commonwealth ceasefire monitoring force and British bobbies. As the ceasefire was gradually implemented the guns were silenced and the country prepared for an election.

There was one pivotal event which happened, and which was to have severe ramifications. It happened on Boxing Day 1979. Josiah Tongogara, the commander of ZANLA, had been one of the most constructive participants in the Lancaster House talks. Smith wrote about how Tongogara had approached him at a social function in London to express the hope that they "could work together in order to build the country, instead of killing one another".[123] ZIPRA intelligence supremo Dumiso Dabengwa later recalled that Tongogara openly expressed a desire at Lancaster House that ZAPU and ZANU contest the elections as one political party and that he always worked closely with ZIPRA commanders.[124] In short, Tongogara was a reconciler, someone who felt the war had run its course and who was determined to work for peace with both ZAPU and the RF. While driving to Chimoio, Tongogara was killed in what ZANU described as a traffic accident. Sitting in the back seat behind Tongogara was Oppah Muchinguri – she was unscathed and said the accident occurred during daytime when the vehicle sideswiped another truck.[125] Another version is that the accident occurred at night when the vehicle went into the back of a stationary truck. The variety of versions has led many to speculate that Tongogara was assassinated by hardliners who did not appreciate his reconciliatory attitude. Whatever the case, his death was remarkably convenient for Mugabe and other hardliners who had no desire to fight the election as one entity with ZAPU. One can but speculate how differently the early post-independence years may have been had Tongogara survived the war.

Inevitably, as the election approached the political rhetoric increased and my parents decided to emigrate in the first few weeks of 1980. While I understood their reasons, I was devastated by the thought of losing my home. In addition, because of the shortage of finance, combined with stringent immigration regulations (originally imposed by the RF to stem the flow of whites leaving the country), which restricted the assets one could take out of the country, my parents had little choice but to emigrate to South Africa. Although in one sense logical, in that my mother at least was returning to her roots, it worried me because I felt I would never be able to live in South Africa.

My final few weeks at the home of my youth in February 1980 were bitter-sweet. In good seasons February is the wettest month of the year, and that month was no exception. It rained every day in my last week at home before I returned to UCT, and the leaden skies reflected my mood as I packed up my room. My earlier understanding and conciliatory attitude to my parents changed as the reality of their decision to emigrate sunk in. In comments I immediately regretted making, I told them that Zimbabwe was my home and that I would only make "token visits" to them in their new home in Port Alfred. In making these statements I caused immense distress and strain to our previously warm and secure family bond.

The country was in similar turmoil. Elements of the Rhodesian security forces made every effort to disrupt the election. On Sunday, 3 February, Selous Scouts, mimicking ZANLA, ambushed a civilian bus, killing sixteen members of a wedding party. The following weekend Garfield Todd (then 72), who had been abroad for the last few months of the war, was detained by police in Shabani under the Law and Order (Maintenance) Act, accused of aiding terrorists. Arraigned in the magistrate's court, bail was denied and Todd was locked up, only to be released a few hours later after the intervention of Soames. That same week several different attempts were made to assassinate Mugabe; through a combination of good intelligence and luck he survived them all. Fuelling the flames were several thousand ZANLA and ZIPRA guerrillas who stayed out of the assembly points and were campaigning vigorously for their respective parties, leaving the electorate in no doubt as to how they should vote, and the consequences of what would happen if they did not vote correctly.

I had to fly to Cape Town for the start of my academic year before the election that was held on 27 February 1980. I was confident enough about the future of Zimbabwe to register for Shona Intensive, a language course offered by UCT. Although many whites were in denial about the result and felt that a coalition of Nkomo, Muzorewa and Sithole would beat Mugabe, all the evidence pointed to Mugabe winning. It was clear to me that the country was tired of the war and wanted it to end; and it would only end if the parties linked to the guerrilla armies won. My white friends in Cape Town were startled to hear me express this view to them; it was the unthinkable scenario. Any doubt was removed when the results were announced at 9 am on 4 March by Registrar Eric Pope-Simmonds: Nkomo's party, ZAPU, which contested under the name Patriotic Front, won 20 seats (all but 5 of them in Matabeleland), the United African National Council, Muzorewa's party, 3, and Mugabe's ZANU PF 57. Smith's RF party won all 20 white seats to complete the 100-seat parliament. ZANU PF benefited from the Westminster electoral system – although it won 63 per cent of the black vote, which would have resulted in only 50 seats, one short of a majority, the first-past-the-post system secured it 71 per cent of the seats, a thumping majority.

Sitting somewhat helplessly in Cape Town, I was alarmed by the size of Mugabe's majority and feared the worst. Within days, though, Mugabe moved quickly to allay fears. He invited Walls to head the army and promised in a broadcast to the nation that there was "no intention to victimise the minority" and that they would "ensure that there is a place for everyone in this country". He promised that property rights would be respected, there would be no nationalisation and pensions would be guaranteed.

At midnight on 18 April 1980 the Union Jack was taken down at Rufaro Stadium and the colourful new Zimbabwean flag raised. In his speech Mugabe was reassuring: "If yesterday I fought you as an enemy, today you have become a friend and an ally with the same national interests, loyalty, rights and duties as myself. If yesterday you hated me, today you cannot avoid the love that binds me to you and you to me." While I remained apprehensive, I wanted to believe that Mugabe meant what he said.

CHAPTER 8

TRANSITIONS
APRIL 1980 TO 1983

"This great Nation will endure as it has endured, will revive and will prosper. So, first of all, let me assert my firm belief that the only thing we have to fear is fear itself – nameless, unreasoning, unjustified terror which paralyzes needed efforts to convert retreat into advance."
– FRANKLIN D ROOSEVELT'S INAUGURAL ADDRESS, 4 MARCH 1933

Any nation recovering from a war is bound to be fragile and Zimbabwe was no exception. The civil war had raged intermittently for fourteen years and claimed in excess of 30 000 lives. Hardly a single family had escaped its horror and its psychological wounds affected virtually everyone. War had become such a way of life that it was difficult to comprehend that it had actually ended. Mugabe's first few acts in office were constructive and designed to consolidate the peace. He met with Smith and indicated that he wanted his counsel; Walls was appointed commander of the armed forces. Nkomo was offered the non-executive presidency and, when he refused that position, was offered the ministry of Home Affairs, which included the Police. This position he accepted. Two of Smith's old colleagues were brought into cabinet, Dennis Norman and David Smith. The former was a highly respected farmer and his appointment as minister of Agriculture immediately settled the white commercial farming sector. David Smith, who had been Finance minister was appointed minister of Commerce.

The opening of Zimbabwe's first parliament on 14 May was symbolically powerful, but also paradoxically bizarre. The new president, Canaan Banana, was driven to parliament in an open Rolls-Royce, accompanied by a mounted BSAP escort similar to the one I had been trained to ride in five years before. The fly past was conducted by Rhodesian Air Force pilots who just months before had used the same aircraft to strafe guerrillas, many of whom were now entering parliament as MPs. The commanders of ZANLA and ZIPRA, Solomon Mujuru and Lookout Masuku, entered parliament, followed by Walls and the hierarchy of the Rhodesian military establishment. Finally, the politicians entered parliament with Mugabe and Smith walking alongside each other; right behind them were Nkomo and Bill Irvine, Smith's old Transport minister who had called Nkomo a "vile murderer" when the Viscounts had been shot down.[126] Amidst all these protagonists was Garfield Todd, who was sworn in as a senator, having been nominated by Mugabe. Todd had called on Mugabe to offer his congratulations on winning the elections, telling Mugabe that in the past there had been a convention that former prime ministers could call on their successors from time to time to discuss matters. However, that convention had been shattered when he tried to call on Smith, only to be refused an audience and subsequently detained. Todd told Mugabe he would like to resuscitate the tradition and, joking, said it would be nice to have an assurance that he would not be arrested and detained again. Mugabe laughed, leaned across and touched Todd's hand, saying, "Garfield, we want you for the senate. We want those who dishonoured you to see you being honoured."[127]

Unbeknown to most of those sworn in that day and the public, all was not as rosy as it seemed. Just a few days before the opening of parliament, on 8 May Mugabe had attended Josip Tito's funeral in Yugoslavia, where he met North Korean president Kim Il-sung on the sidelines. It is suspected that it was during this meeting that Mugabe first discussed the establishment of a special brigade to quell internal dissent, which would be trained by the North Koreans.[128] No doubt what motivated Mugabe in part were the disturbing reports about problems integrating the three armies. Both ZANLA and ZIPRA had agreed to surrender all their weapons held both internally and in neighbouring states to the national army, but only ZANLA had started to comply. Trainloads of ZANLA arms had come in from Mozambique but ZIPRA had been less forthcoming.[129] In one instance they brought in seven truckloads of weapons from Zambia only to cache them in the north west of Zimbabwe. In the latter stages of the war there had been ferocious turf battles between ZANLA and ZIPRA guerrillas, leading to deep levels of antipathy and distrust between the two guerrilla armies. Now that ZANU PF had won the election many ZIPRA guerrillas feared being swamped, or worse. In addition a few bands of dissident ZANLA and ZIPRA guerrillas were rampaging throughout the country. Government responded in a partisan fashion by rounding up hundreds of ZIPRA guerrillas, who were then detained at Khami prison outside Bulawayo, further adding to tensions between the two armies. Mugabe complained in parliament on 28 June that there were ZIPRA "elements" that refused to "recognise the sovereignty of Government" and which were "openly flouting its rule". The situation was further poisoned when ZANU PF hardliners such as Enos Nkala threatened to "crush Joshua Nkomo".

The thin veneer of cohesion was further eroded in July when Walls went on leave, pending retirement. His primary responsibility was the integration of the three armies and it had not gone well. There was a fundamental and irreconcilable dispute between the ZANLA and ZIPRA commanders, with the latter demanding parity and General Solomon Mujuru, the new army commander, insisting that ZANLA forces predominate. Indiscipline at Llewellin barracks outside Bulawayo had led to the detention of several hundred guerrillas, provoking them to issue a statement saying they did not recognise Walls. Walls's departure removed whatever neutrality there was in the integration process, which became increasingly partisan.

With these momentous events swirling around, I travelled up to Zimbabwe for the mid year university vacation with three South African law buddies. In line with my stubborn determination to keep my Zimbabwean links, I drove north from Cape Town in my ramshackle Renault 4 rather than east to see my parents. We were an eclectic bunch: one an ex-war veteran (myself), Derrick Fine, a Jewish student activist (now a leading Aids activist and proponent of the use of simple language), Matthew Walton (who became a leading anti-apartheid lawyer), and Greg Charnock (now a Catholic priest). From the moment we crossed into Zimbabwe there were exhilarating signs of the war's end. A few kilometres outside Beitbridge as we turned west to head to Bulawayo, workers were dismantling the old bunker that had protected a road-block; we had no need to wait for a convoy and joyously drove up to Bulawayo alone. The following day on a visit to Maleme dam in the Matopos I saw an Air Force Allouette helicopter sitting unguarded in a vlei, being used for a new survey of the hills. The thought that this machine, that had wrought such destruction, was now being used for peaceful purposes put a great lump in my throat. I hauled my friends further south – to Kezi – and met some of my old comrades still in the police. My policeman friend Samson Sibanda was still stationed there, promoted to the rank of patrol officer. He spoke positively about the new cooperation which existed between the public and police. The visit to Kezi stirred up deep emotions – I was overwhelmed with a sense of anger and frustration about the futility of the time I had spent there. In a letter to my parents I told them that I felt my *"time at Kezi was misdirected as I was just a puppet"*.[130]

On the way back to Bulawayo we stopped in at a small rural school and were given an impromptu tour by the headmaster. Having been closed for several years, the school had reopened in March; although the buildings were intact, the problems were immense. Several of the children had been out of school for four years, others were unruly, coming from homes broken up by the war, and teachers were few. Presciently, the headmaster told us that foreign aid should be directed towards buying textbooks and school equipment such as desks, words which would stay with me for another occasion much later in life. Despite the pitiful conditions, I came away with a sense of hope.

From Bulawayo we trekked up north west along the glorious teak tree-lined road to Victoria Falls via Hwange National Park. Shortly before the turn off to Hwange we saw an entire section of ZIPRA guerrillas marching in formation down the main road towards us. Much to the consternation of my friends I stopped the car, got out and went to greet them. They were unarmed, although in full uniform. As it turned out they were exceptionally friendly and we had an animated discussion – to a man they said they wanted me home and even suggested that my South African friends should come to Zimbabwe. I came away deeply encouraged. It seemed to me then as if the horrors of war might be easier to overcome than I feared.

Our trip ended in Salisbury (it only became Harare in 1982) where Fine and I met Nathan Shamuyarira, then minister of Information. I had a mandate, in my capacity as vice-chairman of the UCT Zimbabwe Society, to invite the new ZANU PF government to participate in the annual "Focus on Zimbabwe" week. I explained that we wanted to give Zimbabwean students an opportunity to hear from the horse's mouth about future prospects in Zimbabwe; students were wondering whether they would be welcome home, especially those who had served in the military. Shamuyarira was warm and encouraging and we agreed that Justin Nyoka, the director of Information, would come to UCT in August. It was too short notice for a minister to come but we discussed the possibility of ministers coming the following year. I returned to UCT in a buoyant frame of mind, believing that Zimbabwe was off to a good start and on the right track.

My meeting with Shamuyarira energised the Zimbabwe Society committee and soon after the new term started we had arranged a series of meetings around Nyoka's visit. Knowing that the South African government had recently prevented Garfield Todd from addressing students at Wits University, we asked Sir Richard Luyt, the vice-chancellor, to issue the invitation, hoping his gravitas would secure a visa. The SRC threw its full weight behind the week, in marked contrast to what had happened just a year earlier when the SRC had been so opposed to Walls's and Sithole's visit.

Just a few days before the week we were stopped dead in our tracks by the South African government when it refused to grant Nyoka a visa. Mr TJ Booysens, secretary for the Interior, advised that the visit "was not convenient at this stage".[131] This was confirmed by the South African minister of the Interior, Alwyn Schlebusch, who said they had refused to allow Nyoka in because "the time was not opportune".[132] Their action evoked a howl of protest. I said it was "disturbing and astonishing" and the SRC called it "negative and blinkered". Even Pik Botha, the South African Foreign minister, was drawn in, defending their policy as one of "cautious neutrality", which in turn attracted harsh criticism in *Cape Argus* and *Cape Times* editorials.

Unbeknown to us at the time was that the South African government's policy was anything but one of cautious neutrality. In truth it was actively plotting to destabilise Zimbabwe and so the last thing they wanted was a positive view of the country being conveyed to white students at UCT. At the very time we were trying to promote Zimbabwe, disaffected white and black Rhodesian ex-servicemen who had been drifting into South Africa were being organised under Project Barnacle to destabilise Zimbabwe.[133] Their functions were: "eliminations, ambuscades against individuals of strategic importance, gathering of combat information and conducting certain security 'tasks'".[134] One of their specific tasks was to sow animosity between ZIPRA and ZANLA and to build relations with ex-combatants from the former.

The first public inkling of ZANU PF's plans to crush ZAPU was given during Mugabe's address to the first Heroes Day gathering held in Salisbury on 11 August 1980. He spoke vaguely of the intention to deploy former guerrillas into a militia and trained to deal with "malcontents" who were "unleashing a reign of terror".[135] Mugabe followed up that statement of intent when he secretly signed an agreement in October with North Korea's Kim Il-sung "to train and arm a brigade of the defence forces".[136] Ominously, it was to be for "internal defence purposes and not for external operations".

Even with the best will and without external interference from South Africa and North Korea, the slow process of integration was a recipe for disaster. Thousands of young men, with high expectations and heavily armed, were scattered around the countryside. As 1980 drew to an end fewer than 15 000 of the 65 000 ex-ZANLA and ZIPRA guerrillas had been integrated into the national army. Renegades from both armies continued random bandit activity throughout Zimbabwe.

In a vain effort to address the problem some guerrillas were moved in mid October to rural agricultural plots and others to low-cost housing schemes in Bulawayo's and Salisbury's Entumbane and Chitungwiza townships respectively. Almost immediately there was trouble: there was an outbreak of lawlessness around Chitungwiza, necessitating the deployment of combined police and army patrols. Then in the middle of the night of 15 October there was an exchange of rifle fire between the two camps. But worse was to come in Bulawayo.

Trouble started on Saturday, 8 November 1980 when firebrand Finance minister, Enos Nkala, addressed a ZANU PF rally in Bulawayo, virulently attacking and insulting Nkomo and ZAPU. He told the crowd that ZAPU was "superfluous", that all minority parties should be crushed and that the country needed a one-party state. Attendees were urged to support another rally the next day at White City Stadium. Sure enough Nkala continued where he had left off the next day, only this rally was also attended by several hundred ZAPU supporters who had heard about the previous day's vitriol. As Nkala commenced his address his opening remarks were drowned out by these supporters. Nkala responded trenchantly, resulting in a full-scale riot between ZAPU and ZANU PF supporters that had to be quelled by riot police.

After order was restored Nkala was undeterred; he said that ZAPU had become the "enemy of ZANU PF" and said that if the police (which fell under Nkomo, in his capacity as minister of Home Affairs) would not cooperate, "ZANLA troops" would be called in. Several other ZANU PF ministers, including Shamuyarira, spoke in support of Nkala. With temperatures raised among the unarmed civilians, skirmishes occurred in streets outside the stadium at the conclusion of the rally. Inevitably, tension spread and at dusk an all-out battle erupted in Entumbane suburb between several thousand ZIPRA and ZANLA guerrillas, who used machine guns, mortars, grenades and rockets against each other for several hours. Sporadic fighting continued overnight; ZIPRA sent for reinforcements from Gwaai River Mine and a motorised brigade arrived in the early hours of 10 November. Heavy fighting broke out again, which was only quelled later in the day by the arrival overhead of several Hawker Hunter jets flown by white former Rhodesian Air Force pilots. Dabengwa and Solomon Mujuru visited Entumbane and persuaded both sides to hand over their heavy weapons on the understanding that they could keep their light weapons. While the official toll was 58 dead and 500 wounded, the overflowing mortuaries at the nearby Mpilo hospital suggested that many more were killed. Whatever trust had existed between the two armies had completely evaporated; there was a mass desertion of ZIPRA guerrillas who had been integrated into the national army and hundreds in assembly points melted away, taking their personal weapons with them.

I was alarmed by the reports of open warfare in Bulawayo. Although my parents, having emigrated, weren't under threat, the high hopes I had had during the mid year vacation of a peaceful transition were shattered as I wrote my final BA exams that November. I entered a very difficult chapter of my life. It had always been a goal to get a degree and although I obtained it comfortably, including passing Shona with an upper-second, an overwhelming sense of emptiness engulfed me as I received my results. Shortly before I graduated my South African girlfriend of several years broke up with me; I was devastated and thrown into a deep depression. I felt as if all my roots had been severed and my graduation, something I had set as a major goal, was a sombre affair. Christmas was spent with my parents and immediately afterwards I set off to drive the 2 000 kilometres to Zimbabwe in time for New Year.

As I had experienced the previous July, Zimbabwe was full of hope

117

and exhilarating. Although people were worried about the outbreak of fighting in Entumbane, it had all calmed down. Nearly all my schoolfriends were back and we festively celebrated New Year in the Matopos. The war was over and peace apparently prevailed.

UCT's Zimbabwe Society was determined to have a Focus Week in 1981 and in my capacity now as its chair, I drove to Salisbury where I met Ian Smith, Mugabe's principal private secretary, Mr D Van der Syde, the deputy secretary for Information, Ed Moyo, and secretary for Manpower and Development Dr Herbert Murerwa, to see if they would participate.

It was the first time I had met Smith since meeting him as a boy in 1968. He welcomed me into his home, which was right next to the Cuban embassy in the plush suburb of Belgravia. I was struck by the absence of security; his gate was wide open and when I knocked on the door he came alone to greet me. Remarkably, although he expressed some reservations about what Mugabe was doing, he was positive about Zimbabwe and happy to travel to UCT to encourage students to return home. He looked tired but he was determined to make Zimbabwe work. Similarly, my meeting with Harvard-educated Dr Murerwa was constructive; I found a man with a kind face and impressive intellect. Although sceptical about our ability to pull off a Focus Week, given what had happened to Justin Nyoka, he wanted to work with us. We were asked if we could assist government by conducting a survey of the numbers of Zimbabwean students studying in South Africa, which we did that year. I was upbeat when I returned to start my LLB degree at UCT, feeling that despite its manifold problems, Zimbabwe had a bright future.

Within days of my arrival back at university, mayhem erupted again in Zimbabwe. In fact trouble had been brewing for weeks. Mugabe unilaterally sacked Nkomo as minister of Home Affairs when he reshuffled his cabinet on 10 January. Nkomo was appointed as the "politically insignificant"[137] minister of the Public Service and as a sop ZAPU was given two more cabinet posts. Nkomo met with Mugabe and warned him "of the unrest which might arise if ZAPU were stripped of all responsibility for security".[138] Mugabe responded that he could not persuade his central committee to act otherwise but eventually he relented a bit, appointing Nkomo as minister without portfolio – in this role he was to assist the prime minister on defence matters and some public service matters, and he was to remain on the cabinet committee on security. Nkomo complained in his memoirs that in reality all security decisions were made by the ZANU PF central committee and he was not even shown official papers on security.

There were immediate repercussions. On 13 January there was an exchange of fire between National Army troops and ZIPRA guerrillas in Chitungwiza and at the same time some 500 ZIPRA refused to be inducted into the National Army until the political differences between Mugabe and Nkomo had been resolved.[139]

Then on 8 February a major firefight erupted at Connemara barracks between Kwe Kwe and Gweru in the Midlands province between ex ZANLA and ZIPRA guerrillas. Although that fighting at Connemara was quashed within a few days with the intervention of former Rhodesian troops and the Air Force, the fighting spread to Bulawayo. Late in the afternoon of 10 February ZANLA and ZIPRA men exchanged fire at the camp they were based in, situated at Bulawayo's motor-racing circuit in Glenville. In the course of 11 February the old 1 Rhodesian African Rifles Battalion (predominately black, with black and white officers, which had been renamed 11th Infantry Battalion of the ZNA), under the command of Lieutenant-Colonel Mick McKenna, brought the fighting under control. However, that evening fighting broke out in Entumbane, this time a three-way battle involving elements of ZANLA and ZIPRA, who fought each other and who tried to wrest control of an armoury being guarded by a ZNA company under the command of Major Lionel Dyck. Knowing that ZIPRA had heavy armoury at Gwaai River Mine (north west of Bulawayo), and ex-Soviet BTR-152 armoured personnel carriers, and T-34 tanks at Esigodini, McKenna had taken the precaution of covertly deploying early warning teams on Bulawayo's outskirts. Soon after the fighting erupted in Entumbane the early warning team located at the Blue Hills near Esigodini reported that an armoured column was en route to Bulawayo from Esigodini. McKenna responded swiftly, dispatching armoured cars to intercept the column. In the early hours of 12 February the lead vehicle of the ZIPRA column, a BTR-12 carrier, was knocked out on the Johannesburg road opposite the Holiday Inn near Milton School; the remainder of the column, comprising three BTR-12 carriers, was destroyed further out of town near what was then the Hilltop Motel and which is now the Theological College of Zimbabwe.

As day broke, word was received that another column, of twelve BTR-12s and BRDM armoured personnel carriers, was on its way to

Bulawayo from Gwaai River Mine. Once again a company of 11th Battalion was used to set up an ambush, this time at the Umgusa River bridge on the Victoria Falls road. This column did not get close to Bulawayo as several Hawker Hunters buzzed them, causing them to disperse.

Nkomo and senior ex-ZIPRA officers Lookout Masuku and Dumiso Dabengwa were called in; the latter two faced down their own men at considerable risk, ordering them to lay down their arms. Peace was restored finally on 14 February.

Official figures show that some 160 people died in Bulawayo, although some think a figure of 400 is more accurate. There would be no further fighting on this scale. Emmerson Mnangagwa sent McKenna a telegram congratulating him and his men on their "exemplary conduct in stabilising the situation".[140] Several of the white soldiers involved were awarded military medals for their bravery in what was to be called "the Entumbane fighting". Government appointed Judge Enock Dumbutshena to conduct a commission of inquiry; he produced a report which was handed over to Mugabe but never published. Years later the Legal Resources Foundation, of which I was a trustee, brought a case before the High Court compelling its publication; after the order was granted the president's office announced it could not comply with the order because the report had been "lost". One can only presume that the reason for this coyness was because the report showed that white and black ex-Rhodesian servicemen, the ZIPRA high command and the ZAPU leadership acted together to prevent Bulawayo falling.

Safely ensconced in Cape Town, I read of these events with deep sadness. My sense of hopelessness which had started the previous December returned and persisted. Into this void stepped three of my law classmates, Peter Smuts, Barry Jessop and Alastair Wylie. While I had always kept my King James Version of the Bible and sporadically said prayers to a distant God, I did not actually know the meaning of faith. David Watson had stirred me in 1979 and several friends at UCT, including these three, had invited me to a variety of Christian functions over the years. Although I wasn't hostile, I had somewhat contemptuously referred to them as the "God squad" – people who, in my opinion, were overly religious and lacked balance. But they were nothing if not persistent and in February 1981 Smuts invited me to a Bible study group he had started in his digs. There is nobody more arrogant than a fourth year law student and, in keeping with that, I condescendingly agreed to go along, if only to show Smuts that he took spiritual matters too seriously. We started studying the Book of Romans, wonderful for a law student because of its carefully constructed arguments. I had never before been challenged to consider Biblical truths in this fashion and as the weeks progressed I was left increasingly uncomfortable. It would take a separate book to describe the change in my thinking, but suffice it to say that I was deeply challenged. Primarily three things struck me: first, that God's eternal power and divine nature are clearly evident in the world around us; second, that people themselves, all of us, have a natural inclination to turn away from God; and third, that God is not interested in our religious practices but rather in faith, a basic simple trust. Through it all I was challenged to have a fresh look at the historical Jesus Christ and his claims; he was a man who spoke truth to power, who set an amazing example of kindness, wisdom, courage and humility, and yet who also made some rather outlandish claims about who he was, and what he had done.

In particular I battled with the claim of Jesus Christ's resurrection; how could it be that a man could rise again from the dead? How could that possibly be true? I was given a magnificent little book, *Who Moved the Stone?* by Frank Morrison, which challenged me even further. The book lays out a variety of arguments why belief in the resurrection does not defy logic. How could it be that a bunch of frightened common men, fishermen such as Peter, could be transformed on the basis of a lie? If Jesus had just died on the cross and not risen, what caused these men to be transformed from such pitiful, scared men into people who changed the world? Ultimately, while belief in who Jesus Christ actually was remained a matter of faith, the arguments put forward by Morrison gave me confidence that I was not blindly putting my faith in something that was simply illogical. Many weeks of careful study and intense discussions, in particular with Smuts, Jessop and Wylie, followed. By the end of May I was left with clear truths which I did not know how to handle – that a gentle, wise man named Jesus Christ lived two thousand years ago, that he was crucified by the Romans (all verified by independent sources) and that he claimed to be the Messiah, someone in whom I should put my absolute faith. He was either a madman (which was not borne out by his actions and life) or I should take his claims seriously.

After several weeks of inner turmoil, I made a decision in the quiet of my room at 6 pm on 12 June 1981. I had a tiny Gideon's New Testament which I signed: "*Confessing to God that I am a sinner, and believing that the Lord Jesus Christ died for my sins on the cross and was raised for my justification, I do now receive and confess Him as my personal Saviour*". I did not hear angels or sweet music but my outlook on life changed fundamentally from that time on.

As I grappled with Christ's claims, and my reaction to them, during the first half of 1981 I was also thoroughly engrossed in the demands of my LLB degree and running the Zimbabwe Society. My meetings in Salisbury had yielded support from the Zimbabwean government for participation in a Focus Week by a high level group. Given what had happened in 1980, we decided that we had a better chance of pulling off the Week if we invited white Zimbabweans of a more conservative disposition. Accordingly, it was agreed that Senator Dennis Norman, the minister of Agriculture, Brian Grubb, a former president of the Associated Chamber of Commerce and an ex RF MP, Rhodesian arms manufacturer and farmer Andre Holland, would be invited. As in the previous year invitations were issued by the UCT vice-chancellor and extensive preparations made. Grubb was to speak on the topic "Commerce and the New Order", Holland on "The role of white Zimbabweans in the New Order" and Norman would deliver remarks, including a message from Mugabe, encouraging students to return home at the Society's annual dinner scheduled for Friday, 21 August. UCT obtained confirmation from the South African government that there would be no problem and so we hoped it would go off smoothly. On the Monday before the dinner, I was contacted by the Zimbabwe Trade Mission in Johannesburg who advised that Mugabe wanted to know what students would like to hear. I replied that most students wanted to return home but needed encouragement that they would be welcome. On the afternoon before Grubb and Holland were due to leave, 18 August, I received a phone call from Senator Norman telling me that the South African Trade Mission in Salisbury had just told them that their visit was off as, using similar language to the previous year, it was "not opportune at present". Norman also said he had been asked to convey to me that I should "restrain my criticism of the South African government unless I wanted to return home to Zimbabwe earlier than intended"! Norman commiserated with me but there was nothing to be done. He later commented in the press that he was "sad rather than angry"; it had not been convenient for him to come down but he realised that students needed someone to "talk frankly to them" and that he was going to tell students that "if they wanted a challenge … there was place back home and the final rewards would be worth the effort".[141]

The cancellation again made the headlines in South African, Zimbabwean and British newspapers, but that was little consolation to those of us who had worked so hard.

The next day, still irritated by the South African government's action and contemplating how serious their threat was against me, I received a telegram shortly before attending a tax law lecture, which read:

Dear Mr Coltart
Replying to your message of the 17th August – for which many thanks, I am happy and encouraged to learn that Zimbabwean students at Cape Town University are ready and willing to return home upon completion of their studies to serve their country.

As you are no doubt aware, we in government intend to establish a non-racial society based on equality – and the promotion of the well-being of all our people in accordance with our socialist principles.

It is in this connection that we have adopted the policy of reconciliation whereby our people must put aside the hatreds and animosities of the past and approach the future in a positive and constructive frame of mind and with commitment and dedication to the all-round development of the new Zimbabwe.

As we struggle to re-build our country out of the destruction of war we look to young people like yourselves to assist us to achieve our objective of establishing a prosperous and harmonious and humane society in this country.

I call on all of you who have completed your studies to return and join us in the urgent tasks before us. I hardly need to remind you that this is as much your home as it is ours. As so often has been said, in identifying with a returning to the new Zimbabwe you have nothing to fear but fear itself.
Yours sincerely
R.G. Mugabe
Prime Minister of the Republic of Zimbabwe

I was astonished that a prime minister would take the time to write me a telegram. Senator Norman had told me that Mugabe had taken a personal interest in the matter and was saddened about the cancellation, but as a mere student I didn't expect this. I rushed off to my lecture which was about to be given by one of my favourite lecturers, Dennis Davis (then a trenchant critic of the apartheid regime and now a South African High Court judge), and told him about the telegram. Davis enthusiastically said I should read it out to the entire class; it caused a tidal wave of support across the university. The telegram was converted into a poster which was plastered throughout UCT. The contents of the telegram had a positive effect on Zimbabwean students and many, despite the disappointment of the cancellation, felt that perhaps there was a future after all for us in Zimbabwe. Mugabe's use of Roosevelt's phrase of having "nothing to fear but fear itself" came as a particular challenge, and source of encouragement, to me personally.

There was at that time much to fear, however, because Zimbabwe was starting to unravel. Aside from the secret preparations being made by ZANU PF to crush ZAPU and ZIPRA, the South African government's Operation Barnacle was steadily being implemented. On 31 July 1981 Joe Nzingo Gqabi, the ANC's chief representative in Zimbabwe, had been assassinated by a South African hit squad in Salisbury. Then, just days before our Focus Week was due to start on 16 August, a series of massive explosions erupted at Inkomo barracks, north west of Salisbury. The barracks had been the main armoury for the tonnes of military hardware brought in by both guerrillas' armies since the end of the war. In addition the Air Force kept a substantial stock of its bombs there. In a conflagration which lasted hours millions of dollars worth of arms and ammunition were blown up. A subsequent investigation, which included British army experts, concluded that it was caused by "deliberate enemy (i.e. South African) action".[142] What compounded the destruction of the armoury was the realisation that former Rhodesian soldiers and policemen were complicit; a former Rhodesian army engineer, Patrick Gericke, was arrested on suspicion of being involved. Gericke was freed within a few days by the white policeman appointed to investigate the case and both, plus the policeman's entire family, were flown out in South African aircraft in a daring escape mission. That immediately put all the remaining white servicemen and policemen under suspicion.

My term as chair of the Zimbabwe Society came to an end that August. In my meeting with Smith the previous February, when I had asked him what advice he would give students, he had said sardonically: "You are at University to get an education; get on with your studies first, write your exams and then return to worry about the country – it will still be here and will no doubt still give cause for worry when you return!" It was similar advice to what my father had often given and I decided to heed it. There was little point in getting deported from South Africa when I was so close to getting my law degree. Instead I stood for, and was elected to, the Law Students Council and was appointed director of the Crossroads Legal Aid Clinic at the end of August 1981. Sometimes discretion is the better part of valour.

There was also at this time another growing interest in my life which was to have a life-changing affect on me. Earlier on in the year I had met a gorgeous brunette who also hailed from Bulawayo, Jenny Barrett. Although we shared common friends, our paths had not crossed, mainly because she was on the Medical campus studying physiotherapy, which is far removed from the Law Faculty at UCT. In the course of the year our friendship had grown and by September I was head over heels in love with her. Soon after the completion of Jenny's final year exams and my fourth year exams we announced our engagement. Aside from having a deep faith herself, Jenny had a deep-rooted antipathy towards racial prejudice and she also shared my conviction that we should return to Zimbabwe, something she had to do almost immediately to honour the terms of a Zimbabwean government bursary she had obtained to complete her degree. My deep depression I experienced the previous December had lifted totally.

After spending Christmas of 1981 with my parents in Port Alfred, I flew to Bulawayo in early February with the intention of securing employment at the completion of my law degree. Unlike the previous year, I found that many Bulawayo people were pessimistic. My first call was the father of a schoolfriend who was a partner in the firm I would eventually join, Webb, Low and Barry. When I told him I was intending to return at the end of the year he reacted, "You're mad – you want to come and work here?!"[143] I continued the hunt for work in Salisbury, where I found people more positive, and the law firms who interviewed me were more encouraging. I met with Andre Holland again, who felt that whites were needed and wanted.

On Monday, 8 February I stopped by the prime minister's office to drop off a letter thanking Mugabe for his support the previous August. The moment the receptionist saw the UCT logo on the envelope I was ushered through to the prime minister's private secretary (and also then deputy minister of Local Government), Godfrey Chidyausiku. I was somewhat taken aback meeting him because I only knew him as the flamboyant MP who had been an MP in the Rhodesian parliament where he was chastised for wearing a psychedelic suit. Chidyausiku gave me a warm welcome, pumping my hand, and told me how thrilled Mugabe was with the constructive attitude of the UCT Zimbabwe Society. He apologised that I would not be able to meet Mugabe, something I hadn't expected anyway. I was amazed at the reception and wrote to my parents that *"the policy of reconciliation is real for those who want it to be"*.[144] Twenty years later Chidyausiku was to be Mugabe's trump card when he became Chief Justice, providing him with a legal fig leaf in the face of gross violations of Zimbabwe's constitution.

The *coup de grâce* came at the end of the visit: I was invited to attend a law conference at the University of Zimbabwe Law School and here I met Professor Reg Austin for the first time, a ZAPU lawyer, who also encouraged me to return to Zimbabwe. While standing in the rain after the conference, wondering how I would get back into town, the leader of the Nigerian delegation, Botswana's first black Chief Justice and director of Nigeria's Institute of Advanced Legal Studies, Dr Akinola Aguda, asked me whether I would like a lift. No sooner had I accepted the offer than a huge Nigerian embassy Mercedes arrived and whisked us off, the Nigerian flag fluttering in front! In the drive into town Dr Aguda encouraged me to return home and I was touched that this senior, leading African jurist could take such an interest in a white final year law student. For all the negativity surrounding the country, I returned to UCT confident that I could make Zimbabwe our home. In a long letter to my parents I poured out my emotions, telling them how people all over the country had *"fallen over backwards to help me"* and that I was *"convinced that the reason for this was my own attitude"*. My parents were deeply sceptical.

In the same week I was in Salisbury rather momentous events were taking place in the country, but at the time I did not appreciate their significance. In the *Sunday Mail* of 7 February Mugabe announced that a massive arms cache had been discovered on Ascot farm, just north of

Bulawayo, which belonged to a company owned by ZAPU, Nitram (Pvt) Ltd. The cache contained thousands of assault rifles, pistols, mortars, rockets, anti-aircraft weapons and land-mines. Mugabe warned those responsible that "if they wanted to start another war they should be careful". He attacked ZAPU, accusing them of buying farms to be used as arms dumps and of stringing along their partners in government "while planning an eventual takeover".[145] The previous Friday Nkomo had flown to Bulawayo with State Security minister, Emmerson Mnangagwa, without him raising any concerns. Mnangagwa went straight to Ascot farm from Bulawayo airport to address the press which had been summoned there. He told the gathered press that they had uncovered a ZAPU plot to overthrow the government with the help of South Africa.

Action against ZAPU and its leaders followed thick and fast. Nearly all of the properties owned by ZAPU were raided and further materiel was found. On 14 February, Mugabe upped the vitriol, attacking Nkomo by saying "the only way to deal effectively with a snake is to strike and destroy its head".[146] The following day a Government Notice appeared, ironically using a statute first introduced by the Rhodesians, declaring a variety of companies and organisations belonging to ZAPU "unlawful" and seizing their assets. Three days later Mugabe dismissed Nkomo, ZAPU vice-president Josiah Chinamano and Joseph Msika from the cabinet. In a press conference called to explain his decision, Mugabe accused ZAPU leaders and ZIPRA commanders of stockpiling arms to wage "armed struggle". Rhetoric changed to harsh action on 11 March when Lieutenant-General Lookout Masuku – then deputy commander of the Zimbabwe National Army – and Dumiso Dabengwa were arrested and charged with treason.

The events of these few weeks proved to be a harbinger of the genocide which was to follow. While there is no doubt that the arms caches were real, what is equally true is that they were no secret. Both guerrilla armies had held onto weapons and the process of handing them over was ongoing. ZIPRA's arms caches were so large that there was no possibility of them being hidden. Nkomo argued that many of the weapons could have been cached by guerrillas in the aftermath of the Entumbane and Connemara shootouts and that it would have been easy for ZANU PF elements to swell the numbers of weapons. He pointed out that the acquisition of properties had been disclosed to cabinet and he had discussed the plans to use them "in detail with Emmerson Mnangagwa".[147] Both Masuku and Dabengwa had played important, indeed brave, roles in containing the serious outbreaks of violence in the preceding year. Neither Nkomo nor any others of the senior leadership of ZAPU were ever charged with treason. The only senior people actually tried, Masuku and Dabengwa, were acquitted after a lengthy trial, the presiding judge Hilary Squires finding Dabengwa's actions in particular "the antithesis of (someone) scheming to overthrow the Government".

There is one other significant factor which aggravated the discovery of arms caches and that is the involvement of white double agents within the CIO. What is alleged by a number of sources is that former Rhodesian policeman, CIO officer and South African double agent Mac Callaway was instrumental in organising the large arms caches "discovered" in February 1982 and in deliberately misleading government into "believing that ZAPU was engineering a coup".[148] It was certainly in the apartheid regime's interest to stir up tension between ZANU PF and ZAPU. More recent material suggests that ZIPRA cached weapons around assembly points and ZANU/CIO cached some of the weapons on the ZAPU properties owned by its company, Nitram (Pvt) Ltd. Whatever the case, with the exclusion of Nkomo from cabinet and the arrest of the most senior ZIPRA leaders, the scene was set in March 1982 for an escalation of hostilities. Had Mugabe and Mnangagwa in particular been prepared to negotiate, the horror which was to follow could have been avoided.

Relieved of my leadership of the Zimbabwe Society, I got stuck into my final year law studies and at the same time was appointed Director of the Crossroads Legal Aid Clinic, one of several run by the UCT Law Faculty's Legal Aid Committee. I found many of my colleagues on the committee inspirational; in particular Jenny Boraine, the secretary of the committee, who befriended me. Her son, Andrew, had recently been detained by the Nationalist government and her husband, a former Methodist minister, Alex Boraine, was at that time a PFP MP and one of the staunchest white opponents of apartheid. Jenny had been raised on a farm in Rhodesia and to that extent we had common roots. In her gentle manner she enhanced my understanding of the evil of apartheid. Many of my fellow students on the committee were equally inspirational – Wallace Mqoqi (now a leading black advocate in South Africa), Andrew and Peter Corbett, sons of leading South African judge Michael Corbett, Richard Spoor (now one of South Africa's leading labour lawyers), Cathi Albertyn (now a Law professor at Wits University), and many others worked hard to oppose apartheid then, and in their professional lives after graduating from UCT.

At the time all of us were deeply influenced by the work of the newly established Legal Resources Centre and its director, Advocate Arthur Chaskalson. The previous September, Chaskalson had argued and won a case in Johannesburg on behalf of Mehlolo Rikhoto, a black machine operator, entitling him to remain permanently in South Africa. The Urban Areas Act, the principal South African law which governed the rights of blacks to live and work in white areas, allowed black people to obtain permanent rights to live and work in the white areas of South Africa (i.e. outside the homelands) if they could show they had lived and worked in a particular area continuously for ten years. Rikhoto was one of thousands of black people who had to make an annual trek back to their homeland to sign new contracts. The government argued that this broke the continuity, thus denying this right to hundreds of thousands of black South Africans. The court agreed with Chaskalson that the alleged break in the contract was fictional and that Rikhoto should be allowed to remain. The ruling immediately had far-reaching implications for black contract workers across the country, especially in Cape Town, and Crossroads in particular.

Throughout 1982 I spent nearly every Saturday morning during university terms in Crossroads, primarily advising workers of their rights in terms of the Rikhoto judgment. It was frustrating work though. The East Rand Administration had appealed the judgment (ultimately losing when the South African Supreme Appellate Court dismissed the appeal in May 1983) and pending the outcome of the appeal every bureaucratic measure was used to obstruct workers. As I wrote to my parents, *"any attempts to deal with the administration usually (are met) with harsh replies"*.[149] On Saturdays I was removed for a few hours from the beautiful UCT campus to be confronted with the coalface of apartheid – and be continually shocked by the way in which the pass law system disrupted families.

My fiancée Jenny, having graduated with a physiotherapy degree in December 1981, had returned to Bulawayo to work at Mpilo Hospital to fulfil her bursary obligations. I flew up to Bulawayo to spend the last two weeks of July – my mid year vacation – with her. There was important business to be done. We had to finalise our wedding plans for the following year and I needed to secure a job. The former was dependent on the latter both in terms of timing and location. I was still set on working in Harare (the city's name had been changed from Salisbury on 18 April) but the best job offer came from one of the country's oldest firms, established in 1897 – when the railway came to Bulawayo – Webb, Low and Barry. I was interviewed by the senior partner Michael Barry, then in his eighties, the managing partner Bob Cole (who had been part of the 1969 constitutional review committee) and my father's old bridge mate David Ross (one of the three lawyers who first inspired me to do law as a fourteen-year-old). On the final working day of my vacation, Friday, 23 July, I accepted their offer and agreed that I would start work in Bulawayo the following January.

It turned out to be a tumultuous weekend. Although there had been an upsurge in dissident activity in Matabeleland in the preceding few months, it had remained sporadic. There had been a number of ambushes of white farmers but none had been killed. Dissidents had robbed bus passengers and country stores – in other words nothing had happened to capture headlines. That all changed on the eve of my final interview, on Thursday, 22 July. A group of British, American and Australian tourists, travelling from Victoria Falls to Bulawayo in an overland truck, were stopped and abducted by dissidents 73 kilometres outside of Bulawayo. A message scribbled by the dissidents was sent to the police demanding the release of Dabengwa and Masuku and the return of confiscated ZAPU properties. Despite a massive manhunt, headed by 1 Parachute Battalion under Lieutenant-Colonel Lionel Dyck, the tourists were not found and the matter immediately attracted world-wide attention. Eventually, five of the six bodies of the tourists were found close to the scene of the ambush when captured ex-ZIPRA dissidents made indications to police. The same men were hanged in 1986 after they were convicted of the murders. That at face value would appear to indicate that dissidents were responsible for this crime, not pseudo government operators or South African sponsored dissidents. Double agent Kevin Woods insisted that Joshua Nkomo directed dissidents to commit the crime and he asserts that the CIO had plenty of evidence supporting this.[150] However, Nkomo was never prosecuted and one wonders why that was if the evidence against him was so overwhelming; the evidence against the accused dissidents Ngwenya and Mpofu was riddled with contradictions and their death sentences were a travesty of justice. The question as to who actually abducted the tourists remains wide open; it could have been dissidents, or South Africans or Zimbabwean pseudo operators. In any event it provided ZANU with a perfect pretext to intensify their fight against dissidents.

One of my closest CBC and UCT friends, Hans Haefeli, got married that Saturday, 25 July, in Bulawayo. The abduction of the tourists was the focus of discussion; it had happened close to Bulawayo, marked a serious deterioration in the security situation and harked back to the worst days of the war. Many of my schoolfriends were at the wedding, including Napier Avenue friends Rob Nixon and David Bilang. It was the last time I would see David Bilang as he would become a victim of political violence himself before the year end.

Within hours of the wedding a further catastrophic event happened north of Bulawayo at Thornhill air base in the town of my birth, Gweru. In 1980, ZANU PF had inherited the Rhodesian Air Force intact. Nearly all Zimbabwe's fighter jets, including six new British Aerospace Hawk MK60 jets which had been delivered earlier that July, were based at Thornhill. In the early hours of Sunday, 25 July a few South African-backed operatives infiltrated the poorly guarded base, planted bombs with timed detonators on nearly all the fighter aircraft, and withdrew, unharmed and unnoticed, to a nearby place of safety. Just after 3 am the bombs detonated, destroying one Hawk, seven Hunters and one Lynx aircraft and badly damaging several others. The raid instantly destroyed most of Zimbabwe's strike ability both against dissidents and South Africa itself.

The damage went beyond the planes themselves, however, and suspicion turned towards the air force command structure. Unlike soldiers, pilots cannot be trained in a few months and many of the senior officers of the Rhodesian Air Force remained in key leadership positions in the Zimbabwe Air Force at the time of the raid. The ease with which the planes had been destroyed pointed to serious lapses in security and suspicion rapidly developed within ZANU PF that the plan had been hatched with the connivance of the Air Force leadership. Within days over a score of senior airmen were arrested on mere suspicions; most were then subjected to horrendous torture, including electric shocks, which produced "confessions". Any fledgeling trust developing between former Rhodesian officers and the new government was almost totally destroyed and in that the South Africans had struck a double blow.

I flew back to Cape Town a few hours after the Thornhill bombing.

The security checks at Bulawayo airport were far more thorough than when I'd arrived two weeks earlier. The combined effect of the abduction of tourists and the bombing had made all young white ex-servicemen suspect and I was no exception. Although depressed by the resurgence of violence, I resolved to concentrate on finishing my degree. In fact the resurgence seemed to peak at the end of July. *The Chronicle*, a government newspaper, recorded that during this period there were 248 incidents, including 49 murders, attributed to dissidents, but that dissident offences "tailed off dramatically towards the year end".[151] Even the minister of Defence, Sydney Sekeramayi was bullish and in October 1982 he issued a statement that they had "dissidents on the run".[152] So as I wrote my final law exams in November, graduated in December, and prepared to return home, many of my concerns had subsided.

What none of those outside a tight inner ZANU PF circle knew at the time was that the final stages of an evil plan were being implemented. Although *The Chronicle* had reported Mugabe's proclamation on 21 August 1981 of a new unit to "combat dissidents", few had taken much notice and little publicity was given to its development. What we now know is that in 1981 instructors began training a group of ex-ZANLA combatants, who were almost exclusively Shona speaking. Years later the *Zimbabwe Defence Forces Magazine* itself explained that the new unit, known as the Fifth Brigade, was "for internal defence purposes and not for external operations" and for this reason "received special training from instructors of the Democratic Republic of Korea". The brigade "did not use the drill movements and operational techniques that were in use with other existing brigades". For example, whereas in other brigades only officers would be saluted, in the Fifth Brigade "private soldiers saluted each other by hand". Soldiers were trained "to operate as individuals, such as close quarter battle tactics (sic)". In addition "military lessons were delivered together with politics".[153] The Fifth Brigade was not an integrated unit of the ZNA, was not answerable to the normal ZNA command structure and indeed was directly answerable to Mugabe.[154] It was also distinctive – it used different vehicles and uniforms to other units and, in particular, all its soldiers wore red berets. Interestingly it had no military police or provost unit. The Korean instructors "did not for-see (sic) the need" for one as they were "teaching both military and political lessons" and "never envisage (sic) any major indiscipline that would need policing".

Training took place in secret at a base on the banks of the Inyangombe River near Nyanga until 9 September 1982, when Defence minister, Sydney Sekeramayi, announced that their training was complete. The final commissioning parade was held at the base in early December 1982.[155] A brigade flag designed by the North Koreans, with the inscription "Gukurahundi" on it (a Shona expression which in English means "spring rains which wash away the chaff"[156]) was handed over by Mugabe to the brigade commander Colonel Perence Shiri. Mugabe spelt out the duties of the brigade in his speech, saying, "The knowledge you have acquired will make you work with the people, plough and reconstruct. These are the aims you should keep in yourselves."[157] With those words the brigade was "immediately told it was due for deployment".

In isolation the words "plough and reconstruct" seem benign but Zimbabwe was soon to learn how sinister they were as the Fifth Brigade was deployed into Matabeleland during the weeks that followed.

Having graduated from UCT, I returned to Zimbabwe that December to start work and get married, oblivious of these machinations, unaware I was going right into the vortex of a struggle fuelled by the triple whammy of South African destabilisation, ex-ZIPRA dissident activity and ZANU PF's Machiavellian schemes.

CHAPTER 9

GUKURAHUNDI
JANUARY 1983 TO JULY 1984

"Blessed are they who will follow the path of the Government laws, for their days on earth will be increased. But woe unto those who will choose the path of collaboration with dissidents for we will certainly shorten their stay on earth."
– Minister of State Security Emmerson Mnangagwa, 4 April 1983

After spending a very quiet but happy last Christmas as a single man with my parents in Port Alfred, I drove through the night, this time in a somewhat battered old Peugeot 404 (given to us by my parents in anticipation of our wedding), to get home before New Year. The car kept overheating as there had been no rain and it was blisteringly hot. I crossed over the border at Beitbridge with mixed emotions. On the one hand, I was elated to be back in Zimbabwe, law degree in hand, my fiancée waiting in Bulawayo; on the other, there was an oppressive atmosphere in the country I had not sensed since the war. Zimbabwe was in the grip of a drought, fuel was scarce and the 300-kilometre drive from Beitbridge to Bulawayo was almost deserted. Dissidents had ambushed a bus on Christmas Eve, killing several civilians, and this had put a damper on the entire festive season.

Nothing much, though, could put a damper on my reunion with Jenny. Although we were poor as church mice – we both had large post-university debts and, aside from our two old bangers, had no assets – our shared excitement about working to make the new Zimbabwe work was mutually infectious. We also had a deep sense of a calling back to work in Zimbabwe, even though our parents, Jenny's and mine, in South Africa had grave reservations.

Many of my old school and university friends were home too, one of whom was Dave Bilang. Dave went out to spend New Year's Eve on his grandfather's farm at Turk Mine, north of Bulawayo. The whole white farming community was preparing for the New Year's Eve thrash at Turk Mine Club when word came over the agri-alert system just before lunch that Dave and his grandfather, Benji Williams, had been abducted by armed men at Tuf Nut Mine. One of the mine workers had run four kilometres to the Williams homestead at Portwe Estates to raise the alarm. Interestingly, he arrived at Portwe in the company of soldiers, which the family found odd. A local farmer named David Joubert responded immediately and drove to the mine with trackers and militia in tow. Joubert established that when Bilang and Williams had arrived at the mine an armed group of eight to ten men emerged from the bush and captured them. Then they assaulted the two men and forced them to write a note which demanded the return of ZAPU properties for their release. Williams had noted, with question marks, the release aspect and added, "I think we are cold turkey." Joubert saw that the tracks headed off north into a thickly bushed area. The group had left Tuf Nut about three hours earlier and so Joubert decided to drive up a nearby road in an effort to leapfrog the thick bush rather than follow the spoor on foot. After driving about four kilometres they were waved down by a group of ZNA soldiers near Illishe Hill who said they had picked up the spoor of a group of six men crossing the road and heading in a westerly direction. Joubert wondered how these soldiers had got there so quickly as they didn't have vehicles. He was surprised that spoor could be picked up in this manner. There was no indication how the soldiers had been alerted to the emergency, given that the only message that had been conveyed was the one delivered to Williams's wife, and that the first public notice of the abduction was given by agri-alert. Despite these reservations, Joubert offered to help them follow the spoor immediately but the soldiers said their instructions were to await the arrival of army tracking teams. In the midst of the discussions a loud explosion erupted in the north and Joubert saw huge columns of smoke rising from Durban Mine, about four kilometres away. Leaving the soldiers on the road, Joubert's team immediately took off for Durban Mine, fearing for the safety of mining staff. On arrival they found that the store section, fuel tanks and the manager's house at the mine were ablaze, but no one had been injured because the staff had left earlier. Spoor of several men was picked up and followed north but the group bomb-shelled and so Joubert returned to Inyathi, where he found Lieutenant Colonel Lionel Dyck. Dyck said he was confident that Bilang and Williams were with the group heading west and had trackers following spoor from where tracks had been picked up near Illishe Hill.

Early the following morning, New Year's Day, Dyck reported that his tracking teams were on tracks near the Victoria Falls road (close to where the tourists had been abducted the previous July) and they were confident that Bilang was with them because he was plucking out his hair and leaving it as a trail. However, at this time a report was received from one of Williams's workers who said that he had seen armed men north of Tuf Nut Mine, between Tuf Nut and Durban Mine, washing blood from their bayonets in a cattle water trough. Dyck was dismissive of this information. He said his men were close to catching up to the abductees. Dissatisfied with this, another local farmer with tracking experience, Alex Goosen, decided he would backtrack from Durban Mine in an effort to find clues. The trail led Goosen to the water trough where the worker had seen armed men the previous day; from there the tracks were followed up a nearby hill. This was where Benji Williams's mutilated body was found – his throat had been slit and his stomach serially punctured. An extensive search was done of the entire surrounding area, but Bilang's body could not be found.

Early the following morning, 2 January 1983, Goosen, now with assistance from the Air Force and ZNA, picked up spoor north of Durban Mine and followed it, going in a north westerly direction. People who had seen the group along the way reported seeing a light-skinned man in their midst who spoke isiNdebele. This gave hope that the man might be Bilang, which hope was dashed when Goosen spoke on the radio to Phil Williams, Bilang's uncle, who said Dave could not speak isiNdebele. Further enquiries of people revealed that the group was in fact being led by this light-skinned (in Zimbabwean parlance "coloured") man, who was known as "Kiwa". The tracks were followed all the way to the Victoria Falls road where they disappeared – the explanation being that the group had been picked up on the main tar road. It was odd that a heavily armed group like this could get in a vehicle and disappear on a road that was heavily patrolled, with numerous police and army road-blocks.

The discovery of Benji Williams's body resulted in a massive public relations campaign being mounted by the government. Minister of

Agriculture Dennis Norman and Minister of Defence Sydney Sekeramayi came to the Turk Mine district to reassure farmers. The district was courted by the ZNA who convinced them that the only way to protect farmers from further attack was to deploy more troops, which happened within weeks with the arrival of the Fifth Brigade. Exactly the same happened in the Nyamandlovu farming community, to the north of Bulawayo, where a white farming family of six, including two children, had been brutally murdered, ostensibly by dissidents, and also on New Year's Eve.

With the benefit of hindsight the timing of these murders was remarkably convenient for ZANU PF. Dissident activity, by Sekeramayi's admission, had been tailing off, but suddenly, in three highly publicised events, had resurged dramatically. Bilang was the son of a prominent Bulawayo lawyer, Williams was the doyen of the Turk Mine farming community, and the family of six murdered in Nyamandlovu worked for Lonrho, one of Zimbabwe's biggest public companies. The conduct of the military in following up the Bilang/Williams abduction was highly suspicious. At best it was incompetent; at worst it was deliberately designed to put Joubert's team off the scent.

Subsequent events create even more suspicion, however. Bilang's body was found nine months later. Poignantly, the family remembers the length of time well because a week after Bilang was abducted his only sister found out she was pregnant with her first child, and the baby was born a week after the discovery of Dave's body. First was the discovery of a skull, which was found by a herdboy, and then further remains were exposed down an ant-bear hole close to where Benji Williams's body had been found. The skull was taken to John Martin, Bilang's dentist in Bulawayo, who confirmed from dental records that it was Bilang's. It is strange, to say the least, that professional policemen and soldiers did not find his body within weeks of his abduction.

The non-discovery of Bilang's body for nine months fuelled public interest and there were reports of the army insisting it was still looking for him, in the direction of the tracks that allegedly went west from Illishe Hill. The Bilang/Williams family was subsequently told by government that an ex-ZIPRA dissident, Gilbert Satchel Ngwenya, who had been captured, convicted and hanged in 1986 for the murder of the foreign tourists, had confessed to the murder of Bilang and Williams. Curiously, though, despite Ngwenya's "confession", no attempt was ever made to prosecute him for these murders. But most suspicious of all is the fact that "Kiwa" was identified subsequently, is still alive today and has played a major role in ZANU PF land invasions in the Turk Mine area in the last decade.[158] It may be that these were just a series of coincidences but one ironic fact remains: the highly publicised and emotive murders of white farmers and their families on New Year's Eve 1982 provided ZANU PF with the perfect justification to deploy the Fifth Brigade into Matabeleland.

I had spent New Year's Eve with Jenny at a Hogmanay dance in Bulawayo, unaware that evening of the drama unfolding in Nyamandlovu and Turk Mine. We only learnt of Dave Bilang's abduction the following evening and I was deeply distressed by the news. Bilang had been a good friend since junior school, one of the Napier Avenue crowd, and his abduction brought this nasty simmering civil conflict very close to home. I bought the prevailing conventional wisdom, namely, that this was the work of dastardly dissidents, hook, line and sinker.

Although pseudo guerrilla activity had been part and parcel of the Rhodesian war, I did not at the time suspect this. Accordingly, when I started work at Webb, Low and Barry the following Monday, 3 January 1983, my confidence in Mugabe was unshaken.

One of the first actions taken by government in the new year was to impose a dawn to dusk curfew in several Matabeleland North districts, namely Tsholotsho, Nyamandlovu, Lupane, Nkayi, Bubi and Dete. All forms of transport were banned, including scotch carts and bicycles. Stores were closed. Journalists were banned from going into curfew areas and road-blocks were set up on all roads leading into these districts; as a result the flow of information all but dried up. The government had made sure to cover all its bases. The previous July, shortly after the abduction of the foreign tourists, it had re-enacted a highly controversial old Rhodesian Front law – the Emergency Powers (Security Forces Indemnity) Regulations, which granted immunity from prosecution to all government officials and security forces so long as whatever action they had taken was "for the purposes of … the preservation of security of Zimbabwe". Just as they had done in the 1970s, the CCJP complained bitterly but were ignored.

The Fifth Brigade was deployed into the districts covered by the curfew on 20 January 1983, initially into Tsholotsho and Bubi, spreading to Lupane and Nkayi. From the outset it was clear that they were not interested in finding dissidents. Their target was the civilian population. In the only area ever analysed in detail – Tsholotsho – the Fifth Brigade went in systematically and thoroughly. Different units of the brigade were allocated to particular areas covering the entire district and once deployed they went village by village conducting a "grotesquely violent campaign against civilians, civil servants, ZAPU party chairmen, and occasionally, armed insurgents".[159] In 1982, during the arms cache crisis, the CIO, then under Mnangagwa's command, had raided Nest Egg farm and confiscated the entire archive of ZAPU and ZIPRA records, including the names of ZIPRA guerrillas, fallen and living, their families and addresses. It was these records that were used by the Fifth Brigade to "trace former ZIPRA cadres and their families for slaughter"[160]. From late January to mid March 1983, the Fifth Brigade murdered and tortured thousands of civilians, burnt hundreds of villages, and raped and pillaged entire communities. There were horrific public executions, people were lined up and shot in cold blood; on many occasions soldiers would arrive at villages with lists of people affiliated to ZAPU and those found would be assassinated in front of their families. On other occasions, entire families were herded into grass-roofed huts, which were then set alight. Pregnant women were bayonetted, killing the babies in their wombs. Young Ndebele men between the ages of 16 and 40 were particularly vulnerable and were frequently targeted and shot in cold blood. It is difficult in a book of this scope to capture the ferocity and extent of the Fifth Brigade's actions. Suffice it to say that the "actions of all preceding armies paled by comparison".[161]

On 27 January *The Chronicle* had reported that ZAPU MPs had complained in parliament that widespread atrocities were being committed. On 12 February the Catholic bishop of Bulawayo, Henry Karlen, wrote a letter to Mugabe detailing atrocities witnessed by priests and a German Catholic missionary, Dr JF Davis, at St Luke's Hospital in Lupane. Dr Davis later recorded the horrifying incidents she witnessed in the first few days of February:

On Sunday February 6 1983 a crowd of 20 people arrived from Silwane Primary School in the Lupane valley, some 20 kilometres from St Lukes. They had all been severely beaten up; amongst them were 3 lady teachers, one of whom was six months pregnant. They reported that, early that day, 14 trucks had arrived and systematically combed through one homestead after the other, beating and shooting people. From February 6 to 12 we admitted 68 assault cases from the surrounding area covering a 20 kilometre radius. They had been beaten up, some severely, and most of them suffered broken limbs and burns; 34 of them had gunshot wounds, among them a baby of six months. The dead included many young children, women and old men.[162]

Bishop Karlen asked Garfield Todd to deliver the letter. Todd shared the letter with his daughter Judith, who by coincidence saw General Solomon Mujuru, the ZNA commander, on 17 February and told him about the contents of the letter. General Mujuru told Judith he wanted to see the letter and the next day a subordinate, Brigadier Agrippa Mutambara, called by Judith's offices ostensibly to get the information. As things turned out, instead of seeking information Mutambara took Judith to a house and raped her. Judith believes that Mutambara was acting under orders as he was decidedly uncomfortable about the incident.[163] Undeterred, the following Monday, 21 February, Judith handed Mutambara copies of the letter to be given to Mujuru. Garfield Todd himself the same week facilitated the delivery of Karlen's original letter to Mugabe.

I was largely oblivious to the tragedy unfolding in Matabeleland North, although it was on my doorstep. The news blackout was very effective and not having friends or clients who came from the affected areas, all I heard were rumours of mass killings, which seemed unbelievably exaggerated. My first inkling that something was amiss came in February, when I received instructions from a Figtree farmer, June Davies, that on Sunday, 13 February 1983 an "army truck full of soldiers wearing bright red caps" had come to her Woodleigh farm and "arrested" her employee Milos Ndlovu. The soldiers ransacked Ndlovu's home and then drove off with him. Ms Davies reported the matter to the police the next day and was told that the army had evidence that Ndlovu had been involved in "secret meetings" and had been taken to Nyamandlovu for "further investigations".[164] At the same time Ms Davies reported that a bus had been stopped by soldiers wearing red berets near Figtree at Cyrene Mission, men were ordered off it and summarily executed. This was the first time, but by no means the last, that I had to find a "disappeared person". I made numerous calls to the police, CIO and others – none admitted having him, but some gave me the runaround, advising me that he had been detained by another agency, which then proved false.

We reported the disappearance to the International Committee for the Red Cross. Eventually, I wrote a letter, in vain, to the Chihambakwe Commission (set up by Mugabe to investigate allegations of Fifth Brigade atrocities) in November 1983. My letter wasn't even acknowledged. Milos Ndlovu was never found, although later in the year a mass grave was found near Cyrene Mission, not far from Figtree, and remains were removed by Anglican Bishop Robert Mercer, including a skull, which was presented to the Chihambakwe Commission.

For those not in the know the news blackout worked exceptionally well and all we got were snippets of horror stories which seemed too bizarre to be credible. At the time I had personal distractions too. I had applied to be admitted to the Zimbabwean Bar and on 25 February I appeared in the High Court, Bulawayo, a beautiful copper-domed building which dominates 8th Avenue, before Mr Justice Anthony Gubbay to be sworn in as a lawyer. The following day at the Bulawayo Presbyterian church, Jenny and I were married. There was a terrible drought so it was a brutally hot day. Both sets of parents, having emigrated from Zimbabwe, had to fly up; we were both still firmly in the red with student loans and I had to take another overdraft to help pay for the wedding, so it was a modest occasion. We spent the first night of our honeymoon at Maleme Rest Camp in the Matopos. There were hardly any other people there because of the curfew and the drive out was clouded by tension all around us. Several weeks before our wedding Jenny and I had been challenged and encouraged by the prophet Jeremiah and had shared these verses with those invited to the wedding:

> "Blessed is the man who trusts in the Lord, whose confidence is in him.
> He will be like a tree planted by the water that sends its roots out by the stream.
> It does not fear when heat comes; its leaves are always green.
> It has no worries in the year of drought and never fails to bear fruit."[165]

A week after our wedding, on 5 March, the political situation deteriorated further when the Fifth Brigade raided Joshua Nkomo's house in

Bulawayo's Pelandaba suburb. Nkomo himself had been warned of impending trouble so was not present when armed men stormed the house and interrogated staff members about his whereabouts. When they failed to get a satisfactory reply, they shot and killed Nkomo's driver and two other members of his household "out of hand".[166] The soldiers then rampaged through the house, smashing up the kitchen and destroying furniture; as they left, they gratuitously broke all the windscreens of his vehicles and ripped the upholstery of his settees with their bayonets. Nkomo, fearing for his life, was smuggled out of the country by his aides, going into exile.

The same day that Nkomo's house was raided an atrocity occurred in Matabeleland North. Although just one incident, it was typical of many similar attacks on innocent, unarmed civilians. Late that Friday night approximately 100 Fifth Brigade soldiers arrived at a village in Lupane, where only four siblings were present. The four, comprising a 15-year-old girl and her three older teenage brothers, were roughly woken up and then subjected to an harangue that they were all dissidents. They were beaten and then marched in the middle of the night to a camp near the Cewale River. On arrival they had to give their names and were then herded into a building along with others, eventually numbering 62, comprising people from throughout the surrounding area. Once in the building each person was systematically called out of the building, including the 15-year-old girl. Each person was then beaten severely, accused all the time of being dissidents and ZAPU supporters; the girl reported being beaten "with a thick stick about 18 inches long all over the body". Each one of the detained people was beaten continuously until about 3 am on Saturday morning. Then they were marched by Fifth Brigade soldiers to the banks of the Cewale River a few hundred metres from the camp. Here all 62 people, men, women and teenagers, were lined up and gunned down by the soldiers using AK-47 rifles. One of the teenage girl's brothers, who had been standing next to her, was killed instantly; the girl was shot in her left thigh and collapsed among the dead. Miraculously she, her two remaining brothers and four others survived the onslaught and just lay among the dead pretending to be dead. Once the cacophony of firing had died down the soldiers moved among the bodies and "finished off some of the others who had survived". The girl and her brothers lay still until the soldiers left. They then crept away and managed to get home. The two brothers were severely wounded; one had been shot in the chest and arm, the other in the foot. They all survived but one of the youngsters had to have his entire arm amputated, the other his foot.[167] This incident was later confirmed by the missionary doctor Johanna Davis in her autobiography, published shortly before her death, at the age of 97, in April 2015.[168]

The day before the Cewale River massacre happened, on 4 March, two politicians made statements which were diametrically opposed to one another. The first was made by Emmerson Mnangagwa, then minister of State for Security (in charge of the CIO). In a rally held in Matabeleland North, not far from Lupane, he told his audience that government had "an option" of "burning down … all the villages infested with dissidents". He warned that "the campaign against dissidents can only succeed if the infrastructure which nurtures them is destroyed". In a supercilious manner he chillingly described dissidents as "cockroaches" and the Fifth Brigade as "DDT" brought in to eradicate them.[169] The speech was given in the very province where these massacres were taking place and he would have been in possession of intelligence regarding exactly what was going on.

Although the Rome Statute of the International Criminal Court only entered the world's jurisprudence long after 1983, its definition of a "crime against humanity" is relevant in assessing the moral, if not legal, culpability of politicians for their words and actions. Article 7 includes in its definition of "crimes against humanity", "persecution of an identifiable political group", murder and "enforced disappearance", committed as "part of a systematic attack directed against any civilian population" in "furtherance of a State policy to commit such an attack".[170] Mugabe was cunning enough to deny that atrocities had taken place or to couch his language sufficiently ambiguously to avoid a nexus being made between his statements and the actions that followed. Mnangagwa, in these statements and in others he made later, left no room for speculation, but chose to make clear that the actions of the CIO and Fifth Brigade were meticulously planned. In the vortex of the joint Fifth Brigade and CIO actions, he stated plainly that the action against the civilian population of Matabeleland was part of a deliberate state policy.

The same day Mnangagwa spoke, but in a different place, Harare, another politician – a former missionary – pleaded with ZANU PF. Garfield Todd told the senate that anti-dissident action should not involve "the killing of innocents" and stated that "we who are part of the government of this country have a responsibility to demand security for peasants in villages".[171]

Not even Todd, however, knew exactly what was going on. This was the age before satellite television, cell phones and the internet; there was also a rigidly imposed curfew and journalists, under pain of death, were kept out of the areas where the Fifth Brigade was operating. The only papers, TV and radio stations were government controlled. Although I lived in Bulawayo and Jenny was working at the main referral hospital, neither of us understood what was going on. I wrote to my parents at the time that the reports appearing in overseas newspapers about "wholesale massacres" seemed "unfounded". I added: *"Jenny has kept a very close eye on the situation at Mpilo and has treated (since getting back from honeymoon) only 5 new gunshot wound patients – totally inconsistent with reports of war."*[172]

It took the bravery of a few Catholics to first expose the full extent of the horror. Mike Auret, who was then chairman of the CCJP, received a phone call from the head of the CCJP's Bulawayo branch, Joel Simon Silonda, a few weeks after the Fifth Brigade had been deployed. Silonda said that atrocities were taking place and he urged Auret to come to Bulawayo, which he did. After meeting Silonda and Bishop Karlen, Auret was sufficiently concerned to drive out to St Luke's Hospital in Lupane, where he met Dr Davis, who showed him shocking evidence. Auret spoke to injured civilians and listened as he was told horrific stories of mass murder, torture, rape and abductions. The director of the CCJP was dispatched to Matabeleland to investigate further; a comprehensive report was done and approved by the Catholic Bishops Conference, which decided that a delegation should be sent to see Mugabe.

On 16 March, bishops Karlen, Reckter and Mutume, together with Auret, met Mugabe to present him with the report. Mugabe was accompanied by Mnangagwa and Defence minister Sekeramayi who Auret "believed were more aware than Mugabe of the true state of affairs in Matabeleland".[173] Mugabe promised to look into their concerns but said he doubted that "innocent civilians were being violated in any way". The bishops advised Mugabe of their intention to publish a pastoral letter entitled "Reconciliation is still possible", which they did two weeks later over the Easter weekend. It was strongly worded and spoke of the media's failure to reveal the truth about "wanton killings, woundings, beatings, burnings and rapings" of innocent civilians. A few days after the publication of the letter Mugabe reacted angrily, refuting the allegations and calling the authors "a band of Jeremiahs (which) included reactionary foreign journalists, non-government organisations of dubious status in our midst, and sanctimonious prelates".[174] A few days later, however, Mugabe lifted the curfew in Matabeleland North and said that the allegations of atrocities would be investigated and those responsible, if any, brought to book.[175] There was also a change in Fifth Brigade tactics from late March onwards and a "marked decline in atrocities".[176]

In the midst of this I had been focused on two matters. Still wet behind the ears, I had been instructed to defend a young National Parks employee, Bernard McConville, who had been charged with possession of an AK-47 rifle and its ammunition, which he had received in 1980 and, not knowing what to do, had thrown down a latrine. The charge carried a severe penalty – a mandatory five-year prison term – and it was my first experience of having the future of a person in my hands. Alongside this case I had agreed to be the campaign manager for the father of another of my old Napier Avenue friends, Dr Bob Nixon, a local dentist. There was a by-election in one of the all-white (Lancaster House Constitution) seats in Bulawayo and Nixon was standing as an independent against an RF candidate. It was the first public demonstration of my change of political thought since the 1970s. Although I had met Smith as student leader while at UCT, and acknowledged his resolve to make Zimbabwe work, my years at UCT saw a 180 degree change in my attitude towards Smith and the RF. Having had the benefit of studying the RF's conduct through more objective lenses at UCT I had become deeply critical of the RF. In addition to its racist policies, it had negligently squandered several opportunities to avoid war. I felt bitter that so many lives had been lost in a needless war and blamed the entire RF leadership for the loss of friends and even for my parents' emigration. It seemed to me that the RF's hardline policies had radicalised black nationalists and poisoned an entire generation. In my mind we needed to move on and the thought of the RF continuing to be the main representative of white opinion in parliament was anathema to me. Accordingly, when Nixon asked me to help him I leapt at the opportunity. The by-election was for a seat which had been solidly RF for over seventeen years. For the first time, I got drawn into a political battle and had to deal with a sceptical white electorate reeling from the chaos pervading the city.

Ian Smith came to Bulawayo to speak in support of the RF candidate.

He was still a powerful force among whites. Nine other RF MPs had crossed the floor to become independents, including Chris Andersen, one of Zimbabwe's leading advocates, who came to assist Nixon's campaign. Throughout the campaign, Nixon and I stressed the need for whites to play our role in creating an atmosphere of mutual trust among races. I had a good day on April 7; that morning I won my first major case when a suspended sentence was imposed on McConville and that afternoon I was present when it was announced that Nixon had narrowly won the seat by 80 votes. It was a major surprise – the RF had never lost a by-election anywhere in the country – and it appeared to indicate that whites understood the constructive role they needed to play in a new Zimbabwe. Nixon affirmed this sentiment, thanking voters for not wanting to "maintain white superiority" and urging them "to have faith in the future and (to) be positive".[177]

Although April started on this positive note in Bulawayo it soon became clear that out in the countryside there had not been a change of heart by government, but merely a change in tactics. Aside from Mugabe's angry response to the Catholic pastoral letter, Mnangagwa made it quite clear on 7 April that there would be no let up when he told another rally in Matabeleland North that the Fifth Brigade had come to Matabeleland like fire "and in the process of cleansing the area of the dissident menace had also wiped out their supporters".[178] At the same rally Mnangagwa parodied the Beatitudes (the quotation at the beginning of this chapter) promising "woe" to those collaborating with dissidents and "to shorten their stay on earth".[179] At the time Mnangagwa made this statement he must have been in possession of the Catholic Bishops' report presented to Mugabe and him in Harare on 16 March detailing Fifth Brigade atrocities, yet he showed no remorse. All that happened was that the Fifth Brigade and the CIO refined its activities; instead of mass abductions they became more selective. Villagers, mainly men aged between 16 and 40, were "disappeared" from villages and taken to central Fifth Brigade or CIO camps where they were interrogated, beaten and often killed. Men were also "disappeared" from buses, trains and homes, even in urban areas. Many were taken because they were on the lists, supplied to the Fifth Brigade by the CIO, of men who had been ex-ZIPRA or who held some position in ZAPU. These people were, more often than not, never seen again.

In late April Mugabe heard directly from political leaders in

Matabeleland North about atrocities taking place. Cephas Msipa (then a ZAPU cabinet minister) was approached by ZANU PF governor of Matabeleland North Jacob Mudenda, who asked him to arrange a meeting with Mugabe so that rural district chairmen from the province could appeal to him regarding the "intolerable cruelty people were suffering".* Msipa asked Mnangagwa to arrange a meeting, which he did. The meeting was held on the sidelines of the opening of the 1983 International Trade Fair at State House, Bulawayo. A five-hour session ensued, during which the chairmen of Binga, Hwange, Tsholotsho, Lupane, Nkayi and Bubi districts "spoke in graphic detail of the atrocities".† According to Msipa, Mugabe agreed in the meeting to replace the Fifth Brigade with a police Support Unit.

The complaints raised by the Catholic bishops and the district chairmen were reflected in cases that were coming to my attention. In a letter to my parents in May I reported that I now had "5 clients who I am trying to locate ... held by the army". I complained that the army had "no respect for either the rule of law or the sanctity of human life". My law firm had allocated all its security-related work to me and it was taking up most of my time. I met with senior CIO and police officers to complain about these disappearances, pointing out to them that I had been doing the same thing in South Africa for the last few years and did not expect in a "supposedly democratic, progressive, peoples' republic to be doing the same thing".[180] I never managed to find any of the men I had been instructed to locate during this time.

An additional tragedy when there is widespread abuse of human rights is that people become statistics and we forget the personal trauma suffered by families. To counter that it is important to give a glimpse of the personal tragedy. One case I handled at this time illustrates this. I received instructions in early June 1983 from the CCJP concerning the disappearance of an ex-ZIPRA guerrilla, a serving member of 2.1 Battalion of the ZNA in good standing. His name was Toddy Vusumuzi Bhebhe. Bhebhe was arrested while on duty by the CIO on 23 February and taken to Bulawayo. I wrote to the CIO asking after his whereabouts and on 12 July received a letter from the CIO staying that Bhebhe "was released on the 15th March 1983 to members of the 5th Brigade

---

* Msipa, Cephas. *In Pursuit of Freedom and Justice – A Memoir.* Weaver Press, 2015, p 114. Msipa's book was released shortly before this book went to print.

† Msipa, op cit, p 114

based at Lupane". I then made exhaustive enquiries within the Army and eventually, on 30 November, I received a letter from the secretary for Defence stating "5th Brigade members do not seem to remember this insident (sic) at all." The file was closed the following year and the Bhebhe family never found out what happened to their son.

The CCJP continued gathering evidence through April, May and June and in July, Auret and the same three Catholic bishops as before met Mugabe again to present another report of ongoing human rights abuses by the Fifth Brigade and CIO. As before, Mnangagwa and Sekeramayi were present, only this time they were also joined by Army Commander General Mujuru. The report was met with a "stony silence"[181] but Mugabe did promise to establish a commission of inquiry.

The same month I became more aware of the horrendous things happening. Jenny, who was still working at Mpilo hospital, reported that there was a large increase in civilians coming in with gunshot wounds and other serious injuries. One of our friends in church, who also worked with Jenny, was a Scottish orthopaedic surgeon, Ken Rankin. Ken sought advice from me about a dilemma he was facing. Alarmed by the injuries he was having to treat and concerned about his responsibilities to report evidence of torture in terms of the 1981 Handbook of Medical Ethics and UN Resolution 3453 of 1975, he had prepared a detailed report, including photographs, of torture victims he had treated. This had been submitted to Mugabe and Mnangagwa, through the minister of Health. When Mugabe received the report he demanded to know who had taken the photographs and Rankin's name was mentioned. Rankin, although married to a senior ANC leader, Joyce Rankin, living in exile in Zimbabwe, was British, white and on a short-term work permit. Rankin was worried about a threat to deport him and it was on this matter that he sought my advice. In the process he catalogued the gunshot and other serious wounds he had observed on civilian men, women and children. His report, coming from a completely different source independent of the CCJP, containing photographs, removes any doubt that by July, Mugabe, Mnangagwa and other senior leaders knew precisely what atrocities had been perpetrated by the Fifth Brigade.

Shortly after the submission of these reports the Fifth Brigade was withdrawn from Matabeleland North for "retraining", but before they left they committed one further major atrocity. It occurred in Solonkwe, a small village in western Tsholotsho on 10 July; Fifth Brigade soldiers forced 22 villagers, including 9 women and 6 children, into a hut and then set it ablaze burning them all alive.[182]

It was apparent to me that one reason why the CIO and the Fifth Brigade were able to act with such impunity was because most poor people had no way of protecting themselves. Because of years of colonialism the legal system was alien to most poor black Zimbabweans; the police were either fearful or hostile and while the courts were generally sympathetic, the legal profession was urban based and inaccessible. In March 1983 the Bulawayo Legal Practitioners Association (BLPA) had called an emergency meeting to discuss the "threatening attitude of the Police" and its "misuse of Emergency Powers regulations".[183] That meeting was followed by a recognition that there were many people who didn't even have the luxury of legal representation – at the time there was minimal legal aid offered by the state and no organisation which offered free legal advice to those who could not afford lawyers' fees. In early August the BLPA convened a meeting to discuss the problem. At the meeting I volunteered to set up a legal aid clinic, modelled on the one I had run at Crossroads, which would be attended by lawyers in private practice who would give of their time. Within weeks we had a roster of lawyers and secured premises in Charter House, donated to us by Anglo American, then one of Zimbabwe's largest public companies. The Bulawayo Legal Aid Clinic had a trial run in November and opened the following February. It was soon flooded with people suffering from the onslaught wrought by the CIO and the Fifth Brigade. The clinic ended up handling hundreds of cases before it metamorphosed into the Bulawayo Legal Projects Centre in 1986.

Nkomo, partly sensing that the political climate had improved and partly to avoid losing his seat in parliament, returned to Zimbabwe on 16 August, ending his self-imposed exile. However, the Fifth Brigade was redeployed back into Matabeleland North on 29 August and almost immediately disappearances and gross human rights abuses resumed after the brief lull while they were "retraining". There was still no word from Mugabe on the commission of inquiry he had promised. The CCJP kept badgering his office until it was announced on 13 September by Sekeramayi that a commission to look into Fifth Brigade activity in Matabeleland North would be set up under the chairmanship of Simplicius Chihambakwe, a Harare lawyer who had been part of the ZANU PF delegation at the 1976 Geneva talks. Sekeramayi stated that the commission would "report to the Prime Minister and everything would be made known to the people of the country".[184]

The appointment of the Chihambakwe Commisssion appeared to have a sobering effect on the Fifth Brigade because the incidences of abuse reduced dramatically. The conflict in Matabeleland continued to simmer – there was ongoing Fifth Brigade and dissident activity – but overall it paled in comparison to the earlier horror. Attention shifted to a series of political rallies. At these rallies captured dissidents were paraded and forced to declare their allegiance to ZAPU. Civilians were encouraged to disown ZAPU and during this period some 20 000 ZAPU supporters surrendered their ZAPU cards and bought ZANU PF cards as an insurance policy. Reports of killings by both Fifth Brigade and dissidents continued to filter through, but were much reduced.

My own workload continued to grow. The CCJP was channelling more work through to me and I now had the additional responsibility of running the Legal Aid Clinic. As I left the office on 24 October I noticed a personal note addressed to me by Bob Cole, the senior partner of Webb, Low and Barry; thinking it was some instruction for a new case I opened it casually and was pleasantly surprised to read the opening paragraph: "When Mr Barry retires on 31.3.84 we would like you to join the partnership." I discussed the offer with him the next day. Although this conservative firm had deep concerns about my security-related work and its potential to bring me into confrontation with the government, they appreciated that it was a necessary evil; in addition they recognised that with all the turmoil they needed to offer a substantial carrot to ensure that I stayed. The remaining months of the year were a blur, brought upon by an increasing workload, which included representing dissidents for the first time. I still did not fully appreciate the extent of the human rights violations that had occurred that year but that changed when I received instructions from the CCJP to assist them to prepare for the Chihambakwe Commission's hearings scheduled for early 1984.

The brutal reality of genocide confronted me on Tuesday and Wednesday, 6 and 7 December, in the genteel surrounds of St Mary's Catholic Cathedral hall. Bulawayo's 8th Avenue is dominated by the gracious High Court building which sits astride its western end, as is 9th Avenue by the Catholic Cathedral. It was here that the CCJP brought hundreds of Fifth Brigade victims so that affidavits could be recorded from them. I sat before woman after woman (the survivors were overwhelmingly female), recording the most horrendous evidence of crimes against humanity. Sitting at a table in the hall one woman after another told me how her husband, father, brother, son, uncle, grandfather, nephew had been gunned down before their very eyes; how whole families had been herded into huts – men, women and children, even babies – which were then locked from the outside and set alight. It was here for the first time I heard about the Cewale River massacre, the Solonkwe burning and countless other atrocities. It was here that I heard about pregnant women who had been bayonetted; I was told about the systematic rape of others. Independent corroboration of a story gives it credence and taking scores of statements individually from women hailing from all over Matabeleland North left me in no doubt about the veracity of what they were alleging. The systematic and sustained nature of the abuse, which lasted several months and occurred in different areas hundreds of kilometres apart, removed any doubt whether this was a carefully planned, deliberate operation, not some random aberration of a few soldiers on a frolic of their own. I do not use the word "genocide" lightly – it means the act of intending to destroy, in whole or part, an ethnic group through killing, causing serious bodily or mental harm to a group and deliberately inflicting on the group conditions calculated to bring about its physical destruction. That was precisely the evidence presented to me by this benighted group of women.[185] What I heard was about a brigade of exclusively Shona soldiers, backed by the state's intelligence service, who were targeting Ndebele men between the ages of 16 and 40 and entire communities of Ndebele people. Likewise "crimes against humanity" – any widespread or systematic attack directed against any civilian population using murder, extermination, torture, rape, enforced disappearance and other inhumane acts intentionally causing great suffering – fitted the bill.[186]

I was profoundly shocked but moved as well. The quiet bravery of these women, and the Catholic laypeople and priests, was inspirational. It was the first time I met Joel Silonda, Father Pius Ncube and Bishop Henry Karlen and each one of them was utterly determined to speak truth to power. While my confidence in Mugabe himself was shaken, I still entertained the belief that he could not possibly be aware of, or in support of, these dreadful crimes committed by his subordinates.

The Chihambakwe Commission started hearing evidence in Bulawayo on 10 January 1984. The commission, comprising Chihambakwe, retired

Major-General M Shute, Prince Machaya, a government lawyer, and its secretary, CIO operative John Ngara, only expected a handful to appear but instead they were "confronted with hundreds of potential witnesses".[187] Despite aggressive interrogation from Ngara, witness after witness gave evidence of the astonishing brutality visited on them and their families. Looking back, the bravery of these mainly poor rural women was exceptional. The CCJP could offer them no security once they returned to their homes in the rural areas; the Gukurahundi was still ongoing, the Fifth Brigade and CIO still on their murderous rampage – and yet despite this they were determined to tell the commission what they had witnessed, presumably in the belief that something would be done to honour their dead and to stop the nightmare. Overwhelmed by the flood of witnesses the commission adjourned on 14 January, before the CCJP had had an opportunity to present its evidence, advising that it would be back to take more statements. Chihambakwe and his colleagues all returned to Harare and presumably briefed about what they had heard.

An intriguing, but sinister, change in policy was then implemented. Before the Chihambakwe Commission reconvened, a curfew was imposed on the whole of Matabeleland South province on 4 February 1984 and the Fifth Brigade and other army units were transferred there. With the Fifth Brigade no longer in Matabeleland North province, the incidence of abuse in that part of the country tailed off dramatically, almost overnight, but now it was transferred to the people in Matabeleland South. This is arguably Zimbabwe's driest province, an area of 8 000 square kilometres with a population then of 400 000. The province had suffered three successive years of drought and thousands were entirely dependent on humanitarian relief supplies of food. Overnight government closed all stores and halted all food supplies, including drought relief. As had happened the year before in the north, the curfew severely restricted the movement of all people. However, unlike 1983, the Fifth Brigade did not start murdering people in their villages. Instead they occupied an old army barracks at Bhalagwe and began a campaign of abducting people throughout Matabeleland South and detaining them there. As the crow flies, Bhalagwe is fifteen kilometres south of Kezi, five kilometres west of a large irrigation scheme situated near Antelope Dam. The camp was in the centre of a bowl, flanked by two large granite hills and surrounded by thick bush. Even now, three decades on, there are no villages near it in an otherwise crowded Communal Land.[188]

The modus operandi was simple and efficient. The CIO and Fifth Brigade were deployed throughout Matabeleland South and they systematically detained all ex-ZIPRA veterans and ZAPU officials. Other men, women and even children were detained somewhat randomly in sweeps through village lines. Detainees would be taken to the nearest Fifth Brigade base and held until they could fill a truck with some 100 people to transport them to Bhalagwe. Sun Yet Sen police camp, where I had spent the first few months of 1977, was used as a holding camp for up to 800 people in the areas bordering Botswana. People were then brought to Bhalagwe from throughout Matabeleland South, from as far afield as Gwanda and Plumtree. Bhalagwe at the time had some 180 asbestos sheds and these were where the detainees were kept. On 7 February 1984 one early detainee was ordered to count all the inmates there at that time, and he recorded 1 856 people, just under half of them women.[189] It is estimated that at least 8 000 people went through Bhalagwe for the four months it was used as a concentration camp. Detainees were systematically tortured using electric shock; rape was commonplace, as was genital mutilation. Although the murders were not on the scale of what happened in 1983, surviving inmates of Bhalagwe witnessed daily deaths either from people being shot or as a result of the severe beatings they received. Initially, bodies would be buried within the camp but at some point the bodies were exhumed for dumping in local mine shafts, which then became the destination for all those killed in the camp. The key motivation behind the entire new modus was to prevent evidence coming to light. Clearly, ZANU PF was embarrassed by the revelations made so easily from the brazen Fifth Brigade conduct in 1983.[190]

While the Fifth Brigade and the CIO were wreaking havoc at Bhalagwe, the Chihambakwe Commission reconvened in Bulawayo on 23 March and the CCJP, led by Auret, finally was able to present its evidence on 28 March. Evidence was led from seventeen witnesses, including one of the survivors of the Cewale River massacre who had had his left arm amputated. Auret was angered by the callous way in which the CIO representative on the commission, Ngara, interrogated him.[191] Auret gave evidence himself, producing a skull that had been recovered from a mass grave which gave un-rebuttable corroboration – a single gunshot wound in the temple. The mass grave referred to was the one discovered by the Anglican bishop of Matabeleland, Robert Mercer, near Cyrene Anglican Mission, close to where my client's employee Milos

Ndlovu had been disappeared in January 1983.

The commission wound up its work and its members returned to Harare without giving any indication when it would publish its report as had originally been promised. In October 1984 Chihambakwe attended the Law Society of Zimbabwe's Summer School at the Montclair Hotel in Nyanga; I used the opportunity to ask him when the report would be made public. Chihambakwe told me that the publication had been delayed by the printing house which had also printed papers for the August 1984 ZANU PF congress, but assured me it would be made public. That hope was quashed a year later when Mnangagwa announced that it would not be made public. In 1999 Zimbabwe Lawyers for Human Rights (ZLHR) and the Legal Resources Foundation (LRF) brought a case against Mugabe in terms of Zimbabwe's constitution seeking the publication of both the Chihambakwe Commission report and the earlier Dumbutshena Commission report. Mnangagwa deposed to an affidavit opposing the application on the grounds that the findings were "solely for use by the Government" and that because of its "sensitivity" it was not reproduced. Almost four years after the case was brought in November 2003, the Supreme Court, under the now Chief Justice Chidyausiku, agreed with Mnangagwa. In its remarkably brief judgment, the court found the mere fact that the reports were wanted in the "public interest" was not good enough.[192]

No doubt somewhat embarrassingly for ZANU PF, the CCJP had managed to present fresh evidence of what was happening at Bhalagwe when it appeared before the commission in late March 1984. In addition, during this time ZAPU central committee members, including Welshman Mabhena, approached cabinet minister Cephas Msipa again imploring him to arrange a meeting with Mugabe to draw attention to "continuing atrocities".* As had happened in April 1983 the meeting was held at State House in Bulawayo, but this time it was much larger. Msipa records that it was "as if a rally had been called" with people arriving at State House on bicycles and on foot. Once again Mugabe heard chilling evidence for two hours from survivors as many spoke, "some with tears running down their cheeks, saying how many relatives had been lost at the hands of soldiers", how "friends were detained for no reason, tortured, executed". Msipa records that after listening to their impassioned pleas

---

* Msipa, op cit, p 116. Msipa does not say in his book exactly when this meeting took place in 1984 but it appears to have been in the first half of the year.

Mugabe said he "was sorry to hear what was happening" but also implored people to stop "supporting dissidents".† Whether the CCJP's fresh evidence and this meeting influenced the decision to lift the curfew imposed on Matabeleland South, which happened on 10 April, we shall never know, but that is what happened. Coincidentally, the numbers of people detained at Bhalagwe started to reduce and by the end of May the mass detentions ended. Shortly afterwards, in mid 1984, the Fifth Brigade was withdrawn from active duty and underwent five months of "infantry training" at Mbalabala barracks near Esigodini. Although it had one further tour of duty in Matabeleland in 1985 it did not revert to the same level of its 1983/4 criminal activity. It was involved in abductions in the run up to the 1985 elections, but did not engage in the murder of thousands as it had before. Eventually, in 1986 it underwent "conventional training" under the British Military Advisory Training Team and was made a regular brigade of the ZNA.[193]

ZANU PF has largely sought to wipe away the memory of the Gukurahundi. Mugabe later called it an "act of madness" and conceded that they had engaged in a "reckless and unprincipled fight". But then in the same speech he sought to justify it, saying, "we killed each other" and "both sides were to blame".[194] At the time it was justified on the grounds of military necessity, and some even after the Gukurahundi justified it on these grounds. Lieutenant Colonel Dyck, for example, said the following:

> "I support it [deployment of the Fifth Brigade] ... often you have to be cruel to be kind. Had an operation like that not taken place, that battle would have gone on for years and years as a festering sore. The fact is that when Fifth Brigade went in they did brutally deal with the problem. If you were a dissident sympathiser, you died. And it brought peace very, very quickly. When the Fifth Brigade went in they were quite prepared to take that role [i.e. of extra-judicial killings] and they were successful."[195]

The fact is that it did not bring peace and the battles continued for over three more years after the Fifth Brigade had been withdrawn. Government's own figures of dissident activity show no measurable

---

† Msipa, op cit, p 117

decline in dissident activity as a result of Fifth Brigade actions. In the Gukurahundi period of the Fifth Brigade's deployment from January 1983 to July 1984 government recorded 165 murders, 84 rapes and 497 robberies allegedly committed by dissidents. In the two years following, 1985 and 1986, government recorded dissidents being responsible for 264 murders, 184 rapes and 688 robberies.[196] If anything, dissident activity was greater after the Gukurahundi than before.

Hindsight shows that the Gukurahundi primarily sought political rather than military objectives. Mugabe, long before taking power, expressed the view that "the multiparty system [was] a luxury".[197] He often stated that he wanted to bring about a one-party state. He also warned that if Zimbabweans did not like a one-party state "we will have to re-educate them". ZAPU stood in the way of that goal because of its rock solid support in the south west of Zimbabwe. At the time of the Gukurahundi, Mugabe called ZAPU a "dissident party" and like many of his lieutenants vowed to destroy ZAPU. Given the Fifth Brigade's tactics of not going after dissidents, it appears that their primary motivation was to destroy ZAPU's support base; to so intimidate ZAPU followers that they would never support ZAPU again. The message that civilians got in Matabeleland North and South from the Fifth Brigade was "it is impossible to have more than one political party in [Zimbabwe], otherwise you will be punished".[198]

At the time it happened this intention was not as obvious as it is now. In particular, Mugabe at the time was not clearly implicated in the genocide. Auret writes that his "regard for Mugabe was not diminished" by mid 1984. He was "content to lay the blame for the atrocities on the ministers (viz Mnangagwa and Sekeramayi), the military commanders" but not Mugabe.[199] While my own trust in Mugabe had been shaken, I, too, without the benefit of hindsight, still felt then that he could not be aware of all that had taken place.

ZANU PF decided in mid 1984 to change strategy again. One can only speculate that it was the result of a combination of believing that the "shock treatment" had been successfully administered to the public of Matabeleland and the realisation that their crimes against humanity could not be continued indefinitely. The new strategy was aimed at annihilating the second-tier leadership of ZAPU, which in turn would bring me personally into increasing conflict with ZANU PF and Mugabe.

CHAPTER 10

"YOU'LL BE SEEING FIRE" – THE ANNIHILATION OF ZAPU JULY 1984 TO 1987

"We want to wipe out the ZAPU leadership. You've only seen the warning lights. We haven't yet reached full blast. The murderous organisation must be hit hard. I'll lock up more MPs and the leader himself. I've locked up a few honourable members (of Parliament) and I think they will have to rest for a long time to come."[200]
– Minister of Home Affairs, Enos Nkala, 1985

During the last few months of the Fifth Brigade's reign of terror in Matabeleland my legal practice was becoming hectically busy. On becoming a partner in April 1984, I took over the entire case load of a partner who had emigrated. The Bulawayo Legal Aid Clinic (BLAC) opened its doors in February. Some 24 lawyers from Bulawayo had volunteered their time and I was responsible for the general administration of the clinic. In that role, I was invited by the Ford Foundation to a conference hosted in Harare at the end of February to debate the future of legal aid in Zimbabwe. It was to be a pivotal meeting in that it brought together a variety of key Zimbabweans who were to pioneer public interest law in Zimbabwe, including Enock Dumbutshena, Ian Donovan and Eileen Sawyer. Dumbutshena was Zimbabwe's first black High Court judge, who had acquitted the Zimbabwe Air Force officers detained following the 1982 South African attack on Thornhill airbase, thus earning the wrath of ZANU PF. Donovan was arguably Zimbabwe's leading human rights advocate at the time. Sawyer was a long-standing opponent of the Rhodesian Front, an archetypical white liberal who had established both the Harare Citizens Advice Bureau and the University of Rhodesia's Legal Aid Clinic. Later that year, the three became the founding trustees of the Legal Resources Foundation (LRF), modelled on Arthur Chaskalson's South African Legal Resources Centre which had inspired me so much at UCT. Although the BLAC was in its infancy, we had the first tentative discussions of how we might collaborate to establish a national network of clinics.

The difference in atmosphere between Bulawayo and the rest of the country was startling; very few people, even human rights activists, fully understood the trauma the people of Matabeleland were experiencing. Although there were worrying breaches of the rule of law which occurred in Harare, such as the re-detention of people acquitted by the High Court, the rural areas outside of Matabeleland were safe and there were no known torture camps. As the year progressed I received an increasing number of instructions that indicated a change of strategy by the government. It became clear that they were intent on undermining ZAPU structures and any organisations which might come to their assistance. Serious human rights abuses were taking place right on our doorstep, at the Stops Police Camp, not even a kilometre from the High Court in Bulawayo. No one was immune and two incidents involving the Anglican Church in May 1984 illustrate this.

I received instructions to represent Father Ozias Mkhosana, a 55-year-old Anglican priest, who was detained and held incommunicado for allegedly "recruiting dissidents and being involved in subversive activities". Using Rhodesian-era emergency powers regulations, the police were able to detain Mkhosana on a whim without having to produce him in court. It soon became apparent that he was being held simply because he had been rather too outspoken about Fifth Brigade activities.

The same month I received instructions to assist Father JR Milton, the Anglican Vicar General and Archdeacon of Matabeleland, who was receiving threatening phone calls from the police. Father Milton had been horrified by the treatment meted out to a congregant at Stops Camp. The man had been detained by police and in his report Father Milton advised:

"*Using aggressive means the Police forced him to admit. His torturers were armed with aggressive instruments e.g. pick handles, iron rods and sjamboks. The seven men tied the victim's hands and feet. They used bags full of water inserted on the victim's head in order to avoid screaming and halt breathing. He was thrashed thoroughly until one of his arms were broken. They promised to kill him if he didn't react positively.*"[201]

For bringing this complaint to the attention of the police, Father Milton was then himself harassed and had to seek our assistance. A meeting was held with senior police officers in May 1984, which ended the phone calls. The original complaint of torture was never investigated.

These actions targeted against the Anglican Church were simply a precursor to fairly widespread ZANU PF-inspired action against its perceived enemies in the run up to the 1985 election. Concurrent with the training of the Fifth Brigade, ZANU PF had also trained up a Youth Brigade which was unleashed on the public for the first time in 1984. In June, there was a week of violent demonstrations by the Youth Brigade in several cities where ZAPU had support. The most serious riots were in Kwe Kwe, where Youth Brigade members stoned and burned homes of ZAPU and Muzorewa's UANC supporters. (Muzorewa himself had been detained the previous November and spent most of 1984 in detention on spurious grounds – he was never charged with anything.) Then local ZAPU MP William Kona's house and the ZAPU offices were ransacked and burnt.[202]

ZANU PF held its Second People's Congress from 8–13 August 1984. The congress, which was held in the rather incongruous – for a Marxist Leninist party – luxury of Harare's Borrowdale Race Course, demonstrated ZANU PF's political intent with crystal clarity. In his four-and-a-half-hour address Mugabe said that he expected a mandate in the 1985 elections to "proceed towards the full attainment of (their) political goals – the establishment of a one-party state and the fulfilment of the socialist revolution".[203] The main obstacle in the way of that vision was ZAPU.

In the ensuing months a concerted campaign against ZAPU supporters and leaders unfolded in areas where the Fifth Brigade had not operated. It started in October when the ZANU PF governor of Midlands province Benson Ndemera delivered an "incendiary speech" at the funeral of a ZANU PF official killed by dissidents. Six busloads of Youth Brigade responded by rampaging through the Maboleni area of Lower Gweru, beating up ZAPU supporters, torching 64 homes, three stores and six cars.[204] Four people were murdered and several hundred were left homeless. Although this was well organised and committed in broad daylight, no arrests were made and no prosecutions followed.

Just a few weeks later I had my own first-hand experience of the Machiavellian nature of ZANU PF's ploys. On the evening of Wednesday, 14 November I received instructions to represent two members of the Beitbridge Rural District Council, its chairman, a local businessman named Raymond Roth, and its executive secretary, Lewis Watson, who had been detained by the police. Beitbridge, a town bordering South Africa, marked the edge of a political divide; the area to the east of the town towards the Mozambique border was solidly ZANU PF, and to the west was equally solidly ZAPU. This was a legacy of the war and demarcated where the respective guerrilla armies' (ZANLA and ZIPRA) hegemony lay. Early the previous Friday, on 9 November, the local ZANU PF senator Moven Ndlovu had been shot and killed by an unknown assailant in Beitbridge. His murder was followed by an outburst of violence by ZANU PF Youth Brigade members and militia, who roamed through Beitbridge's townships beating up anyone suspected of being a ZAPU supporter; a score of people died and a few hundred were injured. Roth and Watson, along with several others, were detained and accused of being complicit in Senator Ndlovu's murder. I was led up the garden path for a day trying to locate my clients, but early on 16 November I found them at a CIO interrogation centre at Esigodini, some 30 kilometres from Bulawayo. Watson was fine, but Roth had been badly tortured. He had been subjected to water-boarding and electric shock treatment. Roth told me he had been made to lie on the floor and a green canvas duffel bag, full of water, was placed over his head and upended, cutting off his air supply and nearly drowning him. Both had been served with detention orders, accusing them of "being involved in the murder of Senator Moven Ndlovu". The CIO told them they had been implicated by a local ZAPU leader, Joseph Makado, who had also been detained.

According to Watson, Senator Ndlovu was not a firebrand but a moderate who got on with everyone and he was puzzled by the murder. Indeed, Watson believed that the principal suspect was a local ZANU PF leader, Canaan Mbebzi.[205] Mbebzi was wanted for a variety of crimes, had a firearm that he was not shy about using, and had been seen at Ndlovu's house on the night he was murdered. He had played a prominent role at Ndlovu's funeral and was among those who had mobilised the Youth Brigade and militia. As Watson explained his blood-curdling theory it dawned on me that Ndlovu may well have been murdered by one of his own, providing a convenient pretext for the subsequent attack on ZAPU supporters. As I left Watson's cell I realised that a CIO operative had been eavesdropping and had heard the entire conversation. If this was a bizarre ZANU PF plot, I was now the only free person who knew about it. This thought unnerved me. Friday afternoons were notoriously used by the CIO to detain people, knowing a bail application would only be heard the following Monday. When I got home Jenny and I, for the first time, but certainly not the last, decided to go to ground for the weekend to evade arrest or worse. We moved out of our home and sought refuge with a friend.

Over the weekend I got further instructions to represent Joseph Makado himself. His family were distraught because he had been detained for almost a week and no one in his family knew where he was. Once again I was given the runaround but when I found him the CIO refused me access to him. I brought a petition before the High Court on Monday, 19 November against the minister of state in charge of the CIO, Mnangagwa, and was granted an order by Judge John Manyarara, compelling the CIO to grant me immediate access to Makado. Although the CIO continued to act in contempt of court by denying me access, they realised their bluff had been called regarding Roth and Watson's implication in Senator Ndlovu's murder and both men were released a few days later. I never did get access to Makado but he, too, was subsequently released. Charges were brought against some ZAPU officials for the murder but when they appeared before the then Beitbridge magistrate Lawrence Kamocha he refused to confirm their statements confessing to the murders because they had been so badly tortured by the police. No one was ever convicted of the murder.

Mugabe used Senator Ndlovu's murder as the reason for dismissing the remaining two ZAPU ministers in his cabinet, Cephas Msipa and John Nkomo. Msipa recounted that shortly before Senator Ndlovu's murder Mugabe had given him the floor in cabinet to speak about people in Matabeleland "being massacred".[*] Msipa spoke for an hour, providing cabinet with "a list of incidents". Curiously, although some

---

[*] Msipa, op cit, p 118

ministers were provocative, Mugabe "didn't enter the discussion"; he just "listened attentively" without getting angry. When Mugabe later fired Msipa, he explained that it was because while Msipa and Nkomo gave the impression that they were working with cabinet, they were "in fact ... secretly supporting dissidents",* a claim Msipa vehemently denied.

ZAPU dispatched three of its central committee members to Beitbridge to investigate the disturbances. Norman Zikali, Angelina Masuku and Molly Ndlovu didn't get very far. On arrival in Beitbridge they were arrested without warrants by the CIO and taken back to Bulawayo, where they were detained at Khami Prison. Masuku was held until May 1985, the remainder until 1986.

As with the Bilang/Williams murder, Senator Ndlovu's murder raised many questions; again at the very least it provided ZANU PF with the perfect justification for a further crackdown on ZAPU in the run up to the elections.

The year ended with further violence in Plumtree, on the Botswana border. This was sparked by an inflammatory speech given at a rally by the hardline ZANU PF governor of Matabeleland South, Mark Dube, on 9 December 1984. Dube told the crowd, many of whom had been forced to attend, that people in the area were not cooperating with government and that these wrongs must be avenged. The police were also warned not to stand in the way of the Youth Brigade who were in attendance. The speech spawned a similar eruption of violence to that which had been seen the month before in Beitbridge. The Youth Brigade went through Plumtree, dragging people from their homes and assaulting them. Once again hundreds were injured, several seriously, but the perpetrators acted with complete impunity; no arrests were made and no prosecutions followed.

Although the rest of Zimbabwe was relatively peaceful, the new year started with high levels of tension in Matabeleland. While there was sporadic dissident activity, it was overshadowed by continuing violence directed against ZAPU supporters. Using the same modus operandi employed in Kwe Kwe, Beitbridge and Plumtree, ZANU PF's next target was Tsholotsho. Busloads of Youth Brigade invaded villages in the early hours of 27 January, burning huts and stores and beating anyone who failed to produce a ZANU PF party card. Scores of people were injured

---

* Msipa, op cit, p 121

and at least one person killed. That was followed in late February 1985 with the murders of five UANC members in the Matabeland North coal mining town of Hwange. A week later 4 000 troops sealed off working-class townships of Bulawayo and conducted pre-dawn searches of houses for arms. Hundreds of people were detained for questioning.[206] ZANU PF's intent was clear: there was a systematic approach to intimidating as many ZAPU supporters as possible in areas that had not yet borne the brunt of the Fifth Brigade.

After two years of practice I was given a breather; I was selected by Rotary to visit the USA on a Group Study Exchange programme for two months. Our team comprised five Southern Africans, myself, a Zimbabwean banker Joe Sibanda, a Malawian and two South Africans. The trip was novel in many respects. I had not travelled overseas since I was twelve years old. It was also my first trip to the USA and my first experience of snow and a biting cold northern hemisphere winter. News of Zimbabwe was scarce; the age of the internet was far off and I battled to keep up with all that was happening at home. The programme was based in central Pennsylvania and took us to New York, Washington and some of the great American Civil War sites such as Gettysburg. It was my first tangible introduction to Abraham Lincoln's life and I saw the spot where he had delivered his address declaring that "*this nation, under God, shall have a new birth of freedom—and that government of the people, by the people, for the people, shall not perish from the earth*". Up until that point I had not studied the American Civil War much but was inspired by the thought that Lincoln's words equally applied to Zimbabwe. Although the circumstances of that war were different to our own, there were similarities – both were internecine struggles with racism at their core. Both needed a "new birth of freedom" which did not automatically follow the end of wars ostensibly fought to bring liberty.

The US trip marked the genesis of two institutions I would become associated with for many years. When the team arrived at Harrisburg, Pennsylvania airport in the afternoon of Saturday, 2 March I was collected by my first American hosts, Henry and Charley Rhoads, and taken to their beautiful home on the banks of the Yellow Breeches River. Henry, a Harvard-trained lawyer, was then senior partner of a Harrisburg law firm. The next day the two of us canoed down the Yellow Breeches River, which was the start of a lifelong friendship between our two families. Henry, however, also got engaged in the Zimbabwean struggle and established an American Section 501(c)(3) not-for-profit corporation called the Central and Southern African Legal Assistance Foundation (CASALAF), which was to become a funding vehicle for the Legal Resources Foundation and general legal defence work in future.

The second pivotal meeting occurred in early April when I visited a UCT law buddy, Martin Morrison, who was studying at Westminster Theological Seminary in Philadelphia. While there he introduced me to Zimbabweans Mike and Jan Kreft, who were also studying to go into ministry. That meeting spurred them to think of returning to Zimbabwe, which in turn led to the idea of establishing a Christian school in Bulawayo – the seed of the Petra Schools was planted then.

Having been insulated from everything that was happening back in Zimbabwe, I arrived home from the US in late April and was drawn straight into the 1985 general election campaign. Because of the quirks of the Lancaster House constitution, the election for the 20 white seats was set for 27 June and the "common roll" seat election on 1 and 2 July. I was asked by Dr Bob Nixon MP and Senator Max Rosenfels (both independent members of parliament) to assist the campaign of the Independent Zimbabwe Group (IZG) in Matabeleland, who were going to oppose Smith's RF, renamed the Conservative Alliance of Zimbabwe (CAZ). In my absence during March and April, sporadic outbursts of violence had continued. The CCJP on 23 March had sent a report to Mugabe criticising the "brutal bullying" of opposition supporters, deploring the abductions of ZAPU officials and warning that the legitimacy of the elections was threatened by ongoing violence.[207] Early in April, ZANU PF activists started evicting opposition supporters from their homes. A few days later a truck full of armed men arrived at a shebeen owned by the ZAPU candidate for Lupane, Micah Bhebhe, spraying it with gunfire. Bhebhe survived the attack, but both his son and daughter were killed. Despite calls by Mugabe and some ZANU PF leaders for the violence to stop, no arrests or prosecutions followed. However, the violence did decline and the final few weeks in the run up to the elections were relatively calm. In what was to become a typical pattern of Zimbabwean elections, violence was replaced by the use of the law as a weapon in the closing weeks of the campaign.

By June "virtually every urban and rural ZAPU office had been closed";[208] there were systematic arrests of ZAPU election agents and officials in Gwanda, Nkayi, Lupane and Victoria Falls. In many other areas ZAPU candidates found it hard, if not impossible to campaign. Police cancelled all ZAPU election rallies in Beitbridge and candidates in Harare had a torrid time. There were a few forced disappearances conducted by the Fifth Brigade and the Police Internal Security Intelligence unit (PISI) in the weeks running up to the election, which targeted ZAPU leaders. Ozias Muchuchu, a ZAPU candidate in one Harare constituency, was injured and had his house set on fire. A ZANU PF mob told him they "wanted (his) head and that (he) was not allowed to stand as a candidate".[209] Another candidate, veteran nationalist leader Ruth Chinamano, was unable to campaign, had her car stoned and complained that ZANU PF thugs "would not let my car go until they had cut off my head".[210] Curiously, dissident activity during May and June 1985, according to none other than Mnangagwa came down to "almost nothing".[211]

Shortly before the election, I received separate instructions from both ZAPU and ZANU PF to get some of their youths out on bail. The first case concerned a group of ZAPU youths who had been detained by police and were awaiting trial on charges of assault. The case came before Judge Korsah, a Ghanaian High Court judge, and was opposed by the State. Despite my best efforts, the application was dismissed as Judge Korsah felt that it was in everybody's best interests that the youths remain behind bars until the election was over. Within days of failing in that case, on 14 June 1985, I appeared before the same judge, this time representing ZANU PF. Six ZANU PF activists had been found guilty by a brave Beitbridge magistrate named Wilbert Mapombere for the grievous assault of a ZAPU member, Isaac Chibi, and sentenced to one year's imprisonment on 22 May 1985. The court record showed they had battered Chibi with knobkerries, inflicting multiple fractures. I was asked to appeal the conviction and to get them out on bail in the interim so that they could continue campaigning for ZANU PF. Our chances of succeeding in the appeal appeared slight, but ZANU PF was determined to go ahead with the bail application. Surprisingly, when I filed the papers the State advised that it was not going to oppose the application. The application was placed before the same Judge Korsah; normally a judge would grant an unopposed order but he demanded that State counsel and I appear before him. When we did, he quizzed State counsel why the application had not been opposed and then, after hearing argument from me, dismissed the application. In his reasons he said he was "not prepared to release anyone convicted of, or charged with, politically related crime until after the elections".[212] I have never before or since been happier losing a case; justice was done indeed.

The white election campaign in contrast to the brutal battle being waged between ZANU PF and ZAPU was tame and banal. I spoke at house meetings in support of the independent candidates and also attended public CAZ meetings. Our message was that whites needed to move on and that a vote for the CAZ would destroy the influence that people like Dennis Norman and Chris Andersen had exercised since 1980. Smith, sensing that the Bulawayo public was more amenable to his message, chose to stand in the Bulawayo Central constituency and his message was that it was important for whites to vote for the CAZ because they would then be able to form an alliance with Nkomo's ZAPU. This was a message that didn't find much favour in Harare but resonated with many whites in Matabeleland. I found myself a sole voice during question time at the CAZ meetings, questioning Smith from the floor about whether ZAPU would ever agree to such a pact. Smith was forced to concede that it was a mere wish and that no agreement had been struck with Nkomo. The RF had been complacent in the by-election of 1983 won by Nixon; Smith had not campaigned much that year, but in 1985 he fought a spirited battle in Bulawayo and his old charm among whites worked.

On election day the CAZ swept the board, securing every white seat in Matabeleland and 15 out of the 20 seats on offer country wide. The Independent Group were only successful in Harare, where they won the balance of 5 seats. On the common roll, ZANU PF increased their seats from 57 to 64; however, significantly, despite all the violence, intimidation and arrests, ZAPU won every one of the 15 seats in Matabeleland but lost the 5 seats it previously held, located elsewhere, to ZANU PF.

Despite gaining seats, Mugabe was apoplectic about the results. He railed against whites, speaking about "these racists" who had spurned his hand of reconciliation and in Shona threatened to "kill those snakes among us".[213] But his greatest ire was generated by ZAPU's victory in Matabeleland and its retention of pockets of support country wide. On national television, he called once more for the "weeding out of dissidents".[214] Within a day of the broadcast, serious violence flared in several centres, notably Harare and Kwe Kwe. Mobs of mainly ululating, vengeful ZANU PF women attacked the homes of suspected ZAPU supporters, smashing windows, throwing furniture into the streets and declaring the houses ZANU PF property. Three days of mayhem ensued during which some six people were killed, including a losing ZAPU candidate, Simon Chauruka, who was "gruesomely hacked to death with axes" by ZANU PF thugs in the Dzivarasekwa suburb of Harare.[215] Mugabe, having set the violence in motion, remained silent for its duration; a week later, he called the violence "unfortunate" but nevertheless warned that for those who remained "unrepentant", "things will get tough".[216]

Things were indeed going to get tough and the first sign of this was when Mugabe appointed firebrand Enos Nkala to be minister of Home Affairs, in charge of the Police, and retained Mnangagwa in charge of the CIO. Nkala was still smarting from only having obtained 10 per cent of the votes in the constituency he stood for in Matabeleland South, and he had a long history of antagonism towards Nkomo in particular and ZAPU in general. Their first action was to detain ZAPU chief whip Sidney Malunga as he left parliament on 31 July 1985, accusing him of "recruiting dissidents" and "organising meetings". Malunga was not taken to court – he was detained in terms of the emergency powers regulations which empowered Nkala, as minister of Home Affairs, to indefinitely detain anyone "in the interests of public safety". Malunga was well acquainted with detention, having been detained under similar laws by the RF from 1973 until his release to attend the Lancaster House conference in 1979. Two weeks later, in the early morning hours of 16 August, all the black members of the Bulawayo City Council, including the mayor and town clerk, were detained and held at the notorious Stops Camp.

Nkala made no bones about his intention to crush ZAPU and said in Parliament on 22 August that his "instinct" told him that "you have to be ruthless". He boasted that he had "locked up a few honourable members" and thought they would "have a rest for a long time".[217] He was true to his word and by the end of September, Nkomo's brother Stephen Nkomo MP, ZAPU secretary general Welshman Mabhena MP and MPs Edward Ndlovu and Kembo Mohadi had also been detained. I would end up representing all of these MPs and, in the case of Mohadi, obtaining, with other lawyers, damages of Z$14 000 against the government following his torture. At the same time, some 200 other ZAPU middle-ranking leaders and eight high-ranking former ZIPRA officers in the ZNA were

167

detained. Bulawayo whites were not immune either. A former mayor of Bulawayo, Mike Constandinos, was detained at the end of August, and this was followed by the detention of four retired Rhodesian-era district commissioners, all fluent in isiNdebele, including Mike Jacobs from the Estates department of my firm, on accusations that they were "hatching a secessionist plot". At the same time, scores of Bulawayo Council employees, including ambulance drivers, garbage collectors and bureaucrats, were detained at Stops Camp. I had a very busy August and September and was run off my feet representing scores of people detained at Stops Camp.

My legal practice changed dramatically on 8 October 1985. I received a phone call from Richard Majwabu-Moyo, a black lawyer in Bulawayo, who explained that his firm was representing Sidney Malunga, but they had been threatened for doing so; they had discussed the matter with Malunga and he was happy that I be asked to take on the case, which in turn I was happy to do. Malunga was accused of contravening the old Rhodesian Law and Order (Maintenance) Act, it being alleged that he had assisted dissidents. Within two weeks, I had received instructions to represent another high-ranking ZAPU MP, Edward Ndlovu. His Canadian wife, Mary, came in to see me on 24 October – she was anxious because her husband had had a kidney transplant and had been detained since 17 September in shockingly unhygienic conditions at Khami Maximum prison. Mary was a great friend of Judith Todd, who took an interest in the case from the onset – it was the start of a long and good friendship with them both.

I managed to see Ndlovu first when I visited him at Khami Maximum prison on 8 November. He struck me as a thoroughly charming man and we instantly had a good rapport. He was, however, in a bad way, suffering from angina and the danger that his kidney would be rejected. Ndlovu had been served with a ministerial detention order by Nkala and had recently been told that he was to be charged with contravening another old Rhodesian statute, the Preservation of Constitutional Government Act. Relying on a statement extracted using brutal torture from a fellow member of ZAPU (and recanted on), it was alleged that between January 1985 and the date of his detention in September he had "organised a group to overthrow the Government".[218] With no trial in prospect, my first goal was to get him released from detention; in the ensuing weeks I prepared affidavits from a variety of physicians, all of which stated that Ndlovu was in danger of losing his life if he was not released from detention. Ndlovu also prepared a letter addressed to an old friend of his, Deputy Prime Minister Simon Muzenda, which I had typed and delivered. These appeals fell on deaf ears and he remained detained for months in the squalid conditions. I was deeply shocked by the callousness of the government.

The sense of shock and growing revulsion against ZANU PF grew when I took instruction from Malunga for the first time at Kadoma prison on 22 November. On arrival I was ushered into an interview room which overlooked a long corridor leading to the bowels of the prison. Malunga appeared at the end of the corridor dressed in brown prison fatigues, shackled by leg-irons, and flanked by two warders. He shuffled his way down the corridor towards the room in obvious pain. Malunga was a big man, with a broad, round face; he greeted me with a huge grin and shook my hand with both of his as if I was a long lost friend. It was impossible not to instantly warm to him. I spent several hours with him that day and in the course of the afternoon he detailed how he had been tortured by the CIO. He had been blindfolded and subjected to Falanga[219] which had left him unable to walk for weeks. He was accused of giving a man called Ncube Z$90 in 1982 which was then allegedly used to buy clothing and tobacco for dissidents. The only witnesses were two men, Ncube and Dube, both accomplices in the "crime", but whom Malunga had never met before. There had never been an identification parade and the police had dropped the case in 1983 when the head of CID, Bulawayo Superintendent Morgan Sibanda, had told Malunga in the presence of his then lawyer Lot Senda, "there is no case against you". Suddenly the case had been resurrected and the trial was due to start in Gweru on December 1. When I asked Malunga why his case had been resurrected, he thought it was mainly because of ZAPU's continued hold of Matabeleland, but also, as chief whip, he had been at the forefront of using parliamentary privilege to expose the gross human rights abuses perpetrated by ZANU PF. He had spoken against Fifth Brigade atrocities, the detention of Dabengwa and Masuku; he had exposed evidence of police and CIO torture. In his view, it was imperative for ZANU PF to silence him and also to establish a link between ZAPU and dissident activity.

The trial began in Gweru on 1 December 1985 before Magistrate Paddington Garwe. The State prosecutor was Godwills Masimirembwa;

both men were, and remain, ZANU PF favourites – today Garwe sits on the Constitutional Court bench, having been steadily promoted by Mugabe over the years; Masimirembwa likewise, despite being struck off by the Law Society of Zimbabwe on 14 March 1997 for bringing the law profession into disrepute through a variety of misdemeanours, bounced back to head Zimbabwe's Mining Development Corporation in 2009, appointed by minister of Mines Obert Mpofu.

Masimirembwa's opening gambit was to apply for the case to be heard in camera because he said the State's two principal witnesses needed "protection". In the same breath he also asked for one exception regarding those who could be in court: he wanted members of the CIO to be present while his two witnesses gave evidence! I opposed the application and also asked that the trial be moved to Bulawayo where the offence was alleged to have been committed, pointing out that it greatly inconvenienced Malunga and the State with us all having to travel to Gweru, over 160 kilometres from Bulawayo, for the trial. Masimirembwa opposed having the trial in Bulawayo, arguing that his witnesses would be "frightened" if they had to give evidence there. Having heard the arguments, Garwe ruled that the trial would commence in Gweru, where the two witnesses Ncube and Dube would give evidence in camera; the CIO would not be allowed to sit in court. The whole day was spent on this preliminary argument so we could not start hearing evidence and the case was adjourned to the new year.

When we reconvened in Gweru on 6 January 1986 I happened to be outside court when the State's two key witnesses arrived from Bulawayo – handcuffed and locked in a cage on the back of a police vehicle. Ncube and Dube gave their evidence, parroting the State's line that they had received money from Malunga to buy clothing for dissidents. However, under cross-examination their stories fell apart. It came out that both had been illegally detained by PISI, Ncube for a month, Dube for two months, at Stops Camp. Although both denied that they had been tortured, they conceded that their time in detention was "horrible", and they could give no coherent explanation why they were driven from Bulawayo to Gweru in the back of a cage. Their versions contradicted each other and were patently untruthful in many respects. Ncube was adamant that he had first met Malunga in Bulawayo during the 1970s but the lie was given when it was pointed out that Malunga had been detained by the Rhodesian government for the entire period.

Midway through the trial pressure was brought to bear on me. On the second day of the trial, 7 January, I decided to drive to Gweru Golf Course to take my lunchtime break there. While driving out to the course I realised that I was being followed; I took evasive action by taking a circuitous route, but the car behind mine managed to follow me. No threats were issued but for the first time I realised that my movements were being monitored. Then, shortly after the trial adjourned on 8 January, it appeared that there was a concerted campaign to intimidate me. In 1984 the government had passed a new Citizenship Act, which outlawed dual citizenship. In terms of that law, if one was a dual citizen and wanted to keep one's Zimbabwean citizenship, a decision had to be made prior to 30 November 1985 to renounce any foreign citizenship. Because of my father's Scottish birth, I was at that time also a British citizen and so I renounced my British citizenship before the end of November and applied for a Zimbabwean passport. By mid January 1986 I still did not have a passport and it became a major problem when my father took seriously ill and was admitted to hospital in Port Elizabeth, South Africa. I applied for an emergency travel document which was meant to be issued in days but was not. I sought a meeting with the senior passport officer for Bulawayo, who told me that my application was still under "consideration" because I was viewed as "an enemy of the State". I was due to fly on Friday, 24 January but missed the flight. My father's condition deteriorated and it was only when I presented the passport office with a doctor's letter that they finally relented and issued me with a document on 31 January, which limited my travel to South Africa alone. Fortunately, my father pulled through, but it was a very unpleasant episode. Even when I got back, the authorities dragged their feet on issuing me a Zimbabwean passport and I only received it after Malunga's acquittal in July 1986.

Shortly before flying to South Africa, on 21 January I met the governor of Matabeleland North, Jacob Mudenda, with the Anglican bishop of Matabeleland Robert Mercer and his Catholic counterpart Henry Karlen. We (I in my capacity as an elder of the Presbyterian Church) presented Mudenda with a human rights report I had prepared on behalf of the Christian Heads of Denominations in Bulawayo. Mudenda was a client of mine and, using that contact, I had arranged the previous November for Mercer, Karlen and I to meet him to discuss the human rights situation. Mudenda professed ignorance of what was happening in the area of his jurisdiction and so we agreed to provide him with details. Coincidentally, on 29 November 1985, I had been instructed, in my capacity as secretary of the Bulawayo Legal Practitioners' Association, to prepare a report from cases supplied by lawyers documenting recent human rights abuses affecting their clients. The cases formed the basis of two reports – the Churches' one and another which was sent by the association to the minister of Justice. Both reports documented several areas of concern: police/CIO assaults, illegal detentions, lawyers being denied access to their clients, disappearances, a general disregard by the police for basic human rights, conditions in Stops Camp, and the plight of unrepresented people. The conditions in Stops Camp were particularly appalling. At any one time up to 300 people were detained in security cells designed for a tenth that number, which only had two latrines, two urinals and two showers. There were inadequate numbers of blankets and numerous unrepresented people had been detained for months on end. Details of 30 sample cases handled by Bulawayo lawyers since July 1985 were attached, which documented systematic torture carried out at Stops Camp by the police and CIO. Most were horrendous. Case 5 recorded that the client "was stripped and then his head was put into a canvas bag filled with water ... the bag was tied around his neck and then lifted up suffocating him". In Case 8 the unfortunate client was "hung upside down with his feet tied to rafters and his head was placed in a bucket of water suffocating him". The covering letter handed over bearing the signatures of Mercer, Karlen and myself pleaded that the "violations be investigated and stopped forthwith".[220] Mudenda clucked in disapproval and promised that the report would be taken seriously.

We never heard back officially from either Mudenda or the minister of Justice, and Stops Camp continued to be used as a torture base for another two years. In one particularly egregious case, a client of mine, an employee of a Hwange-based safari company who was accused of assisting dissidents, was seriously tortured by PISI while detained at Stops Camp. When I went to take instructions from him I noticed that he was wearing a brand new, clean pair of overalls, which surprised me seeing as he had been detained in filthy cells for days. The police details refused to allow me to see my client alone; when I asked about the overalls my client looked petrified and the police details gave an absurd explanation: his original clothes were soiled and they had replaced them. Suspecting foul play, I then asked that my client take the overalls off, which request was met with the pathetic response that he could not because that would offend the dignity of a woman police officer who was in the interview room! That was the final straw – I demanded that my client should roll up his sleeves which he did, immediately revealing burn marks up his arms. The police realised the game was up – my client took the overalls off. He had been badly burnt by cigarette stubs across his back and stomach. The overalls had been supplied in a vain attempt to hide the torture. As I left the cells my client asked me to contact his family, and the families of his colleagues detained with him, to convey a simple message: *"Sisaphila"* (we are still alive). Survive they did and all were released when his wounds had healed.

I returned from South Africa in mid February 1986. During my absence Malunga was transferred to Chikurubi Maximum Security prison outside Harare and brought before a magistrate's court in Harare to be charged along with Edward Ndlovu, ZAPU chairman William Kona, and seven ex-ZIPRA senior ZNA officers with attempting to mount a *coup d'état*. Having Malunga in Harare made getting instructions from him even harder but nevertheless the trial resumed in Gweru on 17 February. We heard evidence from the remaining State witnesses and at the conclusion of the State case, I applied for Malunga's discharge on the basis that not even a *prima facie* case had been proved. At the same time I argued that the reason for being in Gweru, namely to "protect" the State witnesses, had passed and that in any event the case should continue in Bulawayo. Magistrate Garwe agreed to the latter but reserved judgment, postponing the case to continue in Bulawayo on 21 March. When we resumed in Bulawayo Garwe disingenuously ducked most of my arguments and said that Malunga should be put to his defence. However, no sooner had he handed down his judgment than Masimirembwa and I were called into Garwe's chambers to be told that he now feared for his life and wanted the case continued in Harare.

Malunga and I were disconcerted by this development because we feared it was simply a delaying tactic. The State case was in disarray and we knew that the Harare courts were chock-a-block. When we reconvened, I argued that Malunga's constitutional rights to a fair trial would be undermined if there were any further long delays. The compromise was that we would continue the trial over weekends in Harare if needs be. So it was that we concluded the defence case on Saturday and Sunday, 5 and 6 April, at the aptly named Rotten Row Magistrates Court in Harare. We presented reams of evidence from *Hansard* showing that Malunga was an embarrassment to the government as he had, more than anyone else, exposed the Gukurahundi and other human rights abuses.

Judgment was eventually handed down on 7 July. I didn't know that Garwe was going to acquit until his final few sentences. The bulk of his judgment dwelt on findings that there was substance to the allegations levelled against Malunga; only at the very end did he concede that, because of technical reasons, such as the fact that the main witnesses were accomplices, he could not convict. In reality the State's case was a tissue of lies, concocted in a vain attempt to establish a nexus between ZAPU and dissidents. Our celebration was muted. Despite the acquittal, Malunga was still under preventative detention so he was led away in shackles back to his cell in Chikurubi prison.

My attention turned to the next case my clients Sidney Malunga and Edward Ndlovu were facing, the treason trial involving them, ZAPU chairman Kona and the ex-ZIPRA commanders. It was meant to be the jewel in the crown of all the cases brought against ZAPU. Ndlovu had been released from detention on 29 April 1986, ZANU PF possibly anxious that yet another senior ZAPU leader should not die in prison. Lookout Masuku, the former commander of ZIPRA, had died at Parirenyatwa Hospital in Harare on 5 April. Although technically Masuku had been released from detention on 11 March, he was already dying in hospital and never moved from the same bed he had been detained in. Despite being an icon of the struggle against white minority rule, Masuku was not accorded hero status and was buried in a civilian cemetery in Bulawayo. In a funeral charged with emotion Nkomo said it was "appropriate that the site chosen for Lookout's grave lies near a memorial to those who fought against Hitler" because Masuku had also "fought against fascism, oppression, tribalism and corruption".[221]

Notwithstanding this tragedy and Malunga's acquittal, ZANU PF were hell bent on trying to paint ZAPU in the mind of the public as a party that supported violence. Aside from Ndlovu all the other accused persons were still being held in Chikurubi. They were brought to court on Tuesday, 5 August but the State advised that it was "not yet ready to proceed". We learnt why at the next hearing, on 18 August: their case relied on the evidence of ZAPU Secretary General Welshman Mabhena who, although he was their principal witness, was also being held in detention. His first act when he appeared in court was to tell the Court that his statement implicating all his ZAPU comrades had been extracted from him under extreme torture and was all a pack of lies. The State case fell apart and the charges were withdrawn. The last attempt of ZANU PF to use law as a weapon against ZAPU had failed.

Mugabe put a brave face on it. He called a press conference in September to say that the unity talks had reached a "sufficiently advanced stage" to allow the attorney general, Godfrey Chidyausiku, to withdraw the charges. Mugabe stressed that this was a decision of the attorney general "acting within the exclusive discretion conferred on him by the Constitution",[222] holding on grimly to the fiction that there was no political hand at play. All the senior ZAPU leaders, save for Dabengwa and a few others, were released – Dabengwa was only to be released in early December.

With all my ZAPU clients released I was able to turn my attention back to other projects close to my heart. On 15 May 1986 I had met with Mark Bellamy, the First Secretary of the US Embassy, to discuss how the Legal Aid Clinic run by the Bulawayo Legal Practitioners' Association could be expanded. Although the 24 volunteer lawyers were doing a magnificent job, their role was confined to giving initial advice, not taking on cases. As demonstrated in the human rights report delivered to the governor and minister of Justice in January 1986, unrepresented detainees were being left to rot in Stops Camp. The US Embassy was prepared to help. In July I travelled to Johannesburg to see how the Legal Resources Centre's office operated. Shortly afterwards the Legal Resources Foundation appointed me as trustee and it was then agreed that we would establish a Bulawayo Legal Projects Centre (BLPC). Proposals were sent to the US Human Rights Fund and NOVIB[223] in September – the short-term objectives were to establish a legal aid clinic, a law library and to promote public legal education. Many young black lawyers setting up their own practices in Bulawayo did not have adequate law libraries, which undermined their practice. In addition I was shocked by how few Zimbabweans knew about their basic rights, which had been exploited by the police, resulting in serious human rights abuses. At the same time I approached Anglo American and other companies, who agreed to provide offices in Charter House and to furnish the Centre. Having secured funding, the BLPC was opened by Zimbabwe's first black Chief Justice, Enock Dumbutshena, on 24 February 1987. I became its first director, a post I would hold for ten years. The agreement with my own partners was that I would spend every Friday afternoon working at the BLPC.

Another project close to my heart was the development of Petra School, the seed of which had been sown in my meeting with the Krefts in Pennsylvania in April 1985. On 12 March 1986 I followed that up, moving a motion at the 88th annual meeting of the Bulawayo Presbyterian Church that we establish a Christian school in Bulawayo. The underlying concern was that education standards at former white government schools in Bulawayo were under threat because of the rapid expansion of the number of government schools country wide. Although this tremendous expansion in the early 1980s extended education to hundreds of thousands of Zimbabweans who had not had access to education during white minority rule, it did come at the expense of putting the entire government educational system under strain. The only alternatives were very expensive, and somewhat elitist, private schools, which Christians in full-time ministry could not afford. My vision was of a school which sought excellence, but which was not as expensive or elitist as most other private schools. The proposal was adopted unanimously and we then linked up with the Baptist and Methodist churches to form a steering committee. The vision was taken up and driven in particular by a Bulawayo chartered accountant, John Cuddington, who more than anyone else worked tirelessly to turn the dream into a reality. A multiracial board of trustees was appointed, comprising a broad cross-section of Christian professionals and pastors. One of these was an ex-ZANLA combatant, Lexon Marufu Mugomo, the minister of the Presbyterian church in Gweru. By the end of 1986 we had agreed on a name, secured land on Chelmsford Road and hired our first teacher.

Petra Primary School opened in temporary premises at the commencement of the second term, on 12 May. A year later we moved into our first classroom block built on a barren, dusty stretch of land. Eventually, in the 1990s a high school was built, where all our children have been well educated.

Amid the political trials and other attacks on the ZAPU leadership, dissidents were remarkably quiet during 1986 and the first half of 1987. *The Chronicle* which, as a government-controlled newspaper, used every opportunity to highlight dissident activity, only reported nine murders, 21 losses to property and sixteen assaults attributed to dissidents during 1986. On 29 July Minister of Home Affairs Enos Nkala was able to report to parliament that "security forces (were) on top of the situation" and that "reported incidents (had) gone down by nearly 68%". He boasted that "most of the bandit gangs (had) been tracked own and accounted for".[224]

Despite these claims, there were some strange high-profile attacks which did not tally with the general decline in dissident activity. In May, just outside Gweru, well away from the traditional areas of dissident activity in Matabeleland, four white farmers were shot at the Somabula farmers' club. In June, two German tourists were murdered on the main road to Victoria Falls. In September, six clinic staff were murdered on a remote road near Nkayi, but in a bizarre twist only the Ndebele members of staff on the team were murdered, not the two Shona-speaking members who were in the same vehicle. It seemed odd that Ndebele-speaking dissidents aligned to ZAPU would only murder their own.

Tied to this activity were the unity talks first announced by Mugabe in August 1986, when Malunga, Ndlovu and the other ZAPU leaders were released. They stuttered along in the months that followed: Nkomo announced at a huge rally in Bulawayo in February 1987 that unity was "imminent"; then in April and May respectively Nkomo and Mugabe announced that the talks had broken down. The breakdown caused another surge of attacks on ZAPU. On 20 June 1987 Nkala banned all ZAPU rallies and meetings and in the same breath said he was considering banning ZAPU altogether. In mid September, ZAPU offices in Bulawayo were raided and twelve ZAPU officials detained in Gweru and Kwe Kwe. That was followed by the effective banning of ZAPU by Nkala when he had all ZAPU offices closed and directed that "all ZAPU structures be set aside" because ZAPU should "now be viewed in the same manner as the MNR bandits in Mozambique".[225]

The attacks on senior ZAPU leaders resumed. At 11 pm on Tuesday, 29 September PISI raided ZAPU secretary general Welshman Mabhena's home and detained him. I was instructed to represent him and when I saw him two days later and questioned PISI as to why he had been detained they said they didn't know because they "were acting on the instructions of the Minister [Nkala]".[226] When I asked Mabhena why they had singled him out he replied: "Nkala thinks I am anti unity." Mabhena was suffering from hypertension and when I pleaded with PISI they relented, releasing him that evening.

At the same time other forms of pressure were piled on ZAPU. On 30 September 1987 Mugabe used the notorious Presidential Powers Act to issue regulations to dissolve the Binga, Bubi, Lupane, Nkayi, Tsholotsho and Hwange district councils. These were councils dominated by ZAPU councillors, who were all "discharged" and their seats "vacated".[227] No reasons were given – it was just done.

A few days later I received my first instructions from Nkomo. In a meeting I had with him and Mabhena at his Blue Lagoon offices, Nkomo asked me to examine whether Mugabe had acted constitutionally. Clearly ZAPU was under siege. Every possible means was being used to force them to agree to a unity pact. There was very little we could do to help Nkomo. Our courts had adopted a rather timid stance towards the Presidential Powers Act and were reluctant to interfere with "discretion" exercised by the president. A few days after my meeting with Nkomo, ZANU PF Minister Maurice Nyagumbo announced that the "unity talks were dead".

Although unity talks resumed in mid November, this terrible chapter in Zimbabwe's history was to yield one final unspeakable atrocity, which occurred on two adjacent farms, New Adams and Olive Tree, only 40 kilometres south east of Bulawayo. In 1982 a few white Christian families, including Gerry and Marian Keightley, decided they needed to do what they could to promote reconciliation between races in the aftermath of the bitter war. Gerry had been in the Rhodesian army and his experiences had deeply affected him – "the unethical and morally reprehensible things he saw (showed him) how depraved men can be in their lust for power".[228] He wanted to "bridge the huge chasm of race that had driven Zimbabwe to war".[229] The couple sold up their assets and in 1984 used the proceeds to buy New Adams farm on which they established a Christian community. They subsequently raised sufficient support to purchase a neighbouring farm, which was renamed Olive Tree, named thus as a "symbolic gesture of peace between the peoples of Zimbabwe". Their vision was to work with local black communities to break down walls of suspicion and to build bridges of trust. For that reason they called themselves the Community of Reconciliation. Unlike other whites living in rural areas, they felt they should not bear arms as that would convey the wrong message to the very people they were seeking to interact with.

One of the members of the Community, Gaynor Stewart, who had married a founder member, entomologist Rob Hill, was a good friend of my wife Jenny, both of them having gone to school together and sharing a common faith. Rob was a pacifist and so found his compulsory call-up for the Rhodesian military difficult. His vision was to start a bee colony on the farm and in neighbouring areas in order to create a honey business from which the local communities would benefit. Because of our friendship we went out to see them at New Adams farm on a number of occasions. The community inspired us – they were a model for the future of Zimbabwe, turning a desert into a productive farm and working closely with local black people. At the beginning of 1987, there was great excitement because Jenny and Gaynor found out that they were both pregnant for the first time and that their due dates were close. Our first child, Jessica, was born on 14 September 1987 and the Hills' baby boy, Benjamin, was born a month later.

In the early hours of Wednesday, 25 November a pseudo-dissident known as Morgan Sango (with the *nom de guerre* "Gayigusu") led a group of about 20 drug-crazed armed men to Olive Tree farm. On arrival they separated the white members of the community, men, women and children, including the Keightleys' 18-month-old child Barnabus, from the black members and tied their hands behind their backs with barbed wire. They were herded into a house and then called out one at a time to another house where each was axed in the back of the neck. Gerry, his wife, their two teenage daughters and finally Barnabus were murdered along with a few other members. The group then moved to New Adams farm where the same procedure was followed. They went house by house calling everyone out, corralling them in the community centre. Then one by one they were called out and taken to a house where each was murdered with the same axe used at Olive Tree. After Gaynor had been killed, her six-week-old son Benjamin was ripped out of the arms of a thirteen-year-old daughter of one of the missionaries and thrown cruelly to the floor. When the dissidents realised that Benjamin wasn't yet dead they "picked him up by the feet, swung him around and smashed his head open on the concrete sink".[230] All in all eleven adults and five children were massacred.

The massacre deeply shocked us and the entire nation. The loss of little Benjamin was particularly hard to bear as we had a constant reminder of his innocence in our new baby Jessica. The atrocity appeared to galvanise the unity talks, however, and a clamour reverberated throughout Zimbabwe that peace should come. It culminated in the signing of an accord between Mugabe and Nkomo on 27 December 1987. It wasn't really a unity accord, more a swallowing of ZAPU.

179

After years of coercion, detentions, malicious prosecutions, murders and threats, ZAPU finally succumbed to ZANU PF's desire to forge a one-party state. The name of the "united party" would be ZANU PF, its leader Robert Mugabe, and it would seek to establish a one-party state. Although not formally included in the agreement, crumbs were thrown to ZAPU in the form of one of the vice-presidencies being allocated to former ZAPU members, which office Nkomo took up. The Unity Accord was followed up with an amnesty signed by the president and Mnangagwa, first for dissidents, then later extended to all security forces. There was therefore to be no accountability, no revelation about who did what, no justice for the tens of thousands of victims. In the end only some 122 dissidents handed themselves in, including Gayigusu, who was never held to account for his brutally cruel murders. To this day, because of the amnesty, we do not know under whose instructions Gayigusu was acting. All that one can say is that, as with David Bilang's murder five years previously, ZANU PF benefited enormously from the tragedy.

CHAPTER 11

A DE FACTO ONE-PARTY STATE
AND ALL ITS TRAPPINGS
1988 TO 1990

"Power tends to corrupt and absolute power corrupts absolutely."
– LORD ACTON IN A LETTER TO BISHOP MANDELL CREIGHTON, 3 APRIL 1887

The first act of the new "united" ZANU PF on 31 December 1987 was to amend the Zimbabwean constitution, abolishing the office of prime minister and replacing it with an all-powerful executive president. Having abolished the reserved 20 white seats the previous September, Mugabe moved to consolidate his grip on power even further. With all his political opponents effectively dealt with, he was close to achieving the dream he had spelt out at the 1984 congress. With 99 out of the 100 seats in parliament, ZANU PF could effectively do as it pleased in parliament. Not all former ZAPU members were happy with the developments.

Malunga had become a good friend of mine following his release and he told me privately how concerned he was by the creation of a *de facto* one-party state. At this time my next door neighbour Malcolm King, himself a former ZAPU operative, arranged for Dumiso Dabengwa, his wife Zodwa, and Judith Todd to come for dinner at our home. Dabengwa spoke movingly about his time in detention and the wasted years he had suffered. He questioned whether the war had achieved its objectives and at one point in the evening remarked, "I sometimes wonder whether it (the war) was worth it – have we really liberated Zimbabwe?"

Although dissident activity had all but ceased, the South African government was still furiously defending apartheid and attacks against

ANC activists in Zimbabwe continued. On 15 January 1988 South African agents bombed an ANC safe house in Trenance, a Bulawayo suburb, killing several people, including an innocent Zambian driver, Obert Mwanza, who had been conned into delivering a car (with 100 kg of high explosive hidden in its boot[231]), a Renault 5, to the front door. With callous disregard for life, the agents detonated the bomb from a distance, not checking that the driver had got away. I was shocked by this abominable act and so when I overheard a conversation between two whites a few days later giving details about the matter I had no compunction in contacting a man called Bob Mutare in the CIO to pass on the information. The whites must have assumed that I would be sympathetic, but on the contrary I was appalled. I had got to know Mutare over the years in seeking to get clients released and so I phoned him up to tell him I had information. When he came to my office he seemed very interested in what I had to tell him; I had no idea whether it was useful or not. He offered to reward me, which I declined – in my mind I was doing my duty in trying to see that justice would be done. Within days most of the operatives, including a double agent, Kevin Woods, had been arrested. Whether the information I passed on was the missing link in the chain of clues I do not know, but Mutare later told me it had been critically important. I had never before, and have never since, passed on information to the CIO. Whatever the case, it made the CIO realise, I think, that I was genuinely interested in non-violent resolutions of political problems, for it opened doors with the CIO in the months that followed.

One of the founding objectives of the BLPC was to conduct human rights training courses for law enforcement agents and I have no doubt that this incident secured the CIO's attendance at the courses later in 1988.

With the end of the dissident war and harassment of ZAPU I was able to focus more on regular legal practice and on developing the BLPC. From the initial small legal aid clinic we had begun, by now we had branched out and had set up advice centres, initially in three of the poor working-class areas of Bulawayo. That in turn necessitated the training of paralegals, people who had a basic knowledge of law, who could advise people of their rights and if needs be refer cases to either one of our 24 lawyer volunteers or to our first permanent lawyers, Barney Greenland and Steve Nkiwane, the latter an ex-ZIPRA war veteran. A Test Case committee was established to identify cases that could be taken to the Supreme Court, and which would set new legal precedents promoting respect for human rights. The law library was progressively expanded and by the end of 1988 was one of the most current and best stocked in Bulawayo. It was a time of rapid expansion and the BLPC became a hive of activity – young lawyers were always busy researching in the library, a series of lectures and seminars were held on legal topics, and we started work on simplifying legal topics into easy-to-read pamphlets in Ndebele and Shona. We had also established ties with Columbia and Harvard universities in the US and a steady stream of law interns started to flow. The buzz within the BLPC reflected a broader optimism in Bulawayo – for the first time in a decade there was peace and economic progress in the region. My legal practice at Webb, Low and Barry was also flourishing so in between that, running the BLPC and being a new father, I was kept busy.

In August/September 1988, I and two other Bulawayo lawyers involved in the BLPC, Intikab Esat and Mordecai Mahlangu, travelled to the States as guests of the US government. The three-week trip was pivotal in the development of the BLPC and my own outlook regarding using the legal system to oppose tyranny. Aside from anything else, our visit to the Martin Luther King Center for Nonviolent Social Change in Atlanta broadened my understanding of all that King stood for; I had never studied American history and it was the start of what has become a lifelong interest in King's life and legacy. At Columbia University in New York, I met Professor Jack Greenberg, the legendary white lawyer who was director-counsel of the NAACP Legal Defence Fund. Greenberg had been co-counsel with Thurgood Marshall in the groundbreaking case *Brown v Board of Education* in which the US Supreme Court declared state laws establishing separate public schools for black and white students to be unconstitutional. He inspired me to think of how even an unjust legal system could be used to promote human rights. It was Greenberg, along with Columbia Professor Barbara Schatz, who suggested I set up what the Americans call a Section 501(c)3 non-profit corporation in the USA to support legal work in Zimbabwe.

Through that meeting the Central and Southern African Legal Assistance Foundation (CASALAF) was formed. Henry Rhoads became its president and ex-Zimbabweans Daryl Buffenstein, an Atlanta lawyer, and Trevor Harris, son of former Bulawayo mayor and my father's friend

Ralph Harris, then a New York chartered accountant, joined the board.

It was during this trip that I met Michael Posner, a doyen of the human rights fraternity in the US who was then director of the New York Lawyers Committee for Human Rights. The Lawyers Committee had funded and supported the first investigation into the Gukurahundi, which culminated in a report, *Wages of War*, researched and written by New York journalist Bill Berkeley in 1986. The trip ended at Harvard, where I visited the International Defence and Aid Fund which at the time was playing such an important role in funding the anti-apartheid struggle. Within a few years, come the end of apartheid, it was to close down its defence programme and hand over to the new South African Legal Defence Fund (SALDEF), which would pursue trials still taking place ahead of the establishment of a democratic dispensation. Henry Rhoads eventually joined the SALDEF board, which was to become a critically important channel of funding for the LRF.

Soon after returning from the US, I became personally aware of another murky aspect of ZANU PF rule, and an inevitable consequence of their burgeoning, monolithic power – corruption. The first warnings came from within the party. In July 1988, backbencher Byron Hove created a stir in parliament when he argued a motion about corruption, mismanagement and ministerial interference in Air Zimbabwe, the government-owned national airline. Long-standing ZANU PF stalwart (and the person who had helped Mugabe get across the border into Mozambique in 1975) Edgar Tekere then joined the fray in October, when he told a public meeting in Mutare that "democracy in Zimbabwe is in intensive care and the leadership has decayed". He also expressed the fear that the country was "heading towards the creation of a dictatorship".

There had been a variety of scandals over the years. In 1982 ZANU PF leader Kumbirai Kangai was implicated in a corruption scandal involving the Grain Marketing Board (the Paweni scandal), followed by the National Railways of Zimbabwe (NRZ) housing scandal in 1986, a US$100 million fraud involving the unlawful procurement of Fokker aircraft by Air Zimbabwe, and an exposé regarding ZISCO steel blast furnace in 1987. All had been brushed under the carpet with none of the bigwigs involved being held to account.

In October 1988, a ZANU PF MP, Obert Mpofu, accidentally received a cheque from a car company in Willowvale, an industrial area of Harare. The cheque had actually been intended for Alford Mpofu, a friend of Industry minister Callistus Ndlovu. Obert Mpofu took the cheque to Geoffrey Nyarota, editor of the state-owned Bulawayo newspaper *The Chronicle*. The paper had already built a reputation for aggressive investigations into corruption at all levels of government, and began to investigate. Mpofu had been a ZAPU member but in 1983 had crossed the floor when he was allegedly implicated in a scandal at Harare airport where he worked as a customs officer. He had risen to become the managing director of a ZANU PF-owned company Zimbabwe Grain Bag (Pvt) Ltd, but was fired soon after his revelations to *The Chronicle*.

In the weeks following their receipt of the cheque, Nyarota and deputy-editor Davison Maruziva learned that a variety of ministers and senior officials had been given easy access to buy foreign cars at the Willowvale assembly plant. In some cases, the cars were bought wholesale and resold at a 200 per cent profit. Implicated ministers included Ndlovu, Political Affairs minister Maurice Nyagumbo, and Defence minister Enos Nkala. The scandal went beyond simply ministers making a profit from the sale of vehicles – it was also illegal.

In 1976, as sanctions were gripping Rhodesia, the RF had tightened up a federal law, The Control of Goods Act, tightly regulating goods, such as imported motor vehicles, that were in short supply. ZANU PF continued the law and in 1988 there were stringent laws regulating how much new vehicles could be sold for in Zimbabwe. In all the cases senior ZANU PF ministers had cynically sold the cars they had acquired by virtue of their position, making obscene profits in breach of the law.

On the morning of 9 November 1988 a very worried governor of Matabeleland North, Jacob Mudenda, came into my office brandishing that morning's edition of *The Chronicle* which accused him of on-selling a heavy duty Scania truck he had purchased. It alleged he had bought the truck for Z$338 952 and had sold it to the parent company of Zimbabwe Grain Bag, Treger Industries, for "between $450 000 and $500 000".[232] Although heavy duty trucks were not subject to the Control of Goods (Sale of Motor Vehicle) Regulations, *The Chronicle* story suggested a racket and improper abuse of office.

Mudenda had been a client for a few years. My submission to him of the 1986 churches' human rights report had not ended our professional relationship. Ethics of the legal profession bar me from going into privileged aspects of my instructions, but suffice it to say that I was asked to defend Mudenda on the allegations that he had been involved in corrupt behaviour.

The Chronicle story didn't go away. On 4 January the following year Mugabe appointed a commission of inquiry to look into the "Willowgate" scandal chaired by the then judge president Wilson Sandura. Jacob Mudenda was subpoenaed to appear before the commission in Harare on 2 February and I represented him. Ostensibly, Mudenda was there only to explain the circumstances around the acquisition of the Scania and we thoroughly prepared his answer. He was duly sworn in and the hearing appeared to be going swimmingly until Judge Sandura asked Mudenda whether this was the only vehicle he had acquired. Mudenda said it was. My legal antennae immediately went up and my concern grew as the first question was followed by a flurry of further polite enquiries, such as "Are you sure?", "Did you receive any other vehicle from any other source pertinent to this Commission?" It was clear that Sandura was closing off all possible escape routes. Once they were sealed, he triumphantly produced a piece of paper from his files. Donning his glasses, Sandura slowly read out the contents of the letter which revealed that Mudenda had received another vehicle from another factory. He then glared down at Mudenda, took his glasses off, and asked whether he had perhaps forgotten *this* vehicle. There was nothing I could do but watch my hapless client stammer that the transaction had slipped his mind. It was disastrous. Mudenda lost his job, ironically being replaced by another of my clients, Welshman Mabhena. He was not, however, prosecuted for perjury and lived to fight another day, eventually becoming speaker of parliament in 2013. Others were not so fortunate – Enos Nkala's political career came to an end and Maurice Nyagumbo, who was found by the commission to have received several cars, found the disgrace too great and took his life.

There is one other footnote to this story. Nyarota and Maruziva were forced out of their jobs with *The Chronicle* and kicked upstairs into newly created public relations positions in Harare. Though the men were given pay raises, Mugabe also ventured that their move was a result of "overzealousness", leaving the public in no doubt that they had been removed for their reporting. ZANU PF parliamentarians also criticised Nyarota and Maruziva: the minister of state for National Security, Sekeramayi, while "welcoming" criticism, cautioned, "to the extent that the press now deliberately target Government as their enemy then we part ways".[233] None of those close to Mugabe's inner circle was touched by the commission.

While on the face of it the commission appeared to show a willingness by ZANU PF to combat corruption, in reality it was just a sop. The only politicians held to account were expendable and that realisation further jolted the little confidence I had left in Mugabe.

During this period two further cases I handled exposed ZANU PF's bad faith towards the Unity Accord. The first concerned the district administrator for Nkayi, a rural area north of Bulawayo, Stanley Bhebhe. Following the Unity Accord and amnesty many dissidents and ex-ZIPRA combatants needed to be reintegrated into society. An organisation set up at the end of the war to assist the reintegration of both ZANLA and ZIPRA veterans into civil society, Zimbabwe Project Trust, had done magnificent work under the stewardship of Judith Todd and Paul Themba Nyathi. Zimbabwe Project, continuing its post-war work, had raised money for an agricultural project in the Nkayi district to rehabilitate 43 dissidents and it found an enthusiastic supporter in Bhebhe. This did not go down well with some of the policemen in the district, in particular the shadowy PISI unit, who remained antagonistic towards all ex-ZIPRA combatants. In a bid to undermine the project, they arrested and detained Bhebhe on 29 December 1988 and charged him with the theft of bicycles donated by UNICEF, borehole parts and a water pump donated by Zimbabwe Project.

On 3 January 1989 I received instructions from Judith Todd to represent Bhebhe. Interestingly, none of the entities which had the right to lay charges, viz UNICEF and Zimbabwe Project, had pressed charges against Bhebhe. A PISI section officer, one Shepherd Goto, was on a frolic of his own in bringing the prosecution. During the course of January, I employed vigorous and aggressive tactics to get Bhebhe released and the charges dropped. Bhebhe was finally released on 20 January when state prosecutors in Bulawayo conceded that there was no evidence against him and the original charges would be dropped. Goto, however, said that "further new charges" would be brought and the case was remanded to 3 February. When we appeared in court on that day, Goto advised that Bhebhe would now be charged with theft of a fridge and sand, which we were immediately able to disprove. Receipts were provided regarding both, compelling state prosecutors to drop the new charges. Much to

Goto's fury, the state withdrew all the charges against Bhebhe and he walked away from court a free man.

Undeterred, Goto trumped up fresh charges and, acting unilaterally and illegally, served Bhebhe with a fresh summons the following day, Saturday, 4 February, in Nkayi. Bhebhe arrived in my offices on Monday after the weekend, bearing the new summons, in the company of three Nkayi district employees whom I recognised as state witnesses in the previous cases. Not wanting to be accused of interfering with state witnesses, I immediately asked the three to leave. When Bhebhe and I appeared in court in Bulawayo on 8 February (the date for trial set out in Goto's summons) we were told by the SPP (Senior Public Prosecutor) that Goto's summons was irregular and that the case would not proceed. I was also told that Goto had been reported to his superiors for abuse of process and the SPP recommended that we do the same. The matter appeared to be at an end, although two days later I received word that one of the three Nkayi district employees who had come to my office, John Nkabinde, had been detained, which seemed odd because he was a state witness.

PISI had not given up and their intentions became clear on Sunday, 19 February. Our usual practice at home on a Sunday then was to attend the 8.30 service at the Presbyterian church located in the city centre, which we did on that particular day as usual. As the service ended a friend, Frank Wilmot, came up to me to ask whether I was all right. He told me that he had been moved to pray for me that morning. Thinking nothing of it, I told him I was fine. After church we went to the Bulawayo railway station to collect a young Canadian anti-apartheid activist who had asked to stay with us. As we drove her home she regaled us with her stories of working with the ANC in Lusaka – she was appalled to find that senior ANC leaders drank South African wine and was equally shocked when we got home to find that we offered South African black pepper with her brunch! It was in the course of brunch that the phone rang. The caller identified himself as Inspector A Kambira, who said that he had "got some documents for you regarding the Bhebhe case and I need to bring them to you this morning". I told Kambira that it was most irregular to do this on a Sunday and that he should bring them to my office the next day. He insisted on coming to my home, however, saying that it "would not take long". Sure enough half an hour later Kambira arrived in plainclothes, accompanied by two uniformed policemen.

The civility of the phone call was gone and in a gruff manner he presented a warrant of arrest and said he was arresting me for "attempting to defeat the course of justice". I had a cursory look at the warrant and invited him in to give myself a chance to study it in more detail. Jenny immediately saw what was happening and with a broad welcoming grin invited Kambira for tea. He had no choice but to accept and sat down with Jenny, our Canadian guest and our 17-month-old baby Jessica, while I retreated to an alcove to phone Bryant Elliot, then and now Zimbabwe's finest human rights lawyer, to discuss the matter. Jenny was her most charming self and plied Kambira with tea, scones and discussions about the weather. Our Canadian guest was flabbergasted and watched the events unfolding before her with wide eyes – at one point, she ventured a question, asking Jenny whether this "type of thing was a frequent occurrence"! My scrutiny of the warrant in discussion with Elliot revealed that it was fatally flawed in two respects: firstly, Kambira had not signed his supporting affidavit before a commissioner of oaths and secondly, the warrant had been signed by Chief Superintendent G T Mukosi, the officer commanding Bulawayo *rural* district – Kambira's affidavit alleged that I had called state witnesses to my office in Bulawayo and "advised them to change their evidence in court". The alleged offence had therefore been committed in Bulawayo *urban* district, outside Mukosi's jurisdiction.

Satisfied that I had good grounds to resist arrest, I returned to the happy tea party and told Kambira of the defects in his warrant. I then told him that if he still chose to arrest me unlawfully, I would not bother suing the state but would sue him in his personal capacity. I told him that arresting a lawyer on spurious and illegal grounds would attract a hefty damages award. I would make sure, I added, that the deputy sheriff would come to his home to attach his lounge suite, hi-fi and anything else sufficiently valuable to meet the claim. This threat alarmed Kambira and he anxiously studied the warrant again, mumbling that he would rectify the defects and be back. No sooner had he left than I gathered up baby Jessica and headed off through bush adjoining our home to go to a place of safety. Jenny hurriedly shut up the house, threw a few clothes in a suitcase before leaving in a vehicle to take a circuitous route, ultimately joining up with me in our safe house. Our Canadian guest, by now completely bewildered how such a thing could happen in the free and democratic state of Zimbabwe, was dropped off with friends.

Safely ensconced with my family in our safe house, I began to work the phones. I first spoke to Joshua Nkomo, who was very supportive. Elliot got working too. I had recently been appointed national director (Legal Policy) of the LRF, so our chair and Chief Justice Enock Dumbutshena was informed. He was furious, but for obvious reasons there was a limit to what he could do. Even Garfield Todd was made aware of my plight – a few days before he had been severely burnt while trying to repair his car and was hospitalised in Bulawayo and when we contacted Judith he was fully briefed on the ongoing saga.

The following day the officer commanding police in Matabeleland apologised for my attempted arrest but said that his subordinates were determined to press charges. After a few days I was given an assurance that I would not be arrested and that the attorney general himself would make a decision whether to prosecute in due course. Weeks dragged by. Then in April the Zimbabwean director of Prosecutions, Andrew Chigovera, revealed to Elliot that the police's "star witness", poor old John Nkabinde, had complained that he had made his statement implicating me under duress when detained by the police. However, it was only on 9 September that Elliot received a letter from Chigovera advising that the attorney general had declined to prosecute and the police docket was closed. Although all the facts surrounding the unlawful attempt by the police to intimidate me were brought to the attention of the commissioner of Police, no action was ever taken against either Goto or Kambira. It was the first, but by no means the last time that Police were to attempt to arrest me at home. The incident was a salutary lesson to both me and my wife in how to handle brazen and aggressive policemen in future.

The second case which exposed contradictions in the application of the Unity Accord concerned two captured dissidents, Ndodana Moyo and Nduna Petros Mlilo. In April 1987 Father Pius Ncube had asked me to locate Mlilo on behalf of the CCJP. Mlilo had managed to smuggle a terse note out of the CIO base at Esigodini which said he was detained and "in great need of help". I eventually received confirmation that he was being held and would face criminal charges as he was a captured dissident. My instructions were terminated because the CCJP didn't want to spend scarce resources on dissidents, so Mlilo remained in prison unrepresented until January 1989 when the State decided to prosecute him, Moyo and another captured dissident, Frank Mpofu. The case was unjust in that the three had all been deported to Zimbabwe from Botswana in 1987 where they had been in exile. They had in fact turned their back on violence but were now charged with three murders which had occurred between 1983 and 1986. All admitted that they had been dissidents and were present when the murders took place, but the leaders of the dissident gang, who had actually done the killings, who had remained dissidents, had taken advantage of the 1988 amnesty and were now free men. The greatest irony of all was that several of these men would be called to give evidence that they had committed the murders, not the accused men. Despite these facts, which were largely common cause, the State was determined to proceed and the CCJP, concerned by this injustice, instructed me to defend Moyo and Mlilo.

Taking instructions from Moyo and Mlilo at the dreadful Khami Maximum prison outside Bulawayo was a poignant reminder of the futility of war. Mlilo was a year younger than me, Moyo two years younger. Both had left Rhodesia in 1977 with little education, believing their only hope was to end minority rule. They were both trained as ZIPRA guerrillas; by some quirk the youngest, Moyo, was deployed into Rhodesia and fought in the Gokwe area whereas Mlilo remained outside the country. Moyo was integrated into 1:3 Battalion of the ZNA; Mlilo, presumably because he had not seen active service, was not and was demobilised in 1981. Both were harassed in 1982 – Moyo fled the army fearing for his life and only joined a dissident gang when he saw the atrocities being committed by the Fifth Brigade. Mlilo fled the country to Botswana in 1983 after hearing about the wholesale abductions and disappearances of ex-ZIPRA combatants. On arrival in Botswana, Mlilo was recruited into the dissident ranks and returned to Zimbabwe, where he joined Moyo's gang. Moyo was wounded in a contact with Zimbabwean security forces near Victoria Falls in October 1986 and all three men, Moyo, Mlilo and Mpofu, fled Zimbabwe and handed themselves over to the Botswana police in Kasane. They were all then deported back to Zimbabwe by the Botswana authorities, detained and severely tortured. Their senior comrades, who had remained fighting, were now scot free. It all seemed so utterly bizarre and pointless.

Given that they admitted they were part of the gangs responsible for the three murders, they would be convicted as accomplices to murder. Although their former comrades would confirm that Mlilo and Moyo had not themselves killed anyone, they would confirm their presence.

The only way round the farce was to attempt to extend the application of Clemency Order 1 of 1988 (the original amnesty order which applied to other dissidents) to my clients. The Clemency Order cast a blanket over all offences committed during the Gukurahundi era up to 18 April 1988 and covered the sins of the genocide perpetrated by the Fifth Brigade and CIO, and of course murders committed by dissidents. However, the amnesty only applied to dissidents who were still "at large" and who handed themselves in by 31 May 1988. There was another provision which granted an amnesty to any "former member of PF ZAPU who, as at 19 April 1988, had left or was remaining outside Zimbabwe to avoid criminal proceedings".

I raised three arguments: firstly, that the general amnesty was unconstitutionally discriminatory, in that it favoured those who had managed to evade capture; secondly, that the general amnesty was unreasonable and unjust; thirdly, that the fugitive provision should apply to Mlilo and Moyo – they were former ZAPU members who had left Zimbabwe prior to 19 April 1988 to avoid arrest. I emphasised that the section used the phrase *or was remaining outside Zimbabwe*, rather than *and* – the implication being that they would be covered even if no longer outside Zimbabwe, so long as they had left Zimbabwe prior to the cut-off date. I argued that the order was "manifestly unjust" in that it enabled "those dissidents who held out to the bitter end, including those who committed the heinous murder of missionaries at New Adams farm, to go scot free, yet it condemns those who gave up the fight as far back as October 1986".[234]

The presiding judge, ex-Rhodesian Front MP Justice Fergus Blackie, dismissed the first two arguments but allowed the third, subject to the proviso that we would have to prove in evidence that they were former PF ZAPU members, etcetera. And so the trial started, and continued until 7 August when, at the conclusion of the State case, State counsel suddenly announced that charges were being withdrawn, leading to the acquittal of the three dissidents. A few days later the attorney general telephoned me to advise that he would not prosecute any more dissident-related matters. Although some dissidents who had already been convicted of offences remained in prison a while longer, the Mlilo trial ultimately resulted in this sorry chapter of Zimbabwe's history being closed.

The Unity Accord, dissolving PF ZAPU into ZANU PF, and the 1987 constitutional amendment, eradicating the seats reserved for whites, finally created a *de facto* one-party state in Zimbabwe. With the dissident menace finally ended, the ZANU PF leadership must have thought that a clean sweep in the forthcoming 1990 election would be a shoo-in, but it was not to be.

Jonathan Moyo, then a political science academic, made this profound observation about this period:

> "By removing, or seeking to remove, external obstacles to the establishment of a one party state between 1980 and 1987, ZANU PF rendered itself open to internal criticism following the removal of the external 'enemy'. One consequence of the unity agreement was that ZANU PF came face to face with itself. Groups which had tended to support ZANU PF almost as a ritualistic routine, such as the Zimbabwe Congress of Trade Unions and University of Zimbabwe students, became critical of the authorities."[235]

Two events towards the end of 1988 illustrate this: ZANU PF finally tired of Edgar Tekere's outbursts against corruption, especially when he publicly criticised Mugabe himself, resulting in his expulsion from ZANU PF in October 1988. In September 1988, students at the University of Zimbabwe and Harare Polytechnic organised a demonstration against corruption which was broken up by police using teargas and baton charges. Mugabe shocked students when he returned from an overseas trip and endorsed the harsh police action. To demonstrate they meant business, the government then deported Kenyan law lecturer Shadreck Gutto on the allegation that he helped students draft an anti-corruption petition. That was followed by the withdrawal of government grants awarded to fifteen members of the University Students' Representative Council alleged to be involved in anti-government activities.

The greatest political threat, though, was posed by Tekere who, soon after his expulsion from ZANU PF, established a new political party, the Zimbabwe Unity Movement (ZUM). ZUM got to work quickly and in early 1989 contested a by-election in the Harare constituency of Dzivarasekwa. In what was to become a familiar pattern of electoral fraud, ZANU PF pulled out all the stops to win – Tekere alleged that two ministers intimidated voters and that ZANU PF bussed in party loyalists from neighbouring districts. ZUM rallies were banned by the police and a rally had to be cancelled when a ZANU PF council authority locked

ZUM supporters out of a stadium. While ZANU PF won, ZUM secured 28 per cent of the vote. This remarkable performance so soon after the launch of ZUM led to a further crackdown against the ZUM leadership.

In June 1989 fifteen senior members of ZUM were arrested, detained and then released after a few days. The minister of Home Affairs, Moven Mahachi, defending the detentions said:

> "There is freedom to form political parties but there is no freedom to subvert a legitimate government."[236]

Tekere continued to find that freedom hard to exercise. On 18 July when he tried to address his first public meeting since ZUM's formation, police, using teargas, shut down a rally attended by 5 000 students at the University of Zimbabwe.

Trouble at the university spread. In June 1989 four lecturers, including the acting dean of the Law faculty, Kempton Makamure, were arrested and detained for a week at Harare's Marimba police station. Then, on 29 September, students attempted to hold a seminar marking the anniversary of their 1988 anti-corruption demonstration; it was shut down by 200 riot police and CIO operatives, who called the gathering "illegal". On 2 October the SRC issued a statement protesting the police action as a violation of academic freedom. The authorities reacted to this by raiding the campus in the early hours of 4 October and arresting the SRC president, Arthur Mutambara, and its secretary general, Enoch Chikweche. These detentions provoked a massive protest on campus by thousands of students. Cars were damaged, some further 70 students were arrested and the university shut down. Thirty-day detention orders, using Rhodesian-era emergency powers regulations, were served on Mutambara, Chikweche and other SRC leaders, such as Christopher Giwa, Peter Myabo, Edmore Tobaiwa and Samuel Simango.

Inevitably, the protests snowballed. The detention of Mutambara and other students and the closure of the university led the Zimbabwe Congress of Trade Unions to protest. Its secretary general, Morgan Tsvangirai, issued a short and relatively tame statement asserting the students' right to protest against corruption. This resulted in Tsvangirai's arrest and detention by the CIO on the morning of 6 October. ZANU PF was obviously concerned about the threat he posed, because he disappeared and was denied access to his lawyers. His lawyers were forced to file a *habeas corpus*[237] writ, obtaining an order on 11 October compelling the CIO to give them access to him. Eventually, after being detained for six weeks, Tsvangirai was released without being charged. Following the pattern used against ZAPU leaders, he was re-detained soon after being released and told that he was going to be charged with treason, charges which never materialised either.[238]

Until then, I had never even heard of Tsvangirai, but there was a considerable outcry against his detention and his profile was greatly enhanced.

During 1989, two events happened beyond our borders which impacted the political situation inside Zimbabwe. The first provided a template for the student protests in Zimbabwe. The massive student protest at Tiananmen Square on 27 April that year dealt with issues close to the heart of Zimbabwean students – the Chinese students' "anti-corruption, anti-cronyism" but "pro-party" message delivered that day resonated within the Zimbabwean student movement. ZANU PF and Mugabe himself were still revered by a majority of students in Zimbabwe as those responsible for defeating Smith; most naively believed that Mugabe was also against corruption and cronyism. The bravery of students, especially the heroics of the "tank man" who blocked the passage of a tank at Tiananmen Square, undoubtedly inspired students in Zimbabwe to protest in a similar way. The second incident which captured the imagination of Zimbabweans was the fall of the Berlin Wall on 9 November. Most Zimbabweans then, as now, had limited access to news and so the nuances of the weakening of the Soviet Union were lost on most. An iconic event like this could not be hidden from the public, however, and it acted as a powerful symbol that freedom could even be won in totalitarian regimes. These events, combined with the emergence of ZUM, undermined ZANU PF's quest to move towards a legislated one-party state.

Seemingly unfazed, however, ZANU PF took a major step on 22 December towards consolidating its grip on power when Parliament rushed through the 9th amendment to the Zimbabwean constitution. The ostensible reason for the amendment was to streamline Parliament by abolishing the Senate, replacing it with an enlarged House of Assembly. In reality, though, the amendment diluted democracy, giving Mugabe the power personally to appoint 20 members of Parliament. A further ten chiefs, beholden to Mugabe because he paid them, became MPs, guaranteeing that Mugabe controlled a fifth of Parliament before a single vote had been cast.

The release of Nelson Mandela in February 1990 and the subsequent determination of both Mandela and the ANC to embrace multi-party democracy in South Africa also had a huge impact on the one-party debate in Zimbabwe. In other countries in Africa one-party regimes in countries such as Angola, Kenya, Mozambique and Zambia were under threat. The combination of all these events made ZANU PF's objective of establishing a one-party state all the more difficult, especially as ZUM made it the defining issue in the run up to the election. ZANU PF stated in its manifesto that the "foundation of democracy" would be "firmer in a one party state"[239] but did not actually commit itself in its manifesto to introducing one. ZUM, on the other hand, accused ZANU PF of wanting to convert Zimbabwe into a one-party state, and pledged to fight to secure multi-party democracy.

Despite its appealing promises, ZUM did not get much of a foothold in Bulawayo. At the time I was fully engrossed in expanding the BLPC and so did not get involved in the election campaign as it got under way at the beginning of 1990. From its modest beginnings in 1987, the BLPC two years on boasted two full-time lawyers and three paralegals. During 1988 we opened three paralegal advice centres in the Luveve, Sizinda and Magwegwe working-class suburbs of Bulawayo. One of the paralegals was Chipo Nyathi, the wife of a ZAPU central committee member, Isaac Nyathi; another was Paul Chizuze, a CCJP activist and Catholic catechist, who was to become a pivotal actor in exposing the Gukurahundi in years to come. Our original premises in Charter House were too small and in early 1989 we moved diagonally across the road to a beautiful old Cape Dutch-style building, 94 Fort Street. Its location was perfect, situated right next to the Tredgold Building Magistrates Court and just a block away from the High Court. Despite my clashes with the Nkayi police, I had developed a good enough working relationship with the police and CIO to get agreement for policemen and women, and intelligence operatives, to undergo human rights training courses. Although the CIO participated in just one of our courses (probably to understand precisely what message we were preaching), the police stayed the course and eventually they were conducted countrywide. In my capacity as national director (Legal Policy) of the LRF, I found myself increasingly in Harare and responsible for the national expansion of the organisation with my two colleagues in the executive, Eileen Sawyer and Wilson Manase.

Early in 1990 I was approached by Bulawayo councillor Nelson Sidanile to see whether I would be prepared to stand as an MP for ZANU PF in Bulawayo. Sidanile was an old client; in August 1985 he instructed me to sue the the Police and its PISI unit for unlawful detention and assault. He, like so many ZAPU councillors, had been detained at Stops Camp and was severely tortured by two PISI policemen. He was beaten up, tied upside down and then subjected to water torture with a wet blanket being stuck over his head. Before we could get legal proceedings under way he was detained again, this time on the utterly bizarre allegations that he had "accused the Police for having arrested (him) for no apparent reason" and that "(Minister) Nkala's Policemen were harassing people holding peaceful meetings".[240] It was apparently an offence to claim that the police had acted unlawfully! Unsurprisingly, Sidanile was never charged with that offence, but he continued to have run-ins with the CIO and PISI. His swansong with them before the signing of the 1987 Unity Accord happened when he was detained again on 17 September 1987 on allegations that he "was assisting bandits in Matabeleland North Province". As he was held under emergency powers regulations, there was little I could do to secure his release, but on 1 October I got a message from his wife that he had been refused his Bible by PISI.

That day I had a meeting with Inspector D Chamba, the head of PISI in Bulawayo, who told me, straight faced, that Sidanile was not allowed a Bible because "Jesus wrote politics".[241] My entreaties must, however, have done some good because later that day Sidanile was released, never to be detained again. In all this we had become good friends and I suppose that is the reason he felt I might be a good ZANU PF MP. I was somewhat taken aback by the request as I had never considered standing for Parliament, far less standing for ZANU PF. Without turning him down, I suggested that he first see if there was a consensus within ZANU PF regarding my nomination. He went away to find out. His suggestion apparently went down like a lead balloon within the ZANU PF hierarchy. I was mightily relieved to hear that I didn't have to disappoint him.

That sense of relief grew as the election campaign progressed and as I realised what a minefield I would have got myself into. Although the 1985 election was pockmarked with violence, at least then there was some excuse in that there were still dissidents and South Africa was still destabilising Zimbabwe. There was no such excuse in 1990. There had been no violence for two years and FW de Klerk had breathed a new spirit of reasonableness into South African foreign policy.

The first inkling that the campaign would be bloody came in the form of two ZANU PF campaign messages carried on TV by the ZBC. The first, as Jonathan Moyo recounts, was watched by viewers "in disbelief and astonishment". The message started with a vehicle careening down a hill, screeching its tyres, then crashing into another with a sickening sound of crushing glass and metal, followed by a voice warning harshly: "This is one way to die. Another is to vote ZUM. Don't commit suicide, vote ZANU PF".[242] The second showed a coffin being lowered into a grave with the chilling refrain: "AIDS kills. So does ZUM. Vote ZANU PF". The brazen messages were clear. They were also followed by tangible proof that those who authorised them meant what they said.

The election was marked by widespread and gathering violence, overwhelmingly perpetrated by ZANU PF supporters and operatives against ZUM supporters and candidates. The violence, however, was concentrated in marginal areas where ZANU PF feared defeat. Matabeleland, because of the dominance of old ZAPU support, was largely violence free. In contrast, areas where high-profile ZUM leaders came from became battle zones. There was widespread intimidation of ZUM supporters in Manicaland, Masvingo, Mashonaland West and Midlands provinces. In some constituencies ZUM candidates were seriously threatened. Death threats were issued against the Kariba candidate and in Chivi South (which included Ngundu Halt, where I spent the last few months of 1977) the ZUM candidate was under siege.

The most serious violence occurred in the city of my birth, Gweru. The Gweru Central constituency was contested by two heavyweights, Vice-President Simon Muzenda and ZUM's Patrick Kombayi. Kombayi was a colourful character, one of Rhodesia's first black engine drivers, who had gone into business in Zambia during the war and was a major funder of ZANU PF. Immediately after independence he became Gweru's first black ZANU PF mayor, attracting controversy through his aggressive attacks on many white leaders in the city. He had fallen out with ZANU PF and when Tekere formed ZUM he became one of its leaders. Kombayi was immensely popular in Gweru, especially in the working-class suburb of Mkoba. Just weeks before the election the Delimitation Commission, the body responsible for electoral boundaries, removed Mkoba from the Gweru Central (urban) constituency and allocated it to Gweru South (rural), in a stroke depriving Kombayi of thousands of votes. But that was clearly deemed insufficient by ZANU PF to secure victory. On the afternoon of 24 March 1990 all hell broke loose in Gweru. It started when ZANU PF youths arrived at a store owned by Kombayi singing ZANU PF songs, including one that had the refrain "Kombayi should die". They then stoned and looted the shop before setting it on fire. Shots were fired by someone using an AK assault rifle, wounding three ZUM supporters. Kombayi was alerted and he came to the store, at the same time arranging for the wounded to be ferried to hospital in one of his trucks. As the truck drove towards the hospital, it was fired upon by CIO operatives. Its driver was wounded when a bullet went through his spleen and he lost control of the lorry, only to be set alight by the ZANU PF mob where it came to rest at the side of the road. Kombayi, who had been following the truck, arrived at the scene but before he could even open his door he was fired upon, in the presence of uniformed police officers, by a CIO operative, Elias Kanengoni, and the ZANU PF MP for Chiwundira constituency, Kizito Chivamba.[243] Ten shots in all were fired, six hitting Kombayi, seriously wounding him in his legs, groin and stomach. Kombayi put his hand out the window, shouting, "Okay, stop, you have killed me!", before opening the door and collapsing on the tarmac gushing blood. Remarkably, he lived.

Muzenda won the constituency, as did ZANU PF overall in the general election held on 28–30 March. But as Jonathan Moyo clearly exposed in his seminal book on the election, *Voting for Democracy*, the entire election was mired by violence and serious illegalities. Despite all of this, ZUM managed to win seventeen per cent of the vote country wide (although due to the Westminister-style electoral system it only won two constituencies). Tekere secured 413 840 votes out of the 2.5 million votes cast. As Jonathan Moyo succinctly put it, despite ZUM's defeat the election marked a major victory for democracy: "While ZANU PF's desire for a one-party state remained resolute even after the 1990 elections, the party's ability to act on its desire was greatly diminished by voters who denied it the *total* victory it badly needed."[244]

Mugabe moved quickly to assist those responsible for the violence. Although Kanengoni and Chivamba were prosecuted, convicted of attempted murder and sentenced to seven years' imprisonment, they hardly spent a night in jail and were eventually pardoned by Mugabe. Kanengoni was steadily promoted, ending up as deputy director of the CIO before his death in 2013.

I observed all of this from the sidelines, appalled. Any last remnant of respect for Mugabe and ZANU PF was gone. Little was I to know then that the Kombayi incident would lead to the first death threat levelled against me by ZANU PF operatives four years later.

CHAPTER 12

TRUE PEACE?
APRIL 1990 TO FEBRUARY 1994

"True peace is not merely the absence of tension; it is the presence of justice."
– MARTIN LUTHER KING, MONTGOMERY, ALABAMA, 1955, IN
RESPONSE TO AN ACCUSATION THAT HE WAS "DISTURBING THE PEACE"
BY HIS ACTIVISM DURING THE MONTGOMERY BUS BOYCOTT

ZANU PF's overwhelming majority in parliament in the March 1990 elections and Nelson Mandela's release, heralding the beginning of the end of apartheid, caused many people, especially those in business, to think that southern Africa, and Zimbabwe in particular, was entering a new era of stability and progress. That sentiment also reflected the international euphoria that followed the collapse of the Berlin Wall and the Soviet Union. One of the immediate consequences of both the end of the Cold War and apartheid was the reduction of Western support for ZANU PF. No longer was there a need for the West to look the other way in the interests of keeping Zimbabwe out of the clutches of the Soviet bloc and in persuading white South Africa that there could be life after apartheid. As Western interest shifted towards South Africa, the level of donor support for Zimbabwe waned and concurrently there was increased pressure from the IMF and World Bank for the Zimbabwean government to reform its economic policies.

The first sign of this pressure came in the first budget statement after the election, in July 1990, when the Economic Structural Adjustment Programme (ESAP) was announced. In exchange for economic "liberalisation" (in the form of trade and currency deregulation, devaluation of the Zimbabwe dollar, the lifting of price controls, removal of consumer subsidies and education in social spending), a string of large loans and credit facilities were provided by the World Bank, IMF and international donors. It was estimated that Zimbabwe would need US$3 billion to "spend its way into a new free market economy on borrowed money".[245]

Although business and many economists welcomed the change in direction, I was concerned. The success of the programme required absolute political will to move away from a command economy; and yet at the core of ZANU PF's DNA was desire to control everything from the centre. It seemed to me from the outset that the government, desperate for foreign assistance, would agree to any terms without any real commitment to deregulating society. Everything else spoke of a need to control – increased spending on the military, an ever-increasing size of cabinet and subtle moves to exert control.

One of these subtle moves concerned the retirement of Chief Justice Enock Dumbutshena when he reached 70 in April 1990. The original Lancaster House constitution did not specify a retirement age; in 1984 the constitution was amended to make judges' retirement age 70. This amendment was ironic in light of the subsequent constitutional amendment in 1987, which had greatly enlarged executive powers and created a vastly powerful president with no age or term limits. However, the constitution did allow the president to appoint an acting chief justice for a specified term, and Dumbutshena advised Mugabe that he was willing to stay on in an acting position. Mugabe would not entertain the idea, despite the fact that Dumbutshena was eminently suited to carry on. Dumbutshena and I were fellow trustees of the LRF and, having got to know him well, I appreciated his commitment to democracy and justice. During his tenure as chief justice he completely transformed the judiciary and his retirement came as blow. Ostensibly, Mugabe acted prudently in selecting a replacement. Judge Anthony Gubbay, who had sworn me in as a legal practitioner as a High Court judge in Bulawayo in 1983, was arguably Zimbabwe's finest judge. He had written a string of outstanding judgments sitting alongside Dumbutshena on the Supreme Court. However, Gubbay did not have a political bone in his body to anticipate ZANU PF's machinations and had the additional handicap of being white. In short, he was far more vulnerable to ZANU PF's threats than Dumbutshena ever would have been.

Another worrying development was the rapid assimilation of many former ZAPU leaders into ZANU PF's value system and how this affected their outlook on some of our human rights work.

The BLPC had found its feet and 1990 saw rapid development in a number of areas. The most significant was the opening of the first rural legal advice centre in Zimbabwe at Lupane in July 1990. My friend and client Welshman Mabhena, who following the Unity Accord had been elected deputy speaker of Parliament, enthusiastically agreed to open the centre, which was located at St Luke's Mission. In selecting the location of the first advice centre, I made no secret of the fact as director of BLPC that I chose Lupane because it was ground zero of the Gukurahundi. I knew that there were many unresolved human rights cases in the area and believed that it was important that we try to address them. Mabhena knew this and backed our plans to the hilt. His views were not shared by others, though; I was tackled by several former ZAPU MPs who feared that our plans would simply open wounds. Even when I stressed that our intention was, on the contrary, to heal, they were not satisfied. It became increasingly clear to me that these MPs had no intention to press the issue (of redress for Gukurahundi victims) privately behind the closed doors of cabinet and the ZANU PF politburo. Some had already been wooed by ZANU PF's largesse and had no inclination to rock the boat.

The plight of ordinary people was brought home to me when a poor Bulawayo woman, Musa Sibanda, approached the BLPC in 1989 about her missing husband, Fraser Gibson Sibanda. Sibanda, aged 60 at the time, was employed at Makhalanga Beer Garden as a barman. While he had been involved in ZAPU politics in the 1950s and '60s, he had not been active for some time. On Sunday, 3 November 1985, Sibanda and his wife attended their church, the United Church of Christ, in Mpopoma, where they were long-standing members. Sibanda had a penchant for wearing badges and that day he had on a Christian Service League badge and a "Father of Zimbabwe" badge, which depicted Joshua Nkomo. After the service Mrs Sibanda saw that her husband was in the company of two uniformed policemen and at least one other plainclothes officer. Sibanda told his wife that he had been arrested for wearing a "Father of Zimbabwe" badge and he was then taken away in a police car. She never saw him again. Her frantic searches for him at local police stations in the ensuing months bore no fruit. Some officers confirmed he had been handed over to PISI; eventually, they simply alleged that he had been released and must have fled the country, something she knew her husband would never have done without contacting her. Sidney Malunga managed to get her to the minister of Home Affairs, Enos Nkala, in 1987 but that yielded nothing.

Mrs Sibanda finally came to us for help; we didn't have any public interest case funding at that time, and so we asked the CCJP to take the matter on. Bryant Elliot brought an application in the High Court seeking to compel the police to provide a full report about the arrest and subsequent detention of Sibanda. When pressed in court, the police revealed, for the first time, that on that fateful day Sibanda had finally been released into the custody of Captain Kojak Ngeyi of the Zimbabwe Intelligence Corps (a branch of the ZNA). Prior to this Ngeyi had made "dark threats that he was going to eliminate Sibanda".[246] Sibanda was driven to Brady barracks and the police never saw him again. Conveniently for the police, Ngeyi died in 1988 and so they were unable to shed any further light on Sibanda's whereabouts. Armed with this information, Elliot brought a further case to get an order presuming Sibanda dead, and finally, on 11 December 1991 an order was granted to this effect, six years after he had disappeared. The case came back to me and we sued the police for damages (on 31 August 1994 the government finally paid Z$35 000[247] to settle the claim). Mrs Sibanda was a particularly determined widow and was lucky to live in Bulawayo and to be supported by her church. Most widows, all the more so orphans, were not so lucky; this was a powerful demonstration of how difficult it was for victims to get redress, even with help from the BLPC, LRF and CCJP. The BLPC in particular had limited resources and it was clear that without government creating a mechanism to assist the processing of claims, it would be way beyond our capacity to help all the individual victims. My entreaties to former ZAPU cabinet ministers to address this problem fell on deaf ears and this convinced me that we would have to document the full extent of the suffering. The War Victims Compensation Act was passed in 1980[248] to assist all people who suffered injury during the war and something similar was needed now. I knew that this would not happen unless the veil of secrecy was lifted.

With this in mind we developed a new BLPC human rights report form. We started training paralegals and others in how to document cases. In the course of 1990 we worked towards opening further advice centres in Matabeleland North. Paul Chizuze, with whom I had worked in the CCJP in the 1980s, was brought onto our staff as a paralegal – and he was to play a major role in gathering evidence in the years ahead.

Cases trickled in at first but the numbers grew steadily. For all the progress the BLPC had made since first opening its doors and the improved human rights climate, 1990 still ended on a sobering note. On 3 December 1990 the now retired Chief Justice Dumbutshena opened our new library, named in his honour. In a hard-hitting address he berated government regarding a number of amendments made to the constitution the previous August;[249] he said the amendments (which allowed for hanging, whipping of juveniles and the compulsory acquisition of land without redress to the courts) were retrogressive. Some of them effectively reversed decisions taken by the Supreme Court, decisions which had resulted from test cases brought before the court seeking to expand the ambit of the Declaration of Rights. The Supreme Court, in judgments hailed the world over, had decided that hanging and the whipping of juveniles were "cruel and inhuman punishments" and in violation of the constitution. Dumbutshena was particularly critical of an amendment which removed the right of the courts to review whether any payment made following the compulsory acquisition of land was fair: "(It) flies in the face of all accepted norms of modern society and law. It effectively takes Zimbabwe back to the last century."[250]

Despite the bullish mood in the country at the start of 1991, I still had Dumbutshena's words ringing in my ears. On 6 May I delivered an address entitled "Economic Liberalisation – Political Protectionism?" to a business seminar organised by the chartered accounting firm KPMG Peat Marwick. It was my first overtly political address and my basic thesis was to question whether ZANU PF was committed to political liberalisation as well as economic liberalisation. In the address I noted some positive changes (such as the lifting of the state of emergency first imposed by the Rhodesians and in place for 27 years) but then catalogued all the ways in which government had tightened up its control. The University of Zimbabwe Amendment Act, rushed through Parliament at the end of 1990, gave effective control over the University Council to the president. I repeated Dumbutshena's concerns about the constitutional amendments which had reversed many great decisions of the Supreme Court. I went further than Dumbutshena and accused ZANU PF of intending "to reduce the power of the Court" because it "resented many of the decisions handed down (which had) effectively restrained Government from acting in the way it wanted".[251] I questioned the shockingly low budget provided to the courts and compared it to millions ZANU PF allocated to itself through the ministry of Political Affairs. I suggested that the attempts to rein in the university and courts were because of its need to hide corruption, which was "rife": "Government cannot afford to have students who can articulate concerns (about corruption). Government cannot afford to have a powerful court that will expose and punish corruption at every turn."[252] I concluded by stating that "trade liberalisation and structural adjustment cannot work in a vacuum" and that "economic liberalisation will not work in Zimbabwe unless Government abandons its policy of political protectionism." I urged the business community to "make a bold and public stand", claiming that "if trade liberalisation and structural adjustment are not accompanied by political reform the economy is doomed".

The speech attracted the attention of the independent press and was carried in full by the then leading weekly business paper, the *Financial Gazette*. However, it went down like a lead balloon with government, the business community and international organisations such as the World Bank. Few congratulated me. One notable exception was Sir Garfield Todd, who told me I had hit the nail on the head. It seemed clear to me that we were on the way to ruin, but few appeared to be listening as the economy opened up. We faced such a paradox: the country was the most peaceful it had been in decades and yet I feared we were in mortal peril. My speech did, however, resonate with some of my former ZAPU clients, in particular Sidney Malunga, who came to see me and expressed support for my views.

The relative peace in the country allowed us to expand the LRF rapidly. The BLPC opened legal advice centres in Hwange and Binga in September and October that year, and we identified and trained paralegals to pioneer the opening up of advice centres in Gwanda and Plumtree, our first foray into Matabeleland South province. By the end of 1991 the BLPC and its seven advice centres dealt with over 2 000 cases, most of which involved regular legal issues unrelated to human rights abuses. In my previous capacity as national director (Legal Policy) I had spearheaded the drive to set up Legal Projects centres in Manicaland and Midlands provinces and the fruit of that work was realised in the opening of the Mutare and Gweru Legal Projects centres respectively in

March and May 1991. Although we were unable to persuade the CIO to continue participating in the human rights training courses for law enforcement agents during 1991, we held six courses for ZRP officers. Reports of human rights abuses committed by the ZRP during this period plummeted and a much improved rapport between lawyers and policemen developed. Countrywide people experienced a quality of peace and stability unknown since the early 1950s. It is no wonder that my warnings were viewed by many as a wolf crying foul.

I suppose it was this environment which encouraged Sidney Malunga to invite me as guest of honour to address his end of year Makokoba constituency consultative meeting, which I did on 1 December. The meeting was technically a ZANU PF political meeting because Malunga had been elected to the constituency in the previous year's election on a ZANU PF ticket, but Malunga advertised it as open to all. The meeting was held at MacDonald Hall, near Mpilo hospital in Bulawayo's oldest high-density Makokoba suburb. Malunga invited me to speak on ESAP, rather daunting given that I wasn't an economist, a predicament exacerbated by it being my first political meeting before an all-black, working-class audience. Malunga calmed my fears and gave me complete licence to say what I liked.

Malunga was a much admired and loved politician and so when I arrived the large hall was bursting at the seams. I launched into a critique of ESAP, taking a somewhat different tack to my May speech. The core message was that ESAP would only work if we had a small government in terms of "size and attitude". I argued that "Government and the party (ZANU PF) had become overbuilt", that "ZANU PF had tried to make support for it synonymous with loyalty to Zimbabwe". Government, I said, sought "to control everything from sport to business", and had set up a "plethora of Ministries and Ministers who seem to do nothing other than earn a salary". Drawing on the recently announced budget for 1992, I pointed out that while government was cutting back on spending on social ministries such as Education and Health, it had increased the allocation to the cabinet by 14.35 per cent, increased salaries for its ministry of Political Affairs (from which ZANU PF solely benefited) by 27.58 per cent and was spending millions on renovating and building presidential mansions.

My main attack, however, was reserved for Defence spending, which had risen 11.1 per cent and consumed over 10 per cent of the total budget.

I questioned why this was necessary now in the "post-dissident" era, especially as South Africa had abandoned its policy of destabilisation. I concluded by arguing that if we had "an undemocratic (government) toying with economic reform (it) would fail".[253]

Malunga was unfazed by my attack on ZANU PF and after the meeting he thanked me for being so forthright – "those things needed to be said". The speech made it onto the front page of *The Chronicle* the following day, in a balanced article which included my criticism that it was "useless for leaders to talk of tightening belts when they (were) leading a comfortable life".[254] *The Herald* was more acerbic: two days later in an editorial entitled "Forked tongues in slash Cabinet calls", it "wondered why there were so many Presidents in the country". It decried that I, "a lawyer addressing a two-cent Malunga inspired meeting in Bulawayo", had "found (myself) suddenly an expert in good government" and had "seized upon an opportunity to offer advice on the how-to of running clean government". It concluded by averring that the president would not be "listening to those with political agendas of their own ... or those who speak with forked tongues".[255]

This, my first address at a political meeting – ironically, a ZANU PF one – marked the beginning of my public opposition to ZANU PF and to Mugabe himself.

Another consequence of my heightened profile was an increased number of speaking invitations. One of these happened at the end of January 1992, which is significant for two reasons: firstly, because I was asked to speak at Maphisa, just a few kilometres from the Bhalagwe interrogation camp and just south of Kezi police station, and secondly, because I spoke alongside Jonathan Moyo, then a political science lecturer at the University of Zimbabwe. We were invited by the Danish Volunteer Service to speak about ESAP – I was to explain it and Moyo was to critique its application in Zimbabwe. I warned the participants at the beginning of my speech that they should not attach too much weight to what we had to say for *The Herald* had recently called me a "weekend advisor" and it wasn't the weekend, and Moyo a "fruitcake lecturer". Once again I stressed that for ESAP to work "Government must relinquish a large amount of control over the economy so that the private sector can get to work". I warned that if the private sector was "hindered", the whole process could "break down catastrophically" when "exports required to repay the loans do not materialise and the

My mother, Nora, and me at World's View in the Matobo Hills, 1962.

My father, Bill, and me in contemplative pose during our holiday in Europe in 1969.

My grandfather James Robert Coltart in all his finery as Deputy Lord Provost of Edinburgh, 1938.

Judith Todd with her parents Garfield and Grace Todd at Hokonui Ranch on 23 February 1972, the day after Garfield and Judith were released from detention.

Patrol Officer David Coltart and "Flair", ready for inspection, in training for the BSAP, Morris Depot, December 1975.

The day after I avoided being ambushed on the Berejena Mission road when our armoured vehicle broke down in December 1977. I am in the centre, in the plain shirt, surrounded by my subordinates.

Meeting the minister of Information, Nathan Shamuyarira, to persuade ZANU PF to send government representatives to the UCT "Focus on Zimbabwe Week", July 1980.

Paying my respects at the grave of Dr Martin Luther King Jnr, Atlanta, US, September 1988.

With Chief Justice Enock Dumbutshena at the opening of the Bulawayo Legal Projects Centre's new offices at 94 Fort Street, on 29 March 1989. We are admiring a mural painted by my sister-in-law Sally Barrett depicting the UN Human Rights Charter, which still graces the reception area today.

From left to right: economist Josh Mushure, ZANU PF politburo member Cephas Msipa, me, and Daily Gazette *editor Brian Latham during our Konrad-Adenauer Foundation tour of Germany, Leipzig, September 1994.*

Joshua Nkomo and Sir Garfield Todd celebrating Todd's 80th birthday in July 1988.

MDC Vice-President Gibson Sibanda addressing an impromptu meeting during a "showboat rally" in Bulawayo in June 2000.

Jenny and me outside the Parliament of Zimbabwe, Harare, shortly after I was sworn in for the first time – on 18 July 2000.

Patrick Nabanyama – a key member of my campaign team in Bulawayo South before his abduction on 19 June 2000, never to be seen again.

Me with former ZANU PF cabinet minister Eddison Zvobgo on the Parliamentary Justice Committee tour of Germany, Bonn, July 2001. Although our trip had a rocky start by its end we had established a good rapport.

Still in Zimbabwe... Contrary to propaganda in the Government-owned press, the family of MDC member David Coltart, the MP for Bulawayo South, has not fled the country in the wake of the crackdown on the party following war veteran Cain Nkala's death. Above, Coltart's wife Jennifer is seen with two-month-old Bethany in Bulawayo last week. Her three other children are attending school in the city. She said she and her family had no intention of ever fleeing this country despite their persecution by Zanu PF.

Clipping from the Daily News *of Jenny and Bethany outside the newspaper's offices on 21 November 2001. Jenny went in to prove that our family had not fled the country as alleged by the state-controlled media.*

Morgan Tsvangirai's 2002 Presidential election legal challenge team. Back row, from left to right: Matthew Walton, Adrian de Bourbon, Jeremy Gauntlett and Bryant Elliot; front row, from left to right: Happias Zhou, Paul Themba Nyathi (MDC's Director of Elections) and me.

*Me and advocates Chris Andersen
and Geoge Bizos outside the
Harare High Court at the
commencement of the treason trial
of Morgan Tsvangirai, Welshman
Ncube and Renson Gasela, 3
February 2003.*

*Zimbabwe Test cricketers Andy
Flower and Henry Olonga during
their "black armband – death of
democracy" protest at the 2003
ICC World Cup.*

*The Coltart family taking a break at Hwange Game Park. The photo
was taken at Nyamandlovu Pan on 21 June 2003, shortly after the
attempt on my life. From left to right: Scott Winston, Bethany, me,
Douglas, Jenny and Jessica.*

Handing over a report to the President of Senegal, Abdoulaye Wade, detailing the reasons why the 2002 Zimbabwe presidential election was unconstitutional and illegal. Dakar, Senegal, 24 October 2003. On my left is Hon Idrissa Seck, then prime minister of Senegal.

From left to right: Me, Sekayi Holland, Angela Merkel, Gibson Sibanda, and CDU MP Arnold Vaatz, Berlin, 23 March 2004.

From left to right: Julian Ozanne, me, Chris Martin of Coldplay, Alan Doyle (editor of Zim News), Yvonne Mahlunge (lawyer and member of MDC legal committee), and Henry Olonga. The photo was taken during a fundraising trip to London for the Zimbabwe Defence and Aid Fund Trust, 10 March 2004.

country is left with an economy in the same state it was prior to the implication of ESAP plus a huge foreign debt it has to repay". (This is precisely what happened.)

Moyo focused on the contradictions of a party which had fought the 1990 election on a platform of socialism and was now doing the opposite. Moyo and I sang from the same hymn sheet and pleasantly discussed, and agreed on, a wide range of topics on the drive to and from Maphisa. I find it hard to reconcile that principled Jonathan Moyo with the principal propagandist for ZANU PF we have today, two decades on.

With it being increasingly apparent that ZANU PF was determined to lead the country down the road to disaster, and in the absence of a viable alternative (ZUM had already begun to implode), many concerned citizens felt the need to coordinate the opposition. That sense of desperation was heightened by one of the worst droughts Zimbabwe has ever experienced in the 1991/1992 rainy season. In February 1992, usually Zimbabwe's wettest month, I recorded only 35 mm of rain at my home in Bulawayo. Hundreds of thousands of cattle died and crops failed country wide. Compounding the problem was that maize supplies had run out two months before the harvest was due. I commented at the time: "Someone has made a blunder of monumental proportions. If Mugabe doesn't unravel the mess, he may be forced to hang on to power with the army. People wouldn't be so angry if everyone's belt was tightened at the same time, but while they feel the pinch they watch an increasingly bloated government pass by in grand cavalcades."[256]

On 24 January 1992, ZANU PF published a new Land Acquisition Bill in the *Government Gazette* which for the first time proposed to change the principle of "willing buyer, willing seller" to compulsory acquisition of rural land. While the pressing need to address historical inequities was understood, the bill alarmed many of us as it seemed that if the bill was enacted, and then enforced, it would further compound Zimbabwe's mounting economic problems. It was in this context that a few of us began discussing the need to go beyond mere talk to action. Dr Dumbutshena suggested I develop some constructive policy alternatives and in February I started writing what changes I thought were necessary to Zimbabwe's constitution, and to government structure and policies. By the beginning of March, I had cobbled together what I described as "A Blueprint for Zimbabwe", a 21-page summary of what I thought were the major policy changes Zimbabwe needed. On 11 March I sent them to Dumbutshena for comment and this started a widespread process of consultation. I sent the document to economists, political scientists, lawyers, farmers, industrialists, teachers. Many people, two of them Professor Masipula Sithole and Judith Todd, responded with detailed comments and suggestions. The feedback was overwhelmingly positive and many new ideas and suggestions were then incorporated into revised versions of the original document.

Concurrently, there was an intense debate behind the scenes around the country about how like-minded democrats could promote a different vision for Zimbabwe. The parties that had been in power in the late 1970s got together to form the United Front. An inaugural opposition front meeting was chaired by Ian Smith and attended by ZANU Ndonga leader Ndabaningi Sithole and representatives of ZUM, Muzorewa's UANC and the Conservative Alliance of Zimbabwe. ZUM's involvement was almost immediately put in doubt when Tekere announced that he could not work with Sithole. Many of us also felt that the United Front harked back to the past and would offer little vision for the future. In the result, it was decided, in the first half of 1992, that we would form a new body, a think-tank, not a political party, to be called the Forum for Democratic Reform (FDR) Trust. Dr Dumbutshena and Sir Garfield Todd were approached to be patrons. Both agreed, although Todd withdrew shortly before the trust was officially launched, fearing that it would quickly draw him back into formal politics.

On 30 May 1992 the FDR Trust was launched in Harare. The founding trustees were Eric Bloch, a well-known Bulawayo accountant and economist, Reverend Phineas Dube, Anglican Bishop Peter Hatendi, Theresa Mazoyo, a leading banker, Catholic Bishop Patrick Mutume, former High Court judge Washington Sansole, businessman Tony Tombs, and myself. In advertisements carried in papers the following day, we stressed that we were not a political party, but a think-tank. We noted four ingredients missing from Zimbabwe which prevented "full democracy": the absence of at least one party aside from ZANU PF which could offer the electorate a "competent and reliable alternative Government"; a constitution which encouraged the formation of political parties based on policies rather than "tribal allegiance, personality cult or angry protest"; a better understanding among the public about the "merits and workings of true democracy"; and, finally, the "monitoring and reporting to the public of the actions of elected officials".

The trustees were supported by an executive which included trade unionists (Douglas Mwonzora), academics (Professor Masipula Sithole), liberals who had opposed Smith (such as Diana Mitchell and Eddie Cross), and student leaders (such as Chris Giwa).

Shortly after the launch, the "Blueprint", amended to include the contributions that had come in, was published as a discussion paper and circulated widely. It started with my original sentence: "Many of Zimbabwe's present woes stem from the fact that we have a Constitution which is fundamentally flawed."[257] The Blueprint suggested wide-ranging constitutional changes, a radical reduction in the size of government, new laws to tackle corruption, a long-term commitment to providing title to all people occupying rural land, including communal areas, the developing of a new generation of trained, young black farmers to take over commercial farms, and the removal of all vestiges of Marxism-Leninism.

Just weeks after the FDR Trust was launched tragedy struck. The trust's secretary for Youth Affairs, Chris Giwa, who had participated in many of the student demonstrations at the University of Zimbabwe since 1989, was killed in a car "accident". He had been mobilising support in Marondera, just east of Harare, and when driving back in the evening had rammed into the back of a stationary army truck which had been left in the middle of the main Harare road without its lights on. He was killed instantly. Because the police described it as an "accident", no inquest was held and there was no detailed police investigation into his death. In the weeks before his death, Giwa had received various threats. While there was no evidence that ZANU PF was responsible, as with so many of these accidents, both before and after, it was all too convenient. Giwa was arguably our brightest young leader, a person capable of inspiring a generation. Needless to say, the army driver who had negligently left the vehicle unmarked on a busy main road was never charged.[258]

A few weeks after Giwa's death, I received my first visit by the CIO. Three men in civilian clothes pitched up in the reception area of Webb, Low and Barry demanding to see me. When the receptionist asked them to make an appointment, they said they were from the President's office and needed to see me immediately. I agreed to see them and they were duly ushered into my office. Keeping my cool, I discussed the weather with them before they launched into a cross-examination of my life history, seemingly wanting to know every last detail of my past. I replied patiently, but as things started to drag on a bit I suggested that they look in my CIO file where, I assured them, they would find most of the answers. I then told them that I would not be intimidated and asked them how they were coping with a dollar that was buying less and less. I spoke about rampant corruption in the country and suggested their time might be better employed investigating those who were bleeding the country to death. The meeting ended when I told them the FDR Trust was committed to non-violence and total compliance with the law, so they had no business taking up any more of my time. We parted amicably. I have never been visited by the CIO since.

In September 1992, I travelled to Europe and America. In the Netherlands I addressed an Amnesty International conference on political killings and disappearances and I met US government officials in Washington. I came away from Washington with mixed feelings. On the one hand the visit was deeply frustrating, particularly my meetings in the State department, where I expressed concern about the manner in which ESAP was being implemented. Repeating what I had said in by now many public meetings in Zimbabwe since 1991, I argued that it was wrong for the IMF and World Bank to be pouring money into Zimbabwe without making such loans conditional upon the liberalisation of the political environment. I questioned the wisdom of not insisting as conditions for assistance that defence spending be reduced and the media opened up to independent operators. All I met with was condescension verging on racism – "this is Africa, you know" – and appeared rooted in arrogance ("we know exactly what we are doing in supporting the World Bank and are satisfied it is acting in everyone's best interests.") On the other hand I met a variety of Americans who were deeply interested and concerned about Zimbabwe, people closer to my age, and who remain friends to this day, particularly Walter Kansteiner III, Jim Dunlap, Michael Miller and Ed Stewart. All were relatively young and at that time not particularly influential, save for Kansteiner, but a decade later their friendship would be critical in changing Washington's foreign policy towards Zimbabwe.

My concerns about political killings were highlighted again shortly after I returned from the US. One of our sister organisations, the Open Forum, a Bulawayo-based pressure group which was eventually to join the Forum Party in 1993, had organised public meetings which were highly critical of ZANU PF and the Gukurahundi. In March 1992 two of its members, Amos Dlamini and Kenneth Ncube, had been killed in a suspicious hit and run accident. Then, on 25 October 1992, one of its leaders, Mthandazo Ngwenya, a lecturer in adult education at the University of Zimbabwe, and a colleague, Themba Nkabinde, died in another suspicious traffic accident. Ngwenya was a talented isiNdebele writer and a vociferous critic of ESAP; just days before his death he told friends that he was being trailed in Harare and that he was "marked for death".[259] Curiously, three survivors of the accident were held in hospital under "police protection". Although there was no conclusive evidence that they had been murdered, once again ZANU PF benefited from the deaths, in suspicious circumstances, of two vociferous critics. Albert Nyathi, one of Zimbabwe's best known poets, and one of Ngwenya's protegés, wrote the following tribute, which vividly captures the belief that murky forces used "road accidents" to eliminate opponents:

> Only in dead dreams
> will we talk to him again,
> see echoes of that lovely smile
> and whisper Ndema.
>
> Mthandazo I see the wind
> wielding lethal swords
> and our necks
> have no feet to run away
> brother we await
> in the scowling darkness
> sentence of death never heard in court!
> brother the wheels of these cars
> display no respect for human rights
> all dreams broken
> now not at gunpoint but crashpoint
>
> Now Ndema, Themba, our
> voices are silent,
> no saliva wets the throat,
> our lips move worlds for you
> but no word comes out.[260]

Despite these threats, we believed that we needed to keep speaking out, especially regarding the disastrous implementation of ESAP. On 29 October I spoke at the University of Zimbabwe, making five points on the subject. We needed to change our attitude to foreign investment; ZANU PF needed to realise that we were up against fearsome competition throughout the world. I pleaded for "trade not aid" and criticised the World Bank and IMF's policy of granting massive loans to the government without directing it towards the private sector. I returned to my political liberalisation mantra, arguing that we were trapped by our own fears, which manifested in tight controls, a massive cabinet and army. Without measures to promote domestic investment, such as a reduction in taxes, incentives to industry, the cutting of red tape, the flotation of the Zimbabwe dollar and the tackling of corruption, I said, we could not expect foreigners to want to invest in Zimbabwe.[261] ZANU PF was part of the problem, not the solution, I concluded. Once again it all fell upon deaf ears in government, the business sector and among most diplomats.

One of the results of my September visit to Washington was an invitation to observe the December 1992 Kenyan elections as part of the International Republican Institute's mission. Christopher Hope, in his classic book about tyrants *Brothers Under the Skin – Travels in Tyranny*, observes that "it is as if absolute power turns those who possess it into brothers under the skin … (t)hey begin to impersonate each other, no matter how far apart they be in time or culture or politics"[262]. Kenya brought that home to me. There were startling similarities between Kenya/Zimbabwe, Moi/Mugabe and KANU/ZANU PF. It seemed as if Moi and Mugabe had swapped notes – there was no opposition representation in the electoral commission, millions of Kenyans had been excluded from the voters' roll, the opposition press had been clamped down upon, national days such as Independence Day had been hijacked, and the police and army were partisan. In short it was a carbon copy of Zimbabwe. What differed in Kenya, though, was that the opposition, despite all these obstacles, could have still defeated KANU if they had not been so seriously divided (opposition presidential candidates Matiba and Odinga's combined votes of 2.9 million easily surpassed Moi's 1.9 million).

In a harbinger of what was to befall Zimbabwean opposition politics, there were lessons to be learnt. In a speech to FDR Trust members in

January 1993, I warned that we needed to guard against leaders who put their personal interests ahead of national interest. I felt we needed to be wary of those who wanted to exploit ethnic or racial divisions and argued that competence and integrity should be the two most important criteria in selecting our leaders. The "temptation to unify with other groups simply for the sake of unity" was a mistake, I said; it was important to "agree on policies before unifying".[263]

These comments were made in the knowledge that the FDR Trust's plans to promote the formation of a new political party were well advanced. My original Blueprint of proposed policies had been widely circulated and I spent the first few months of 1993 incorporating all the ideas that had come in, culminating in the consolidation of all our policy papers into one document. On 27 and 28 March 1993, I returned to MacDonald Hall in Makokoba to attend the launch of the new Forum Party of Zimbabwe, formed out of the merger of the Open Forum and the FDR Trust. Dumbutshena was elected interim president, Washington Sansole vice-president, and Dr Themba Dlodlo (who had headed the Open Forum) secretary general. Included in the provisional executive were several people who would become leading lights in the Movement for Democratic Change (MDC). Three of these were Douglas Mwonzora, Lovemore Moyo and Trudy Stevenson. There was also a good sprinkling of professionals and academics, including leading Bulawayo lawyer Nomsa Ncube and Professor Masipula Sithole. I did not contest for any position because I still felt that I could best serve in an advisory capacity behind the scenes.

The policy papers were adopted without amendment. They presented Zimbabweans with classical-liberal policies rooted in a commitment to small government and devolution of power. For example, we proposed to cut the size of cabinet (which in 1993 was in excess of 40) to just fourteen. On the critically sensitive issue of land we committed ourselves to land redistribution, but in terms of a process that would not unduly disrupt production. The policies envisaged "orderly and planned settlement" in which "all necessary infrastructure including roads, schools, clinics and water (were to be) put in place prior to families being resettled".[264] In a radical departure from ZANU PF's policy, we proposed the granting of title to all land holders, subject to provisions designed to protect the current generation of communal land dwellers from losing their rights of occupation for a period of 20 years.

The wide-ranging document suggested significant changes to education, labour, health, housing, transport, energy, environmental and foreign policy. A commitment to far-reaching constitutional changes was made, reducing executive power and devolving more power to provinces and local authorities. A leading Zimbabwean weekly at the time described the collection of policy papers as "a cogent document that addresses in unambiguous terms the problems and issues the ruling party is currently seeking to circumvent" and which "proposed concrete steps by which Zimbabwe could be restored to democracy and economic profitability".[265]

In keeping with our commitment to freedom and transparency, all the sessions were open to the press and police. Despite this, shortly after lunch on the first day the pastor of my church, Ian Spence, who was there observing proceedings, noticed a small microphone hanging from the ceiling close to the podium. On closer inspection he realised that it was in fact a listening device which had been tucked into a crack. I was called and I decided to remove it. The British-made device was almost new, date stamped 1991, and had a powerful transmitting mechanism. A few plainclothes police observed what we had recovered and approached me, asking that it be handed over, which I refused. We told the police and the press that if the owner was prepared to come forward to claim it and give an explanation for why it was there, we would release it. "Finders, keepers", was the succinct declaration of Washington Sansole when asked about it. The device was never claimed, although I received several phone calls from senior police officers demanding that it be handed over. I still have it – and to this day I hope that British aid money was not used to purchase it.

The planting of the listening device was an early indication that ZANU PF would not treat the new Forum Party kindly. Action was quickly taken against vulnerable people who had been elected to leadership positions. For example, within a few weeks Dr Dlodlo was dismissed as deputy chairman of the government parastatal the Cold Storage Commission.[266] Shortly after that, Agrippa Madlela, elected national chairman of the Forum Party, and who was also the chief planning manager of the National Railways of Zimbabwe, was denied permission by cabinet to travel to a meeting of Southern African railway general managers in Beira.[267] Not even the private sector was immune from ZANU PF pressure – Washington Sansole, since he had retired from the bench, had been on the board of Zimbabwe's largest public company, Delta, but soon after being elected vice-president of the Forum Party he was asked to resign, which he did.

ZANU PF need not have got in such a fluster because, in truth, the Forum would always battle to attract grassroots support. Shortly before the launch, Morgan Tsvangirai, then secretary general of the Zimbabwe Congress of Trade Unions (ZCTU), had been approached to see if he would get involved. Tsvangirai declined. The policies were too liberal to attract the trade unions, he said. The same *Financial Gazette* article that had praised the policy document had some telling caveats. "Liberal values in Central Africa rarely constitute a seductive political challenge; they are notoriously difficult to explain to the poor and hungry." It further questioned whether Dumbutshena had "the ruthlessness to make it in politics where nice guys come last". Although the Forum had "set out an impressive agenda for reform", to succeed it would have to "establish an unambiguous connection between bread and democracy".[268]

For its part, ZANU PF seemed determined to pursue policies diametrically opposed to the Forum. For the first time I felt compelled to criticise Joshua Nkomo as well. At the opening of the Zimbabwe Trade Fair in April, Nkomo announced that ZANU PF would take over white- and Asian-controlled businesses if "they were not shared". In response, I said that Nkomo and ZANU PF were dangerously out of touch with what was needed to attract international investment. Nkomo, in my view, "could not have chosen a worse occasion to make his statement" and "any talk of compulsory acquisition of any business (made) foreign investors look elsewhere". I pointed out that ZANU PF and multinationals, indirectly or directly, now owned most businesses in any event. The economy was "terminally ill", and ZANU PF's promises to deal with the malaise could only be taken seriously when spending was "slashed from the top down", starting with the ministry of National Affairs, the cabinet and the president's office.[269]

Compounding the problem was the growing incidence of corruption, a topic I turned to later in the year which aroused Nkomo's wrath. On 27 October I condemned ZANU PF's double-speak on the issue. The previous week Vice-President Simon Muzenda had strongly condemned corruption when opening a conference devoted to the problem. The previous September, Nkomo had condemned corruption in the civil service. Now I took both of them to task, questioning why they thought corruption only existed in the civil service. I listed a variety of scandals that had been swept under the carpet and questioned how it was that the ZANU PF hierarchy had become so fabulously rich, some in a short space of time.[270] This obviously touched a nerve because the very next day I received a call at my law firm from none other than Nkomo himself. He was very angry with me. He told me that I was a racist and that I "should get out of the country". I told Nkomo that his words saddened me and reminded him how we had worked together in darker days. But that phone call also signalled to me that there would be little help forthcoming from most of the former ZAPU leaders now in cabinet.

The violence of the 1990 elections came full circle in the first few weeks of 1994, and with it came the realisation that the West adopted a cynical approach towards human rights abuses perpetrated by ZANU PF. In mid January the Supreme Court handed down its judgment in the appeal by Elias Kanengoni and Kizito Chivamba against their conviction and sentence for the attempted murder in 1990 of ZUM leader Patrick Kombayi. As a result of some amazingly brave legal work done by a government lawyer, Kumbirai Hodzi (who had investigated and prosecuted the case brilliantly), Kanengoni and Chivamba had each been sentenced to six-year jail terms for their brazen attempt to kill Kombayi. Their appeal was dismissed by Chief Justice Anthony Gubbay and a full Supreme Court bench, who were not impressed with their claim that they were acting under the impression that they had "Vice President Muzenda's authority for the shooting".[271] Within hours of the judgment being handed down Mugabe pardoned both men; in fact the word was that neither man had spent even a night in prison since the shooting.

The human rights community was apoplectic. Director of the CCJP Mike Auret observed that this meant that "from the lowest cowardly ruling party riffraff to the highest party thug any sort of political crime can be committed on behalf of ZANU PF and a pardon will be forthcoming".[272] When I was interviewed, I recalled the wave of intimidation that marred the 1990s polls and noted how ZANU PF had ignored a "series of high court orders protecting the urban poor from illegal evictions". In my view we had a major constitutional crisis between the judiciary and the executive and I called upon the international community to exert pressure to preserve the rule of law.[273]

I was profoundly shocked when, two weeks after the pardoning, the Conservative British government prevailed on Queen Elizabeth

II to invite Robert Mugabe on a state visit the following May. At the time it was also announced that Mugabe would be awarded the Knight Grand Cross of the Order of the Bath by the Queen for "significant contributions" to relations between Zimbabwe and Britain. Both the honorary knighthood and the state visit were rare honours – in 1994 the only other person invited on a state visit was King Harald of Norway.

The government-controlled media trumpeted the invitation and used it to ridicule those of us who had spoken out against the pardons. They boasted it was a clear endorsement, that the British government did not share our concerns about the assault on the judiciary. Although the government media did not crow about this, many of us were deeply troubled that the British government would confer the knighthood knowing what we also knew about the genocide of the 1980s. British intelligence must have known of Mugabe's personal complicity in the Gukurahundi, and yet the British government was prepared to allow the Queen to award their highest honour.

On 3 February 1994, I was able to voice my concerns on an international stage. As a member of the Forum Party I was invited to participate in a conference entitled "Networking for Democracy". The conference, which was held in Botswana, focused on the Southern African Development Community's (SADC's) electoral systems and all the major political parties in the region were represented. ZANU PF was represented by the then deputy minister Oppah Rushesha (now minister of Water, Environment and Climate – she has changed her name to Muchinguri-Kashiri) and the registrar general, Tobaiwa Mudede. The conference was opened by a US senator who spoke about the need for African nations to embrace democracy. While I welcomed the remarks, I was incensed, with the remarks coming so soon after Britain's invitation to Mugabe, and the implied endorsement of his own government's conduct. Accordingly, during the plenary session I stood up and spoke about the need for Western governments to be consistent. Patrick Kombayi happened to be part of our delegation and so I used the occasion to refer to his injuries and expressed my deep concern that Britain had invited Mugabe for a state visit so soon after he had pardoned Kombayi's assailants. I argued that actions like that undermined Zimbabwe's judiciary and respect for the rule of law. Kombayi, sitting next to me, graphically demonstrated the reality of ZANU PF's violence; he was still grievously injured and hobbled into the meeting, in obvious pain four years after he had miraculously survived being shot six times in the groin and stomach. Unsurprisingly, my comments created a stir – not only with the hosts but also with Rushesha and Mudede, who were sitting close by.

That evening we all converged on the hotel patio for a drink. Rushesha and Mudede came across with two Zimbabwe embassy officials to the table I was sitting at alone, waiting for my colleagues. They were all very aggressive and asked me why I had "denigrated the President" and embarrassed the government. They were dissatisfied when I responded by pointing out that my criticism was directed at the British government, not at Mugabe. When it was clear I would not back down, one of the embassy officials menacingly said: "Don't worry, Coltart, when we kill you here we will make sure we get your body back to Zimbabwe." I was shocked by the brazenness of the threat and immediately asked Rushesha whether she was going to reprimand the official. She was very angry and replied that she would not, justifying herself by arguing that I had provoked it. This was no idle threat so I left the table, joined my colleagues and told them what had happened. We were all in a foreign country and to that extent all vulnerable. I didn't sleep easily that night, despite bolting my door and making arrangements with colleagues for them to come to my rescue if necessary.

Still troubled by the death threat when I woke up the next morning, I sought comfort from the Bible in my quiet time. In the preceding few weeks I had been working through a favourite book, Jeremiah, and that morning I got to Chapter 15. When I got to its end, I felt as if the Lord was speaking directly to me:

> *Therefore this is what the Lord says:*
> *"If you repent, I will restore you*
> *that you may serve me;*
> *if you utter worthy, not worthless words,*
> *you will be my spokesman.*
> *Let this people turn to you,*
> *but you must not turn to them.*
> *I will make you a wall to this people,*
> *a fortified wall of bronze;*
> *they will fight against you but will not overcome you,*
> *for I am with you to rescue and save you,"*
> *declares the Lord.*

"I will save you from the hands of the wicked
and redeem you from the grasp of the cruel."[274]

The words came like a bolt from the blue. Although deeply encouraging, they also contained a challenge – the promise was conditional on my repentance and use of "worthy words". We all know the state of our own hearts; I knew in my case that the years of privilege under white minority rule had bred attitudes in my heart that were not God honouring. Overwhelmingly, though, these scriptures have been a source of deep comfort for two decades. On that day, alone in my Gaborone hotel room, they consoled me that a wall of bronze would protect me, and they have ever since. Personally, I experienced, in a new way, what true peace really means.

CHAPTER 13

BREAKING THE SILENCE
1994 TO 1997

"Untruthfulness destroys fellowship, but truth cuts false fellowship to pieces and establishes genuine brotherhood."
        – GERMAN CHRISTIAN MARTYR DIETRICH BONHOEFFER,
                                THE COST OF DISCIPLESHIP

Any hope I had had that former ZAPU leaders would take a strong stand to promote respect for the rule of law and basic human rights further evaporated in mid 1994. Of particular concern was a remark made by Vice-President Joshua Nkomo, and supported by a deputy minister, Simon Khaya Moyo, at the beginning of June, warning of "civil war" between whites and blacks if whites "did not associate themselves with the ruling party ZANU PF". Nkomo warned that those whites who did not identify themselves with ZANU PF should "move out of our country now before it is too late".[275] He was making the remarks in reaction to news that an old white Zimbabwean family, the Rosenfels, planned to celebrate the centenary of the arrival of their ancestors from the Orange Free State in 1894 into Matabeleland by re-enacting the ox-wagon trek through the Mangwe pass south of Bulawayo. Nkomo described the family's plans as a "declaration of war". Ironically, the organiser of the trek was not a die-hard unrepentant Rhodesian but Max Rosenfels, who had stood against Smith in the 1985 election and was at the time a ZANU PF MP. Far from trying to provoke a racial incident, the family was planning a low-key event in the middle of the bush; it was intended to be a family celebration not a statement.

Rosenfels immediately offered to cancel the event, but despite this, the government sent Lands department officials to Rosenfels's farm to advise him that the farm was going to be compulsorily acquired. Judith Todd scorned Nkomo's "civil war" threat, remarking that it would be "very one sided and of extremely short duration" given that it would be waged between 9 million blacks and about 80 000 whites.

Distressed by Nkomo's statement, I wrote a letter to the *Daily Gazette* on 7 June 1994. I reminded Nkomo that history was "replete with horrifying incidents where minorities have been castigated as a group, used as scapegoats by powerful politicians and oppressed."[276] While conceding that racism still abounded in the white community, I said that the proposed gathering had been blown out of all proportion "for political ends". I concluded by quoting Martin Luther King: "Like life, racial understanding is not something that we find, but something we must create." Behind my public sentiment was a feeling that the absence of a truth commission at independence had locked us all in the past. Whites had not had to confront their complicity in historical injustice and black politicians were wont to dig up that past to further partisan ends.

This incident convinced me that if Nkomo had resolved to act expediently regarding whites, there was little hope that he would be a strong advocate for the victims of the Gukurahundi. I had always hoped that the Unity Accord would result in some form of compensation or redress for the thousands of families affected by the genocide. Partly with that in mind, we expanded the BLPC's paralegal programme as far as we could in the areas affected by the Gukurahundi. The LRF had limited funding to expand and because of this we were restricted to establishing a maximum of three advice centres per province. By the end of June 1994, we had established centres in Hwange, Binga and Lupane in Matabeleland North; in Plumtree, Gwanda and Beitbridge in Matabeleland South; and in Gweru, Kwekwe and Gokwe in Midlands. By the end of June 1993 the BLPC was handling the bulk of the LRF case work country wide, with 3 811 of the 6 913 cases.[277] Although the majority of these cases were routine matters unconnected to the Gukurahundi, a steady flow of reports from that era continued to come in. It became apparent, however, that without increased funding, and a specific programme, it would be difficult to understand the full impact of the Gukurahundi, let alone seek redress for its victims. It was difficult to gather data because most of the surviving victims were in remote, inaccessible rural villages. In addition many people were still petrified of saying anything, and even if brave enough to speak up, did not know what their rights were or think that anything could be done. Another major obstacle was the time lag – the Gukurahundi had happened a decade earlier. Many of the victims fled the country to escape the wrath of the Fifth Brigade and were still in exile in South Africa; many had died or were too old and crushed to do anything about the abuse they had suffered. In short we needed access to contemporaneous reports because what the BLPC had uncovered was insufficient. The Fraser Gibson Sibanda case had shown that even where a victim was brave and determined enough to seek redress, the process of getting compensation was slow and cumbersome. That case had come to our attention in 1989, but as at June 1994 we had still not received payment of damages from government.[278] Neither the LRF, nor any other human rights organisation, had the capacity and resources to bring legal actions on behalf of the thousands of victims.

Conscious of this, I sought a meeting with Mike Auret in late June. I suggested that the LRF and CCJP embark on a joint project to address the issue. I followed up with a letter to Auret on 4 July, expressing my view that until there was some acknowledgement that the atrocities occurred, some form of apology and compensation paid, there would never be genuine reconciliation between victims and perpetrators.[279] I pointed out that calls for compensation had "fallen on deaf ears" and hopes that the unity agreement would secure compensation "had come to naught". My proposal set out a six-point strategy:

1. The CCJP and the LRF, working through the BLPC, work on a joint proposal which may include other human rights organisations.
2. The CCJP and BLPC would "collate and computerise on a standard format" all the existing cases and then analyse where the human rights violations had occurred. The purpose was to understand "the pattern" of violations so that teams going into rural areas would have "a reasonably clear idea where the principal violations occurred".
3. Once the initial work had been conducted, teams would be deployed into the affected areas. The BLPC would supply people with legal knowledge, Amani Trust[280] people with "medical, psychological or psychiatric expertise" and CCJP

people capable of providing "spiritual and pastoral input". At the conclusion of this stage the goal was to have "as complete a picture of all human rights violations committed during the period 1982–1988 by both Government operatives and dissidents".

4. The next stage would involve the quantification of damages, which would include input from medical professionals regarding the psychological or psychiatric treatment (and its cost) required. The report would not mention victims' names, but would "summarise the types of human rights violations, the units responsible and the total quantum of damages suffered collectively by all the victims".

5. Once compiled, the report would be submitted to government, including a proposal to establish a "reconciliation trust" which would be the channel of compensation.

6. The "reconciliation trust" would establish educational scholarships for children, arrange for the reburial of remains in mass graves, and build "symbols of reconciliation" such as clinics and schools. Where people continued to suffer because of the "loss of breadwinners, some form of pension could be paid out of the trust". I referred to the KTC squatter case brought by the South African LRC which saw some R5 million being paid into a trust fund for the benefit of those who suffered.

I was concerned that government should not "perceive the project having a political agenda". For this reason, no work would be started in the rural areas until after the 1995 elections and then should be done in a "low key and confidential manner". Likewise the final report was to be kept confidential until government had had an opportunity to consider it and set up the trust. Ultimately, the report should be published to prevent the abuses "from happening again in future". Again this proposal was premised on what was happening in South Africa, where their minister of Justice, Dullah Omar, had set up a truth commission.

The proposal was accepted by the CCJP but it took several months to get permission from the Catholic Bishops Conference to release their contemporaneous historical data to us. Agreement was reached that the CCJP material be made available to the BLPC on condition that the bishops approved the final content of the report before it was published.

Agreement having been reached with the CCJP, we then set about the task of raising funds to expand our work and complete the task.

At the time, the LRF was mainly funded by Canadian, Swedish, British, American and Dutch governmental and donor organisations, so naturally we turned first to them to see if they would support the initiative. It became clear, however, that although most were sympathetic, none of them wanted to fund the exercise. Given the funding problem, a decision was made to use BLPC core funds to support the initial stages of the project. Existing staff were redeployed to focus on the first stage of consolidating existing data plus the CCJP data, once it had been delivered to us. In fact there was a long delay in getting the CCJP data, which was only accessed late in 1995. The data included some of the statements I had recorded from witnesses at the Catholic St Mary's Cathedral in 1983 and other documents that had been submitted to the 1984 commission of inquiry. There was plenty of material I had never seen before, including detailed hospital records from mission hospitals, letters written by priests recounting their horror, and the general reports which had been submitted to Mugabe when the bishops met with him in 1983.

At the time we had a number of interns working for the BLPC and they were tasked with going through *The Chronicle*'s archives to extract all the contemporaneous media reports of the disturbances between 1982 and 1988. *The Chronicle,* being a government mouthpiece, focused almost exclusively on dissident atrocities but nonetheless it provided some interesting insights. There were some 1 500 media reports which documented over 500 offences. And so the project began in 1984 – a slow, woefully underfunded project which was done largely under the radar screen. We didn't tell *The Chronicle* what we were looking for and the LRF annual reports themselves during this period were cryptic about what was being done. The only inkling given in our annual reports at the time were paragraphs regarding "disappearances" of people during the 1980s.

The only former ZAPU leaders I was in contact with during this period were Welshman Mabhena and Sidney Malunga. They were critically important advisers as I waded through this political minefield. Malunga in particular encouraged me to go ahead with the project and so it came as a great shock when he died in mysterious circumstances in August 1994.

On Saturday, 20 August, Malunga had a lunchtime meeting with Bulawayo-based ZANU PF MPs at Bulawayo's city hall. There had been an argument between Malunga and some of the MPs, one of whom was Dumiso Dabengwa. After the meeting, as Malunga was about to leave for his farm in Nyamandlovu, his long-standing driver, one Nhliziyo, suddenly advised that he was not prepared to drive, but that his son would replace him. Later that afternoon on Malunga's return to Bulawayo, there was an accident on a deserted road in which Malunga apparently died instantly. His body was ferried to Mpilo hospital mortuary. Close family members inspected the body and immediately foul play was suspected. The younger Nhliziyo claimed that a dog had run out in front of the car and he, acting on Malunga's instructions, had swerved to avoid it, causing the car to overturn. However, the driver was unscathed and the car virtually undamaged; in fact, according to a close relative who went to the scene, Jabu Xaba, it looked as if the vehicle had just been manually turned over. Malunga's body only had one wound – a 10-cm indentation on the left side of his forehead, which looked as if it could have been inflicted by an axe or similar weapon. The injury didn't match the damage to the car. Malunga's body was mysteriously whisked away to the mortuary and there was a minimal police investigation of the accident. The younger Nhliziyo was sickly and, in a further twist to the story, died shortly after Malunga died. Close family members to this day believe that Malunga was murdered earlier on that afternoon, and that the car was simply turned over to give the impression of an accident. Sadly, at the time the family did not have the means to conduct an independent investigation and post-mortem so they have never been able to confirm their suspicions.

Malunga was declared a national hero and buried at Heroes Acre, alongside several other ZANU PF leaders who had died in mysterious circumstances. Whether this was just an accident or whether he was murdered we shall never know; but what we do know is that Malunga was the most outspoken of Nkomo's heirs apparent, and his death shut an annoying and embarrassingly critical mouth within ZANU PF.[281]

In early September 1994 I travelled around Germany as a guest of the Konrad-Adenauer-Stiftung (KAS) with Dr Reg Matchaba-Hove, a medical doctor who was also chair of Zimrights (then Zimbabwe's pre-eminent secular human rights organisation), Brian Latham, the editor of *The Daily Gazette*, Cephas Msipa, a former ZAPU member and ZANU PF cabinet minister, and Josh Mushure, an economist. Our host, the director of KAS Zimbabwe, Burkhard Hinz, was particularly concerned to show this diverse group of Zimbabweans the stark contrast between East and West Germany soon after the fall of the Berlin Wall. Accordingly, while the trip started in the former West, the bulk of our time was spent in Berlin and the former East. Although Germany had been pouring 180 billion marks a year into the East, the difference between the developed, vibrant West and decrepit East Berlin was astonishing. It made a deep impression on each one of us. If ever there was a practical demonstration of the effect of different ideologies on the same people, with the same language and culture, here was it. From Berlin we travelled to Dresden. One of our meetings there was with Hans Herzberg, the chief constable of the Free State of Saxony, who described how the East German police, the Stasi, had destroyed families and sown so much suspicion among people. In the interests of transparency they had made all Stasi's files on some 12 million East German citizens available, and many were shocked when they inspected their own files. One husband discovered his wife had been spying on him for twelve years; a daughter found out her father had been reporting on her for years. I wrote to my parents: *"A culture of fear pervaded the entire nation and there was much to be scared about."*[282] The Stasi stories poignantly reflected Zimbabwe's CIO, a subject we discussed that evening. A bond developed among us, particularly between me and Cephas Msipa who, despite his high position in ZANU PF, has remained a good friend ever since.

Our next stop was Leipzig, a typically rundown Eastern city but not as badly devastated by World War II as Dresden had been. It was here that I had one of my most inspiring dinners ever, with a Reformed Presbyterian pastor, Vicar Roland Schein, who described the role the church had played in bringing the Wall down. He told us of the ideological vacuum caused by the loss of the War and the demise of the Nazis, a vacuum that was filled by communism. Leipzig had suffered decades of loss. The Nazis' treatment of the Jewish community had delivered a cultural and economic blow to the city, even before the War. The War had physically destroyed vast areas of it, which was followed by the Russians chasing out many of its prime citizens. Communism, Schein said, had a voracious appetite – he likened it to sitting on a raft on which a fire has been lit in the centre, with the people on board using the planks of the raft to feed the fire. The Eastern German regime responded to the collapsing economy by allowing disaffected people to apply to leave, but the moment they did so they were ostracised.

Schein responded by starting a small Monday prayer group for eight of these people. It was designed to provide spiritual and emotional support to them, but rapidly became the focal point for dissent. Numbers grew quickly and the group metamorphosed into a service, which eventually spilled out onto the streets. The Stasi did all they could to stem the outpouring of dissent, but more and more people came and the sermons got all the more critical. On 2 October 1989, 25 000 people arrived for the service at St Nicholas, forcing another seven churches to open to accommodate the flood. The next week over 100 000 people arrived. The church's core message *"keine Gewalt"* (no violence) never changed and people who gathered around responded by telling the Stasi: "We are not vandals, we are the people." The events in Leipzig resonated and reverberated throughout East Germany and culminated in the Wall coming down.

Schein had some profound insights regarding our situation. Although Zimbabwe was, and remains, very different, there were also many parallels. In my mind, the main lesson was to remember Jesus' parable of the mustard seed – that the Lord uses the weak and small to achieve great things in the face of oppression. Importantly, the lessons I had learnt in Atlanta in 1988 about Martin Luther King's teaching on non-violence were now complemented by this stirring tale of how a small, resolute, principled prayer group could be used by God to transform an entire nation.

The trip was a watershed for me in another respect: it marked the beginning of my appreciation of German people, especially those from the East. I discovered that many Germans, having lived under two forms of totalitarian rule, had a deeper appreciation and empathy for our struggle than people from other democracies, who had never personally experienced fascism or Marxism-Leninism. What I term my "body of brothers" developed. This was a group of German friends – Burkhard Hinz, Arnold Vaatz, Willy Pabst, Wolf Krug and Anton Boesl – who have provided me with the deepest friendship and moral support ever since. God works in strange ways. My father, who fought Germany for six years of his life, would never have imagined that Germans would become such admired, cherished and respected friends of mine.

A few weeks after we returned from Germany, Dr Reg Matchaba-Hove had an opportunity to interrogate ZANU PF's policy towards compensation for the victims of the Gukurahundi. During our trip there

229

had been opportunities to share the LRF/CCJP project. Even well-meaning human rights activists like Matchaba-Hove hadn't appreciated what had happened during the Gukurahundi – and of course he didn't know what we were doing now. Without going into detail, I explained to him the need for, and great difficulty to obtain, compensation for victims. On 28 September, Matchaba-Hove participated in a Meet-the-President programme and used the opportunity to ask Mugabe whether he would consider setting up a fund to "assist victims of the Matabeleland dissident war" to help in "restoring their dignity". A visibly angry Mugabe responded by chastising Matchaba-Hove for "preoccupying (himself) with victims of the dissident war only and ignoring thousands of liberation war victims". Continuing his rant, Mugabe told Matchaba-Hove not to "highlight problems for political reasons beyond reasonable proportions".[283]

Mugabe had now made it crystal clear that no compensation would be paid. His arguments were also disingenuous because he knew very well that there was already a War Victims Compensation Act[284] in place which provided compensation for those who had suffered during the war between ZANLA and ZIPRA and the Rhodesian security forces.

Not long after Mugabe's proclamation, we finally received payment from government of Z\$35 000 to settle Mrs Musa Sibanda's damages claim following the murder of her husband. I decided that we needed to use the case to publicise the plight of innocent people who were still suffering from the Gukurahundi. Accordingly, on 8 November 1994, we had a handover ceremony at BLPC. Joel Silonda, the regional director of the CCJP, handed the cheque over to Mrs Sibanda and I issued a press statement in which I pointed out that Mrs Sibanda was the first (and remains the only) "victim of the dissident war to receive compensation".

"It was deeply saddening to read that President Mugabe recently said that his Government would not compensate victims of the dissident war," I said. I asked if there was "any reason why innocent Zimbabwean citizens should not be compensated in similar fashion" to those who could claim under the War Victims Compensation Act.[285] "Compensating innocent victims of this unhappy chapter," I said, would "facilitate meaningful emotional healing and reconciliation."[286] The handover ceremony made it to the front page of *The Chronicle* and featured prominently in other papers, but our plea was ignored by government. No change was made to the War Victims Compensation Act as I had suggested it should; indeed events in the years following exposed that the act was abused and its funds looted by top-ranking ZANU PF leaders.

In November 1994 I wrote an open letter to Mugabe in response to a call he had made to the Church for it to give government "moral direction". In a speech he gave to a Presidential Prayer Breakfast, which had been organised by South African evangelist Dr Michael Cassidy's Africa Enterprise organisation in Harare on 15 October, Mugabe had told Christian leaders that "the ship of State looks to you (Church leaders) for moral and spiritual direction".[287] He went on to tell them that they had "the message of life" and that they should "not be afraid to deliver it".

I waited a few weeks to see whether Christian leaders would respond to the invitation and point out some of the grave issues confronting Zimbabwe. When it appeared that they had not taken up the offer, I felt I should write to Mugabe. Although not a Christian leader in the conventional sense, I was someone who believed in Jesus' promises and I was also an elder of the Presbyterian church. After much thought and prayer, I completed a five-page missive, which I arranged to have delivered to Mugabe personally on 1 November. When, after a few weeks, I had not received any reply I sent it to Brian Latham, who gave it front page coverage in *The Daily Gazette* on 21 November. The letter started by bemoaning the fact that the church had, with a few exceptions, failed in its prophetic role for decades, both in Rhodesia and Zimbabwe. I listed several concerns: corruption, the failure to compensate the victims of the Gukurahundi, the perversion of justice in pardoning Kombayi's assailants, and Mugabe's failure to distance himself from those in his party who had likened him to Christ. The letter concluded:

> "All the points of concern have nothing to do with party political matters. They deal with the essence of God's standards of justice and morality. The Church has a duty to speak out whenever biblical standards of justice are being ignored or flouted. You have challenged the Church to give direction and this is right. But the Church, I think, in many ways has failed you and Zimbabwe as it has been too timid. I trust it will start to recognise its responsibilities. Daniel helped the ruler he served not by bowing to his desires but by fearing God before the King. In nearly all the verses I have quoted [I had drawn heavily on Amos, Isaiah and Micah] there are strong warnings which you need to heed.

One of the principal roles of the Church is to be salt and light in society. Salt, so that the decaying process can be halted. Light, so that the Church can show the way out of a path which leads to our destruction. However, if we all do not heed these warnings and act, both the Bible and history show us that the ship of State is on a perilous course."[288]

The new year, 1995, was an election year and in February Mugabe issued a proclamation setting the dates for a general election on 8 and 9 April. The opposition, including the Forum Party, was in a chaotic state. The previous year, two senior Forum leaders, Themba Dlodlo and Agrippa Madlela, had purported to replace Dumbutshena as president, resulting in unseemly litigation in the High Court barring them from representing the party. Compounding matters was the party's failure to excite working-class and rural Zimbabweans. ZUM was in a similar state of disarray, as were all the other opposition parties. In short, unlike the previous election when Tekere and ZUM had posed a real threat to ZANU PF's hegemony, in 1995 ZANU PF had no cause to fear that their grip on power would be affected. I was asked by Washington Sansole, who was standing for the Forum Party in the Bulawayo South constituency, to be his campaign manager.

No sooner had the campaign got under way than I was distracted by my involvement in what the ZANU PF-controlled press described as a kangaroo court. On Sunday afternoon, 26 February 1995, I received a call at home from a friend, Peter Brodie, asking me to represent a highly successful white Nyamandlovu dairy farmer named Jeffrey Swindells, who had been arrested. Swindells's usual lawyer was unavailable and so when he was picked up by the police on allegations of receiving stolen property he had no one to turn to. I phoned the officer in charge of Nyamandlovu police and requested that he release Swindells on bail, pointing out that as a prominent farmer he was unlikely to abscond. The request was refused. Cognisant of section 107 of Zimbabwe's Criminal Procedure and Evidence Act, which states that an accused person may "*at any time*" apply for bail, I phoned the senior Bulawayo High Court judge, Justice Fergus Blackie, to find out who the duty judge was. He told me that there was no duty judge, but said he would try and help. Having explained that I needed to make an urgent bail application, Blackie asked me to get the officer in charge to telephone him so that he could assess the police's attitude. When I asked the officer to contact the judge he refused; advised of this, Blackie then telephoned the officer himself, but the man would not accept his word that it was in fact Justice Blackie on the line. Blackie got back to me and explained that the only way he could verify his identity would be for us both to travel to the police station, which we then did. On our arrival bail was agreed to and at the same time I was asked to represent three other people who had been arrested on similar charges, Romeo Tommy, Shawn Tommy and Isaiah Ndiweni, none of them white. They, too, were released on bail.

Although unusual, there was nothing unlawful in the granting of bail in this manner and there the matter should have rested. However, on 28 February *The Herald* carried a story on its front page beneath the headline: "Night Kangaroo Court by Judge Sets Four Free". It conveniently ignored the fact that three of the men freed weren't white and was followed by a flurry of editorials in *The Herald,* including one which posed the question "would (the judge) have displayed the same enthusiasm if (he had been approached) with a similar request on a Sunday night to free a black client from custody?" and answering the question itself – "We doubt it very much." The editorial concluded: "We expect the Law Society to interest itself in the case and haul (before it) … Mr Coltart who, until now, had been one of the most respected lawyers in the country." [289]

The intention of ZANU PF was clear – it was determined to paint me as an arch racist who went to extreme measures to release white clients. Pressure was brought on both the Law Society and the chief justice to investigate Blackie and myself. Chief Justice Anthony Gubbay wrote to Mugabe on 7 March 1995, asking that a tribunal be appointed to investigate Blackie's behaviour. I was informed by the Law Society that I, too, would be investigated. In the interim, the government-controlled press continued to milk the story and despite letters sent to them pointing out the facts, these were simply ignored. The entire episode was very stressful, as up until then I had had an unblemished professional record, which was now being impugned on allegations that I had acted in an improper and racist fashion. Fortunately, the Law Society investigated the matter promptly and I was exonerated in a letter I received from the Law Society secretary, Wilbert Mapombere, on 18 May advising that the matter did not involve "any wrong doing on (my) part". [290]

Blackie was not so fortunate. Pending the outcome of the tribunal he was suspended, which suspension was only lifted by Mugabe on 20 March 1996 when the tribunal found that while the "adverse press reports (had) greatly damaged" Blackie's integrity, on the facts "misbehaviour" (had) not been established. Astonishingly, although the tribunal had submitted its report to Mugabe on 28 November 1995, he allowed Blackie to stew under suspension for another four months.[291]

The episode consumed my attention, and I was not a particularly useful campaign manager for Sansole. Jenny stepped into the breach by organising the campaign for part of the constituency. Our home became the communication centre for the entire election and family members had to be roped in to take care of our three young boisterous children, who were all under seven. Sansole performed well in the context of the overall annihilation of the Forum Party at the polls. He secured 35 per cent of the vote in Bulawayo South, the highest percentage any Forum candidate achieved anywhere in the country. The elections, which were remarkably violence free, resulted in ZANU PF winning every seat on offer, bar two in Chipinge, which were won by Ndabaningi Sithole's ZANU Ndonga party. The elections were characterised by massive voter apathy; tens of seats in rural areas weren't even contested and there was a low turnout. Country wide, ZANU PF, despite its absolute control of the electronic media and other arms of state, only received 1 142 560 votes. It was worse for the Forum Party, though – it only received 88 223 votes, 6.28 per cent of the votes cast. The results sounded the death knell of the party.[292]

Despite the lack of violence and their dominance, ZANU PF apparatchiks could not resist employing their usual tricks in subverting the electoral process, but ironically it took an ex-ZANLA war veteran, Margaret Dongo, to expose them. Dongo had co-founded the Zimbabwe National Liberation War Veterans Association (ZNLWVA) in 1989 to promote the rights of marginalised veterans and in 1990, supported by the ZNLWVA, had won Harare East on a ZANU PF ticket. She proved to be a real thorn in ZANU PF's side in a parliament they otherwise dominated. She used her parliamentary privileges to speak out on human rights issues, making herself sufficiently unpopular with the ZANU PF leadership for them to ensure she didn't secure nomination in their primary elections. As a result she stood as an independent candidate in the Harare South constituency, but lost by a narrow margin. Convinced that the election had been rigged, Dongo sought the services of a bright, energetic young Harare lawyer, Tendai Biti, to challenge the result. Biti exposed serious defects in the ensuing case: many non-resident voters had been registered and some 41 per cent of the names on the voters' roll were inaccurate. The High Court overturned the result in August 1995 and Dongo comprehensively won the re-run, securing almost double the number of votes than her ZANU PF opponent, becoming one of only three opposition MPs in parliament. The case opened everyone's eyes to the extent of electoral fraud perpetrated by ZANU PF, laying the foundation for a host of challenges which were to follow the 2000 elections.

With the elections past we, that is the BLPC, were able to increase the pace of research into the Gukurahundi but we were still hobbled by the lack of funding. I had worked closely with Amnesty International in the 1980s, in particular in the Malunga trial, in which they had helped pay Malunga's legal fees. Now, in desperation, I approached them for funding. In the second half of 1995, they agreed to provide the princely sum of £6 000, which converted into Z$61 375, to fund the project. It seems remarkable now but the entire *Breaking the Silence* report, including all the research, collation of evidence and writing of the report, was done on that tiny budget. With this limited funding secured, we were able to start our field research.

We decided to start with Tsholotsho because Joel Silonda, who had been such a key informant in 1983, knew that that was where the Fifth Brigade had first been deployed. Silonda and another former CCJP worker, assisted by paralegal Paul Chizuze, commenced gathering information in Tsholotsho (which includes Nyamandlovu, which is the name used in the report). They made some twelve visits to Tsholotsho in the latter half of 1995, at great risk to themselves, and it was a traumatic process for them. They investigated ward by ward, interviewing people, recording evidence and mapping where atrocities had occurred. Local councillors were roped in and asked to identify people who had suffered injuries or losses, "whether at the hands of security forces or dissidents".[293] Many people were still deeply scarred by what had happened, while others were still too afraid to come forward. Some agreed to speak but backed out at the last minute, fearing they might face further retribution for speaking out. I monitored the process carefully, very anxious about our researchers, that they would be attacked or "disappeared".

The research was not exhaustive as we were severely limited by finance and so we did not manage to get to every area and certainly did not get statements from all the victims. Despite this, by the end of the year we had a total of 910 named victims in just one district. When that figure was extrapolated to the other thirteen administrative districts of Matabeleland North and South provinces, and the adjoining seven districts in Midlands province, the enormity of what had happened started to sink in. Although Tsholotsho and Lupane had been ground zero of the Fifth Brigade, we knew they had been deployed throughout Matabeleland.

Soon after securing the Amnesty International funding in September 1995, I contracted a Bulawayo-based academic, Shari Eppel, to oversee the data collection and to begin the process of bringing order to the masses of horrifying memories that were flooding in. One of her first tasks, with the help of interns, was to conduct a thorough search of all the newspaper articles in *The Chronicle* from that era as a counterpoint to the CCJP and BLPC data. *The Chronicle* gave the state version of events. Eppel set up two databases – the Human Rights Database, into which was entered all the information about atrocities coming in from our interviews and other civic collections, and *The Chronicle* Database, which captured every murder of that era, with perpetrators and victims as claimed by the state. In the final report, the findings of both data sources were meticulously and impartially included, in graphs and tables. This was done to ensure that the government could not say that we had ignored crimes committed by dissidents and had focused simply on the Fifth Brigade killings. The complete dissonance between the two databases has surprisingly seldom drawn any commentary: there was so clearly only a small and highly manipulated reality being portrayed in the government media, at a time when tens of thousands of ordinary citizens were facing daily terror, beatings and murders at the hands of a voracious, cruel state machinery.

Only a tight circle of people knew what we were doing in Tsholotsho in 1995, so few appreciated the conflict I faced when I was asked to propose a vote of thanks at the LRF's 10th anniversary dinner held on 10 November 1995. The guests of honour were the recently appointed president of the South African Constitutional Court (also former head of our sister organisation, the Legal Resources Centre), Arthur Chaskalson, and the head of our relevant government ministry, the minister of Justice, Emmerson Mnangagwa. Chaskalson presented no problem, but I was troubled about what I should say about Mnangagwa, who had been one of the architects of the Gukurahundi, a subject I was deeply immersed in at the time. In fairness to Mnangagwa, he had been very supportive of the LRF's less contentious projects, such as our publishing of the Zimbabwean law reports. I also did not want to spoil a celebration by being contentious so I resorted to humour, claiming that the LRF could take "credit for the Minister's legal prowess" because Mnangagwa had served his articles under "our most eminent Trustee Dr Enock Dumbutshena in the 1970s in Zambia before qualifying as a Barrister in 1976".[294] All the same it was a curious position to be in, sitting between one lawyer partly responsible for the Gukurahundi and two other world-acclaimed jurists.

Given our tiny budget, a decision was made at the beginning of 1996 to limit our further data collection to one district in Matabeleland South province, Matobo, which we knew was the location of the biggest concentration camp, Bhalagwe. Only ten weeks was devoted to this exercise and so it was not as thorough as the one in Tsholotsho. ZANU PF was also now more aware of what we were doing and we faced subtle opposition: many local ZANU PF councillors were unsupportive and some were even actively opposed, ordering people not to come forward. The CIO also started appearing at some of the interview sessions. Notwithstanding this, we still gathered some 350 named victims and thousands of others were brought to our attention.

While this was taking place in the rural areas, Eppel started the process of examining the archival information, partly from the BLPC reports, but predominantly from the CCJP. Their Catholic missions and St Luke's Hospital in Matabeleland North had received many accounts of atrocities and had treated many patients during 1983–5. There were shoe-boxes and files bursting with letters from parishioners, priests, even bishops, as well as St Luke's Hospital's extensive medical records, some of which were listed in the final report as an appendix. In many ways, the archives made for more shocking reading than the 1995 interviews, having "the edge of immediacy, the confusion, the terror, captured in between the lines".[295] They were entirely disordered, and sifting through them and trying to see where and how they overlapped with the 1995 interviews became a huge challenge. Ultimately, the solution to this came with a decision to analyse the data in the form of "village by village summaries": the names of villages seemed to be the best common denominator to work with, to prevent counting victims twice and to get a better idea of the chronology of events that had unfolded. The 1995 interviews named victims, which was often not the case in the CCJP archives – which tended to take the form of a priest recording "5 shot dead in Sikale, 1 Feb 1983", for example, with no names of victims. So the village Sikale would become the common reference around which to cross-compare the 1995 interviews.

Using this process, we were able to arrive at a figure of over 3 500 separate victims who were murdered. The figure of 20 000 deaths which is regularly ascribed to the *Breaking the Silence* report is nowhere to be found in the report. However, 3 500 victims is clearly a partial figure, arrived at via a very limited number of interviews, in a limited timespan, conducted in only two of the 20 districts directly affected by the Gukurahundi. Clearly the scale of the killings and other abuses was massive during that era, although a precise number may never be arrived at. It is clear that thousands of people perished, with tens of thousands more suffering beatings and property losses. In that context the figure of 20 000 people killed is not unreasonable. Most were killed in the first half of 1983. Put in further context some 35 000[296] people lost their lives during the period of war which spread throughout Zimbabwe and engulfed neighbouring states between 1973 and 1989.

With the data having been collected and analysed by mid 1996, we turned to the compilation of the report itself. The bulk of the report, including the explanation of the methodology used, the historical overview, the two administrative district case studies and the analysis, was written by Eppel in consultation with Auret and myself. Writing the historical overview in the report was challenging. There were limited sources available at that time, as there were very few extant writings in the public domain analysing the causes of the massacres, or even acknowledging them, such was the silence around the events. Once more newspaper articles, including Terence Ranger's useful summaries of what was said at rallies during those days by ZANU PF, and discussions with key informants, helped to build a sense of how things had happened. We had to be careful to portray an unemotional and balanced history, as our intention always was that the report be read by Mugabe and the state, and it would draw a reaction if anything claimed in it could be shown to be inaccurate or exaggerated or a misrepresentation.

Eppel travelled to South Africa and spoke to a commissioner of the Truth and Reconciliation Commission, then operative, in the hope of discovering something about Super Zapu and South Africa's role in this – which she was unable to do.

We drew in other organisations with specialised knowledge. Our preliminary findings were shown to Amani Trust whose director, Tony Reeler, wrote the chapter on the psychological consequences entitled "Organised violence: the implications of the 1980s disturbances for its victims". A group of LRF lawyers helped me write the chapter setting out the legal damages which victims could claim. Visits were made to rural Matabeleland to see what belongings might be found in a hut, to assess damages in relation to the many hut burnings of the 1980s. Contact was made with the Argentinean Forensic Anthropology Team (EAAF) who sent out Argentinean forensic anthropologist Mimi Doretti to assist us. Doretti was taken out to look at mass graves and the Bhalagwe Concentration Camp and it was she who wrote the chapter that makes recommendations for the recovery of human remains – something very dear to the hearts of the survivors.

As the enormity of what had happened, and its ongoing consequences, sank in to the few of us involved, we became aware of how important it was to get the final report right, and in the final months of 1996 it became all consuming. Eppel, who prior to being contracted by me had not been involved in human rights work, found the compilation of the report "intense and emotional". Verity Mundy, another employee of BLPC, who had started work on the project before Eppel was appointed, found the "horrific accounts in the files completely overwhelming". She "crumpled under the shock (and) suffered a nervous breakdown which ended up in her being hospitalised".[297] Eppel found that "at times it was hard to believe what (she) was hearing and reading, so much cruelty was being recounted. The report and the responsibility of doing justice to it became an obsession – in the final few months, (she) worked 80 hour weeks, writing, checking and rechecking the information to ensure that what was in that report could withstand any verification check that might be thrown back at it."[298]

At the very end of the process, having studied the findings, in particular the sentiments expressed by survivors, I wrote the Introduction and the Recommendation chapter. What came through strongly from the statements of victims was that they did not want a witch hunt, just a chance to be heard. Whether that was because they were resigned to the fact that the perpetrators of the violence were still in power I do not know, but it was clear that the overwhelming sentiment was that the country needed to move on. In broad terms victims wanted three things:

acknowledgment that what had happened *had happened*, an apology, and communal reparations. Accordingly, eight recommendations were made, namely that:

1. *There be official acknowledgement of the suffering through publication by Government of* Breaking the Silence *and the earlier Chihambakwe report;*
2. *All those members of the security forces and dissidents responsible for atrocities and still serving should be removed from positions of authority;*
3. *Amendments to a variety of Acts should be passed, including the War Victims Compensation Act, to assist victims obtain compensation;*
4. *Mass graves and unmarked graves should be professionally exhumed, the remains identified and reburied;*
5. *Specific funding be obtained to deploy professional teams of counsellors/psychologists and doctors to work in the affected communities;*
6. *A Reconciliation trust be established to effect communal reparations in the form of educational scholarships for orphans, irrigation schemes in affected areas and financial help to help communities conduct traditional ceremonies to appease the dead and the missing;*
7. *An urgent debate be started by Government and civil society to consider Constitutional amendments to prevent widespread human rights abuses ever happening again;*
8. *All parties including Government, civil society, churches and political parties should refrain from making inflammatory statements and work towards constructive dialogue.*

Despite the overwhelming evidence of crimes against humanity, even genocide, having been committed, we deliberately took a conservative, conciliatory line to ensure that *Breaking the Silence* would see the light of day. The final draft was completed by the end of November 1996 and I reported this to a meeting of LRF trustees in Harare on 6 December 1996. In August I had released a press statement confirming that a report was being prepared. This was in response to enquiries from journalists who had heard what we were doing. My statement caused considerable disquiet and a *Sunday Mail* opinion piece published on 29 September 1996 alleged that the "CCJP (sought) to divide people in Zimbabwe".[299] The CCJP worked under the broad jurisdiction of the Catholic Bishops Conference and while Auret was committed to seeing the report published, we were advised at the LRF meeting that the bishops were not. Prior to our meeting, the Bishops Conference had met and divided three to three on whether to publish. Archbishop Chakaipa, who had performed the marriage ceremony for Mugabe and his secretary, Grace Marufu, in a Roman Catholic Mass at Kutama Mission a few months previously, on 17 August 1996, was the one most opposed to publication. Auret, who attended, recounted that as he was leaving at the end of the meeting, he heard Chakaipa say under his breath "never". On begging his pardon Chakaipa said emphatically to Auret: "This will never be published."[300] Because of their division the bishops would only support a reconciliation trust and that an abbreviated version of the report be sent to Mugabe.

The bishops' opposition placed us in a considerable quandary, so we resolved to lobby Bishop Mutume, the president of CCJP and a former trustee of the LRF. When we did so, he explained that some of the bishops were implacably opposed to publication and that the Conference would not allow itself to be divided on the issue. The LRF trustees met again on 7 February 1997 and decided to publish alone if it came to that and an order was put in for some 500 copies to be printed, but embargoed. Finally, at an urgent meeting convened on 5 March, we resolved to present *Breaking the Silence* to Mugabe, but in deference to the bishops we would not distribute it before receiving a response from the office of the president. Dumbutshena was asked to meet the bishops to explain our viewpoint and to persuade them to present the report themselves, as this remained our preference. Surprisingly, Dumbutshena broke through and as a result of his meeting, Bishop Mutume and Auret together delivered a copy of *Breaking the Silence,* plus a covering letter, to Mugabe's office on 17 March.

The covering letter had asked Mugabe to respond to the report by 7 April. Not surprisingly, the day came and went and by the end of the month it was clear that government's strategy was going to be to ignore it. My presumption was that Mugabe was aware of the bishops' determination not to publish, and believed he could just sit it out. Both Auret and I had our hands tied because of our fiduciary responsibilities to our respective organisations. Knowing our frustration, Shari Eppel, without discussing her intentions with us, decided to take matters into her own hands. After consulting with Judith Todd, she arranged for copies of the original computer disks, containing substantial data and the final version of the report, to be sent to veteran journalist Peta Thornycroft in Johannesburg. Thornycroft passed on this information to David Beresford, who broke the details about the report in a story that was carried on the front page of South Africa's *Mail & Guardian* on 2 May 1997. Two days later Zimbabwe's *Standard* Sunday newspaper published an article containing excerpts from the report.

Mugabe reacted furiously. At the burial of former ZAPU veteran politician Stephen Vuma on 10 May he remarked "as we lay Vuma to rest let us remember that there are those bent on mischief making", people who "preferred to wear religious garb and publish reports that are meant to divide us".[301] He opined that "the wrongs of the past by whoever should not be allowed to come into the future of the Nation".[302] The only positive things said were that the Fifth Brigade atrocities were "a mistake"[303] and while ZANU PF had "sworn not to go by the past except as a record or register" that record "will remind us what never to do". "If that was wrong, if that went against the sacred tenets of humanity, we must never repeat it ... never oppress man nor allow oppression of man by man," he said. Ironically, that was precisely what *Breaking the Silence* was intended to be – an accurate record which would assist in preventing atrocities happening again in Zimbabwe.

The revelations in the *Mail & Guardian* led to demands from the independent press in Zimbabwe that the full report be released. We still hoped that the bishops would consent to releasing the report, which in turn would place pressure on the government to participate in the proposed reconciliation trust. Because of this, we did not release the report, but at a meeting of LRF trustees on 17 June we decided to write to Mugabe to tell him that we were going ahead with setting up a trust and inviting government to nominate two representatives. Concurrently, we wrote to the bishops advising them of the letter to the president and asking them to instruct the CCJP to nominate two representatives to the trust. In the same letters we informed Mugabe and the bishops that if we did not hear from them by 4 July we would go ahead with the distribution of the report.

July 4 came and went without any response from either Mugabe or the bishops, so we distributed copies of *Breaking the Silence* at all the LRF's Project Centres on 9 July, and to the media, diplomats, vice-presidents, ministers and governors two days later. The bishops responded immediately, with Mutume writing and expressing "sadness that the bishops commissioned the report and that the LRF was to collaborate with the CCJP" but had "seen fit to unilaterally publish it without the approval of the Bishop's Conference".[304]

Government and its media studiously ignored the report, a stance it has maintained to this day. No one has ever challenged the findings, basically because they are indisputable. If anything, the report was written too conservatively and history may well show that it underplayed the gravity of what happened. It was only some 18 months later that Mugabe vented his wrath against Auret and me, believing that the two of us were primarily responsible for *Breaking the Silence*.

CHAPTER 14

PRELUDE TO MAYHEM
1997 TO 1999

"The likes of ... the Aurets and Coltarts of our society, who seem bent on ruining the national unity and loyalty of our people and institutions, have got to search their consciences. Why are they day in day out working to destroy the unity of our people to promote strife amongst us ... let them be warned therefore that unless their insidious acts of sabotage cease my government will not hesitate in taking very stern measures against them."

– PRESIDENT ROBERT MUGABE'S ADDRESS TO THE NATION,
TELEVISED ON ZTV, SATURDAY EVENING, 6 FEBRUARY 1999

Following the Forum Party's annihilation at the 1995 polls, and being preoccupied with *Breaking the Silence,* I did not pay much attention to partisan politics during the period 1995 to 1997. Indeed the political environment in Zimbabwe in 1997 was depressingly sterile. ZANU PF dominated parliament and the March 1996 presidential election had been a non-event. In their 1989 amendments to the constitution, ZANU PF had staggered the holding of parliamentary and presidential elections and given the president a longer term of six years. The Forum Party had been so shocked by its poor showing in the 1995 parliamentary elections that Dumbutshena was not put forward as a presidential candidate. Only Muzorewa and Sithole were nominated to stand against Mugabe. The electoral process was even more farcical than 1995: the media bias was even more pronounced and Mugabe stretched the privileges of incumbency to new limits. He flew around the countryside in no fewer than three helicopters, one of which had just been purchased for

Z\$150 million. All the electoral bodies were manned by people appointed by Mugabe.

Despite all of this ZANU PF were determined not to take any chances. They trumped up against Sithole the now typical charge of wanting to assassinate the president and arrested him on 12 October 1995. Although he was released on bail, one of his bail conditions was that he should not travel abroad, which bar persisted until the election. Sithole and Muzorewa both withdrew from the race, the latter on the eve of the election, leaving Mugabe as the sole candidate, prompting him to give an angry national televised address urging people to vote "in their millions". Although Mugabe won a "resounding victory" in the elections, which were held on 16 and 17 March 1996, polling 92.49 per cent of the vote, embarrassingly, only 29.5 per cent of the electorate turned out to vote. It was the lowest poll since independence. But the bottom line was that by mid 1996 Mugabe had achieved almost absolute control.

As if to confirm that all was not well after the elections, the public service held a massive strike in August/September that year. Although there had been widespread strikes between 1980 and 1982, the trade union movement had then gone into a period of decline. In 1985 a new Labour Relations Act was introduced, severely restricting the right to strike, which was compounded by the emergence of a weak labour leadership, more interested in pursuing ZANU PF patronage than standing up for workers' rights. In 1988, however, a new secretary general, Morgan Tsvangirai, was appointed who worked with other key figures, such as Gibson Sibanda, to revitalise the ZCTU. By 1990 the labour movement had changed from "being a pliant wing" of ZANU PF to a "more autonomous force".[305] The ZCTU fought hard in the early 1990s to improve the collective bargaining rights of its members; this, together with its strident criticism of ESAP, brought the ZCTU into increasing conflict with the government. The 1996 public service strike consolidated the ZCTU's relations with civil servants, further strengthening its urban base. In addition, the hitherto close relationship between ZANU PF and civil servants was seriously undermined.

Serious divisions within ZANU PF itself emerged in 1997 when war veterans turned against the party, demonstrating for better conditions. At the root of their protest was the War Victims Compensation Fund. The original Victims of Terrorism (Compensation) Act had been passed by the RF in 1972 to compensate for death, injury and damage caused by an act of terrorism post 1972. In 1980, ZANU PF amended the act, setting up a fund to assist those negatively affected by the war during the period March 1962 to March 1980. The majority of war veterans were eligible for compensation, but they were neither aware of the act's existence nor its provisions. High-ranking politicians and officers, however, had drawn benefits from the fund, and in fact had drained it of "millions of dollars through inflated compensation claims".[306] Some war veterans working in the pensions office observed who was benefiting and got the word out to other veterans to apply for compensation. A flood of applications followed, with the bulk of the injury or disability assessments being done by Dr Chenjerai Hitler[307] Hunzvi, then a doctor at Harare Central Hospital. The *Zimbabwe Independent* first exposed the scam in 1996, but ZANU PF only acted in April 1997, when there was public outcry over the obvious looting of the fund. Mugabe established a commission of inquiry, which was chaired by then judge president Godfrey Chidyausiku, and suspended all payments from the fund.

The inquiry finding shocked Zimbabweans: hundreds of false claims had been submitted in which many injuries were grossly exaggerated. At the centre of the scandal was Hunzvi, who had signed medical certificates for veterans and inflated the percentage disability. In addition he had deliberately disguised his handwriting, favoured his relatives and even signed his own disability certificate. But senior ZANU PF members were also implicated, including Joice Mujuru (awarded a 55 per cent disability and Z$389 472 payout), Oppah Rushesha (65 per cent and Z$478 166), Perence Shiri (50 per cent and Z$90 249), and Grace Mugabe's brother Reward Marufu (95 per cent and Z$821 668). Despite these revelations, none of those responsible was brought to book and there were no prosecutions for fraud. The fund itself, though, was drained and so there was no money left for genuine claims.

Compounding the fury of innocent veterans were the revelations around what came to be known as the "VIP Housing scandal". Thousands of civil servants had been contributing to a fund which was designed to assist them purchase their own homes. This "pay-for-your-house" scheme was irreparably undermined when millions of dollars were diverted from it to pay for senior government and political leaders, including Grace Mugabe (who had a mansion built for herself at 221 Armthwaite Road in Harare) and then Judge Paddington Garwe (who had been the presiding magistrate in the Malunga trial). Although Grace

Mugabe subsequently repaid the money, the damage was done. The perception was that senior figures were on the take at the expense of common people.

The shutting down of the War Victims Compensation Fund was the final straw. Tensions between the ZNLWA and the ZANU PF leadership grew, with the former interpreting the inquiry as a device to disguise the looting of the fund by politicians and an attempt to discredit the foundation. Despite Hunzvi being exposed as a fraudster, he was elected chairman of ZNLWA and used his new position aggressively to tackle the ZANU PF leadership.

In July 1997, Hunzvi demanded a meeting with Mugabe, which demand was ignored. Veterans then took to the streets for three days of rowdy protests, following Mugabe around the capital and noisily disrupting his speeches. On Heroes Day, 11 August, veterans drowned out Mugabe's speech by shouting and banging iron bars on the bonnets of ministerial Mercedes Benzes, "making such a din that Mugabe folded up his notes and left".[308] Veterans then invaded the ZANU PF headquarters. They ran from floor to floor, overturning filing cabinets and furniture. Things deteriorated further, with veterans holding ministers hostage and finally besieging State House itself.[309] Mugabe was forced to capitulate. Although the inquiry had by now revealed Hunzvi's fraud (which resulted in him being paid over half a million dollars for loss of hearing and a leg wound – although he had never fought a day in battle during the war), these salacious facts were more than set off by the embarrassing revelations about Joice Mujuru and Mugabe's brother-in-law, Marufu. Hunzvi demanded that each veteran receive a one-off payment of Z$50 000, land and a monthly, reviewable, pension of Z$2 000 per month. Although there were only about 32 000 guerrillas at the end of the war, Hunzvi claimed that their numbers stood at 50 000. None of this was budgeted but Mugabe had no choice but to yield to their demands. A prodigious package was announced: each veteran would receive lump sum payments of Z$50 000 (then worth about US$3 500),[310] a monthly pension of Z$2 000 (about US$142), and land. The immediate total cost was a shocking Z$4.2 billion (over US$300 million).

To fund this, it was announced that sales tax would be raised from 15 per cent to 17.5 per cent, a surcharge of 20 cents a litre would be raised on fuel, and the cost of electricity would go up. This was followed with the listing for the first time of 1 471 white-owned farms for compulsory acquisition. In issuing notices of acquisition, ZANU PF knew they would never be able to pay for the farms they wished to acquire.

Almost overnight my workload doubled as I prepared to defend numerous farmer clients.

On 5 November 1997 the newly appointed British Labour Party secretary of state for International Development, Claire Short, had written to Zimbabwe's minister of Agriculture, Kumbirai Kangai, placing conditions on British support for land purchases. She wrote:

> "(W)e do not accept that Britain has a special responsibility to meet the costs of land purchases in Zimbabwe. We do, however, recognise the very real issues you face over land reform. We believe that land reform could be an important component of a Zimbabwean programme designed to eliminate poverty. We would be prepared to support a programme of land reform that was part of a poverty eradication strategy but not on any other basis."[311]

Zimbabwe's own coffers were dry, and ZANU PF could not meet the British terms of a gradual and orderly transfer of land. War veterans, in their anger over the widening wealth gap between the ZANU PF elite and themselves, had demanded land immediately – a demand that could not be met in any other way than a populist announcement that whites' land would be seized without any means to pay compensation. The payouts to veterans, combined with rumours of land acquisitions and word that Treasury was printing money, precipitated what is known in Zimbabwe as "Black Friday", 14 November 1997, when the Zimbabwe dollar crashed, losing 73 per cent of its value, eroding in a stroke much of the real value of the payments to veterans. Workers, who were already reeling from inflation and the general decline of the economy, received the news angrily. Morgan Tsvangirai, as secretary general of ZCTU, called for a general strike on Tuesday, 9 December 1997.

The previous October I had stood down as director of the BLPC, after ten years at the helm, and simultaneously taken up the role of senior partner of my law firm Webb, Low and Barry. This new responsibility had somewhat desensitised me from the mood of the public and so through a combination of being immersed in the firm's work, ignorance of the growing strength of the ZCTU and scepticism, I was totally unprepared for what I witnessed in the centre of Bulawayo that Tuesday. At lunchtime

I had given a lecture to the Theological College of Zimbabwe (which then had its campus on Lobengula Street), ironically on the topic "How the Church can promote social justice and human rights". As I left the TCZ campus, I saw hundreds of workers streaming in towards the city centre and so, curious, I rushed back to our firm's offices, which at the time were on the fourth floor of the Haddon and Sly Building. The building overlooked the city hall and its carpark. I struggled to park my car because 8th Avenue was a sea of people. When I got up to my office I was amazed to see thousands of workers gathered in the city hall carpark, overflowing onto 8th Avenue to the south, and Takawira Avenue to the north. The peaceful mass meeting, punctuated with songs and hymns, was being addressed by the president of ZCTU, Gibson Sibanda, who was also then a train driver in the National Railways of Zimbabwe. I couldn't hear what Sibanda was saying, but the mood of the crowd was electric and its size unprecedented. The meeting dispersed peacefully and I left the office that evening hopeful that the emerging tensions in Zimbabwe could be resolved without bloodshed. Sadly, the situation was completely different in Harare, where riot police using teargas had been deployed to block the demonstrations, which then turned violent, with cars being overturned and some shops looted.

ZANU PF responded in their typical, time honoured fashion. Within days Tsvangirai's ZCTU office on the tenth floor of Chester House in Harare was raided by war veterans, who tried to throw him out of his window. Tsvangirai screamed for help, fought them off with the aid of colleagues, but suffered a variety of injuries and ended up in hospital. Mugabe blamed "whites and foreigners" for inciting the riots. Instead of admitting that the crisis had been started by corruption in his own ranks, indeed in his own household, Mugabe played the race card. It was clear as 1997 drew to a close that ESAP had utterly failed. My warnings made six years previously had all come to pass. Zimbabwe was now in a catastrophic downward economic spiral, heavily indebted to the World Bank and IMF, so much so that she would soon be suspended from both organisations for failing to meet her obligations. Economic liberalisation without political liberalisation was indeed doomed to fail.

The economic consequences of the decisions made in November 1997 became apparent in the first few weeks of 1998. The cost of staple goods rocketed, including cooking oil, soap and sugar. But it was the price of maize meal that hit hardest, when it rose by some 36 per cent.

When the government announced a further 21 per cent increase in this staple, it precipitated the calling of a three-day strike by the ZCTU from 19 January. Although once again Bulawayo was relatively orderly, the strike in Harare degenerated rapidly. On the first day, black working-class townships were cordoned off by police; the crowds responded by setting vehicles alight and chasing the police. Looting followed and even central Harare had a pall of teargas hanging over it by the end of the day. An announcement that the increase in the price of maize meal would be reversed didn't stem the riots, causing Mugabe to deploy the military the next day. Armed with whips, batons and assault rifles, soldiers went from house to house, often dragging out their occupants and randomly beating people. The show of force ended the strike. Once again Mugabe took to state media, blaming whites for being behind the ZCTU. This time he also belittled the ZCTU leadership, including its train driver president, Gibson Sibanda:

> "You have the mistaken belief that you are more powerful than the government. People must weigh themselves and see what they are good at. Some drive trains, some are foremen, but people who witnessed the liberation struggle will not accept you."[312]

Sibanda's witty retort to Mugabe was: "At least I, as a train driver, keep my train on its tracks."

More sinister was the legal action taken against some of the rioters. Some 2 575 youths, women and children of school-going age were detained and vigorously prosecuted. Harsh sentences were imposed. In one case, a first offender young single mother caught stealing a 5 kg bag of mealie meal from a Chitungwiza shop was sentenced to two years with hard labour. In the context of the War Victims Compensation Fund scandal revelations, where senior ministers had got off scot free despite defrauding the state of hundreds of thousands of dollars, the sentences were outrageous. I criticised the treatment being meted out, pointing out that "these were people with pent up anger", and that "first offenders should be treated differently from hard core offenders".[313]

With an uneasy peace restored, it became increasingly clear that the root of the problems facing Zimbabwe was its deeply flawed constitution which vested far too much power in the executive. The seventh recommendation in *Breaking the Silence* was that "Government, citizens of Zimbabwe and civil society begin an urgent debate to consider what constitutional safeguards are necessary to prevent widespread human rights violations occurring again". That recommendation reflected a growing consensus in the human rights community that our focus needed to be trained on constitutional reform. This resulted in the launch of the National Constitutional Assembly (NCA) on 31 January 1998, under the chairmanship of Tsvangirai. The NCA was an initiative by churches, civil society and human rights organisations, trade unions, student movements and political parties to "conscientise Zimbabweans through broad debates on the need to make a new Constitution".[314] Although largely a Harare-initiated body, it rapidly drew in activists and organisations from throughout the country.

Personally, I was delighted by the new focus on the constitution. Ever since Dumbutshena's inspirational speech at the opening of the BLPC library in 1990 about the need for constitutional reform, the issue had been close to my heart. When I drafted the Forum "Blueprint" in June 1992 my opening sentence identified that many of Zimbabwe's woes stemmed from the fundamentally flawed constitution.[315] In 1996 I was incensed by the 14th Amendment to the constitution which removed birth rights, diluted the right to privacy, and the right citizens had to have their non-citizen spouses live with them. The last change was particularly galling, because it reversed a Supreme Court decision the BLPC had won in 1994, establishing the right of Zimbabwean women to have their non-citizen husbands live with them.[316] The Immigration Department had adopted a discriminatory practice in which female citizens were not entitled to have their non-citizen husbands reside with them, but male citizens could. Our argument was straightforward: women also had the right to marry and if they were not entitled to live in Zimbabwe with their husbands, they faced the dilemma of either having to live apart or outside Zimbabwe. The Supreme Court agreed with us and went further in a subsequent case[317] to rule that foreign husbands also had the right to work in Zimbabwe. Amendment 14 reversed all of this. In a speech I made to Rotary in Bulawayo in August 1996, I emphasised that the amendment underlined "once again the need to hold a Constitutional Conference in Zimbabwe". I said that our constitution was "being butchered by a small clique of ZANU PF males who have shown no respect for human rights in the last 16 years and show no intention of respecting them in future".[318]

The launch of the NCA instantly opened up the debate and I participated enthusiastically. My opening gambit was an opinion piece published on 6 February in which I argued that we had paid a heavy price for our "flawed Lancaster deal". Although I believed there was "not the slightest chance that the regime (would) go along with the idea" of a Constitutional Conference, I felt it was important that we had "a positive and peaceful goal to focus on".[319] This article led to a flood of invitations to speak on the the subject, and 1998 was dominated by speaking engagements with a diverse array of organisations. Two of these invitations led to interesting exchanges involving former ZAPU politicians who now held senior positions within ZANU PF. In the first, on 20 February, I shared a platform with Minister Joseph Msika and former minister Enos Nkala to debate the "Way forward regarding the Gukurahundi atrocities". A massive crowd of some 4 000 in Bulawayo's large city hall booed Nkala and Msika when they tried to absolve themselves of responsibility. To his credit, Msika condemned what he termed "a dark cloud in the Nation's history" but he angered the crowd when he argued that "we should not open up old wounds". Interestingly, Nkala denied knowledge of the massacres, "shifting the blame to Mugabe, late Minister Ernest Kadungure and Justice Minister Emmerson Mnangagwa whom he said should face the public and answer for their sins".[320] Quoting Martin Luther King's point that the absence of tension did not denote peace, I argued that justice needed to be done and one of the ways was by compensating victims. In the second meeting, in April, I found myself up against Dabengwa; we had both been asked by the Christian Communicators Association to debate the controversial new Public Order and Security Bill which was soon to be tabled before parliament. Dabengwa argued that it was "not intended to suppress" Zimbabweans, rather to "protect them". I begged to differ, arguing that the bill remained "draconian and unacceptable", that its "intended effect (was) to deter people from demonstrating" and that it would not "resolve the anger felt by people". I spoke of a "tidal wave of discontent" and said that if "Government wanted to prevent disorder" it should "tackle the fundamental complaints of the people" rather than "impose draconian laws which ultimately would not stop the process of change".[321] In both meetings, the spectre of Mugabe's former protagonists converted to his main apologists intrigued me.

In some 26 speeches that year I addressed churches, women's groups, the Law Society, the media, estate agents and insurance institutes, and

NCA meetings themselves on the need for constitutional reform. Of course, many others were doing the same – Morgan Tsvangirai, Professor Welshman Ncube, Lovemore Madhuku, Tendai Biti and others spoke country wide, galvanising the public. Even when the topic was not strictly on the constitution, I found ways of diverting the debate that way. My central theme was that our constitution was "an expedient document of compromise designed to end a war, drafted in a hurry by foreigners and agreed upon by elderly male politicians".[322] My principal complaint, "the most serious flaw", was that the present constitution "totally subverted the concept of separation of powers" in that "the Executive (was) overwhelmingly powerful at the expense of both the Legislature and Judiciary". It was a theme I was to come back to time and time again. The Zimbabwean presidency simply had far too much power and that, in my view, was at the root of Zimbabwe's crisis of governance.

Almost as if to highlight this flaw in our body politic, in August 1998 Mugabe committed Zimbabwe to war in the Congo, propping up Laurent Kabila, without seeking approval from parliament and much against the public's will. Kabila, with assistance from the Tutsi-dominated Rwanda government, Uganda and Burundi, had started a rebellion against Zairean dictator Mobuto Sese Seko in October 1986, eventually overthrowing him and declaring himself president of the newly renamed Democratic Republic of the Congo on 17 May 1997. There was a conspicuous Rwandese presence in Kabila's new administration, but that relationship cooled to such an extent that at the end of July 1998 Kabila unceremoniously expelled all his Rwandan military advisers, and Rwandan and Ugandan troops. On 2 August the Banyamulenge people mutinied in the eastern town of Goma and within weeks a well-armed rebel group, the Rally for Congolese Democracy (RCD), backed by Rwanda and Uganda, started to advance across the country. By mid August even the capital Kinshasa was threatened and an urgent meeting was held in Harare on 19 August to assist Kabila. Mugabe immediately committed Zimbabwe to back Kabila, along with Angola, Namibia, Chad, Libya and Sudan. Thus started the Second Congo War which lasted five years and cost the lives, conservatively estimated, of at least 860 000 people.[323] It became the deadliest war in African history, eventually involving nine African countries.

But none was more committed to war than Zimbabwe. Some 3 000 ZNA troops, supported by combat aircraft and armoured vehicles, were deployed immediately under the leadership of former Fifth Brigade commander Perence Shiri, who by then had been promoted to Air Marshal. Although the Zimbabwean forces prevented rebels from overrunning Kinshasa, Kabila and his new allies suffered a series of setbacks. On 22 October, after an eight-day battle, the Rwandan and Ugandan-backed rebels captured Kindu, a strategic town on the Congo River. Numerous Zimbabwean troops were killed and captured. Reinforcements and additional troops had to be sent, with some reports estimating that at times there were as many as 13 000 Zimbabwean troops in the DRC.

Inevitably, the government could not keep a lid on what was happening. Even though it imposed a news blackout, pictures emerged in independent newspapers of Zimbabwean prisoners of war in chains and the number of body bags with dead troops returning to Zimbabwe increased. Even Dabengwa incurred the wrath of mourners when he tried to defend Zimbabwe's involvement at the burial in Bulawayo of two soldiers killed in action. What also irritated the general public was the cost of the war, which rapidly escalated; the government admitted at one stage that it was costing Z$1 million a day but the figure was more like US$1 million per day. Whatever the actual cost was, the effect of the war on the economy was clear – this further un-budgeted expense fuelled inflation, then at about 30 per cent per annum and rapidly rising. The war was the final straw in Zimbabwe's relationship with the IMF. A standby facility of US$176 million was suspended after only one draw-down of US$53 million, with the IMF complaining that the Zimbabwean government had "failed to cut its spending deficits to within agreed parameters".[324] Several years earlier the World Bank had already suspended ties with the government when it failed to keep its budget deficit in check. Now Zimbabwe was firmly on its own, suspended from both the World Bank and IMF.

With the war degenerating into a bloodbath, South Africa's Nelson Mandela made frantic efforts to broker peace. Employing shuttle diplomacy, he met with rebel leaders, Mugabe, Namibia's President Nujoma and Rwanda's then military strongman, Paul Kagame. By November 1998 it emerged that Mandela's "efforts (had) been stalled by Mugabe's apparent determination to punish the rebels". Mugabe's "belligerence" had "turned a localised rebellion into a fully-fledged regional war".

When I was asked to comment I pointed out that all the countries "fighting in the Congo (had) no moral standing to preside over peace negotiations" and that we needed a "peace force whose position (was) not compromised by vested interests". I argued that there was no legitimate government in the Congo: "Kabila, exalted by Mugabe and his allies as the legitimate leader, was not lawfully elected. He is only a *de facto* President who came to power through the barrel of a gun." Finally, I had a direct dig: "Countries with blood on their hands should not lead peace negotiations because they are heavily compromised. Maybe a peacekeeping initiative by the UN, OAU and SADC might succeed; certainly not peace talks led by Mugabe."[325]

The growing disquiet regarding Zimbabwe's involvement within the DRC blew into the open on 10 January 1999. The *Standard*, then the only independent Sunday paper, published a story alleging that 23 ZNA officers had been arrested over a plot to oust the government. The editor, Mark Chavunduka, was arrested by the military on 12 January and denied access to his lawyers, who obtained a High Court order two days later on the basis that the military had no right to detain civilians. However, the military refused to abide by the High Court order, saying that civilian courts had no jurisdiction over military camps, where Chavunduka was being held. A second order, demanding that the minister of Defence produce Chavunduka by 10 pm on 18 January, was also defied. Ray Choto, the journalist who had written the story, was being hunted down and so he handed himself over to the police on 19 January, only to be handed over to the military. Eventually, on 21 January both men were released on bail. Both had also sustained serious injuries as a result of torture (which included electric shocks to their genitals) inflicted on them by military police.

Outraged by the blatant disregard shown by the military for the High Court, and the disregard shown by government, three Supreme Court judges, Nick McNally, Simba Muchechetere and Wilson Sandura wrote to Mugabe complaining that "the army can operate with impunity in breach of the law",[326] and asking the president to make a statement confirming "that the rule of law is accepted as a necessary ingredient of a democratic Zimbabwe". The letter was followed by a petition from Judge Adams on behalf of all the High Court judges supporting the Supreme Court. The first sign that ZANU PF would not respond positively came when the minister of Information, Chen Chimutengwende, issued a statement saying that government would soon introduce stringent media regulations, adding they were "working flat out to bring sanity to the media".[327]

But the real punch came the following day when Mugabe delivered a live television address at 9.30 pm on Saturday, 6 February 1999. He said the judges had "shocked us by behaving in a manner we regard as unbecoming". He described their actions as unconstitutional and "an outrageous and deliberate act of judicial impudence", bringing into question their independence and suggesting they go into politics. Inevitably, he turned to whites, arguing that ZANU PF had forgotten the whites' "iniquitous past" and allowed "Ian Smith and those like him (to) enjoy the comforts and freedoms" of Zimbabwe. Without any sense of irony he then said:

> "The whites of our community must play an even greater part in order to atone for the sins of their evil pasts. The likes of Clive Wilson and Clive Murphy [two of the proprietors of the *Standard*] complemented by the Aurets and Coltarts of our society, who seem bent on ruining the national unity and loyalty of our people and institutions have got to search their consciences and ask themselves whether in fact they belong to Zimbabwe and share the same philosophy, sentiments and feelings as the rest of our people. If they do, why are they day in and day out working to destroy the unity of our people to promote strife amongst us, to cause disaffection among our forces and to undermine a legitimately established government of this country. Let them be warned therefore that unless their insidious acts of sabotage cease my government will not hesitate in taking very stern measures against them."[328]

Aside from the fact that Wilson, Murphy and Auret were all outspoken opponents of Smith, Auret and I had had nothing to do with the journalists' detention and the furore surrounding it. Two weeks earlier, I had responded to a statement made by Dabengwa, in his capacity as minister of Home Affairs (in which he had said that government would neither make an apology nor compensate civilian victims of the Gukurahundi). Dabengwa had argued that the amnesty for dissidents was sufficient, but I insisted "there must be an apology to the innocent citizens who had suffered".[329] Whether this statement aroused Mugabe's ire again I do not know, but whatever caused it, the fact remained that Auret and I were in his focus, and we were drawn into the worst constitutional crisis since independence. I was shocked at being identified in this manner and, knowing how Chavunduka and Choto had been tortured, made precautions. I prepared to go into hiding and went to the extent of identifying escape routes and safe houses with friends. Interviewed at the time, I said I took Mugabe's threat "very seriously" given that it was coming from someone who was "embattled" and who was going "to rely on the military to remain in power".[330]

The threat did not materialise and it appeared that ZANU PF were themselves shocked by the widespread condemnation of Mugabe's remarks. During February, it emerged that ZANU PF had decided to counter the NCA's growing traction for a new constitution by initiating its own process. I received a letter from ZANU PF's secretary for Legal Affairs, Eddison Zvobgo, inviting me to become a commissioner on a proposed national commission of inquiry into a new constitution. In fact a number of us in the NCA received similar invitations. At first glance, it appeared to be a positive step and an intensive debate began within the NCA, and other related organisations, about whether we should participate or not.

On 11 March I took part in a debate on the subject, called by the NCA, at Bulawayo's large city hall. I was in two minds: on the one hand my inclination was to accept the invitation so that I could work from the inside to influence matters, and yet on the other I had a real fear that ZANU PF would subvert the process. Both Mugabe and Justice minister Mnangagwa had proclaimed that they saw no need to debate a new constitution; their statements were borne out by the fourteen amendments to the Lancaster constitution which had nearly all served to consolidate power. I asked, "How can we trust the people who 18 months ago said they were comfortable with the present constitution to spearhead its reform?"[331] This would be a commission appointed by Mugabe and therefore controlled by him. Could it really be trusted to take on board the views of the public and would it be truly representative? Seeking to be positive, though, I suggested that a retired judge should head the process, that the commission should be representative of all major reputable organisations, that public hearings should be conducted, and a constitution reflecting the views of the people should finally be subjected to a referendum.

My attention was then diverted by the rapidly deteriorating condition of my father in South Africa, which took me to his bedside. Aged 88 he had had a good innings but my concern was that he still battled to reconcile a just, sovereign God with one who had allowed all the suffering he had witnessed in World War II. Throughout our relationship we had always enjoyed a good argument on any topic but especially politics, and so when I found my faith in Jesus Christ at UCT, religion became a new topic he enjoyed to canvas. He accepted that Christ lived as a historical fact but felt he was just a good man, not divine. It was important to me that I could be with him during his last few days and it gave me great comfort that my father allowed me to pray with him, something we had never done before. On the final weekend before he died on 12 April, his beloved Scotland beat France to clinch the 1999 Five Nations Rugby Championship; although very ill, he still managed to celebrate. It was my father who had imbued in me both my love of sport and interest in politics, and right until the end our debates continued. Appropriately, my mother and I spread his ashes in a bunker at Royal Port Alfred Golf Club before I returned to Zimbabwe to take up the cudgels again.

While I had been away, the government-initiated constitutional reform process had got off to a bad start. It appeared as if divide-and-rule strategies were being employed. Invitations had been sent to individuals rather than asking organisations such as the NCA to nominate representatives to participate. A meeting had been held with Zvobgo on 16 March, which appeared to be constructive but did not result in agreement. A major bone of contention was that Mugabe intended using the Commission of Inquiries Act, which gave him unacceptably wide powers, to interfere with the process. The following day the NCA and other organisations resolved not to participate and so the battle lines were drawn. On reflection, those weeks marked a critical turning point in Zimbabwe's history because an opportunity to forge a consensus was lost. Both sides dug their heels in and there was no compromise.

Mugabe went ahead with his own plans, establishing a national commission of inquiry[332] on 28 April, through presidential proclamation. Our fears that Mugabe was not committed to genuine inclusivity appeared justified; he appointed his go-to judge Godfrey Chidyausiku as chairman and the 241 delegates were dominated by ZANU PF members and apologists. There were some neutrals and opponents: ironically, several former RF MPs were included, among them Chris Andersen,

Bill Irvine, Mark Partridge and Gerald Smith. There were a few human rights activists, too, such as Dr Reg Matchaba-Hove and Jessie Majome, but they constituted a tiny minority. Not taking any chances, Mugabe added all the current MPs, all but three of whom were ZANU PF, in addition to the 241 named commissioners, ensuring that the party would enjoy an overwhelming majority in all decisions taken. Revelations followed that the constitutional commission would have a budget of some Z$300 million, including a massive media campaign, costing Z$37 million, and hefty allowances for all commissioners and staff.

When the chairs of various sub-committees of the commission were announced in June, it became even clearer how tightly controlled the exercise was going to be: Chidyausiku would chair the executive committee, ZANU PF MPs Rita Makarau and Patrick Chinamasa would chair the critically important separation of powers and legal committees, and independents such as Eric Bloch would chair relatively insignificant committees like public finance. One surprising appointment was that of Jonathan Moyo, who had been such a virulent critic of Mugabe, as chair of the media and public relations committee. It was only as the work of the commission unfolded that we realised how much his loyalties and thinking had changed. Moyo was transformed from one of Mugabe's staunchest critics into one of his closest aides.

In stark contrast, the NCA had a minuscule budget and we all volunteered our time. As had happened in 1998, I threw myself into a demanding speaking schedule and delivered over 20 speeches on the constitution during the course of 1999. Our focus was on explaining the deficiencies of the existing constitution, criticising the process employed by the commission, receiving the views of people, and developing a consensus about what was needed in a new constitution. On the weekend of 18 and 19 June a constitutional convention was held at the Chitungwiza sports complex, attended by delegates and representatives of a wide array of political parties, churches, trade unions, civic associations and human rights organisations. The meeting resolved to reject the government's commission and to work towards drafting a "working draft constitution". The following week, on 23 June, I was elected to the legal committee of the NCA which was charged with providing legal input to the entire process. The committee was chaired by Lovemore Madhuku and included Tendai Biti, Brian Kagoro, Professor Geoff Feltoe, Professor Welshman Ncube, Douglas Mwonzora and Yvonne

Mahlunge. I had up to this point worked with lawyers older than myself, such as Dumbutshena and Sansole, but now I got to work with a new generation of exceptionally bright lawyers who were all Harare based. The realisation that they shared a similar vision for Zimbabwe's new constitutional order as I did was exhilarating.

Joshua Nkomo died on 1 July 1999. It did not come as a shock because his health had been in decline for some time. However, his death was the catalyst for two significant political developments. The first concerned ZANU PF's hold on the Matabeleland provinces. On the day he died I commented that "just as Mugabe is the cement that holds ZANU PF together, Nkomo was the cement that held ZAPU together"; and I predicted that his death "could speed up the disintegration of the party in the region".[333] Less than a year later ZANU PF was swept away in Matabeleland; whether it was Nkomo's death alone which caused this is debatable, but there is no doubt it was a major factor. The second concerned ZANU PF's land reform policy, which changed after Nkomo's demise from one which tried to work within the law to one that was unlawful, chaotic and violent. Many former ZAPU members such as Dabengwa, Msika and Msipa did not fully embrace the new land policies driven by Mugabe in the 2000s; their voices would have been much stronger had they been supplemented by Nkomo's. Despite my clashes with Nkomo, I recognised that he had been a restraining force against the excesses of ZANU PF hardliners.

Unbeknown to me, behind the scenes the ZCTU leadership was steadfastly making plans to form a new political party to oppose ZANU PF in the 2000 general elections. Although a National Working People's Convention (comprising trade unions, churches, human rights groups) held in Harare in February 1999 had focused primarily on the need for a new constitution, delegates came away understanding that a new political formation would also have to be constructed to challenge ZANU PF. Likewise, while there was no explicit resolution that the ZCTU would take up the task, there was "a tacit understanding"[334] that it would do so. The establishment of Mugabe's constitutional commission, and its shenanigans made it clear that there was no genuine desire in government to bring about democratic reform, which in turn fuelled the drive for a new party to oppose ZANU PF. Quiet preparations continued within the ZCTU, culminating in it holding an extraordinary congress on 7 August, which resolved to sponsor the establishment of a new political party.

The resolutions included commitments to allow those in leadership who would take positions in the new party to retain their offices until the election. ZCTU president Gibson Sibanda concluded the meeting observing "(a)lthough our child is still to be born, that baby is expected to learn to crawl, to stand, to walk and to run. Change is coming to Zimbabwe."[335] ZANU PF's propaganda has always described the MDC as a concoction of the West and whites, but nothing could be further from the truth. It was a party rooted in the Zimbabwean trade union movement and not a single white was present when this momentous decision was taken.

Shortly after the ZCTU congress I received a call from Sibanda, who asked me, with Tsvangirai's concurrence, if I would consider becoming the interim secretary for Legal Affairs of a new party to be formed called the Movement for Democratic Change (MDC). I was somewhat taken aback for a number of reasons. My firm had represented the National Railways of Zimbabwe (NRZ) since its establishment in 1897 and I had argued numerous cases on behalf of the NRZ against its unions, so the invitation was unexpected and complicated. More perplexing was the decision whether to take up formal political office for the first time. While I had been involved in politics and had represented numerous politicians and parties, it was quite another thing to actually enter the fray. I had only recently assumed the role of senior partner of my firm, I had a young family and my wife, unlike me, was not a political animal. Although Jenny had a deep interest in politics, she had no political ambitions either for me or for herself. Another concern was race – although we were nineteen years on from independence, I knew that the wounds of decades of racial discrimination and a ghastly war had not healed. I had fought under the RF and wondered how the Zimbabwean electorate would view that. However, against all of this was the realisation that unless we brought about change in Zimbabwe, ZANU PF would destroy the country. The economy was in ruins, corruption was rampant, we were involved in a terrible war in the DRC, and there appeared to be a cynical attempt to subvert the constitutional reform process.

I discussed the request with Jenny and we prayed about it. Although seriously concerned about the ramifications for our family, she appreciated the need for us to be involved. With my wife's support, I sought the counsel of my fellow elders in the Presbyterian church, who enthusiastically felt I should take up the offer. Finally, I broached the matter with my law partners. Remarkably, they backed my decision to go into politics, knowing full well how it would affect the firm. Not only would my leadership in the firm be lost, but they appreciated how we might also lose clients. Indeed, within months of my entry into politics, government ordered the NRZ board to terminate our century old mandate. With the endorsement of my family, church and law firm I met with Sibanda to advise him that I would take up the post.

The MDC was launched at Rufaro Stadium on 11 September 1999, the same place where Prince Charles had handed over power to Mugabe nineteen years earlier. Having been at the modest launch of the Forum Party at MacDonald Hall, I was unprepared for the massive rumbustious crowd of 20 000 workers who turned out to celebrate. An electrifying atmosphere built up as the party manifesto, flag and slogans were unveiled. I had to quickly learn the new slogans, the principal one "*chinja maitiro, guqula izenzo*" ("change your deeds") drawing roars of approval from the crowd. Then all the interim leadership was introduced, me included, culminating in Tsvangirai and Sibanda, the latter as interim party leader. For the first time I experienced the intoxicating applause of thousands of black Zimbabweans. Paradoxically, I knew that the greater the applause, the greater the hostility ZANU PF would direct towards me. I had seen first hand how ZANU PF responded to the threat posed by ZAPU, but this gathering posed a far greater threat to their hegemony. However, for all the mixed euphoric and fearful emotions raised by the launch, my first task for the MDC was banal: I was tasked with drafting the MDC constitution.

ZANU PF responded predictably to the launch. Its propaganda machine downplayed the size of the crowd and described the MDC as a small grouping of disgruntled workers and whites backed by the West. There was one intriguing reaction, though, from Mugabe himself. On 17 October he addressed a memorial service for the late ZAPU politician Sikhwili Moyo in Bulawayo. Flanked by my old friend and client Welshman Mabhena, Mugabe lambasted me while describing Gukurahundi as "regrettable".[336] Repeating his mantra first used in his 6 February national address, but reversing its order, he criticised "the Coltarts and Aurets of our society" for having the temerity to tell government what should be done for victims. For the first time, Mugabe said that government would compile a list of those affected and would "explore ways of compensating them". Admitting that the Gukurahundi had "caused a lot of suffering, some of which persists today", Mugabe said "people out to promote disunity made it appear as if the Government was not aware of the need to help those affected by the atrocities". The most intense irony was that these words were translated into isiNdebele by Mabhena, who had himself been severely tortured, had never received compensation and indeed never did prior to his death. History shows that the promised lists were never prepared, nor did Mugabe ever make any effort to compensate the victims. It was political posturing at its worst.

As the year drew to a close, the national constitutional commission became increasingly farcical. With a vast budget at its disposal, it had successfully conducted meetings country wide and recorded the views of ordinary Zimbabweans. Interestingly, these meetings revealed a remarkable consensus and understanding of constitutional issues by the public. One dominant concern was abuse of power which "resulted from too much power being placed in one person's hands".[337] An overwhelming majority insisted on a more accountable system of governance; in particular they wanted a non-executive president, an executive prime minister, who would be accountable to parliament, and a system of proportional representation which would allow greater representation of opposition parties in parliament.

Commission chair Chidyausiku delivered a draft of the constitution to Mugabe towards the end of November, who then ordered that it be changed to suit his wishes. Things finally came to a head on the morning of 29 November when Chidyausiku "railroaded and bulldozed" the adoption of a draft constitution which was "at significant variance with the expressed wishes of the population".[338] Several of the independent commissioners, including chair of the finance committee Eric Bloch, resigned in protest. Bloch accused Chidyausiku of preventing debate and of being determined to "let the draft be adopted irrespective of the will of the Commission". Bloch felt that "a magnificent opportunity for the development of a bright future for Zimbabwe (had) been destroyed".

All my worst fears were confirmed when I read the draft constitution. In a lengthy critique of the draft published on 3 December 1999, I described it as a "smoke and mirrors constitution".[339] Far from reducing the power of the executive, the latter's power was to be enlarged. Chillingly, it proposed that the president would be given explicit powers to deploy the military within Zimbabwe "in defence of Zimbabwe" without parliament's consent.[340] In the same chapter, the president was given the sole power to "determine (the military's) operational use". Even the bill of rights bore the mark of executive intervention – there was a new "right to dignity and reputation", protecting people whose reputation was "injured by an inaccurate or offensive statement" published by a newspaper.[341] We were left in little doubt that this was in reaction to the independent media's exposés of senior ZANU PF leaders, including Mugabe. There was a new clause reducing government's obligation to pay compensation for agricultural land (which was further changed later by cabinet, removing government's obligation completely if Britain would not pay compensation). I concluded that "the draft (was) a very cunning deception. It appears to provide a check on Presidential power but will not be an effective check at all. All told the President will be just as powerful. What is horrifying is that in some ways he will be more powerful in that he will have tighter control over Parliament and better defined powers to use the military within Zimbabwe."

As 1999 drew to close it was announced that a referendum to decide on the constitution would be held on 12 February 2000. While the rest of the world fretted about Y2K, and what the new millennium would ravage on their computers, those Zimbabweans yearning for a new dawn of freedom wondered how we could defeat the passage of the new constitution. I spent that New Year's Eve camping with my family in the Matobo Hills. As the new millennium dawned, on a beautiful sunny morning, I was confident we could secure a majority "no" vote. As things turned out that was the easiest task which lay ahead. Few of us appreciated then that ZANU PF's determination to remain in power would wreak far more havoc than any millennium bug ever could have done.

CHAPTER 15

STRIKE FEAR INTO THEIR HEARTS
THE 2000 REFERENDUM AND ELECTION

"The State is an instrument in the hands of the ruling class, used to break the resistance of the adversaries of that class."
— JOSEPH STALIN, 1924

Two major events loomed in the opening weeks of 2000: the constitutional referendum and the first MDC congress, and I was caught up in a flurry of activity around them. Our efforts to secure a "no" vote intensified and reached a crescendo in the run up to the 11 and 12 February vote. In the last week of January, I spoke every day, sharing platforms with Lovemore Madhuku, Bishop Pius Ncube and lawyer Brian Kagoro. As David Blair observed, it was a "fight between an elephant and a mouse".[342] The national constitutional commission used its massive budget to dominate the airwaves and government-controlled press. Their message presaged what was to come in any event after the referendum – it was promised that a "yes" vote would see white farmers lose their land. The NCA campaign, in contrast, was poorly funded and faced obstacles at every turn. The ZBC refused to air NCA television adverts until compelled to do so by a High Court order.

In the midst of the campaign, final preparations were being made for the MDC congress which was scheduled to be held at the Chitungwiza aquatic centre on the weekend of 29 and 30 January. The question regarding who was going to lead the MDC dominated discussions. Gibson Sibanda, the interim leader and president of ZCTU, had broad appeal and impeccable credentials, having been detained by both the RF and ZANU PF in the 1970s and '80s. However, he was Ndebele, and the fear was that this would count against him in a country that was predominately Shona. In addition, although a strong leader, Sibanda was a quiet, reserved man; he did not have Morgan Tsvangirai's charisma. Many in Bulawayo argued that the MDC needed to move on from ethnic considerations, but eventually a consensus emerged that the election would be hard enough to win and that it would be easier to mobilise Ndebele support for Tsvangirai than Shona support for Sibanda. In the week before the congress that consensus was relayed to Tsvangirai by Paul Themba Nyathi; Sibanda indicated that he would not contest the presidency and was happy to deputise Tsvangirai. My admiration for Sibanda grew. He could have demanded that a natural progression be followed, but he willingly stood down in the national interest. It was one of many selfless decisions Sibanda would take.

I didn't make the first day of the congress because I had already committed to speaking to the Evangelical Fellowship of Zimbabwe about why evangelical Christians should vote "no" in the referendum. All the key votes for positions took place that day and part of the method in my madness (i.e. about missing that day) was to put down a fleece. I was still unsure about whether I should seek political office and so was content to be excluded from the MDC's national executive. As it turned out a remarkable consensus emerged amongst the 14 000 delegates that first day: Tsvangirai and Sibanda's leadership positions were unanimously endorsed by all the provinces and a superb national balance in the top leadership was agreed to. Ndebele leaders Welshman Ncube and Fletcher Dulini Ncube secured the key secretary general and treasurer positions. Their election was balanced by the election of Shona leaders, former ZCTU vice-president Isaac Matongo, as chairman, and fellow trade unionist Gift Chimanikire, as deputy secretary general. Nyathi was elected director of elections, a job he had last performed for ZAPU in the 1980 elections.

When I arrived at Chitungwiza early the next morning, I was advised that I had already been elected to the national executive[343] but would have to be introduced to the delegates. The hall was packed to the rafters by a massive, boisterous crowd which erupted as I came on to the stage. With my heart in my mouth, I bellowed the MDC slogans and thanked the crowd for electing me; far from being swept away by the euphoria, however, I felt a deep dread about what lay ahead. We were entering wild, unchartered territory and I knew the nature of the beast we would have to confront. ZANU PF would use every possible means to destroy us.

Our first political test came quickly in the form of the constitutional referendum, which was held over the weekend of 12 and 13 February. In the two weeks following the MDC congress all our energies were focused on securing a "no" vote and I addressed several more meetings in Bulawayo. It became increasingly clear that the referendum was going to be more a test of public confidence in the government than on the constitution itself. The draft constitution was a complex document, and both the "yes" and "no" campaigns were relatively superficial, which made it difficult for lay people to make informed decisions on its merits. Only a tiny minority were able to attend meetings where the merits of the proposed constitution were debated. The ZBC had refused to allow debates to be broadcast and most of what came across the airwaves were one-sided political messages directing people to vote "yes". I had been tasked with monitoring the vote in Bulawayo and as I drove around the city on the Saturday morning there was a surreal calmness. Although the turnout was quite high in the constituency (I had focused most of my time on Bulawayo South), reports came in of a low poll elsewhere which made me fear that apathy would win the day.

When counting began after the polls closed on Sunday evening it was immediately clear in Bulawayo South that the "no" vote was overwhelming. Not only had more people turned out there to vote "no" than anywhere else in the country (17 961) but it was also the second highest margin against the proposed constitution (80.7%). The next day as results came in a pattern emerged – there had been a relatively large turnout in urban areas, with crushing victories, in excess of 70%, for the "no" campaign, and low turnouts in most rural areas, with marginal majorities for the "yes" campaign. Finally, on Tuesday, 15 February, the registrar of elections, Tobaiwa Mudede, glumly announced the final result: 578 210 people had voted "yes" and 697 754 had voted "no", with 54.7% of those who voted rejecting the constitution. The overall turnout of 1 312 738 was, however, very low. Bulawayo, Harare, Mutare, Gweru and Kwe Kwe had delivered a damning defeat for Mugabe; substantial majorities in Matabeleland North, South and Manicaland provinces had also voted "no". Indeed the only province that delivered a substantial "yes" vote was Mashonaland Central.

I had to pinch myself. I was incredulous that ZANU PF had finally allowed a free vote, and I waited with bated breath for Mugabe to respond, which he did that evening in a national broadcast. Mugabe did not spew out vitriol this time. Rather he was calm and deliberate. He told us that "Government accepts the result and respects the will of the people" and concluded saying, "The world now knows Zimbabwe as a country where opposing views and opinions can be found alongside each other peacefully. Let us all, winners and losers, accept the referendum verdict and start planning our way for the future."

Several supporters and friends had joined me at home to celebrate and after watching the broadcast they asked me what I thought. I didn't believe for a moment that Mugabe had changed and that ZANU PF would take the loss lying down. The key was in his final phrase – how would ZANU PF start "planning (their) way for the future"? Although the referendum victory gave the MDC superb momentum in the run up to the election, with hindsight it was a critically important wake-up call for ZANU PF, which in turn enabled it to devise a violent strategy that would ensure that it would not lose the coming election.

The real ZANU PF response to the referendum result came the very next day, Wednesday, 16 February when "war veterans" invaded Dothan farm in Masvingo province. Their leader, Eston Mupandi, made the connection to the referendum, telling journalists "those who voted 'no' do not need the land. We will invade the farms until we have enough land. This is war and we have started another phase of the liberation struggle."[344] The day after this invasion was reported in the press Mugabe was interviewed on the eve of his 76th birthday and was now far more menacing than he had been only a few days before, warning that "nobody should rejoice" over the defeat the Government had suffered. He then announced that the constitution would still be changed by inserting the land seizure clause. "We will take the land, make no mistake about that," he said. Then came the chilling message: "The people are angry and if we let the people vent their anger they will invade the farms."

Mugabe's message was contradictory, making clear on the one hand that government would take land, and yet suggesting somehow that this was a people-driven movement. Any doubts about whether this was a grassroots-driven exercise were removed in the days following Mugabe's statement. Within a week invasions commenced across the country. The invaders were transported to farms in Government District Development Fund vehicles and Police Land Rovers. By the end of February, some

70 farms were occupied with the number of new invasions increasing daily. Then came the news that Dr Chenjerai Hitler Hunzvi had been placed in charge of the invasions with a substantial budget at his disposal. "War veterans" (described as such despite the majority of those moving onto farms being far too young to have ever been guerrillas) were being supplied with food from government vehicles and were being paid a daily rate. Hunzvi, for his part, started to travel the length and breadth of the country, employing inflammatory anti-white racist rhetoric, while the police stood idly by.

Curiously, despite this rhetoric, and the threats directed by the invaders against white farmers, there were few efforts made to physically force whites off their land. A common pattern emerged country wide: farmers could lessen the fervour of the threats by signing scraps of paper agreeing to relinquish their land; the "war veterans" would then set up camp on the farm and turn their attention to what, as became increasingly apparent, was their real target – the farm workers. ZANU PF had done its homework in analysing the results. The body of some 500 000 farm workers constituted a crucial swing vote which would determine the election result. There was little they could do about the urban electorate and those from Matabeleland, and to a lesser extent Manicaland, who would vote against ZANU PF come hell or high water. Likewise the referendum results showed that their support in communal areas outside Matabeleland and Manicaland was still sufficiently solid. What had swung the referendum against them was the block of commercial farm workers living predominantly on the labour-intensive tobacco and horticultural farms in the Mashonaland, Masvingo and Midlands provinces who had voted "no". White farmers had greatly assisted the "no" vote by encouraging their labour to vote "no" and by transporting them to the polls. In addition, many white farmers started funding the MDC, demonstrating to ZANU PF that this block would vote against them in the election. Some farmers went to the extent of taking leadership positions in rural structures of the MDC. In doing so white farmers, as a block, became associated with opposition politics in the mind of ZANU PF. Reports started to flood in of a systematic campaign to "re-educate" farm workers. Farm workers' villages were invaded at night and hundreds were assaulted. Known MDC activists were identified and dealt with severely. ZANU PF's intention was clear – they needed to break the back of MDC support on these farms and disrupt the MDC's organisational structures on them. If ZANU PF could claw back this vote, they would be able to reverse the 5 per cent majority which secured the "no" vote.

The expectation in the country was that the elections would be held in April. The last general election had ended on 9 April 1995, and before that on 30 March 1990. Section 63(4) of the then Zimbabwe constitution stated that parliament automatically dissolved within five years of its commencement, and the assumption because of this was that the election would be held before the end of April 2000. The Electoral Act also required the president to give notice of the dissolution of parliament; in 1995 Mugabe had issued his proclamation on 27 February, dissolving parliament on 7 April and scheduling the elections for 8 and 9 April. He had acted similarly in 1990, and so the expectation was that by mid March 2000, Mugabe would issue a proclamation setting the electoral process in motion.

Weeks dragged by and still there was no sign of a proclamation. All the while the numbers of farms being invaded increased, as did the intimidation of farm workers. ZANU PF had obviously decided that they needed more time to soften up the electorate.

In the absence of an election date the MDC started campaigning and preparing for the election. On the weekend of 11 and 12 March, Tsvangirai, Welshman Ncube and I travelled to South Africa to rally support among the huge expatriate Zimbabwean community there. We spoke at rallies in Soweto and Sandton where we urged Zimbabweans to return home to vote and to use their financial muscle to back the MDC. With the benefit of hindsight it was probably a mistake to have included me in the delegation. ZANU PF's propaganda line was that the MDC was the brainchild of white farmers and the British. My presence would have undoubtedly buttressed that line in the minds of some, especially among African politicians outside of Zimbabwe who would have had no knowledge about me. That fear didn't cross the minds of Tsvangirai or Ncube at the time, because they weren't racist and knew the genesis of the MDC.

I returned to the news that I would be standing in Bulawayo South constituency. Originally, my home was in this constituency, but it was subsequently gerrymandered to exclude my home and a block of middle-class suburbs by shifting the boundaries west to include entirely black working-class suburbs. The result of the redrawing of the boundaries had the effect of transforming the original constituency from one that was overwhelmingly middle class to one that was approximately 60/40 per cent working class/middle class. The final racial composition was approximately 90 per cent black with the remaining 10 per cent white, coloured and Asian.[345] ZANU PF presumably thought that black working-class people would never vote for me.

My selection was immediately criticised by the president of a ZANU PF-aligned group, the Affirmative Action Group (AAG), Matson Hlahlo, who "castigated the choice of a white man" to stand in Bulawayo South. He also asked an all-black audience in Nketa, a working-class suburb of Bulawayo South: "… are you the type of people who can be represented by a white man?"[346]

Despite this rhetoric things remained calm in Bulawayo and most urban areas, but not so in Zimbabwe's commercial farming districts. At the beginning of March, Dabengwa, then minister of Home Affairs in charge of the police, issued a statement recognising "that farm owners enjoy as much right to protection as any other citizens" and declared that he had "decided to instruct war veterans to withdraw from farms with immediate effect".[347] Hunzvi, one of Dabengwa's lowly juniors in ZIPRA, who had never seen action, immediately countered him. He held his own press conference to announce that invasions would continue. Mugabe himself appeared on ZTV that night, backing Hunzvi and in the process humiliating Dabengwa, announcing they would "not put a stop to the invasions" which he claimed were "a peaceful and lawful demonstration by ex-combatants".[348] That set the seal on the matter and invasions rapidly increased in the ensuing days, rising to 450 farms by 12 March, including for the first time some in Matabeleland. The Commercial Farmers Union (CFU), desperate to help its members, took the matter to court and on 17 March obtained an order from Judge Paddington Garwe declaring "every occupation unlawful" and ordering all persons who had "taken up occupation" to "vacate within 24 hours". The order was made with the consent of both Hunzvi and Augustine Chihuri, the commissioner of Police, who had been joined as respondents. Both then wilfully proceeded to ignore the judgment, and by 21 March the number of invaded farms had leapt to 742. It marked the beginning of a long battle fought in the courts by farmers who obtained judgments which were rarely honoured. Any semblance of the rule of law disappeared in Zimbabwe from this time.

I addressed my first campaign meeting at Nketa Hall on Sunday morning, 26 March 2000. Nketa is a typical Bulawayo working-class township – rows and rows of dusty streets with small but neat detached bungalows surrounded by vegetable gardens and durawalls. Nketa Hall is a community centre which adjoins the ubiquitous football fields found throughout the townships. I was unsure as to what reception I would receive or even how many people would be present and so was pleasantly surprised to find the hall full to overflowing. Although in my capacity as director of BLPC I had spent time in working-class suburbs developing our advice centres there, I had never before addressed a public political meeting, aside from Sidney Malunga's Makokoba meeting in 1991. I was acutely aware of my inability to speak either chiShona or isiNdebele fluently. Although I had studied Shona at university, I had an academic, not practical or conversational, knowledge of the language. Furthermore I had never been a good linguist and all court proceedings in Zimbabwe were in English. I feared my lack of fluency would be a massive handicap, but in this meeting I had no cause to. On arrival I was greeted by Patrick Nabanyama, a former ZAPU stalwart, who had joined ZANU PF on the unification of the two parties but had now crossed the floor to the MDC. Nabanyama was a slight man, short and slim; he had a ready grin and an engaging manner. Using his great sense of humour he got the crowd in a good mood before introducing me, detailing the work I had done for the BLPC and ZAPU. Nketa Hall is near the Botswana road and so I spoke about the difference between Botswana and Zimbabwe, pointing out that Botswana used to be Zimbabwe's poor cousin but now Zimbabweans went there for employment and to shop. The reason for our differing fortunes was because Botswana didn't concentrate too much power in a single individual, respected the rule of law, and tackled corruption. I apologised for my inability to speak isiNdebele or chiShona but asked them to consider my track record. During question time I was asked about how the MDC would respond to the threats of war that had been made by war veterans. I called for people to be courageous, but stressed that a commitment to non-violence was essential, at which a murmur of approval rippled through the crowd. It was a modest start but the warmth of the crowd was palpable and at the end I was overwhelmed by the swell of people who gathered around me to tell me how much they appreciated me standing. A few of my white friends had come along in support and they, too, were amazed by the friendliness of the crowd. If this was to be the tenor of the campaign, it would be a breeze!

The reality of opposition politics in Zimbabwe struck home the very next day when the first MDC supporter was murdered by ZANU PF thugs. Edwin Gomo, aged only sixteen, was killed on 27 March near Bindura. He died while travelling to an MDC rally after being hit on the head by a stone thrown by a ZANU PF mob. The day after that another MDC supporter, Robert Musoni, was murdered – also in Bindura. The police did nothing to bring the culprits to book, even though both victims were murdered in broad daylight. In response to the growing incidences of violence around the country, the NCA organised a "March for Peace" in central Harare on Saturday, 1 April. Although the police had initially refused to allow the march, necessitating a court order compelling them, the 1 500 marchers were pleasantly surprised when riot police allowed them to form up and march that morning and a carnival atmosphere developed. This came to an abrupt end when several hundred "war veterans", armed with pick-axe handles, iron bars, sticks and clubs, were allowed past riot police to attack the marchers, who included elderly people, priests and nuns. Hundreds of people were injured, some seriously, in full view of the police. Not a single "war veteran" was arrested, despite video evidence captured by journalist Edwina Spicer showing the mob arming themselves and leaving the ZANU PF headquarters. When challenged about the attacks, the Information minister, Chen Chimutengwende, said that the veterans had been provoked and were "incensed". Such a brazen demonstration of brutality in the middle of Harare gave unlimited licence to Hunzvi and all those perpetrating violence. Increasingly brutal assaults were meted out and, for the first time, white farmers themselves were targeted in addition to their workers.

On Sunday, 2 April, a liberal white farmer, Iain Kay, was surrounded by invaders on his farm Chipeza near Hwedza, east of Harare. Kay's father Jock had been an independent in the 1985 election, opposed to Smith's CAZ party, and his wife Kerry was renowned in the community for her work combatting AIDS. Kay himself was someone fluent in chiShona and he had a good relationship with his workers and surrounding communities. This all meant nothing now, and Kay was almost clubbed to death by ZANU PF thugs armed with axe handles and fan-belts tied to sticks. The mob was distracted by the approach of Kay's son, which allowed Kay to flee by diving into a dam and swimming across to safety. He was rushed to hospital in Marondera, severely injured, with deep lacerations on his back and face. The local police, including a Constable Finashe Chikwenya, acting on an old-fashioned principle, namely, that crime was crime, irrespective of who committed it, arrested three of those responsible for Kay's attack. The invaders had the last laugh, however. The very next day Chikwenya was back on Chipeza farm where he was ambushed by other thugs, who stole his pistol and shot him dead. None of those responsible for Chikwenya's murder was arrested and those who were already under arrest for Kay's assault were released. The message was clear – there would be complete impunity for those doing ZANU PF's bidding. Even the police were now subordinate.

If there was any doubt about the complete and absolute licence given to "war veterans", it was dispelled by Mugabe himself at a rally he addressed in Bindura on 7 April. Repeating that government would not remove "those who invaded farms", Mugabe turned his attention to whites. Speaking about how whites were "campaigning for money through the internet for the MDC", he asked whether they were "determined to fight against Mugabe and his Government?"[349] and declared "the fight to be on". Turning his attention to Tsvangirai, he called him a "puppet and traitor" and then, incredibly, blamed Tsvangirai for the violence, menacingly warning: "Tsvangirai is inviting fire for himself and it burns you."

In the week that followed, there was a strange interregnum of Mugabe's policy. Firstly, on 10 April the attorney general, Patrick Chinamasa, appeared in court on behalf of the Police to argue that Garwe's 17 March order directing the eviction of all invaders was impossible to enforce because of a lack of resources. It was an argument founded on the propaganda line that these were spontaneous demonstrations. Advocate Adrian de Bourbon, representing the CFU, asked Chinamasa: "Why can't the same official transport that took the invaders to the farms be used to take them out again?" The presiding judge, Moses Chinhengo, dismissed Chinamasa's application, confirming that the farm invasions were illegal and that the ZRP had "a public duty to enforce" the law of Zimbabwe. It was an intriguing application – a futile attempt to give some respectability to lawlessness.

Then the following day cabinet met in the absence of Mugabe, who had flown to Cuba to attend the South Summit in Havana. Joseph Msika, the new former ZAPU vice-president who had replaced Joshua Nkomo, chaired the meeting, which resolved to send three ministers – Dabengwa, John Nkomo and Sydney Sekeramayi – on a tour of invaded farms.

Their purpose was to "talk to the war veterans on the need to end the invasions". On 13 April, Msika held a press conference, confirming this cabinet decision, in which he announced "it was no longer necessary to continue with these demonstrations".[350]

Other forces, however, were at work because the tour never took place and within days the battle took a further ugly turn. A few weeks earlier, the MDC national executive had resolved that Tsvangirai should contest Buhera North, a seat near his rural home. I had unsuccessfully argued that Tsvangirai should rather contest a safe (both politically and physically) seat in Harare, but a majority felt that it was more important to convey a confidence-building message by taking on ZANU PF in the rural areas.

On the morning of 15 April, a Saturday, three MDC activists, Sanderson Makombe, Talent Mabika and Tichaona Chiminya (who was also Tsvangirai's personal driver), were driving to Murambinda, a town in the centre of Buhera North, when their vehicle was overtaken and forced to a halt by another vehicle with "ZANU PF Manicaland Province" stencilled on its side. Makombe, who was sitting in the back, was able to flee, but Mabika and Chiminya were trapped in the vehicle. They were beaten and then had petrol poured over them and were set alight. With the two left aflame and writhing in pain, the assailants, led by CIO operative Joseph Mwale and the ZANU PF MP candidate's election agents,[351] drove off. Makombe rushed out of his hiding place to rescue them but Chiminya was already dead; Mabika died in hospital a few hours later. Although the police were provided with Mabika's eye-witness evidence, Mwale was never prosecuted for this heinous crime.

At the same time this was happening, about 100 kilometres north of Murambinda in Macheke, another message was being sent to white farmers who supported the MDC. David Stevens, who farmed tobacco at his Arizona farm, made no secret of his support for the MDC, unlike many farmers who quietly did so but never let on. A huge crowd of invaders arrived at Stevens's farm gate that morning in high dudgeon. The previous day they had assaulted some of Stevens's workers who had had the gall to retaliate and it was time for revenge. Stevens came to his gate where he tried to negotiate, but within moments he was pounced upon and thrown into his own Land Rover. A convoy formed which roared off with Stevens bound within. Stevens had earlier called for help from neighbours and five of them saw him being driven past. They gave chase and ended up in another small village, Murewa, where they saw the Land Rover parked outside the local war veterans' office. Having been shot at as they approached, they drove to the police station nearby to report the matter and seek help. The police wouldn't intervene and even when a gang of ZANU PF supporters arrived at the station and hauled the men out "with constant assurances (they) were going to be killed", the police did nothing. Stevens's neighbours were then split up – with one taken to the war veterans' office and the rest to the ZANU PF offices. Stevens was at the war veterans' office where he was "beaten over and over again" and finally shot dead. All the rest were severely beaten at the various locations they were taken to. Eventually, one group was bound by wire, blindfolded and driven out of Murewa. At one point the vehicle stopped and "a heavy object was thrown on top of them". It was David Stevens's body. All the survivors and Stevens's body were eventually dumped. Some succeeded in walking to safety on their own; others were found by search teams. No effort was made by their assailants to hide Stevens's body – it seemed part of their plan to parade his utterly battered corpse to the world. It was designed to send a chilling message to every farmer in the country regarding what would happen if their support for the MDC continued. The press unwittingly did ZANU PF's job for them as horrific images of the brutalised men were posted on the internet.

Early on the following morning, as the full horror of the Macheke abductions emerged, Mugabe flew into Harare International airport on his return from Cuba. He was met by a large cheering crowd of ZANU PF supporters, cabinet ministers and Hunzvi. The minister in charge of the CIO, who must by then have been fully briefed on the Stevens murder, Sekeramayi, spoke first, blaming the MDC for the violence. He concluded before handing over to Mugabe: "The MDC have slapped a lion in the face and they will be devoured."[352] Mugabe took the rostrum and immediately made it clear that Vice-President Msika had acted without his consent – he would not order the "war veterans" off the land. He repeated his warning to white farmers, first mentioned the previous week at Bindura, as well as his previous mantras: the MDC had started the violence and ZANU PF supporters should "defend themselves". He was utterly contemptuous of the High Court, dismissing the "little law of trespass". Drawing laughter from the crowd, he parodied Jesus' injunction to turn the other cheek by saying, "Some say, you must turn the other cheek, but I have only two cheeks: after I have turned both, which one do I turn?" The speech dispelled any doubt that Dabengwa and Msika's efforts to moderate the chaos and violence were an aberration. Hunzvi and the security apparatus apparatchiks gathered by now knew they had a clear mandate to continue their murderous programme.

Bulawayo and the south of the country in general had not experienced the terror of Mashonaland, and our hope was that we would avoid it because of the relative moderation of former ZAPU leaders who were now in cabinet. That hope was shattered in the early hours of Zimbabwe's 20th Independence anniversary when word came through of an attack on a client of mine, Martin Olds, who farmed in Nyamandlovu not far from Bulawayo. The first I heard was when Nigel Yates,[353] another farming client of mine, arrived at my home, greatly distressed, early on Tuesday, 18 April. Olds's wife had contacted him to tell him that a large group of armed men in a convoy of vehicles had driven down to Olds's Compensation farm. When they arrived at the farm, Olds thought they were the usual invaders come to make noise and he went out to speak to them. What he didn't realise was that this group was operating with military precision. Along with the group of invaders were some 20 men in concealed positions armed with AK-47 rifles. As Olds got to the gate he was shot in the leg. Badly wounded, he managed to get back to the house where, at 6 am he phoned his wife and sent out a distress call on radio ("I've been shot and need an ambulance"), before firing back. His neighbours immediately called an ambulance from Bulawayo and reported the gunfight to the police, which could now be heard – Nyamandlovu police station is only a few kilometres from Compensation farm. The police made no attempt to help; on the contrary they threw up road-blocks across all routes between Nyamandlovu and Bulawayo. Even the ambulance called from Bulawayo was turned back.

It was with this news that Yates came to me for advice. He wanted to mobilise a group of men to go in to save Olds. While deeply sympathetic to the need to save Olds, I expressed my fear that, aside from it being too late to save the man, this was a trap designed to escalate the crisis. If farmers reacted en masse, this would provide ZANU PF with an excuse to widen their attacks on white farmers and Mugabe with "evidence" that the MDC and farmers were indeed provoking violence. Yates was appalled by the thought of abandoning a fellow farmer and felt that he must at least try to save Olds – but he didn't get further than the police road-block.

As the morning wore on a clearer picture emerged of what had happened. Shortly after the gunfire stopped, the convoy of thirteen trucks carrying the attackers drove back through the police road-blocks, which they were let through without hindrance. In fact they were so brazen that they stopped at a bottle-store in Nyamandlovu to noisily celebrate their kill. Only then were Olds's neighbours and friends allowed back to the farm, where they found a terrible sight. Olds had put up a courageous fight against his attackers. It was apparent they were highly trained – they had fired AK-47s from several carefully prepared firing points strung around the house. Olds only had a shotgun and 9mm pistol, but despite the massive disparity in fire power he held out for about half an hour. This had been the gunfight that could be heard by his neighbours. Petrol bombs made in beer bottles were then thrown into the house, causing an inferno; they literally smoked Olds out and the mob then surrounded him, shooting him over and over again and hacking him with knives and axes, leaving his battered body lying outside his home.

Curiously, the police made no attempt to prevent the press from going in and soon graphic pictures of Olds were published. In Stevens's murder it could be argued that the crime had been committed by civilians on a frolic of their own. Olds's murder pointed to state action. Although all the assailants were dressed in civilian clothes, they had used military weapons and acted with military planning and discipline. The attack was also carefully coordinated. The police knew to prevent help getting to Olds and to allow the murderers to leave.

Once again there was a cursory investigation with no follow up for a crime committed in broad daylight within earshot of a police station. The gratuitous violence and truly shocking state of Olds's body was designed to send a fearsome message to farmers in the south, as had been the intention with Stevens's murder in the north. Why they chose to make an example of Olds is not entirely clear. What is clear is that Olds knew his life was under threat. The weekend before he was murdered, he had asked his wife Kathy to make a note of a police report number – he had received an anonymous death threat which he had reported to Nyamandlovu police.[354] Olds had told his wife who he suspected was behind the threat: a local politician with whom he had clashed on many occasions. Olds was someone who spoke his mind and when this politician came to his butchery a few weeks before asking to put up posters, Olds replied that that would be fine so long as he could also put up MDC posters in the candidate's store. Most farmers would not have disclosed their political affiliations, but Olds had no such qualms. He was by nature a courageous man. Ironically, ten years before to the day, on Independence Day 1990, he had been decorated with Zimbabwe's Bronze Cross by Mugabe for bravely saving a friend from the jaws of a crocodile.

Just a few hours after Olds was murdered, Mugabe gave an interview to the ZBC's Reuben Barwe which was later televised. As he had done at the airport the previous Sunday, but now on a much larger stage, Mugabe removed any doubt about what was happening or who was responsible. Turning to farmers, he said:

"For them to have banded together to a man in opposition to government, to have gone much farther in mobilising their labour forces on the farms, to support the one position opposed to government, has exposed them as not our friends, but our enemies. Our present state of mind is – you are now our enemies, because you have behaved as enemies of Zimbabwe and we are full of anger."[355]

That night I was asked to address a gathering of anxious farmers at a Bulawayo restaurant. Unfortunately, there was little I could say to encourage them because there was no one they could turn to for help. The police were looking the other way and any attempt to defend themselves would provide just the pretext Mugabe needed to train more violence their way. All I could do was remind them that until democracy was rooted in Zimbabwe they would always be held to ransom; to that extent we all had no choice but to soldier on.

With violence breaking out all over the land, I found that I couldn't focus on my own campaign, but needed to speak in fragile communities who were terrified by what was happening around them. This commitment took me out of my constituency to towns across the country – to Chiredzi, Gweru and Chipinge, among others. Many communities beyond Matabeleland were bewildered. They had never experienced or even knew much about the Gukurahundi and so had not seen that side of ZANU PF since the war. Somewhat paradoxically, my standard message was one of hope. Although I warned we had "a long, hard and rocky road to travel on",[356] I reminded people that in the euphoria following the referendum I had warned that ZANU PF would fight dirty. In fact, the principal reason ZANU PF was resorting to violence was confirmation that they feared losing. I said that the level of violence would increase in direct proportion to their fear. Martin Luther King's speeches inspired me as ever and I reminded my audiences of his injunction: "When evil men plot, good men must plan. When evil men burn and bomb, good men must build and bind. Where evil men would seek to perpetuate an unjust status quo, good men must seek to bring into being a real order of justice."

As I gave these speeches, there were the first rumours of threats planned against me and in response a group of friends volunteered to guard me. They installed an electric fence around my home and chipped in to provide me with a security guard 24/7. At the same time our entire family life changed and we all, even our children, had to follow rigid new disciplines. Assuming that all my calls were monitored, we learnt never to discuss travel plans on the phone. Jenny and I would speak in code; it was almost impossible for friends to decipher our gobbledygook. Jenny developed new daily routines, including evacuation packs for each of the children containing essential clothing, toothbrushes and chocolate bars. For me she prepared a "detention pack". This included warm clothing and prison "currency" – cigarettes, matches and chocolate. Where possible I would not travel at night and I also started changing cars so that there was no predictability in our movements. A bullet-proof vest was bought for me, which I started wearing, under my shirt, at all public events. At this time we even changed our church. We had worshipped at the Bulawayo Presbyterian church in the centre of the city since returning to Zimbabwe in 1983, but my security team felt that the routine of going there at 9 am every Sunday was dangerous. So we moved to another church closer to home, Whitestone Chapel, which was a much shorter route in more familiar territory.

Across the country, ZANU PF thugs rampaged and in early May they started targeting MDC candidates. The first, on 2 May, was Bindura MDC candidate Elliot Pfebve, whose rural village was attacked by ZANU PF thugs wielding axes, iron bars and pangas. Pfebve was away campaigning so they abducted five men, including his father and brother Matthew; both were severely beaten and Matthew died. This was followed on 9 May by an attempt to murder Blessing Chebundo, the MDC candidate for Kwe Kwe who was standing against Mnangagwa. Chebundo was surrounded at a bus stop by five men who poured petrol over him and attempted to set him alight. He was only saved by the match failing; he then had the presence of mind to grab one of his assailants, shouting out that if they burnt him their comrade would burn as well. Despite his bravery that day, ZANU PF did not give up and a week later a 50-strong gang threw petrol bombs in his house, razing it to the ground. On 10 May ZANU PF supporters arrived at MDC Chimanimani constituency candidate Roy Bennett's home, forcing his pregnant wife and workers to chant slogans. Bennett had been a ZANU PF member, but had recently joined the MDC and agreed to be their candidate. Bennett was forced off his farm and his wife Heather was so badly roughed up that she tragically suffered a miscarriage. Like Pfebve, Bennett was fortunate not to have been at home as he would otherwise, in all likelihood, have been murdered.[357] By mid May neutral human rights organisations estimated conservatively that the violence engulfing the country had resulted in 19 murders, 1 012 assaults and 8 rapes, almost all clearly committed by ZANU PF supporters, or "war veterans".[358]

Although Mugabe had launched ZANU PF's manifesto on 3 May, a date for the election had still not been announced. It appeared as if ZANU PF thought they had still not softened up the electorate sufficiently.

We felt defenceless. As legal secretary of the MDC there was nothing I could do to protect our candidates and supporters. The international community appeared paralysed and although I had a stream of concerned diplomats calling on me, there was little they could offer. We had taken some heart from an oblique attack on Mugabe by Nelson Mandela on 6 May. Addressing a UNICEF meeting in Johannesburg, Mandela criticised African leaders who "had once commanded liberation armies" but thought it "a privilege to be there for eternity".[359] However, by then Mandela was no longer president of South Africa and President Mbeki remained mute. Our hopes got up when Don McKinnon, the secretary general of the Commonwealth, arrived in Zimbabwe on 15 May; diplomats had promised that he had come to deliver a stern message to Mugabe. McKinnon was provided with detailed reports prepared by human rights organisations and the MDC, leaving him with no room to doubt the catastrophic situation. However, after two days in Harare and a meeting with Mugabe, McKinnon left us enraged. Shortly before flying out he held a joint press conference with ZANU PF Foreign minister Stan Mudenge when he astonishingly said that he believed it was "possible to have free and fair elections". This naïveté was based on his meeting with Mugabe, who "genuinely want(ed) to see violence *lessened*", with McKinnon opining that "the violence needed to go *downwards*".[360] I wanted to ask McKinnon what level of violence would be acceptable to the Commonwealth but had no opportunity to do so. The only positive thing that came out of McKinnon's trip was an announcement by Mnangagwa a few hours after he left that the election would be held on 24 and 25 June. Although the Commonwealth had turned a blind eye to ZANU PF's savagery, we now at least had a timeframe within which to work.

Of immediate concern was how to defend ourselves, especially our leaders Tsvangirai and Sibanda who were so vulnerable to attack. People within the country were fearful of openly assisting the MDC in case they themselves were targeted. But there were indications that Zimbabweans in the diaspora would assist and so I flew to Cape Town to set up a legal mechanism to receive funds. I approached my closest friend from my school days, Mark Gilmore, who was an accountant, and another good friend from university, the former anti-apartheid lawyer Matthew Walton, to set up a trust compliant with South African law. That trust has been used ever since for the promotion of democracy in Zimbabwe. Our first task was to secure funding to purchase armoured vehicles for Tsvangirai and Sibanda to travel in, so that they could campaign around the countryside. Both men were under such threat that they took their lives in their hands if they ventured out of urban areas. Two Nissan vehicles were modified in South Africa; from the outside they appeared to be regular twin cabs but they had bullet-proof glass and armour plating which would see them through small arms fire. There were no reports of any harsher weapons, such as rockets, being used and our calculation was that ZANU PF would maintain the pretence that the attacks were spontaneous civilian protests, not state-organised ones.

While the MDC was effectively prevented from campaigning in wide swathes of the rural areas, it was difficult for ZANU PF thugs to mobilise within cities and towns, especially Bulawayo. I decided, however, that I would restrict the number of public meetings I had and concentrate on small house meetings. Given that the majority of voters were in the high density suburbs of Nketa, Nkulumane and Emganwini, I focused most of my time there, which meant that I would have to have meetings in the small houses of relatively poor working-class people. So began a series of almost clandestine meetings. Using a variety of subterfuges, we would arrange with our local structures to meet in peoples' homes, usually at night after work. Patrick Nabanyama had brought the entire ZANU PF structures across with him which meant that there were ready-made party branches to tap into. These meetings turned out to be some of the most heartwarming times I have ever experienced. I was quite overcome by the warmth of the welcome I received and it gave me a new appreciation of how wonderfully hospitable black Zimbabweans are. By the end of May, after several of these sessions, I was quietly confident that my race would not be a factor in the election.

ZANU PF must have had the same intelligence, because on 28 May I learnt of a new ruse they had decided to employ. The Bulawayo *Sunday News* carried a front page story that day entitled "Coltart not eligible for polls?" The opening paragraph stated that I would not be eligible for public office as I still held British citizenship.[361] The paper, obviously with inside "knowledge", informed the public that those who had not renounced their British citizenship automatically lost their Zimbabwean citizenship, the inference being that I was one of those. It was indeed true that I had never renounced my British citizenship (originally acquired by virtue of my father's birth in Scotland) in terms of Zimbabwean law, but what the registrar general didn't know was that I had anticipated this years before, in 1991, and had renounced my British citizenship in terms of British law, so I had nothing to renounce when the Zimbabwean law came into effect.

Nomination day was 2 June, and when I arrived at the nomination court to submit my papers to stand in Bulawayo South the local registrar triumphantly announced that my papers would be rejected because I was not a citizen. Fortunately, the *Sunday News* article had forewarned me and I had come armed with all the original papers I needed, but particularly the blue declaration of renunciation of British citizenship that I had submitted to the British Home Office in June 1991. The production of the document took the registrar by surprise and his jaw dropped as he studied the document. I was asked to accompany him to his office where he phoned the registrar general Tobaiwa Mudede. I was of course only party to one side of the conversation, which went like this: "Sir, I have Mr Coltart in my office – when he submitted his nomination papers he produced a British Form RN1 which appears to show that he renounced his British citizenship in 1991." He then paused as Mudede spoke back and as he did so he turned it over, holding it up to the light saying, "No – it appears to be the original and it is stamped on both sides by the Home Office and British passport registry." He then described the document in detail to Mudede – what colour it was, exactly what was written on it and who it was issued by. Eventually, he said, "Yes, sir", put the phone down and turned to me to tell me that his office had not been aware of my renunciation and that I would be able to stand for election after all. I went outside where my campaign team was waiting anxiously. When I told them that I would be standing after all they burst out into ululations. Remarkably, despite the fact that numerous rural constituencies were no-go areas for the MDC, we managed to nominate candidates in all 120 constituencies.

The final few weeks of the campaign were a blur of meetings. We tried to lighten the mood and organised what we called "showboats" – a cavalcade of brightly coloured trucks and cars festooned with Zimbabwe flags and MDC paraphernalia. We all clambered aboard the open-backed trucks and drove around Bulawayo South, and the city centre, with music blaring, stopping every so often to have impromptu meetings at shopping centres or wherever people were gathered. These displays must have sent shivers running down ZANU PF's back, because the response we got from people was overwhelming, even joyous. The MDC used the friendly open-handed symbol and people responded without having the fear which accompanied attending political meetings, vigorously waving back at us. Inevitably, in the final weeks my focus was on Bulawayo South alone and it was deceptive to the extent that few of my colleagues elsewhere were able to campaign as freely as I was.

The sense of euphoria in Bulawayo reached its climax on the evening of Wednesday, 14 June when we held a meeting in Bulawayo's gracious city hall. The occasion was used to introduce all the MDC Bulawayo candidates and by 7 pm when the meeting was due to start there was an expectant, heady atmosphere. A huge crowd had packed the hall and speakers had to be set up outside to cater for the thousands who could not get in. All of us candidates lined up in an ante-room and started to walk in down the main aisle behind Gibson Sibanda, as Phil Collins's anti-apartheid anthem "Colours" began blasting out of the speakers. The words poignantly captured many of the issues Zimbabweans had to grapple with. At one point, the song diverts to an African drumbeat as it builds to a crescendo, and we organised our arrival on the stage to coincide with this moment. Collins's reminder of how life never got better for people living without their rights drew shouts of approval from the crowd. The song eventually questions arrogant leaders who, as demi gods, sit in judgment over the people, warning them that the day is soon approaching when the buck would stop with them.

Collins's lyrics were scrolled on a huge screen behind us on the stage and every time a question was asked Mugabe's portrait flashed up, causing a deafening roar in the crowd. We had asked Sir Garfield Todd to say a few words, introducing him as Zimbabwe's "oldest living freedom fighter". He joked with the crowd, telling us, "If I was 50 years younger I'd be 41, not 91, and I'd be asking you to vote for me. Instead I'm asking you to vote for the MDC." He then asked us "to think of all those who've died, of the teachers who've had to run away, of all those who've suffered in these hard times".[362] He concluded by condemning all the "evil that was taking place", describing the ZANU PF leadership as a "cabinet of jellyfish". I had a huge lump in my throat as the crowd cheered Todd off the stage and for a moment allowed myself to lapse into the dream that Todd's vision of a free, multiracial Zimbabwe was now within our grasp. I spoke after Todd, and before Gibson Sibanda, praising him: "This country has never known true freedom; we had a glimpse of it under Todd's rule, but we have since relapsed. But there comes a time when people get tired of being trampled upon by oppressors – now is that time."[363]

I flew to Harare the weekend before the elections to attend the MDC's final rally on Sunday, 18 June at Rufaro Stadium. The previous day Mugabe had held a poorly attended rally at the scene of his triumphal return to Zimbabwe in 1980, Zimbabwe Grounds. In 1980 hundreds of thousands had thronged the venue but only a few thousand turned up this time. In contrast, Rufaro was packed to the gunnels by an exuberant 45 000-strong crowd. One could be forgiven for thinking that ZANU PF were set to be swept away, but I knew that the situation was far different in the rural areas, where the majority of the seats were.

Soon after I was introduced to the crowd, I received a call from my anxious wife in Bulawayo to say that we had received a threat that thugs were on their way to burn down our home. Jenny and the children were immediately evacuated by friends. My old CBC buddy Rob Nixon followed them, quickly rummaging through the house and removing sentimental items such as photographs. As things turned out the threat did not materialise but as a precaution the family remained in a safe house until after the election.

Others were not so fortunate. At 4 pm on 19 June, some ten ZANU PF activists knocked on the door of Patrick Nabanyama's[364] home in

Nketa 6 suburb, asking for him. The child who answered the door innocently called to her father that some people had come to see him. When Nabanyama came to the door, the mood changed instantly and the men grabbed him and started pulling him out of the house. Nabanyama's wife Patricia screamed for help but was powerless to prevent the men from dragging him away and bundling him into a waiting vehicle. It was the last time she and the children saw Patrick. She did, however, recognise one of the men, as did neighbours. His name was Simon Rwodzi and he was a former ZIPRA guerrilla.[365] The previous month, on 19 May, Nabanyama had been threatened with death by a group of five war veterans. Believing that the police wouldn't do anything, he reported the matter to the press.[366] A second threat was made against Nabanyama in early June by another war veteran, Ephraim Moyo. Moyo told Nabanyama that he would "make him disappear". Nabanyama reported this threat to a Police Inspector Gwenzi on 13 June, but nothing was done, leaving him dreadfully exposed. A few days before, Nabanyama's house had been daubed with the words "MDC", undoubtedly a threat similar to the way Nazis painted yellow Stars of David on Jewish homes, but he felt there was no point reporting the matter to the police. On Sunday, 18 June, he received a threat that his house would be burnt down and so he had gone into hiding for the night, tragically deciding to go back to his home the following day, where he was found. Just hours before he was kidnapped he wrote a letter, which I still have in my possession, detailing the threats. In it he bravely stated: "… killing me will not stop the change – MDC is daily gaining support, by beating people they're de-campaigning themselves".[367]

When I received the report of Nabanyama's abduction I went to all the local police stations to make sure they had received a report of the abduction and to enquire what they were doing to find him. Nabanyama's fears about the police were justified because they didn't lift a finger to investigate the matter. Furious, I demanded that they at least give me a constable so that I could go to the homes of the former guerrillas we knew had been involved, Simon Rwodzi and Ephraim Moyo, to see if I could find Nabanyama. Reluctantly, the officer in charge allocated a constable to accompany me and we set off for their homes. It was all in vain; the men were not around and all I could do was leave messages telling them that we knew they had kidnapped Nabanyama and that justice would take its course if any harm came to him. It was a vain, pathetic threat, but all I could do. The last few days of my campaign were not spent on the hustings but searching for Nabanyama. ZANU PF's violence had come right to my doorstep.

We never saw Nabanyama again. There are various rumours about what happened to him, the most credible being that he was taken to a CIO safe house in Bulawayo where he was severely tortured and died from his injuries. Nabanyama was but one of some 37 murdered, 2 466 injured and 27 people raped in the run up to the election. Altogether 617 people were abducted and some 10 000 people displaced.[368]

We had one final closing rally for Bulawayo South at Bulawayo's Centenary Park amphitheatre on 21 June. Once again the venue was packed, only this time by a majority of white people, most of whom had not come to the rally at the city hall the week before. Most had not heard about Nabanyama's abduction and there was a sense of euphoria. Urban middle-class people in Bulawayo had little idea of what was happening in the rural areas and their presumption was that this was going to be a landslide and Mugabe was about to be swept away. I decided I needed to use the opportunity to tackle a prickly subject, namely, our collective responsibility as whites for the chaos that had befallen Zimbabwe. I spoke against racist attitudes and said the derogatory terms that some whites used to refer to blacks was as repugnant as blacks calling whites "mabhunus".[369] I spoke about the need for a truth commission which should go back to 1965 so that we, as whites, as well as blacks, could "face up to our past".[370] It wasn't what many were expecting and one of my white campaign staff contacted me the following day to complain. He told me that I was wrong to resurrect what whites had done in the 1960s and 1970s, because they were under attack now and needed support, not criticism. All I could do was reiterate the belief I expressed in the meeting – that whites were also complicit in the poison engulfing the country. We had enacted unjust laws, which caused a war and much bitterness – which was now being regurgitated by ZANU PF. I expressed my fear that if ZANU PF was removed without an understanding of how all sectors of society had to change, it could still be a false dawn.

Zimbabwean election days are usually peaceful and orderly. Ever since independence, although ZANU PF has brutalised the electorate in the run up to elections, it has always understood the need to be on its best behaviour come election day, and 24 and 25 June were no exception. These were bitter-sweet days. While there was tremendous excitement in the air, for me it was tinged with deep sadness as it increasingly seemed that Nabanyama had been murdered. I had hoped that he had just been abducted to prevent him from campaigning for me during the last few days of the election, but that hope faded as election day dawned and there was no sign of him. Most of those who were voting didn't know about Nabanyama's fate and so their enthusiasm was undiminished as I visited polling stations. They couldn't openly demonstrate where their loyalties lay but on countless occasions as I entered stations I was given coy thumbs up, winks and broad grins.

Polling stations closed on Sunday evening and counting began immediately; I decided to stay at Nketa Hall, which was both a polling station and the command centre for the entire Bulawayo constituency. I anxiously watched as the first boxes were opened but it soon became apparent that it was a landslide; ballots for the MDC and ZANU PF were separated and within minutes the MDC pile was four times the height of ZANU PF. When the count was concluded late that evening I had won with 20 781 of the 24 756 votes cast. The margin of victory, 84.7%, turned out to be one of the highest in the country, and the second highest of all seats won by the MDC. My main opponent, former ZANU PF cabinet minister Callistus Ndlovu, received 3 193 votes. Interestingly, I received a higher proportion of votes in the completely black working-class areas than I did in the middle-class areas. While there is no doubt that I benefited enormously from being on the crest of the MDC tidal wave, the margin of the win demonstrated that the people of Bulawayo South had not allowed race to be a factor. Because of the wide margin and urban location (which enabled quick collation of votes from all stations), we finished our count long before most constituencies so I went to bed that night hopeful that I would wake up to a new dawn of freedom.

CHAPTER 16

PARLIAMENTARY BATTLEGROUND
JULY 2000 TO FEBRUARY 2001

"For I have neither wit, nor words, nor worth,
Action, nor utterance, nor power of speech,
To stir men's blood; I only speak right on;
I tell you that which you yourselves do know."
– SHAKESPEARE, *JULIUS CAESAR*, ACT 3, SCENE 2

Despite our optimistic hopes of winning the election, in reality ZANU PF had stitched up their hold on power when they had amended the constitution years before. Firstly, the election was only for parliament, not president, and Mugabe's term continued until 2002. With vast powers at his disposal he could appoint his own cabinet, and control the security forces and the courts even without a majority in parliament. Secondly, Mugabe had the power to appoint 30 non-constituency members of parliament in addition to the 120 who were elected. This meant that to control parliament we would have had to win 76 seats – a landslide – and to achieve that would have to secure far more votes in the rural areas than the NCA had achieved in the referendum. Our hope was that if we obtained a majority of the elected seats in parliament, we would be able to block oppressive legislation and force ZANU PF to cooperate. At the very least our hope was that even if we were only able to win the election, but not an absolute majority in parliament, this would provide the necessary momentum to win the all important 2002 presidential election. It would also expose the fundamentally undemocratic nature of the constitution, which in effect would prevent the majority party from governing.

But it was not to be and ZANU PF's brutal campaign in key rural seats won the day for them. Although we took all the urban seats by wide margins, nearly all the Matabeleland seats, many rural seats in Midlands and Manicaland, we lost seven seats that had voted "no" in the referendum: Marondera East, Chinhoyi, Chegutu, Goromonzi, Bindura, Makoni East and Masvingo North. All of these were located in commercial farming areas and all had been subjected to extreme violence and nearly all won by ZANU PF candidates, who used inflammatory language. All were lost by small margins, some agonisingly narrow: CIO minister Sekeramayi won Marondera East, where Iain Kay had been so brutalised, by a mere 63 votes. Shadreck Chipanga, former head of the CIO, won Makoni East by 118 votes. Despite all the violence meted out, thousands of brave voters had withstood the barrage and still voted the way they wanted to. However, a sufficient number of voters buckled under pressure and as a result ZANU PF "won" the election with 62 seats against our 57 (1 seat went to ZANU Ndonga). The critical seven seat swing transformed a comfortable 65/55 majority over ZANU PF in parliament into an election "victory" for them. As the Commonwealth observer team under Nigerian former military ruler General Abdusalam Abubakar noted, "the violence which disfigured this campaign was employed systematically as part of a strategy to diminish support for the opposition parties".[371]

Although we were crestfallen about the overall result, there was still much to celebrate. The MDC controlled all the cities and major towns and numerous excellent candidates had won their seats. I was delighted that some of my fellow lawyers had won: Innocent Gonese, a former director of the Mutare Legal Projects Centre, Tendai Biti and Welshman Ncube would form a critical core of legal expertise in parliament. Some feisty human rights activists also won, notably Mike Auret, Trudy Stevenson and Paul Themba Nyathi. There were also some remarkable victories, bravely achieved in the face of terror, in particular Blessing Chebundo, who beat Mnangagwa in Kwe Kwe, and Roy Bennett, who won in Chimanimani.

One vital seat was lost, that of Buhera North, the constituency contested by Tsvangirai. The decision to have Tsvangirai stand there would prove to be a critical error. Tsvangirai would not be in parliament and as time wore on a dangerous gulf grew between him and many of the MPs, which would play a role in the split of the MDC five years later.

My immediate concern after the election was to locate Patrick Nabanyama. We had received no word about him and as the days went by my fears grew. I contacted people I knew in ZANU PF, former ZAPU clients and the church, asking them all for help. Then on 5 July I received a call from Ian Beddowes, a white ZANU PF activist, who asked for a meeting on behalf of the War Veterans Association to discuss the matter. Suspicious about their intentions, I agreed to meet at the Presbyterian church, in the presence of my pastors, Kevin Thomson and Victor Nakah, the following evening. We prepared thoroughly for the meeting and my entire security team, plus back-up, were strategically deployed around the church in case they had sinister motives. Beddowes arrived with four war veterans, but only one of them, Aleck Moyo, introduced himself. They alleged that an office used by the War Veterans Association in Nketa had been burnt; in response I said the MDC was committed to non-violence and we would support the prosecution of anyone identified as the culprit. They then told me that they were equally concerned about Nabanyama's abduction, but that they were not responsible for his disappearance. I told them that we knew that at least one ZIPRA veteran, Simon Rwodzi, had been present when Nabanyama was dragged from his home, and I found it difficult to believe that they didn't know what had happened to him. I pointed out that another veteran, Ephraim Moyo, had threatened, on 11 June, to "disappear" Nabanyama. They appeared shocked that I had this information but maintained their innocence and the meeting ended with an agreement that we all "abhorred" violence and would work together to "restore peace in Nketa".[372] To this day I don't know what they hoped to achieve in the meeting, but it showed me that they were troubled by Nabanyama's continued disappearance, a factor which was to become significant a year later.

The same day that I met with the war veterans, Tsvangirai announced a fifteen-member shadow cabinet, in which I was appointed shadow Justice and Constitutional Affairs minister. The MDC's purpose in quickly naming a small shadow cabinet was to demonstrate how Zimbabwe could be run efficiently by far fewer than the massive cabinets routinely appointed by Mugabe, whose last government had consisted of 49 members, including two vice-presidents, 20 full cabinet ministers, six ministers of state, eight provincial governors, and thirteen deputy ministers! The shadow cabinet included several of my close friends. Nyathi, Biti, Chebundo and Welshman Ncube were there, and Gibson

Sibanda was appointed leader of the opposition in parliament. We had decided that we should use parliament to grow democratic space and I was confident we had a superb team to do so.

Mugabe convened parliament on 18 July 2000. In the previous parliament, ZANU PF had secured 118 of the 120 contested seats and dominated all proceedings. We decided from the outset to use every opportunity to remind ZANU PF that they could no longer do as they chose. Although I had visited parliament as a student, I had only been as far as the visitors' gallery and so this was the first time I was able to walk through the entire building. It was virtually unchanged from Rhodesian days. The building itself is nondescript, a pitifully modest building, itself a reflection on the minor role that the legislature has played in the governance of the country for decades both pre- and post-independence. The chamber itself was barely able to squeeze in all 150 MPs; but what intrigued me most was that the decorations were virtually unchanged from Rhodesian days. The walls there were bedecked with photographs of MPs going back to Federation days, including pictures of the almost all-white RF-era parliaments. There were even some pictures of a much younger looking Queen Elizabeth. In the midst of these colonial relics we were all sworn in.

This was followed by our first contest.

ZANU PF had decided to nominate Mnangagwa as their candidate for speaker. Mnangagwa, who had suffered a humiliating loss against Blessing Chebundo in Kwe Kwe, was kept out of cabinet by Mugabe, presumably so that he had a strong, trustworthy pair of hands to take care of the unruly MDC mob in parliament. Although Mnangagwa's election as speaker was a shoo-in, we felt that it should be challenged. Accordingly, our newly appointed chief whip, Innocent Gonese, nominated a former moderate ZANU PF MP, Michael Mataure, as speaker, forcing the issue to a vote. We secured a small moral victory when the secret ballot result was returned: Mataure received 59 votes, meaning that at least one ZANU PF MP had not voted for Mnangagwa. The same process followed to elect a deputy speaker, only this time I nominated Paul Themba Nyathi, pointing out that he was "a freedom fighter whose fight for freedom and democracy did not end in 1980".[373] Predictably Nyathi lost as well but we picked up another ZANU PF vote with 60 MPs voting for him. Two days later, with all the traditional pomp and ceremony, Mugabe arrived to open parliament in a Rolls Royce.

We filed in together, with many MDC MPs alongside ZANU PF MPs who had secured their seats by violence. Mugabe had the gall to open his address by congratulating the electorate, who, he said had, in casting "their votes, shamed those who had wished for an atmosphere of violence and mayhem to mar the electoral process".[374] As he said this I wondered what Patricia Nabanyama would think, and I glanced over at Blessing Chebundo, who would have to sit under a speaker whose supporters had tried to burn him alive and had succeeded in razing his home to the ground.

Parliament began in earnest on 1 August, and the very next day we got our first taste of how democratic it would be. Tendai Biti brought a motion petitioning parliament to set up a committee to investigate the electoral violence and make recommendations about compensation for victims, legal action against perpetrators and actions to prevent recurrence. Eddison Zvobgo immediately stood up on a point of order, saying that the civil actions the MDC had brought in the High Court to challenge a variety of results in some 39 constituencies across the country made the matter *sub judice*. Mnangagwa immediately agreed and ruled the motion inadmissible, shutting Biti's protest down with the words, "You only speak if I recognise you. I have not recognised you and have made my ruling." Undeterred, Welshman Ncube leapt into the fray, using a craven ZANU PF motion praising the presidential address, to voice concern about violence, the Gukurahundi and attacks made against the judiciary by some ZANU PF MPs. It set the tone for the entire parliament.

I delivered my maiden speech on 9 August, when I moved a motion calling for parliament to agree on a process that would resuscitate constitutional reform. My critique of the existing constitution was a red rag to a bull and attracted a stream of invective from the ZANU PF benches. I commenced by suggesting that parliament's most important task was to pass into law a new democratic constitution. I ended by quoting from Martin Luther King again, and favourite passages in scripture – the true fast in Isaiah 58. Warning that we should avoid what King described as "a long and desolate night of darkness", I reminded MPs of God's promises in Isaiah: if we "loosened the chains of injustice", and "set the oppressed free", then our "light (would) break forth like the dawn and (our) healing (would) quickly appear".[375] My appeals fell on deaf ears. No sooner had I sat down than Zvobgo moved an amendment to my motion calling upon government to consider "mechanisms for making it possible to revisit the necessity for a new democratic constitution".[376] Instead of ducking the issue completely, ZANU PF's intention was to move any decision on the matter away from parliament to cabinet.

As the dust settled on the elections, information regarding serious irregularities flooded in from all over the country. Losing MDC candidates brought in evidence of rampant intimidation and other irregularities. Some ZANU PF candidates had actively participated in intimidating the electorate. In other constituencies hundreds of voters were turned away for spurious reasons. The voters' roll was in a pitiful condition and had been used to prejudice MDC candidates. There was such a consistent pattern of gross abuse of the Electoral Act that we decided to institute legal proceedings to challenge the results in 39 constituencies. As legal secretary, the organisation of these cases fell to me. Aside from clogging up the courts with the flood of cases, our action also caused extreme consternation within ZANU PF. Not only was their MPs' sense of security shattered but they were faced with the prospect of daily disclosures in open court of widespread abuse of the electoral process. ZANU PF MPs who had just been sworn in to parliament were summonsed and faced the prospect of being cross-examined in court about their nefarious activities. I worked closely with the LRF which had public interest/test case funds available to pay for the various private law firms that acted on behalf of our candidates. The LRF made no secret of the fact that it was funding the test cases, using funds provided by the US International Republican Institute.[377] It was at this time that ZANU PF got wind of a move by the US Congress to introduce a new "Zimbabwe Democracy Bill", which proposed the application of sanctions for the first time and more support for institutions that promoted democracy. ZANU PF made the incorrect assumption that US government monies would be used to fund the civil cases brought against their MPs and my counterpart, the ZANU PF legal secretary, Eddison Zvobgo, (whose election was one of those challenged) tabled a motion expressing, among other things, outrage that the US government had "pledged to pay all the legal expenses to the opposition in all and any litigation they might want to bring in our courts on spurious or flimsy grievances".[378] In fact there was no such undertaking by the US government to pay "all expenses" and the test cases were run on a shoe-string budget. For 20 years and four previous elections ZANU PF had got away with murder – opposition parties had complained bitterly about irregularities but had never done anything about it. We were determined to end this culture of impunity, by using every non-violent tool at our disposal, especially the courts, to expose electoral fraud.

Zvobgo's motion was eventually debated on 12 September. His aim was to portray us as lackeys of the Americans but we turned the debate on its head. The late MDC MP Learnmore Jongwe in particular was stunningly effective in using the debate to do what Biti had been prevented from doing by the speaker, Mnangagwa, a few weeks earlier – systematically cataloging the pre-election incidents of murder, arson, assaults and rape. Jongwe showed that ZANU PF had poured coals on its own head and, after a sombre speech, brought the house down with his conclusion saying, "What Hon Zvobgo is suggesting reminds me of a man who murdered his parents and was convicted of murder ... before sentence was passed he pleaded for mercy on the grounds that he was now an orphan".[379]

I used the debate to document what had befallen Patrick Nabanyama. Without mentioning Nabanyama's name, I said, "this afternoon I want you to look into the face of a Zimbabwean"[380] and produced a picture of Nabanyama. I then recounted the long history of activism of the man in the photograph, that he had been detained by the RF and was a loyal member first of ZAPU, then ZANU PF. Finally, naming Nabanyama, I said he had been disappeared and that "when we talk about falsehoods and spurious allegations, that is the reality". Mnangagwa immediately took exception, saying that if I was making an allegation against the government, then "you are really out of order". I moved on but shortly afterwards quoted Mugabe from *The Herald*, where he had been reported as saying "opposition people should watch out, otherwise they will die".[381] The interjections from the ZANU PF benches gradually dried up as a succession of MDC MPs movingly spoke of the most horrendous atrocities. It was the first time ZANU PF MPs had ever been confronted with unassailable evidence of their handiwork. Most did not know where to turn.

It was the beginning of many debates on prickly issues. Biti brought a motion on Zimbabwe's ongoing involvement in the DRC war, I asked that all parliamentary proceedings be filmed live, and all of us contributed vigorously to motions brought by ZANU PF MPs. Debates often went late into the night that September, as we used every parliamentary custom and rule to expose ZANU PF's misrule.

Outside of parliament the MDC was under as much threat as ever. On 7 September, MDC offices in Harare had been bombed and that had been followed by a police raid on three offices on 14 September to search for arms of war! The police were as partisan as ever – not investigating serious crime committed against us, but raiding our offices and arresting our members on spurious charges. Towards the end of the month I addressed a protest rally on the steps of Bulawayo's city hall, which had been organised to bring pressure to bear on the police to investigate the Nabanyama disappearance. The meeting was held at the public venue closest to the police headquarters in Bulawayo with the hope that our loud calls would be heard. Seven war veterans had been arrested on charges of kidnapping Nabanyama, but they had been released on lenient bail conditions. The men arrested were Cain Nkala, Ephraim Moyo, Simon Rwodzi, Aleck Moyo, Howard Ncube, Stanley Ncube and Julius Sibanda. The attitude of the police was symptomatic of their conduct everywhere in the country and it led to massive discontent within the MDC and among the party's supporters.

An intense discussion was taking place within the MDC about how to address the growing concerns of our supporters. Those of us within parliament felt we had no choice but to continue to use parliament, the courts and the media to pursue our agenda of democratic change. Many of those outside of parliament, however, especially trade unionists and Tsvangirai himself, felt that this was insufficient. The first indication of this difference of opinion came on 30 September, when Tsvangirai addressed another huge crowd at Rufaro Stadium in celebration of the first anniversary of the MDC's founding. He told the crowd "the time for mass action is now" and then added, "what we say to Mugabe is 'Please go peacefully. If you don't want to go peacefully, we will remove you violently.'"[382] I was in Bulawayo at the time and within minutes of the remark was phoned by several journalists wanting comment, which placed me in an awkward position. I understood Tsvangirai's frustration with all that was going on, but the words at face value contradicted our commitment to peaceful, non-violent change, and to boot were a propaganda gift to Mugabe, who had falsely claimed the MDC was violent. Not very convincingly, I explained the MDC's position as "Tsvangirai … warning Mugabe to consider history", to consider the "long line of dictators who have refused to go peacefully" and the spontaneous actions of "the people (who) have removed them violently".[383] I emphasised that the MDC national executive had never discussed anything about the violent overthrow of the regime, and our unequivocal policy was never to engage in violence.

On my 43rd birthday, 4 October, my family personally experienced the police's partisanship for the first time since the raid on our home in February 1989. I had spent 3 and 4 October in Harare in several meetings coordinating our electoral challenge cases. On the afternoon of my birthday, I was preparing to travel home from Harare airport when I received a frantic call from Jenny, telling me that she had returned home to find several truckloads of armed police parked outside, demanding to search our home for "broadcasting equipment". When they arrived only the children were at home with our domestic worker, Agnes Mukosera, who had kept the police at bay, aided by our Fawcett Security guard, James Makoni.[384] An Austrian friend, Rita Ruf, heard about the raid and drove down to rescue the children. When she arrived the police initially refused to allow her to go inside the house. Ruf lost her temper and shouted, "For goodness sake leave the children out of politics." Suitably chastened by this angry woman, the police allowed her in. While driving the children back to her home our youngest son, Scott, who was then aged seven, was utterly distraught and screamed, "They are going to kill my dad, they are going to kill my dad!"[385]

Jenny herself was calm when she telephoned me but wanted to know whether she should relent and let the police inside. I encouraged her to keep them at bay as best she could and boarded the plane. I knew exactly what the matter was about.

For many years I had felt that the government monopoly over broadcasting, inherited from the RF regime, was unconstitutional and needed challenging. When ZANU PF took power in 1980 it simply changed the name from the Rhodesia Broadcasting Corporation (RBC) to the Zimbabwe Broadcasting Corporation (ZBC) and nothing else. The ZBC slavishly followed the ZANU PF line, as the RBC had followed the RF. No other independent radio or TV stations were allowed and Section 27 of the Broadcasting Act gave the ZBC the sole right to broadcast. In my view this offended Sections 11, 19 and 20 of the Lancaster House constitution, which in theory allowed freedom of expression and conscience. In June 1994, as director of BLPC, I had met with Richard Carver of Article 19, the International Centre against Censorship, to see if we could get funding to challenge the ZBC monopoly. It was easier said than done because the Supreme Court would not entertain an academic challenge to the legislation. A real broadcasting organisation would have to be established with a genuine intention to broadcast, which naturally would cost money. When I travelled to Germany in August 1994 with the editor of the *Daily Gazette*, Brian Latham, we discussed setting up a radio station company with a view to challenging the legislation. Following that discussion, Latham applied for a broadcasting licence, but on 21 February 1996 received a letter from Bornwell Chakaodza stating that, while government had "decided to liberalise the airwaves", it was still "working on amending the existing Act" and as a result "no application can be considered at the moment".[386] Armed with the refusal letter we decided to take it further and in March 1996 I met with two DJs, Simon Parkinson and Gerry Jackson, both of whom worked for the ZBC at the time. We agreed to set up a company, Capital Radio (Pvt) Ltd, which was incorporated by me in July 1996. The original directors of Capital Radio were myself, Latham, Parkinson and Jackson. Parkinson was going to raise funding but had difficulties doing so and so the project went into hibernation until 2000, when Mike Auret's son Mike Jnr got involved. He managed to mobilise sufficient funding, and in April 2000 filed papers in the Supreme Court challenging the constitutionality of the ZBC's sole right to broadcast. The government, in opposing papers filed in May, admitted that the sole right offended the constitution but argued that the granting of a broadcasting licence should await a regulatory framework, suggesting that it would do so by "not later than the end of the second session of the Fifth Parliament", i.e. after the presidential election scheduled for 2002. Dissatisfied with that, Capital Radio went back to the Supreme Court on 22 September 2000, obtaining an order allowing it to "import broadcasting equipment and to operate a commercial radio station".[387]

With the order secured, Capital Radio moved swiftly, imported the equipment and on the morning of 4 October 2000, started broadcasting from offices at the top of the Monomotapa Crowne Plaza Hotel in central Harare. Although the first broadcast was relatively bashful, it announced in no uncertain terms that Capital Radio was an independent station and would broadcast news and music without fear or favour. The moment they went on air all hell broke loose. Riot police and CIO agents descended on the studios, closed it down and started dismantling equipment. Simultaneously, raids were conducted on the homes of all the directors, including Jackson's, Latham's and mine.

When I arrived home from the Bulawayo airport I found my wife, several well wishers and two truckloads of heavily armed police locked in a standoff outside my gate. As I approached the officer in charge he angrily said to me, "Hon Coltart – your wife is even more cheeky than you!" and it soon became apparent why he felt this way. Jenny had stood her ground for several hours. She had refused to accept the facsimile copy of the search warrant because it was cut off at the bottom and bore no signature. She had cleverly managed to get all the children out of the gate and whisked away by friends, then got herself ensconced behind the gate. Our ridgeback got very excited and added a further deterrent. I had a look at the warrant. It authorised the police to search my home for "vehicles, vessels, aircraft, broadcasting equipment and any related items". With as straight a face as I could muster, I told the officer we had difficulty landing aircraft in our one-acre plot and the only vessel I had was a decrepit Fireball dinghy in our backyard. I assured him that we had no broadcasting equipment, and that in any event the warrant was defective. After another two hours of haggling outside the gate and with the AK-47-armed police surrounding me getting increasingly agitated, I finally relented and allowed them to search my home. I proudly took them to the Fireball lying in the back yard but they were not impressed. They proceeded to go through our entire home, including rifling through my then fourteen-year-old daughter Jessica's personal effects, which incensed her. Much to their disappointment they didn't find a broadcasting studio and left.

Capital Radio urgently obtained an interdict from High Court Judge Ishmael Chatikobo barring the police from searching the station's studio or seizing equipment, which the police promptly disregarded. A further order was obtained from Judge Elizabeth Gwaunza ordering the police to return equipment that had been seized and compelling the police commissioner, Augustine Chihuri, to appear before the court "to show cause why he should not be imprisoned for contempt of court".[388]

Jonathan Moyo, the minister of Information, responded by producing new laws – the Presidential Powers (Temporary measures) (Broadcasting) Regulations.[389] The 68-page document was a bureaucrat's dream, with enough red tape to ensure nobody would be able to broadcast for years. Rather than embrace the right of expression, it sought to restrict it through numerous provisions which made it well nigh impossible to get a licence. Only one other national broadcasting service would be allowed. If the broadcasting licence was to be held by a company, its "controlling interest" had to be 100 per cent Zimbabwean, thus blocking any foreign investment. A provision which appeared to apply to me was a bar on any MP or office bearer of a political party being a director. There was a rigorous code of conduct protecting "national security", ensuring discreet "coverage of civil and public disorder" and, in a clause harking back to the rejected constitution, "the reasonable protection of an individual's name and reputation". Clearly, any licence would be subject to tight controls over what could be put out on the airwaves. The regulations must have been in preparation for months, but were now sprung upon the public, without going through parliament, to prevent Capital Radio from broadcasting. Capital Radio never broadcast again. Chihuri never went to prison for contempt. Fifteen years on, there is still not one single radio station in Zimbabwe that operates independent of ZANU PF control or majority influence.

The deliberate policy of impunity, implemented through a long line of amnesties, was continued by Mugabe within days of the Capital Radio raid. On 6 October, he announced an amnesty[390] which pardoned everyone involved in political violence in the run up to the election. Although murder was excluded from the amnesty, this was meaningless in the absence of a single serious murder investigation by the police. Kidnapping was one of the crimes covered by the amnesty which immediately emboldened the war veterans who had disappeared Nabanyama. Aside from my statements made in parliament, I had been lobbying the attorney general and an old client Kembo Mohadi, who was minister of Home Affairs, to bring charges against the men we knew had dragged Nabanyama from his home. To give credit to both, Cain Nkala and his six fellow war veterans had been charged for the kidnapping and murder of Nabanyama, albeit on pathetically lenient bail conditions. A few days after Mugabe announced his amnesty, I went to Western Commonage magistrate's court to attend the remand proceedings of the war veterans. I wanted to know when their trial would begin. As it turned out the court was advised that the police were not yet ready to proceed with the trial and so the accused were remanded again. When walking out of the court with fellow MP and MDC treasurer general Fletcher Dulini Ncube, one of the accused men shouted out in isiNdebele: "*Umkhiwa lo ka nanzele, ngoba sizamthola!"*, meaning "this white man must watch out because we'll get him".[391] We were both shocked by the brazenness of the threat and immediately made a report to the police. Nothing was done to arrest or charge the man.

The Clemency Order made by Mugabe was the final straw for the MDC. The violence meted out against our members was bad enough, but the realisation that Mugabe was determined to ensure that none of the perpetrators faced justice deeply angered us all. The MDC national executive met on 16 October and I was mandated, as legal secretary, to draft a parliamentary petition to impeach Mugabe. We always knew that it was purely symbolic: while the constitution only required one third of MPs to initiate impeachment proceedings, it required two thirds to complete the process, something we knew would never happen. However, we were desperate to make a point that Mugabe's conduct the entire year had been unacceptable. The constitution[392] allowed three grounds for impeachment: wilful violation of the constitution, physical or mental incapacity, or gross misconduct. Citing Mugabe's brazen support of the military who ignored court rulings in the 1999 Choto/ Chavunduka journalist case, his failure to uphold judgments in land cases, and his inflammatory speeches inciting violence, we argued that he had wilfully violated the constitution. The petition recorded some of his statements and listed 35 MDC members or supporters who had been murdered in 2000. To show that he was guilty of gross misconduct we focused on his "systematic abuse of the prerogative of mercy", his decision to deploy Zimbabwean troops in the DRC and his "failure to deal with corruption".[393]

All 58 MDC MPs then signed the petition, which was presented to the speaker and tabled in parliament on 25 October. ZANU PF leader of the house Chinamasa was apoplectic when Sibanda spoke, but Mnangagwa kept his cool, advising that he would set up a committee, in terms of the constitution, to investigate the matter and report back to parliament. Mnangagwa's sting was in the tail – he directed that the "document not be published and any media which publish it will be in contempt of law".[394] Chinamasa latched onto that and in a menacing tone made "it very clear that if there is any publication of this document in the newspapers I will move to hold those newspapers in contempt of this Parliament".[395]

The petition was never published in *Hansard* and while a committee was set up (which included me), it never met. We had posted the document on the internet before Mnangagwa's ruling and the *Daily News* bravely published large extracts from it the next day. Mnangagwa subsequently ruled that the *Daily News* was in contempt of parliament but, probably fearing that contempt proceedings would bring unwanted public attention to the contents of the petition, no further action was taken against the newspaper.[396] They had other more effective ways of silencing the newspaper altogether.

Although both Chinamasa and Jonathan Moyo described the petition as "frivolous and vexatious", ZANU PF was deeply embarrassed by it. Mnangagwa went to the extreme length of ejecting the British and South African ambassadors who had come to listen, Richard Longworth and Jeremiah Ndou, from the Speakers' Gallery[397] on the flimsy grounds that they were there without his knowledge. As Sibanda tabled the petition ZANU PF organised hundreds of its supporters to stage a demonstration outside parliament. Mugabe later addressed thousands of supporters outside ZANU PF headquarters, furiously advising that government was "considering revoking the policy of reconciliation so that those involved in war crimes during Zimbabwe's war of liberation stand trial".[398] As he was wont to do, Mugabe reverted to race – "Ian Smith and his fellow whites committed genocide" and would "stand trial for their crimes". He went on to observe that "in Europe they (were) still hunting for those behind Nazi war crimes and Zimbabwe (could not) be an exception". Chillingly, he concluded by generically focusing again on Mike Auret and me, saying, "They (i.e. whites) must take note that the Coltarts and Aurets and the rest of them will not be free from arrest."[399] While inflamed by the impeachment petition Mugabe didn't mention it once. It was clear, though, that he held me responsible for it; as author he was in one sense correct, but in every other sense he was wrong because it reflected a deep-rooted fury within the MDC.

This was the fourth time that Auret and I had been personally identified in Mugabe's mantra, so we decided to issue a press statement. On 1 November 2000 we addressed a press conference in Harare in which we said the personal attacks were "unjust and uncalled for". We were at a disadvantage because the constitution made it "impossible to take legal action against the President". The president's attacks on us and "on a tiny ethnic minority (were) shameful and a total negation of a President's role in any nation".[400] When asked by the press about what should be done, I responded that "the time (had) come for organisations like SADC, the EU, the Commonwealth and the UN" to "rein in Mugabe".[401] Reminding the press of the "consequences of hate speech from what happened in Yugoslavia … the international community must ask: what is the difference between Slobodan Milosevic and Mugabe?" I questioned why "travel bans (were) not imposed on Mugabe", and also why "The Hague (was) not investigating Mugabe for crimes against humanity". Auret, who was then aged 64, spoke about ZANU PF's long and "well documented history of political violence", expressing concern that the threats were real and imminent.

Less than a fortnight after the press conference, I had an opportunity to raise these issues in Washington. The International Republican Institute invited an MDC delegation, led by Fletcher Dulini Ncube, to visit the US for meetings with members of Congress and the State department. The delegation, which also included lawyers Brian Kagoro, Yvonne Mahlunge and myself, trade union leader Lucia Matibenga and student leader Nelson Chamisa, met a wide variety of Republicans and Democrats, including Congressman Donald M Payne, chair of the Congressional Black Caucus, Susan Rice, President Clinton's assistant secretary of State for Africa, and Andrew Young. In all the meetings we argued that Zimbabwe was in danger of unravelling and that a carrot-and-stick approach should be used, to encourage Mugabe back towards constitutionality. It was particularly important that African Americans take the lead because the bulk of human rights abuses were being perpetrated against black Zimbabweans, not whites. White casualties captured the international media's headlines but the reality was that whereas a few whites had been affected, serious human rights violations had been committed against thousands of black Zimbabweans. Many African Americans had a nostalgic view of Mugabe, justifiably connecting him to the overthrow of Ian Smith. In addition, because of the Western media's focus on white farmers they viewed the current struggle as an extension of the 1970s war, not a struggle between black trade unions and a corrupt, rich ruling elite. Kagoro, Mahlunge and Chamisa, all highly articulate young black activists, were particularly effective in swaying their opinion. Had the job been left to me alone, as a white person, I have no doubt that their attitude towards Mugabe would not have changed.

Two key meetings were with my old friend Michael Miller, who was by then Senate Majority leader Bill Frist's legislative assistant, and Michele Gavin, an Africa specialist with Senator Russell Feingold. Frist and Feingold were to become the authors of the Zimbabwe Democracy and Economic Recovery Act 2001, and both Miller and Gavin were already working on the idea and sought our advice. I have often been accused by ZANU PF of authoring this act, which is false. While we all stated forcefully that those responsible for human rights abuses should be held to account, and while no doubt some of our arguments carried weight, the final act was not of our making and was solely crafted by the US Senate in the months that followed, before being tabled on 8 March 2001 by Frist and Feingold. The act eventually received widespread support from the Congressional Black Caucus, including Congressman Payne, and the likes of Hillary Clinton and Joe Biden.

Within a week of our return to Zimbabwe, ZANU PF's official organ *Zimbabwe News*'s November edition was published with my picture on the front cover and the headline "Treason and Treachery by MDC members".[402] The article said our actions (lobbying "racist organisations") could be "categorised as treason",[403] but conveniently omitted any mention of our meetings with Congressional Black Caucus members, and others who had traditionally supported ZANU PF. It alleged that we wanted "to remove the Government by force" and "were appealing to a foreign power" to assist us. Treason in Zimbabwe carries the death penalty so this was a serious shot across our bows.

While we waited to see if ZANU PF would follow through on its threat to charge us with treason, our attention shifted to the courts. After filing the 39 petitions on behalf of losing MDC candidates, our legal teams had spent several months compiling evidence and preparing cases. By November we were ready to start the trials in several of the matters, which caused extreme concern within ZANU PF. The first sign of trouble came when one of the defendants, Phillip Chiyangwa, the ZANU PF MP for Chinhoyi, indicated that he was preparing a motion to impeach Chief Justice Anthony Gubbay[404] on the grounds that he had "usurped his powers". At the same time Information minister Jonathan Moyo called for Gubbay's resignation. The reason for their angst was made clear when the full bench of the Supreme Court unanimously ruled on 10 November 2000 that the fast track land programme was unlawful. The Supreme Court was then comprised of Gubbay and Nick McNally (both white liberals who had opposed Smith), an Asian, Ahmed Ibrahim, and two black judges, Wilson Sandura and Simbarashe Muchechetere. All had been appointed by Mugabe well after independence; all had impeccable credentials and fine legal careers.

In the past ZANU PF had just defied the courts; on this occasion they upped the ante. On 24 November a mob of some 200 "war veterans" led by Joseph Chinotimba raided the Supreme Court just as it was about to start a session. The justices fortunately were not in court when police allowed the crowd to surge in and dance on the benches shouting, "Kill the judges!"[405] Aside from the police's inaction, no condemnation was forthcoming from the minister of Justice or the attorney general and no action was taken against the culprits.

Remarkably, the Supreme Court stood its ground. The intention of the mob was apparently to frighten the judges into resignation but none did, a particularly troublesome prospect for ZANU PF just as the 39 electoral petitions were about to commence in the High Court, all of which in theory would end up in the Supreme Court. Having failed to frighten the judges, ZANU PF took another tack. On 8 December Mugabe issued a new statutory instrument which read:

> *"Recognising that the general elections held following the dissolution of Parliament on 11 April 2000 were held under peaceful conditions and that the people did so freely … the election of a Member of Parliament shall not be rendered void."*[406]

It went on to declare that even if there were contraventions of the act, "in the interests of democracy and the peace, security and stability of Zimbabwe", they would be "deemed not to be such a contravention". The intention was to nullify all the petitions just three weeks before the first were due to start in the High Court. I addressed a press conference a few days later. Flanked by Tsvangirai and Learnmore Jongwe, I advised that the Electoral Act did not give Mugabe the right "to condone breaches of the Electoral Act and Constitution",[407] and confirmed that we had filed an urgent application to the Supreme Court to set the notice aside.

The day after our press conference was held, Mugabe addressed the ZANU PF congress and provided the nation with one of his worst quotes ever. Another white farmer, 70-year-old Henry Ellsworth, had been gunned down on his farm near Kwe Kwe on 12 December, in a barrage of automatic gunfire. It was another well-planned execution carried out with ruthless military efficiency. When he had addressed the ZANU PF central committee meeting on 13 December, Mugabe had repeated his criticism of the CFU, which he accused of having "declared war against the people".[408] But he quite outdid himself at the congress the following day when he said "(o)ur party must continue to strike fear into the hearts of the white man, our real enemy".[409] In doing so, he broadened his attack beyond farmers and the likes of Auret and me; clearly Gubbay was now in his sights too.

A few days before Christmas, Hunzvi entered the fray, giving the Supreme Court fourteen days to resign "or else"; in the context of a year of murders conducted with absolute impunity, it was a fearful threat levelled against the judges. Despite that, the judges persevered and our case was argued before them in early January by advocates Chris Andersen and Eric Matinenga. Possibly in anticipation of the judgment about to be handed down, Gubbay wrote to Vice-President Muzenda on 18 January, telling him they were fearful of their safety and the safety of their families.[410] The letter resulted in a meeting with Muzenda, but Gubbay was just subjected to a torrent of abuse. The meeting ended with Gubbay, utterly exhausted, remarking that he should perhaps resign, without saying that he would.

Judgment in our constitutional challenge against Mugabe's Electoral Notice, barring our court challenges, was handed down on 30 January 2001. In a unanimous decision the Supreme Court ruled that we had the "right to partake in an election that was free and fair and devoid of illegal practices ... and to challenge the result of an election". In the landmark decision the judges stated that "the right of full and unimpeded access to court is of cardinal importance for the adjudication of justifiable disputes".[411] It was the final straw for ZANU PF and three days later minister of Justice Chinamasa strode into Gubbay's chambers to tell him that his "resignation" had been accepted. Flabbergasted by Chinamasa's brazenness, Gubbay agreed to go on leave on 1 March and formally retire in June. But Chinamasa was not done yet: a week later he went to see judges Nick McNally and Ahmed Ibrahim and, mafia-like, told them: "... the President does not want you to come to any harm".[412] Neither judge was intimidated, however, leading to further apoplexy from ZANU PF. On 22 February, their chief whip Joram Gumbo moved a motion in parliament calling upon Mugabe to set up a tribunal to remove the Supreme Court judges under attack. Chinamasa spoke and justified his conduct on the basis that Gubbay and his colleagues were racists. In a heated exchange with Chinamasa I pointed out that Gubbay had opposed Smith and had been lead counsel in the defence of the late ZANU PF chairman Herbert Chitepo. "If this is a racial issue," I asked, "then why are you seeking the removal of (black) Justices Sandura and Muchechetere?" Reminding Chinamasa that he had "no right to initiate the removal of the Chief Justice", I concluded that his "intense move against the Judiciary only came after the Supreme Court ruled that the President had acted contrary to the Constitution (enabling) the MDC to carry on with its electoral challenges".[413]

Although he didn't participate in the Parliamentary debate, Jonathan Moyo waded in, telling *The Herald* that it was unjust for Zimbabweans "to expect as judges former Nazis and their collaborators".[414] Not satisfied with his cabinet colleague's slur, and ignoring the unfinished debate in parliament, Chinamasa unconstitutionally wrote to Gubbay on 26 February, summarily ordering him to vacate his office within 24 hours and his official residence in thirteen days. Astonishingly, Gubbay didn't even get the letter before he read all about it on the front page of *The Herald* on 27 February. This was a bridge too far for Gubbay, and he wrote to Chinamasa withdrawing his resignation and advising he would stay on until his original retirement date in April 2002. Inevitably, this stirred up the most vile response, including anti-Semitic sentiments being expressed in parliament by a ZANU PF minister. War veterans, including Chinotimba, pitched up at the Supreme Court threatening war. Gubbay took the unprecedented step of having a bodyguard accompany him, but eventually the pressure got to him. Late on 2 March, Gubbay's lawyers brokered a deal in which he would leave office immediately and retire in July on condition no further judges would be "hounded out of office".[415] Within days Mugabe's trusted Judge Chidyausiku was appointed chief justice over the heads of the remaining four Supreme Court judges. Ever since the courts have generally been subservient to the will and whims of ZANU PF.

Concurrent with this attack on the judiciary, ZANU PF was equally focused on the Fourth Estate – the media – and by February 2001 had inflicted near fatal blows on the only independent daily newspaper, the *Daily News*. While ZANU PF retained a tight control over the electronic media, it had allowed some independence in the print media. Two weekly financial papers, the *Zimbabwe Independent* and the *Financial Gazette*, had operated profitably for years and were tolerated by the regime because they had limited circulation and preached to the converted in any event. They also provided a convenient example of how ZANU PF "respected freedom of expression". The proprietors of the *Financial Gazette* had started a sister paper, the *Daily Gazette*, but had closed it in the mid 1990s. In March 1999 the *Daily News* was launched, with the feisty Geoff Nyarota (former editor of *The Chronicle* who had broken the Willowgate scandal story in 1980s) as editor. Thousands of Zimbabweans starved of news took an instant liking to the paper and its circulation soared. An unsuccessful attempt was made to shut it down in April 2000 when a bomb took out much of its ground floor, destroying a curio shop and ethnic art gallery directly beneath Nyarota's office. As 2000 wore on the *Daily News* boldly published stories about the unfolding horror, including details of Mugabe's impeachment petition. Despite being found guilty of contempt by speaker Mnangagwa in December 2000, no action had been taken against the paper until, on 23 January 2001, a shrieking mob of ZANU PF supporters, led by Hunzvi, assembled outside the *Daily News*'s headquarters. Three days later *The Herald* published an article by Jonathan Moyo, in which he wrote: "It is now only a matter of time before Zimbabweans put a final stop to this madness in defence of their cultural interest and national security."[416] The pretext for his attack was a story the *Daily News* had published which suggested that some Zimbabweans had greeted the 16 January assassination of DRC leader Laurent Kabila with "joy and jubilation". According to Moyo, this put Zimbabwean troops still deployed in the Congo "at risk" and compromised Zimbabwe's national interest.

It was indeed only a very short time before an attempt was made to put a final stop to the *Daily News*. Within 36 hours of Moyo's article appearing in *The Herald*, at 1.45 am on Sunday, 28 January a powerful explosion destroyed the *Daily News*'s printing press. The *Africa Defence Journal* opined that only "the Zimbabwean army ... has access to the type of explosives used in the blast or the professional acumen to completely wreck the machinery".[417] Whoever was responsible made sure that Moyo had made no idle threat. Despite the blast, Nyarota and his team demonstrated exceptional bravery and ingenuity – the *Daily News* published on Monday, 30 January, relying on another printing press. Although not fatal, the blast did inflict long-lasting damage – before the bomb the *Daily News* "often ran 48 pages and sold up to 120,000 copies"; after the blast it could only print "a maximum of 24 pages and 70,000 copies".[418]

One year on from the triumphant defeat of ZANU PF in the February 2000 constitutional referendum, it had held onto control of parliament, all but destroyed the judiciary, snuffed out any prospect of an independent radio station and done all in its power to close down the remaining independent daily. ZANU PF's purpose in all of this was obvious: it reflected a determination to whittle down whatever democratic space was left in the country. With the all important presidential election a year off we knuckled down to prepare for another brutal election campaign, knowing that some of our principal means of waging our non-violent struggle had been weakened. We could *only speak right on*.

CHAPTER 17

TERRORISTS AND "TERRORISTS"
MARCH 2001 TO DECEMBER 2001

"We agree with President Bush that anyone who in any way finances, harbours or defends terrorists is himself a terrorist. We too will not make any difference (sic) between terrorists and their friends."
– ANONYMOUS ZIMBABWEAN GOVERNMENT SPOKESMAN,
QUOTED IN *THE HERALD*, 23 NOVEMBER 2001

While ZANU PF were constitutionally able to delay the date of the 2000 parliamentary general election, they had no such wriggle room regarding a presidential election. Section 28 of the constitution made it quite clear that the election would have to be held by not later than 31 March 2002, and in March 2001 that date loomed large. Committed as we were to working within the law, it fell to me to develop legal strategies to ensure that Tsvangirai, our presidential candidate, would have the best possible legal support. Given ZANU PF's record since taking power, it was inevitable that it would bend, manipulate and break the rules and we needed to counter that. Early in March I developed a strategy which focused on the following areas: the parliamentary electoral challenges, the voters' roll, postal votes by non-resident Zimbabweans, the machinations of the Electoral Supervisory Commission, the mayoral elections for Bulawayo and Harare, and the legal defence of MDC members who were being arrested and detained.

The Supreme Court judgment overturning Mugabe's attempt to stop the 39 challenges to the 2000 parliamentary election resulted in the resuscitation of the cases, but with that, increasingly large lawyers' bills too. Most of the cases could only be fought effectively if large numbers of witnesses were brought to give evidence in court, which was an expensive exercise. In addition, one thing we had learnt from the June election was the importance of the voters' roll and how it had been manipulated by the registrar general. We were aware that he held it in electronic format and there was no reason why we should not have access to it in that format as well. The paper version of it could not be easily searched and analysed. With this in mind I had written asking for an electronic copy and we anticipated that we would have to go to the Supreme Court to compel its production. Other challenges were contemplated to allow non-resident Zimbabwean citizens to vote and to keep the Electoral Supervisory Commission honest. ZANU PF had been dragging its heels regarding mayoral elections for Harare and Bulawayo; we had already gone to court to have the Harare election held and needed to do the same in Bulawayo. But my biggest headache related to ensuring that MDC members were adequately represented. The law was being used as a weapon by ZANU PF and an increasing number of our members were being arrested on spurious charges. All needed legal representation and the bills were mounting.

Not even our high-profile leaders were exempt from this type of harassment. Gibson Sibanda had been arrested on 6 February 2001 on a charge of "inciting public violence". The police had arrested him on the basis of an unsubstantiated report in *The Chronicle* which said he had incited MDC members to beat up ZANU PF supporters. I was at the rally where Sibanda was accused of having made the threat and heard no such thing. Notwithstanding that there was not a shred of evidence, aside from the newspaper report, that is, Sibanda was still arrested and hauled before court. Then in March, Tsvangirai was charged under the Law and Order (Maintenance) Act for an "act of terrorism", namely his warning given to Mugabe (that he should leave peacefully rather than be removed violently) at the September 2000 Rufaro stadium rally. These were the high-profile cases, but my office was inundated with reports of our members being arrested and detained countrywide. We simply didn't have the funds or structures to provide adequate legal assistance. The need to address this pulled me away from parliament and drew me into a hectic schedule of foreign travel to raise awareness and funds.

The first of these trips was to the UK and US in March 2001. I was relieved to get away because on 6 March I had received the most explicit death threat yet. It came by text message to my cell phone and stated that I, and my family too, would be killed. At the same time MDC colleagues became aware of a document that detailed a plan to eliminate our four white MDC MPs; I was at the top of the list with Auret, Roy Bennett and Trudy Stevenson. Finally, on 7 March I received a letter which stated "from a source who has given accurate information in the past I am told that the powers that be intend celebrating Independence Day 18 April by killing one or more people – please take care."[419]

I flew to London on 11 March with Sekai Holland, Paul Themba Nyathi and Roy Bennett. There we split up, enabling me to focus on institutions that historically had helped fund legal cases. I met with Lord David Shutt of the Joseph Rowntree Foundation (who described to me how the apartheid-era legal defence organisations such as the International Defence and Aid Fund had worked), Amnesty International and the Department for International Development (DFID). On 13 March I addressed the Law Society of England and Wales on the topic "Attacks on the Judiciary and their Implications for Zimbabwe", closing with the remarks that "our resolve (was) undiminished but we need(ed) assistance from the international community". I was very specific: we did not want "general sanctions", but needed "travel bans and asset seizures against those responsible for human rights abuses".[420] During the same trip I made a fleeting one-day visit to New York which initiated a series of later meetings with potential funders there.

I came home again only briefly before embarking on another trip to Europe in mid April. It started with a few days in Geneva visiting a variety of UN missions there, most importantly the UN Commission for Human Rights, to speak about the gross violations our members and supporters had suffered. From there I flew to New York with Paul Themba Nyathi. We had received advice that George Soros was sympathetic towards our plight and was prepared to meet us. Prior to the meeting Zimbabwean businessmen based in New York advised us of the New York business culture – there should be no beating around the bush; people appreciated straight talk, facts and figures. Armed with this advice, Nyathi and I met Soros on 25 April at his luxurious apartment overlooking Central Park. We had been told that he could only squeeze in half an hour because he was due to have lunch that day with Mikhail Gorbachev. Nyathi, being the leader of our delegation, found it difficult to break with his Ndebele tradition of very courteously commenting on the weather and speaking in general terms about the situation in Zimbabwe. After 20 minutes of chit-chat we were no closer to the nub of our visit, namely, our acute need of finance, and so I, heeding our New York friends' advice, cut to the chase. I explained to Soros that serious human rights violations were taking place in Zimbabwe, that law was being used as a weapon and that without legal assistance the struggle for democracy and freedom would be seriously weakened. The MDC was also being called upon to provide medical care and support for people who had been brutalised. Foreign governments were reluctant to fund the party and without assistance from NGOs and individuals, ZANU PF would simply grind us into submission. I said that as a lawyer responsible for trust accounts I had set up systems to ensure that monies donated would be handled by third parties and properly accounted for, and joked that neither Nyathi nor I would get our grubby paws on any of it. This took me less than five minutes, whereupon Soros responded: "Fine – you clearly need help. I will contribute US$500 000 from my personal funds and my assistants will make all the necessary arrangements. All the very best for your struggle; I admire what you are all trying to do and am pleased to help." The meeting ended and we were ushered out. I was somewhat shellshocked – I had never raised so much money in such a short space of time and was staggered by Soros's generosity. When Nyathi and I got back down to the street we let out a whoop and did a jig together, much to the amusement of the taxi driver who had come to collect us.

Washington was our next stop. It was the first time I had been back to the city since George W Bush had won the 2001 presidential election. A few of my old friends had been appointed to key positions. In particular, Walter Kansteiner III had recently been nominated by President Bush as assistant secretary of State for Africa. Michael Miller had been appointed director for African Affairs in the National Security Council and other friends from my 1992 Kenyan observer mission were in key positions. Although we now had an open door to the new administration, we were anxious to ensure that we had bi-partisan support and so we also had a series of meetings with Democrats, including Gregory Craig (special counsel in the Clinton White House and Foreign Policy adviser to Senator Ted Kennedy), and Africanists such as Leonard Robinson, then president of the Africa Society. Our task was to build cross-party support for the freedom struggle in Zimbabwe and to mobilise support for the MDC.

This second visit impressed on me that, even with a new administration and friends in high places, there would be no quick change to US foreign policy. However, every visit built further awareness of Zimbabwe's crisis and we came away encouraged that the nostalgic attachment to Mugabe's defeat of Smith's Rhodesia was evaporating.

Back home again I was thrust into a variety of parliamentary debates. ZANU PF had tabled a series of bills to consolidate their position. A Rural Land Occupiers Bill sought to protect people who had invaded farms illegally; another amendment to the Land Acquisition Act sought to bring legality to what the Supreme Court had ruled as illegal the previous December. Finally, a Citizenship Amendment Bill was tabled to tighten up rules against dual citizenship and to strip Zimbabweans who had been out of the country of their citizenship. In all these debates we made valiant attempts either to defeat or whittle down objectionable clauses, often debating well into the night. Always, though, ZANU PF had their substantial majority and while we had minor victories, their effort to provide a cloak of positivistic legality to their brazen flouting of international norms and human rights proceeded swiftly. I was always struck by minister of Justice Chinamasa's determination to plug all the legal loopholes, often through patently unjust laws, seemingly in the belief that these unjust laws would redeem Zimbabwe in the eyes of the international community.

In September the previous year I had been appointed chairman of the Justice, Legal and Parliamentary Affairs committee, alongside veteran human rights activists Mike Auret and Innocent Gonese. All parliamentary committees were evenly composed of ZANU PF backbenchers and MDC MPs and we were fortunate to have relatively moderate ZANU PF MPs, such as Eddison Zvobgo. Accordingly, when we first met it didn't take much persuasion to agree that we would focus our work on the operations of Zimbabwe's prisons, the administration of justice, particularly the non-prosecution of certain cases, and the operations of the judiciary. Using our powers to summon people to give evidence, we arranged for Chinamasa, the attorney general Andrew Chigovera, the commissioner of Police Augustine Chihuri, Sternford Moyo, president of the Law Society, and others to appear before us. Our attempts to summon Chinamasa in February 2001 regarding his threats levelled against Supreme Court judges failed; he provided a range of excuses why he couldn't attend. Others were reluctant to appear and were very prickly when they did, but the hearings resulted in us reaching a consensus regarding a wide number of recommendations, which I presented to parliament on 24 May 2001, the last day of the parliamentary year. We delved back into the past and brought to the fore corruption in the courts, particularly through criminal dockets going missing, and the non-prosecution of high-profile politicians in a variety of corruption scandals such as the VIP Housing scheme and War Victims Compensation Fund. We found that the "inaction of the Police and Attorney General (in prosecuting these cases where the culprits were known) is inexcusable".[421] A major concern related to the non-prosecution of murders. The report made the finding that "(t)he Commissioner of Police was not able to explain satisfactorily the non prosecution of numerous politically motivated murders especially where the perpetrators were known". We expressed our "deepest concern at what appears to be an effort by the Police to obstruct the course of justice".[422]

The report was ignored by the ZANU PF leadership and the government-controlled media and to that extent was academic, but it did show me that there were some within ZANU PF, such as Zvobgo, who didn't approve of violence, corruption and subversion of the rule of law. It appeared to me that they were trapped within a ruthless party they didn't know how to get out of.

With the first year of parliament over, time opened up for other pursuits. In discussions with the director of the Konrad-Adenauer Foundation, Anton Boesl, I had expressed a desire to consolidate the growing consensus within the Justice, Legal and Parliamentary Affairs committee. Boesl suggested a study trip to Germany, which would focus on how Germany had dealt with its past horrors and transitional justice issues. Agreement was reached, resulting in me leading a team to Germany in late June, equally made up of ZANU PF and MDC MPs, including Zvobgo. Boesl organised a fascinating mix of terror and harmony and the trip had a profound effect on all of us. It started by us being brought face to face with the brutality of Germany's past. Incongruously, on a beautiful summer's day we were taken to the Berlin-Hohenschönhausen prison, used by the East German Stasi secret police from 1951 onwards. It comprises 200 cells and interrogation rooms where political prisoners were taken to, secretly, in trucks purposely designed to disorientate prisoners so that they didn't know where they were. We clambered through one of the old prison trucks, which had several sealed holding cells on its back, and imagined how people were picked up and driven around in the dark for hours, before being driven behind the closed doors of the prison, which gave no hint of its location. Although the prison is in the north east of Berlin, it was never raided after the Berlin Wall came down precisely because prisoners never knew where it was located. As we were shown torture cells and the instruments of torture, I commented that it was not dissimilar to the 1980s CIO torture facility at Esigodini outside Bulawayo, where many of my clients had been held. The next day we were taken to the Nazi Sachsenhausen concentration camp where thousands of political prisoners were incarcerated, including Lutheran pastor Martin Niemöller, from 1938 to 1945. Niemöller's post-war statement was particularly poignant and apt for Zimbabwe:

> *"First they came for the Socialists, and I did not speak out—*
> *Because I was not a Socialist.*
> *Then they came for the Trade Unionists, and I did not speak out—*
> *Because I was not a Trade Unionist.*
> *Then they came for the Jews, and I did not speak out—*
> *Because I was not a Jew.*
> *Then they came for me—and there was no one left to speak for me."*

I was particularly moved by a visit to Dietrich Bonhoeffer's cell at Tegel prison in Berlin later on in the week. Bonhoeffer had long been one of my heroes and his letters from prison (many of which were written from Tegel when he was there during 1943 and 1944)[423] are a remarkable testament to his trust in God in the most adverse circumstances. Sitting in his cell, I tried to imagine how he kept his equanimity and even managed to win over many of his prison guards in the face of such a ruthless regime.

Inevitably, the trip included sessions with German parliamentarians and bureaucrats, and in the first of these the underlying tensions between us came to the fore. We were asked about the current human rights situation in Zimbabwe and, as chairman, I had the first say. I took the opportunity to detail the ongoing abuses in our country, before opening up to other members of the committee. Zvobgo, as the senior ZANU PF MP, was embarrassed by my report and politely disagreed with my take on the situation back home. However, after the meeting when we convened at our hotel Zvobgo took me to task and threatened to return home. He was angered by my criticism of the Zimbabwean government, which he felt was out of place on a foreign trip. I asked whether he disputed any of my allegations, which he could not, and I suggested that he should speak out in meetings if anything I said was untruthful. This got us back on an even keel and he agreed to stay on. By the end of the trip we had established a good rapport, which grew into a friendship lasting until his death in 2004.

Although Zvobgo crafted many of the amendments to the Lancaster House constitution which consolidated Mugabe's power, he and Mugabe subsequently fell out. In 1996 Zvobgo, a Harvard-trained lawyer, was seriously injured in a traffic accident, itself "considered suspicious by many".[424] Mugabe then demoted him, dropping him from cabinet altogether in 2000. This German trip consolidated the unity of our committee; the realisation that human rights abuses are universal took the racial sting out of our partisan differences of opinion.

Within days of my return to Zimbabwe we held a memorial service for Patrick Nabanyama at the Bulawayo Presbyterian Church. The service was preceded by a march from St Mary's Catholic Cathedral through the city. Archbishop Pius Ncube spoke on behalf of the wider church, condemning violence and political intolerance in all its forms. I spoke about the culture of impunity which perpetuated disappearances in Zimbabwe. Tracing the history of activists who had been disappeared, such as Dr Edson Sithole and Fraser Gibson Sibanda, I said that what made Nabanyama's case worse was the brazenness of his abductors. We knew who they were, they were unrepentant, and they had the temerity to threaten people interested in their trial. Knowing that my words would get back to them, I warned Nabanyama's abductors that God loved justice and would secure it in the end. Citing the handing over of former Yugoslavian president Slobodan Milosevic to The Hague a few days earlier, on 28 June, I said, "The world is changing and there are few places left to hide."[425] Buttressing my point that we served a God of justice, I quoted extensively from the Book of Amos, concluding with the injunctions to "hate evil, love good; maintain justice in the courts" and I implored everyone to "let justice roll on like a river, righteousness like a never failing stream".[426] My remarks fell on some deaf ears because soon after I spoke a group of CID officers tried to come into the service to arrest people. They were barred from coming into the church by the crowd, who recognised them as the same men who had arrested MDC MP and treasurer general Fletcher Dulini Ncube the previous day.[427] Without any sense of irony the local government-controlled *Sunday News* criticised us, saying we were "too big for our small shoes" and claiming that the police had "the right to pick up suspects" any time, neglecting to comment that the entire service had been held because of a fundamental injustice.

It concerned me that the Nabanyama story, and others involving black Zimbabweans, got such little currency in the international media, which tended to focus on the ongoing harassment of white farmers. This moved me to write an opinion piece for *The Sunday Telegraph* entitled: "Whites are not the main target of the thugs".[428] I wrote that Mugabe "was perfectly happy for coverage in Western newspapers of the detention of 20 white farmers and the random beating of white women in Chinhoyi". I argued it suited "him to have the violence continuously (committed) against thousands of black Zimbabwe pass unnoticed" and said that if "all the world sees is his attacks on whites that makes him look like a liberator". Specifically urging that the West should not impose "blanket sanctions" or the "cancellation of sporting links", I wrote, "the only thing which will hurt are sanctions targeted at the people who order the violence ... targeted against the cronies who are profiting from Mr Mugabe's rape of Zimbabwe". Presumably to nail my colours to the sanctions mast, the government-controlled *Chronicle* printed my article in full and it invited unprecedented vitriol in the government-controlled media.

On 28 August *The Herald* published an opinion piece entitled "Coltart has no place in Zimbabwe" – because I had "called for sanctions".[429] The ire against me increased even more that week when the *Daily News* announced it was going to serialise *Breaking the Silence*. One ZANU PF supporter interviewed said "if the whites in the MDC want to rule this country again they must go back to the bush and fight", followed by the opinion that "if we had our way there would be no presidential elections next year because that is what is causing all these problems. President Mugabe should be made life president to stop all this nonsense."[430]

"All this nonsense" in Bulawayo was in fact the mayoral election scheduled for 8 and 9 September. Chinamasa had done his best to postpone the election indefinitely in June 2001 through an extraordinary *Government Gazette*, claiming that the voters' roll was in a shambles.

We went to court and obtained a judgment from Judge Kennedy Sibanda (the same person who had spoken on behalf of ZAPU to UCT students in 1979), overturning Chinamasa's notice and ordering Registrar General Mudede to hold the election in the shortest possible time.[431] I was drawn in to support the MDC candidate, Japhet Ndabeni-Ncube, but it soon became apparent that, if anything, our support had grown since the June 2000 general election. Tsvangirai came to Bulawayo the weekend before the mayoral election for one of the largest rallies ever held at White City Stadium. In contrast ZANU PF attracted a tiny crowd at the same venue.

On Saturday morning, 8 September, the first day of the election, while driving in the city centre with my security team we noticed a string of buses laden with young people arrive at the city hall, where they were dropped off. Concerned by the number of buses coming in, we drove in the direction they were coming from and observed that there were more Kukura Kurerwa buses driving into Bulawayo along the Harare road, from outside the city limits. We turned around and followed them back into town, but as we did so our vehicle was followed by a Land Rover with civilian number plates. As we got to the city hall carpark and started photographing and videoing the buses discharging their loads of young people, the same vehicle tried to block us off. Evading the Land Rover, we then started a comical Keystone Cops routine, driving around the buses as the Land Rover followed us around, its occupants remonstrating and shouting abuse at us. We continued filming. We noticed that as they left the bus each person was given a piece of paper. With the occupants of the Land Rover becoming increasingly hostile, and not wanting to have our photographic evidence destroyed, we drove off with the Land Rover in hot pursuit. My sedan easily outpaced it, however, and, after downloading what we had filmed at a safe house, we continued our tour of polling stations without further incident until later that day. As the polling stations were about to close, I received a report that our MDC Bulawayo headquarters was being raided by the police and there was need for legal representation, which necessitated me going there. I was dropped off by my security team, but as they left my vehicle was spotted by police, presumably aware of the description of my vehicle from the morning's charade. They were cut off and my entire security team was arrested.

Leaving other lawyers to deal with the unlawful search of our headquarters, I made my way to Bulawayo Central police station "Law and Order" department offices, where I found Detective Inspector Martin Matira and my three security men, Craig Edy, Hedley Quick and Craig Biddlecombe. When I asked what they were being charged with, Matira said they had been found in possession of a walkie-talkie radio and were going to be charged for possessing a radio without a licence. I pointed out that the charge was defective in that the walkie-talkie could be, indeed had been, bought in a supermarket, and that low-power devices, such as the one seized, were exempt from licensing.[432]

Matira wasn't going to let legal trivialities get in the way of a good arrest. The video camera had been seized as well and although Matira couldn't think of an appropriate charge in that regard, he refused to return it to me. The police were anxious to know where the morning's footage had got to and had interrogated the three men prior to my arrival. Despite not having a shred of evidence, and after several hours of arguing in his office, Matira advised me that he was going to detain the men. The following morning the police went on a fishing expedition at their homes – searches all done illegally without search warrants. All three men were highly competent marksmen and skilled practical pistol shottists. Biddlecombe was also a government-licensed small arms dealer who operated a registered company called Safari Arms (Pvt) Ltd. It was not surprising, then, that the police found numerous hunting rifles and other firearms in their homes. Not satisfied with that, the police also gathered some of Biddlecombe's clients' rifles which had been surrendered to the police armoury the previous April pending the acquisition of licences, and added these to the pile of weapons found at their homes! We immediately provided all the government-issued firearms licences for the weapons, but once again the police were determined not to let facts impede their mission. That Sunday evening Senior Assistant Commissioner Albert Mandizha convened a press conference where he paraded all the seized rifles which he alleged were unlicensed "arms of war". *The Chronicle* dutifully took up the story the next morning with a headline "Arms Caches found at MDC Officials' Offices"[433] and quoting Mandizha as saying "all are specified weapons used only by the Police and army; all were unlicensed". Augustine Chihuri got in on the act next, alleging that the "three men were part of a group on a mission to track down and hunt ZANU PF supporters".[434]

I felt exceptionally vulnerable without the protection of my three bodyguards. A few days before, on 5 September, my wife Jenny had given birth to our fourth child, Bethany, which, while a joyous event, severely restricted our mobility. In addition, soon after Mandizha's triumphant press conference that Sunday evening, unknown gunmen had sprayed automatic gunfire at Gibson Sibanda, Paul Themba Nyathi, Welshman Ncube, Fletcher Dulini Ncube and two independent journalists, Mduduzi Mathuthu and Loughty Dube, who were interviewing them at the MDC headquarters. Although no one was injured, the incident had deeply shocked us all. The shooting had been reported to the police but was dismissed by them as "stage-managed to divert attention from the discovery of (the) massive arms caches".[435] In reality all this did was divert attention away from the fact that the MDC won the Bulawayo mayoral election handsomely, with Ndabeni-Ncube polling 60 988 votes to the ZANU PF candidate's 12 783.

My bodyguards were finally taken to court on 11 September 2001. The police attempted to throw the book at them, but the presiding magistrate, John Masimba, was immediately unimpressed, telling the state counsel in granting bail that "the case (was) not as serious as the State (was) making it appear – actually there was a lot of panel-beating in a bid to enable the State to prosecute the accused". He observed that "most of the evidence in this case (was) incoherent".[436] Most of the charges, including the original allegation of being in possession of an unlicensed radio, were thrown out there and then as the gun licences and relevant law were produced in court. The state's case was reduced to a few trivial allegations, such as that Edy had been found in possession of a CZ pistol which was licensed for "self protection", which the state argued did not include protecting himself when in my company. One .22 rifle's licence had expired five days before the arrest, a technical offence at best, concerning a weapon that was hardly an "arm of war". Edy, Biddlecombe and Quick were released on a token bail payment and we all went home. As I collapsed before a TV in my study after a manic few days, the first image I saw was that of a Boeing 767 crashing into one of the Twin Towers in New York. It was so surreal that I checked whether I was on CNN, thinking someone may have changed to a movie channel. But the grim reality soon set in. The world was about to change and with it pressure on the ZANU PF regime. The 9/11 act of terror was to prove the ultimate diversion which, ironically, would benefit those responsible for terror in Zimbabwe. In a bizarre twist of fate those of us pursuing non-violent change would be accused of terrorism by the perpetrators of terror. Compounding that irony, the Western world became so compelled by the need to hunt down the terrorists responsible for 9/11 that, understandably, much of its attention was diverted away from Zimbabwe.

Throughout this period I continued to organise and monitor the 39 MDC electoral challenges that were before the High Court. Despite ZANU PF's best efforts to intimidate potential witnesses (for example, in Chiredzi North witnesses' homes were burnt down and in Mount Darwin South a key witness was abducted, never to be seen again), judgments were being handed down in our favour. In April 2001, Judge James Devitte had ruled that ZANU PF's Kenneth Manyonda's victory over Tsvangirai was illegal[437] and his election was set aside. In the initial thirteen cases the results in seven constituencies were set aside and the seats declared vacant. Those cases alone in theory gave the MDC a majority in parliament but in all of the ultimate sixteen High Court judgments in favour of the MDC the ZANU PF respondents appealed to the Supreme Court. The appeals suspended the High Court judgments and all the ZANU PF MPs affected retained their seats. It soon became clear why ZANU PF had been so anxious to hound judges Gubbay and his fellow Supreme Court judges out of office earlier in the year. The new chief justice, Chidyausiku, who had taken office in July 2001, was joined by several other new appointments to the Supreme Court, ensuring that the court was controlled by more sympathetic elements who were happy to allow the electoral appeals to gather dust.

I criticised these appointments in parliament, pointing out that judges Sandura and Muchechetere (both black Zimbabweans) were far more experienced judges. Minister Chinamasa responded with a remarkable volley on 27 September, telling me to "stop casting racist aspersions on members of the Judiciary who cannot defend themselves".[438] Chinamasa argued that Chidyausiku was more experienced than Sandura and Muchechetere, which prompted an angry public response from the latter, who wrote that he had graduated from law school long before both Chidyausiku and Chinamasa had even started their studies.[439] Quite how suggesting that two more experienced apolitical black judges were preferable to other black judges, who had shown political bias, is "racist" still eludes me. Chinamasa was right in one regard – the new chief justice was vastly more experienced in the political realm than his predecessors and he made sure that not one single electoral appeal case was heard by the Supreme Court prior to the expiry of that session of parliament in 2005. Although the electoral challenges brought by the MDC exposed massive electoral fraud and violence they did not succeed in dislodging a single ZANU PF MP.

As the 2002 presidential election drew ever closer my thoughts and work were drawn towards developing a transitional justice plan for the MDC in the event of Tsvangirai defeating Mugabe. In August 2001, I had attended a civic society workshop in the Matopos to discuss what was needed to redress the terrible human rights abuses Zimbabweans had suffered for decades. South Africa's Truth and Reconciliation Commission provided a recent regional template for Zimbabwe and we heard from some of its commissioners about its successes and flaws. One of the presenters was Priscilla Hayner of the New York-based International Centre for Transitional Justice (ICTJ), who suggested the MDC apply for assistance in developing a detailed transitional justice policy. This suggestion led to a series of planning meetings at the ICTJ in downtown New York just weeks after 9/11.

New York was a war zone: the fires at the base of the Trade Centre were still burning and an awful smell of kerosene and rotting flesh still pervaded lower Manhattan. As I sat in the 33rd floor offices of the ICTJ to begin the delicate process of planning a process of transitional justice in a post-Mugabe era, I was confronted with the poignant reality of 9/11. My attention kept being drawn to pieces of paper fluttering by my window, which had been pushed up by the Trade Centre fires. I am rarely moved to write poetry, but on 7 November 2001 wrote this.

Ground Zero – 120 Broadway

A bitter wind drives
The sweet, acrid stench,
The work of hateful men,
Deep into my soul

Fires, burning deep within
Yield papers swept away, heavenwards
The forlorn remains
of ideas crushed

Somebody's "vitally important" memo
Now irrelevant

Fluttering by the 33rd floor
Defying the pull of Wall Street
Hustling below

Sharp shards of steel
Greet the eye
Burnt, twisted, fragile
Grotesquely straining upwards
Towards what might have been
And what was

White angels dancing
In the air
Strangely liberated
Not bound now by files,
Convention, form and time.

As I wrote that poem other hateful men were at that moment working within Zimbabwe to foment further evil plans. Before leaving for New York I had read a report that Cain Nkala, one of the war veterans responsible for Patrick Nabanyama's disappearance, was getting agitated over the pending High Court trial for Nabanyama's murder. According to reports, he was tired of being the scapegoat for Nabanyama's disappearance and was threatening to spill the beans. Nkala told his war veteran colleagues he was going to hold a press conference and reveal the truth.[440] Relatives later told a local weekly that Nkala "had opposed the use of violence during ZANU PF campaigns"[441] and "wanted to leave the country because his life was in danger". Whatever the case, on the evening of Monday, 5 November Nkala was abducted from his home in Magwegwe, Bulawayo by a group of about ten men armed with AK assault rifles who used a similar *modus operandi* to that employed in Nabanyama's abduction. As Nkala was dragged away a neighbour "heard him call out the names of his kidnappers".[442] Shortly after the abduction Nkala's wife, who had witnessed the crime, was warned "not to speak to journalists" and placed "under police guard".[443]

Curiously, the Police Diary Log of the investigation[444] omits any mention of the neighbour's evidence about the names of the kidnappers. Instead within a day it records a "report" submitted to the military

Joint Operations Command (JOC), listing MDC youth "linked to the offence".[445] Within hours of this "information" Deputy Commissioner Mpofu, on the evening of 7 November 2001, coincidentally at almost the same time as I was writing "Ground Zero" in New York, ordered that I and my parliamentary colleagues Paul Themba Nyathi and Moses Mzila-Ndlovu be "questioned".[446]

Unaware of this instruction, I flew back to Zimbabwe via London and Johannesburg on 10 November. While I was in transit in London I was briefed by Alan Doyle regarding all that had been happening in my absence. Doyle, an old Bulawayo friend, had given up his job to devote all his time to create *Zimnews*, a daily internet-based compilation of the most pertinent news coming out of Zimbabwe. One of the unsung heroes of this time, Doyle methodically worked for years from a small house near Heathrow trawling through international papers and posting articles on Zimbabwe. He had an uncanny ability to get to the nub of an issue. Doyle warned me that it appeared there was a concerted campaign brewing against me. When I got to Johannesburg I received a warning there from ex-ZIPRA war veterans that I was going to be detained and charged with Nkala's murder. I had every opportunity to remain in South Africa but decided that if I did so it would give credence to the allegations, so I flew home on the final leg to Bulawayo. The tension was palpable in Bulawayo and grew in my own household on Sunday evening, 11 November when Vice-President Joseph Msika appeared on national television accusing the MDC of murdering Nkala (clairvoyantly two days before Nkala's body was found), threatening "if they (the MDC) are looking for a bloodbath they will certainly get it". In the same news report, Matabeleland North governor, Obert Mpofu, blamed a "third force of former Rhodesian troops" which, he said, was "working to destabilise the government".[447] The following day I received separate reports from three different sources that senior ranking ex-ZAPU cabinet ministers had resolved that my "elimination was a necessary piece of the ruling party's Presidential campaign".[448] I decided to continue with my normal routines and went in to work at my law firm on Monday morning, although fully expecting to be detained at any moment.

In a remarkably deft and swift piece of policing, Detective Inspector Matira arrested MDC members Khetani Sibanda and Remember Moyo the same morning and by that evening had extracted "confessions" from them both. That very afternoon, in a blaze of publicity, including ZTV cameramen, Sibanda and Moyo were taken out to a lonely field outside Bulawayo where they "showed" police a shallow grave where Nkala had been buried. The entire event was tragi-comically stage managed; aside from the miraculous confessions extracted in such a short space of time, the confidence exhibited by the police that the body would be found (demonstrated in the presence in advance of news television cameras) was unprecedented. One of ZTV's top reporters, Reuben Barwe, was so confident of a find that he had come down to Bulawayo that morning to record the event before a "confession" had even been extracted from Sibanda. In a bizarre *faux pax*, video footage recorded by the ZTV showed a uniformed policeman standing guard over the grave before it had been pointed out by Sibanda! Within a week of Nkala's abduction, his body had been "found" and "confessions" extracted from his murderers. In any professional police force this would have been exceptional detective work; in the context of Zimbabwe, where the abductions and murders of tens of opposition supporters had gone uninvestigated for months, it was completely implausible.

That evening the "discovery" of Nkala's body was prime time news on ZTV with detailed and gory footage shown. Minister of Home Affairs John Nkomo was interviewed, fulminating that the MDC leadership was responsible for the murder. Early that morning my election campaign manager Simon Spooner had been detained as well. In the middle of the news I received a call advising that Spooner's lawyers had been denied access to him and that they had no idea where he was being held. The net was slowly tightening. Over time Jenny and I had developed a number of routines to cater for the various threats levelled against us. In the event of us having to go into hiding the children and Jenny had a pack with essential clothing in it. I had a separate bag containing the essentials I would need in prison – warm, old clothing, basic toiletries, a Bible, and writing materials. Expecting to be detained that night, I checked my bag.

For some inexplicable reason I was not detained the next day, although two parliamentary colleagues, Fletcher Dulini Ncube and Moses Mzila-Ndlovu, were arrested. I decided to be more proactive by flying to Harare where I had a series of meetings with the MDC leadership and diplomats, advising them of the credible intelligence I had received of a plan to eliminate me. On the morning of 15 November I chaired the parliamentary Justice committee meeting on the same day *The Herald* suggested I was a wanted man. The previous evening, in discussions with Roy Bennett and

Morgan Tsvangirai, we had agreed that for my own safety I should go to ground for a few days as the inflammatory rhetoric around the discovery of Nkala's body had raised the possibility of a random attack against me. Bennett organised a charter flight for me to travel down to friends in Gweru without having to risk driving and he took me out to catch the flight after my committee meeting ended. On arrival at Charles Prince airport I saw a client of mine, Simon Rodgers, who said he was flying back to Bulawayo in his own light aircraft and that I was welcome to fly down with him. We cancelled the charter flight and I waited for Rodgers to fuel his aircraft before four of us, Rodgers, Max Rosenfels, myself and one other clambered aboard. We taxied out to the runway, having obtained clearance, to take off. As the plane took off I settled down in my seat, happy that I was at least going to have a few days' break from the unrelenting tension. We took off in a northerly direction and as we banked left back over the airfield to head south to Gweru the radio crackled into life. Rodgers had earphones on so I could not make out what was being said. He replied, "But you gave me clearance – if I turn back now, I am going to miss my daylight window to get back to Bulawayo before sunset." I then saw him visibly blanche and say tersely, "Roger wilco, permission to land I take is granted?" He immediately reduced throttle and told us that he had been ordered to return immediately. When he had questioned the order he was told: "If you do not comply Zimbabwe air force jets will be scrambled and you will be shot down."

The plane landed without incident and we taxied to an apron close to the control tower. As we approached I noticed several truckloads of policemen armed with rifles arriving and as Rodgers shut down the engine they spread out, surrounding the aircraft. Rodgers and his friends were shocked. They hadn't a clue what was happening. I assumed that for some bizarre reason the police had waited to arrest me in a spectacular fashion. As we disembarked I sought out the commanding officer and asked what the problem was. He didn't seem to know and said he was awaiting instructions. We all stood around for about an hour until the officer in charge told Rodgers he could go but that I would have to remain. It was too late for Rodgers to get back to Bulawayo before dark but they were so rattled that he took off anyway and flew across to Harare International airport to wait until the following morning. By the time Rodgers took off again a press retinue had gathered, including my friend Brian Latham. Still the police just stood around; I was not under arrest but I couldn't leave until eventually just before dusk word came through that they should return to barracks and I could go. Thoroughly bemused, I decided that I should still go to ground for a few days. I had received word that Jenny and the children had made it to a safe house in Gweru and so when Latham offered to drive me through the night I leapt at his offer.

There was one other fascinating twist to the Charles Prince airport incident. Just half an hour after its control tower told Rodgers that his plane would be shot down if he didn't return, the Civil Aviation Authority of Zimbabwe issued the following "new permanent Notam":

> *"All non scheduled flights operating into or out of any airfield in Zimbabwe (manned or unmanned) are required to submit flight plans for each leg of the flight at least 24 hours before the flight. Filing of flight plans by radio is no longer permitted. This includes the use of the Harare briefing frequency 122.5MMZ. Emergency cases will be treated on their own merits. Any aircraft that does not comply with the above requirements will not be allowed into the airspace."*[449]

This Notam persists to this day. It completely changed the prevailing flying practices in Zimbabwe, which had operated efficiently for decades, and has caused considerable inconvenience to businessmen and tour operators ever since.

It was just as well that I went to ground because that weekend ZANU PF leaders stoked the fires. On 16 November some 400 war veterans (most of whom had travelled down to Bulawayo from Harare overnight by train) and ZANU PF leaders gathered in Bulawayo and, armed with axes, sticks and whips, marched to the city hall under a three-vehicle police escort. In full view of the police they assaulted bystanders, especially whites. One old woman had her windscreen smashed, resulting in her later having to have glass surgically removed from an eye. A German aid worker was dragged from his vehicle and beaten in front of his terrified children.[450] At the city hall the mob was addressed by former Home Affairs minister Dumiso Dabengwa and local war veterans' leader Jabulani Sibanda, who spoke out against "terrorism". The city hall and mayor's office was then raided. Japhet Ndabeni-Ncube, the MDC mayor, had already fled his office, leaving the crowd to ransack it, destroy papers and steal his briefcase. Still the police did nothing to prevent these crimes perpetrated in urban government offices. Confident that they could act with complete impunity, the march resumed and ended up at the MDC regional headquarters building on Herbert Chitepo Street. On arrival, once again in the presence of a substantial police presence, the ZANU PF supporters broke down a portion of the outside wall of the building, smashed windows and broke in. A 20-litre container of petrol was carried inside and swished around before the building was set ablaze, and eventually razed to the ground. Far from doing anything to prevent the arson, the "Police formed a barricade to prevent anyone from dousing the flames".[451] Incensed by this brazen attack, some MDC supporters retreated and walked a few blocks to a building owned by one of the ZANU PF leaders who had addressed the crowd, Sikhanyiso Ndlovu, and set it on fire. The nadir I feared had happened – with virtually our entire leadership either in safe houses or in prison there was no one to restrain our apoplectic young supporters.

It was announced that Cain Nkala, a relatively junior war veteran, was to be accorded National Heroes status and on Sunday, 18 November he was buried in Heroes Acre, Harare, after a state funeral addressed by Mugabe himself. Paraphrasing President George W Bush's remarks made after the 9/11 attacks, Mugabe declared that Zimbabwe, like America, would not tolerate "acts of terrorism on its soil". Describing the MDC as "terrorists" throughout his speech, Mugabe accused us of "political violence and crimes against humanity" and warned that our "days were numbered". He said that Nkala's murder was a terrorist attack by "former Selous Scouts making a come-back on the political scene".[452] Removing any doubt about who Mugabe was talking about, Information minister Jonathan Moyo, irritated by my public accusation that Nkala's murder had been an "inside job", said "what David Coltart and MDC terrorists are saying in the media about this inside job is pure Selous Scout fiction". He went on to say that "as the President has said the Selous Scouts are back at it again. Coltart is leading the pack as a former Selous Scout."[453]

Despite the virulent accusations, I recognised I couldn't afford to give any credence to the ZANU PF propaganda line that I was on the run. Accordingly, we drove back to Bulawayo the next day and I went into my office. Despite this, *The Chronicle* ran a story entitled "Coltart's Family Evacuates?" The opening paragraph suggested that as "police investigations into terrorism" widened, my family was "understood to have evacuated to

South Africa".[454] It was hard even for ZANU PF propagandists to suggest that I had gone into hiding because I flew up to Harare that morning and spoke in parliament, at one point looking directly at the ZANU PF front bench with the following challenge: "I ask my Hon friends on the other side to look me in the eye – are you really interested in our nation or are you just interested in the retention of power?"[455]

Jenny, keen to set the facts straight, marched into *The Chronicle* offices with our two-month-old baby Bethany in a carry-cot, announcing to the editor: "I am Mrs Coltart and my children are at Petra School and you can confirm that."[456] She also told him, which went unreported in *The Chronicle,* that she "and her family had no intention of ever fleeing Zimbabwe despite (our) persecution by ZANU PF".[457]

Back in Bulawayo, and with the detention threat against me lowered, I was able to turn my attention to the plight of the various MDC members who were in detention. Spooner had been held incommunicado in the Esigodini CIO detention centre for a few days before another prisoner, about to be taken to court, had scratched Spooner's wife's telephone number on his skin and phoned her, revealing Spooner's whereabouts. In the interim Spooner had been interrogated but never about Nkala's murder, just about his involvement in the MDC. When he was finally taken to court and remanded in custody he was incarcerated in Khami maximum security prison. On Spooner's arrival at Khami word soon spread among the inmates, bringing tears to his eyes when three floors of prisoners erupted into MDC political songs, slogans and chants. His bail proceedings, which started in the High Court on 22 November, were an immediate revelation. The state case against Spooner, as explained by Detective Inspector Matira, was that he had masterminded Cain Nkala's murder and given explicit instructions to Khetani Sibanda. State counsel initially told the court that Sibanda and Remember Moyo would be called to give evidence but then she inexplicably changed her mind, forcing the presiding judge, Judge Kamocha, to call them himself. Sibanda and Moyo gave evidence of excruciating torture suffered at the hands of the police, but denied that they had ever implicated Spooner. Judge Kamocha concluded that Matira's evidence implicating Spooner appeared "to be false"[458] and ordered Spooner's release on bail on 6 December. Despite the state case being a tissue of lies, Kamocha's order was appealed against. Just before Christmas, 35 days after Spooner had been detained, Supreme Court Justice Muchechetere dismissed the appeal, heavily criticising the police's conduct. Muchechetere was so outraged that he arranged for his wife to phone Spooner's wife, passing on a message that he wanted to know immediately if Spooner was maltreated again.

Although fellow MP Mzila-Ndlovu was released in November, Fletcher Dulini Ncube was not as fortunate. He, Khetani Sibanda, Remember Moyo, director of MDC security Sonny Masera, Sazini Mpofu, and Army Zulu were formally charged with Nkala's murder. Ncube in particular was subjected to harsh treatment, no doubt because he was also MDC treasurer general and privy to information regarding MDC funding sources. In addition to being severely tortured, police deprived Ncube, a diabetic, of vital medicines, causing him to lose the sight of one eye during his imprisonment that November and December.

There are three important footnotes to the Nkala murder which provide overwhelming evidence that it was an inside job. The first occurred in May 2002 when Nkala's six surviving war veteran colleagues were tried for Nabanyama's murder in the Bulawayo High Court before the same judge, Kamocha, who had released Spooner on bail. The state's case, to put it mildly, was lacklustre and seemed designed to secure the accused's acquittal. No effort was made to prove that Nabanyama was in fact dead, or at least had been declared dead. Moreover, and shockingly, the state did the defence's work by calling two war veterans, Ngoni and Flackson, who obligingly told the court that the last person with whom Nabanyama had been seen was none other than Cain Nkala. Although Judge Kamocha found parts of their story "highly improbable",[459] in the absence of any evidence that Nabanyama was dead the judge had no option but to acquit all the accused persons. Without so much as a whimper the state "agreed with the defence that the State had not made a *prima facie* case".[460] Even more conveniently, the accused could not be charged with kidnapping or assault because those offences were covered by Mugabe's 2000 amnesty. As a result all the ZANU PF operatives responsible for Nabanyama's disappearance walked out of court scot free, and have never been held to account for their crime. Nkala's murder was a critical component of their acquittal.

The second footnote is provided in the trial of Fletcher Dulini Ncube, Khetani Sibanda and the other four MDC activists who were charged with the kidnapping and murder of Nkala. The trial began in October 2002 and, unlike the Nabanyama matter, was pursued vigorously by the state. However, in March 2004 Judge Susan Mungwira courageously threw out all the "confessions" extracted from the six MDC members, stating that fourteen out of the fifteen police witnesses had "shamelessly lied".[461] Mungwira, who at the time was receiving chemotherapy for cancer, and on one occasion nearly collapsed leaving the courtroom, found that the police had assaulted the men and their relatives, deprived them of sleep and threatened them with guns. Her most damning finding was that the police had "visited (Cain Nkala's) grave the night before" Khetani Sibanda was "supposed to have guided them to the site". Judge Mungwira called the investigation into Nkala's death an "appalling piece of fiction". It was no wonder that Detective Inspector Matira was confident enough to get ZTV reporter Reuben Barwe down from Harare before Nkala's body had been been pointed out by Khetani Sibanda. In her final judgment, delivered on 5 August 2004, Judge Mungwira acquitted all the MDC men, finding there was "no evidence whatsoever that (Khetani Sibanda) made indications to the police which led to the discovery of (Nkala's) body".[462]

I only became aware of the final footnote in 2015 after my relationship with Dabengwa had come full circle. From having had dinner in my home after his release in 1986, to me being branded a terrorist by him in 2001, Dabengwa and I once again have a cordial relationship. In 2015, when he became aware that I was writing this book, he gave me sight of a memo he had in his possession, which records a version of what happened to Nkala. According to this document, when it became apparent that Nkala was going to "expose about [sic] abductions" he "was abducted by a operations team dispatched from Harare by a Intelligence Head M" comprising six operatives namely C, SD, FZ, KT, M and M".[463] Nkala was then "taken to the same safe house" Nabanyama had been taken to, where he was tortured and murdered prior to being "driven near Solusi where he got dumped in a shallow grave". The operatives then "in turn went after MDC operatives and security officers" who were "brought to book for (sic) murder of Cain Nkala".

However, all this was unproven as 2001 came to an end. With the 2002 presidential election just months away, the MDC leadership were branded as "terrorists" by the very people who had ordered Nkala's murder. Our presidential candidate, Morgan Tsvangirai, had not been targeted in the Nkala operation, but an elaborate plan had already been hatched to ensnare him and our secretary general Welshman Ncube.

CHAPTER 18

THE 2002 PRESIDENTIAL ELECTION
AND ITS AFTERMATH
JANUARY TO JUNE 2002

"But let us not forget that violence does not exist alone and cannot survive in isolation: it is inevitably bound up with the lie. Between them there is the most intimate, most natural, fundamental link; violence can only be concealed by the lie, and the lie can only be maintained by violence."
– ALEXANDER SOLZHENITZYN, *ONE WORD OF TRUTH*

As we battled to defend ourselves against the trumped up charges brought against our members in the last few months of 2001, ZANU PF was systematically preparing for the presidential election which Mugabe proclaimed in early January would be held on 9 and 10 March. The September 2001 mayoral election in Bulawayo had shown that the MDC urban support was rock solid. Intimidation in communal areas had continued, meaning that the swing vote of commercial farm workers, so crucial in the June 2000 parliamentary election, would decide the election. In the course of 2001 ZANU PF had continued the process of advertising the farms that government had "acquired" in terms of the Land Acquisition Act. By mid 2001 a total of 4 493 farms had been listed for acquisition, about 90 per cent of all white-owned farms. At the same time mob violence had forced about 25 per cent of them to close down altogether. But remarkably, despite all the threats, a majority of commercial farms still continued to operate, albeit under difficult conditions, and therein lay a major problem for ZANU PF. For so long as white farmers were still on the land the possibility existed that their workers would vote MDC rather than ZANU PF.

On 7 September 2001, at a meeting of Commonwealth foreign ministers in Abuja, ZANU PF had agreed "to restore the rule of law to the process of land reform" and "take firm action against violence and intimidation". This was just another ruse, though, because in the closing months of 2001 ZANU PF implemented a variety of policies and decrees designed to do the reverse.

In fact ZANU PF did just the opposite of what it promised the Commonwealth by moving against nearly all of the remaining white commercial farmers. A mere two months later, on 9 November, Mugabe issued a decree amending the Land Acquisition Act. The new "law" compelled all farmers in receipt of a "Section 8 occupation order" to pack up and leave their farms within three months. It was worded to apply retroactively. The immediate consequence was that farmers were barred from working on their farms and confined to their homes, and so resettlement could begin right away. This decree was followed on 4 December by a new Supreme Court ruling which reversed all the previous judgments and gave government full authority to proceed with the dispossession of white farmers. Chief Justice Chidyausiku, with the support of three new Supreme Court judges, but with a dissenting judgment from the sole survivor of the previous court, Judge Ahmed Ebrahim, declared that land was "a matter of social justice and not, strictly speaking, a legal issue".[464]

Due to a combination of a drought and the ruinous land reform policies, maize production fell by 42 per cent in 2001 and by the end of the year Zimbabwe faced a shortfall of 800 000 tonnes which, paradoxically, provided ZANU PF with an opportunity to intimidate rural voters through control of food. Hunger became an important weapon in its arsenal. The World Food Programme warned that some 500 000 people faced starvation and ZANU PF cynically exploited the disaster.[465] In December new regulations were published, giving the state-controlled Grain Marketing Board (GMB) the sole right to import, buy, sell and stockpile maize and wheat. In January 2002, commercial farms that had been stockpiling maize to feed pigs and poultry were raided and their maize confiscated. Unable to feed their animals, farmers sent them to slaughter, further undermining their ability to survive. But the action ensured that the last independently held stocks of grain had been seized.

With absolute control over maize supplies, ZANU PF could now control food aid in rural areas, a powerful inducement for famished people to support the party. This was particularly so in drought prone areas, such as Matabeleland, which had voted against ZANU PF so heavily in 2000.

Another key facet in the ZANU PF election strategy was to control and limit the number of new voters, by making the registration process cumbersome. In November 2001, it had given notice to amend the Electoral Act, creating unprecedented requirements for voter registration. Aside from stripping Zimbabweans living abroad of the right to vote, city dwellers would have to produce proof of residence, in the form of utility bills and the like, something well nigh impossible for the growing number of people living in shacks. One of the consequences of the land reform programme was that thousands of displaced farm workers had been forced into towns and these measures were designed to ensure they would not be able to vote. In addition, new provisions ordered village headmen and chiefs to vouch for everyone registering to vote. This provision, combined with ZANU PF's control of food aid, gave the party enormous power to control the rural vote. Other amendments banned independent election observers and voter education programmes run by civic groups.

Minister of Justice Chinamasa had introduced the measures in parliament in an unorthodox fashion, using a General Laws Amendments bill to amend the Electoral Act. On 18 and 19 December 2001, before parliament adjourned for Christmas, several MDC MPs, including me, fought a spirited battle against the measures and the manner in which they had been introduced, but we were consistently outvoted by ZANU PF. When parliament reconvened in its first sitting of the new year on 8 January, all that was left for it to become law was a debate regarding a few amendments and the final third reading of the bill. Continuing where I had left off in December, I argued that the provisions contravened the plain requirements of the constitution which allowed all citizens over eighteen to be registered without restriction. I concluded by complaining that Chinamasa was "distorting the Constitution and this provision remains unconstitutional no matter what gloss (he) puts on it".[466]

We had extracted one concession from Chinamasa. This allowed voters to make a "sworn statement confirming his/her place of residence" and when that amendment came for a vote we supported it. What followed was the one victory we achieved that entire parliament. Chinamasa, obviously believing that he had worn us down and we would acquiesce to the entire bill, called for the third reading of the bill. When he called for the reading only a handful of MDC MPs were in the house, and it appeared the ZANU PF benches had an easy majority. What Chinamasa didn't realise was that there were more MDC MPs outside. Because we opposed the bill we objected to the third reading and the bells had to be rung. To Chinamasa's horror, in marched the other MDC members, giving us a majority; despite a last ditch attempt to find other ZANU PF members when the house was divided, we outvoted ZANU PF 36 to 23. It was a disaster for Chinamasa. Much of ZANU PF's election strategy was based on preventing as many new MDC voters from registering to vote as possible, which could not be implemented with the defeat of the bill.

The next day Chinamasa made no mistake with the next leg of ZANU PF's electoral strategy. Virtually the entire ZANU PF caucus rolled up to parliament to debate the Public Order and Security Bill (POSA). POSA was designed to replace the draconian Rhodesian Law and Order (Maintenance) Act (LOMA), but did so only in style not form. In many ways it was a refinement on LOMA, better suited to the current conditions prevailing in Zimbabwe. The RF had not feared criticism of the prime minister in the same way as ZANU PF feared criticism of Mugabe. Accordingly, a key focus of the new law was to outlaw "undermining the authority of or insulting the President" – designed to prevent the MDC from criticising Mugabe's track record in the run up to the election. Another key provision to counter the MDC's successful use of public meetings was to give the police wide powers to regulate them. Permission had to be sought to hold meetings and another raft of offences was created to punish those who did not secure this permission.

On the afternoon of 9 January we gathered in parliament to debate the Bill. ZANU PF steamrolled the bill through parliament and despite our best efforts to block it (a sixteen-hour debate that went through the night) the third reading was finally won by ZANU PF at 4.10 am on Thursday morning, 10 January.

That afternoon Chinamasa came back to parliament determined to overcome the defeat of the General Laws Amendment bill. To our astonishment he sought to "rescind (the) decision on the Third reading" of the bill, accusing the MDC of "treachery". Despite the fact that the Zimbabwean constitution, parliamentary standing orders and international parliamentary practice clearly prohibited the reintroduction of a defeated bill in the same session of parliament, Chinamasa, aided by the deputy speaker, nevertheless forced a vote on the issue. The ZANU PF caucus had been fiercely whipped into line and voted 62 to our 47. The "recision" achieved, Chinamasa moved the third reading of the bill again. We were so outraged by this brazen abuse of parliamentary law and procedure that the entire MDC caucus knelt down and commenced praying. Our action infuriated ZANU PF members, with one MP, Paul Mangwana, shouting out: "Speaker, please march them out, this is not a chapel."[467] The house divided again and ZANU PF "passed" the bill. Another key leg of ZANU PF's strategy had been achieved by hook or by crook. The lengths they went to demonstrated how important these measures were to prevent all Zimbabweans from exercising their vote.

A few days later the minister of Labour, July Moyo, unveiled a further line of attack when an amendment to the Labour Relations Act was moved. The bill, among other things, redefined and tightened up "unlawful collective job actions" in an effort to emasculate a key constituency of the MDC, the trade unions. It also sought to deregister "troublesome unions". Zvobgo, in his capacity as a member of the parliamentary legal committee, to his credit agreed that elements of the bill offended the constitution. On 15 January the matter was debated in parliament and I could not resist the opportunity to expose some of the hypocrisy displayed by a party that called its leaders "comrade" and yet did all in its power to undermine workers' rights. I quoted from Jonathan Moyo's book *Voting for Democracy,* written in 1991 before he had had his Damascene conversion to ZANU PF, in which he identified the start of the falling out between ZANU PF and trade unions. Moyo had written that "groups which tended to support ZANU PF, such as the ZCTU, became critical ... and held them responsible for ills such as inflation and unemployment".[468] I went on to complain about legislation being moved by non-constituency MPs who didn't have to report back to the electorate, a dig at Moyo and others, who had been appointed by Mugabe.

This was the final straw for Moyo, who had been stewing across the way from me on the opposite benches. He shouted out that I was a "*murungu*[469] bastard". My colleague Paul Themba Nyathi objected in his inimitable, humorous fashion, saying, "Even if Hon Coltart is a *murungu* he is not a bastard in this House. He is an Hon member."[470] When questioned by the speaker, Moyo denied the accusation. I continued my speech, opened the copy of the book Moyo had given me in front of the house, and said, "I would be very much surprised if my Hon friend would say such a thing because I will repeat what is written by him at the front: 'To my dear friend David, with all the best wishes in the hope of a better future for all of us. Jonathan Moyo, 23rd July 1993.' So I would be surprised if he called me a *murungu* bastard."[471] It brought both sides of the house down, and even Moyo was forced into a wry smile. For reasons only known to them, ZANU PF did not pursue the bill any further.

The final leg of ZANU PF's electoral strategy was contained in the misleadingly named Access to Information and Protection of Privacy Bill (AIPPA), which the minister of Information, Jonathan Moyo, conjured up, and which was debated in parliament in the last week of January 2002. Moyo immediately ran into problems, however, with his own caucus and in particular Eddison Zvobgo, for whom the bill was a bridge too far. Debating the bill on 29 January, Zvobgo said, "… this Bill in its original form was the most calculated and determined assault on our liberties in the 20 years I served as Cabinet Minister" and called it "ill-conceived and dangerous".[472] Zvobgo questioned why Moyo, as minister, sought "such overwhelming power from Parliament", including powers to investigate and spy.

Given Zvobgo's opposition, the bill was watered down and Moyo's investigative powers were removed. The amended bill allowed journalists to criticise Mugabe, even though POSA prohibited it. Media licences would no longer be issued by Moyo himself, but by a commission appointed by him. Existing investors in media companies would be exempt from a clause requiring new media ventures to be 51 per cent Zimbabwean owned. Nonetheless when the revised bill was presented to parliament on 31 January, it remained draconian. Quoting the prophet Isaiah again, I spoke at length in opposition to the bill, arguing that contrary to its name it was designed to "curtail the rights of Zimbabweans to information" and would be used to "close down institutions like the *Daily News* and others which are exposing the truth".[473] Once more we debated well into the night but ultimately ZANU PF had its way and the bill was passed.

With ZANU PF having achieved the coercive legislative environment it desired for the presidential election, parliament was adjourned to 28 May. We still held out hope that, despite the massive obstacles placed in our path, Tsvangirai might yet be our new president when parliament reconvened.

With the election campaign now in full swing ZANU PF and Mugabe revealed the main planks of their message. If the old South African Nationalists had used *"swart gevaar"* (Afrikaans for "black threat") to terrify white South Africans into voting for them, ZANU PF was determined to use *"wit gevaar"* ("white threat") to terrify black Zimbabweans, and I was a major component of their strategy.

On 1 February they released Mugabe's manifesto – "22 reasons for voting ZANU PF". Reason 1 was to combat terrorism – whites were attempting to "rule again and bring back racism, terrorism and suffering". On the same page was a photograph of me (presumably found in police archives) when I received my "Best Recruit" award at my passing out parade in January 1976, with a sub-title explaining that "Selous Scouts are back at it again" and that the manner Cain Nkala was killed "was similar to methods used by the Selous Scouts". Reason 3 was to combat racism, accusing the MDC of being "bent on bringing back racism". It went on to allege that "former Rhodesians, including notorious ones like David Coltart who worked for the Rhodesian Special Branch, are abusing youth by giving them small change, drink and drugs, turning them into terrorists trained to fight for white interests only".[474] Reason 20 was to "promote racial reconciliation" and Mike Auret and I got it in the neck again. Racists, naming the two of us, who were "fuelling conflict", were not going to be tolerated and would be "soon thrown in jail where they belong". Whites were right, left and centre of ZANU PF's propaganda campaign. Morgan Tsvangirai, according to them, was just their puppet.

In early February I flew to New York with my LRF colleague and MDC chief whip, Innocent Gonese, to continue our legal preparations in anticipation of Tsvangirai winning the presidential elections. A new president would have the power to appoint eight new provincial governors, which would potentially give the MDC a majority in parliament – but even this was subject to chiefs deciding to take orders from a new president other than Mugabe. This would have enabled the MDC to implement a raft of new legislation to promote democracy. Since starting work with the New York-based International Centre for Transitional Justice the previous year, we had done a vast amount of thinking and work in creating a legal framework for a peaceful transition to democracy. With the backing of ICTJ president Alex Boraine, who was also a former deputy chairman of the South African Truth and

Reconciliation Commission, the ICTJ enabled a Zimbabwean legal draftsman to work on a wide array of new legislation. Now it needed to be finalised. ZANU PF's contempt for the rule of law, its widespread corruption, and the politicisation of the judiciary, police force and armed forces had severely compromised institutions. Likewise ZANU PF's creation of youth brigades had created a culture of violent deviant behaviour which would be difficult to root out. We recognised that the rebuilding of a democratic order, in which there would be respect for the rule of law, would be a complex process.

In the course of an intense week in New York we completed a 225-page Justice Policy document,[475] designed as a template for a new Zimbabwean order. It detailed our policy regarding the judiciary, attorney general's office, police, prosecution policy, prison reform, a new constitution and parliament. The document recognised that wholesale changes to institutions would destabilise the country and so it set out a gradual process of reformation. Key to the transition would be the promotion of new principles which would underpin the civil service, including selflessness, integrity, objectivity, accountability, openness and honesty. Included in the document were several new draft bills including Anti-Corruption, Truth Commission, Whistleblower, Administrative Decisions, Freedom of Information, Media Complaints Council, and Independent Broadcasting bills. There were also policy papers dealing with a wide variety of issues such as vetting human rights offenders, judicial reform, prosecutions strategy, reparations, human rights training for police and prison officers, guidelines for election broadcasting and minimum electoral standards. ZANU PF propaganda has always falsely claimed that the MDC hasn't got any policies. The fact is that since early 2002 the MDC has had comprehensive policies and draft legislation available which, if implemented, would completely transform Zimbabwe's legislative environment and lay the foundation for its transformation into a democratic state.

I arrived home from New York at midday on Saturday, 16 February into the midst of a firestorm. Ever since the announcement of the election in January, all over the country violence had surged. Although ZANU PF youth brigades, called "Green Bombers" (because of the green military fatigues they wore), had been on a rampage against suspected MDC supporters for months, a new tactic was employed in mid January targeting MDC MPs who were at the forefront of Tsvangirai's election campaign. It commenced with a savage attack on MDC Lupane MP David Mpala on 13 January – he had been abducted by ZANU PF supporters and Green Bombers, had his abdomen slit open and skull crushed. He had not died but was seriously injured.[476] Shortly after Mpala's abduction, the homes of four Harare MDC MPs, Chaibva, Munyanyi, Mhashu and Makuvaza, were attacked. On 20 January ZANU PF supporters had violently disrupted an MDC campaign rally at White City Stadium in Bulawayo; instead of arresting them the police had cordoned off the stadium and fired teargas at MDC MPs and their supporters who were trying to get in. Beatings and violence spread and by the end of that month the MDC could not campaign in at least 40 out of the country's 120 constituencies.

The day before I left for New York, on 7 February MDC MPs Abednico Bhebhe and Peter Nyoni were ambushed by military personnel and ZANU PF militia on their way to a presidential campaign rally in Nkayi. Militia and soldiers opened fire on the convoy of cars, puncturing tyres. Bhebhe and Nyoni, along with 34 supporters, were dragged out of their vehicles, beaten up and then detained in the local police station.[477] They were only released from detention on 13 February. I had managed to evade these attacks but as I drove in from the airport my wife told me that Green Bombers had been deployed that week to the suburb we lived in; the previous day they had stoned three cars on Circular Drive, just a kilometre from our home.

After resting at home, Jenny, our children Douglas (then aged 11) and Bethany (six months old) and I left to drive into town at 4 pm to collect our daughter Jessica, who had been attending a birthday party. Shortly after leaving our home I noticed a crowd of about 100 ZANU PF youths dressed in Robert Mugabe T-shirts straddling the main connecting road into town, Northway. Concerned for the safety of my family, I took another route. About an hour later, having collected Jessica, we returned but found the ZANU PF youth still blocking Northway. As I turned into Northway I noted a beige Toyota pick-up, registration number 450-260M, with a man standing next it who appeared to be directing the youths. I drove on and took the indirect route we had left on, but as I approached our house I realised that there were more ZANU PF youths blocking the road, about 50 metres from our home. I turned the car around and drove to a friend's house, where I phoned the police to report that I was being prevented from getting home by ZANU PF youths. The police were decidedly uncooperative and advised me that they might have "difficulty in attending the scene as they had transport problems". I waited half an hour and then ventured out with my friend, leaving Jenny and the children behind, to check to see if the youths were still barricading my home; they were not – although they were still in the vicinity, we observed them walking away. The coast clear, I collected my family and drove home. About an hour later a police vehicle arrived with three uniformed officers in it; they advised me they were responding to my report made two hours earlier. I told them that the youths had moved off and they left.

Just as we were putting our children to sleep, at 8.45pm, three more police vehicles arrived, this time packed with armed uniformed officers and men in plainclothes. I went out to the gate and, through it, spoke to an agitated officer who told me that a report had been made that I had fired a shot in the presence of ZANU PF youths. Pointing out that I had never possessed a firearm, I asked when the shot was fired and was told "between 4.30 and 5pm". I told the officer that I hadn't even been in the vicinity at that time and gave them the names of the people from whom I had been collecting my daughter. That suggestion didn't appeal and an angry demand was made that I let all of them inside to search my home. I refused to allow them in in the absence of a search warrant, which got them even more agitated. With weapons being brandished in my face, I said I would be happy for the senior uniformed officer to conduct a search. I had nothing to hide but I didn't know who the plainclothes men were and my fear was that they would plant a weapon. Subsequently, I learnt that the ZANU PF operative in the beige Toyota pick-up I had seen earlier had in fact fired a shot in the air in the vicinity of my home. A young man living near our home was abducted and assaulted by the ZANU PF youths that afternoon. He was bundled into the same Toyota and witnessed this ZANU PF operative, who was in charge and called by the youths "Majuzi", let off a couple of shots that afternoon.[478] While I didn't have this information that evening, I knew, from my years as a lawyer, how easy it was to plant a weapon and then "link it" to an expended cartridge left at a scene by an operative.

The police remained adamant that they should all be allowed to conduct a search. When I refused I was advised that I was under arrest. Telling them that they had no right to arrest me, I refused to go (I was standing behind our locked gate), which invoked a furious reaction from one of the men in plainclothes, who told me "they would be back to get me". Surprisingly, instead of breaking down the gate and coming after me, they left. Once again the family was hurriedly packed into a car and we all went into hiding. Because we feared that a road-block may have been set up, I got into the boot of my parents-in-laws' car, had them cover me with a blanket and take me to a safe house. My father-in-law, then aged 79, a North Africa and Italy veteran of World War II, was delighted by all the excitement, and I think saddened that he never had to bluff his way through a road-block with me in the boot.

The following Monday morning I presented myself to the local Hillside police station in the company of my legal partner, Josephat Tshuma. Parked at the station was the same beige Toyota pick-up I had seen the previous Saturday afternoon, indicating connivance between the police and ZANU PF, which I pointed out to Tshuma. I was immediately arrested and taken into the "Law and Order" section at Bulawayo Central police station, where Detective Inspector Matira advised me that I was going to be prosecuted for discharging a firearm in a public place. Once again I went through the entire sequence of events, giving him the names and telephone numbers of people he could interview to confirm my alibi. I invited him to check that I had never held a firearms licence, and that I had made a report to the police. None of this interested him; I was fingerprinted and locked up. Shortly after lunch a junior officer advised me that they wanted to search my house and I should accompany them. My cell phone had been taken off me and I was denied the right to phone Tshuma. As I was getting into a Land Rover in the courtyard of the station Matira stuck his head out from a first floor window, instructing the junior officers to take a bakkie[479] and that I should be handcuffed and held in the back of it. The vehicle was then driven out of the police yard with me sitting on the back in my suit in handcuffs. Instead of taking the quickest, direct route to my home, the officers drove the vehicle slowly through the centre of Bulawayo, making sure I was on full display. Several people recognised me and soon there were scores of people waving at me, using the open-handed MDC slogan. My Presbyterian pastor Kevin Thomson had staked out the police station ever since Tshuma had departed that morning, fearing that I would be disappeared by the police, and I saw his car following the police vehicle at a distance, which was a great comfort. We eventually got home and the search was conducted but they found nothing. There was one complication during the search – our daughter

Jessica was so infuriated by a previous raid on the house, when police had rifled through her personal effects, that she had locked the door to her room, determined to prevent a search there. Fortunately, the police relented and didn't break the door down! Two of the junior officers were clearly embarrassed about what they had been ordered to do and when they had a chance with me alone, they apologised.

As I was climbing into the bakkie, at the end of the search, the surly officer in charge noticed our neighbour, Jeanette Cross (the wife of fellow MDC national executive member Eddie Cross), taking photographs of me from across the road. The officer was enraged: he stormed across to Jeanette, snatched the camera from her, and told her she, too, was under arrest. She was ordered into the back of the bakkie and so off we went together, back to Bulawayo Central.[480] Given the experience of representing countless detainees as a lawyer, I knew that this was just the beginning of my ordeal and so I was bracing myself for a few nights in the squalid Bulawayo Central cells or worse. Much to my surprise, soon after getting back to Bulawayo Central I was told the police docket for my prosecution was ready and that I was being taken to court. It was the first time I had appeared on the accused's side of the dock and as I came up from the prisoner's well beneath the court the presiding magistrate, before whom I had appeared as defence counsel numerous times, looked shocked. To his relief the state prosecutor, who had already told Matira how unimpressed he was with the charges, advised the court that bail would not be opposed. The magistrate ordered that I pay a peppercorn bail and I was released. Jenny, who had already started preparations for a long haul of my imprisonment, couldn't believe her eyes when I walked in the front door. It was, however, to be a disruptive long haul before the courts; despite not having an iota of evidence against me, I kept having to appear in court on remand until June 2003, when the charges were finally withdrawn.

While I was in New York that February a small Australian television channel, SBS TV, was used by ZANU PF to unveil a new line of attack against Tsvangirai and the MDC. On 13 February, it alleged that Tsvangirai had been conspiring with a Canadian public relations company, Dickens & Madson, to assassinate Mugabe. They were in possession of a video tape recording of portions of a meeting that had been held between Tsvangirai and an alleged Israeli con artist, Ari Ben-Menashe in Montreal on 4 December 2001. Inevitably, the next day the

Zimbabwean government-controlled media splashed selected details of the recording, which had been made using cameras hidden in the ceiling. The soundtrack was poor, requiring sub-titles to explain what was being said. Although Ben-Menashe tried to get Tsvangirai to discuss Mugabe's assassination, Tsvangirai never suggested that Mugabe should be murdered. It remains unclear how SBS got hold of the video tape, although the lead journalist behind the story, Mark Davis, had been to Harare shortly before the programme was broadcast. The fact that the ZBC already had a copy of the tape the day after it was aired in Australia suggested collaboration between SBS and ZBC. SBS, on being pressed about the matter, conceded that Ben-Menashe had been contracted by ZANU PF and had sent it a copy of the tape. Knowing that the story would lack credibility if broken by the ZBC, it appears that ZANU PF operatives ensured that it be broken in Australia to make it seem as if the matter was not contrived. The choice of an Australian TV station was also deliberate – the Commonwealth Heads of Government Meeting (CHOGM) was scheduled to be hosted by Australian Prime Minister John Howard at Coolum in March 2002 and ZANU PF's intention was presumably that the story would sway their thinking against Tsvangirai.

The ZBC and *The Herald* produced further details of the alleged plot, implicating Welshman Ncube and the secretary for Agriculture, Renson Gasela as well. Tsvangirai's arrest was called for and the police duly obliged by charging Tsvangirai with treason on 25 February. Curiously, though, Tsvangirai was not taken to court and the police advised that the trial would not start until after the presidential election. Given the seriousness of the allegations, a person charged with treason would normally have been detained and bail refused, but that would not have looked good in Tsvangirai's case. Right from the beginning of the saga ZANU PF's intention was clear: it was designed to cast Tsvangirai in a bad light and to confuse the electorate.

Some of the excerpts of the tape recording, although not criminal, were damaging. They made it obvious that Tsvangirai had been caught up in a sting operation in Montreal. Not knowing anything about the matter, I asked for details and was told that Tsvangirai, Ncube and Gasela had met Ben-Menashe in London and that the MDC had paid his firm US$100 000 to lobby for the MDC in North America. While I understood that such a lobbying contract could not be discussed within the national executive (given the extent of our infiltration by CIO operatives), I was surprised by the amount of money paid and that no background checks had been made. A simple Google search at the time revealed that Ben-Menashe was an unsavoury character, and so I was concerned that this had not been done. It also seemed unwise for Tsvangirai to have met Ben-Menashe alone in Montreal, making him vulnerable to this type of scam. However, knowing how ZANU PF twisted facts, I thought that this was simply another warped electioneering tactic which would not be pursued. Only time would show that it had other deeper objectives: to divide the MDC and drain it of resources.

With less than a month to go to the election, I threw myself into the campaign and criss-crossed the entire country in support of Tsvangirai. In the last two weeks of February I spoke at meetings as far flung as Victoria Falls in the west to Rusape in the east. On two occasions in this campaign Roy Bennett and I had near escapes, one an accident, the other contrived. The first occurred when we were flown in a light aircraft to speak in Karoi. As we approached the rough landing strip from the south west the pilot misjudged his speed and came in too fast. At the north-eastern end of the strip, next to Ridings School, there was a copse of trees, giving pilots very little leeway. As the pilot battled to get the plane settled, the trees appeared to be rushing up on us. Once the pilot got the aircraft down he braked vigorously and the aircraft came to a halt just metres from the trees. Nothing was said but I made a mental note to drive in future. Shortly afterwards Bennett and I drove from Harare to a campaign meeting near Chegutu. The meeting ended in the late afternoon and we got back in our car soon afterwards to commence our return drive. It wasn't long before we noticed that we were being followed by a car with three people inside it. Bennett tested their intent by speeding up and then slowing down, but still they stuck behind us. By now dusk was falling and we began to worry that this was a prelude to an "accident" – with us driving into a stationary army truck, perhaps, conveniently parked on the road, with the tailing vehicle advising others of our precise location and ETA. Bennett sped up as fast as he could but the car, leach-like, stuck to our tail. Coming onto a straight stretch of road he suddenly rammed on brakes, completely taking the driver behind us by surprise, who then lost control of his vehicle, causing it to spin across the road behind us. Although the tailing vehicle didn't crash, it ended up in bush alongside the road where it stuck. We were able to continue our journey back to Harare unimpeded. We both realised that it had been imprudent to travel alone together as we presented too tempting a target.

A key component of our campaign was to use the courts as best we could to level the electoral playing field. The MDC legal affairs committee, which I chaired and which included Innocent Chagonda, Advocate Adrian de Bourbon, Innocent Gonese and Yvonne Mahlunge, brought some fourteen cases, mostly in Tsvangirai's name, to the High and Supreme courts in the run up to the election. Our main concern related to the registration of voters. On 19 December 2001 we obtained an order preventing the registrar general (RG) from closing the registration of voters.[481] On 31 December, the High Court ordered the RG not to remove illegally names from the common voters' roll and to reinstate those names he had already removed illegally. The same judgment ordered the RG to supply us with the common voters' roll up to 2 January 2002 in electronic format which, surprisingly, was complied with.[482] On 25 January the High Court ruled in our favour, ordering the establishment of the common roll, the right of permanent residents to vote, and the right of voters to vote anywhere in the country. The same judgment found the RG in contempt for not having kept the voters' roll open as previously ordered.[483]

Government immediately appealed that order to the Chidyausiku-led Supreme Court, which promptly reversed the 25 January High Court judgment, thereby disenfranchising thousands of voters. Only Judge Sandura, a remnant of the Gubbay-led Supreme Court, supported the original High Court order, giving a dissenting judgment in our favour.[484] On 19 February we instituted proceedings in the Supreme Court to have the General Laws Amendment Act, unlawfully passed by parliament through Chinamasa's guile in January, ruled illegal. This time we were fortunate: on 27 February the Supreme Court, with another Gubbay remnant, Judge Ebrahim (who was acting chief justice in Chidyausiku's absence) set aside the act because of the procedural irregularities in the passage of the bill through parliament.[485] This was a particularly sweet victory, vindicating our debate against Chinamasa when he had ridden roughshod over parliamentary rules and procedure.

Our celebrations were short lived, though, because a few days later, on 5 March 2002, Mugabe published a decree reinstating all the provisions which favoured him and validating all acts done in terms of the General Laws Amendment Act, which had just been declared invalid by the

Supreme Court![486] The decree also revealed for the first time that a secret supplementary voters' roll had been compiled. We had been told that the voters' roll had been closed on 10 January, so we had no idea who had been allowed to register in this manner. A further supplementary list was prepared of people who had been unilaterally taken off the voters' roll and would not be allowed to vote, targeting whites and other minorities, who lost the right to vote in droves. Mugabe's farcical decree drove us back to the Supreme Court two days later to seek a ruling declaring his decree unconstitutional. The matter was argued before a Chidyausiku-led Supreme Court on the eve of the election. Despite the obvious urgency of the matter, judgment was reserved and only handed down well after the election, on 4 April, when a majority of the court ruled that Tsvangirai did not have *locus standi* to bring the case, in a stroke ducking all the serious breaches brought before the court.[487] All our efforts to use the legal system to secure a level playing field came to nought. Aided and abetted by the Supreme Court, Mugabe had created an electoral playing field to his liking, which enabled him then to subvert the will of the people in the ensuing election.

Despite all the pitfalls and obstacles thrown in our way, as voting began on Saturday, 9 March we remained optimistic that Tsvangirai could still win. Opinion polls had shown that he was well ahead of Mugabe. I was Tsvangirai's election agent for Bulawayo South, my own constituency, and as polling started long queues formed and it looked as if there would be an excellent turnout. However, as the day wore on reports came in from major cities across Zimbabwe of a deliberate attempt to thwart urban voters. One of the decrees introduced by Mugabe on the eve of the election was to reduce the number of polling stations in urban areas, in some cities by as much as 60 per cent. Harare, with nearly a third of all voters, was only allocated 164 polling stations. By contrast the number of polling stations in ZANU PF strongholds was increased by 644. As a result rural voters found it easy to vote but by 3 pm that Saturday the lines at some stations in Harare were over three kilometres long, with tens of thousands patiently waiting to cast their votes. So strong was the determination to vote that thousands remained in these queues overnight when polling closed at 7 pm that evening. Even on the biased Registrar General of Election's figures the official total number of registered voters in Harare was 722 918, but by the end of the day only 148 409 had managed to cast their vote. An urgent application was prepared that evening and filed at the home of the duty High Court judge for Harare at 3 am on the morning of Sunday, 10 March, seeking an extension of polling. When the matter was eventually heard at 2 pm that afternoon, Minister of Justice Chinamasa surprisingly appeared on behalf of the electoral bodies we had sued – the Registrar General of Elections, the Electoral Supervisory Commission and the Election Directorate. All were meant to be independent of the minister and government, but the lie to that was given in Chinamasa's appearance. Chinamasa assured the judge that while there had been a problem the previous day, it had been rectified. Knowing that if anything the situation was far worse than Chinamasa let on, our legal team pressed for a physical inspection, which resulted in the judge inspecting polling stations in Harare that afternoon by helicopter. It didn't take long for him to see from the air long queues snaking throughout Harare. As a result Judge Hlatshwayo made an order[488] extending polling by one day to 7 pm on Monday, 11 March. Although more people voted that Sunday in Harare (176 722) some 55 per cent of the electorate had not yet managed to vote.

The euphoria we felt over securing an extra day of voting was misplaced because ZANU PF brazenly subverted the order. The first sign was when Chinamasa announced later in the evening, on ZTV, that voting would only be extended in Harare and Chitungwiza, despite the clear dictates of the order which extended throughout the country. However, not even that restricted opening was complied with – the polls in Harare and Chitungwiza only opened at midday. When they did some polling stations were attacked by mobs of ZANU PF supporters, causing many voters to flee. The final breach occurred when polls closed at 7 pm. Despite a clear right to vote given to voters still in queues at close of polls,[489] voters were turned away. In some cases police used teargas to disperse them. Only 43 898 managed to vote in Harare that Monday, in total only 369 029, 51 per cent of those eligible to vote in an election where there was massive interest. Outraged, we went back to court, asking for registrar general Tobaiwa Mudede to be held in contempt and seeking a further day of polling the next day. Judge President Paddington Garwe decided to hear the case himself. He adjudged that Mudede was not in contempt and refused to extend the polling to another day.[490] We and the electorate had been outdone by a ZANU PF coterie of lawyers, judges and civil servants.

As we waited for votes to be counted, reports came flooding in of massive electoral fraud and abuse throughout the country. More than

1 400 people, mostly MDC polling agents, had been arrested over the three-day election, preventing them from being at their posts. In other areas polling agents had been abducted by ZANU PF militia. The voters' roll was in a shambles and many people registered in our strongholds had been left off it. In many stations ballot boxes had gone missing for hours at a time, and in some cases when our polling agents complained they were arrested. Strangely, in a country with a literacy rate in excess of 90 per cent, thousands of people claimed to be illiterate and needed to be "helped" in casting their vote. There were massive anomalies in voter turnout – in ZANU PF strongholds such as Uzumba-Maramba-Pfungwe, a remote rural constituency, the turnout was 73.5 per cent, whereas in the Harare constituency of Dzivarasekwa only 32.3 per cent had managed to vote.[491]

On 13 March the official results were announced by Registrar General Mudede. Mugabe had "won" the election, with 1 685 212 votes to Tsvangirai's 1 258 401. In the 2000 election ZANU PF had secured 1 203 263 votes (48.32 per cent of the vote) against the MDC's 1 171 656 (47.05 per cent). Miraculously, Mugabe had managed to secure another 481 949 votes out of thin air.

We were incredulous when some organisations such as the OAU described the election as "transparent, credible, free and fair" and wondered which election they had been observing. Fortunately, some leaders and parties saved Africa's blushes. The leader of the Commonwealth observer group, Nigerian General Abdusalam Abubakar, recommended that the Commonwealth should not accept the result. The presidents of Ghana and Senegal also condemned the poll. While the ANC delegation described the election as "credible", they could not call it "free and fair". Critically, though, President Mbeki, the most influential African leader, covered up for Mugabe. Mbeki had sent two South African judges, Sisi Khampepe and Dikgang Moseneke, to report on the elections. In a damning 27-page report delivered to Mbeki they found that violence, including 107 politically motivated murders, was the "hallmark" of the election. ZANU PF's militia had been the "primary perpetrators of violence". They found that the electoral laws had been "amended dramatically and manipulated by executive decrees", that government had "discarded the rule of law by failing to give effect to High Court decisions", and that police treatment had been "partial". They concluded that "having regard to all the circumstances, and in particular the cumulative substantial departures from international standards of free and fair elections found in Zimbabwe ... these elections cannot be considered free and fair".[492] Mbeki, however, refused to release what became known as the Khampepe Report, which only saw the light of day when a South African newspaper, the *Mail & Guardian*, won a Constitutional Court challenge compelling the South African government to release it in November 2014. Until then the official South African government position reflected the findings of the South African observer mission which disingenuously found the election "legitimate". That stance bought ZANU PF and Mugabe breathing space and betrayed the will of the Zimbabwean electorate.

While it had been obvious that ZANU PF would do everything necessary to win the election, I was still stunned and depressed by the result. The prospect of six more years of tyrannical rule was hard to stomach. It also wasn't surprising that there were elements within the MDC who now felt that non-violent tactics would never defeat ZANU PF's machinations.

On 19 March both the MDC parliamentary caucus and national council met in Harare to conduct a post-mortem of the election. Everyone was angered by the blatant theft of the election and some argued that it was pointless challenging the result – fire should be met with fire. I, along with others, argued passionately that we needed to remain true to our founding principles and that, while challenging the result through court was fraught with problems, we had no option but to remain committed to the use of non-violent tactics. This view prevailed and the legal committee was mandated to challenge the result on behalf of Tsvangirai. We set to work, gathering and collating evidence of electoral fraud and malpractice, but had hardly started when Tsvangirai, Welshman Ncube and Gasela were formally indicted in the High Court and charged with treason. We had our work cut out for us. In the space of a few days I took responsibility for a presidential election challenge and the defence of our president and secretary general.

Tsvangirai's court application against Mugabe, filed in the High Court on 12 April, immediately evoked a hostile response from him. The South African government had been trying to broker a negotiated settlement of the political crisis and we had appointed a team, which included Welshman Ncube, to conduct secret talks. However, Mugabe had been insisting that we first recognise him as head of state. The moment the court papers were filed, he berated Tsvangirai for challenging his victory and called off the talks. With Tsvangirai's court challenge finalised, and given the political stalemate and parliamentary recess, I decided to get my family out of the country for a break and we flew to Cape Town.

While there I consulted a broad cross-section of people who would be best suited to represent us in both the electoral challenge and the treason trial. While Zimbabwe had outstanding advocates, I felt it necessary to internationalise the cases as best we could. Both cases were intensely political and we needed top lawyers with high international credibility and profile to conduct them. It was particularly important to engage lawyers who enjoyed the ANC's respect. Two names came up – Jeremy Gauntlett and George Bizos. Gauntlett, aside from being one of Africa's foremost constitutional lawyers, had represented President Mandela, Archbishop Tutu, the ANC and the Namibian government. I met Gauntlett in Cape Town on 19 April and he agreed to lead the presidential challenge case alongside Zimbabwean advocates Adrian de Bourbon and Happias Zhou. Although I was unable to meet Bizos, Mandela's legendary treason trial lawyer, on that trip, I returned to Zimbabwe convinced that he would be the best person to lead the treason trial defence team.

Parliament resumed briefly on 7 May, which gave the minister of Finance, Simba Makoni, a chance to address us on the state of the economy. It was the first statement made by a ZANU PF minister post the presidential election and it was remarkably candid. Makoni told the house that inflation was running at 112 per cent. His report, he said, was "another instalment to the accumulating record of economic decline"; he stated that farmers should be able to "farm without disruption" and that there should be an "end to violence".[493] He could have been speaking for the MDC.

His remarks regarding violence resonated with me as I had just received word of yet another death threat. A well-placed and trusted source had warned that a hit squad had been formed to eliminate me and three other white members of the MDC, Auret, Bennett and Cross. I commented at the time: "I am by no means paranoid, I have had death threats more direct than this before, but what's alarming about this case is the identity of the source."[494] Makoni's comments regarding farmers were pertinent too – since the election there had been a more intensive effort in many parts of the country to force farmers off their land. My interpretation at the time was that ZANU PF had been shocked by the resilience of the MDC's support, especially in commercial farming areas. Despite all the violence, threats and murders, thousands were still voting for the MDC in these areas. Without the massive rigging Mugabe would have lost by a country mile; ZANU PF recognised that without destroying white commercial farmers once and for all, they would be hard pressed to win the next parliamentary election, which would take place in 2005. Makoni's speech, although welcomed by us, set him on a collision course with Mugabe, resulting in his removal from cabinet a few months later.

Having sat for only two days, parliament was adjourned to August. In the two years since our election Zimbabwe was in a greater crisis than ever. Parliament itself had been undermined; our failed attempts to persuade MPs in the government benches to change course gave rise to growing cynicism among our supporters about the value of pursuing change through the legislature. Likewise our inability to use the legal system and courts to secure justice made many question this non-violent method. At this time I was interviewed by Philip Gourevitch, author of the book *We Wish To Inform You That Tomorrow We Will Be Killed With Our Families*, which tells the story of the 1994 Rwandan genocide. I told him of the growing desire for revenge expressed by our supporters: "What we hear at many political meetings is people saying, 'Will you please just look the other way for 48 hours?'"[495] I felt that we could still prevent revenge attacks "if a firm, clear message of change (was) articulated", which should include a truth commission going back to UDI, 11 November 1965, as "many of the crimes committed since then (were) better understood in that context". I spoke of the "miracle" that had happened regarding race relations in Zimbabwe. Despite Mugabe's attacks on whites, who in turn had been "disengaged from black people", there was an irony in that it had "taken this drama for (some white) people to realise that there (were) outstanding black people". In the same article Judge Washington Sansole agreed, saying, "That race thing is just a red herring." For all ZANU PF's racist invective and violence directed against whites, there was little chance of racial conflagration. Rather our growing challenge was to retain the commitment of our supporters, especially young black people, to the path of non-violence. The greatest threat to our pursuit of non-violence was ZANU PF's own violence directed against our supporters, and our inability to protect them. As Solzhenitzyn postulated, "violence does not exist alone and cannot survive in isolation: it is inevitably bound up with the lie". In my view the best method of exposing the lie remained in speaking truth to power through parliament and the courts, compromised as these were.

CHAPTER 19

TREASON AND OTHER NEFARIOUS ACTIVITIES
JULY 2002 TO MARCH 2003

"We are mourning the death of democracy in our beloved country."
– STATEMENT BY ANDY FLOWER AND HENRY OLONGA
10 FEBRUARY 2003

As the third session of Zimbabwe's fifth parliament approached, nearly all the senior leaders of the MDC were facing some charge or other. President Tsvangirai, Secretary General Ncube, and secretary for Agriculture Gasela were facing treason; Vice-President Sibanda, for "inciting violence"; Treasurer General Dulini Ncube, for Cain Nkala's murder, and so the list went on. I, responsible as legal secretary for their defence, was facing my own charge of "discharging a firearm". And that was just the tip of the iceberg. Many of our MPs and hundreds of our rank-and-file members were facing similar charges. The legal costs of these cases, together with the civil electoral challenges and Tsvangirai's presidential election case, were draining the MDC of its resources. This necessitated me travelling to Canada, the UK, US, Germany and South Africa during the parliamentary adjournment to fundraise for the Legal Defence Fund.

Back in the country as the opening of parliament by Mugabe on 23 July 2002 loomed, I attended an MDC caucus meeting with all of us feeling besieged. The election had been brazenly subverted and law was being used as a weapon against us. In that atmosphere we resolved not to attend Mugabe's address. We didn't recognise him as *de jure* president and the only "peaceful, non violent way"[496] of expressing that position was by walking out for the duration of his attendance in parliament. Mugabe duly opened parliament but spoke to a half-empty house. Save for one reference to the fact that 6.1 million Zimbabweans faced "some hardships",[497] reading Mugabe's speech afterwards one would think that Zimbabwe was in no trouble at all.

The first motion filed in the new parliament was one proposed by me, condemning the attorney general for his "selective application of the law" and demanding the prosecution of serious crimes. Before we could get the debate under way, though, ZANU PF adjourned parliament to mid September. They were in no mood to have us document in *Hansard* all the abuses being suffered.

The figure of 6 million Zimbabweans facing "hardships" alluded to by Mugabe was in fact a figure used by the World Food Programme at the time, when it warned that this number would soon face starvation. The figure was bad enough but it was compounded by ZANU PF using starvation as a political opportunity. On 12 July the minister of Home Affairs and ZANU PF MP for Beitbridge, my former client Kembo Mohadi, had addressed a meeting in the province that was facing the greatest threat of starvation. This was Matabeleland South, in which "a clear objective to control NGO feeding programmes was evident".[498] Mohadi aggressively told the meeting that because NGOs were there at government's invitation, they would have to follow government directives and announced that government would "take over" all food distribution. Other, similar reports filtered in, and by late July it was obvious that ZANU PF intended using food as a weapon. On 7 August the *New York Times* carried a long op-ed written by me entitled "Zimbabwe's Man-made Famine", with the sub-heading: "Mugabe's regime will pay any price to keep in power". The piece was accompanied by a stark drawing of a maize cob comprised of skulls drawn by award-winning Ukrainian cartoonist Igor Kopelnitsky. Citing the WFP's 6 million figure and the WHO's estimate that 25 per cent of Zimbabweans were HIV positive, I argued that some 300 000 Zimbabweans could die as a result of the "combination of famine and AIDS".[499] Pointing out that most of our reservoirs still had water, I argued that "had experienced farmers been allowed to plant their crops Zimbabwe would not have had to import any food at all". I concluded that Zimbabwe was "becoming a police state" and that "the Mugabe regime may be counting on catastrophe for its own salvation".

The United Nations-sponsored Earth Summit on Sustainable Development was held in Johannesburg a few weeks after the op-ed was published. Mugabe attended the summit, along with 100 world leaders. One of the main aims of the summit was to reconcile development with environmental sustainability, with particular emphasis on food security. It seemed that my op-ed, published in a newspaper well read in the United Nations, may have embarrassed Mugabe because when he got back from the summit, he went on another rant.

Soon after Mugabe's plane touched down at Harare airport on his return from Johannesburg on 4 September, he launched into another attack against me: "… *whites who have been asking Britain to impose sanctions … do not deserve to be in Zimbabwe. These like Bennett and Coltart are not part of our society. They belong to Britain and let them go there. If they want to live here, we will say 'stay', but your place is in prison and nowhere else. We say no to beggars, no to puppets. We have puppets here in the MDC led by their leader. Even in Parliament they will listen to what their white master, Coltart, tells them to do. We said we don't want that type of partnership.*"[500]

Although Mugabe's threat was not the first, in the context of all that was going on around me, it was more earnest than ever. The best form of defence being attack, we arranged for full-page advertisements challenging Mugabe's statements to be published in the remaining independent newspapers. In particular we decided to use the telegram Mugabe had sent to me back when I was at university in 1981. Dated 19 August 1981 we reproduced the telegram alongside Mugabe's statement. One of the advertisements asked Mugabe what had changed since 1981.

Several of my black friends came to my assistance. The most poignant was an open letter to Mugabe written by Siphosami Malunga, Sidney Malunga's son, then a trial attorney on the special panel for serious crimes in East Timor. The letter traced the work that I had done to secure his father's release from detention and reminded Mugabe of his obligation to respect and protect all Zimbabweans' rights of freedom of speech.[501]

In the weeks following Mugabe's statements I had a succession of meetings with advocates Adrian de Bourbon and Chris Andersen, the Zimbabwean senior counsel handling Morgan Tsvangirai's civil electoral challenge against Mugabe and his criminal defence respectively. In the meantime George Bizos had agreed to defend Tsvangirai and I met him for the first time on 19 September. Having been in the pressure cooker environment of the Zimbabwe legal system for so long it was deeply encouraging to have Bizos on our team.

The state was dragging its feet on the treason trial so most of our focus was on the civil challenge to Mugabe's election. We knew he had only won through massive fraud but because of the tight circle of Mugabe supporters who controlled the electoral process it was important that we get access to what was at the core of the electoral fraud – namely, the voters' roll. The Electoral Act entitled all contesting parties to a copy of the roll but all that we had managed to get out of the registrar general's office was a paper version of it, which was almost impossible to audit. As a precursor to the main case we had applied to the High Court for an electronic copy of the roll but the presiding judge, Rita Makarau, a person with strong links to ZANU PF, dismissed the case, disingenuously ruling that "copies" in this digital age could not possibly include electronic copies.[502]

Jeremy Gauntlett argued before the Supreme Court on 1 October 2002 that the High Court ruling was wrong for three reasons. Firstly, it ignored that the registrar had previously been ordered by a different court to provide the roll on compact disc, and the registrar could not now renege on this order. Secondly, "copy" under the Electoral Act clearly meant any form of a copy, just as "writing" in old laws included typewriting. It was common cause that the voters' roll was stored in electronic form, and could easily be copied on discs. It was pointed out that if the roll was not made available on disc, the task of analysing a voters' roll containing some five million voters and 120 constituencies would, as the government well knew, be close to impossible. Finally, we argued that the registrar had been evasive and obstructive and was patently acting in bad faith. Even though the High Court had confirmed that we were entitled to a paper copy of the roll the registrar had even refused to provide us with *that* copy. In a remarkable feat of jurisprudential gymnastics the Supreme Court, under Chidyausiku, contrived to find reasons why we should not receive an electronic copy of the roll. To this day it remains a major issue which dogs the electoral process in Zimbabwe.

In among the various legal proceedings was the ongoing need to use parliament as a forum to expose the ongoing horrors within Zimbabwe. On 15 October 2002, I debated a motion on the ill-treatment, including torture, of suspects and ordinary members of the public by the Zimbabwe Republic Police. Ironically, my address had to be directed to the speaker,

Emmerson Mnangagwa, one of the key architects of the Gukurahundi which resulted in wholesale torture. I commenced by acknowledging that the root of torture was to be found in the methods used by the BSAP. I pointed out that in the early 1980s many former members of BSAP had remained in the police force and were responsible for much of the torture. I reminded the minister of Home Affairs, Kembo Mohadi, that I had represented him in the case, concluded on 4 July 1986, in which we had obtained on his behalf $14 000 worth of damages after he himself had been tortured by the police. This caused quite a stir and the interjections started to flow freely, especially from the minister of Justice, Patrick Chinamasa. Despite these interjections I exposed several current examples of police using torture and concluded by arguing that Amnesty International's 12-point programme for the prevention of torture should be implemented. I pointed out that the International Convention against Torture had been ratified by all our neighbours and if ZANU PF persisted in its refusal to ratify the convention, it could be argued that it had acquiesced or condoned the ongoing acts of torture.[503] Not surprisingly, both the speaker and the ZANU PF front bench studiously ignored my arguments; if anything, the incidence of torture grew in Zimbabwe during the years that followed.

Shortly after this debate we witnessed the end of a chapter in Zimbabwe with the death of one of my heroes, Sir Garfield Todd. His wife Grace had died the previous December and they were such a team that I think he lost the will to live. On Sunday, 27 October 2002 thousands of us congregated at Dadaya Mission again to pay our last respects. As Judith Todd wrote subsequently, the event was more like a wedding than a funeral because it was a celebration of a person who had had a consistent vision for many decades of a moderate, tolerant and democratic Zimbabwe. At the urging of Eddison Zvobgo, at the graveside Judith Todd read out a personal letter to her sent by Queen Elizabeth, which caused a rumble of contentment throughout the massive crowd.[504] I was left wondering what Zimbabwe might have been had Garfield Todd not been deposed in February 1958.

On my return to Bulawayo I received a sharp reminder that Zimbabwe was some way off Todd's vision of a benign state. On the drive back from Dadaya the brakes on my vehicle appeared to be playing up and so I had it checked. It was discovered that one of the brake lines had been deliberately severed. It was the first, but not the last, attempt on my life in the ensuing months. Although I had been threatened several times before, this was the first actual attempt; I was immediately forced to increase my security, which included a new routine of checking my brake lines after any of my vehicles had been left in a public place.

Fortunately, I was due to fly abroad again, which provided a welcome break from the increased pressure brought about by this unwelcome discovery. At the end of October, I visited Canada and the United States. The main purpose of this trip was to address a meeting of Parliamentarians for Global Action in Ottawa on the role of parliamentarians in developing the recently announced United Nations principle of the "Responsibility to Prevent". The opening address at the meeting was delivered by Bill Graham, the Canadian Foreign minister, who spoke on the topic "The State's Responsibility to Protect as the New Governing Principle of International Affairs". The principle, first developed by Kofi Annan, held that where a population was facing serious harm as a result of state failure, and the state in question was unwilling or unable to act, the general and historical principle of non-intervention yielded to an international responsibility to protect. There was broad support for the notion and my speech on the topic was supported by positive interventions from MPs from Tanzania, Senegal, Burundi and Panama. This new principle potentially gave us a very useful lever to argue that the international community should not just sit aside and observe anarchy taking place within Zimbabwe.

From Canada I flew to Washington for another series of meetings, including one with Kofi Annan and US Secretary of State Colin Powell on 12 November. Walter Kansteiner III, then assistant secretary of State for Africa, set up the meeting on the sidelines of a UNA-USA International Visionaries dinner. Having just had the benefit of hearing the Canadian Foreign minister's views, I argued that the responsibility to protect doctrine should be invoked in respect of Zimbabwe. I stressed that I was not advocating any form of invasion but believed that the United Nations in particular should play a more active role in trying to resolve the Zimbabwean crisis. Continuing a theme I had first raised in the *New York Times* op-ed, I argued that there needed to be more bilateral engagement with the South African government. Once again I expressed the fear that the ZANU PF regime was using food as a weapon. Both men were deeply sympathetic towards our plight but were pessimistic about what could be achieved to bring about change without more regional support. I got word later that evening that Annan had agreed to raise the issues in the UN.[505]

Shortly after my return to Bulawayo in November, I had a stark personal reminder about how ZANU PF was able to use law as a highly effective weapon against us when I appeared again in the remand court at Tredgold Building. It was almost nine months since I had first been arrested and my legal team argued that the state had had more than ample time to prepare its case. However, the prosecution argued that they needed "more time"; their case, they claimed, was not yet ready. The presiding magistrate agreed with the state and ordered that I be remanded out of custody again pending a new court date, which would be given in the new year. It was an effective tactic to keep me distracted when I wanted to be focused on Tsvangirai's treason defence and the case against Mugabe.

Back in parliament on 14 November, I listened to the new Finance minister Herbert Murerwa's budget speech. It was a catalogue of disaster: he conceded that the country "was facing severe economic difficulties", that "output had declined 19.3 per cent in three years", and that inflation had "accelerated to 144.2 per cent by end of October".[506] Murerwa, always a moderate in my view, tried to conclude on a positive note, quoting from Jeremiah 29:11: "For I know the plans I have for you, declares the Lord. Plans to prosper you and not to harm you. Plans to give you a hope and a future."

I responded to Murerwa in parliament on 26 November:

"These are verses I hold very close to my heart and often turn to. But there is a real danger if we take scriptures like that out of context. If you read the whole of Jeremiah we see that the Lord abhors murder, rape, deceit, lies and corruption. Yet when we speak about these issues we have been met by giggles on the other side – by people who condone murder, kidnapping and other crimes. We must not ever live as though God does not know and see." I concluded: "… if we acknowledge that people have been murdered and bring those responsible to justice, if we restore democracy, respect the judiciary, apply the law equally to all, stop using food as a political weapon, then those promises will become a reality, but not before."[507] For once I was listened to in silence by the ZANU PF benches. There was none of the usual heckling.

By the end of the year, as much as they tried, ZANU PF could not inveigle the international community into accepting that Mugabe had been lawfully elected. That must have been painfully obvious to both them and the ANC. While I was in North America a Catholic priest, Fr Fidelis Mukonori, a confidant of Mugabe, had called on Tsvangirai, to tell him Mugabe wanted to meet outside the country. This was followed by an approach to Tsvangirai by Colonel Lionel Dyck, who had gained the confidence of ZANU PF when he successfully led an army brigade against dissidents during the Gukurahundi in Matabeleland. Dyck told Tsvangirai that he had met the then commander of the Zimbabwe Defence Forces, General Vitalis Zvinavashe, and Mnangagwa, who said they were concerned about the worsening situation in Zimbabwe. Dyck said he had met periodically with Zvinavashe and Mnangagwa over a period of four months before he offered to put them in touch with Tsvangirai. When they agreed, he contacted a former Rhodesian army colleague who knew Tsvangirai, and so the meeting took place. According to Tsvangirai, Dyck told him that Mugabe had agreed to retire but said nothing about holding elections.[508]

It was in this context that on 5 December I received a telephone call from a prominent South African businessman who had close links to the ANC, asking me to fly to Johannesburg urgently to meet an ANC emissary. I flew down and, on Sunday, 8 December, I met with the man, who introduced himself to me as Patrick Moseke. He said that he had been instructed to meet me on behalf of the ANC and went on to tell me that Mnangagwa had led a delegation of ZANU PF members to South Africa the previous week for talks with the Mbeki government. I was asked to spell out the MDC position regarding a settlement of the political, economic and humanitarian crisis. I said there would have to be some form of transitional authority which would be of limited duration and which would have a limited mandate restricted to governing the country during the transitional period, securing food and medicines to avert famine, stabilising relations with the international community and agreeing on and passing new laws dealing with the electoral environment. This would have to culminate in a fresh election for president. Of particular concern was a report that had been presented to the UN Security Council on 16 October implicating senior ZANU PF leaders, including Mnangagwa, in various shenanigans that had taken place in the DRC. Moseke said that some form of amnesty would have to be considered as both Mugabe and Mnangagwa were fearful of prosecution.[509] I said I understood why an amnesty might have to be considered, but pointed out the difficulties surrounding such a decision.

The next day I met Moseke again. He told me that he had spent the previous evening conveying what I had said to the Mnangagwa delegation, who were staying in a Johannesburg hotel. ZANU PF did not want another election and they wanted Mugabe to remain on as a ceremonial president, with Mnangagwa taking on the role of prime minister. According to Moseke, Mnangagwa would adopt a more pragmatic approach to a range of issues, including that of commercial farmers. The MDC would be offered several cabinet positions and there would be a lessening of political tensions. There was also a sting in the tail – if we did not accept their entreaties, Mnangagwa would crush the opposition more completely than Mugabe had sought to do. Moseke showed me a document analysing the situation which he told me had been prepared by the ANC, aided by their intelligence services. He said the document had been given to President Mbeki who had embraced its recommendations. On reading the document I found the analysis of Zimbabwe's economic crisis, and its causes, comprehensive and perceptive. But its recommendations made no reference to elections or a transition to democracy. Instead the document referred to the need for a "leadership succession plan" and dismissed the MDC as a "rudderless party, lacking both policies and unity".[510]

I returned to Zimbabwe and conveyed details of the meeting to Tsvangirai. On 18 December he in turn revealed all the details of these different approaches to an MDC national executive meeting. The feeling within the MDC was that the approaches were designed to co-opt the MDC as a minority player in a process to sanitise the ZANU PF regime and leave it in power, with no prospect of a new election until Mugabe's term of office ran out in 2008.

The unanimous view was that the MDC should have no part in such an arrangement.

The very next day, 19 December, Mnangagwa was presented on stage at the ANC's national conference in Stellenbosch where he was given a standing ovation. When the story broke publicly in mid January 2003, it was met with a series of swift denials from Zvinavashe's, Mnangagwa's and Mbeki's offices, with each denying that there was any such plan. The clear impression left in my mind, though, was that Mbeki and Mnangagwa were jointly trying to organise a takeover by the latter.

In the midst of all this political chicanery, I started 2003 keenly anticipating the cricket World Cup which was due to be held in South

Africa and Zimbabwe in February. Aside from my desire to see all the top players in the world perform at home, I saw it as an opportunity to expose to the world what was happening inside Zimbabwe. Accordingly, a group of us met secretly to plan a series of peaceful demonstrations within the cricket grounds, and advertisements to be placed in Southern African newspapers exposing human rights abuses. Just as our plans were coming to fruition I received a call from Zimbabwe's first black test cricketer Henry Olonga. He told me that he and Andy Flower were very distressed about what was going on in the country and that he had suggested to Flower that they meet with me to discuss their concerns.[511] I invited them round for dinner, much to the delight of my children, who hero-worshipped them.

After dinner we went up to my study where they told me all about the dilemma they were facing. Andy had been approached by an old friend and fellow Zimbabwean player, Nigel Hough, who felt that the Zimbabwean cricket team had a God-given responsibility to challenge what was happening in the country. In essence he wanted the whole Zimbabwean cricket team to boycott the forthcoming World Cup; he had suggested that the entire team should go to the opening ceremony in Cape Town and then announce that it would not take part in the World Cup. Having listened to the plan, I offered my opinion. While it was right to protest because of the terrible things taking place in Zimbabwe, I agreed, in my view it remained important to protest in a way that would garner support and sympathy. If it was too disruptive of the World Cup, it might actually lose them support. For that reason I suggested that they wear black armbands, similar to those commonly worn by test cricketers when icons of the game have died. In their case they would be wearing them to mourn the death of democracy in Zimbabwe, which in my view would be a peaceful, non-disruptive and yet highly poignant and effective protest. They thought about the idea and said they would come back to me.

A few days later they returned to tell me that they were going to adopt the idea but they felt that they also needed to release a statement to explain what the armbands meant. They asked me to help them draft the statement. We spent an evening hunched around my computer and came up with the following:

"It is a great honour for us to take the field today to play for Zimbabwe in the World Cup. We feel privileged and proud to have been able to represent our country. We are, however, deeply distressed about what is taking place in Zimbabwe in the midst of the World Cup and do not feel that we can take the field without indicating our feelings in a dignified manner and in keeping with the spirit of cricket.

"We cannot in good conscience take to the field and ignore the fact that millions of our compatriots are starving, unemployed and oppressed. We are aware that hundreds of thousands of Zimbabweans may even die in the coming months through a combination of starvation, poverty and AIDS. We are aware that many people have been unjustly imprisoned and tortured simply for expressing their opinions about what is happening in the country. We have heard a torrent of racist hate speech directed at minority groups. We are aware that thousands of Zimbabweans are routinely denied the right to freedom of expression. We are aware that people have been murdered, raped, beaten and had their homes destroyed because of their beliefs and that many of those responsible have not been prosecuted. We are also aware that many patriotic Zimbabweans oppose us even playing in the World Cup because of what is happening.

"It is impossible to ignore what is happening in Zimbabwe. Although we are just professional cricketers, we do have a conscience and feelings. We believe if we remain silent, that will be taken as a sign that either we do not care or we condone what is happening in Zimbabwe. We believe that it is important to stand up for what is right.

"We have struggled to think of an action that would be appropriate and that would not demean the game we love so much. We have decided that we should act alone without other members of the team being involved because our decision is deeply personal and we did not want to use our senior status to unfairly influence more junior members of the squad. We would like to stress that we greatly respect the ICC and are grateful for all the hard work it has done in bringing the World Cup to Zimbabwe.

"In all the circumstances we have decided that we will each wear a black armband for the duration of the World Cup. In doing so we are mourning the death of democracy in our beloved country. In doing so we are making a silent plea to those responsible to stop the abuse of human rights in Zimbabwe. In doing so we pray that our small action may help to restore sanity and dignity to our nation."

The statement was embargoed. All I knew was that it was going to be released before Zimbabwe's first World Cup game against Namibia in early February. Unbeknown to Henry and Andy was my involvement with others, including the Catholic archbishop of Matabeleland, Pius Ncube, in the planning of protests. Having been sworn to secrecy, I was unable to tell the rest of my colleagues about Henry and Andy's plans but was able to use my knowledge of them to ensure that the protest plans of the churches and civil society dovetailed with what they were planning to do.

A week before the commencement of the World Cup the treason trial of Tsvangirai, Welshman Ncube and Gasela got under way before Judge President Garwe in the Harare High Court. As I was responsible for the coordination of the defence team – comprising George Bizos, Chris Andersen and Eric Matinenga – I attended the opening day of the trial on 3 February. It was almost sixteen years to the day since I had last appeared before Garwe in the Sidney Malunga trial and I had an overwhelming sense of déjà vu. Back then Judge Garwe was a magistrate who had presided over a political trial designed to crush ZAPU. This was yet another political trial presided over by Garwe, but this time designed to decapitate the MDC. Although privately I felt that Tsvangirai had been foolhardy in his December 2001 meeting with the Canadian agent provocateur Ari Ben-Menashe, I recognised that the full force of ZANU PF's cunning and deceit had been used to entrap him. On a grand stage ZANU PF was once again using law as an instrument of injustice, not only to distract the leadership of the MDC but also to drain it of resources. Bizos was the perfect foil against the Machiavellian machinations of ZANU PF. Not only did he understand the political dimensions of the case but he was fearless. In time he also proved to be an exceptionally useful ally in persuading elements within the ANC about the true nature of ZANU PF. The commencement of the trial, however, also marked the beginning of intense efforts to raise sufficient funding to pay for the criminal defence, and also to keep the civil electoral challenge against Mugabe going.

With the treason trial defence under way, I flew to Cape Town to attend the opening of the World Cup, scheduled for 9 February 2003.

Andy Flower and Henry Olonga had been asked to meet with the English cricket team the day before the opening ceremony as England were debating whether to fulfil their fixture against Zimbabwe. Flower and Olonga wanted me to attend the meeting with them. On the afternoon of 8 March, we met the English team captain, Nasser Hussain, coach Duncan Fletcher and David Morgan, then chairman of the England and Wales Cricket Board (ECB) at their hotel, The Cullinan. Hussain explained that he and his players wanted to know what we thought about them playing in Zimbabwe. While they were worried about safety and security issues, their primary concern was how they would be perceived by the people of Zimbabwe and whether we felt there was a moral case for staying away. They were particularly concerned about their own media which, Hussain said, would "crucify us if we play". Flower and Olonga took them into their confidence about their armband protest that coming Monday and the revelation clearly stunned Hussain. They told Hussain they felt that boycotting the England/Zimbabwe match was the right thing to do. Confusing matters, I disagreed with that view and tried to persuade the English to come to Zimbabwe. Once again, aside from my desire to see them play against Zimbabwe, I knew that England would bring a much bigger press contingent than any other team and to that extent the various protests planned would get much more publicity if they came. I was not at liberty to reveal anything of what was planned, but in any event I feared that knowledge of the protests might in itself deter the English from coming. They all kept their cards close to their chest and at the end of the meeting we didn't have any idea what their decision would be. In the end England decided not to travel but, fortunately, the English press came anyway.

I remained in Cape Town to watch the opening game between South Africa and the West Indies while the Zimbabwean team flew back to Harare. The following morning I was glued to my television, watching the opening match between Zimbabwe and Nambia played in Harare. My heart filled with pride to see Flower and Olonga's bravery as they implemented their plan. Shortly before they walked onto the field they issued the statement we had prepared to the press contingent and donned their black armbands. Zimbabwe thrashed Namibia but the story that grabbed the world's attention was their peaceful protest. At the same time civil society in Harare had organised to get protesters into the ground; placards were unveiled and peaceful protests held. Some spectators,

367

hearing of the black armband protest, donned black armbands themselves.

Both Zimbabwe Cricket and the government reacted furiously. The protesters were identified and arrested as they left the ground, the police trying to ensure this was not done in the glare of TV cameras. The matter was referred to the ICC, which wrote to the two players on 14 February, telling them that while they had not broken any rules, they should "adhere to (the) guidelines" Zimbabwe Cricket had imposed. Olonga's cricket club, Takashinga, took the most strident action against him. Its chairman, ZANU PF loyalist Givemore Makoni, said that Olonga would be called before a disciplinary committee and expelled.[512] (Olonga denied them the pleasure by resigning of his own volition.) Having been expressly banned from wearing black armbands, both Flower and Olonga wore black wristbands in the next match against India.

Zimbabwe's remaining World Cup matches were scheduled to be played in Bulawayo, starting with a match against Australia on 24 February. Our little informal group of activists had been planning protests for weeks. Under the banner of "Zimbabwe Cricket Supporters for Democracy", with a logo of three cricket stumps transmuted into prison bars, we had published a series of advertisements giving reasons why the political situation in Zimbabwe was "just not cricket". They included several witty cartoons and statements such as "Robert Mugabe was clean bowled by Morgan Tsvangirai in the 2002 Presidential election but he refuses to walk!" In anticipation of the Bulawayo matches, we bought up tickets and distributed them to activists. We had several thousand pamphlets produced secretly which were smuggled into the grounds and distributed to the foreign press and visiting teams' hotels. On the morning of the Australia game, hundreds of activists used cunning tactics to smuggle protest banners into the ground, which were then unveiled during the course of the match. Some of the banners were ingenuous – most protestors had small banners hidden on their bodies, one letter or word each. Some had a letter on their shirts, which when displayed together with others spelt out a phrase such as "ZIMBABWE NEEDS JUSTICE". The police and Zimbabwe Cricket were apoplectic and comical scenes resulted. As the match progressed there were cat-and-mouse antics between the police and protestors as the former sought to confiscate the banners and arrest those unveiling them, beyond the view of TV cameras and the international press. Archbishop Pius Ncube joined the protests, thereby placing the police in a quandary. Some fifteen activists, including several friends of mine, were arrested but in the process numerous messages condemning human rights abuses were beamed out to the international community, in particular the Commonwealth. Six of the people arrested were severely assaulted by police, some badly beaten on their backs with sjamboks and batons. Flower and Olonga were innovative yet again: both players wore red sweatbands, having been barred from wearing black.

When the next match was played, against Holland, the police were there in full force, but still banners were smuggled in. At a pre-arranged time a group stood up together, singing protest songs and waving their banners. The protesters tried to remain in a group and when the police came for them they linked arms to make arrest more difficult and obvious. At one point all the fuss they were making attracted the attention of TV cameras, causing the police to back off. The protesters spoke among themselves and made a decision to make a dash for it. Everyone rushed off in different directions, followed by comic scenes of policemen chasing activists who ducked and dived and hid among the crowd. However, many were arrested beyond the gaze of cameras and taken to the Law and Order section of the police where some, including some women, were badly beaten. As in the Australia match most detentions took place "unobtrusively, this time of 42 activists".[513] Having made the mistake after the Australia game of releasing activists prior to the Holland match, the police took no chances and all 42 people arrested, several friends of mine among them, were still in detention five days later when the final match against Pakistan was due to be played.

Despite this, further activists were mobilised, resulting in 23 mostly young people being arrested at that match. Although Zimbabwe couldn't afford to drop Flower for the matches, being their best player, they took the precaution of dropping Olonga and barred him from appearing in public.

The ZANU PF regime was deeply embarrassed and angered by the protests. Although there was never any collusion between our group of Bulawayo activists and Flower and Olonga, the two players bore the full wrath of the regime's fury. After the World Cup neither ever played for Zimbabwe again. It was something I had warned them about and counselled them on when we first met. I have a deep love of cricket and had somewhat ambivalent feelings about both our and their protests. Although morally it was the right and courageous thing to do, I also recognised that it could result in a witch hunt and the undermining of cricket in Zimbabwe. However, with democratic space being shut down, it seemed to me that all forms of non-violent protest had to be employed.

ZANU PF's wrath was about to be turned against me with a ferocity I had never experienced before. The first attempt on my life occurred shortly after the Zimbabwe/Australia match. I was driving out of town when, providentially, I drove over a broken bottle lying on the road. Concerned that it may have cut a tyre, I stopped my vehicle and inspected the inner sides of my tyres. This inspection revealed that the inside of one of the tyres had a circular burn on it. It looked as if someone had used a car cigarette lighter to burn a neat hole on the inside of the tyre where it couldn't be seen. Had I travelled much further on the tyre there is no doubt that it would have burst. Experts who examined it later confirmed that someone had deliberately burnt it in a place that was not easily visible and in a manner that would inevitably cause it to blow out.

The second incident was carefully planned. The first hint that something was afoot came on Saturday, 1 March 2003. On that day I was away from home enjoying a break with my family over a school exeat weekend. My home security team reported on my return that on the Saturday afternoon a white Land Rover Defender station wagon vehicle (of the type used by the CIO and the police "Law and Order" section) with several plainclothes occupants drove slowly past our house (which is in a cul-de-sac) and back again, with the occupants taking a detailed interest in our house. It did not stop and appeared merely to be on a surveillance mission.

Then, on Monday lunchtime, 10 March, a green Land Rover pick-up vehicle, with four plainclothes policemen inside it (one woman and three men), arrived at my gate. I was at the office and Jenny was out. They demanded to be allowed into the yard but were refused entry by our trusty Fawcetts Security guard. They told the guard that all they wanted to know was what vehicles I had and was using – an odd question as this information could easily be supplied by the Central Vehicle Registry (CVR). In other words these plainclothes people wanted to know what vehicle I was *using* at the time, not so much the vehicles I *owned*. I asked my law partner Josephat Tshuma to telephone the police to find out what they were after. The police feigned ignorance but did confirm that the "Law and Order" section had a green Land Rover pick-up, which was allocated to Detective Inspector Taderera. Furthermore our domestic worker, John Tlou, who had himself been recently detained by the "Law and Order" section during the World Cup cricket protests, identified one of the policemen in the vehicle as being Sergeant Ngwenya, of the "Law and Order" section.

I flew to Harare the following morning to attend parliament and only returned on Friday, 14 March. In my absence a sinister chain of events had unfolded in the vicinity of my home. On Tuesday night, 12 March, two men, Charley Mackay and a local veterinary surgeon, Gerrard Stevenage, were robbed of a brand new vehicle about two kilometres from my home. Mackay was admitted to hospital with fractured ribs and a ruptured spleen, having been beaten by his assailants. Shots were also fired by one of the hijackers from an AK-47 rifle; the cartridge casings recovered from the scene of the crime were clearly marked as being manufactured by the Zimbabwe Defence Industries (ZDI). Ammunition of this type is only available to the police and the military.

The following evening a Matabeleland farmer, Jimmy Goddard, went to the hostel of Whitestone Primary School (which is adjacent to my home) to take his young sons some ice-cream as a treat. Goddard had sent one of the boarders to fetch his children and while he was waiting for them he took a call on his cell phone. Suddenly he saw a vehicle hurtling towards him at breakneck speed. The white Isuzu twin-cab sped past a group of young children, among whom was one of Goddard's sons, and screeched to a halt. Three hijackers leapt out while the driver remained in the vehicle. One of the men pointed a camouflaged FN military assault rifle (also a government weapon) at Goddard, who was then hit on the head with a heavy object. He dropped to the ground. When the hijackers realised the keys to his Toyota Land Cruiser were not in the ignition, one of the hijackers pushed his rifle into Goddard's chest, demanding the keys. Goddard handed the keys over and the men took his vehicle and fled.

Then on Thursday evening, 13 March, Barry Dakin and his daughter were cutting long grass for horse fodder on a verge near their home not far from ours. Both were caught unawares and assaulted by four hijackers. Dakin, in trying to protect his daughter, was cracked on the head. Again the men got away with their vehicle. Reports of all the incidents were made to Hillside police station, but by Friday afternoon a report had still not been submitted to the Zimbabwe Republic Police Traffic Division.

On Friday afternoon I was informed about these incidents by my security team and warned to be extra vigilant. While hijackings per se were not completely unusual in Bulawayo, my constituency had never known such a spate of them, nor had government-issue weapons been used before. Furthermore, the police response to the hijackings was pathetic. All of these factors were taken into account in leading to the assessment that there was a deliberate pattern which in turn could well be a precursor to a targeted attack on me.

On the Saturday morning I had a meeting with a client of mine at home. Jenny and two of our children had left home early to attend a school athletics day. After concluding my meeting I left home with our younger son (aged 9) and baby daughter (aged 18 months). As I drove out of the gate and I stopped to speak to the security guard, I noticed a light blue Mazda truck parked further up the cul-de-sac. It started moving slowly towards me and as it drew level with me I noticed that its occupants were three young men, with shaven heads, in plainclothes. The man in the middle was holding an AK-47 rifle upright between his legs. The vehicle crept past me and then turned right into another street, ostensibly driving towards town. Given all the goings on that week, I was very concerned so I waited a few minutes with the guard before driving off myself, keeping a good lookout.

When I reached the intersection where the Mazda had turned up, I saw it parked some 150 metres from the intersection on the left-hand side of the road. Now fearing the worst, I drove straight on instead of turning up the same road they were on, as had been my original intention. I drove up a road parallel to the one they were on as fast as I could. However, as I turned up another road, still taking evasive action, I observed in my rear-view mirror the Mazda racing up behind me. I increased my speed even further and made the decision to turn back towards town where I would have more escape options.

It was technology and the bravery of friends that saved me. Trying to sound as calm as possible, so as not to scare the children, I phoned the head of my security team, Craig Edy, and told him I was being chased. We agreed that I would try to take evasive action and rendezvous with him near a safe house. Maintaining cell phone contact with Edy, I travelled down Burnside Road towards town and tried to get away from the Mazda, but it kept a distance behind me of approximately 70 metres. As I approached an intersection near our agreed rendezvous point I sped up as fast as possible and then braked at the last minute and turned left, without indicating, into a side road. Sure enough the Mazda kept pace, although it delayed a bit in turning into the side road, dropping back approximately 100 metres behind.

I sped along a few blocks and then, thankfully, I spotted Edy parked on the right-hand side of the road outside the Church of Ascension Anglican church. I accelerated to create more space between myself and the Mazda. As I passed Edy I saw him pull out onto the road and intercept my pursuers. I drove another few blocks before turning into a safe house, with Edy following close behind. The electric gates started to shut right behind Edy, effectively blocking the Mazda and he leapt out of his vehicle pistol in hand. The occupants of the Mazda were at a disadvantage because their weapons were in the car, whereas Edy could take a clear shot at them, so they didn't try to follow him into the yard, but stopped outside.

Reinforcements had been called for and initially they were tasked with driving past unobtrusively to ascertain whether or not the Mazda was still in the vicinity. When the first security detail arrived he confirmed that the Mazda had parked some 50 metres beyond the gate facing back towards the gate from the direction it had come from. When further security personnel arrived they told us that the Mazda was still there – and when the last person came past he reported that the three men were standing outside their vehicle. None of the security personnel was able to get a registration number for the vehicle as it had been obscured. Soon after the fourth member of my security team arrived in the vicinity the Mazda finally drove off. It was just after 11 am – the ordeal had lasted two hours.

The security team made a decision not to attempt to arrest the men as they had no idea how well armed they were. A decision was also made by me not to report the matter to the police – the memory of the last time I had reported an incident resulting in me being arrested was still fresh! The safe house was only a block away from Hillside police station. The men had staked out the house for nearly an hour, clearly confident that they had nothing to fear if a report was made to the police. They only ended their malevolent vigil when it must have been clear to them that they were outgunned.

On reflection there is no doubt that this was a detailed plan by state agents to assassinate me under the pretext of a criminal hijacking. Nearly all hijackings in Zimbabwe during that period commenced with high-value vehicles being trailed from town, businesses or shopping centres. The *modus operandi* used by the gang in my neighbourhood that week was unprecedented. In this case my home and I had been targeted specifically. I was driving an old ramshackle Nissan 2.7 pick-up – hardly a vehicle desired by criminal hijackers. My wife had driven out earlier in a far more valuable vehicle, as had my client only minutes before I left.

Several days before the incident I had been asked specifically to meet a councillor in one of Bulawayo's townships that morning. At the time the meeting was arranged I was surprised by his insistence that we meet. The councillor was subsequently exposed as a CIO operative. The plan was no doubt to get me to a remote venue on my own and to assassinate me under the pretext of a routine criminal, as opposed to political, hijacking. Surveillance had been conducted at my home weeks before the incident and information had been sought regarding what vehicles I was currently using. The argument that the action was criminally, not politically, motivated would have been buttressed by the spate of hijackings near my home in the days preceding my doomsday. After the attempt against me the spate of hijackings miraculously dried up, and the gang responsible was never caught. As it turned out I was probably saved by the presence of my children and my cell phone. I immediately went into hiding until my security had been further strengthened. A few hours after the incident, I was surprised to be telephoned, out of the blue, by a white Harare businessman with ties to ZANU PF. He asked me how I was. I don't know whether he had any idea what I had been through that day, as I didn't let on, but in my mind the series of coincidences was uncanny. It may well have been that he had been unwittingly used by ZANU PF to extract key intelligence about me.

Weeks before this incident the MDC had decided to engage in mass action, a means of non-violent protest. Together with our trade union partners, a nationwide stayaway in protest against ZANU PF was planned for 18 March. Although I wasn't at home (still being in hiding) an unmarked police Land Rover took up a watching position for the entire weekend prior to 18 March outside my home, presumably waiting for me to return home. In a way it brought the story full circle, with the role of the police completely subverted – they were present only to acquire information for nefarious purposes. However, the publicity[514] which surrounded the attempt on my life appeared to give pause to those who had thought to silence me that way and had already made several attempts.

No further attempt on my life would be made for another nine years, presumably because of the feeling that their cover had been blown. Whether these attempts had been made at the express directive of Mugabe, following his threat made six months previously, or whether they were a Thomas Becket-ian "ridding of a turbulent priest", I will never know.

CHAPTER 20

UNDERGROUND – A TRIUMPH
OF COURAGE OVER FEAR
MARCH 2003 TO DECEMBER 2003

"One who never turned his back but marched breast forward; Never doubted clouds would break; Never dreamed though right were worsted, wrong would triumph; Held we fall to rise, are baffled to fight better; Sleep to wake."

– ROBERT BROWNING, "EPILOGUE"

On the evening following the attempt on my life two men I had worked with on the World Cup Cricket protest came to see me at the safe house where I had taken refuge. They were shocked by the brazen attempt to kill me, but understood that, paradoxically, the attempt was an act of desperation by an increasingly paranoid regime. The cricket protests had exceeded our expectations. They had attracted the attention of the world and had deeply embarrassed the regime. The MDC, on the other hand, was embattled – a ready and easy target. While we might have been hopeful that public protests would bring the ZANU PF regime to its knees, we all appreciated their massive capacity to unleash further barrages of brutality. Organisations with formal structures such as the MDC and trade unions were easy to infiltrate, which gave the regime good notice of their plans and who the kingpins were. The MDC was already riddled with spies and agents provocateurs, the latter stirring up trouble and promoting violence within the organisation – creating the very justification needed to crack down further. The beauty of the cricket protests was that they had caught ZANU PF by surprise and, because they had been organised by a tight group with no public profile, were difficult to stop.

One thing we had noticed during the events was the ravenous demand for printed materials. In a country starved of information the public snapped up our pamphlets. There were things we wrote that even the independent papers would have been fearful printing, knowing that POSA could be employed against them. All of us were committed to non-violence and had been inspired by Martin Luther King's "letter from Birmingham Jail" which defended the use of non-violent resistance to oppression. It argued that people had a moral responsibility to break unjust laws, and to take direct action rather than wait for justice to come through court or parliament. Our attempts to use conventional means had only resulted in more oppression. There was a need to obtain more quivers to our bow, without compromising on our unwavering commitment to non-violence.

We spent that evening brainstorming and finally came to an agreement: we would set up an underground organisation that would use unconventional means to support what was being done by the MDC, churches and other civic bodies. What was most needed was a means of communicating down to grassroots and up again. We knew that the internet had not been exploited fully. Although at the time there was limited access by Zimbabweans to the internet, we recognised it as an important means of safely spreading information. That meeting was the genesis of an organisation we called "Waterfowl". It was run for a decade by a small eclectic group of activists, most of whom were based in Bulawayo. Within a few months of setting up we had a few secret printing presses which would generate hundreds of thousands of pamphlets over the years. The presses were complemented by websites established off shore by the Zimbabwean diaspora. A network of activists was established countrywide who distributed non-partisan pamphlets and fed back information to us for publication. Our group met every Monday evening to consider information that had come in and to decide on the content of forthcoming pamphlets. When church or civic groups needed sensitive pamphlets printed we would use a variety of ploys to get thousands of copies printed without them knowing where the extra copies miraculously came from. Using encrypted web-based software, we were able to convey information to our off-shore colleagues, who then posted articles on Zimbabwean websites. A critical component of our work was to feed verified information to local and international media organisations. Through this we succeeded in developing links with journalists the world over and when some of them visited Zimbabwe we helped them with vehicles and other logistics.

Although we came from a variety of backgrounds, and frequently had differing political views, our collective commitment to non-violence bound the group together. We were never exposed but we did have some narrow escapes. Eventually, "Waterfowl" had to be wound up when funding dried up. One day when democracy finally comes to Zimbabwe the full story must be written for the majority of the group are unsung heroes and heroines. Indeed, in the group I had by far the highest profile, which was a mixed blessing – I was privy to useful information, but also the most susceptible to arrest, torture and spilling the beans at the time when "Waterfowl" was operational. To minimise the threat posed to the organisation in the event of my arrest, I never knew the location of the printing presses, nor the names of those who operated them. I only knew the core group and they all had plans to go to ground the moment I was arrested.

At the same time that "Waterfowl" was being set up in 2003 the work of the Legal Defence Fund (LDF) was expanding. It had got to the stage where it needed a full-time coordinator. While I was still in hiding I approached a retired man in our church, Martin Lightfoot,[515] who had good administrative skills and a history of activism, with a mandate to transform the LDF. It had been operating on an ad hoc basis but with the numbers of people being detained growing, it needed full-time management and structure. The aim of the LDF was to provide a rapid response for activists arrested on politically motivated charges, to ensure they were legally represented, and that all associated costs, including bail, travel expenses, lodging and subsistence, were met. Lightfoot was mandated to establish a database of lawyers in Zimbabwe who were willing to provide services to activists at discounted rates. He also needed to be in touch with the MDC's branches countrywide plus other activist groups to get instructions as soon as anyone was arrested. Finally, Lightfoot had to document all proceedings from the time of arrest to release or judgment date.

Lightfoot started work on 1 April 2003, but for statistical purposes we took on cases backdated to 8 February. In that short time the LDF provided legal representation to 743 people arrested, of whom 144 had ongoing cases and 298 suffered abuse such as an assault or illegal detention at the hands of the police.[516] Although I controlled and supervised the LDF, it provided legal representation for all people, whether they were members of the MDC or not. Many clerics, human rights activists and members of other opposition parties benefited from the fund, and most didn't know where the support had come from. Lightfoot operated from home, with no back-up staff, using an untraceable cell phone number to make contact with lawyers, MDC branches and civic organisations. Eventually, 34 legal firms and some 63 lawyers from many parts of the country became part of the underground network. Using the right of legal privilege, the confidentiality of attorney/client correspondence, lawyers were able to protect Lightfoot's identity and hide the existence of the fund itself.

With Lightfoot's appointment the huge burden of running the nascent LDF was lifted from my shoulders; from then on my task was to give broad legal direction and to raise sufficient funds domestically and internationally to sustain the LDF, funds that were channelled through our Cape Town-based trust. The trust itself had grown to such an extent that it required the services of a South African chartered accountant. To ensure accountability, and to protect it in the event of my arrest, no donated money ever passed through my hands and I was not privy to the means Lightfoot used to secure the funds in Zimbabwe and pay law firms. In September 2007 a Bulawayo pastor, John Knox,[517] took over the running of the LDF from Lightfoot. Despite it being an underground organisation, it was subjected to stringent audits and operated with an absolutely clean financial record. Between 2000 and December 2013 the LDF handled thousands of cases, protecting the rights of hundreds of activists. It is still in existence but has not handled any cases since December 2013 as a result of a shortage of funding.

While I worked from the comparative safety of a safe house after the attempt on my life, setting up these underground organisations, the MDC leadership, Tsvangirai and Sibanda in particular, were at the vanguard of the nationwide stayaway from work which took place on 18 and 19 March 2003. We had no idea how successful the call would be but we needn't have been worried because the whole country shut down. While government departments and schools remained open, all other sectors ground to a halt. Although ZANU PF put a brave face on it, they were shocked. On the second day of the stayaway, by sheer coincidence, the US-led bombardment of Baghdad began, which also rattled Mugabe. While we had never called for an invasion, and never have since, Mugabe was not to know this, and the thought must have crossed the minds of the ZANU PF hierarchy that they might be next.

On 6 March President George W Bush had signed an executive order blocking the assets of Mugabe and 76 other ZANU PF cabinet ministers, politburo members and the commanders of the army, air force and prison service.[518] Bush had "determined that (their) policies had undermined Zimbabwe's democratic processes, contributing to the breakdown of the rule of law, to politically motivated violence and to political and economic stability in the southern African region". While we had not called for the order, Bush's assessment of what was happening in Zimbabwe was correct. Coming so close to the invasion of Iraq, it must have sent shivers down the spines of the ZANU PF hierarchy. Perhaps because of this concern there was no immediate backlash from ZANU PF against the MDC leadership following the stayaway, but by the end of the month they were sufficiently composed again to take action.

On 1 April MDC Vice-President Gibson Sibanda was arrested under POSA for "seeking to overthrow a democratically elected government during the 18 and 19 March stay-away". Why they only took action against Sibanda remains a mystery. Virtually all the other MDC leaders were facing other serious charges so one can only assume ZANU PF felt they had no one else they could harass. Sibanda was held for seven days in police custody before we finally managed to get him out on bail. His bail payment itself told a story about the economy. When I had been granted bail on 18 February 2002 I was ordered to pay Z$2 000. Sibanda was ordered to post bail of Z$1 million just thirteen months later!

Rank and file members of the MDC were also targeted by the police at this time. Many members whose only crime was to be associated with the MDC were arrested. Sheila Atkinson's[519] story is typical of what many of my support team went through during this period. Shortly after the stayaway in March, Atkinson's house was raided by police at 5 am one morning. The house was difficult to get into so Atkinson kept all the lights off and remained quiet, hoping that they would go away, but they persisted, eventually throwing rocks on her roof. Atkinson and her sixteen-year-old daughter hid in the pantry until the police eventually left. They weren't finished with her yet, however, and came back to the house time and time again, causing Atkinson to play a cat-and-mouse game with them. On one occasion when she was out the police raided and bullied her housekeeper into letting them into the home so that they could see a photograph of her – they obviously only had her name and didn't know what she looked like. Eventually, after weeks of harassment, Atkinson handed herself in. She was a nurse, a mother of two teenage children, who had never had any brushes with the law, so she was unprepared for and terrified by the prospect of being locked up. Everything was taken off her, including her bra and glasses, before she was locked up in a squalid cell. She was taken from the cells to be interrogated at Bulawayo Central. No allegation of any crime was put to her – the sole purpose of the exercise was to extract from her details of fellow activists.

On her second night in detention Atkinson heard the agonising screams of someone in a neighbouring cell being tortured, something which haunted her. Finally, two and half days after her arrest, she was taken to court and charged with trying "to coerce a constitutionally elected government to stand down". Stringent bail conditions were imposed, requiring her to report weekly to the police. In addition her passport was seized, preventing her from being able to visit her aged and sickly parents in South Africa. After frequent remands in court the charges were eventually dropped ten months later.

Prior to the advent of the MDC the Atkinsons had not been involved in politics or activism at all – they were a normal urban family, who just happened to feel strongly about the gross human rights abuses happening around them. Atkinson's husband, Trevor, had been detained in the aftermath of the Holland/Zimbabwe World Cup cricket match. He had not even been part of the demonstrations, but had tried to help activists there being brutalised by the police, who rewarded him by arresting him and detaining him for four days. Before the Atkinsons knew it the entire family had been sucked into the dangerous game of politics in Zimbabwe. As traumatic as their experience was, they had a strong network of friends who could step into the breach and they had money to sustain them while their lives and business were disrupted. Black working-class families who chose to oppose the regime faced greater challenges; poorer people tended to be detained for longer and treated worse than whites.

With a death threat still hanging over me and our legal bills mounting, I went on another fundraising mission – to South Africa, Canada and the US – in April 2003.

Buoyed by the success of the first stayaway, the MDC started working on what it dubbed "the Final Push". With pressure ratcheting up, it was felt that ZANU PF could be brought to the negotiating table, if not to its knees, through further industrial action.

I arrived back home in time to commence my trial on 8 May. The state was still not ready to proceed, fifteen months after the commission of the alleged offence. Despite our protestations, the presiding magistrate gave the state one last chance to proceed, warning that if they were not ready by the next court date I would be discharged for want of prosecution. I was remanded to 9 June. The date was deliberately chosen because I knew that the MDC's "Final Push" was scheduled for the week before. The few weeks in the run up to 2 June were frenzied. Effectively, I was wearing five hats: I was working with party structures, the "Waterfowl" team, and the LDF, aside from parliamentary duties and the burden of my legal practice.

"Waterfowl" produced thousands of pamphlets advising people of the impending mass action and encouraging all to join and these were distributed all over the country. Anticipating a massive crackdown on the protests, it was also necessary to have legal teams ready. The plan was that Tsvangirai would lead a march in Harare and Sibanda would follow suit in Bulawayo.

Predictably enough, the afternoon before the Final Push began, Sunday, 1 June, police commissioner Augustine Chihuri secured an order in the High Court barring the MDC from going ahead. We immediately filed an appeal against the decision and continued our preparations to join the marches the following day, while the police did all they could to thwart our plans. Two Bulawayo MDC MPs who had not gone into hiding, Milton Gwetu and Esaph Mdlongwa, were picked up by police, and another two, Abednico Bhebhe and Thoko Khupe, narrowly avoided arrest.

On the morning of 2 June I met with my security team in a safe house in central Bulawayo, prepared to join Sibanda. It was a solemn moment. I had left Jenny and the children to go into hiding the previous evening with a heavy heart. We all had bullet-proof vests on but knew they would be little help if the police laid into us. Being one of the few whites, and a particularly disliked one at that, I knew I would be targeted for special treatment. The plan was that Sibanda was going to start walking with the local MDC leadership from a high-density suburb into town, but first we had to wait for Tsvangirai to start in Harare. Time ticked by and then word came through that the plan had been abandoned. Tsvangirai had spent Sunday night in a safe house but early Monday morning he had returned home to get changed. Within minutes of arriving home police arrived to arrest him. It appeared that someone in his close inner circle had betrayed his movements because the police's timing was perfect. Leaderless, the Harare march collapsed, and they had no alternative plan. Instead of going ahead in Bulawayo, Sibanda decided to sit tight. I have no doubt that his decision was also influenced by the presence of helicopter gunships and troops deployed in Bulawayo.

Our safe house was close to local army barracks and as we waited for instructions air force helicopters repeatedly flew over the house, patrolling Bulawayo's streets from the air. Reports came in that pockets of protesters in Harare had been brutally crushed by police, using teargas, backed by the army. The sentiment in Bulawayo was that the lead had to come from areas outside Matabeleland and when it became apparent that it would not, we were all stood down. Although Tsvangirai was released on bail later that day, the momentum for protest marches had been lost. Despite massive repression, the stayaway went ahead, however, and this aspect was highly successful – Zimbabwe was shut down for a week. But a key moment had been lost and ZANU PF lived to fight another day – and fight they did.

Several MDC supporters were murdered, the police arrested several hundred MDC activists, including key organisers, and finally, on the last day of the stayaway, Friday, 6 June, Tsvangirai was rearrested and charged with another count of treason. Initially denied bail, Tsvangirai spent two weeks in Harare remand prison until bail of Z$20 million was ordered by Judge Susan Mavangira.

Mugabe, shaken by the success of the stayaway, responded vitriolically: "Let the MDC and its leaders be warned that those who play with fire will not only be burnt, but consumed by that fire."[520] In fact Mugabe had no cause to fear because hindsight has shown that the only thing "final" about the "push" was that it was the last countrywide public protest the MDC was able to muster.

The brutal undeclared war being waged against us started to take its toll. Human rights veteran Mike Auret resigned his parliamentary seat that June and emigrated from Zimbabwe. He had courageously stood up against the RF and exposed the Gukurahundi but the pressure of decades of struggle finally started to affect his health.[521]

The original treason trial resumed but on the sidelines it appeared as if ZANU PF was looking for ways out of the mess. Chinamasa approached Welshman Ncube to see if they could settle the political impasse, which resulted in informal talks between them, and ultimately a document signed by the two of them outlining their points of convergence. Whether this was by design one doesn't know, but a consequence of these meetings was the start of a wedge being driven between Tsvangirai and Ncube. That burgeoning state of distrust accelerated as the treason trial against them both progressed. In mid July the state closed its case in the treason trial, causing Bizos to apply for Tsvangirai, Ncube and Gasela's discharge on the basis that there was no evidence upon which any of them could be convicted.

Judge Garwe delivered his judgment on the application on 8 August,[522] acquitting Ncube and Gasela but ruling that there was evidence against Tsvangirai he would have to answer – namely, the video of the Montreal meeting that Tsvangirai had attended alone. Although we felt Garwe was wrong in not acquitting all three, the existence of the video, poor as it was, gave him the justification he needed to put Tsvangirai to his defence. That decision contributed greatly to divisions emerging within the MDC. Tsvangirai, already cut off from the parliamentary caucus, now faced serious criminal charges alone. Unlike the charges most of the rest of us faced, Tsvangirai's treason charge carried the death penalty, was being heard before one of the regime's favourite judges, and was being pursued with maximum vigour by the state. Ncube and Gasela could now travel out of the pressure cooker that Zimbabwe had become; Tsvangirai was trapped, his passport held by the High Court as part of his bail conditions. That isolation was compounded by the growing influence of a small group of people around Tsvangirai, some of whose motives in time would prove to be suspect.

At the end of August 2003, local council elections were held in Zimbabwe. Before the poll ZANU PF controlled every municipality save for Harare and so, although councillors as individuals wielded little power, collectively in cities like Bulawayo they had been able to out-vote our MDC mayor. Two wards were up for election in my constituency, contested by MDC members Angilacala Ndlovu and Litshe Keswa. We campaigned together and it soon became clear that we still enjoyed overwhelming support, which must have been apparent to ZANU PF because it showed greater desperation than ever before. A day before the election piles of maize bags, guarded by ZANU PF operatives, appeared in open areas close to polling stations. Upon enquiry we were told that if the electorate "voted the right way" the maize would be released to local residents. In the context of extreme food shortages and a rapidly depreciating currency, the sight of so much food was a powerful inducement, but this didn't sway the voters of Nketa, Emganwini and Nkulumane suburbs, who voted for Ndlovu and Keswa with thumping majorities. The next day all the maize bags had been removed, no doubt the penalty for voting MDC. Despite all the threats, violence and electoral fraud the MDC swept the election. Prior to the election we only controlled Harare; after it we controlled every major city and town in the country, including Bulawayo, Gweru, Mutare, Masvingo, Victoria Falls, Kariba, Gwanda, Ruwa, Zvishavane and Hwange. Writing about it shortly afterwards, I described it as "a triumph of courage over fear".[523]

In September minister of Information Jonathan Moyo's stated intention of shutting down the *Daily News* was finally achieved. With the bombing of the newspaper having failed to silence it, Moyo used AIPPA, the 2002 law that compelled media to register, to finish the job. The *Daily News* argued that the requirement to register was unconstitutional and refused to register. On 11 September the Supreme Court ruled that if the newspaper wanted to challenge the media law, it had to register first. A week later the paper did register – and it was promptly denied a licence to operate. The police then moved swiftly to close the newspaper. The Supreme Court's judgment had cynically worked in tandem with government to silence a critical newspaper. There was no reason why the Supreme Court could not have ruled on the fundamental constitutional point without requiring the paper to register first.

One of our concerns at this time was for African governments to appreciate the nature of the political struggle in Zimbabwe. ZANU PF, through its ambassadors spread throughout the continent, and through heads of state meetings attended by Mugabe himself, had numerous opportunities to preach their propaganda line. They were also consistent and clear about their message: our complaints about violence were exaggerated, and in any event theirs was a legitimate struggle against colonialism, racism and neo-imperialism. Tsvangirai, according to ZANU PF, was just an unprincipled puppet who was prepared to use any means to acquire power. We had limited means to travel in Africa and there was a limit to the role I could play. ZANU PF used race and land as powerful symbols to convince African leaders that the MDC was merely a front to return Zimbabwe to Rhodesia. My and other whites' profiles were of enormous benefit to ZANU PF in Africa. We were described as unreconstructed Rhodesians, hardline racists who dreamt of Ian Smith regaining power. Because of this we decided it was prudent for our top black leaders to play the major role in disproving this propaganda.

However, in October 2003 an opportunity presented itself for us to meet a wide range of African leaders when Liberal International held its 53rd congress in Dakar, Senegal. Tendai Biti and I were selected to represent the MDC. While we were there we had a private meeting with Senegalese president Abdoulaye Wade. We handed him a dossier cataloguing human rights abuses and electoral fraud in Zimbabwe. Being a lawyer himself, Wade was interested to hear the views of two Zimbabwean lawyers. He was sympathetic, and he told us that he would do what he could to get sense to prevail. In the years to come Wade became critical of Thabo Mbeki's failure to be more proactive in Zimbabwe.[524] In 2009 he offered Mugabe asylum, saying "My friend Mugabe does not want to make concessions, we are at a dead end, he can no longer govern the country alone."[525]

On my return home I stopped off in Johannesburg to meet with Bizos to plan for the next phase of Tsvangirai's defence. When I told him about my meeting with Wade, Bizos said that he was sure "Madiba" (President Mandela) would appreciate a briefing, and then and there he arranged for the two of us to meet Madiba at his home in Houghton that evening. When I arrived at 5.20 pm, Bizos was already there. I was immediately struck by the minimal security. I was not even searched going in and was taken by a solitary policeman around the front of the house to large double teak doors. I was greeted at the front door by a secretary and ushered into Madiba's living-room to the right of the entrance hall – a large, stately, elegant room painted in soft pastel, beige and pink colours. Madiba was seated at the far end of the room with his legs up on a stool, dressed in a silk dressing-gown. His legs were obviously swollen and he was rubbing them.

Not knowing me from a bar of soap, Madiba gave me a warm welcome as if I was a long lost friend. Bizos, who had been sitting on a seat to his right, got up and moved to a sofa to Madiba's left so that I could sit right next to Madiba and talk to him. Then he formally introduced me as a colleague from Zimbabwe who was concerned about the situation and had a message to convey. The mention that I had just arrived from Senegal prompted Madiba to speak of his need to speak to President Chirac regarding support for South Africa's bid to hold the 2010 Soccer World Cup – saying that Morocco was closer to Europe than the rest of Africa in outlook and that holding the World Cup there would not fully meet Africa's demand to have the games in Africa. He was cautious about not undermining Mbeki's role as president and said he would not speak to Chirac on a formal basis, but as a friend, to seek France's support for South Africa's bid. In making the introduction Bizos had stressed that more needed to be done regarding Zimbabwe, a point Madiba agreed. He said he was pleased to have me come and would be interested in hearing my point of view.

I started by explaining a bit of my background. I told him that I was born in Zimbabwe, studied law at UCT, had at one stage been an admirer of Mugabe – I mentioned Mugabe's telegram and my tax lecturer, Dennis Davis, whom Madiba knew. I explained how shocked I had been when I returned in 1983 into the vortex of the Fifth Brigade and the Gukurahundi. I spoke about the fear that the Gukurahundi had instilled in black lawyers and about my transition into representing ZAPU MPs, including Edward Ndlovu and Sidney Malunga (both of whom he knew). I spoke of my work with Enock Dumbutshena in the formation of the Forum Party, and then concluded my brief biography by explaining that I represented a predominately black constituency and my current role (Bizos having earlier introduced me as Foreign Affairs spokesman so I had to set the record straight!) as legal secretary. Moving to the current situation, I voiced concern that since July, when presidents Bush and Mbeki had discussed a "quiet diplomacy" strategy for Zimbabwe, the objective facts on the ground showed that no progress was being made. I pointed out four objective facts:

1. The August supplementary budget in which the vote for the CIO was doubled and the vote for the Youth Brigade more than doubled – a clear indication where their intentions lay;
2. The new food distribution policy announced in August giving distribution power to ZANU PF agents rather than NGOs, which had given the WFP so much heartache – and explained how food had been used as a political weapon;

3. The banning of the *Daily News* in September;

4. The ongoing suppression of the MDC, including the treason trial, fresh charges levelled against MDC leaders, and the shooting of MDC workers ten days previously (which Madiba acknowledged he had read about).

I posited that these facts were indisputable, were evidence that quiet diplomacy had not yielded any fruit and that far from the political environment loosening up, it was becoming more draconian. Anyone mediating the Zimbabwean crisis also needed to understand the ongoing ramifications of the Gukurahundi – anyone who felt that Mugabe would negotiate his way out of power did not understand Mugabe's true fears. I said the only people who understood were the actual victims, Mugabe and his inner circle. Only they knew the true extent and true horror, and the possible consequences, of that period. Because of his deep-rooted fears, Mugabe was unlikely to give up real power through dialogue. This, I said, was something President Mbeki needed to appreciate.

Madiba responded by saying that Mbeki was a shrewd politician who understood Mugabe, but that he was also in danger of losing Africa on the issue – something he could not afford. He spoke at length about his own clashes with Mugabe and how as president he had threatened to walk out of SADC if Mugabe was allowed to continue his antics. He said that other regional leaders, save for President Muluzi, feared Mugabe and would not stand up to him, complicating Mbeki's ability to deal with the situation. At this juncture I stressed that there was a dangerous political vacuum. I then went on to speak about the grave catastrophe facing Zimbabwe, referring to WFP figures regarding starvation and institutions collapsing (I spoke about a third of the medical school professional staff leaving, the subversion of the judiciary and the consequences of economic collapse). Bizos chipped in at this point to reinforce what I was saying (as he in fact did at several stages, all of which contributed enormously to the force of the "argument"). I spoke of the urgency of the situation and said that it should not be left to spiral out of control. Quiet diplomacy, as presently conducted, would not work.

I told Madiba that his counsel about Mbeki's difficulty in Africa tallied with what Fink Haysom and Alastair Sparks had said to me in previous conversations about Mbeki's problems in dealing with the situation. That was why we had approached President Wade with a specific request that he rally presidents Kofuor, Kibaki, and Mogae and that they in turn approach Mbeki in a supportive and understanding manner to strengthen his arm in dealing with Mugabe, without alienating Mbeki from the rest of Africa. I expressed the hope that Madiba could encourage that process and joked that collaboration with Wade may also get his vote in securing South Africa's bid to get the World Cup. With Wade's support he might get Francophone Africa and France on side as well!

Madiba said that the idea merited consideration but he repeated his concern that Mbeki might rebuff him because of his past history of confrontation with Mugabe. Both Bizos and I then stressed that his role was best behind the scenes and George said that he should be involved in "quiet diplomacy" within the ANC! Madiba agreed that the crisis needed urgent action and that the situation was desperate, but he feared that Mugabe was not susceptible to any pressure. Mugabe, he said, "didn't appear to care about his people or the economy". I responded by saying that I understood his concerns and that their fears about Mugabe were well founded. I referred Madiba to Christopher Hope's book *Brothers Under the Skin* and said I found it fascinating how dictators shared the same traits no matter what colour they were or what era they lived in. Madiba took particular note of the book and asked me to repeat the author and title. Bizos chipped in about a story concerning Idi Amin who he said was proof that dictators did not have to be white!

By this stage the conversation had already lasted about 40 minutes and as Bizos had only asked for five minutes in his phone call that morning, I felt that I had already overstayed my time, although Madiba gave no indication of this. Preparing to leave, I said that was all I had come to request of him and the only remaining thing was to leave him with a copy of the heads of argument in the presidential election challenge case, presenting him and Bizos with a copy. As I was about to get up Madiba asked me about the state of the judiciary. I explained that the Supreme Court had been subverted, save for Judge Sandura, and that only about 40 per cent of the High Court judges were professional and independent. Bizos broke in to talk about Judge Susan Mavangira's judgment in Tsvangirai's second treason charge bail application, telling Madiba that, despite obvious pressure, she had done the right thing. In contrast, Bizos complained, Judge Garwe, when presented with an unarguable point, would rule correctly, but given any latitude whatsoever would rule in a partisan way.

I explained why we had chosen the legal route in the face of obvious bias. It was done cognisant of many problems but was an attempt to stop the cycle of violence that had afflicted Zimbabwe since 1890. I explained that there were hawks and doves in the MDC and that my argument to proceed with the court proceeding had only just won the day in April 2002, when hawks within were calling for action in the streets. I said the MDC was determined to pursue peaceful, non-violent means but that the danger of a political vacuum was real and that they grew when non-violent, peaceful means of bringing about change were frustrated. I said that while we expected the court challenge to be frustrated we hoped if it was complemented by strong international pressure a peaceful transition could still be secured.

Madiba then said that it was important to continue with that agenda and that it was important for internal pressure to be maintained and for people like me to remain in the country fighting for justice. He said he greatly appreciated my coming to see him (which I thought was ironic, given that I was in awe of him) and I responded that the reverse applied. He said that his children and grandchildren were telling him that he was "past it" and that he appreciated that people "of my calibre" had taken the time to come and brief him, stunning me with his graciousness. I told Madiba my children also had to fight for my time and they also wished that I did not have so many meetings; that I suspected that Madiba's family were just saying that to him because they had missed him so much in the many long years when he had been unable to see them at all. I said I had had a deep hope to meet him but had never thought it would become a possibility and that I greatly appreciated him spending so much of his time to listen to me.

When I finally got up to go, not wanting the time to end, I mentioned my hope that I would see him again. Mabiba replied that he did not think he would be "very welcome in Mugabe's Zimbabwe". I responded by saying that tyrants come and go and that I looked forward to the opportunity of welcoming him to my constituency one fine day. Bizos then encouraged the positive sentiment, saying, "in 1964 the prospect of seeing freedom during his lifetime in South Africa seemed remote" but that it had happened and that so it would happen in Zimbabwe.

Wishing Madiba well and good health, I left. On leaving I noticed that his dinner place had been set at the end of a long baronial dining room table (in a room leading from the living-room) – alone. Solitude, I suppose, must be nice when there are so many pressures thrust on one, but for a person who was kept away from his family for 27 years, the scene was poignant, to my mind at least. As I left the room Madiba gave me a hearty smile and a wave of both his hands, saying how nice it was to meet.

Bizos walked me out to the security gate, venturing that the meeting had gone well and that I should now leave it for Madiba to work out a plan. The time was 6.25 pm when I left. I had been just over an hour with one of the greatest men who ever lived. It remains the most remarkable meeting I have ever had. I was treated with humility, compassion and empathy by a man who had suffered so much.

On 4 November, we finally managed to get the presidential electoral challenge under way. It had been a battle just to get to that point. Having filed the petition on 12 April 2002, Mugabe, the registrar general of Elections, Minister of Justice Chinamasa and the Electoral Supervisory Commission dragged their feet. It took them months to file opposing papers. Despite being required to in terms of the Electoral Act, the registrar general had failed to move all voting materials into Harare, frustrating our need to audit them. We were also denied access to the original voters' rolls. All this necessitated a plethora of side applications in our attempts to get them to comply. The registrar of the High Court, getting in on the act too, was dilatory in setting the case down, despite provisions in the Electoral Act which stated that petitions should be dealt with urgently. Eventually, we had to go to court in May 2003 to compel the registrar to set the matter down, resulting in an order granted on 4 July. In doing so Judge President Garwe, so often at the centre of these legal battles, ordered that only the legal arguments would be dealt with initially. Evidence of electoral fraud could only be presented later once the legal arguments had been decided upon.

Our legal team, comprising advocates Gauntlett, De Bourbon and Happias Zhou, filed a 158-page heads of argument. There were ten broad issues, the most important being the contention that Section 158 of the Electoral Act (introduced in 1990), giving the president power to make electoral law by regulations, constituted a "dispensing power, invalid for four centuries". It vested in the president a legislative power which made him the framer of rules for an election "in which he himself was a contender – a judge in his own cause".[526] The remaining issues were all weighty and included the failure to hold the third day of polling as

391

ordered, the illegality of changing the rules at the eleventh hour, and the failure to permit postal voting. None of these arguments even touched on the evidence of electoral fraud, which was yet to come, but they were overwhelmingly powerful on their own. It took Gauntlett more than a day to argue all these points before the presiding judge, Ben Hlatshwayo. The learned judge had been rewarded with his own land, taken in 2003, when "he arrived at (commercial farmer) Vernon Nicolle's 580 hectares in Banket, snatched the keys from the maid and declared the place his".[527]

Mugabe's lawyer, Terrence Hussein, replied cursorily to Gauntlett. I was gobsmacked listening to his arguments. He basically gave a political speech, insinuating that Tsvangirai was part of a British plan to remove Mugabe from office. In conclusion he said it was "inconceivable" that the election of president should be set aside simply because of the "flowery language of three lawyers".[528] Gauntlett responded to Hussein's "argument", barely concealing his contempt for his unprofessionalism. He concluded by reminding the court how important the case was and asked the judge to rule as urgently as possible.

It was a waste of breath. Hlatshwayo took seven months to hand down his judgment, showing utter contempt for the rules of court which required election petitions to be dealt with urgently. His response to the 158-page heads of argument prepared by arguably Southern Africa's finest constitutional lawyer was a one page judgment, summarily dismissing Tsvangirai's claims. I suppose in reality Hlatshwayo could not afford to do anything else; the reason Hussein replied with political bluster was because Gauntlett's arguments were unassailable. No doubt Hlatshwayo realised he couldn't find any coherent legal reasons to dismiss the case either, so relied on brevity.

In the week following the presidential case argument, there was a sinister turn in our struggle. On 13 November 2003, British human rights campaigner Peter Tatchell showed an 18-minute video at the Institute of Contemporary Arts cinema in London, which featured two men in balaclavas and camouflage. Tatchell, who had tried to effect a citizen's arrest of Mugabe for torture when he last visited London in October 1999, claimed that one of the men was the commander of a new underground movement, called the Zimbabwe Freedom Movement. He said the Movement had a network of cells throughout the country and thousands of members, "primarily members of the security forces disillusioned with Mugabe". They had access to arms dumps and were serving notice on Mugabe to "resign or face removal by judicious use of appropriate force".[529] The video, which Tatchell said had been smuggled out of the country, was farcical. In my mind this was either a CIO ploy or an inane scheme. Aside from the principle of remaining committed to non-violence, it seemed absurd to even consider whether armed struggle was practicable. None of Zimbabwe's neighbours would consider providing bases for guerrillas and within the country any armed movement would be overwhelmingly outgunned by an army well practised in the art of guerrilla warfare. What shocked and worried me most about the incident was the reaction to the video by a few of my MDC colleagues. While the majority dismissed the video as a prank, one or two expressed the view that armed struggle might be the only way to remove ZANU PF. As it turned out nothing further was heard about the Zimbabwe Freedom Movement, but it was another reminder to me that our commitment to the use of non-violence was under threat.

In fact ZANU PF was undermining Zimbabwe at a rate far quicker than any armed struggle could do. On 20 November that year, I was in parliament to hear the minister of Finance deliver his depressing budget speech. He estimated the economy had "contracted 13.2%" that year and inflation was to "peak at 600% by December".[530] We started to hear the sanctions mantra sounded more often. He blamed the collapse of the economy on sanctions and the HIV/AIDS pandemic, studiously avoiding the real reasons for collapse: violence, the destruction of our largest foreign exchange earner and employer, commercial agriculture and the exiling of thousands of our best brains.

There was further bad news in early December. Zimbabwe had been suspended from the Commonwealth on 19 March 2002, and the decision was due for review at the next Commonwealth Heads of Government Meeting (CHOGM) scheduled to be held in Nigeria in December 2003. Australia's prime minister, John Howard, was particularly proactive in encouraging Commonwealth leaders to stand firm against Mbeki who had wanted Zimbabwe readmitted. In the run up to the meeting, Nigerian host President Obasanjo had refused to invite Mugabe. Zimbabwe dominated CHOGM's agenda. The discussions were marked by Mbeki's attempts to have Zimbabwe's suspension lifted, but his efforts were foiled. To resolve the impasse that had developed around the issue, Canada and Kenya proposed a committee to resolve the issue of whether to lift Zimbabwe's suspension. The committee, composed of the heads of government of South Africa, Mozambique, Nigeria, India, Jamaica, Australia and Canada, ruled by six-to-one (South Africa being the odd one out) against lifting Zimbabwe's suspension. In response, Mugabe announced, on 7 December, that Zimbabwe was withdrawing from the Commonwealth, marking only the third occasion (after South Africa in 1961 and Pakistan in 1971) that a country had withdrawn voluntarily.

The MDC leadership were appalled by Mugabe's unilateral decision. When the matter came up for debate in parliament on 10 December, I described the decision as "wrong, illegal, foolish and selfish".[531] I challenged ZANU PF "to put this to a referendum (to) see whether (it enjoyed) the support of the Zimbabwean people". All Minister of Foreign Affairs Mudenge could argue, conveniently ignoring Mozambique, India, Jamaica and Nigeria's stance, was that the Commonwealth was now dominated by "racist bullies". In withdrawing from the world, Mudenge sounded increasingly like the RF had done when it declared UDI. The action was, he said, "guided by principle", "historic" and meant to "uphold our independence and sovereignty".[532] Ironically, just as South African Prime Minister Vorster had been Smith's principled friend, so, too, was Mbeki saluted "for his resolute stand in defence of cherished principles". Quite what those "principles" were eluded us. Presumably, they didn't include the principles set out in the Harare Commonwealth Declaration signed by Mugabe on 20 October 1991, which included "the individual's inalienable right to participate by means of free and democratic political processes in framing the society in which he or she lives".[533]

On the weekend before Christmas the MDC held its second National Conference at the Harare showgrounds. I presented the MDC Justice policy document, which had been first developed with the help of the ICTJ in the run up to the 2002 presidential election, but never made public. The document, which was ratified by the conference, included a commitment to a new constitutional reform process, the establishment of a truth commission and major changes to our anti-corruption laws. The endorsement of the truth commission proposal was particularly satisfying because of its specific nuances. I was determined that we should have a victim-orientated policy which sought to ascertain the views of victims before going on to formulate policies about justice and reconciliation. The naming of it, i.e. a "Truth Commission", itself was significant. It was not to be a "Truth, Justice and Reconciliation" commission because the policy envisaged that victims would define what laws should be implemented to achieve the latter two objectives. In our studies of similar commissions the world over it had become clear that too often politicians had predetermined what consequences should await the perpetrators of human rights abuses, rather than the victims themselves. For that reason the policy set out a two-stage process, starting with an opportunity for victims to tell how they had suffered, and giving them an opportunity to explain how they believed justice and reconciliation could be achieved. The justice and reconciliation policy formulation would then be based on the victims' views and requests, not on the whims of politicians and lawyers. Finally, the process would start with UDI, 11 November 1965, which I hoped would help address historical injustices under white minority rule.

The year ended with an event which, although very sad in itself, would eventually also contribute to the breakup of the MDC in 2005. Zodwa Sibanda, MDC Vice-President Gibson Sibanda's wife, died over Christmas. She was a seasoned politician in her own right and had endured detention as a ZAPU member under both the RF and ZANU PF. Zodwa was a tower of strength behind her husband, a reliable counsellor and friend, whom he trusted implicitly. Critically, she also enjoyed the trust and ear of Tsvangirai's wife Susan; together, as only trusted spouses can do, they helped keep their respective husbands' relationship strong. Her death removed that channel of communication with deleterious consequences in future. At the time, though, it was a just another cruel blow. She had been a warm, motherly figure to a political organisation that had tried to do right, but was under siege from all directions.

CHAPTER 21

"CONTEMPT OF PARLIAMENT" JANUARY 2004 TO MARCH 2005

"Zimbabweans are suffering. There are numerous cases of human rights abuse and torture. It is a situation where we cannot stand by watching a tragedy unfold without becoming complicit through our apathy."
– Archbishop Emeritus Desmond M Tutu, in a letter written on behalf of the Zimbabwe Defence and Aid Fund, March 2004

I started 2004 plagued by concern over how I would find sufficient money to keep our various cases going. The most expensive aspect of the presidential election challenge (gathering and presenting evidence of fraud from throughout the country) was still ahead, and hundreds of our leaders and members still faced criminal charges. Although some funds had come in, we faced massive shortfalls. Jenny, knowing that I was burdened by this, arranged for the family to have a break together at a lodge in the Matopos. We were lounging around the pool, on a Friday in early January, when Julian Ozanne saw me and came over to us. Jenny, being protective of me and our family time, was not particularly welcoming and gave him a bit of a cold shoulder. Ozanne had interviewed me a few years before when he was the *Financial Times* African bureau chief. He explained that he had recently got married in Kenya and was on honeymoon and taking his new wife to many of his favourite haunts in Africa. We were amazed at the coincidence of our being at the same rather remote lodge on the only day he was passing through Matabeleland. Inevitably, we got round to talking about the state of Zimbabwe and I mentioned my funding dilemma. As I impressed on him how ZANU PF were succeeding in using law as a weapon he said that he might be able to help. His wife, he explained, was the actress Gillian Anderson and she was "well connected". Later on we met Anderson, who agreed to help, but I, not being a movie buff, remained blissfully unaware about who she was or what movies she was famous for until I went home and googled her.

In the weeks that followed we agreed that if I could persuade two credible patrons, Ozanne and Anderson would use their contacts to establish and fund a new organisation to fund victims of human rights abuses in Zimbabwe. That chance meeting led to two entirely new funding organisations, the Zimbabwe Defence and Aid Fund and the Zimbabwe Benefit Fund, being set up in the UK, which although linked administratively to the Cape Town trusts, drew on an entirely new set of individual donors. I approached Archbishop Pius Ncube to be a patron. With him on board, Archbishop Desmond Tutu was approached to be the other patron and much to our delight he agreed to help.

Parliament resumed on 20 January 2004. One of the first orders of business was to debate a further amendment to the Land Acquisition Act. Commercial farmers had used every possible legal argument to prevent their land being taken, much to ZANU PF's annoyance; this new legislation was to remove the loopholes they'd been using, but the proposed bill was found to be unconstitutional by the Parliamentary Legal Committee. On 21 January, after Welshman Ncube had laid out the committee's objections, Justice minister Chinamasa rose to argue that the bill complied with the constitution. Anticipating that this would happen, I immediately raised a point of order, objecting to Chinamasa speaking. I argued that it was a crime for any MP to participate in a debate if he or she had a direct pecuniary interest in the matter.[534] Tabling a list of 37 ZANU PF MPs, together with the farms they had acquired in terms of the fast-track programme, I argued that all those on the list were precluded from debating. It was a particularly embarrassing for some of the MPs who were listed as having several farms and were thus in contravention of ZANU PF's professed policy of one farm per person. In fact some were listed as having as many as four farms allocated to them. Those who were listed as having multiple farms included minister of Information, Jonathan Moyo (3), minister of Agriculture Joseph Made (2), Saviour Kasukuwere (4), governor of Matabeleland North Obert Mpofu (3), and Mugabe's sister Sabina Mugabe (5).

Chinamasa's name was on the list too. He and his wife were listed as having acquired a farm known as Lawrencedale 4 in Headlands, plus three others. Consequently, I argued, he would be committing a criminal offence if he debated and should be barred.

All hell broke loose. My fellow MDC MPs demanded that a ruling be made but this only resulted in two of them, Gabriel Chaibva and Tendai Biti, being thrown out. Chinamasa shouted out that I was "a racist liar", that he had been "allocated Lawrencedale 3, not Lawrencedale 4"[535] and that he hadn't been allocated four farms. His principal concern appeared to be the allegation that he had received several farms, which totally missed the point, namely, that even with only one farm he had a pecuniary interest in the matter. ZANU PF steamrolled over my objection, as well as the constitutional points raised by Welshman Ncube, ably assisted by Speaker Mnangagwa. At the end of the debate that day the ZANU PF chief whip Joram Gumbo asked Mnangagwa to investigate whether I was guilty of contempt of parliament in that I had "presented false documents with intent to deceive Parliament". Mnangagwa said he would study the matter and make the ruling the following day.

Although I didn't realise the full gravity of the situation at the time, things got very nasty the next day. Before even dealing with my point of order regarding Chinamasa's breach of parliamentary privilege, Mnangagwa dealt with the allegation levelled against me. He found that there was a "*prima facie* case of breach of privilege and that an enquiry" was necessary to establish whether I was guilty of "contempt of Parliament".[536] Turning to my original point of order, Mnangagwa found that my claim that ZANU PF MPs had "a direct pecuniary interest as beneficiaries of the Land Reform programme (was) mischievous, frivolous and devoid of legal logic and validity".[537] It was another classic case of facts being turned on their head, the accuser becoming the accused. Buoyed by the rulings, ZANU PF rammed through its amendments to the Land Acquisition Act. While annoyed by Mnangagwa's rulings, I was not too fussed as I had done my homework in the preparation of the list and was confident I could prove it was correct. What I didn't appreciate at the time was ZANU PF's intentions behind trying to hold me in contempt of parliament. It was only when the ZANU PF caucus voted to have MDC MP Roy Bennett imprisoned for contempt in October that I realised my narrow escape. What they had not been able to achieve, namely my imprisonment, through the courts, they would now attempt through parliament.

The same day Mnangagwa ordered that I be investigated for contempt, I met with Bizos, who was in Zimbabwe for Tsvangirai's treason trial. Welshman Ncube and Gasela had been the first defence witnesses and their evidence drove a coach and horses through the state's case. Ncube was able to show that Menashe had refused to return US$100 000 paid to him by the MDC on the grounds that he had fulfilled his lobbying contract. This contradicted his evidence in the criminal trial in which he said he had done nothing to help the MDC. Bizos had insisted that a few men who had been in the Montreal meeting with Tsvangirai be called, but the state had been unable to compel them to come to Zimbabwe. All the state relied on was the totally discredited evidence of Ben-Menashe himself. On that note, the case came to an end on February 26.

In his closing argument Bizos accused the "ZANU PF regime" of entrapment; Ben-Menashe was paid to entrap Tsvangirai and obtain testimony against him via the video. "The temptation to lie, the temptation to please (his) paymasters must have been overwhelming," Bizos told the court. The state's lawyers had claimed the video recording resulted in Mugabe's "elimination", or murder, being discussed. But Bizos argued there was no clear or unambiguous reference to a murder, assassination or coup. "How bad has the State case got to be in order to be thrown out? How bad does a witness have to be to be disbelieved?"[538] he asked during his summing up. Judge Garwe was unmoved in reserving judgment, telling our defence team that there was "a lot of evidence" which would have to be gone through. There was a lot of evidence, but it was all highly suspect and we expected Tsvangirai to be acquitted within a few weeks.

Soon after the end of Tsvangirai's trial, The Zimbabwe Institute finalised a report entitled *Playing with Fire*, which documented all the human rights abuses that had been perpetrated against MDC MPs and candidates since 2000. The report, prepared in advance of the parliamentary elections due to be held in March 2005, and based on mounds of evidence the MDC Legal Committee had supplied, made the point that MDC MPs were "amongst the most persecuted in the world".[539] The findings were horrifying: 90% of MDC MPs reported violations which directly affected their person, such as attempted murder, torture, assault or detention; 42% reported being physically assaulted and 16% tortured; 44% of MPs had had their homes vandalised; 60% reported attacks or threats against family members.[540] The 92-page report provided graphic evidence backing the findings. Its key message was that "conditions were far worse than they were in 2000", especially considering the draconian legislation introduced since that election.

Playing with Fire was released in Johannesburg on the eve of my trip to Europe on 9 March to set up the Zimbabwe Legal Defence and Aid Fund (ZLDAF). At the same time, Archbishop Tutu issued a letter encouraging people to support ZLDAF, making the point that "Nelson Mandela himself might not have been saved from the gallows without the effort of the international community and those who selflessly strove to see that justice prevailed".[541]

I arrived in London to a hectic schedule of meetings with MPs, Lords and journalists, centred around the *Playing with Fire* report. I also addressed the England and Wales Bar Human Rights Committee, which was the start of a long and fruitful relationship between that committee and the legal profession in Zimbabwe. Ozanne had pulled out all the stops. He had arranged for me to meet people who would run ZLDAF, which would be modelled on the apartheid-era International Defence and Aid Fund (IDAF). They included solicitor, Bill Frankel OBE, the so-called "Mr X" in the IDAF,[542] Mark Katzenellenbogen, a London banker and nephew of South African anti-apartheid icon Helen Suzman, and British human rights lawyer Mark Muller Stuart QC. The irony of Frankel's involvement was not lost on us – the IDAF had played an important role supporting Mugabe and other detainees in Rhodesia in the 1960 and '70s, and here he was back again involved in helping people whose rights were being abused by the very people who had received IDAF help before.[543] The ZANU PF propaganda machine has always portrayed the MDC as a British government project, which isn't true; aside from it being a home-grown party, the vast majority of funding for the two trusts, the LDF and ZLDAF, which funded most of our cases, came from similar sources to those that had funded ZANU PF and ZAPU during the 1970s, namely private individuals and the Scandinavians.

With the trust in the process of being set up, we turned our attention to fundraising. This is where Gillian Anderson came into her own. She arranged for me and fellow MDC Legal Department committee member Yvonne Mahlunge to meet a number of celebrities she knew personally, including Coldplay's Chris Martin and Sir Bob Geldof. We asked Henry Olonga, who by then was in exile in the UK, to join the ZDLAF board and he came along to these private meetings, forming a trio. Olonga was not just a superb cricketer but a marvellous singer, too, who enjoyed enormous respect in the UK for his black armband protest. I think the bait of knowing that they would meet Olonga encouraged some of the celebrities to make time to meet us. All were concerned about what was happening in Zimbabwe and willing to help. Martin had a strong Zimbabwean connection – his mother was born there and his grandmother still lived in Harare. Geldof had a long-standing interest in Africa and an inherent dislike for dictators; he issued a statement not long after meeting us, publicly endorsing ZLDAF, in which he described Mugabe in his typically brash fashion as "a scar on the face of Africa".[544]

During the same trip, I flew to Copenhagen and Berlin, once again speaking to *Playing with Fire*. In Berlin I joined forces with fellow MDC national executive members, Vice-President Gibson Sibanda and Sekai Holland, for a series of meetings with German ministers and parliamentarians. Once again we were amazed by the great empathy shown towards us by German leaders who had suffered under the East German regime. On our first evening, we met with one of the heroes of the autumn 1989 uprising in Dresden, Arnold Vaatz. It was immediately apparent that Vaatz understood our plight better than most leaders we had met world wide. He was so concerned about our situation that he arranged for us to meet then Christian Democratic Union (CDU) leader Angela Merkel the next day. We struck an immediate rapport with Merkel, who ever since has remained a steadfast supporter of the Zimbabwean democracy struggle. While most politicians throughout the world have been sympathetic towards us, most simply don't understand the battles we face. Many of our experiences are so incredibly bizarre, truths stranger than fiction, that they are hard to comprehend. Presumably, because Merkel and Vaatz had themselves lived through similar injustices, they immediately understood our plight.

For some reason Zimbabwe was remarkably placid on my return from Europe that autumn season. It may have been because ZANU PF's ploy to convict Tsvangirai of treason was in disarray. The prosecution of MDC Treasurer General Fletcher Dulini Ncube for the murder of Cain Nkala was floundering too. Whatever the case, the calm was broken on 18 May. The first I heard of trouble was when Tsvangirai phoned me in Bulawayo to tell me that I would probably have another case on my hands because MDC MP Roy Bennett had attacked Justice Minister Chinamasa in parliament. As it turned out Chinamasa, in debating a proposal to impose a mandatory prison sentence for stock theft, said that Bennett had forgotten that "his forefathers were thieves", and that what he owned was not "because of his intelligence but was a legacy … an inheritance of stolen wealth accumulated over a century and a half".[545] The accusation blew a fuse, causing Bennett to charge at Chinamasa and push him to the ground. In the ensuing fracas, ZANU PF MP Didymus Mutasa kicked Bennett before he was escorted out of the chamber by the sergeant-at-arms. Having recovered his composure, Chinamasa remarked that "at least the events that have just happened show to which extent Whites treat Africans". It was this statement that was to underpin how ZANU PF would exploit Bennett's loss of temper. Inevitably, at the close of the day the minister of Labour, lawyer Paul Mangwana, moved a motion that a Committee on Privileges be appointed to investigate Bennett's contempt of parliament. The next day the deputy speaker, Edna Madzongwe, duly obliged, advising that a committee similar to the one dealing with my alleged contempt, comprising the speaker, Mnangagwa, Joice Mujuru, Chief Mangwende, and MDC MPs and lawyers Tendai Biti and Welshman Ncube, would investigate Bennett.

Two of the three remaining white MPs were now under investigation. At the time I didn't appreciate the full ramifications of what had happened. Although Bennett's action had certainly humiliated Chinamasa, it also played into ZANU PF's propaganda line that we were all just a bunch of unreconstructed Rhodesians. Henceforth it served their purposes well to focus all their hatred on Bennett and, in doing so, their portrayal of me as the principal bad egg waned.

My own case before the Privileges Committee was already well under way; the committee had interviewed the permanent secretary for Lands, Land Reform and Resettlement and some of the ZANU PF MPs who had been on the list I'd tabled. The committee had also received written submissions from other MPs either "confirming or denying the information".[546] I received a letter from parliament summoning me to appear before the committee on 12 August with my lawyer, but before I could do so providence intervened again. Biti and Ncube had told me that things were not going well for many of the ZANU PF MPs listed by me because the committee's enquiries had opened a can of worms. The permanent secretary for Lands, under cross-examination by committee members, had confirmed that many of the MPs had indeed occupied several farms, some vicariously through family members. Concurrently, the matter had come to the attention of the minister of Lands, John

Nkomo, who also at the time happened to be chairman of ZANU PF, resulting in him issuing withdrawal letters to those MPs mentioned on my list as multiple farm holders, including a few cabinet ministers. The media got wind of the withdrawal letters and even the ZANU PF mouthpiece *The Voice* got in on the act, condemning *mafikizolos*[547] within ZANU PF who were holding on to multiple farms against both government and party policies.[548]

Matters came to a head on 25 July when an anonymous writer, using the pseudonym Lowani Ndlovu, published a lengthy article in *The Sunday Mail* criticising Nkomo. Using language that was routinely part of Jonathan Moyo's lexicon – "neocols, Rhodies and mumbo jumbo" – the letter alleged "evil collaboration between Coltart and officials in the Ministry of Lands".[549] It also accused Nkomo of signing withdrawal letters that were "scandalously false and malicious". Interestingly, it confirmed that the withdrawal letters had been served on "three or four Cabinet Ministers" without mentioning names, "lest (the readers) become unnecessarily excited". Nkomo immediately hit back, stating that he would not be "intimidated, perturbed or frustrated by those causing this hullabaloo".[550] The "angry obfuscations by those defending the indefensible would not scare (him in his) efforts to retrieve farms from land grabbers". It was confirmed that Nkomo had taken back land from several cabinet ministers, three of whom were Moyo, Chinamasa and Made. Moyo, found to have had three farms, was quoted as saying the withdrawal letters were "preposterous and annoying".[551] With all these internecine battles erupting within ZANU PF, my hearing before the Privileges Committee on 12 August was called off. I was never summoned again and the matter was allowed to die quietly.

The same day that "Lowani Ndlovu's" vitriolic article appeared in the Zimbabwean press I happened to be in Boston, attending the Democratic Party's national convention. There were many side events which provided outstanding opportunities to network. In the space of a few days I met a diverse range of people, including Kerry Kennedy, Robin Cook, Bono's manager Paul McGuinness, and African Foreign ministers. But the highlight was listening to the keynote address delivered by a 42-year-old Illinois state senator on the evening of 27 July in the massive FleetCenter auditorium. His key message was "hope" and much of it resonated with me. He spoke of "the hope of a skinny kid with a funny name who believes that America has place for him, too". Every time he mentioned the word "hope" thousands of signs were waved by delegates emblazoned with the word. He persisted with the theme: "Hope in the face of difficulty! Hope in the face of uncertainty! The audacity of hope! In the end, that is God's greatest gift to us, the bedrock of this nation. A belief in things not seen. A belief that there are better days ahead." The speech energised the entire convention and became the most important political springboard of its deliverer – Barack Obama. Although his speech was not directed at Zimbabwe, it encouraged me to keep going in the face of difficulty. At the end of the evening I made sure to grab one of the signs the delegates had been waving. It is still fixed to my study door and reads "Hope is on the way".

I got back home to two pieces of bad news. Firstly, Judge Hlatshwayo had dismissed all our legal arguments in the presidential election challenge case in a cursory one-page judgment. This meant that we would now have to prove electoral fraud, many of the details of which were being tenaciously held onto by the registrar general's office. Secondly, despite Judge Garwe advising that he was going to hand down his judgment in the Tsvangirai treason trial on 29 July, at the eleventh hour the matter was inexplicably and indefinitely postponed.

As months dragged on without a judgment in the treason trial, tensions rose within the MDC. Given ZANU PF's undemocratic nature, its military past and the seamless relationship between party and state organs, it was apparent from its inception that the MDC had been infiltrated by CIO operatives at every level. The ongoing struggle, with its unrelenting pressures, provided fertile ground for agents provocateurs, no more so than in the unsettled environment created by the uncertainty of Tsvangirai's fate. In his book *At the Deep End*[552] Tsvangirai writes of how people around him sowed seeds of doubt in his mind about what even his closest colleagues like Sibanda were up to. Implicit in this "intelligence" was that a plot was brewing to replace Tsvangirai, creating a web of suspicion. Compounding this destructive whispering in Tsvangirai's ear was a growing lawlessness among the young men who provided security for the party.

One of the consequences of five years of unlawful detentions, beatings, torture and struggle was that our young people had been brutalised. Since the launch of the MDC in September 1999 our young party activists had been in the equivalent of an undeclared war; many had died but hundreds had been locked up and subjected to the most shocking treatment.

Inevitably, this hardened most of them and, in some cases, twisted their minds. This body of men, too, was infiltrated. Agents provocateurs found easy prey, young men who were receptive to suggestions that violence be used to settle scores. The same people exploited fault-lines within the party, particularly ethnicity, background and funding shortages, to drive a wedge between Tsvangirai and other senior leaders. Nearly all the young activists were unemployed and in the collapsing economy desperate for money. Welshman Ncube, the secretary general, was particularly vulnerable to attack – he was Ndebele, an academic (rather than a trade unionist) and controlled the party's scant finances. He had also been acquitted of treason charges by Judge Garwe, itself a source of suspicion for those with malevolent intent. It was in this environment that a deadly phenomenon erupted within the MDC through the course of 2004: the use of violence.

The first stirrings of violence within the MDC had occurred much earlier, in 2001, when fights had broken out in Chitungwiza, causing an internal inquiry to be held. The inquiry found that two MDC groups "were involved in a bitter power struggle"[553] and as a result some of the MPs involved were severely censored. Recommendations were made that some of them even be suspended, but in fact very little action was taken. This set an early bad precedent within the MDC. Although there had been sporadic outbursts of violence within the party since then, none had shaken the very core of the MDC. This changed in late 2004.

Earlier in 2004, on two occasions, the MDC's director of administration, Khazamula Chirilele, had been threatened by a group of youths who had not been paid after by-election campaigns. On both occasions Chirilele had been held hostage. Although he was not Ndebele, he worked under Ncube and was seen as a "sell out to Ndebeles".[554] Various threats had continued but they metastasised into an ugly incident that occurred on 28 September 2004, just weeks before Tsvangirai's judgment was handed down. A group of 25 youths surrounded Peter Guhu outside his office on the six floor of the MDC headquarters building, Harvest House, in Harare. Guhu had been appointed by Ncube as MDC director of Security in 2003. He had reported this troublesome group to the MDC leadership, including Tsvangirai, calling them "thugs". Somehow this report had got back to the young men and they were incensed. The entire group laid into Guhu, severely assaulting him before trying to throw him down the stairwell. Guhu managed to grip onto the railing and screamed for help. He was rescued by an MDC MP, Paul Madzore, who happened to be close by. Guhu was taken to hospital suffering from a ruptured ear drum, two cracked molars and numerous bruises and abrasions. He was, however, lucky to be alive because the intention to kill was obvious. On hearing of the assault Tsvangirai asked that a report not be made to the police;[555] the matter would be investigated and dealt with in house. Shockwaves reverberated throughout the embattled party, but many of us were distracted by the broad assault on the party by ZANU PF.

Our entreaties to Judge Garwe to hand down his judgment in the treason trial finally bore fruit when we were advised that he would do so on Friday, 15 October, nearly eight months after the trial had ended. Bizos flew up from Johannesburg, as did I from Bulawayo. Remembering how Garwe had ruled in the Malunga case, ultimately doing the right thing, I was confident that he would not convict. Bizos was equally confident. As recorded in his memoirs, where he quotes retired South African Constitutional Court judge Johann Kriegler, "(i)n a high profile case with the leader of the opposition being defended on a capital charge by a world-renowned human rights advocate, Mandela's lawyer and friend, and with the diplomatic community and the world media watching closely, a verdict of guilty would have called for convincing or, at the very least, credible reasons".[556] Garwe knew this. He had delayed giving his judgment as long as he could but now he had to acquit, which he did before a packed court.

The political damage had been done, however. Tsvangirai had been kept from travelling for over two years and the uncertainty of a death penalty hanging over the head of the MDC leader had driven a wedge deep into the party. After the judgment, Bizos and I drove to the South African embassy for a meeting with the ambassador, Jeremiah Ndou, and his deputy, Kingsley Sithole. Ndou was pleased with the acquittal, expressing the hope that it might lead to rapprochement between ZANU PF and the MDC. Bizos shared my scepticism – we both felt that Mugabe knew he couldn't go into another general election with charges hanging over Tsvangirai. The entire sordid affair had served its purpose. Ben-Menashe had earned his ill-gotten gain at the expense of Zimbabwean taxpayers.

The real nature and intent of ZANU PF was shown soon afterwards, on 27 October, when the Privileges Committee presented its report on the alleged contempt of parliament by Roy Bennett. Using its ZANU

PF majority, it found that Bennett's "conduct was the worst (inflicted) on the dignity of Parliament known in the history of Parliament" and recommended that he be "found guilty of contempt and sentenced to fifteen months imprisonment with labour"[557] with three months suspended, an effective sentence of a year. It brushed aside the provocation that Bennett's wife had miscarried after she had been threatened, that Bennett had been illegally detained and tortured, and that all his property had been taken from him without a cent in compensation. We were profoundly shocked as Paul Mangwana read out the recommendation. As a lawyer, Mangwana knew that in a criminal court a first offender accused, who had pushed over another man under severe provocation, would never get a custodial sentence, never mind a year's imprisonment. Bennett, upon hearing the recommendation, asked for time to read the report and respond. The speaker, Mnangagwa, agreed, telling Bennett that he would have to respond the following day.

That evening I met with Bennett, his wife and a few of their friends. It was obvious that ZANU PF were determined to be as vindictive as possible; what they hadn't managed to achieve through the courts, the conviction and imprisonment of MDC members, they would now achieve through parliament. They knew there would only be muted criticism from Africa because a white man had assaulted a black man. Bennett was in a Catch-22: if he remained in the country, he would be imprisoned for a year; if he fled the country, ZANU PF would be handed a propaganda coup and Bennett would never be allowed back in. It would end his political career and ability to represent his constituents. Friends offered to drive Bennett overnight to a remote border where he could walk across to safety. After hours of agonising we came up with a plan we knew was highly risky, but if it worked would enable him to leave the country without breaking the law. That at least would enable him to get out until the dust had settled, when he could return. Calls were made to travel agents and he was booked on an early flight to Johannesburg with a return booking that would get him back in time for parliament the following afternoon. If it worked, we could negotiate an assurance that he would not be imprisoned and he could fly back. If no assurances were given he would remain in exile until an assurance had been given. We knew it probably wouldn't work but he had no option but to try it. Bennett checked in at Harare airport early the next morning but did not get past the security checks. He was arrested by a CIO operative. The arrest itself was illegal as Bennett had not committed any offence but those legal niceties were ignored and Bennett was driven under guard back to parliament to await his fate that afternoon.

Virtually the entire Parliamentary session on the afternoon and evening of 28 October was devoted to debating Bennett's contempt of Parliament. It started with Bennett himself responding to the Committee's report and recommendation. He apologised to Parliament and to Chinamasa, pointing out the enormous stress he had been under. Interspersing his address with comments in chiShona, Bennett pointed out that before buying his farm he had sought the blessing of traditional leaders and had worked closely with local black communities. As a former member of ZANU PF he had worked with local communities with commitment. He was driven by his love of Zimbabwe. After reading out a detailed legal response to the charge, which had been prepared by his lawyers, Bennett concluded with some pungent remarks: everything he owned had been taken or looted; two of his workers had been murdered; many of his female workers had been raped and their homes burnt. There had never been any investigation into these crimes, let alone justice. Nevertheless he was "ready to go to jail".[558]

Mnangagwa then ordered Bennett out of the chamber, to enable the debate to begin. It started with Wilson Kumbula, the sole MP from the small ZANU Ndonga Party, telling parliament that if it sentenced Bennett in this manner it would be "tantamount to a kangaroo court".[559] The MDC caucus had decided that the only other white MPs, Trudy Stevenson and myself, should not speak because of the racial undertones of the matter. Priscilla Misihairabwi-Mushonga commenced with an impassioned plea that a sentence of this nature would only create "further acrimony". She was followed by Paul Themba Nyathi, who employed all his wit to break the tension, explaining how he felt angered and insulted when he, a war veteran who had been imprisoned by the RF, was called a puppet of Tony Blair. Nyathi also withdrew "any insults in advance that (he was) likely to direct in this House", which caused even Chinamasa to laugh. Speaker after speaker from the MDC benches pleaded. Welshman Ncube told the house he had researched similar incidents the world over and couldn't find any precedent for such a punitive penalty. Even one brave chief, Chimombe, pleaded that the sentence be reduced. There was a stony silence from the ZANU PF benches, save for two speeches, one by Lazarus Dokora, another from Olivia Muchena, highlighting the aggravating features of the matter. Muchena, a professing Christian, said a "child should not go scot free. We instil discipline by punishing people and deter others from doing the same wrong".[560] The last person to speak was leader of the opposition, Gibson Sibanda. Telling the house that the sentence appeared to be motivated more by "vindictiveness than justice", he implored that it be focused on what would "heal the nation", suggesting that an appropriate penalty would be a six months' suspension from parliament and a heavy fine.

The whole thing was a futile exercise because ZANU PF had already made up its mind. Paul Mangwana, chair of the committee, wound up the debate ironically arguing that the sentence was appropriate because Bennett's action was an "attack on the dignity" of parliament. In fact the gravest attack on parliament's dignity was the vote that followed. The ZANU PF caucus and chiefs had been whipped into line; even Chief Chimombe, who had pleaded for leniency, voted with ZANU PF in the division, securing the original, unaltered motion by a margin of 53 to 42. Judges in their own cause, Chinamasa and Mutasa voted without any qualms for the motion. Bennett was called back to be told smugly by Mnangagwa that he had been found guilty and sentenced to a year's imprisonment with labour.

As I sat in the chamber quietly listening to the debate and praying, I was struck by the bitterness washing over from the ZANU PF benches. Bennett had become the object of their wrath; while some were embarrassed and would not look me in the eye, many smirked, consumed by the *schadenfreude* of Bennett being exiled to some decrepit prison. As we filtered out of the chamber our MDC women MPs were utterly distraught; many of them were in floods of tears. My only consolation was the spirited defence our black colleagues had put up in a matter with fearsome racial overtones. For all the decades of racial oppression wrought by successive colonial governments and all the attempts by ZANU PF to play the race card, it was profoundly moving to see how MDC MPs had risen above the hatreds of the past to defend a colleague with a short fuse, who happened to be white. This injustice marked another watershed in my interaction with Mugabe. For years Mike Auret and I had been portrayed by the ZANU PF propaganda machine as the incarnation of Rhodesia. In the 2002 election that changed to me alone. In September 2003 Roy Bennett was named with me by Mugabe for the first time. However, from October 2004 onwards, Bennett became the sole incarnation of Rhodesia in Mugabe's mind. I would be mentioned in dispatches every so often, but Bennett would henceforth bear the full venom of ZANU PF's wrath.

For all the apparent unity demonstrated by ZANU PF when Bennett was sent to prison, in fact deep divisions within it were soon to emerge. The death of Vice-President Simon Muzenda in September 2003 had sparked a vigorous contest within the party, splitting into two camps around Emmerson Mnangagwa and former ZANLA commander Solomon Mujuru,[561] for a replacement. In the course of 2004, the Mnangagwa faction developed and reached agreement around four principles, which would later become known as the "Tsholotsho Declaration", namely that:

1. there should be ethnic and regional balance in the party's four top leadership positions;
2. the office of President and First Secretary should not be reserved for one ethnic group but should rotate among Zimbabwe's major ethnic groups;
3. that these top positions should not be imposed but elected; and
4. that the party's constitution and the rule of law within the party should be respected.

Behind these "principles" was a concern that one ethnic group, the Zezurus, dominated all the top leadership positions within ZANU PF and government.[562] Mugabe, Vice-President Msika, the chief justice, the commissioner of Police, and the commander of the Armed Forces were all Zezuru. Other ethnic groups, particularly Mnangagwa's Karanga ethnic group, felt that this should end and the principles provided a means of achieving that goal.

Mnangagwa, as ZANU PF secretary for Administration, was in a key position to promote the principles. He also stood to benefit enormously if the principles were adopted as he would become vice-president. A series of meetings were held countrywide, culminating in a meeting on 30 August in which eight of the ten provincial chairmen indicated that they would "vote in favour of the principles".[563] Having secured the support of a majority of provincial chairmen, Mnangagwa wrote a letter to party structures on 11 November, detailing nomination procedures for any of the top four positions which was due to be held at ZANU

PF's December congress. Solomon Mujuru's faction, having got wind of a meeting of Mnangagwa's supporters in Tsholotsho on 18 November, through John Nkomo and Nicholas Goche, persuaded Mugabe to call an emergency Politburo meeting the same day, which amended the party's constitution to mandate that at least one of the vice-presidents should be a woman. The amendment effectively scuppered Mnangagwa's hopes of becoming vice-president.

The politburo meeting also prevented Mnangagwa from attending the event planned in Tsholotsho, but on the evening of 18 November, an informal meeting was convened. Those who attended included Moyo, Chinamasa and six provincial chairmen. That meeting resolved that Joice Mujuru's candidacy for the vacant vice-president slot would be opposed. In addition it was agreed that they would retain Mugabe as president, but nominate Mnangagwa for the other vice-president slot instead of the incumbent Msika. Finally, Chinamasa would be proposed as party chairman.

Mugabe and the Mujuru faction, however, thwarted these plans. When the December congress was held the Mnangagwa faction was sidelined; Mugabe and Msika held their positions and were joined by Joice Mujuru and John Nkomo as vice-president and chairman respectively. Jonathan Moyo, in a series of articles published after the congress, vented his anger against Mugabe. His final article had a deadly sting in the tail. He concluded that "the current political and economic problems facing Zimbabwe (were) due to the fact that the country (was) being ruled by a hopelessly clueless, tired and terrified undemocratic clique which desperately (wanted) to cling to power by fair means or foul at the clear expense of national interest".[564] Moyo was subsequently expelled from ZANU PF and Mnangagwa demoted to the lowly position of minister of Rural Housing.

Moyo's article also mentioned the "collapse of the economy with inflation of 913.6% galloping towards 1 000%", which was a fair assessment.

By the end of 2004 the nation was in an extreme crisis. In a report published at the year end, it was estimated that there was 70% unemployment, 80% of people were living below the poverty line, 27% of adults were HIV positive, key industries had contracted between 40 and 60% and 25% of Zimbabwe's population (some 3.4 million people) had gone into economic or political exile.[565] Despite this, ZANU PF kept

411

digging in. The last few parliamentary sessions of 2004 were dominated by further draconian legislation. Although we fought long into the night, on one occasion pushing debate until 5.45 am, ZANU PF pushed through measures to control NGOs and tighten its control over the electoral process. In the early hours of 17 November, I said what "a great honour it was to stand here at 4.05 am to oppose the (NGO) Bill." Our opposition was "symbolic of a non-violent struggle against fascism", exemplified in a bill that was "fascist in its content and application".[566]

My last formal engagement that year before taking a Christmas break in Malawi was to attend an MDC national executive meeting in Harare. It was the first one since Tsvangirai's acquittal and to that extent should have been joyful, but was not. Rather the simmering tensions created by Guhu's assault had escalated. In October, Ncube had found the situation so intolerable at Harvest House that he moved the Administration department to offices in the same building as his legal chambers. When the underlying friction erupted into an acrimonious debate I felt constrained to speak. I reminded the meeting that we had endured five years of oppression, that tension was inevitable, that *agents provocateurs* were having a field day. We needed to remember where we had come from, I said, and what we had achieved. Tsvangirai and Sibanda were sitting together at the other end of the table from where I was sitting. I engaged them both, saying "the two of you are the heart of the party; if you stick together, the rest of us will find that there is no oxygen outside your combined orbit; our ability to keep the party together depends on your partnership".

On my way back from Malawi on 5 January 2005, I stopped in at Mutoko prison to see Roy Bennett. Although by no stretch of imagination pleasant, the prison was more like a heavily guarded school than the sombre grey edifices of Khami and Chikurubi prisons. My arrival, unannounced, caused quite a stir among the officers. I was neither family nor Bennett's stated legal representative. Despite explaining that I was MDC secretary for Legal Affairs, and ultimately responsible for Bennett's defence, the officer in charge was too scared to allow me in. A few hurried phone calls, presumably to Prison HQ, resulted in a firm refusal. Fortunately, the prison was so small that word got back to Bennett that I had visited. Legal proceedings had been instituted in the High Court to review parliament's decision but failed. Determined to use every possible means to correct the injustice, we instructed Jeremy

Gauntlett to take Bennett's case to the Supreme Court, but that too was delayed. And so Bennett remained in prison.

Although the general election was only due in June 2005, Mugabe suddenly announced on 1 February that the election would be held on 31 March. The previous August SADC had agreed on new electoral principles, which included "equal opportunity for all political parties to access the State media", "impartiality of electoral institutions", and "an accessible voters' roll".[567] Optimistically, we had hoped that Mugabe's peers would encourage him to bring our electoral environment in line with these fundamental principles, but the new Electoral Act gazetted on 21 January and the Zimbabwe Electoral Commission Act were just a disingenuous attempt at compliance. In reality all the electoral bodies were appointed by Mugabe. New laws effectively banned NGOs from conducting voter education. The registrar general persisted in refusing us access to an electronic copy of the voters' roll and demanded Z$12 million for an unsearchable paper copy of the roll.

Research teams working for the MDC legal department had conducted a constituency audit on the rolls we had and had established that there were up to 1 million "dead" voters, 300 000 duplicate entries and that in total some 2.6 million of the 5 658 637 registered voters were "ghost" or false or incorrect entries.[568] The Delimitation Commission, chaired by a Mugabe appointee, had presented its report to him in December 2004, dramatically reducing constituencies in MDC urban strongholds in favour of rural areas where ZANU PF held sway. The excuse that there had been urban to rural drift contradicted not only African trends but Zimbabwe's own 2002 census. If there had been any drift, it was from Zimbabwe in general to South Africa and Botswana, but contrary to both the SADC Principles and the practice of all our neighbours, the estimated 25 to 30 per cent of the Zimbabwean population who had left Zimbabwe since 2000 would be denied the right to vote. One crucial aspect of the electoral environment, first introduced by the RF in the 1960s, hadn't changed one iota – the electronic media was as biased as ever. The report showed that the sole broadcaster, the state-controlled and funded ZBC radio and TV brazenly promoted ZANU PF.

One lesson ZANU PF had learnt was that it did not need to use violence to win a majority as it had in 2000 and, to a lesser extent, in 2002. This understanding was consolidated by the declining influence within ZANU PF of the hardline Mnangagwa faction, post the Tsholotsho

Declaration. By the beginning of 2005, the vast majority of white farmers had been forcibly evicted and their workforces dispersed, in the process destroying the informal opposition political structures on farms. The critical swing vote of the 500 000 commercial farm workers no longer existed as a cohesive block. The bar against "foreigners" had excluded thousands of Zimbabwean farm workers from being included on the voters' roll, so even if they were of a mind to vote, they couldn't. The number of urban seats had been reduced. But, ironically, ZANU PF's greatest weapon was the unintended consequences of the chaotic land reform programme, namely, starvation. In the past when drought affected the communal areas' dry-land maize crop, irrigated maize, produced by commercial farmers, would fill the gap. With those reserves gone, and the massive silos located in former commercial farming areas such as Banket empty, Zimbabwe was now experiencing severe food shortages. Food distribution became the ultimate political weapon. The starvation of rural Zimbabweans was not so much a strategy to starve people to death, but to trade food for votes. Despite critical shortages, ZANU PF ministers denied that there was a crisis. For example, minister of Labour and Social Welfare, Paul Mangwana, announced in August 2004 that Zimbabwe didn't need any food donors because "we have harvested enough food". WFP was not asked to provide food on a large scale and other smaller NGOs involved in food distribution were stopped. Those policies left millions of Zimbabweans, urban and rural people, at the mercy of the ZANU PF-controlled GMB, which had a near monopoly over maize supplies. In the few weeks preceding the election threats by ZANU PF operatives persuaded voters that support for the MDC would result in starvation.

The only benefit for me was that the 2005 election campaign in Bulawayo South was almost violence free. Law, however, continued to be used as a weapon. Soon after the election date was announced we started our campaign in earnest with door to door visits of constituents. Knowing that the voters' roll had been tampered with, we wanted to ensure that as many people as possible were on the roll. One team, under the leadership of Sam Maponde, was arrested by the police on the grounds, in the words of the officer commanding, Bulawayo Chief Superintendent Muzambi, that "the action they were taking was illegal as they should confine their campaigns to political rallies".[569] Astonishingly, police spokesman assistant commissioner Bvudzijena supported Muzambi's stance, arguing that door to door campaigns were "a recipe for political violence". The police stance was so extreme and indefensible that we managed to get an urgent interdict in the High Court barring them from interfering any further.[570]

A day after obtaining the order, ZANU PF made one further attempt to prevent my nomination as an MP, on 18 February. In the 2000 election officials had tried to use my rights to British citizenship to bar me from standing. This time they tried to use my tentative rights to South African citizenship. Contrary to ZANU PF's approach to citizenship in Zimbabwe, which sought to exclude as many people, especially minorities, from citizenship, the ANC had enacted liberal laws in South Africa in 1995[571] which enabled children of South African citizens to apply for citizenship, even if they had been born outside South Africa. Technically this applied to me and to many Zimbabweans. The attitude of the registrar general's office was that if you were potentially an opposition supporter and had the potential to be a citizen of another country, this was sufficient to strip you of your citizenship and take you off the voters' roll. Knowing that this was being done systematically and that it would be employed against me, I had taken the precaution of getting a letter from the director general of the South African department of Home Affairs confirming that I was not a citizen.[572] Adopting a belt-and-braces approach, I also had an affidavit from my mother confirming that she had never registered my birth in South Africa, and an opinion[573] from JG Dickerson SC, a South African silk, advising that I "was not a South African citizen, had never held citizenship and was not entitled to it". Armed with all of these documents, I presented myself to the nomination court. As anticipated, the officials raised the question of my citizenship; once again, as had happened in 2000, I pulled out all the papers I had. Much to their consternation they were forced to concede that I was not a South African citizen after all, no matter how hard they tried to bestow that privilege on me. My nomination was accepted, as were the papers of my principal opponent, ZANU PF cabinet minister Sithembiso Nyoni. Despite the beatings, arrests, murders and torture, the MDC managed to nominate 120 candidates countrywide. Bennett, still in prison, was unable to stand for Chimanimani and so his wife, Heather, courageously stood in his place.

Although the campaign was peaceful in Bulawayo South, I was pessimistic about the overall election. On 19 March, just ten days before the election, I gave an interview to *The Sunday Telegraph* in which I spelt out ZANU PF's plan. They had "simply switched tactics … learned their lesson", I said. They understood that they couldn't have "images of people being shot, so the methods of intimidation (were) more insidious". I also pointed out that three years after the presidential election we hadn't yet been able to audit a "single ballot", despite extensive litigation, which indicated that ZANU PF knew they could rig with impunity.[574] Not one of the 39 electoral challenge cases we had brought after the 2000 election had been concluded, rendering each one of them academic. ZANU PF had even less to fear from the courts in 2005 than they had in 2000. They didn't care too much about urban seats; they would lose them but it didn't matter because they could comfortably control parliament with the majority rural seats and the 30 presidential appointments.

Even so, I was amused to see the lengths ZANU PF were prepared to go in Bulawayo South. Just days before the election it was announced that a new suburb, Emganwini, would be electrified if ZANU PF won. A huge electricity transformer was even moved into position, presumably to tempt voters as the party had done with food in the 2003 local government elections. It didn't work, though, and the day after the election the transformer was taken away.

Although my percentage of the vote dropped from 84.7% in 2000 to 75.8% in 2005, I still won by a comfortable majority of 8 343. Of concern, though, was that the overall turnout dropped from 24 526 to 15 981, a pattern repeated all over the country. Hundreds of thousands of our supporters had left the country and were unable to vote. In a cruel paradox, ZANU PF's destruction of the formal economy had helped them.

When the official results were announced ZANU PF had "secured" 1 569 867 votes, a 59.6% majority, with 78 seats, against the MDC's 1 041 292 votes, constituting 39.5% and 41 seats. The results showed a similar overall pattern to 2000. The MDC won virtually all the seats in the main cities, Harare and Bulawayo, where our organisation and good communications were able to reduce electoral manipulation. The MDC also won a majority of seats in Matabeleland. But in rural Mashonaland, in central and northern Zimbabwe, where the majority of the population lived, ZANU PF won all but one seat.

Although we were not surprised by the results, they were nevertheless a crushing blow. After five years of struggle we had gone backwards in parliament. ZANU PF, with the 30 presidential appointees, now had the two thirds majority they needed to change the constitution at will. Gone were the days when they had been forced to whip their entire caucus to get a simple majority. The courts had been almost completely subverted, so little could be achieved there. Although substantial evidence rolled in of brazen electoral fraud, there was neither the money nor the appetite to go through another pointless, academic exercise in court. The results also showed that our porous borders with South Africa and Botswana had acted as a safety valve. Young people, the vanguard in uprisings against other totalitarian regimes the world over since 1989, had left Zimbabwe in droves. Nearly all the non-violent methods of struggle used by us had been cynically trashed, leaving us vulnerable to those opposed to ZANU PF who had lost patience, and to those within ZANU PF still itching for a fight.

CHAPTER 22

THE MDC FALLS APART
APRIL 2005 TO JUNE 2006

"I am convinced that if we succumb to the temptation to use violence in our struggle for freedom, unborn generations will be the recipients of a long and desolate night of bitterness, and our chief legacy to them will be a never ending reign of chaos."

– MARTIN LUTHER KING

While we were not surprised by the results of the 2005 elections, we were nevertheless stung by the comments of certain ANC ministers in South Africa who endorsed the results. In particular President Mbeki had given a strong inkling of where his sentiments lay just before the elections, when he said he had "no reason to think that anybody in Zimbabwe will act in a way that will militate against the elections being free and fair". His belief was that "things like an independent electoral commission (and) access to public media (had) been addressed".[575] Mbeki's ministers assigned to monitor the elections followed suit after the election: South African Labour minister Membathisi Mdladlana found that the elections "by and large" complied with the SADC guidelines and "reflected the will of the people". Minister Phumzile Mlambo-Ngcuka was equally gushing, but conceded that she had "received complaints".

In the run up to the elections we had painstakingly explained to observers, including the South Africans, how the Zimbabwean electoral system breached the SADC guidelines. Some such breaches should have been obvious to them, even in the comfort of their hotel rooms, such as the extreme ZANU PF bias of the only television and radio stations, the ZTV and ZBC. So much hung on the South African government's viewpoint; with the country in such dire straits economically, ZANU PF could not survive without the cover provided by the ANC.

Flabbergasted by the ANC's whitewashing, and without any other means of exposing electoral fraud, we decided we would have to speak out in their back yard. Paul Themba Nyathi, MDC director of Elections, and I addressed the press corps in Johannesburg on 12 April. Much of what we said was old hat: there was no independent electoral commission, an accessible voters' roll had not been made available, the state-owned media, including the largest circulating papers and the only TV and radio stations, were blatantly biased. But in addition we had new evidence about what had happened on election day itself.

Many MDC election agents had been denied access to polling stations; 133 155 voters (10 per cent of the total) were turned away, almost all of them young people, and the total individual votes-cast tallies finalised by the Zimbabwe Electoral Commission (ZEC) on election night did not match the collective count announced later. Astonishingly, between close of polling and the announcement of the results in the ensuing 48 hours, a further quarter of a million votes appeared out of the ether in the 72 constituencies in which votes-cast figures were announced. Two weeks on from the elections, on the day we held the press conference, ZEC had still refused to announce the total-vote figures for the remaining 48 constituencies. Despite vigorous efforts made by us to have access to the original polling station returns in these same constituencies, this had been denied. In short it was a brazen cover up.

ZANU PF knew they could do this with impunity for so long as the ANC in particular looked the other way. History had come full circle. Just as the Nationalists had allowed the RF to frustrate the democratic will of the people, the ANC was doing the same for ZANU PF. The MDC did not lose the election on 31 March. The people of Zimbabwe had lost the right to elect a government of their choice.

We got a good press but it made no difference – the ANC was determined to look the other way.

Although it was pointless going to court regarding the 2005 election's irregularities because of the biased judiciary, we still saw merit in finalising the original 2002 presidential election challenge. Given that Mugabe still had another three years of his term to run, we considered it worthwhile to focus on it again. Judge Hlatshwayo, having taken seven

419

months to hand down his cursory one-page judgment in July 2004 on the legal issues argued in November 2003, had still not given us the full reasons for his ruling. This made it impossible for us to appeal those issues to the Supreme Court (he eventually handed down his reasons, two years after the matter had been argued, in November 2005). Given the media focus on Tsvangirai's challenge, and the fact that we thought we were close to exposing electoral fraud, it made sense to push on with the case. However, at that time all we could concentrate on were the allegations of electoral fraud which depended on our ability to inspect the original voting materials. In a High Court judgment granted on 15 October 2003, registrar general Mudede had been ordered to produce the polling records in their sealed packets as was required by law. Mudede didn't bother to comply with this, and other orders, necessitating us going back to court to compel him. On 27 May 2005 we obtained two fresh orders[576] which found Mudede guilty of contempt of court for failing to produce the voting materials. The same judgments fined him and committed him to 60 days jail unless he delivered the required sealed records within ten days. Initially, Mudede ignored the judgments and the police did nothing to enforce the contempt orders. Eventually, after nine opposed applications and eleven court orders, voting records were produced for inspection, in June 2005 – over three years after the election.

In May 2005 I finally managed to see Bennett in Mutoko prison. By some quirk this time I was allowed in, but the authorities reacted to my visit and within days Bennett was moved to the more austere Chikurubi facility. While that was closer for his wife to travel to, the conditions were far harsher and I regretted that I might have been the reason for the move. Bennett had spent his first month in Harare Central prison before being moved to Mutoko, resulting in a five-hour round trip for his family for a 30-minute visit once every two weeks. Although conditions in Mutoko prison were far from good, Chikurubi was, and remains, notorious among Zimbabwean jails for its harsh treatment of prisoners and the appalling health and sanitary conditions. Diseases such as tuberculosis were rife, the water supply was often contaminated, and severe overcrowding assisted the spread of infection.

On 28 June 2005 Bennett was released from Chikurubi after spending eight months of his twelve-month sentence in custody. It is standard prison procedure to commute a third of any sentence for good behaviour. He subsequently revealed that when he arrived in jail he had been made to stand naked in front of prison guards and was then given a prison uniform covered with human excrement and lice. He denounced prison conditions generally in a press conference after his release, saying, "The inhumanity with which the prisoners are treated and their total lack of recourse to any representation or justice combined with the filth and stench of daily life is something I will never forget and I will not rest until their conditions are improved."

Bennett's case, although one of the most egregious, was but one of hundreds the LDF was handling at the time. Between April 2003 and September 2005, the LDF handled a total of 497 cases, involving 2 595 individuals arrested, most of them MDC activists. Of these individuals, 635 reported some form of abuse, including torture, while under arrest.[577]

POSA was proving to be a useful weapon for ZANU PF because, by some margin, the highest number of arrests was for POSA offences, mostly around the issue of getting permission to hold political meetings. In fact in Bulawayo over 75 per cent of arrests were for POSA "offences". Perhaps the most compelling statistic, though, was the pitiful number of convictions the police obtained during this period. In only four of the 497 cases were the accused found guilty of an offence. In nearly all the cases handled the charges were eventually withdrawn, with ZANU PF's interests being neatly looked after from every angle. The POSA restrictions made it difficult for the MDC to campaign. Hundreds of our activists were locked up in the process of what would be normal democratic activity in most countries, and the massive legal costs drained the party of scarce resources. Any doubt about the partisanship of the police was removed with one remaining statistic – no ZANU PF loyalist was ever (indeed has ever been) arrested, let alone prosecuted, for a POSA offence since the law was enacted in 2002.

The sheer number of people needing support, however, meant that the LDF's funding needs were more acute than ever. Fortunately, ZLDAF was working well by then and it had some high-level support. In May 2005, Archbishop Pius Ncube flew to London to speak at a variety of fundraisers. One such event was a tea hosted by Prince Charles. Although I was in the UK at the time, I did not attend the tea because we felt it would be imprudent. Prince Charles was apparently very gracious. Over Scottish shortbread and tea, he reminisced about how he had been the Queen's representative in Zimbabwe at Independence, when the Union Jack was lowered and the Zimbabwean flag was raised for the first time in Harare. He remained very fond of Zimbabwe, and had had high hopes for what seemed to be a promising nation. He listened attentively while Archbishop Pius and human rights campaigner Shari Eppel explained the situation in Zimbabwe, describing widespread human rights abuses and poverty, and he said what a tragedy it was that such great potential in a nation had not been realised, and that Robert Mugabe had become such a dictator.[578]

In the midst of our efforts to defend our members from unlawful arrests and detentions, serious crimes were being committed within our own ranks with impunity. On 12 May 2005, the same group of youths who had beaten up Director for Security Peter Guhu in September 2004 demonstrated at Harvest House, demanding that MDC MPs boycott parliament and alleging that party resources had been misused. Over the next few days the situation deteriorated: party vehicles were confiscated from staff; on Sunday, 15 May administrator Frank Chamunorwa was abducted and beaten; the following day Diamond Karande was roughed up. Finally, on 17 May, Z$21 million was stolen from an administrator accused of being sympathetic to the secretary general, Ncube. The same day the ringleader of the youths, the same person who had led the attack on Guhu, fomented the stoning and theft of party vehicles.

The police did nothing to arrest those responsible for creating mayhem within the MDC, raising suspicions that a hidden hand was at work. The attacks came at the time we had finally started to investigate the Guhu attack internally. The national executive had appointed a commission of inquiry, comprising a group of ZANLA, ZIPRA and Rhodesian war veterans – Dr Tichaona Mudzingwa, Moses Mzila-Ndlovu MP, and Giles Mutsekwa MP – and they had started interviewing all those involved, perpetrators and victims. Our own action to get to the bottom of the September violence had, however, stirred up a hornet's nest.

As these disturbances within the MDC were simmering, ZANU PF unleashed an unprecedentedly harsh assault against our urban support base. It started in Harare on 25 May and was carried out with military efficiency throughout Zimbabwe. On 1 June I was working in my law office in Bulawayo when constituents phoned me to say that the police were systematically clearing out informal traders in town. Several years before, when Zimbabwe's formal sector started to contract, the Bulawayo municipality had designated several areas in the city, including 5th Avenue, which runs past the Bulawayo Presbyterian church, where informal traders and vendors could establish stalls. At 5th Avenue it was done efficiently: bays were painted on the tarmac, licences were issued and the road was made a one-way street. Over the years it had flourished. It became a good place to buy fresh vegetables, second-hand clothes and knick-knacks.

I was horrified when I inspected 5th Avenue that day. Armed police had arrived without warning, systematically "cleansing" the area, expelling all the vendors and, at the same time, confiscating their wares. One shocked vendor who was standing by told me that the police had looted Z$2.5 million worth – his entire stock had been taken. He was poor and tearfully explained that he had no other income. I remonstrated with the police, but all I got was that they were following orders. Over the next few days it became evident that this was a national campaign directed by Mugabe. It had even been given a name – Operation Murambatsvina (Shona for "drive out rubbish"), chillingly similar to the meaning of Gukurahundi. In the first week of June the police drove out every last informal trader in Bulawayo with ruthless efficiency. The furniture and mattress makers of Makokoba, the malls at Lobengula Street, Entumbane and Renkeni were all shut down, leaving piles of rubble lying on the streets. As the police went through, destroying everything in their path, they also looted goods and dumped them in their trucks. Stalls were burnt down, leaving smoke wafting everywhere. The same was happening throughout the country. Although we organised a successful two-day national stayaway on 9 and 10 June, coinciding with Mugabe's opening of the new parliament, there were so many ructions within the MDC we were unable to do anything more as the scale of Operation Murambatsvina escalated.

With the vending sites cleared up, the police, joined by army and ZANU PF youth brigades, next turned their attention to informal settlements on the periphery of cities and towns. With the collapse of commercial agriculture, thousands of destitute farm workers had flooded urban areas and constructed shacks on vacant land. In existing suburbs unemployed workers had constructed lean-tos, which were rented out as another source of income. These became the target, in mid winter, of teams of police, army and youth brigades, supported by bulldozers. Without notice, without provision of alternate accommodation or even tents, without regard for women with young children, bulldozers moved street by street, field by field, systematically destroying all these structures.

I spent the weekend of 11 and 12 June in Killarney, an informal settlement on Bulawayo's north west boundary, and witnessed police systematically razing shacks, leaving their occupants in the freezing cold. That Sunday evening I spoke to a woman in her seventies, sitting shellshocked in the smouldering ruin of her home. Holding her seven-year-old grandson, she explained that her husband had died five months previously; her daughter, aged 28, had died the previous Friday of AIDS and she had come back from the funeral to find her home destroyed with all her meagre belongings burnt. She was petrified because the police had told her on arrival that if she was "still there by Monday they would be back with dogs and horses".[579]

Churches stepped into the breach to assist the thousands of people thrown out in the open in mid winter: in my constituency, church halls were opened as places of refuge. As people were screened, several appalling facts became clear. Nearly half the people originally came from neighbouring countries and had no rural homes they could go to; most were already undernourished, and many had AIDS. It was a recipe for disaster, but a disaster that could easily be swept under the carpet. There wasn't any blood on the streets – the victims would simply fade away and die quietly in their thousands.

On 23 June MDC MP Edwin Mushoriwa tabled a motion in parliament condemning Operation Murambatsvina. Speaker after speaker from the MDC benches related what was happening all over the country, demonstrating that what I had witnessed in Bulawayo was part of a well-coordinated national action. The three ZANU PF ministers responsible for the exercise didn't bother to justify their actions. The only response we got was from ZANU PF MP Walter Mzembi, who callously argued that they had "wanted to restore dignity to (our) supporters".[580] Infuriated, I interjected: "Is there any dignity in freezing to death?"

When my turn came to speak I documented everything that I had seen, before suggesting two motivations: fury, caused by ZANU PF's loss of every urban seat bar one, and fear, a "pre-emptive strike to intimidate people who may rise up in protest". Hoping that scriptures might jolt the architects of this atrocity, even if our words would not, I quoted from Psalm 7:14:

Whoever is pregnant with evil
conceives trouble and gives birth to disillusionment.

Whoever digs a hole and scoops it out
falls into the pit they have made.
The trouble they cause recoils on them;
their violence comes down on their own head.

My concern was not only the "humanitarian catastrophe" but for the future of a country where "young children see policemen, who are meant to be respected members of society, burning their homes down, treating their grandmothers as if they are dogs".[581] Questioning the values this conduct built "in this generation of children", I begged "rational, sober-minded members of Government" to stop the policy immediately before further harm was done to our nation.

Although ZANU PF dismissed our complaints, they could not ignore the United Nations. Kofi Annan appointed UN-HABITAT's under-secretary-general and executive director, Tanzanian Anna Tibaijuka, on 20 June 2005, to lead a fact-finding mission to Zimbabwe. The team arrived on 25 June, which slowed down the operation as ZANU PF tried to put its best face forward. Despite the UN team's presence, Operation Murambatsvina continued and was not over by the time Tibaijuka left Zimbabwe on 7 July, seven weeks after it started. The UN's report, issued a few weeks later, was utterly damning, and it bears repeating:

> "It is estimated that some 700,000 people in cities across the country have lost either their homes, their source of livelihood or both. Indirectly, a further 2.4 million people have been affected in varying degrees. Hundreds of thousands of women, men and children were made homeless, without access to food, water and sanitation, or health care. Education for thousands of school age children has been disrupted. Many of the sick, including those with HIV and AIDS, no longer have access to care. The vast majority of those directly and indirectly affected are the poor and disadvantaged segments of the population. They are, today, deeper in poverty, deprivation and destitution, and have been rendered more vulnerable. Operation Restore Order took place at a time of persistent budget deficits, triple-digit inflation, critical food and fuel shortages and chronic shortages of foreign currency. There is no doubt therefore that the preliminary assessment contained in this report constitutes but a partial picture of the far-reaching

and long-term social, economic, political and institutional consequences".[582]

The long term consequences could not be fully spelt out then, but it is not unreasonable to speculate that Murambatsvina probably killed more people than the Gukurahundi because of the fatal combination of displacement, HIV/AIDS and poverty. The report noted that 24.6 per cent of Zimbabweans were infected with HIV/AIDS at that time and estimated that "over 79,500 persons over 15 years of age living with HIV/AIDS (had) been displaced".[583] It expressed concern that "immediate consequences likely include(d) shortened life expectancy and death owing to lack of treatment and care in a situation where life expectancy has already dropped to only 33 years, malnutrition and exposure to the elements."

In the months and years following Murambatsvina Zimbabwe's economic collapse escalated, the supply of drugs declined and only a fraction of the 700 000 people displaced ever had their homes replaced. It is likely that tens of thousands of people had their lives cut short as a result of Murambatsvina. The UN never followed up on its mission and the architects of this Faustian bargain have never been held accountable for what it was – a crime against humanity, the "forcible transfer", which is part of "a widespread or systematic attack", of "a civilian population", which "intentionally causes great suffering".[584]

Aside from our parliamentary debate and a meeting a group of our women MPs held with Tibaijuka, the MDC's response to Murambatsvina was relatively mute. The main reason for this was the growing internecine struggle within the party. On 25 June I attended a national executive meeting that had been called to consider a report prepared by the management committee (comprising the so-called "top six", which included Tsvangirai, Sibanda and Welshman Ncube) regarding the attack on Guhu and the May violence. The report, which did not include the commission of inquiry's own report, recommended that the youths responsible be expelled from the party. But there was an elephant in the room: the identity of senior members of the party who were behind the attacks and what should be done to them. Allegations were made that a few men who worked in Tsvangirai's office were, at the very least, sympathetic to the youths. Tension rose and it was impossible to get a consensus; all that was resolved was that the youths would be expelled from the party. The meeting ended with Tsvangirai suggesting that the management committee should be dissolved. Although at the time I did not understand all the dynamics going on, the friction within the management committee was palpable.

A further national executive meeting was convened on 15 July, which I could not make as I was about to leave on a speaking tour of Australia. I was so concerned about the ruction that I prepared a five-page statement which Innocent Gonese tabled and spoke to. It argued that our "commitment to non violence (had) earned us deep respect" but the attempted murder of Guhu and the May assaults had "seriously undermined (our) credibility". If we did not "send out a clear and unequivocal message that violence (would) not be tolerated", we would "reduce the standing of the MDC to that of ZANU PF". The expulsion of the youths was not enough, in my view, and there had been "an inadequate investigation into who was behind the violence". This could only be addressed by establishing a disciplinary committee. Once again, in an echo of the comments I had made the previous December, I stressed the critical role Tsvangirai and Sibanda played in "uniting the Management Committee". My statement concluded with a personal appeal to Tsvangirai: "The present dispute in essence is rooted in the allegation that your presidency is under threat. Ironically the greatest threat to your presidency comes from the very people who are apparently suggesting that somebody else wants the job."[585] Pointing to the widespread support Tsvangirai still enjoyed among the electorate and within the MDC leadership, I felt that support would "only be undermined if (Tsvangirai failed) to act in a determined fashion to root out those responsible" for the violence. Behind these words was my belief that a group of people within Tsvangirai's inner circle were not only behind the violence, but also poisoning his view of many people who had made massive sacrifices in his quest to become president of Zimbabwe. Sadly, neither the statement nor the discussion that followed it resolved the impasse, which continued to fester. Although the youths were expelled, within weeks Tsvangirai re-employed them in his personal security team, arguing that it was his right. Likewise the influence of the people suspected of being behind the attacks, in his inner circle, grew.

On the same day the inconclusive MDC meeting was held, 15 July, Constitution Amendment Bill number 17 was gazetted. Mugabe had spoken in the 2005 election campaign about his desire to secure the two thirds majority necessary to amend the constitution, which by hook and crook ZANU PF was now able to do. The new amendment bill envisaged two major changes – the entrenchment in the constitution of the draconian land acquisition provisions and the reintroduction of the senate. At the time it was introduced I didn't sense any danger for the MDC; rather I saw it as an opportunity to debate constitutional amendments that we wanted introduced. It had been impossible in both parliaments, since the MDC's formation, to introduce constitutional amendments because of parliamentary rules. Now, because ZANU PF had introduced the topic, the door was opened for us to suggest wholesale amendments to the constitution. Accordingly, as soon as I returned to Zimbabwe from Australia, I secured agreement from the MDC Legal Committee to have comprehensive constitutional amendments drafted. Zimbabwe's best legal draftsman was contracted to incorporate all the principles that had come out of the NCA process into a new draft constitution. Simultaneously, the draftsman was told to consider the positive aspects that had come out of the government's 1999/2000 Constitutional Commission, in particular its report entitled "What the People Said", which contained a remarkably frank diagnosis of the country's ills and unflinching prescriptions for their cures. Our thinking was that we would stand a better chance of convincing ZANU PF MPs of voting for our amendments if we could show that they in fact stemmed from the government's own constitutional outreach. This exercise resulted in a 125-page "Notice of Amendments", which in fact was an entirely new constitution for Zimbabwe.

From the outset we knew that ZANU PF MPs would be whipped into line and that our amendments would never pass, but we felt we should not let the opportunity go by to at least debate what a new, democratic constitution could look like. Our amendments suggested a non-executive president with an executive prime minister. There was also a comprehensive bill of rights and numerous other provisions to entrench and enhance democracy. ZANU PF's bill was read a second time on the afternoon of 24 August, opening up the committee stage of the bill, at which point I tabled our lengthy amendments, seconded by Tendai Biti.[586] In tabling our amendments we made it clear that we did not agree with the process of changing the constitution in parliament without first having canvassed the views of Zimbabweans and having obtained a broad consensus, but seeing as ZANU PF was determined to push ahead with amending the constitution, we would use this opportunity to have a wider debate. Parliament was adjourned that day with the understanding that debate on the amendments would happen the next day.

As parliament adjourned I received a call from Tsvangirai. He asked me to meet him urgently at his home. When I arrived he told me he was unhappy with one aspect of our notice of amendment relating to the qualification of the president. In the original document received back from our draftsman, a new Section 29 set out three qualifications for the non-executive president: that he or she be a citizen by birth or descent, be at least 40 years old, and have a university degree. The latter was a novel requirement, which had come out of the Constitutional Commission's "What the People Said" document. Eight of Zimbabwe's ten provinces had said "that the head of State must be the holder of a university degree".[587] Our draftsman, wanting to incorporate as much of the Constitutional Commission's content as possible, had included this provision. Given the rush in getting our notice of amendment ready we had not managed to go through the document prior to it being circulated among the MDC leadership. However, prior to the filing of our notice of amendments we had decided to delete clause 29(1)(b), the provision relating to the university degree, because we felt it unfair to people who had, through no fault of their own, been denied a university education. Accordingly, when the notice was duly filed by Biti and myself, that clause had been deleted and the amendment signed by myself. It was this clause that was giving Tsvangirai concern because he felt it was targeted at him. I explained how the clause had come about and that it had in fact already been removed, and I showed him my own amended copy. In any event I pointed out that it would not have excluded him from office because he was not interested in a non-executive position, but rather the executive prime ministerial post.

Although Tsvangirai understood the issue, it was clear that he was under the impression that this was some underhand plot to subvert him. Once again I was at pains to reassure him of my own support. I emphasised that I would not countenance such devious means of undermining his leadership of the MDC. Our meeting ended on that note but next morning I received a call from Sibanda advising me that Tsvangirai remained unhappy about our constitutional amendments and saying that we would have to withdraw them.

When parliament reconvened the next day, to ZANU PF's astonishment, I withdrew all our proposed amendments. Chinamasa, delighted with the development, stepped in and moved his amendments, every one of which we opposed, including the provision reintroducing the senate. ZANU PF's overwhelming majority in parliament meant that they would have got their way in any event, but I did think that the MDC had lost an opportunity to paint a vision of what a new democratic constitutional order would look like.

The recreation of a senate ignited a robust debate within the MDC about whether we should participate in it or not. Mugabe had pushed for the senate mainly as a means to provide jobs for those who had lost out in the March parliamentary election. Although it wasn't a body to which we had objection in principle, the senate was a luxury Zimbabwe couldn't afford at the time. To this extent there was consensus within the MDC; we all agreed that we would rather not have it. However, its establishment was a reality and ZANU PF announced that elections for the senate would be held soon. The question was: should we participate in those elections or not?

In this context the senate issue became a lightning rod for another ardent debate which took place within the MDC. Six years on from our establishment we were no closer to rooting democracy – the Movement for Democractic Change had not changed anything. Many felt that our participation in parliament had achieved nothing other than great suffering for all who had stuck their necks out in support of the party. The violence directed against Guhu and our staff, although no doubt stirred by *agents provocateurs,* resonated with many young people who felt that the only way to meet fire was with fire. The senate debate provided both the *agents provocateurs* in our midst, and those who had grown weary of non-violent methods, with an opportunity to push for a change in strategy. There was no consensus within the national executive either. Because of this it was agreed that we would need to consult with our grassroots. Throughout September this process took place, culminating in the convening of our National Council in Harare on 12 October.

The National Council meeting attended by provincial council representatives from throughout Zimbabwe was held at Harvest House. The meeting started with representatives from each of our twelve administrative provinces reporting back on their respective results. A pattern soon emerged. The southern, central and eastern provinces of

Bulawayo, Matabeleland North and South, Midlands North and South, and Manicaland were overwhelmingly for participation in the senate, with the northern provinces of Harare, Chitungwiza, Mashonaland West, Central and East, and Masvingo against. Delegates from Matabeleland and Midlands, who had suffered under Gukurahundi, were vehement in their views – they had no desire to give ZANU PF any foothold again and they argued that every seat should be contested.

Manicaland had a slightly different view, which emanated more from our own internecine battles. Roy Bennett, recently released from prison, explained that while he personally was against participation he was appalled by the conduct of some MDC leaders who had threatened delegates to vote against participation. Manicaland province, which Bennett represented, and which had been ambivalent regarding participation in the senate, was now firmly for participation as a result. Bennett himself was for participation. It became apparent that the same group had threatened others – the Mashonaland West delegation spoke of the same group going around threatening members not to participate.

The main reasons the northern provinces advanced was that participation in parliament had yielded nothing. However, in most of these provinces the sentiment against participation was not overwhelming. The Bindura district in Mashonaland Central had voted for participation, Harare had reached a "consensus" on the issue, and in others the "no" vote was won narrowly. Our Youth and Women's leagues then gave their views. Both were stridently against participation, with the Youth League spokesman saying that "revolutions were inevitable" and the women arguing that "action was needed to remove ZANU PF".

A rational debate followed with views expressed both for and against by members of the national executive. When I spoke, I said that whatever decision we made, the economy would decide the fate of the country. Although I was for participation, I understood the views of those who were against this – the key was to "devise alternate non violent strategies whether we participate or not". At the conclusion of the discussion no obvious majority view was apparent. This prompted Bennett to suggest that the management committee should decide the issue, which we would all then accept. This proposal was accepted and the six committee members retired to deliberate in a separate office. After a while they came back, having failed to reach a consensus.

It was then that MDC chief whip Innocent Gonese suggested a secret ballot. This was accepted by all, including Tsvangirai. It was implicit in our acceptance of a ballot that we would all abide by its result. In terms of the MDC's constitution the National Council was comprised of the national executive and the chair, secretary and treasurer of each province, and the Women's and Youth executives. Decisions had to be passed by a simple majority and there was no constitutional provision for a proxy, not that any person claimed to exercise a proxy vote. Given the tight margin revealed by the provincial reports, and the good turnout at the meeting, ballots were prepared and distributed. After the ballots had been counted it was announced that the "no" vote had prevailed by 33 to 31. Tendai Biti, who was firmly against participation, was so overjoyed that in his exuberant celebration he broke the plastic chair he was sitting on and went clattering to the ground. We all laughed but were interrupted by the chair, Isaac Matongo, who apologetically explained that he had miscounted. The result was in fact 33 to 31 *for* participation.

The mood changed immediately. Tsvangirai, who had made clear his views against participation, was angered by the result. He gathered up all his papers and strode out of the room. I was deeply shocked. When the first, wrong, result was announced, those of us *for* participation had accepted it as the view of the majority, and so I expected a similar response at the correction. I had no idea that Tsvangirai had such strong views; even less that he would not accept the result. In my mind, if we were a democratic party, it was critical that internal votes be respected, but I recognised that perhaps Tsvangirai saw this as a vote of no confidence in his leadership. For that reason I proposed that all the remaining five management committee members should follow Tsvangirai immediately and counsel him to accept the result of the council vote, and then report back to us as council. This motion was adopted, and we dispersed at around 4 pm, having started at 10 o'clock that morning.

The management committee's efforts failed and the rift between Sibanda and Tsvangirai widened. Desperate to persuade Tsvangirai, Sibanda, Ncube and other members of the committee flew to South Africa to seek President Mbeki's help. A phone call by Mbeki to Tsvangirai only exacerbated matters, convincing Tsvangirai that there was some nefarious plot to unseat him. I spoke to many people during the ensuing weeks and it became apparent that what had underpinned the "for" vote was the disquiet about violence creeping into the party, plus the feeling that non-participation in the senate heralded a revocation of the MDC's

MDC supporters outside Nketa Hall, Bulawayo South constituency, days before the 2005 election, 28 March 2005.

With then Australian Prime Minister Kevin Rudd at Consilium, Coolum, Australia, 2 August 2008. We met to discuss the growing crisis in Zimbabwe.

Welshman Ncube and me standing outside the State Department in Washington after another round of lobbying meetings in 2006.

From left to right: Douglas, Jessica, Scott Winston and Bethany in my campaign T-shirts for the Khumalo Senatorial constituency, March 2008.

I was sworn in as Minister of Education, Sport, Arts and Culture at a ceremony in Harare on 13 February 2009. Immediately behind me, partly obscured, is Arthur Mutambara. Sitting just to the right of the flag, also partly obscured, is then South African President Kgalema Motlanthe. Standing behind Mugabe looking to his left is Morgan Tsvangirai. The photo captures the moment when I took out my own pen to sign, cracking the "joke" that I only trusted my own ink, which didn't impress Mugabe.

Bethany at home in Bulawayo, recovering from the lioness attack. With her is our friend and owner of Antelope Park, Andy Conolly who lost his left arm following a lion attack in similar circumstances.

Meeting with former Australian prime minister John Howard to discuss his candidacy for ICC president. Sydney International Airport, 18 June 2010.

Opening a new block at Helen McGee School, Masvingo, 14 October 2010, flanked by the headmaster, parents and local education officials.

Zimbabwe's cricket captain, Elton Chigumbura, and me on the sidelines of the ICC Cricket World Cup. Nagpur, India, March 2011.

With Archbishop Desmond Tutu, patron of the Zimbabwe Defence and Aid Fund Trust, Johannesburg, 10 November 2011.

From left to right: Mary Ndlovu, educationalist and widow of the late ZAPU leader Edward Ndlovu, me and Judith Todd in 2012.

Founding BLPC paralegal, veteran human rights activist and friend Paul Chizuze, who disappeared on 8 February 2012 and has never been seen again. With his death went much of the knowledge regarding where Gukurahundi-era mass graves are located in Matabeleland.

Being introduced to parents and children at the ministry of Education annual awards ceremony, Binga, 1 July 2011.

Zimbabwe's greatest Olympian, Kirsty Coventry, and me at the 2012 Olympics in London.

Informal meeting on 5 August 2012 with British Foreign Secretary the Rt Hon William Hague on the sidelines of the Olympics in London.

Vice-President John Nkomo and me outside the primary school he attended in 1944 prior to the opening of the John Nkomo High School, Tsholotsho, by Robert Mugabe on 13 July 2012. Scores of people were massacred within a 10-kilometre radius of this school by the Fifth Brigade in February 1983.

Me with some members of my 2013 campaign team.

Morgan Tsvangirai and me, after meeting at my home on 22 October 2014 to discuss the state of opposition politics.

With Joel Silonda (aged 92), former chairman of the Catholic Commission for Justice and Peace, Matabeleland, and brave researcher into the Gukurahundi. Bulawayo, 22 October 2015.

Meeting children at a ceremony marking a new investment in the Education Transition Fund at Mutasa Primary School in Harare, 27 March 2012 – hope for the future.

commitment to non-violence. At the core of the debate was the MDC's failure to deal with the youths responsible for violence and their handlers. Those who had been the architects of violence inside the party were the same people who had been using threats to secure a "no" vote regarding the senate issue, thus conflating the two issues.

On the other hand it appeared to me that Tsvangirai felt besieged and many of the architects of the violence were also the only people giving him succour. It became equally clear that there were *agents provocateurs* and ambitious people on both sides, who were determined to widen the gulf. Some of these people, on both sides, were close friends. I spoke to them, wrote to them, and phoned them, pleading with them to desist. Sadly, most continued, some writing and speaking publicly, and destructively. Professor Brian Raftopoulos managed to get the two sides together and persuaded them to agree to desist from attacking each other in public, while preparing for a second meeting at which some agreement might be reached. He then shuttled between the groups to come up with a four-point agreement, which, if accepted by both sides, would unblock the impasse:

1. The Sibanda faction would withdraw from the Senate election.
2. Tsvangirai would re-convene National Council, apologise for overturning its resolution and accept whatever sanction if any was meted out.
3. Tsvangirai would renounce violence and remove those members and employees who had been reinstated unconstitutionally after being expelled/dismissed for violence by National Council.
4. Tsvangirai would disband his "kitchen cabinet", who were involved in violence and who habitually overturned resolutions made by elected party structures.

Sibanda's faction agreed to withdraw from the senate election, provided Tsvangirai kept his side of the bargain. Sadly, it came to naught. In early November an illegally constituted meeting of council members opposed to participation in the senate was called, purporting to rescind the valid 12 October decision, further driving a wedge between the two factions. When press reports emerged, falsely suggesting that the meeting had been properly convened, I expressed my frustration by writing to one of the people quoted as follows:

"I remind you of the scriptures you shared with me a few weeks ago – Ezekiel 13:10–12: 'Because they lead my people astray, saying "Peace", when there is no peace, and because, when a flimsy wall is built, they cover it with whitewash, therefore tell those who cover it with whitewash that it is going to fall.' The people of Zimbabwe are being led astray – they do not know about the intra-party violence and have been conned into thinking that this is only about participation in an election. This resolution does purport to convey that there is 'peace' – there is no peace because there are still violent men in the organisation whose positions are now stronger than ever. There has been a whitewash – the issue of violence is not mentioned anywhere in any of the resolutions, public or private. My suggestions [to address the violence] have not been taken up, nor does it appear that they ever will be."[588]

On 12 November I met with Tsvangirai to try to persuade him to consider my suggestion to address the violence issue. My idea was that the MDC should appoint an independent inquiry comprising two lawyers I admired greatly – Innocent Chagonda, Tsvangirai's lawyer, and retired judge Washington Sansole. Tsvangirai was interested enough in the suggestion to speak to Chagonda, who phoned me in early December. Following the call I wrote to him, elaborating on my suggestions for a neutral commission, which I suggested should include other prominent, respected lawyers such as Sansole and Beatrice Mtetwa.[589]

In the midst of these efforts to reconcile the two factions the senatorial election went ahead on 26 November. Without the support of a major faction of the MDC, many constituencies were not contested and the entire election was marked by apathy. Only 600 000 people bothered to vote, a 19.5% poll, with ZANU PF garnering 73.71% and the MDC 20.26%. The MDC only won seven of the 50 seats on offer; all of the five seats in Bulawayo and two in Matabeleland South. As we had feared, ZANU PF got significant toe-holds in former MDC strongholds such as Harare, Matabeleland North and Manicaland. These sobering facts did nothing, however, to quell the burgeoning divisions within the MDC.

In early December the faction under Sibanda's leadership applied to the High Court for an interdict seeking to restrain Tsvangirai from conducting business on behalf of the MDC. At the time I wrote that "the decision to take Morgan to court, while justified in law, (was) a serious political error".[590] Tsvangirai responded by convening a press conference on 20 December, accusing Sibanda and others of "plotting to kill him in order to form a government of national unity with ZANU PF".[591]

I was deeply saddened that in one year the relationship between these two men had collapsed. I felt at the time that had Zodwa Sibanda still been alive, she and Susan Tsvangirai would have been able to help their husbands reconcile. My distress increased when I heard that Gonese had switched his allegiance from Sibanda to Tsvangirai. Shortly after this, Bennett told me that he had been persuaded to take over the chairmanship of Manicaland for Tsvangirai's faction. Both had voted for participation in October and were concerned by the breach of our constitution. My hope was not that they would join Sibanda's faction, but that they would assist in attempts to bring the two factions together.

As the new year started I found myself increasingly isolated. At that time I wrote to exiled *Daily News* editor Geoff Nyarota expressing my sense of isolation:

> "At present I do not have a happy home anywhere. In any event I have felt that it is necessary for some of us to stay out of the fray in the hope that we can speak to both sides. You say I must get off the fence. I do not believe there is any fence – it feels more like being a political wilderness, a desert, between the two sides. I strongly believe that the two sides cannot be effective acting independently of the other; Morgan undoubtedly has majority support of party members but virtually all the leadership talent, acumen and integrity lies in the other side".[592]

The division between the two factions became final on 6 January 2006, when a National Council meeting called by the Sibanda faction resolved to expel Tsvangirai. My letter to Chagonda, suggesting an independent commission of inquiry, was never responded to but, in fairness to Chagonda, it had been rendered academic. Although I met Tsvangirai again in Bulawayo on 27 January in an effort to persuade him to agree to a commission of inquiry, it was clear that too much water had flowed under the bridge. Both factions were now preparing for their own congresses to elect new leaders. I did, however, get Tsvangirai's agreement to allow me to try to broker an "amicable divorce" between the two factions.

I performed one final task for Tsvangirai. Following the May 2005

High Court order compelling registrar general Mudede to provide us with the 2002 presidential election materials, our investigative team under Topper Whitehead had finally conducted an audit of materials from twelve constituencies, between 10 August and 15 December. During January 2006 we, under the guidance of a chartered accountant, Lucy Hollands, collated the evidence and prepared a report. Hollands was a most unlikely activist, being a quiet, reserved lady in our church who shunned publicity. But she was scrupulously thorough and played a major role in assisting us produce a 103-page report into the electoral fraud that had taken place. We found that there had been "systematic and secretive tampering to the lists of registered voters", done by "means of illicit removals from the rolls, questionable numbers of additions to the rolls, and numerous duplicate voters on the roll".[593] The audit also revealed "widespread fraud perpetrated using various means, including voters voting more than once, and manipulation of results at the National Command Centre". According to the official results Mugabe had won by a margin of 418 809 votes. Our audit showed that, conservatively, 286 196 votes had been "fraudulently included in the count". When one added the numbers of voters "illegally prevented from voting, the total fraud, on a most conservative basis, was in excess of 490 000 votes".

Aside from the massive obstacles in trying to get the electoral challenge trial under way, I was to play no further part in it. Another legal secretary was elected when Tsvangirai's faction of the MDC held its congress on 18 March. Tsvangirai's case was to suffer a further blow on 13 June 2006, when Whitehead was arrested in Registrar General Mudede's office and deported to South Africa the following day. Whitehead, who was born in Harare in 1940, had been declared an "undesirable inhabitant" by Home Affairs minister Kembo Mohadi the previous December, but presumably the authorities hadn't known where to find him to execute the deportation order until he presented himself in the registrar general's office. The deportation was an effective way of ensuring that no further incriminating evidence against Mugabe would be produced in court. Little further effort was made to pursue the case, allowing Mugabe to see out his term unflustered by any niggling court proceedings.

In February 2006, I started to experience the consequences of not casting my lot in with the Tsvangirai faction. The first wind I got of it was when I was told that one of our major funders would no longer fund the LDF because of the split, and that funds already allocated would be shifted to Zimbabwe Lawyers for Human Rights. In a meeting with the ambassador of the donor country on 8 February, I questioned the decision, pointing out that ZLHR didn't have either the national network of the LDF or the ability to stay below the regime's radar screen. Although ZLHR was ostensibly non-partisan, it and other civic groups were already aligned to the Tsvangirai faction of the MDC. The ambassador's response, "that it was in the MDC's own interest that it did not have financial ties to foreign donors",[594] was diplomatic but unconvincing. I told him that without foreign support we would be hard pressed to keep the LDF running, which in any event was not an MDC organ and had been used to defend activists across the political and human rights spectrum on a non-partisan basis. Concerned that the decision was based on a fear that I would act in a partisan manner (in favour of the Sibanda faction), I stressed my commitment to human rights for over two decades – in my view legal defence should be provided to *all* who were suffering abuse. I pointed out that because of the LDF's low public profile, it was less susceptible to being closed down by the regime than an organisation like the ZLHR.

The ambassador was unmoved and stuck to his guns. In the same meeting when asked which faction I was likely to join, I said the outcome of the two congresses "would determine (my) ultimate allegiance".[595] "If Tsvangirai dumped his kitchen cabinet (which I viewed as responsible for the violence), I said, I "might side with his faction". Tsvangirai's kitchen cabinet was a group of colleagues, not all of whom had an elected position in the party, whom he regularly seemed to turn to for advice. On occasion he had acted on their advice in conflict with resolutions of the party, such as the re-employment of those expelled from the party for their involvement in the Harvest House violence. Leaders like Biti and Bennett also had qualms about the kitchen cabinet and wanted Tsvangirai to put the views of the national executive ahead of it.

When I got back to Bulawayo I was confronted by further fallout. One of the principal members of my campaign team told me that I needed to heed "the big picture" – Tsvangirai was the most popular opposition leader and I needed to subordinate my concerns about violence to that political reality. If I did not make that decision, he said, he would no longer back me. When I explained how important the pursuit of non-violence was, I was told that this "could be addressed once Mugabe has been removed". Over the next few years my failure to grasp "the big picture" would be used incessantly to criticise my decision to remain with the smaller faction of the MDC. I came to understand that the "big picture" actually meant "the end justifies the means". ZANU PF was violent so a bit of violence to remove it was justified. My argument that, aside from the moral principle of using non-violent methods, it was foolish to play to ZANU PF's strongest suit, violence, fell on deaf ears.

It was the beginning of a withdrawal of support from some friends and comrades. This withdrawal would later develop into outright hostility, hate speech and my being ostracised by some. Although my closest friends stuck by me, I was crestfallen at losing the support of some key members of my team.

However, my greatest concern related to the massive cut-back in funding for the LDF. Although the country which had withdrawn support was by no means the only donor, the withdrawal of its funding knocked a huge hole in our budget. Between February 2003 and the end of January 2006 the LDF had handled 668 cases, involving 3 468 victims. Most of those cases were still in the courts and needed support. The crisis demanded urgent action so I flew to the funding nation's capital for meetings with a wide range of people. I met with parliamentarians and government officials: much to my relief the decision to cut LDF's funding was reversed.

While I was abroad the Sibanda faction of the MDC held its congress on 25 February, resulting in the election of Arthur Mutambara as its president, with Sibanda remaining vice-president and Ncube secretary general. Shortly before leaving for Zimbabwe to travel overseas on 20 February, I had written to both Sibanda and Tsvangirai advising that I would not be attending either congress and setting out suggested terms for the "amicable divorce" I had discussed with Tsvangirai in January. There were six contentious issues, including the party's name, slogan, physical assets and members of parliament. Section 41 of the constitution stated that if a political party gave written notice to the speaker that an MP "ceased to represent its interest" the relevant seat could be declared vacant by the speaker. This provision could be a wonderful gift to ZANU PF if both factions wrote seeking the expulsion of MPs from the opposing faction. ZANU PF's speaker would no doubt gleefully oblige if given half a chance to do so. Accordingly, my letter suggested an agreement that neither faction would seek to expel the other faction's MPs. The letter concluded that once the amicable divorce had been agreed to I would have to decide which faction to join. Although the MDC faction now led by Mutambara (MDC-M[596]) responded to my suggested settlement, by the time the Tsvangirai faction (MDC-T) held its congress in Harare on 18 March I had not heard back from Tsvangirai.

Shortly before the MDC-T congress, ZANU PF resumed its persecution of Roy Bennett. Mutare gunsmith Michael Hitschmann was arrested in connection with an alleged plot to overthrow the government, along with MDC-T MP Giles Mutsekwa and the party's Manicaland treasurer, Brian James. Inevitably, Bennett was high on the government's list and a manhunt followed. The allegations soon multiplied: Bennett, Hitschmann and others were said to have planned to assassinate President Robert Mugabe when he travelled to Mutare in late February to celebrate his 82nd birthday. Bennett and Hitschmann were also alleged to have prepared for acts of sabotage. Minister of State Security Didymus Mutasa appeared on ZTV and said that

> "[Zimbabweans] are absolutely secure. The only people who may not be secure … are those people who are causing these problems because we will not spare them. And if it came to a position where we have to eliminate them physically because of what they are doing, then it is their fault, that is what they are looking for, and we will not hesitate to do that."

Bennett fled to South Africa and was elected treasurer of the MDC-T *in absentia*. Although Biti was also elected to the senior position of secretary general, many of the architects of the intra-MDC violence retained influential positions. Biti and Bennett were people I trusted in MDC-T, but it seemed to me that they were a tiny minority and would be overwhelmed by others.

Through April I agonised over which party to join. Having still not heard from Tsvangirai, I wrote to him on 8 April asking for a reply to my suggested terms for an "amicable divorce". None was forthcoming although I was told by some MDC-T leaders that they had rejected the offer but would not go public. Knowing that Bennett shared my concerns about the intra-MDC violence, I wrote a long 18-page letter to him in exile on 26 April, setting out the recent history, which included the following:

"What concerns me is what future we are creating in Zimbabwe for our children. Are we now just going to perpetuate ZANU PF's legacy of violence, deceit and corruption? Are we going to simply change rulers but not change the way we govern?

"Herbert Agar once wrote: 'The truth which makes men free is for the most part the truth which most men prefer not to hear.' Fundamentally the issue at stake is truth. You know the truth about what has really happened in the MDC as well as I do. However it is not easy to go against the flow."[597]

In May I had a meeting which decided me. Two well-known and trusted journalists[598] came to see me at home, having asked to meet me in a secure location. They told me that they had filmed a "training camp" for MDC operatives in South Africa. The training was being done by ex-South African policemen under the supervision of an ex-Rhodesian soldier. There was confusion as to whether the training was "offensive" or "defensive" but weapons were clearly involved. The South African National Defence Force had been bribed to allow these trained men back across the border. The journalists were not going to write the story because they feared that if they did innocent people would be harmed, but they felt I needed to know. They had told me this because they were utterly appalled, and so was I – even if the training was defensive, it was a propaganda gift to ZANU PF. It also appeared to be chronically amateurish. While I understood the desperation and helplessness that many felt in the face of ZANU PF's oppression, this was, in my view, a foolhardy response. Even if one believed in a violent solution, the training was on such a small scale that it could never mount a serious challenge to ZANU PF's hegemony. What it would provide was the ideal excuse to crack down even harder on the MDC. The revelation was the final straw. Principle aside, I was unwilling to have any part of an organisation that was prepared to take such risks. I wrote a circular letter to my constituents on 23 May, telling them that because the MDC-T had "shown no inclination to deal with violence" I could not join that party. Without disclosing what I had been told about the training camps, I wrote that "leadership is ultimately about taking responsibility for the welfare of others. Good leaders are obliged to ensure that people who repose faith in them are not unnecessarily endangered".[599] All that was left for me to do now was to decide whether to stay in politics and, if so, to get assurances from MDC-M that they would root out "the scourge of violence".

An overwhelming majority of constituents I spoke to at that time wanted me to remain in politics, albeit many wanted me to join MDC-T and still didn't fully understand why I felt so strongly about the violence issue. It was difficult explaining my position because I could not reveal what I had been told for fear that innocent people would get caught up in the ZANU PF purge that would surely follow. While the intra-MDC violence had never up to that point been perpetrated on the scale of that by ZANU PF, I feared that if we didn't draw a line in the sand to stop it, the party would be sucked into a cycle of violence, which ultimately could lead to yet another war. Finally, on 15 June I called a press conference, where I announced that I was joining the MDC-M, which had committed itself to a "zero-tolerance" disciplinary approach to violence. I knew it was politically suicidal to join a relatively small party but stated: "I would rather lose my seat in Parliament than compromise certain principles which are fundamental to my belief system."[600]

CHAPTER 23

A HELLHOLE IN THE WILDERNESS
JUNE 2006 TO JANUARY 2008

"The political conditions that sustain dictatorship also poison the opposition."
— NEW YORK TIMES EDITORIAL ENTITLED "THE CONTAGION OF DICTATORS" 11 OCTOBER 1997

I was not in a celebratory mood when I joined the smaller MDC-M party. Although many of its leaders, particularly Nyathi, Mzila-Ndlovu, Sibanda, Ncube, Trudy Stevenson, Priscilla Misihairabwi-Mushonga and Abednico Bhebhe, were good friends, the MDC split was a gift to tyranny. Our rank and file supporters had made enormous sacrifices, many with their lives. A poignant reminder of this came a few days after I had announced my decision. I was attending a memorial service at the Presbyterian church on 19 June commemorating the sixth anniversary of Patrick Nabanyama's disappearance. I picked Patricia Nabanyama up from their home in Nketa and during the drive to the church explained why I had joined the MDC-M. Patricia nodded sympathetically but I realised that despite all the violence that had ruined her life, her focus was trained on removing Mugabe. Tsvangirai commanded the support of most people opposed to Mugabe and was best positioned to end his rule. My concern about growing violence within the MDC did not affect her whereas Mugabe's continued rule did. Patricia's attitude reflected the views of many people. They needed a vehicle to end tyranny. All that the split had done was put its wheels in a ditch. My concerns about perpetuating the cycle of violence and its legacy did not address Patricia's immediate problems.

The split also confused many MDC supporters who could not understand why the leadership simply couldn't get on with each other and get on with the job. Tragically, I found that in Nketa people divided along ethnic lines, with most Ndebele-speaking people in support of my decision, and most Shona people against. Some of my most ardent Shona-speaking supporters, Sam Maponde, for example, who had been arrested just a year before while campaigning on my behalf, were devastated by my decision. I was between a rock and hard place, rather like a child whose parents have divorced and who has to choose which house to live in. Many close friends, colleagues with whom I had been in the trenches, such as Biti, Bennett, Lucy Matibenga and Tsvangirai himself, were now in a different camp. In truth the split was, I suppose, inevitable. Aside from everything else, seven years of struggle against a brutal regime had yielded very little. The strain had taken its toll. The MDC from its beginning was such a broad church; its only common objective was to end tyranny and beyond that there was very little consensus. From its inception it had significant fault-lines of ethnicity, class and ideology, which were easy for ZANU PF *agents provocateurs* to exploit. Ironically, because the MDC was committed to democratic practice its infiltration was easy.

As the years of struggle wore on everyone became increasingly suspicious of others' actions and motives. With the split cemented, ZANU PF's propaganda and security wings did everything in their power to sustain the division. Their propaganda machine painted the MDC-T as evil reactionaries, the MDC-M as good, obedient moderates. Their security apparatus turned its full attention to the MDC-T. While there was sporadic harassment of MDC-M members, it was nothing like the treatment meted out against MDC-T colleagues. The threat level against me personally dropped dramatically, even though I remained just as outspoken as ever. It served ZANU PF's purposes to deepen the divisions between us. The rift was also fuelled by certain irresponsible remarks made by former MDC colleagues on both sides. An old Christian friend of mine in the MDC-T publicly referred to Nyathi, a democrat if ever there was one, as a "dissident", an especially outrageous description in the context of the Gukurahundi. It became part of a general campaign to vilify the MDC-M. A workshop was held in Johannesburg which had the specific agenda of devising a strategy for the MDC-T to crush the MDC-M. Instead of focusing on ZANU PF, both MDC parties became introspective. The combination of ZANU PF and MDC-T propaganda worked – my in-box was soon full of hate mail. Former colleagues, even some clients, wrote harshly. Some of the printable monikers were "white dissident", someone who was "living in utopia" and who was "trying to live a normal life in an abnormal society". Interestingly, virtually all the worst abuse came from whites.

By early July relations between the two MDC factions appeared to have reached rock bottom. This was demonstrated to me by an incident that happened on Sunday, 2 July. One of my oldest political friends, going back to the Forum Party days and MDC MP for Harare North, Trudy Stevenson, had been campaigning in Mabvuku suburb of Harare when the car she was driving in with two colleagues was waylaid by thugs. There were about 40 of them blocking the road. As the car approached they threw rocks at the windscreen and when the vehicle was brought to a halt, they smashed the vehicle and dragged the three hapless people out, severely assaulting them with stones, iron bars and sticks. The thugs also stole their cell phones, Z$20 million in cash and other valuables, including wedding rings, before fleeing. All three victims were rushed to hospital. Stevenson was the worst injured, suffering a broken wrist and severe head injuries. According to press reports only seven of the thugs were positively identified: Wilson Goliath Munyaradzi aka Lecturer, Petty Zambezi aka Mai Danken, Norman Hanyani and Tendai aka Chigubhu, Tonderai Ndira and his brother Barnabas Ndira.[601] All those identified were members of the MDC-T. Barnabas Ndira was one of the fourteen members who had been suspended by the MDC national executive in June 2005, who had been re-employed as part of Tsvangirai's personal security team.

Shocked by the brutal attack perpetrated by its members, MDC-T established an independent commission of inquiry to investigate the matter. When the commission of inquiry's detailed 123-page report was produced a few months later it concluded that the CIO's security apparatus was most likely responsible for the assault. It noted that the MDC's internal failings and divisions had made both factions susceptible to CIO infiltration. The report credited Tsvangirai and the MDC-T leadership for having established the commission and for their public commitment to non-violence. However, it faulted them for failing to follow through on the recommendations of previous commissions, especially with regard to disciplining violent party members.[602]

On 26 September Biti expressed his disappointment to US embassy officials that Tsvangirai "did not directly address the MDC's deficiencies, specifically its failure to deal with violence".[603] Some of those members who had been implicated in the assault on Guhu in September 2004 were still in party structures. The report was subsequently effectively buried and many of those implicated in Stevenson's assault remained within the MDC-T. For example, one of the young men found by the commission to be "an interested party",[604] Tonderai Ndira, was himself abducted from his Mabvuku home by ZANU PF supporters on 6 June 2008 and murdered for being an MDC-T operative.[605]

This environment made it exceedingly difficult for me to continue writing and speaking as positively as I had in the past. Ever since going into politics I had concentrated on conveying positive messages. In my regular report-back meetings and circular letters I had focused on hopeful developments. Even in the darkest days of 2000, I felt that good would prevail over evil, eventually. Now with the MDC sullied and divided it was harder to proclaim this with the same conviction. Paradoxically, the only factor that provided hope that the status quo could not persist was the economy. My mantra every time I spoke during this time was "the laws of economics are as inviolable as the law of gravity – drop a stone, it will hit the ground; fuel inflation and the economy will collapse".

ZANU PF, ably assisted by the governor of the Reserve Bank, Gideon Gono, was busy fuelling inflation, primarily by printing money in ever increasing volumes. Gono had been appointed governor in November 2003 of a bank that was already being grossly mismanaged. The Reserve Bank building, constructed in the 1990s on Samora Machel Avenue, Harare, is a monument to ZANU PF's profligacy. It is Zimbabwe's tallest building and no expense was spared in its construction. For a country with such a relatively small economy it ridiculously dwarfs the United States' Federal Reserve building. Gono's predecessor in September 2003 had responded to the bank's inability to print money fast enough by issuing "bearer cheques" in denominations ranging up to Z$100 000. The cheques looked like banknotes; they had serial numbers but they also had expiry dates. Through 2004 and 2005 Gono got the printing presses churning out ever increasing numbers of these bearer cheques, such that by 2006 one had to pay for groceries with wads of Z$100 000 cheques. He then extended the expiry date on cheques indefinitely. By mid 2006 the system couldn't cope and in July 2006 Gono announced

"Project Sunrise", the demonetisation of the old notes and cheques, at the same time removing three noughts from the currency. He claimed this was necessary because the bank could only account for Z$10 trillion of Z$43 trillion in circulation; the rest, he said, was being held in mini "central banks".

On 1 August a new currency was introduced and companies were given 48 hours to change all their prices. This was a mammoth exercise. The old currency would only remain valid for 21 days (later extended by another 14 days to allow rural people to swap their old money). From the very first day the new currency was unsuitable. The notes ranged from one cent notes to Z$100 000 notes and did nothing to stem inflation; in fact it merely fuelled it. Alongside the new notes came a marketing campaign in which Gono promised single digit inflation, a strong currency, repayment of IMF loans, and that Zimbabwe would be the most "attractive investment destination" by December 2008.

The reality was in stark contrast to Gono's promises. With parliament hardly sitting and the opposition in disarray, I concentrated most of my time during this period in Bulawayo. Running the law firm was an increasing challenge. Issuing fee notes was highly problematic in a hyper-inflationary environment because if clients delayed even a week in paying the original bill, it would only be worth a fraction. We started with a warning on each bill that if it was not paid by a fixed date, it would be revised. It was difficult to understand the real current value of money because the official exchange rate of the Z$ declared by the Reserve Bank bore no relation to a parallel or black market rate. With increasing frequency we would have to consult with businessmen clients who knew the current parallel rate, so that we could equate our fees with the real value of the Z$. It was illegal to charge in foreign exchange and being lawyers we could not afford to run our firm as many businesses were doing, through undercover foreign exchange transactions. At the same time we faced growing logistical difficulties. Our offices had been located in the top floor of the Haddon and Sly Building since the 1950s, but it was becoming difficult to use the lifts because of frequent power cuts. Fuel was also short and many hours had to be spent away from the office sitting in queues to buy fuel. We took the decision to move to an industrial area, to a double-storey building with no lifts and in an area where there were fewer power cuts.

Things were increasingly difficult on the home front too. In August

Jenny and I made our first trip to Botswana to grocery shop. Bulawayo's supermarkets were running out of most supplies and the only way to ensure that basic needs were in the larder was by making the 400 km return trip across the border. Hyper-inflation hit us all hard. I received a letter from Old Mutual advising me that my pension policies would be paid out prematurely. Having agonised over policies two decades before and painstakingly saved to pay premiums for years, the Old Mutual offered payment of an amount which equated to a month's grocery shopping. From that time on, the words "pension" and "retirement" were deleted from my lexicon.

Our strictures were nothing compared to those suffered by the vast majority of my constituents, however, especially those who lived in the high-density suburbs of Nketa, Nkulumane and Emganwini. In an effort to assist them I had established the Bulawayo South Constituency Development Trust and in August 2006 we started working with a local orphanage, Loving Hand, on a new project in Nketa. Two old CBC schoolfriends of mine, Hans Haefeli and another who wishes to remain anonymous, contributed generously to the trust, enabling us to drill a borehole and install a new drip irrigation system on land allocated to the trust by the city council in Nketa. My attention had been drawn to the pioneering work of Brian Oldreive. Years previously Oldreive was managing a maize farm in the north of Zimbabwe which was nearing bankruptcy. Burning and deep soil inversion were common practices on the farm, causing terrible sheet erosion to occur, resulting in loss of seeds and water. Increasing amounts of money were being spent on the machinery required for ploughing and double rollings of the lands, and yet yields continued to decline. Being a man of faith, Oldreive prayed for solutions. He noticed that in virgin bush there was no deep soil inversion and that a thick "blanket" of fallen leaves and grass covered the surface of the soil. This led him to research how he could apply these ways of nature to his farming. He began to experiment with zero-tillage, using a simple hoe on two hectares of land. The results were outstanding and so he had the faith to increase the hectarage under zero-tillage. Within six years the whole farm of 1 000 hectares was under minimum tillage and in subsequent years, with healthy yearly profits being made from then on, other farms were bought. He eventually oversaw the farming of 3 500 hectares under minimum tillage.

In the early 2000s Oldreive was evicted from these farms as a result of

447

ZANU PF's land policies. The farms around Bindura had served as the nucleus for a new national project called "Farming God's Way", which promoted zero-tillage prior to Oldreive's eviction. With no farms to work on, Oldreive decided to expand the teaching of zero-tillage principles countrywide. My attention had been drawn to his work through another CBC schoolfriend of mine, Alan Norton, who worked with Oldreive. I was struck by the amazing yields obtained on non-irrigated (dry) lands and felt that although my constituency was urban, the principles of zero-tillage could be applied usefully. Not only could the land supply fresh vegetables to the orphanage, but also I hoped the principles of zero-tillage would be taught to the entire community.

On 7 April 2006 the World Health Organisation had released a report stating that Zimbabwe had the world's lowest life expectancy, 34 for women and 37 for men,[606] a statistic that was painfully obvious in Nketa, and other working-class suburbs of Bulawayo, where graveyards were filling up rapidly. The death rates were the result of a perfect storm – the combination of HIV/AIDS, poverty and starvation. Something had to be done and this was a small start in my constituency.

On 12 October 2006, when I was interviewed in Johannesburg by Stephen Sackur on the BBC's Hardtalk he asked how bad I thought things could get in Zimbabwe. I replied:

"It can get far worse. One of the tragedies of not doing this interview in Zimbabwe [the BBC was banned from Zimbabwe at the time] is that you don't see for yourself what is going on. Life for the average Zimbabwean is sheer hell now with rampant inflation, food shortages and an increasingly authoritarian and paranoid regime. It's a hellhole at present. But unfortunately when we look elsewhere in Africa, if you take the extreme examples of Somalia and Liberia, (we see) it can go a long way down. One just hopes that because Zimbabwe is situated in the middle of Southern Africa, regional leaders will understand that this is a cancer in our region and that they need to take stronger measures to reign in this regime so that we can negotiate a way out of this mess."[607]

Four days after my BBC interview, as if to confirm my assertion that the regime was increasingly "paranoid", I got a call to assist Paul Themba Nyathi, who had been arrested. Nyathi had been found in possession of an anonymous pamphlet entitled "Message to our Armed Forces". The pamphlet asserted that the police and army were also "suffering as a result of economic collapse", "were struggling to pay for food" and needed "help, to help themselves". The public were called upon to "help them to find the courage to say enough is enough".[608] Nyathi was charged with "causing disaffection amongst the police force". The prosecution was not pursued with any vigour as most in the justice system quietly lauded Nyathi, even though he wasn't the author of the offending document.

As 2006 drew to a close, there was growing appreciation among genuine democrats in both the MDC-T and MDC-M that Zimbabwe was hurtling towards becoming a failed state and that our division was only compounding the deepening gloom. Our friends in the international community had rallied round to assist in a process of reconciliation between the two parties. On the weekend of 25 to 27 August, a small group of leaders from both parties had gathered at Irene Country Club outside Pretoria to explore whether at the very least we could agree on a code of conduct to regulate our interaction. The meeting was mediated by Professor Brian Raftopoulos, Dr Kofi Apraku, a charismatic leader in the Ghanaian New Patriotic Party, and Lord John Alderdice, a politician from Northern Ireland who, in helping broker the Good Friday agreement, had been willing to talk with Sinn Féin after the IRA called a ceasefire in 1994, when others in the unionist community had regarded such discussions as unacceptable.

They approached the meeting with a mixture of sympathy and admonition. When Apraku in his opening remarks said "if you are still fighting each other in 2008 then you will hand election victory to ZPF on a platter", I felt like hugging him. Although in my mind he was stating the obvious, there were many in both parties who saw no need to unite or reconcile. Alderdice talked about the Northern Ireland experience and how it was necessary to be realistic. He told us that it was "too much to ask Gerry Adams and Ian Paisley to like each other – so we asked them to respect the institution they represented, if not respect the individual".[609] He urged us to consider "some reasonable guidance of conduct" which then became the focus of the meeting. Apraku, my former BLPC colleague and lawyer Jessie Majome, Isaac Maphosa and I were delegated to draft a code of conduct, while another group under Alderdice debated outstanding areas of dispute between the two parties. It was agreed that we would take the code back to our respective national executives for endorsement.

I came away feeling encouraged. Tendai Biti in particular had led the MDC-T team in a constructive spirit. But even in that small meeting there were people with different agendas. One of the MDC-M participants was the party's spokesman, Gabriel Chaibva, who had been elected as MDC MP for Harare South and had impressed me in parliament. Chaibva, however, was not all he appeared and in the meeting made several unhelpful comments which annoyed people. In the years to come he would have a volte-face, becoming a prominent ZANU PF apologist, making me wonder today whether his role then was to do everything he could to maintain the gulf between the two factions.[610] Whether he was a CIO operative then I do not know. There were one or two others on the MDC-T team who were also abrasive in public, and their statements exacerbated relations between the factions.

The negotiating teams congregated again over the weekend of 25 and 26 November at The Grace hotel in Rosebank, Johannesburg. This time only Raftopoulos was there to mediate. He cut to the chase immediately, asking both teams whether there were "any other committees". I was nonplussed by the question, but understood why it had been posed when Biti confirmed that MDC-T had appointed another team, which was dominated by divisive elements. He was at our meeting, he acknowledged, "incognito (and) treading a dangerous path and if news (of our meeting) got out it would empower the group that (was) against the process of unity".[611] He went on to explain that it had been a "major battle to get Tsvangirai to sign (the code of conduct)" and that he would not attend a joint press conference. Biti suggested that the code be implemented in any event, explaining that he had been "engaged in wheeling and dealing of 'Bismarckian' proportions even to get to the meeting". When we questioned him about Tsvangirai's attitude he was more positive. Tsvangirai "himself (did) not have a problem" but was "not confident about getting National Executive authority". Bemoaning "corrosive elements" in the MDC-T, Biti sighed. We in the MDC-M had "been liberated from some of the elements in our group", he said.

After this sobering start we got down to business and made good progress on outstanding issues in dispute, the composition of a commission of inquiry and how we could implement other confidence building measures. We agreed on "compliance committees", bodies from both parties that would work to implement what had been agreed. I and

Abednico Bhebhe would be on ours; Innocent Gonese and Gertrude Mthombeni would be on theirs. Both were people I knew I could work with. After two days the meeting ended on a constructive note, with a joint discussion on how we could rein in our respective fiery spokesmen – Chaibva (MDC-M) and Nelson Chamisa (MDC-T). Raftopoulos, quoting Amilcar Cabral, urged us on: "*Tell no lies. Expose lies whenever they are told. Mask no difficulties, mistakes, failures. Claim no easy victories …*"

After a negative hiatus of a year, I felt more encouraged, but my optimism was tinged with concern all the same about what Biti had told us. In addition the suffering of poor people all around us was hard to bear, and yet many continued to inspire with their indefatigable attitude. Their example enabled me to strike the following positive note in my circular year-end letter to friends:

> "We have also had some profound insights this year – the most important being that God usually uses the weak and seemingly hopeless situations to achieve great things – the most important example of course being Christ on the cross. Towards the end of the year I was reminded of this encouraging verse from 1 Corinthians 15:58:
>
> 'Stand firm. Let nothing move you. Always give yourselves fully to the work of the Lord, because you know that your labour in the Lord is not in vain.'
>
> That is what we intend doing in 2007 – with great expectation."

The first few months of 2007 were marked by increasing signs of ZANU PF's paranoia. Parliament didn't sit at all in January, partly because government was battling to source sufficient fuel for parliamentarians. Then, on 16 February, the minister of Home Affairs announced a general ban on all political meetings "due to the volatile situation prevailing in the country".[612] In compliance with this diktat the police banned a meeting we tried to organise at Bulawayo city hall on 17 February, necessitating an urgent court application. Similarly in Harare MDC-T meetings were shut down. When parliament finally convened on 20 February, ZANU PF were focused on a new National Incomes and Pricing bill introduced by Minister of Industry Obert Mpofu. The bill sought to force a lid on the rapidly escalating prices of all goods brought on by hyper-inflation.

The minister of Finance in his budget speech the previous November had conceded that inflation was running at 1 204.6 per cent,[613] which in fact was a conservative figure. Government just couldn't keep up and in a knee-jerk reaction, without addressing the root causes of inflation, it came up with this draconian bill which was intended to criminalise retailers who were trying to remain afloat. When I opposed the bill in a debate on 21 February, I pointed out that government was "trying to control market forces" but "had failed and would fail". For the first time I sensed a note of panic in the ZANU PF benches; they knew what we were saying in opposition was correct but they didn't know what else to do.

On Saturday, 10 March I flew into Helsinki to observe the 2007 Finnish general election. The following day I found an English-language church to attend and when I got back to my hotel room a flurry of messages came through about further chaos at home. The Christian Alliance, a grouping of Christian churches, had organised a national day of prayer for Zimbabwe to be held at Zimbabwe Grounds in Highfield, Harare. The leaders of a variety of mainline denominations and political leaders, including Tsvangirai and Mutambara, had tried to attend. As had happened a few weeks previously in Bulawayo, however, the police pre-empted the prayer meeting by cordoning off the Christian Alliance offices, shutting down all church services in Highfield and sealing off Zimbabwe Grounds. On their way to Zimbabwe Grounds Biti, Mutambara and a host of leaders from both MDCs were intercepted, arrested and taken to Machipisa police station. Tsvangirai, on hearing of these arrests, bravely drove to Machipisa where he was dragged out of his car by police and thrown into a fenced courtyard. Men and women in police uniforms were systematically brutalising the MDC leaders and activists already there, laying into them with whips, iron bars, wooden planks and boots. The police soon turned on Tsvangirai himself. They beat him across the head with an iron bar and continued to assault him for 20 minutes, leaving the man battered and bleeding profusely.

Not even women were spared on this brutal occasion. Sekai Holland, a grandmother, and Grace Kwinjeh were severely beaten and both subsequently had to be flown to South Africa for specialist attention.

That Sunday evening scores of detained MDC leaders (from both factions) were farmed out to various police stations and detained. Lawyers and doctors were denied access to them. Because so many of the usual spokespersons were behind bars, the media had difficulty getting comment, resulting in my phone ringing ceaselessly in Helsinki. It was all rather surreal sitting in the benign Finnish environment commenting on torture being inflicted on my colleagues thousands of miles away. I issued a statement quoting the UN Convention against Torture and focused on my former client, Kembo Mohadi, the minister responsible for the police, accusing him of having "failed to prevent torture being used by the police". Mohadi, I said, was "deeply aware of the issue because it (had) been raised on several occasions with him in Parliament". Calling upon him to resign, I argued that "he should also be acutely empathetic because he himself suffered torture at the hands of this regime in the 1980s".[614]

As usual my words fell on deaf ears, but there was one silver lining, something I mentioned in an interview on the ABC's Lateline programme. The events had raised Tsvangirai's profile once again in the international community "and in that there was some safety".[615] In truth it turned out to be a public relations disaster for ZANU PF. Images of Tsvangirai emerging from court on 14 March, battered and bandaged, flashed around the world. The same images showed Mutambara at his side conveying a sense of solidarity among the Zimbabwean opposition. Although the regime had cynically targeted Tsvangirai for torture and had not touched Mutambara, both had been held for two days. In fact the torture backfired spectacularly: three days after the MDC leaders were released, the president of Tanzania, Jakaya Kikwete, met with Mugabe to express SADC's disapproval, prompting an ever defiant Mugabe to tell the West "to go hang" for daring to criticise his treatment of the "violent MDC". Belligerently, Mugabe at the same time warned the MDC they would "get arrested and will get bashed by the police".[616] Western diplomats, who had gone in force to the court hearing when the MDC leadership were released on bail, were also the focus Mugabe's wrath. They were told "to behave or else we kick them out of the country".

Still in Finland, I spent the rest of the week experiencing the alien environment of a democratic election. The Finnish election concluded at 8 pm on Sunday evening, 18 March, whereafter we were taken to the election results centre. All the leaders of the nine competing parties gathered by 10 pm when the results were announced. They convened in an auditorium to engage in a debate, moderated by independent journalists, about the results. Parties on the left had suffered losses and their leaders candidly admitted their reasons for their declining support, at the same time congratulating the victors. At the end of the debate the protagonists shook hands, kissed and hugged. I may as well have been on Mars as I thought of my colleagues back home nursing their injuries.

Following the assault and torture of MDC and human rights activists there were a string of Molotov cocktail attacks around Harare. Three police stations, a supermarket and a passenger train were attacked by unknown assailants. Some 40 MDC-T leaders were arrested in early April and charged with conducting a terrorist campaign. Government produced a dossier of photographs, including some of victims of the attacks, which it posted on the internet. The case was to drag on for months. In typical fashion the police were unable to produce sufficient evidence to back their claims. In June the prosecution announced that the police needed to travel to South Africa to investigate what they claimed were MDC-T terrorist training camps established there.

From a distance at the time I wondered who was behind the attacks. ZANU PF had a long history of pseudo-attacks which were then used as the pretext for arresting members of the opposition, so it seemed plausible that the prosecutions were baseless. However, because of what I had been told about weapons training in South Africa, I wondered whether the police might have received similar information to that which I'd received, but were struggling to prove that the training itself was taking place or that the training went beyond self-defence and was done with the intention of waging armed struggle. Whatever the case, all the arrested MDC-T leaders were released by August and none was ever convicted.

One positive result of the renewed attack on both MDC parties was that it reinvigorated the negotiations between MDC-T and MDC-M, which had stagnated since we had last met in November. A few weeks after I returned from Finland we reconvened at Irene Country Club. Biti was still hobbling from the injuries he had sustained and he described the vicious attack that had rained down on him. After two days of discussions the eight of us present arrived at what I thought was a superb draft coalition agreement. Firstly, we would jointly agree on whether or not to contest the 2008 general and presidential elections, so as to preclude one party competing alone and dividing those opposed to ZANU PF. Secondly, if we agreed to compete, the MDC-T would choose the presidential candidate and MDC-M would choose his or her running mate. As regards the parliamentary election, the party holding an existing seat would put forward a candidate "after consultation with the other formation (party)".[617] If existing seats were not held by either party "an equitable formula for deciding which formation would contest" would be agreed upon, considering such things as "the prospect of winning the seat in question". Senatorial seats would be shared and 50 per cent of our candidates would have to be women. The agreement also dealt with post-election matters such as the formation of a cabinet in the event of victory. The agreement would still have to be ratified by the national executives of both parties but I came away from the meeting with high hopes that sense would prevail.

Sense was the last thing on the ZANU PF politburo's mind. Parliament was hardly sitting and when it was the focus was on pushing through further draconian legislation. On 13 June I spoke against another new law – The Interception of Communications bill – describing it as "a fascist piece of legislation",[618] which immediately incurred the wrath of the minister of Agriculture, Joseph Made, who protested that Zimbabwe was not a fascist country. This prompted the Speaker to demand that I withdraw the heinous remark. The bill was designed to facilitate the CIO's snooping on private conversations without any independent judicial permission. Despite our objections, the bill was easily passed with ZANU PF's crushing majority.

Two years of my second parliament had passed with the house being reduced to a rubber stamp of the politburo. Shortly after parliament had been adjourned for another lengthy period, ZANU PF's paranoia was in evidence again. On 25 June Obert Mpofu, the minister of Industry and new chair of "The Cabinet Taskforce on price monitoring and price stabilisation", issued a shrill statement that government was "aware that escalating price increases (were) a political ploy engineered by our detractors to effect regime change against ZANU PF following the failure of illegal economic sanctions".[619] Prices of goods were to revert to what they had been on 18 June. Mpofu complained that, for example, bread had rocketed up from Z$22 000 a loaf on 18 June to an "unjustified" price of Z$45 000 on 24 June. This was followed by further panicky directives over the next few days: on 29 June all goods and services were to be charged at the rates they had been on 18 June and could not be raised without approval from the "National Incomes and Pricing Commission", chaired by none other than lawyer Godwills Masimirembwa. Mpofu had resurrected Masimirembwa's career. From the lofty heights of prosecuting Sidney Malunga in 1986 he had subsequently fallen on hard times, and in 1997 had been struck off the roll by the Law Society of Zimbabwe for abusing trust funds.[620] Now he was to play a pivotal role as ZANU PF strenuously tried to stem the inflation tsunami.

Mpofu's directive caused pandemonium in the retail sector. News of what was effectively a 50 per cent price slash was announced on ZTV and ZBC, before official communication of it was made to retail businesses. Many of the larger businesses, with stores countrywide, only received official notification several days after the announcement and it took a few days more for them to implement the directive. Mpofu and Masimirembwa were determined to make a point, which they did on Friday, 6 July. Fridays had for many years been a favourite day for the police to detain MDC activists because they could be held over the weekend as an extra punishment before being bailed by a magistrate on Monday. Now the same treatment was meted out to company directors and managers across Zimbabwe. The police swooped on them across Zimbabwe, accusing them of not reducing prices "in line with the government directive".[621] In Bulawayo directors from big companies such as Jaggers, Makro and Edgars were arrested and guarded by "heavily-armed machine-gun-toting troops".[622] In all some "1 850 managing directors or senior employees of companies"[623] were arrested and detained that weekend.

The crackdown was hailed by the government-controlled media as a victory against "economic saboteurs". These "saboteurs" were hauled before courts on Monday, 9 July. Eventually, all the cases were thrown out when it emerged that the statutory instrument, giving legal force to Mpofu's fiat, had only been printed on 7 July and distributed in Bulawayo on 10 July. It was, however, just the beginning of the chaos. With inflation surging well above 2 000 per cent and shops forced to keep their prices at 18 June levels, unscrupulous people exploited the situation to secure bargains of the century. Top army, police and prison officers, along with other senior government and ZANU PF officials, and anyone with cash, cleaned out shops selling TVs, fridges and other white goods.

One of Gono's directives was to limit how much ordinary people could withdraw from their bank accounts. Even though an ordinary person might have billions of Zimbabwe dollars in his or her account, they couldn't access hard cash. This rule was arbitrarily applied and didn't apply to those in the ZANU PF hierarchy, who used their cash to demand that goods be sold to them. The message got out to people lower down the ZANU PF ladder and shops were soon besieged by war veterans, Youth Brigade members and others, demanding goods. By the end of July shops, large and small, had been looted of goods. Some large clothing retailers, such as South African-owned Power Sales and Edgars, were completely cleaned out. In the former's case "80% of stockholding was wiped out at a 50% discount in a two-month period".[624] With hyper-inflation and a plummeting Zimbabwe dollar, it was impossible to restock. By mid August shops, supermarkets and clothing stores across the country were empty and would remain so until the advent of the inclusive government in 2009. "Empty" is no exaggeration: even supermarkets would only have a few items for sale, sparsely sprinkled along hundreds of metres of bare shelves.

In mid July 2006, ZANU PF trained its venom on Archbishop Pius Ncube. Ncube, a stalwart of the Catholic church, CCJP and ZLDAF, had become the biggest thorn in Mugabe's side. It was intensely embarrassing to have one of the only two archbishops in Zimbabwe as his, a Catholic, principal critic. While people like me could be dismissed in Africa as an unreconstructed Rhodie racist and Tsvangirai as a Western stooge, Archbishop Ncube's clarion calls against gross human rights abuses could not be ignored by African leaders. Archbishop Ncube, in many ways consistent with his earthy soul, succumbed to temptation of the flesh and Mugabe leapt at the chance to exploit it to the full. State operatives became aware that Archbishop Ncube was having a dalliance with a married Bulawayo woman, Rosemary Sibanda. Cameras were secreted in Archbishop Ncube's bedroom at Bishop's House at St Mary's cathedral, which filmed him *in flagrante delicto*. By some means this was brought to the attention of Sibanda's husband, who sued Ncube for adultery, claiming Z$20 billion damages. The assistant sheriff of the High Court obliged by arriving at Bishop's House to serve the summons in the company of *The Chronicle* and ZBC news teams and photographers, on 16 July. The story was emblazoned across the front page of *The Chronicle* the next day, together with semi-pornographic pictures of Archbishop Ncube and Sibanda strewn across a full inside page. The pictures were in chronological order and captioned with cynical and suggestive remarks. That night the ZBC dispensed with its normal puritanical policy regarding pornography by showing lurid video clips on the main news. The following morning *The Chronicle* purported to claim that this wasn't a state operation by revealing the identity of the "private eye", one Earnest Tekere, who had conducted the sting. It was an elaborate ruse to convince the public that ZANU PF had had nothing to do with the revelation. However, the end of the article revealed that Tekere had, prior to forming his company, been in the CID for 20 years. It made no mention of how he had been able to rally *The Chronicle* and ZBC so effectively, nor did it mention how he had evaded arrest for unlawful trespass at Bishop's House or being in possession of pornographic videos.

Be that as it may, the revelations shattered Archbishop Ncube and overnight ended his ability to speak out against the excesses of the regime. I had dinner with him on the evening of 17 July to console him and give whatever legal advice I could. There was very little that could be done, in fact, as he had admitted the affair. On 11 September 2007, it was announced that Pope Benedict XVI had accepted "the resignation of Archbishop Ncube from the pastoral government of the Roman Catholic Archdiocese of Bulawayo". For once Mugabe had not had to resort to blood to silence an opponent. Personally, I was deeply saddened by the matter. Archbishop Ncube was never a pretentious bigot. On the contrary, he was, and remains, a brave, humble, principled patriot who spoke truth to power for decades. Long before he came to high office he risked his life in exposing genocide and never stopped speaking out in support of the weak and voiceless. When he did this he was often isolated; without a family to support him he even found himself alone within the Catholic Church as his peers were either too scared, or too compromised, to criticise the regime.

With nearly all Zimbabweans, outside the ZANU PF elite, that is, doing whatever necessary to keep body and soul together in the vortex of a nation falling apart it was important to use every opportunity to highlight the growing crisis. Ironically, because most white farmers had been evicted already, and given there was little blood in the streets following the March assaults, the foreign press began to lose interest in Zimbabwe. The country was sliding inexorably towards another flawed election in 2008, a situation compounded by ongoing disagreements between the two MDC parties.

In the middle of September an opportunity was presented for us to raise Zimbabwe's profile again when the British organisation Intelligence Squared arranged a debate on the topic "Has Britain failed Zimbabwe?"

at the Royal Geographic Society in London. The academic RW Johnson, author Peter Godwin, and Tendai Biti were asked to support the motion; Zimbabwean author Chenjerai Hove, political science academic John Makumbe and I were asked to oppose it. As is their custom, Intelligence Squared took a pre-debate poll which showed that a substantial majority of the packed hall felt that Britain had in fact "failed Zimbabwe". Johnson, Godwin and Biti had a wonderful time identifying all the errors of British foreign policy over decades, encouraged by roars of approval from the crowd. Although Hove wowed everyone with his literary genius and Makumbe, using his inimitable wit, entertained us all, the audience remained unconvinced. When it was my turn to speak I found myself trapped between the knowledge of Britain looking the other way during the Gukurahundi and my conviction that a succession of Rhodesian, followed by Zimbabwean, leaders were primarily to blame for the crisis in which we found ourselves.

I started by using the title of Ian Smith's book *The Great Betrayal* to show that while Smith would have energetically supported the motion, UDI was arguably the principal reason for Zimbabwe's fall from grace. Likewise Mugabe's racist jingoism, I pointed out, would also hold Britain responsible for our demise, but it simply wasn't true. Finally, I argued that if any foreign countries had failed Zimbabwe these were South Africa and the SADC bloc. These were the countries that had had the opportunity to restrain ZANU PF but they had failed to do so. I couldn't let an opportunity pass to plead for help, whoever was to blame. Quoting French Foreign minister Bernard Kouchner's contemporaneous comments that "the international community has a humanitarian duty to intervene where tyrants brutalise their people",[625] I said I hoped that this would not remain an academic debate. Zimbabwe was in deep trouble, floundering, and if the international community didn't act it was in danger of becoming a failed state.

Although we narrowed the margin, we still lost the debate.

Back home the state of paralysis continued. In the last quarter of 2007, parliament only sat on some twelve days and most of the sessions only lasted an hour. At the end of September ZANU PF demonstrated its paranoia again, rushing through a new "Indigenisation and Economic Empowerment" bill, which decreed that all foreign owned businesses would have to have 51 per cent indigenous ownership. Mugabe warned "profiteering businesses" that the bill would be used "to seize companies".[626] Price controls hadn't managed to stem inflation and so in ZANU PF's mind the next step was to seize companies. On 30 October there was light entertainment when both the speaker and deputy speaker were away and an acting speaker had to be elected. ZANU PF had hardly any MPs in the house and so Gibson Sibanda nominated me. The nomination failed by a narrow margin (28–22) but it was refreshing to see MPs from both MDC factions pulling together.[627] The budget speech which followed on November was a fairytale that bore little resemblance to the reality of the economic chaos besieging Zimbabwe. A salient point, however, made by the minister of Finance regarding the inflation rate was truth stranger than fiction: "Year on year inflation has been rising rapidly from 1 593.6% in January 2007 to reach 7 983% by September. Figures for October are not available because many items included in the consumer-basket have not been available in the shops."[628]

Parliament sat once more that year, on 5 December, and then adjourned. At the time none of us on the MDC benches realised it would not sit again for another eight months, given the turmoil that was to follow. As the year ended, many hours every week were spent sitting in fuel queues or chasing off to some store which had a scarce item for sale. Prices of the few goods that were available had reached ridiculous levels. A pair of men's briefs, manufactured at a cost of US$1, could sell for anything between Z$10 and Z$70 billion. Money had to be carried around in shopping bags. At our law firm we started getting a daily rate of exchange to judge how much our fees in Zimbabwe dollars would have to be adjusted by. Fees would then change literally from one day to the next, going up billions of dollars at a time.

Politically, the year ended in limbo. In June 2007 I had been appointed by the MDC-M to chair a constitutional technical team which was to assist a secret mediation process initiated by Mbeki and SADC. Behind the scenes a small group of lawyers, Chinamasa, Biti and Ncube, had negotiated a new draft constitution in Kariba which was signed by the three of them on 27 September. But after signing off on it, the entire process ground to a halt because of Mugabe's intransigence. Although the presidential election was looming in March 2008, our parliamentary terms still had another two years to run, so none of us anticipated a general election in the new year.

Christmas 2007 was the quietest we have ever celebrated as a family. It seemed almost obscene to be celebrating. Although in my Christmas letter I praised Jenny in a lighthearted manner – "she has now got her full 'Huntin' and Gathering' colours and is highly proficient in travelling to Botswana and further afield in search of such luxuries as flour and sugar … she has now added bread making to her string of talents"[629] – life for old and poor people had become almost unbearable. In 2007 we saw all our Zimbabwean life savings evaporate before our eyes. As tough as this was for us, it was nothing compared to the lot of pensioners and the unemployed. Following a report-back meeting for my constituents at the end of the year an old man came up to me bearing his latest monthly NRZ pensioner's pay advice, which notified him that Z$475 had been deposited in his bank account. This was not enough to buy a match, let alone the taxi fare needed to draw the money out.

The new year started as the old ended. Everything was dominated by inflation. Gono responded on 18 January 2008 by announcing new Zimbabwe dollar notes in Z$1 million, 5 million and 10 million denominations. All it did was fuel inflation more and further collapse the dollar: on 11 January the Z$/Rand exchange rate was Z$350 000 to the Rand; by 19 January "it had shot up to Z$700 000 to the Rand".[630] Prices in stores started going up 200 per cent every fortnight. Even if one had cash, it was difficult to get it out of one's bank. Gono had imposed a cash withdrawal limit of Z$5 million a day, which was the equivalent of the cost of a litre of diesel. And yet if one didn't get one's money out of the bank, it would halve its value every week.

Mugabe ambushed everyone, even Mbeki, when on 25 January he announced that a general election, i.e. both a presidential and parliamentary election, would be held on 29 March. All the secret talks brokered by Mbeki came to naught – the election would be conducted solely on ZANU PF's terms. Our terms of office as MPs were to be cut short by two years. The constitution allowed for parliament to be dissolved in this manner so there was nothing to be done but prepare for another election. Both MDCs were completely taken by surprise; our assumption was that only the presidency would be contested, a far easier political prospect than a general election. Of immediate concern was the fact that the MDC coalition agreement negotiated in April 2007 had stalled. Hawks within the MDC-T felt it granted the MDC-M too many concessions and so they refused to ratify it. We faced the prospect of handing the election to ZANU PF and Mugabe, to use Apraku's warning, "on a platter" by dividing the vote. Those opposed to tyranny had been so poisoned by its bile that we were in danger of perpetuating the regime because of our inability to get on with each other.

CHAPTER 24

SAY NOT THE STRUGGLE NAUGHT AVAILETH
JANUARY 2008 TO FEBRUARY 2009

"Say not the struggle naught availeth
The labour and the wounds are not in vain
The enemy faints not, nor faileth,
And as things have been they remain.

If hopes were dupes, fears may be liars,
It may be, in yon smoke conceal'd,
Your comrades chase e'en now the fliers,
And, but for you, possess the field."
— ARTHUR HUGH CLOUGH, 1855

Well before Mugabe announced the dates of the 2008 election the perennial debate about whether to contest had resurfaced within the MDC-T. The general state of depression among MDC supporters generally, beset as they were by economic problems and disappointed by the ongoing divisions, caused many to think that the elections were unwinnable. In early January MDC-T supporter and political scientist John Makumbe reflected the views of many when he stated: "It is obvious that any opposition political party participating in this election will be legitimising the Mugabe regime. It will obviously lose the elections. Under the current constitution, only Mugabe's party, ZANU PF, will win."[631]

The unexpected announcement of a general election, combined with the real prospect of the two MDC factions dividing the vote against each other, focused the minds of its leaders. After a few preliminary discussions a meeting was convened at Pandhari Lodge in Harare in late January. It was attended by senior leaders of both MDC factions, including Tsvangirai, Biti and Lovemore Moyo from the MDC-T, and Mutambara, Sibanda and Welshman Ncube from MDC-M. The draft coalition agreement, which we had agreed upon the year before, was reviewed and adopted with a few minor changes. The MDC-M would back Tsvangirai's candidacy for president. As a *quid pro quo* Mutambara would be appointed vice-president in the event of Tsvangirai winning. Existing parliamentary seats held by the respective factions would be solely contested by the respective faction. It was complicated by the fact that the Delimitation Commission had gerrymandered old constituencies to suit ZANU PF and many constituency boundaries, and their names, had changed. My old constituency, Bulawayo South, was virtually unrecognisable and the original old area was now split among three different, newly named constituencies. To counter this, Clause 8.3.2. of the agreement stated:

> "Each sitting Member of Parliament will choose which constituency he or she wishes to be a candidate in, having regard to the new delimitation of constituencies provided that such selection shall be of a constituency which contains a part of his or her previous constituency."[632]

One thing that the April 2007 agreement had been vague about was who would contest seats currently held by ZANU PF. The new agreement decreed that ZANU PF-held constituencies in the Matabeleland and Midlands provinces would be equally shared between the two factions. In all the other provinces ZANU PF-held constituencies would be shared on the basis of two thirds MDC-T and one third MDC-M. All those present signed up to the eminently sensible deal. Although the MDC-M benefited by having an opportunity to contest in areas in which it had minimal presence, this was more than balanced by Tsvangirai having a clear run at the all important presidency. Furthermore, the respective strengths of the two factions had never been tested in a general election and the state of the country was too dire for experiments. Finally, both factions would benefit from the surge of optimism among opposition followers when they realised that our differences had been put aside in the national interest. All that remained was for the agreement to be ratified by the two respective national councils.

I was not present at the Pandhari Lodge meeting. Several months before I had agreed to several speaking engagements in the US and had left Zimbabwe before Mugabe had even sprung the election surprise. On 21 January I spoke in Georgia at a Martin Luther King memorial event on the subject "The power of dreams". Regretting that King's non-violent philosophy had gained little traction in Rhodesia, I spoke about the cycle of violence in Zimbabwe spawned by a brutal war to end racial discrimination. The battle to break that cycle of violence was now being waged within the opposition and I told the audience how important King's pledge designed for volunteers at the Birmingham, Alabama, protest in 1963 was. Clause 8 of the pledge compelled volunteers to "refrain from the violence of fist, tongue, *or heart*";[633] the latter was all important, especially for leaders. The commitment to non-violence could not be sustained if it was superficial, temporary and not heartfelt. From Georgia, I travelled to Washington and New York. Seeking to address all shades of American political opinion, I gave a wide-ranging speech about the political environment in Zimbabwe at the Heritage Foundation on 25 January. My central message was to quote President Clinton's 1992 campaign cry, "It's the economy, stupid". I used it to reinforce my theory that no matter what ZANU PF did to subvert the electoral process, the collapsing economy would force them to negotiate. I was upbeat about the chances of an MDC coalition because my colleagues had communicated encouraging details of progress being made back home. In fact, I was still in this optimistic frame of mind when I boarded the return flight to South Africa at Dulles airport on Saturday afternoon, 2 February.

When I arrived at OR Tambo International airport in Johannesburg the first thing I did was turn on my cell phone. Hoping to get news of the finalised coalition agreement, instead I received only bad news. While I had been in the air the national councils of both MDC factions had convened in Harare to consider the coalition agreement. Despite some objections and concerns, the draft agreement was agreed to by the MDC-M which was conveyed to the MDC-T negotiators at Elton Mangoma's office. In the first meeting of the negotiators MDC-T advised that their executive demanded certain specific seats in Harare and Manicaland. After consultation with the MDC-M executive, this was agreed to and our negotiators shuttled back to Mangoma's office to convey the news. However, when they met again it was clear there was a major problem. Elements of the MDC-T from Bulawayo, whose lowly positions in the MDC prior to the split had been elevated to lofty ones following the split, had told the MDC-T council meeting that they were not prepared to accept the provision (Clause 8.3.2 mentioned above) that existing MPs would retain the right to contest their seats. A few of these people argued that there was no need for a coalition agreement as they would win their seats in any event. Both Tsvangirai and Biti argued strongly that the agreement should be accepted but it was to no avail.[634] Tsvangirai himself wrote that the MDC-T council "resolved to go into the election alone despite (his) spirited appeals and arguments for unity of purpose".[635] All our hard work painstakingly to knit together a coalition agreement foundered because of the selfish interests of a few people who put their own interests ahead of the national interest.

That Sunday evening, still in Johannesburg, I expressed my grave concern about the failed coalition to a major supporter of the opposition. He told me that the previous evening he had been contacted by the MDC-T to see if he would still support them if the coalition talks collapsed. Although he was concerned about the collapse of the coalition talks, he sought to console me by telling me he had received a "prophecy" recently that Tsvangirai was going to sweep the board, so felt comfortable about what had happened. Although this man was the only one relying on a prophecy, others in the MDC-T camp had a similar optimistic outlook. A senior member of the MDC-T national executive told me in December that they were going to take "every seat in Matabeleland".

On the evening of 3 February, back in Bulawayo, I attended a meeting that had been called to discuss the election. Two MDC-T supporters were there, both supremely confident that the collapse of the coalition would not matter. When I pointed out the dangers of splitting the vote they were dismissive – the MDC-T was going to win convincingly. The MDC-M, they told me, wouldn't win a seat. I left the meeting very depressed. It seemed clear to me that their confidence was baseless and misplaced; we were going to hand victory to ZANU PF again through our own foolishness.

Everything was thrown upside down the following day when former ZANU PF minister of Finance Simba Makoni held a press conference in Harare to announce that he was planning to contest the presidential election against Mugabe and Tsvangirai. Makoni, who was rumoured to have the backing of retired general Solomon Mujuru, enjoyed considerable respect among the business and diplomatic community so the announcement sent tremors through Zimbabwe's body politic. ZANU PF responded in alarm. War veteran Joseph Chinotimba threatened Makoni with violence. *The Herald* opined that he was a "pawn of the United Kingdom", designed to split the ZANU PF vote to secure Tsvangirai's victory.

Makoni's announcement immediately electrified a lacklustre campaign, however. Prior to the announcement many people aside from me were depressed by the general electoral environment, now made worse by the MDC factions' inability to form a coalition. Overnight Makoni opened up an entirely new and unexpected prospect – a divided ZANU PF. Suddenly defeat of ZANU PF became possible again and this energised people across Zimbabwe.

Before Makoni's announcement, Mutambara had privately expressed his reluctance to stand for president. Since the April 2007 MDC reconciliation meeting our party's mindset had been that we would support Tsvangirai's candidacy and we did not anticipate the collapse of the coalition talks. Following Makoni's declaration, discussions commenced between his new party and the MDC-M, resulting in our national council being reconvened in Harare on 10 February to consider a novel proposal. Mutambara told the meeting that he didn't want to stand for president as this would further divide an existing three-way race. There could be mutual benefit if we supported Makoni's candidacy; we didn't have a presidential candidate to support and Makoni's party had few grassroots political structures. An intense debate followed with most of those taking part focusing on what Makoni's entry might do to Tsvangirai's prospects. In the end a broad consensus emerged: the MDC-T had rejected the reasonable coalition terms and the advice of its own leader; irrespective of our decision Makoni was already contesting the election and we had no candidate; in those circumstances it seemed logical that we should support Makoni who was prepared to work with us.

Personally, although still distressed about the collapse of the coalition, I was happy with the decision. Aside from having little other option, Makoni had always impressed me in the two years we had sat in parliament together. He had always been decent and told the truth about the state of the economy. In his 2001 budget address he hadn't minced his words about what the country needed to do. He had never participated in the unlawful and violent land grabs; although he owned a farm, he had bought it honestly with his own money years before the land invasions began. Finally, he had bravely stood up to Mugabe resulting in him losing his cabinet post in 2002. Critically for me, Makoni had never been implicated in any violence or corruption, even when he was a member of ZANU PF.

A few days after our decision to back Makoni's candidacy, I submitted my nomination papers to stand in the Khumalo senatorial constituency. The MDC-M had decided that I should contest this seat for a variety of reasons. My old house of assembly Bulawayo South seat had been split up, gerrymandered beyond recognition, into three new seats. The intention appeared to be to divide my existing support. In addition the Khumalo seat spanned two house of assembly seats and the party hoped that I might lend support to our two MP candidates, especially as the Khumalo constituency included the area where I had lived ever since returning to Zimbabwe in 1983.

Remarkably, although I had stood and won in two prior election campaigns and had been an MP for eight years, the nomination court *still* queried my citizenship, although on this occasion it was perfunctory. I had come armed with all my papers, which satisfied the officer. At the end of the day ZANU PF, MDC-T and MDC-M (although the official name for the purposes of the election, indeed, which it has remained ever since then, was MDC[636]) all fielded candidates in all 210 constituencies. There was one exception: MDC-T, astonishingly, negotiated a deal with the architect of the Access to Information and Protection of Privacy Act and the man behind the *Daily News*'s demise, Jonathan Moyo, not to oppose him in Tsholotsho, where he stood (still out of favour with ZANU PF) as an independent against ZANU PF and MDC-M candidates.

The Khumalo constituency comprised some three fifths of Bulawayo. If one pictures Bulawayo as a clock face, with 12 o'clock as north, the constituency spanned around clockwise from 11 o'clock in the north west, to 6 o'clock in the south – in other words the entire central and eastern portions of the city, bounded by the Victoria Falls, Lobengula and Matopos roads in the west and the city limits to the east. It was a massive urban constituency, extending from the airport in the north to the Criterion waterworks in the south. Although it had far fewer working-class people, the racial composition was not that much different to my old Bulawayo South constituency; it was overwhelmingly black, with some five per cent of the electorate made up of minorities.

However, we started the campaign with three major problems. Unlike 2000 and 2005, this was not going to be a straight fight against ZANU PF as I also had an MDC-T opponent. Secondly, one or two of my key campaign team were now with the MDC-T and would be campaigning against me. With some of my key supporters from previous elections now openly hostile towards my campaign, I relied, as I had done so many times before, on a few loyal friends. When I established the BLPC I relied heavily on a succession of outstanding women, such as Rosanne Hendry, Deborah Barron, Mary Ndlovu, Jessie Majome and Eileen Sawyer. This time I turned to two women in particular, Ceri Cox and Stella Allberry, who worked miracles. My long-standing law partner, Josephat Tshuma, joined the team as campaign manager.

A third major obstacle was created by our decision to support Makoni's presidential candidacy, which infuriated many people who didn't know or understand the background, in particular the MDC-T's decision not to ratify the coalition agreement. This situation was compounded on 19 February when Roy Bennett, who was still in exile, wrote a hard-hitting letter that was published in the *Cape Argus*. Among other things, he said:

> "Makoni has been a loyal, long standing member of ZANU PF's politburo. His record is there for all who care to see. He was silent at the time of Gukurahundi and his overall backers are all the key perpetrators of that massacre. He was complicit and silent at the time rampaging mobs ran through our High Court rendering the rule of law obsolete. He was silent when the *Daily News* was shut down and the owners and employees were hounded and humiliated. Makoni even sat in on political discussions and never once raised his voice when defenceless Zimbabweans were rendered homeless, in that shameless act of cruelty, Operation Murambatsvina. He was silent when business leaders were assaulted and small businesses bankrupted through price controls. The time for opportunism is not now. Makoni and his own are seeking a soft landing for ill gotten gains and human rights abuses, and are now attempting to believe in a need for change."[637]

As reluctant as I was to tangle publicly with a friend, especially one who had been through the mill, I felt I had no option but to set the record straight. Bennett enjoyed the respect of many voters in my constituency, who would take his allegations seriously. Pointing out the fact that Bennett and I had both served in the BSAP, and had been forgiven by the thousands of black Zimbabweans who had voted for us, and Mandela's spirit of forgiveness in South Africa, I argued that "our problems (were) so grave and seemingly intractable that we (would) not be able to save our land unless all responsible and patriotic Zimbabweans display a similar spirit of forgiveness and turning away from evil". I concluded:

> "We may criticise (Makoni) for staying within Zanu PF for so long but it is an unjustified cut to say that he has agreed with all that has happened in Zimbabwe since independence. Even if I am wrong in my assessment of Makoni's past, what we know for certain now is that he has broken from Zanu PF in an astonishingly brave move. His manifesto indicates that he stands for the right things, including national reconciliation and a new democratic constitution.
>
> "In my view this courageous move should be supported, not criticised. Now is the time for us all to display the same degree of forgiveness afforded Roy Bennett and me by black Zimbabweans. The quid pro quo is that Simba Makoni must show that this is a genuine turning away from Zanu PF's evil past – but I think he has already demonstrated that through his actions and words of the last few weeks.
>
> "Now is also the time for all patriotic Zimbabweans to work together to bring Robert Mugabe's ruinous and brutal dictatorship to an end."[638]

My letter evoked two types of responses. Many Zimbabweans wrote to thank me, but others wrote furiously criticising me for suggesting that service in the Rhodesian forces was anything that needed forgiveness for.

The letter aside, in the weeks that followed it became increasingly apparent that Makoni's campaign was floundering. Although he had turned his back on ZANU PF, he fell between two stools: in his attempt to encourage high-ranking ZANU PF leaders to support him, he remained relatively mute in his criticism of ZANU PF's past. This tactic didn't work. General Mujuru and other heavyweights kept their power dry and never gave him the endorsements he desperately needed.

As Makoni's campaign petered out Tsvangirai's gathered momentum through March. There was palpable excitement that ZANU PF was on the ropes, an emotion bolstered by the relatively peaceful atmosphere in which the elections were conducted. Knowing I had a battle royal, I focused most of my attention on my own Khumalo constituency, which was peaceful save for two incidents. In the first, my two sons Douglas and Scott, and some of their schoolfriends, under the charge of an employee, John Tlou, were putting up posters near my home when two carloads of ZANU PF supporters stopped near them. Anxious that they meant trouble, and separated from Tlou, who was putting up posters elsewhere in another vehicle, my boys kept their distance, but the ZANU PF supporters approached in an apparently friendly manner to ask whether they could use a ladder our team were using. With their guard down my boys let them use the ladder, at the same time entering into some friendly banter. What they didn't realise was that some of the ZANU PF supporters had sneaked around the back of one of our campaign vehicles and let the air out of a tyre. The deflated tyre was only discovered when the ZANU PF group drove off. Now worried, they decided to return home, but no sooner were they back on the road than they realised they were being followed. A car chase ensued, causing the deflated tyre to shred and the vehicle to be abandoned. Fortunately, no one was injured and we managed to recover the vehicle later that evening. In the context of Zimbabwean elections the incident was child's play, but it was nevertheless a reminder that even in the relatively benign environment of our home suburb we had to be on our guard.

The second incident involved pulling down posters rather than putting them up. One of our campaign teams caught an MDC-T MP candidate red handed pulling down my posters; when they challenged her she responded belligerently: "Shut up or I will hit you with my wheel spanner."[639] It was bad enough having to deal with ZANU PF's antics, but shocking to realise how far tyranny's poison had permeated the opposition.

However, the hardest thing for me to stomach in the March 2008 election was the partisan nature of much of civil society, including the church. The donor community traditionally did not provide direct support for political parties; support for democratic governance matters was channelled through civic groups such as Bulawayo Agenda and the Christian Alliance, many of which were blatantly partisan in favour of MDC-T. Although there was no evidence of these bodies providing direct financial support to MDC-T, they provided platforms and other opportunities to MDC-T candidates that were not afforded to me and my MDC-M colleagues. Likewise the independent media, including papers such as *The Zimbabwean* and the *Daily News*, and radio stations such as SW Radio Africa and VOA's Studio 7, were partisan in favour of the MDC-T. Often it was done in subtle ways – the MDC-M was usually referred to pejoratively as the "breakaway faction", which was not factually correct. I could live with the factual description of the MDC-M being the "smaller" faction, but the constant inference that somehow we were renegades, and in cahoots with ZANU PF, was simply false. Our concerns regarding violence and breaches of the MDC constitution were usually ignored.

The stance taken by civic groups dovetailed neatly with more hostile rhetoric coming from many MDC-T leaders, who constantly suggested that we were sell-outs and somehow had done a deal with the devil. In my mind the stance adopted by civic groups amounted to a fundamental compromise of their *raison d'être* – the promotion and protection of human rights. It concerned me that by turning a blind eye to intra-MDC violence, civic groups and church groups undermined their moral high ground to condemn ZANU PF's human rights violations.

The election, which was held on 29 March, realised the concerns I had expressed when the coalition talks failed in February. The election itself went smoothly. In addition, soon after counting began it was clear that I had a comfortable majority. But word started to filter in that my MDC-M colleagues contesting seats elsewhere had been heavily defeated, except for ten seats in Matabeleland North and South provinces. Stalwarts such as Sibanda, Ncube and Nyathi had been swept away. It was no wonder the Bulawayo MDC-T candidates had fought so tenaciously against the coalition agreement, because their arguments that they would win their own seats were vindicated. My own victory in Khumalo was tempered by the realisation that I was the only MDC-M candidate who won an urban seat anywhere in the country. The MDC-T, however, had done superbly, winning every seat in Bulawayo, Harare and gaining a majority of seats in Masvingo, Manicaland and Matabeleland North.

However, as the parliamentary results started to flow in over the following days the pyrrhic nature of the MDC-T victory emerged. Further amendments by ZANU PF to the constitution had increased the number of house of assembly seats from 150 to 210 and the senate from 60 to 93. In the senate only 60 seats were directly elected, the remainder being elected by chiefs or appointed by the president, meaning that if the presidential election was lost, a simple majority win in the senate would be insufficient. Legislation had to be passed by both chambers to become law.

The good news was that for the first time since independence ZANU PF had lost their majority in the house of assembly, with MDC-T winning 99, ZANU PF 97 and MDC-M 10, with 42.88%, 45.9% and 8.39% of the vote respectively.[640] Jonathan Moyo won his seat as an independent, narrowly beating the MDC-M candidate. The bad news was that ZANU PF had effectively captured the senate, taking 30 seats against the MDC-T's 24 and MDC-M's 6, with a similar percentage of the vote. The 18 chiefs elected as senators would vote with ZANU PF because of Mugabe's patronage. While of course these figures were produced by the partisan ZEC, and as such were highly questionable, even based on their figures the results illustrated the enormity of the MDC parties' collective folly. In some 20 senatorial and house of assembly seats ZANU PF won with a minority; the two MDC parties had split the vote, handing control of the senate to ZANU PF. In the house of assembly a thumping majority was reduced to a narrow majority. While it goes without saying that the entire electoral process was flawed, had the MDC parties acted sensibly, and agreed on a coalition, the parliamentary elections would have been won by a country mile.

Our attention turned to the presidential election results, but from the outset skulduggery was at play. The first harbinger was that ZEC took several days to announce the house of assembly results, and even longer to announce the senate results. Biti held a press conference in Harare, claiming victory for the MDC-T and Tsvangirai, based on their own returns, which precipitated a furious response from ZEC and threats of arrest, which sent Biti into exile. The MDC-T unsuccessfully brought an urgent court application trying to compel ZEC to release the results. Outside the prescribed 48-hour window ZANU PF announced it would seek re-counts in a number of constituencies. This was accepted by ZEC, prompting me to complain that "the delay between the expiry of the 48-hour period and the writing of the letters of complaint by ZEC is inexplicable, unreasonable ... the only inference one can draw from the delay is that the commission has connived with ZANU PF and therefore acted illegally".[641]

Days went into weeks and still there was no sign of the presidential results coming out. Eventually, on 2 May, five weeks after the election, ZEC announced that Tsvangirai had won 47.9%, Mugabe 43.2% and Makoni 8.3% of the presidential vote. Zimbabwe's constitution required a 50 per cent plus 1 majority. Tsvangirai's percentage was therefore insufficient and a run-off election between Tsvangirai and Mugabe would have to be held. This was scheduled for 27 June.

No one outside of Mugabe's inner circle knows exactly what was discussed between the date of the election, 29 March, and the final announcement of the presidential result on 2 May, but we get some idea from circumstantial events. Some ZANU PF politburo members who have since fallen out of favour with Mugabe, such as Didymus Mutasa, have spoken about the confusion within ZANU PF when it became clear that Mugabe had lost the election. At some point some people rallied around Mugabe. Mnangagwa was Mugabe's election agent and, accordingly, would have been central to the discussions. The first public sign that something sinister was afoot was a meeting of senior members of the police, army, prison service, CIO and war veterans. This took place at Nkayi Business Centre on 14 April. A source at the meeting revealed (weeks before it was announced officially by ZEC) that there would be a presidential run-off and that "violence would be a central pillar of Mugabe's campaign".[642] Unambiguous calls to engage in violence were made, with one senior officer stating: "If the country is given away through the ballot, we will not hand over power, but rather go back to the bush and start another war."[643]

Presumably, similar meetings explaining the plan were held in other parts of the country because within days of this meeting reports started to come in of a dramatic upsurge in violence right across Zimbabwe. Between January and the conclusion of the election human rights organisations reported 63 violations which leapt tenfold to 618 in April.[644] By mid May doctors in Harare reported having treated 1 600 victims that month alone. Most of the violence (46 per cent) was concentrated in the rural Mashonaland provinces where the MDC-T had made surprising inroads, winning twelve seats in what was traditionally ZANU PF's stronghold. Matabeleland was only minimally affected and a strange reversal of fortunes took place; whereas in 1983 the rest of the country was blissfully untouched by the Gukurahundi, now we in Matabeleland listened to horrifying reports of what was happening in the north.

The violence was systematic and well coordinated. In rural areas men, acting with military efficiency, went village by village telling people not to "make mistakes voting again". MDC supporters were identified, beaten, tortured, abducted. At the same time operatives systematically decimated MDC-T's youth leaders. Many of those who had been implicated in the assault of Guhu in 2004 and Stevenson in July 2006 were targeted. Godfrey Kauzani, who had led the assault on Guhu, was abducted in Murewa and found shot dead on 14 May; the same day, Better Chokururama, one of those expelled by the MDC national executive in June 2005, but subsequently re-employed, was found murdered; Tonderai Ndira, accused of being part of the mob that had assaulted Stevenson, was abducted from his home in Mabvuku on 6 June and found murdered in Goromonzi a week later.[645] Those who survived abductions and beatings "identified the perpetrators either as war veterans, armed security force members or ZANU PF youth militia or varying combinations of the three".[646]

At the same time the brutal campaign was started against MDC activists, the regime did everything possible to stem the flow of information about these incidents, as it had done during the Gukurahundi. Although it was impossible for them to announce a curfew this time – because that would have swept away any possibility of maintaining a pretence that this was to be a "free and fair" run-off election – the authorities clamped down on journalists across the country. For example, on 10 April 2008, 30 armed policemen raided the Bulawayo home of Margaret Kriel and detained her. Kriel, who had years before worked as a radio presenter at ZBC, and was a blogger, was flattered to be mistaken for her daughter Robyn, a foreign-based TV journalist, who had been conducting a variety of interviews, including one with me. Kriel's crime was that she had breached Jonathan Moyo's AIPPA law, practising journalism without accreditation.

The clampdown fuelled international media interest and my assistance was sought by many journalists and organisations who wanted to report from inside the country. One of these organisations, Sky TV, secretly imported broadcasting equipment, including satellite feeds, which we kept, spread over several different locations. Sky's Emma Hurd and Stuart Ramsey then brazenly broadcast live reports from within

Zimbabwe, infuriating the government who did not know where they were broadcasting from, or how they had achieved the feat.

On Friday, 23 May 2008, Sky decided to take the equipment out of the country and contracted three South Africans to transport it to South Africa. On their way out the three were stopped by police and some of the equipment was discovered. Their arrest led the police back to Bulawayo, where they raided the home of our close friend Rita Ruf and found a Sky generator there. This in turn led to the business premises of another friend, Craig Edy, being raided, where the bulk of the remaining Sky equipment had been left. Both Ruf and Edy were arrested in scenes reminiscent of the 2000 raids on my home when Capital Radio started broadcasting. When Edy's business was searched the warrant declared that the police were looking for "broadcasting equipment suspected to have been unlawfully used before, during and after the March harmonised elections".[647] Edy ended up languishing in jail for a few days before being granted bail. The attorney general then maliciously used a draconian RF-era law to overrule the bail order, resulting in Edy's detention for another fortnight.

On 30 May the government-controlled *Chronicle*'s headline trumpeted: "Mischievous Foreign Journalists Warned" and the report advised how the government was "concerned about the rate of smuggling of equipment into the country by Western journalists who broadcast illegally from Zimbabwe".[648] Similar arrests of pesky foreign journalists and photographers took place in a number of areas in the country, exhibiting a determination by ZANU PF to conceal the reign of terror spreading throughout Zimbabwe.

Tsvangirai, fearing for his own life as this violence unfolded, fled the country. He went into exile in Botswana, where he was protected by President Ian Khama.

Much to my relief, Tsvangirai and Mutambara had announced at a joint press conference held in Johannesburg on 28 April that MDC-M would back Tsvangirai's candidacy in any run-off election.[649] Buoyed by that agreement, I embarked on a series of overseas trips to alert the international community about what was taking place in Zimbabwe and to mobilise resources. Between 5 May and 14 June I flew overseas three times, speaking in Washington, New York, London, Stockholm and Copenhagen about the grave crisis at home. My message to senators, congressmen, parliamentarians, church leaders, and journalists was that ZANU PF's latest purge "bore all the marks of Gukurahundi". It was well organised, I said, and individuals had been targeted (77 per cent of all victims were from the MDC). There was pre-meditation, an effective curfew and a media blackout; the violence was gratuitously vile, deliberately done to instil fear, and was accompanied by public denials from the regime's leadership.[650] I argued that crimes against humanity were being committed and called for the prosecutor of the ICC to get involved. At the same time further resources were organised for the LDF, which was inundated with calls to represent hundreds of MDC activists detained countrywide. Between January 2008 and February 2009, the LDF arranged for the defence of 1 212 activists, the vast majority of whom were detained and prosecuted during April, May, June and July 2008.[651]

By this time the administration of the LDF had been taken over by "John Knox", a local Bulawayo pastor. Just as Pius Ncube had put his life on the line in the 1980s, so during this period Knox worked tirelessly, often alone, traversing Zimbabwe to ensure that activists were defended and looked after. Given the great risk to his life during this frightening period, he remains one of the struggle's unsung heroes.

I returned home from the last trip to Denmark and Sweden on 14 June to a country wracked by violence. Although Matabeleland remained relatively peaceful, the rest of the country was like a war zone. Aside from the curfew most rural areas had military or ZANU PF militia bases. The north and north east had become no-go areas and it was well nigh impossible to campaign for Tsvangirai. Some 200 of Tsvangirai's own electoral agents had been abducted and murdered in the preceding six weeks.[652]

Faced with this impossible situation, Tsvangirai announced on 22 June that he was withdrawing from the run-off, describing it as a "violent sham", and saying that his supporters risked being killed if they voted for him.[653] On the same day that Tsvangirai pulled out, Mugabe confirmed the futility of his staying in the race by declaring: "… the MDC will never be allowed to rule this country – never ever … only God, who appointed me, will remove me – not the MDC, not the British … only God will remove me".[654] Mugabe, no doubt disappointed that Tsvangirai's withdrawal had stripped away the last vestiges of legitimacy, went ahead with the election, which he won "convincingly" with 85.5 per cent of votes cast. Within days it became apparent that Mugabe would not receive the same uncritical African support he had in the past. SADC, the Observer Mission of the AU and the Pan African Parliamentary Mission all condemned the election results, saying that they "did not represent the will of the people',[655] "fell short of accepted AU standards",[656] and were not "free, fair and credible".[657]

Any thoughts Mugabe had had that he could avoid criticism by his peers had been removed two days before the election, on 25 June, when a SADC Troika meeting was held in Swaziland. The meeting, which included Tanzanian president Kikwete, noted that the conditions in Zimbabwe were not "conducive for holding free and fair elections".

Mugabe reacted angrily on 27 June:

"We are surprised by what some SADC leaders are saying. Some are even calling for President Mbeki to stop current mediation efforts while others want him to be replaced. These reckless statements being made by some SADC leaders could lead to the break-up of SADC."[658]

Mbeki had provided Mugabe with enormous cover during his mediation, which started in 2007, but this was now under threat with Zimbabwe falling apart. With a growing chorus of states expressing concern about the unfolding events, Mbeki pushed for negotiations. In mid July he tried to get the two MDCs and ZANU PF to sign an inter-party agreement that would pave the way for power-sharing talks. Tsvangirai refused to attend the meeting unless certain pre-conditions were met. These included the cessation of violence, the release of 1 500 or so political detainees, and the swearing in of the new parliament which, three months after the election, had still not happened. Without these conditions being met, Mbeki nevertheless finally managed to get Mugabe, Tsvangirai and Mutambara to meet on 21 July to sign a Memorandum of Understanding. The MOU committed all three parties to dialogue. None of the parties was to take precipitous action, such as forming a new government. All necessary measures were to be taken to end violence.

Although the incidence of violence had decreased after the run-off election, the country remained on a knife edge. On 7 June, while passing through Johannesburg on my way to Sweden, I had met with a person close to the MDC-T who warned me that a plot was being hatched by some people to assassinate certain key people deemed responsible for the violence in Zimbabwe. Such was the frustration with the undeclared war being waged against the MDC, that this group felt the only way to end it was to eliminate its architects. I was profoundly shocked by the news and when I got back to Zimbabwe in mid June I raised my concerns with party leaders and diplomats. No one else had received this intelligence, so I hoped that it was no more than a rumour. However, on 28 July, while stopping over at Johannesburg airport, this time on my way to Australia, I received another identical report from a South African-based writer who also had close links to the MDC-T. The writer told me that the plans were well advanced and that he was telling me so that I could exert whatever pressure I could to scupper them. There was no possible connection between the two sources, which convinced me that this was more than rumour.

On 2 August I had dinner in Queensland with Prime Minister Kevin Rudd, on the sidelines of a Consilium organised by the Sydney-based Centre for Independent Studies. Although I didn't feel comfortable about raising the assassination plot with Rudd, I spoke generally about the exceptionally grave crisis in Zimbabwe. I said that the country was a time-bomb waiting to explode, with disastrous consequences for the region. Rudd was receptive and promised to raise the alarm within the Commonwealth.

Meanwhile intensive negotiations, involving ZANU PF, MDC-T and MDC-M negotiators, had begun in South Africa on 24 July, building on previous agreements and draft legislation, including the so-called Kariba constitution that had been signed by all the negotiators on 30 September 2007. Under pressure from SADC good progress was made, including agreement on a new inclusive constitutional reform process and a mechanism to achieve national healing and reconciliation. The result was the signing, on 28 July 2008, of an agreement entitled "Framework for a New Government". In terms of this document Mugabe would continue in office as president. He would appoint three deputy presidents, two nominated by ZANU PF and one by MDC-T. Tsvangirai was to become prime minister and there would be three deputy prime ministers, one each nominated by the parties. It was agreed that there would be a cabinet made up of 38 ministers, comprising seventeen from ZANU PF, sixteen from MDC-T and five from MDC-M. The negotiators adjourned on 6 August with the understanding that certain outstanding issues, including the powers and duties of the president and prime minister respectively, would have to be resolved by the "Principals", comprising Mugabe, Tsvangirai and Mutambara.

Mbeki and his team of mediators arrived in Harare on 9 August to clinch the deal but the negotiations immediately ran into problems around the role of the prime minister. Over the course of the next few days there were intensive discussions around this issue, which culminated in Mbeki's team tabling a document dealing with the prime minister's role on the afternoon of 12 August. Considerable debate followed and in the course of the afternoon and early evening the original document was amended several times. The debate had narrowed down to two critically important MDC-T demands, namely, that the prime minister should be "Head of Government" and should chair cabinet.

In the belief that all had been agreed upon, a final draft was prepared by Mbeki's team. Assuming that this was acceptable to the MDC-T and Tsvangirai, Mutambara indicated that he would agree to what was set out in the final document. However, Tsvangirai, after consulting his colleagues, advised that the final document was unsatisfactory and so the meeting ended.

The following morning *The Herald* carried the false story that Mutambara had entered into a bilateral agreement with Mugabe. The story was picked up by many international papers. Mutambara immediately convened a press conference and put the record straight by stating unequivocally that he and the MDC-M would *not* enter into a bilateral agreement with ZANU PF. Despite this, the belief that somehow MDC-M was prepared to do a deal with ZANU PF stuck. ZANU PF's self-serving propaganda, designed to split those opposed to it, worked very effectively. I immediately saw the effectiveness of their strategy as my in-box filled with angry mail – one writer saying how "sickened and disgusted (he was) by the conduct of the MDC breakaway faction"; another from a long-standing client of mine told me that I was "a disgrace to the people of Zimbabwe". Even a long-standing member of our administrative staff phoned me and asked me aggressively whether I was pleased about "getting into bed with ZANU".

With the talks deadlocked around the issue of the role of the prime minister, ZANU PF employed another ruse to divide the two MDCs further by announcing that parliament would finally be opened by Mugabe on 26 August. The first act of any new parliament is to elect a speaker, which ZANU PF correctly guessed would exacerbate the rift between the two MDCs. In the negotiations with ZANU PF and the MDC-T in late July, we had suggested that agreement should be reached that an MDC-M nominee should be the speaker. The suggestion was not made from any sense of entitlement, but purely from a belief that a relatively neutral person might be better able to bridge the huge gulf that would exist in the new parliament, primarily between ZANU PF and MDC-T. But this was rejected by both parties. During discussions regarding who would be acceptable as a speaker, the MDC-T negotiators eventually indicated that they would prefer to nominate Dumiso Dabengwa than people nominated by the MDC-M such as Gibson Sibanda or Paul Themba Nyathi. In other words, notwithstanding our joint history and the support given to Tsvangirai's candidacy in the run-off, much of the focus of the negotiations was on the intra-MDC party dispute, rather than on presenting a common front against ZANU PF. Convinced that, aside from our right to nominate someone, it would be in the nation's best interest to have a neutral speaker, the MDC-M national executive agreed on 20 August to nominate Nyathi as speaker. Nyathi, a founder member of the MDC and its first director of Elections, enjoyed respect across the political divide: a war veteran, who had been detained for years by the RF, with an ability to make even his fiercest adversary laugh.

The day before the vote for speaker was to be held, Sunday, 24 August, the MDC-T parliamentary caucus was called to a meeting. Knowing Nyathi's popularity and that several of its members would vote for him, MDC-T MPs were threatened with expulsion if they voted for him. Despite the parliamentary standing orders requirement for a "secret ballot",[659] MPs were told that they would have to show their ballot to MDC-T MP and its vice-president Thoko Khupe prior to voting. In the same meeting MDC-T MP Lovemore Moyo was elected as their nominee for speaker. Moyo, a relatively junior member of the MDC prior to 2006, had sided with the Sibanda faction after the October 2005 split but had then crossed the floor to the MDC-T shortly before its congress in March 2006, securing in the process the senior position of chairman. Unbeknown to us at the time, Moyo and Khupe had also recently met with some nine MDC-M MPs in Gaborone, Botswana, where a secret deal was struck for them to vote for Moyo as speaker in return for positions and other incentives.[660] This, too, was an offence in terms of Zimbabwe's Parliamentary standing orders and international parliamentary practice.[661]

There was a further twist on the morning of 25 August prior to the vote, when ZANU PF cunningly announced that it would not propose its own candidate but would support Nyathi. They had correctly assessed that their nominee would split the vote, allowing Moyo to win; in any event it suited them to fuel speculation that some nefarious deal had been done between MDC-M and ZANU PF, which was not in fact the case. Accordingly, when nominations were called for the speaker that afternoon it came down to a straight contest between Nyathi, nominated by MDC-M's Njabuliso Mguni, and Moyo, nominated by MDC-T. When voting began several MDC-T leaders, including Khupe and Moyo himself, displayed their ballot papers before depositing them in the ballot box,[662] encouraging their subordinates to do likewise. The combination of the threats levelled against their own MPs and the inducements offered to some of the MDC-M MPs worked. When the ballots were counted Moyo had secured 110 votes against Nyathi's 98. Mguni, the very MDC-M MP who had nominated Nyathi, voted for MDC-T's Moyo. The entire episode left a very bad taste in my mouth and further undermined relations between the two MDC parties.

Fortunately, the distrust generated by these machinations did not derail the talks brokered by Mbeki, which continued behind the scenes. Mugabe employed brinkmanship as August drew to a close, threatening to form a cabinet if agreement wasn't reached by 4 September. With no breakthrough in sight, and to quell false allegations that were resurfacing, the MDC-M reiterated on 8 September that it would not participate in any government with ZANU PF if the talks were deadlocked. Without MDC-M support in parliament ZANU PF could not govern. This realisation played a major role in the resumption of formal negotiations the following day. Once more Mbeki flew in to Harare to mediate.[663] He tabled a fresh proposal which would make Tsvangirai an executive prime minister. The proposal, which created a Council of Ministers to be chaired by Tsvangirai, resolved the impasse. Mugabe would chair cabinet which would decide government policy while the Council of Ministers, presided over by Tsvangirai, would implement those agreed policies.

On 15 September 2008, Mbeki finally presided over the signing of the "Global Political Agreement" (GPA) which would govern a ZANU-PF, MDC-T and MDC-M "coalition". Mugabe, Tsvangirai and Mutambara signed the document at a lavish ceremony held at the International Conference Centre in Harare. Although there were many smiles, handshakes and shows of goodwill, in reality there was still a huge reservoir of mistrust and ill will.

The next day I flew to Washington to give a speech at an event organised by the Inter-Parliamentary Union which focused on the problems of unlawful detentions, torture and assassination of opposition leaders around the world. I spoke alongside parliamentarians from Haiti, Afghanistan, Liberia, Ecuador and Timor-Leste. Their testimonies were depressingly similar to mine. A key question was how to steer undemocratic regimes on a reform path in the face of outright violence and oppression. Once again I took aim at the World Bank and IMF for supporting undemocratic regimes that had a record of serious human rights abuses, a theme I had first taken up in Washington sixteen years earlier in 1992. I argued that a carrot-and-stick policy should be applied universally – if governments showed a genuine desire to respect human rights, they should be rewarded; if not, then support should be terminated immediately.

While I was in the US, I received a call from Welshman Ncube, secretary general of the MDC-M, advising me that the party wanted me to be part of the cabinet. Ongoing negotiations after the signing of the GPA regarding the composition of the unity government meant that the MDC would be entitled to three cabinet seats. The party leadership had met and decided that I should be one of the three nominees. Ncube asked me which portfolios I would be interested in. I suggested Justice, Environment or Education. Justice because law was my forte and I had been shadow Justice minister for eight years after being elected to parliament in 2000; Environment because of my passion for Zimbabwe and its beautiful national parks; Education because of my interest in the Petra Schools and children. I knew that Justice would be a long shot because it was such a strategically important and powerful ministry. Likewise I was aware that Environment was a ministry ZANU-PF would want because it provided much scope for arbitrage and rent seeking (through the corrupt discretionary awards of lucrative hunting concessions either to cronies or to hunting operators who were prepared to pay bribes).

As it turned out neither MDC-T nor ZANU PF were interested in Education because it was not a politically powerful ministry. If anything it was viewed as a poisoned chalice – the education sector was in such a mess that no one wanted to take on the headache. Instead the two dominant parties were locked in a struggle to split the ministries that controlled the main levers of power – Defence, Security, Home Affairs, Justice and Finance. After considerable wrangling and horse-trading ZANU PF was left with almost all the "coercive" ministries – Defence, Security and Justice. The MDC-T got Finance, Constitutional Affairs and would share control of Home Affairs (Police) with ZANU PF. So, without disclosing who would be selected as minister, our leadership negotiated with minimal effort for Education to be allocated to the MDC-M. The split of these ministries was to prove crucial in the years ahead.

I returned home, just two weeks later, to a Zimbabwean economy that was falling apart faster than ever. Through all the political wrangling that year hyper-inflation had really gathered steam. In just the fourteen days I was away, I was shocked to see how much further the Zimbabwean dollar had tumbled. In August 2008, Reserve Bank Governor Gono had released new Zimbabwean banknotes, lopping off a further ten zeros from the currency in the process. The previous currency had become uneconomical to print and was becoming worthless, with inflation running at in excess of 2 000 per cent per month. To take an example: a ladies' skirt, which in February 2008 was priced at Z$19.6 million, would now cost Z$12.6 trillion (Z$12 600 000 000 000). With the new currency and the dropping of ten zeros the same skirt cost only Z$1 260. But within days of stock being re-marked with the ten zeros taken off, two zeros were back.[664] By 8 September, the same skirt cost Z$21 600 and just three days later was selling for Z$43 200. By 20 October the price had risen to Z$414 million. Accordingly, in the course of the year the price of the skirt jumped (without the ten zeros taken off) from Z$19.6 million to Z$4 140 quintillion or, in figures Z$4 140 000 000 000 000 000 000)! By the year end, the Reserve Bank issued a Z$100 trillion note. It barely bought a loaf of bread. That note was arrived at after a total of 21 zeros had been taken off the original currency since 1997, a totally incomprehensible figure.

The impact on all Zimbabweans, except the ruling elite, was severe in those closing months of 2008. It had become virtually impossible to run our law practice – we had to adjust our fees twice a day to keep up with the real value of our original work. Supermarkets became empty caverns; rows and rows of empty shelves with just a smattering of some goods that were so over-priced they were simply unaffordable to most.

In August, cholera had broken out in parts of Harare and spread quickly to other cities, towns and villages. The ministry of Health announced on 1 December that there were 11 735 cases identified and that fatality rates were as high as 30 per cent in rural areas. It rapidly got out of control and by the end of December thousands had died. It is estimated conservatively that around 98 585 people were infected and some 4 287 people died during the epidemic. Zimbabwe was more in danger than ever of becoming a failed state.

Despite hyper-inflation and cholera rampaging through the country destroying the lives of ordinary Zimbabweans, the political wrangling continued, but by the end of January 2009 it was patently clear that there was no other viable option but to implement the GPA signed in September. Tsvangirai had objected to a variety of unilateral acts by Mugabe, including his reappointment of various people – Gideon Gono, the Reserve Bank governor, for example. Eventually agreement was reached at a SADC Heads of Government meeting in Pretoria on 26 January 2009. Constitutional amendment 19, which facilitated the GPA, was expedited through Parliament on 5 February. Such was the rush to get the bill passed, only three people spoke in the senate that afternoon – Chinamasa for ZANU PF, Sekai Holland for MDC-T and me for MDC-M. Asking where "violence had ever got our nation", I argued that the GPA and the constitutional amendment we were debating enabled us "to draw a line in the sand … to commit ourselves henceforth to use non-violent means to transform our nation".[665]

With the constitutional framework in place, the three Principals, namely Mugabe, Tsvangirai and Mutambara, then met to agree on the names of the actual cabinet ministers. When Mugabe was told by Mutambara that I was the MDC-M's pick for minister of Education he was extremely unhappy. He used the excuse that it was inappropriate to select a lawyer for this position. Mutambara stuck to his guns over a few days of haggling and Mugabe eventually relented. I was to become a minister in a cabinet led by Mugabe. I received the news with mixed emotions. The thought of working with a group of people responsible for so much suffering, some of whom were guilty of crimes against humanity, appalled me. Against this I knew that Zimbabwe faced total collapse and there were no viable – that is, peaceful, non-violent – alternatives at hand. My wife, my church – all the people around me whom I trusted – encouraged me that it was the right thing to do.

CHAPTER 25

DRAWING BACK FROM THE BRINK
FEBRUARY 2009 TO MAY 2010

"If you want to make peace with an enemy, one must work with that enemy and that enemy becomes your partner."
– NELSON MANDELA, *LONG WALK TO FREEDOM*

The swearing in, or rather, as I think more appropriate, the "swearing at", ceremony for the new cabinet by Mugabe was held on Friday, 13 February 2009 at State House, an archetypal colonial building in Harare. It was the first time I had been to State House and I was intrigued to see it had been preserved in all its traditional splendour. Unlike most government buildings of that era, it was immaculately maintained – the lawns were all manicured, the roads pothole free, and the building itself gleamed from a recent coat of white paint.

On arrival, I found a gaggle of my prospective cabinet colleagues from all three parties. I was the only white cabinet minister and there were just five women due to be sworn in. The entire place was crawling with security agents, police and army, and the atmosphere was tense. The ZANU PF members were particularly excited to be there because, unlike prospective cabinet members from the two MDC parties, they had been chosen by Mugabe himself and had only just been advised of their inclusion the previous evening. They knew they were going to be in cabinet, but not what position they would fill. There were several animated discussions among them as to how they would each benefit from Mugabe's largesse. At least one of them was told, on arrival, that actually, he was no longer going to be in the cabinet. One of these unfortunate souls hung around, I suppose hoping that there had been some mistake.

As a result, the ceremony was delayed for nearly three hours because of last-minute in-fighting within ZANU PF to determine which of the 22 top party officials, gathered there for the ceremony, would be formally appointed. ZANU PF was allowed fifteen cabinet posts and the two MDC parties together had sixteen. Mugabe had had difficulty squeezing all the people he wanted to appoint into ZANU PF's allotment. Prospective ministers from both MDC factions refused to be sworn in until the matter had been sorted out. Mugabe, Tsvangirai and Mutambara held a rushed closed-door meeting in the State House dining room with SADC chairman and South African president Kgalema Motlanthe and, as mediator, the now former South African President Mbeki (who had recently been voted out of office by the ANC). Mugabe's chief of protocol, Samuel Kajese, came out at one point and begged us to join Zanu PF MPs in the ceremonial rituals, but we all refused to budge until the three principals had reached a workable solution.

Several marquees had been erected in the gardens in front of State House and we were seated in one adjacent to where Mugabe and visiting dignitaries, including Mbeki, were to be seated. The event finally started but not without further controversy. Without consulting his fellow principals, Mugabe had invited the self-proclaimed Anglican Archbishop Nolbert Kunonga to open the proceedings with a prayer and homily. Kunonga had been excommunicated by the Anglican Church of Zimbabwe and its mother body, the Church of the Province of Central Africa, the previous May for harassment and violence perpetrated against Anglicans. Kunonga had called Mugabe "a prophet from God" and had received a farm from government. At least two of the MPs due to be sworn in, Tendai Biti and Eric Matinenga, had borne the brunt of Kunonga's actions, in that they had been unlawfully and violently prevented from worshipping in their home Anglican church, St Luke's in Harare. Unsurprisingly, both the prayer and homily were decidedly uninspiring.

While waiting for the swearing in ceremony to begin news filtered through that Roy Bennett, who was due to be sworn in as deputy minister of Agriculture, had been arrested while trying to fly out of the country to South Africa. Bennett had been given assurances that he could return to Zimbabwe from exile in South Africa. We were told that the police had acted malevolently by whisking him away and denying him access to his lawyers; indeed it took some time for Bennett to be located and several weeks before he was eventually released on bail. The news cast a pall over the event. It was clear this was a provocation by hardliners, designed to scuttle the inauguration of the cabinet at the last minute. There was a general discussion among many of us. Despite our anger, however, we felt we should not succumb to the schemes of hardliners.

We then all congregated to take the oath of office in front of Chief Justice Chidyausiku, the man who had been responsible for so many curious interpretations of the Zimbabwean Constitution since Gubbay was hounded out of office in 2002. I lined up with several of the men who had threatened us for a decade; some of whom had been behind the murders of friends; others in all likelihood had been involved in the planning of my own arrest and attempted assassination. After taking the oath verbally, each one of us went up to sign the oath before Mugabe, in the presence of presidents Motlanthe and Mbeki. It was the first time since the 1980s that I had met Mugabe. He was very tense as I came up – a photograph taken of the moment shows him glowering as I signed the oath. When I was offered a pen with which to sign I declined, joking that I would use mine as I only trusted my own ink. Mugabe didn't appreciate the humour and gruffly shook my hand before I moved off.

After we had all been sworn in, Mugabe retired to his office and each of us, in no apparent order, was summoned individually to see him. When my turn came, I was ushered into a huge office with a red carpet and high ceilings, rather like a naughty schoolboy before a headmaster. Mugabe was sitting behind a large teak desk with vice-presidents Joice Mujuru and Joseph Msika to his left. To Mugabe's far left, stretched out on a chaise longue, was his wife Grace Mugabe, listening intently to the proceedings. The atmosphere was very tense but Mugabe attempted to break it by saying, "Ah, Mr Coltart – welcome. I see that you have decided to exchange *mens rea* for the three R's" as he pushed my letter of appointment across the desk. It was a witty crack, *mens rea* being the Latin term used in Roman Dutch law to describe criminal intent and the three Rs refer to education – reading, (w)riting and (a)rithmetic. I laughed in agreement and he then began a rambling exposition on the state of education in Zimbabwe. His opening comment, that the education sector was in "some difficulty", was a ludicrous understatement. Prior to my appointment, I had arranged a series of briefings from respected educationalists who told me that the sector was in a severe crisis. In fact most schools had not even opened at the start of the school year in January and tens of thousands of teachers were on strike.

When he had finished I reminded Mugabe of the telegram he had sent me eighteen years before in 1981, particularly the last sentence – namely that "in returning to Zimbabwe I had nothing to fear but fear itself". I said: "Mr President, I took you at your word and returned. I am now here to work in the national interest to restore excellence to education. Whatever has passed before between us should not be allowed to distract us from our joint task to act in the best interests of Zimbabwean children." On that relatively benign note, the meeting ended. The only surprise was contained in my letter of appointment; all along I had been told I would be allocated Education and that was what I had been preparing for. Mugabe's letter to me advised that I was to be minister of Education, Sport, Arts and Culture. Although it meant more work, I was pleased about the additions.

After the swearing in ceremony I returned home to Bulawayo for the weekend to tidy up my affairs. I had been uncertain whether I would ever be sworn in, so I had to make last-minute arrangements with my law firm to hand over work. After 26 years in the firm my partners had agreed to give me indefinite leave of absence, without pay, to serve the nation. I flew back to Harare on Tuesday, 17 February, wondering what I would find.

The permanent secretary for Education, Dr Stephen Mahere, collected me from the airport. He, rather like Mugabe, underplayed the crisis in education during our drive into the city. However, from the first moment I walked into the headquarters of the ministry in Ambassador House, an eighteen-storey building in the centre of Harare, it was apparent that a catastrophe awaited me. The ground floor had a long passageway which led to the reception and the stair (and lift) well; as we walked down the passageway, it became steadily darker; at the end the stairwell we found ourselves in near total darkness. Through the gloom I could see several well-dressed female civil servants waiting for the only working lift, with buckets of water balanced on their heads, in the style typical of rural women who walk kilometres each day to get water for cooking and cleaning. I asked Dr Mahere what this was about. He told me the building had been without water for about eighteen months and the women had to carry water up to their offices to make tea and flush the toilets. We waited a bit but after a while it became apparent that the remaining "working" lift had failed too. The only way up to my ministerial office on the fourteenth floor was to walk up the stairs. Being reasonably fit, the climb wasn't that much of a challenge – what was, though, was the gagging stench: none of the toilets, which were off the stairwell on each floor, had been flushed in weeks. The entire walk up was rather like wading through a sewage pond.

When I got to my office, the thing that struck me first was that there was no internet; indeed not even a computer. I asked about this and was informed that my predecessor had not been computer literate so there'd been no need for the internet. Within minutes of being ushered into that office, the ministry's Transport manager came rushing in, somewhat breathless, to inform me that I needed to get down quickly to the government Transport office to collect my brand new white Mercedes Benz, which the ministry had reserved for me.

At this time I was aware that there were some 90 000 teachers on strike because they hadn't been paid for months. Nearly every government and local council school – 8 000 of them – was closed, and those that were functioning had hardly any textbooks. And there was no money to remedy the situation. Because of this I felt it would send all the wrong messages to the teachers' unions if my first act as Education minister was to secure a luxury Mercedes Benz limousine. So I declined the offer. In addition I didn't want to face the wrath of my old friend Paul Themba Nyathi; we had entered into a mutual pact prior to the 2000 election never to drive a Mercedes Benz if we ever got into office. While neither of us disliked the marque per se, in Zimbabwe it had become synonymous with ZANU PF's profligacy, and we did not want to be associated with that. When Tsvangirai heard about our pact he told us that we were being presumptuous thinking either of us would ever make it to cabinet in any event! I later decided to use a Nissan Pathfinder 4x4, which was far better suited for driving to schools through the country, especially seeing that 70 per cent of them were in the rural areas.

My inaugural week was a blur of meetings. The first was cabinet which met in the Munhumutapa Building adjacent to Ambassador House. The portion of Munhumutapa Building where cabinet meets is one of the oldest buildings in Zimbabwe, a two-storey colonial complex which also houses the president's and vice-presidents' offices and, before the advent of the presidency, successive prime ministers' offices. I arrived that first morning, on Tuesday, 17 February, just before 9 am to get accustomed to my surroundings. I used a side entrance for ministers, where I was thoroughly searched with metal detectors, a routine which continued for the duration of the Government of National Unity (GNU). No cell phones, tablets or laptops were allowed into the meeting. As I trudged up the stairs to the cabinet room past the president's office I thought of all the decisions that had been taken in that building during my lifetime: the decision to remove Todd as prime minister just after I was born in 1958, the decision Smith had made to declare UDI, the meetings to confront the guerrilla onslaught in the 1970s, the planning of Gukurahundi, Murambatsvina and everything else that had befallen Zimbabwe since 1980.

Cabinet meets in a large, almost square room with a single entrance on its northern aspect. The western and eastern walls have windows; the southern wall is blank, wholly covered by an enormous gold curtain, with a portrait of Mugabe as its centrepiece. The room was dominated by a huge single oval ribbon-table which ran, two metres wide, around the entire room, with a massive carpeted area forming no man's land in the middle. A small, separate table occupied the centre of no man's land. This, I came to discover, was always bedecked with a beautiful flower arrangement.

The cabinet room had pre-assigned seats with our names. Mugabe's was in the centre at the southern end, flanked by Mujuru, Msika (the two ZANU PF vice-presidents), Tsvangirai, Mutambara and Khupe (the two deputy prime ministers) to his right, and Dr Mischek Sibanda (chief secretary to cabinet) and Johannes Tomana (the attorney general) to his left. The rest of us were spread somewhat randomly around the rest of the table, although there did appear to be some attempt to put the more senior ministers closer to Mugabe. My seat was on the western flank in the third of the room closer to Mugabe, my immediate neighbours being Foreign minister Mumbengegwi to my left, and minister of Tertiary Education Mudenge to my right. An eclectic bunch of political heavyweights sat to my right, between where I sat and Mugabe, including, two down from me, Defence minister Mnangagwa, Finance minister Biti, State Security minister Sekeramayi and Justice minister Chinamasa. My MDC-M colleagues, Mutambara, Ncube and Misihairabwi-Mushonga, were nowhere close; they were all seated opposite me on the eastern flank of the table.

Mugabe arrived promptly at 9 am, and, as proved to be his custom, moved around the western flank of the table to his chair, shaking the hands of each minister, and having short chats with many, cracking jokes with some, on his way. He shook my hand solemnly, greeting me tersely "Mr Coltart", the term he would use throughout the GNU. I replied, "Good morning, Mr President", which, although correct and respectful, no doubt jarred because he was used to being called "Comrade President". It was the first time I had stood next to him (on both occasions at the swearing in ceremony he had been seated) and I was struck by how short and frail he seemed. However, from the very first day it was clear that ZANU PF ministers were in awe of him. Aside from reverently referring to him always as "H.E." (His Excellency), they were painfully obsequious.

Having taken his seat, Mugabe made some conciliatory remarks about the challenges facing the country and the need for us all to work together. All the same that first meeting was tense, stilted and short – but it was functional and I came away thinking that there was a chance that we could make the GNU work. Although I was uncomfortable being in a room with so many who had caused so much harm, from the outset I was aware that there were a range of people from all parties who appeared to want the GNU to succeed. In one sense, I stood out in the room, being the only white person, but aside from a few who would routinely issue subtle reminders of my colour, I quickly came to understand that battle lines would be drawn on principle, not race.

That afternoon I had my first detailed briefing by senior management regarding the state of education. A shocking, depressing picture was painted. Relations between the ministry and the teachers' trade unions had broken down completely. One immediate crisis was that the public O and A level examinations written the previous November had not been marked yet and there was no money to pay the markers. There had only been a total of 27 teaching days during the whole of 2008; 20 000 teachers had left service, most of them because they couldn't survive the hyper-inflationary environment – by the time their pay arrived at month end it was worthless. When I asked for accurate data, I was told that the ministry's data collection system had broken down and that there was no data available since 2006. I asked for handover notes from the previous minister only to be told that there was nothing. Indeed when I started going through the various files I discovered that all the previous correspondence and other papers were unavailable. In short, the education system was close to collapse. There was also a palpable sense of fear among the senior civil servants; that I was an unknown quantity would have contributed to this, but it was also apparent that they were paralysed by a rigid, uncompromising system.

In a bid to encourage them I reinforced three points: that their job was to facilitate, not obstruct; that the ministry of Education, Sport, Arts and Culture should be the least partisan of all ministries; and that my door would always be open and they were not to call me "Honourable" – plain Minister Coltart, or Senator, would do just fine.

My first task in the ministry, though, was to address our own working conditions. I contacted an engineer friend and asked him to investigate why there was no water in our headquarters building. It turned out that a US$800 sump pump, which pumped water up to storage tanks at the top of the high-rise building, had failed. As I knew Biti had no money, I looked elsewhere for assistance. The Australian ambassador responded positively to my request for help and within a few weeks water was flowing throughout the building and the stench had gone, along with the need for water buckets. The same generous Australian grant also, in time, got all our lifts working and the entire building habitable again.

My top priority was to persuade teachers to return so that we could at least open schools. That afternoon I met with Biti to explore what capacity government had to pay teachers. Shortly before the formation of the GNU, Mugabe's interim Finance minister, Chinamasa, had finally accepted the reality that the Zimbabwe dollar had died by legalising the use of foreign currency, particularly the use of the US$. Although for months foreign currency had been used openly for business transactions, this was done in defiance of stringent laws that outlawed this. The Reserve Bank no longer had the capacity to print banknotes which were worth less than the paper they were printed on. Biti's headache inheriting this mess was that he had little currency with which to pay salaries, so I found small comfort in his office. Biti's eminently sensible solution was to order that all civil servants, be they sweepers or ministers, should receive a salary of US$100 per month until the coffers had filled a bit.

The next day I met with the two biggest teacher unions, the Zimbabwe Teachers' Association (ZIMTA) and the Progressive Teachers' Union of Zimbabwe (PTUZ), to explain the crisis and what Biti was proposing to do. We desperately needed to get teachers back in schools but I was frank with them – there would be little money in the short term and their work would have to be for the love of children. My door would always be open and my cell phone on, as this was a crisis we could only resolve together. On Monday, 23 February, I met with UNICEF country representative, Roeland Monasch, and secured his commitment to mobilise international stop-gap funding. This was followed by a series of meetings that day with trade unions, which culminated in agreements being reached. That evening I held a press conference announcing that trade unions supported a call for teachers to return to schools the following Monday. I would declare an amnesty for all teachers who had left their posts for "political or economic reasons"[666] between January 2007 and March 2009. And the next two school terms would start a week earlier to enable children to catch up.

True to their word the unions mobilised their members and a week later schools opened across the country. Aside from the 90 000 teachers who returned to work, a further 20 000 teachers had left Zimbabwe since 2007. The amnesty worked and in the course of the next few years some 15 000 teachers were attracted back into service. This happened despite the best efforts of certain apparatchiks who did their best to frustrate the amnesty by placing a series of bureaucratic obstacles in the way of teachers trying to return. In the 2008 election teachers had been targeted by ZANU PF supporters throughout the country as they were viewed collectively as MDC supporters; that attitude towards them had not changed and most returning teachers were viewed with suspicion by some.

A few days after taking office, former ZANU PF minister of Education, Fay Chung, came to see me with the suggestion that I activate a little known clause in the Education Act which allowed the minister to appoint a National Education Advisory Board (NEAB). I leapt at the opportunity. While I had told my senior staff that what I knew about education was limited and that I would need their professional advice at every turn, I feared that some of my senior staff were either so fearful or so partisan that I would need a more objective source of guidance, which NEAB provided. Within days I appointed a wide spectrum of educationalists. Among them were my friend and LRF colleague Mary Ndlovu, the head of the body governing private schools, the Association of Trust Schools (ATS), Neil Todd, and Chung herself, to sit on NEAB. I appointed a former permanent secretary of Education and former cabinet secretary Dr Isaiah Sibanda as chair. NEAB proved to be an invaluable source of wisdom during my entire tenure.

Tragedy struck on the first Friday of March in a manner that threatened the livelihood of the GNU. Tsvangirai's wife Susan was killed in a road accident, which also injured Tsvangirai himself, while driving to their rural home in Buhera. Given that so many political leaders from Tongogara to Malunga had died in suspicious circumstances, when I received the news my first thought was that foul play was at work. In the immediate aftermath conspiracy theories abounded, but as the dust settled it appeared that this had in fact been an unfortunate accident. Tsvangirai and his entourage had been travelling south towards Masvingo when a truck, travelling north, had veered into their path, sideswiping Tsvangirai's vehicle, which in turn caused it to overturn. The truck driver claimed that he had hit a bump in the road which made him lose control of the vehicle. I frequently drove the road where the accident occurred so on my first opportunity I stopped to inspect the scene, which was close to the Ngezi Dam turn-off on the Harare to Masvingo road. The section of road where the accident occurred was in very poor condition and close to the point of impact there was a large bump in the road, consistent with what the driver alleged. The driver himself did not have any political history and appeared genuine. It would have taken intricate planning, and split second timing, to have engineered that the truck reach that particular point at the very moment Tsvangirai's vehicle approached from the opposite direction. For once it seemed that ZANU PF were not to blame but suspicions at the time ran high.

The fledgeling GNU was already under massive strain. Much to both MDCs' dismay Bennett was still in detention in Mutare several weeks after being arrested. We had been told about his conditions, which he later described as "40 days (spent) in unspeakable squalor and filth, surrounded by walking corpses, surreal apparitions of skin and bone, men whose bodies barely clung to their souls".[667] In addition Mugabe was meant to appoint governors to Zimbabwe's ten provinces in accordance with a formula which had been agreed to. For example, Paul Themba Nyathi was meant to be appointed governor of Matabeleland South as the MDC-M's sole governor. Mugabe resisted this, arguing that because sanctions hadn't been lifted by the US and the EU he was not obliged to comply with that side of the bargain. In addition, during the hiatus between the signing of the GPA in September 2008 and the formation of the GNU in February, Mugabe had unilaterally re-appointed Gono as Reserve Bank governor and Tomana as attorney general, in breach of the GPA terms, which stated that he should do so in consultation with Tsvangirai. At an extraordinary meeting of SADC heads of state held in Pretoria on 26 January it was agreed that these "appointments would be dealt with by the inclusive government after its formation",[668] which hadn't happened.

Aside from these political tensions the pressure mounting on me was considerable. The biggest immediate headache was that O and A level public examination papers, written the previous year, remained unmarked. UNICEF came to our rescue by providing us with emergency funding to pay for markers and by mid March I was able to report that "80% of the papers had been marked".[669] Thousands of children waiting for O level results were still waiting at home, though, so I made the decision to allow them back into schools to start the new year based on their mock results, if not their actual final marks. I was plagued by the realisation that if we didn't maintain teacher morale and provide them with teaching materials, the quality of education would continue to plummet. Further meetings I arranged between trade union leaders and Biti demonstrated that government would not be able to pay anything more than their US$100 per month salary. I could empathise with union leaders because my sole income at the time from government was also US$100. My law firm wasn't paying me anything because I was on extended leave without pay; indeed without the gifts of one particular Bulawayo friend, who supplemented my income at that time, I would not have been able to continue in government. At this juncture I latched onto a policy which had been implemented at the height of hyper-inflation. My predecessor had allowed parents to pay teachers "incentives" to keep them in the classroom. In rural schools teachers were particularly hard hit because by the time they got their salaries they were worthless; the only way to keep teachers was to provide them with food and other incentives. I announced that incentives would continue to enable parents to supplement the meagre salaries teachers received. Although this move wasn't popular with everybody, the vast majority of parents responded positively.

While the payment of incentives secured the attendance of teachers, I was unable to address the acute shortage of teaching materials. Preliminary surveys done by both ministry staff and NEAB illustrated the crisis: on average there was only one textbook available for every fifteen children. In many rural schools the only textbook was the one used by the teacher. Without textbooks children struggled to learn, no matter how good their teacher was. Armed with this information I turned once more to the donor community. April and May was dominated by a series of meetings with ambassadors, UNICEF, UNESCO and others, in which I explained the crisis in education. I argued that if the problem was not addressed, an entire generation of children would have a deficient education, with dire consequences for the country and region. Zimbabwe had been an educational powerhouse; our schools had in the past produced top students, but this ability was now under serious threat. Given that most Western ambassadors were sceptical about the GPA and concerned about ZANU PF's control of the civil service, it was a tough sell. Although they were sympathetic to the plight of children, they needed encouragement that money donated would actually go to children, not into some corrupt politician's bank account. Following these meetings a plan evolved that would ensure that funding would go to the intended beneficiaries – a fund would be set up and administered by UNICEF, but chaired by me. Donors would be consulted in all decisions taken by the ministry regarding our funding priorities and methods. I had to strike a delicate balance between respecting the right of donors to ensure that their money was well spent, and the need for educationalists within the ministry to determine what our funding needs were.

It was difficult to keep body and soul together at this time. Apart from my primary responsibility to restore education for over three million Zimbabwean schoolchildren, other pressures were mounting. The MDC-M had appointed me as co-chair of the Constitution Parliamentary Select Committee (COPAC) which had begun its work to reform Zimbabwe's constitution, one of the principal objectives of the GPA. In addition the Sport, Arts and Culture components of the ministry required attention. The former was an aspect of the job I relished as I have always been a keen sportsman, but the resuscitation of sport soon proved as difficult as funding education.

One of my first tasks as minister was to secure funding to enable our national football team to travel to meet a FIFA commitment. Within a few weeks of taking office I turned my attention to one of my passions, cricket, which was in the doldrums. The Zimbabwe Cricket Board had been audited in 2007 by the ICC following allegations of corruption but the audit report had never been made public. In addition, the CEO of the ICC, Malcolm Speed, had allegedly been put on paid leave until his contract ran out in 2008 after a serious falling out with Ray Mali, the ICC president, following the ICC executive's decision not to take any major action against Zimbabwe Cricket, which further fuelled my suspicions. I called for the audit report which, although unsatisfactory, did not provide me with sufficient evidence to act against the board. I would have to work with the existing board. I called a truce and commenced a process of trying to help them restore links with Test playing nations.

Partly because of my love of cricket and partly because of its symbolic significance, I was convinced of the need to get Zimbabwe's Test status back. Historically, Zimbabwe had always punched well above its weight and was just one of nine Test playing nations in the world. However, in the aftermath of the Flower/Olonga episode, cricket had fallen apart. Aside from the loss of these iconic players, ZANU PF-connected administrators had turned on the remaining white players, making conditions so unpleasant for them that most of them left Zimbabwe. By 2005 the team was a shadow of its former self. Although the remaining talented young, predominantly black players tried hard, without the experience of the older white players, the team started losing heavily, and embarrassingly. Our play got so bad that Zimbabwe Cricket had unilaterally withdrawn from playing Test matches in 2005. Having received assurances from the Zimbabwe Cricket Board that teams would be elected on merit and their finances properly managed, I agreed to lobby the international community to get Test teams touring Zimbabwe again. My first effort at this happened on 17 June 2009, when I met with the MCC and Andy Flower, who was then England's coach, in London to persuade England to restore ties. It was the beginning of a sustained effort which bore mixed results.

Clouding all these efforts at this particular time was the knowledge that my mother was seriously ill. She had been diagnosed and treated for breast cancer several years before; I thought she had been cured, but late in 2008 we learnt that the cancer had metastasised and in June she started to deteriorate. In early July I flew to her hospital bedside in Port Elizabeth; the advice from doctors was grim and my mother and I made a decision to return home to Zimbabwe together. She had always been plucky but she excelled beyond her own high standards in her last few days. Dressed exquisitely, she stoically flew back to Bulawayo with me on 6 July. All our children bar one were at home and we spent a precious final few days together before she died. Bulawayo's crematorium was unserviceable, having also suffered the ravages of hyper-inflation, so we decided to bury her at Shalom in the Matopos in the shade of a kopje overlooking Silozwe mountain. As the few close friends and family helped me lower the coffin into the grave we heard the beautiful haunting cry of a fish eagle patrolling the nearby Maleme River. In my mind, it was the good Lord's reminder to me of my mother's character – a beautiful, graceful person with a steely spirit.

Inevitably, most of my time continued to be absorbed by the education sector. In early September the new country representative of UNICEF, Dr Peter Salama, reported that there was sufficient donor support to launch the Education Transition Fund (ETF). We agreed on this name to emphasise that it was designed as a short-term stabilisation strategy rather than a long-term funding channel. In my speech at the ETF launch on 14 September I said that the ETF was to assist the ministry meet the first of three short-term policy objectives, which were:

1. to restore a basic level of education urgently for as many Zimbabwean schoolchildren as possible;
2. to devise and implement a scheme to ensure that disadvantaged talented children were identified and nurtured so that their talents were not lost to the nation;
3. to allow non-government schools to operate without any hindrance.[670]

Our primary objective was to "produce several million textbooks" which would involve local publishers and printers in a "national emergency effort". I spoke of meetings with these companies in which I had stressed this wasn't "an opportunity for companies to make windfall profits".[671] This was to become a vexing issue in the months that followed.

Cabinet and the council of ministers' meetings at this time resembled the early rounds of a boxing match when boxers tentatively jab at each other but do not try knock-out blows. All the MDC ministers were new in their posts and we were finding our feet in a hostile environment. While there were some heated debates in cabinet, most issues were skirted around, making it difficult to get anything done. Within my own ministry, I found many colleagues who wanted to assist me but were too scared to give me open support. In addition, bureaucratic wheels turned slowly, frustrating my reform efforts. One example of this was the problem I faced appointing a new board for the Sports and Recreation Commission (SRC). The old board's tenure had lapsed and in terms of the SRC Act I was empowered to appoint a new board, in consultation with the president. Having got the consent of new prospective board members, I wrote in August to Mugabe seeking his consent but the issue got bogged down in his office. Not wanting to raise the matter in cabinet, I requested a private meeting with Mugabe on 20 October, which he agreed to. When I was ushered into his office, alone in the same office Todd, Smith and others had used, he asked me matter of factly whether the meeting was "private or business". On being told it was "business" a secretary was called to take minutes. I started by explaining my short-term educational goals, summarising what I had said at the ETF launch. Then I elaborated on my proposal to establish special academies for talented disadvantaged children and said I believed that we needed to allow private schools to operate freely. I was concerned about the number of academically, athletically or artistically talented poor children who were dropping out of school. We had old former white boarding schools, with magnificent, but run-down facilities which I wanted to rehabilitate into centres of excellence for these talented children. Regarding private schools, some ZANU PF ministers had recently spoken disparagingly about them in cabinet; I argued that they should be left alone as they were doing an excellent job. Our goal should be to bring government schools up to the standards of private schools, not vice versa. After some discussion, Mugabe said he supported the idea of academies and acknowledged the constructive role that private schools played in the country. I then turned to my main reason for meeting: the SRC board. Mugabe seemed surprised when I told him that I could not appoint the board because his office had taken over two months to respond to my letter. He called a senior secretary in and ordered him to investigate. I had thought that the delay was political – and had something to do with the fact that I had nominated an outspoken former president of the Law Society, Joseph James, as chairman of the board and had wondered whether Mugabe was unhappy with this. However, there was no sign of any displeasure and as things turned out, a few days later I received a letter from Mugabe agreeing to the entire board I had proposed.

With the official business dispensed with, Mugabe showed no

inclination to end the meeting so I seized the opportunity to address two further issues not related to my ministry. Firstly, I spoke about Bennett. Mugabe had steadfastly refused to swear Bennett in as deputy minister of Agriculture. Although Bennett was out on bail, charges were also still pending against him. Expressing concern about Bennett's treatment, I told Mugabe that he was someone "who loved Zimbabwe deeply" and the portrayal of him as a racist was a caricature. I said to Mugabe that no matter what had happened in the past it was time for the "Nation to move ahead".[672] Mugabe didn't respond; he just listened from his side of the desk. I then moved to the issue of whites and land in general and explained how the issue was hindering my efforts to raise funding for education. I had recently held meetings with the French and Finnish governments, both of which had raised the issue. I told Mugabe that the unrelenting drive to force whites off all rural land was perceived as ethnic cleansing, not only by the British and Americans, but also by governments which the state media had portrayed as sympathetic to ZANU PF. This angered Mugabe and he launched into a lecture on the history of land. Not wanting the meeting to degenerate, I reminded him of his 1981 telegram when he had inspired me with his vision of a "multi racial, democratic society". There were many white Zimbabweans, I told him, who had a deep knowledge of, and passion for Zimbabwe but who had been left without even a few hundred hectares to farm. While I recognised that Zimbabwe couldn't go back to the inequitable land holdings which existed pre 2000, I urged that there should be no further racial discrimination in the allocation of land. My mention of the telegram and his original vision appeared to calm him down, because Mugabe quietly listened to the remainder of what I had to say and the meeting ended on a cordial note. Aside from securing Mugabe's agreement for the new SRC board, the meeting achieved nothing tangible. However, the ice between us was broken and, surprisingly, from that moment on Mugabe started supporting me on educational issues, if little else.

Prior to meeting with Mugabe, I had met with Tsvangirai and Mutambara, the other two GPA principals, to get their buy-in for my short-term education policies. With Mugabe on board I felt more confident to press ahead with my plans. The following week, on 28 October, I launched "Teach Zimbabwe", a new NGO headed by Guyanese-born Kojo Parris, who was a Cambridge-educated banker. Teach Zimbabwe would spearhead the academies project, which was to be a public/private initiative. I met with Neil Todd, the CEO of the Association of Trust Schools and told him that so long as private schools did not become islands of privilege, I would give them a free hand. My main focus, however, was the textbook programme. Our fundraising efforts had been successful and $70 million had already been pledged to the ETF by Australia, Denmark, Finland, Germany, Netherlands, Norway, New Zealand, Sweden, the United Kingdom, and the European Commission on behalf of the European Union. I found that certain countries were exceptionally receptive – in one short meeting alone in Finland, on 28 September 2009, I had raised $7 million. With the money secured, UNICEF director Peter Salama and I intensified our efforts to secure reasonable deals with the three main Zimbabwean educational publishing companies.

Regrettably, despite my calls made at the launch of the ETF that the textbook programme should not be seen as an opportunity to make windfall profits, it became clear that these companies had formed a cartel. From an educational perspective, our ideal was to purchase replacement textbooks from all three publishers to meet the individual preferences of schools and teachers. Try as we might to get them to lower their prices, we failed and we faced the prospect of the three companies making windfall profits of approximately $10 million, solely for the primary school phase of the programme. I was left with no option but to authorise Salama to arrange an international commercial tender for the primary school textbooks. Instead of buying textbooks from all three publishing houses, the ETF would grant a contract to the publishing house that submitted the lowest tender. It was controversial because it went against the educational ideal of providing individual schools with their preferences, but I felt I had no choice. The second phase of the programme, to provide secondary textbooks as well, was dependent on making every saving possible in the first phase. The decision taken, UNICEF went ahead with an international tender, which was eventually adjudicated in Copenhagen in January 2010 and awarded to Longmans Zimbabwe. The contract for some 13 million textbooks, which brought down the average price of a primary school textbook from $5 per copy to $0.70, was to be used as a stick to my back in the months that lay ahead.

As 2009 drew to a close, the GNU remained on shaky ground, with some 27 outstanding problems to be dealt with, including Mugabe's continued refusal to swear in Bennett, and sanctions. The prospect of

another election at some unspecified point in future had led to continued
tensions and grandstanding between the two dominant MDC-T and
ZANU PF parties. In late October 2009 the MDC-T decided temporarily
to withdraw from parts of the inclusive government because "outstanding,
non-compliance and toxic issues continue to impede the inclusive
government".[673] In his statement announcing the withdrawal, Tsvangirai
advised they would "disengage from ZANU PF and in particular from
Cabinet and the Council of Ministers until such time as confidence and
respect (was) restored among us".[674] Although sympathetic towards the
MDC-T, the four of us MDC-M ministers resolved to remain in cabinet
to prevent ZANU PF from acting unilaterally and to keep channels of
communication open. Once again our decision was criticised by many
people, including some from within the MDC-T, who suggested we had
"reacted (to the MDC-T boycott) with glee". I responded by writing that
"cheap political points don't help the nation" and that statements like
those were "false and destructive to the fragile process"[675] we all were
in. As things turned out the MDC-T cabinet boycott only lasted a few
weeks. For all its imperfection, the GNU remained the only reasonable
way ahead. However, 2009 ended with the GNU hanging by a thread.

Aside from the textbook contract, several other key events happened
in the opening months of 2010. Much to my delight, the first post-
independence minister of Education, Dzingai Mutumbuka, had made
contact with me in 2009 to offer whatever assistance he could to resuscitate
the sector. Following his resignation from government, he had taken on
a succession of senior posts in the World Bank. The bank was unable to
fund the Zimbabwean education sector because of Zimbabwe's ongoing
default on its loans. Notwithstanding this, Mutumbuka had used his
influence to encourage the bank to help in whatever way it could. He
found an enthusiastic supporter in another senior World Bank education
specialist, Susan Hirshberg. Their efforts resulted in a key retreat being
held at Leopard Rock resort in the Eastern Highlands in January. Both
were aware of subtle attempts by certain senior civil servants designed
to disrupt and obstruct my work within the ministry. With this in mind
the retreat was designed to build a broad consensus within the ministry
in support of a strategic plan. For the first time we brought together
provincial education directors from throughout the country. I left the
retreat exhilarated: the experience had revealed to me that there was a rich
vein of competence within the ministry. The further down the ladder one

went, it appeared the more non-partisan, committed and professional the civil servants were. Indeed, by the end of the retreat it was apparent that our plans were being held back by a tiny handful of senior civil servants who were determined to put partisanship ahead of children's interests.

A few days after the Leopard Rock retreat I flew to Washington with my MDC-T cabinet colleague and fellow Christian, Eric Matinenga, to attend the annual National Prayer Breakfast. On the sidelines, we met a broad spectrum of American politicians, including senate majority leader Harry Reid and senators Inhofe and Coburn, to lobby for support for the GNU and the removal of sanctions. I also had time to meet the former director of the New York Lawyers Committee for Human Rights, Mike Posner, who had been appointed by President Obama as assistant secretary of state for Human Rights. In all these meetings Matinenga and I argued that while the GPA was flawed and there was no guarantee it would work, it was all we had and it was incumbent on everyone to make it work. While I was under no illusions about the machinations of hardliners within ZANU PF to derail the GNU, I was concerned that the retention of sanctions would assist the hardliners. It was already providing them with a convenient excuse not to comply with key aspects of the GPA such as the appointment of governors. I also felt that the remaining sanctions were past their sell-by date; while they were undoubtedly effective in stigmatising those responsible for gross human rights violations in years gone past, they no longer had any practical impact. The measures seizing assets had been circumvented by wily ZANU PF leaders in any event, who had moved their assets to the Far East years before. Not even the travel bans had much impact because Mugabe, and others who had had travel bans imposed on them, were able to travel wheresoever they chose whenever they were invited by the UN. Our task, however, was hampered by disparate voices within the MDC-T, some of whom were quietly encouraging the Americans and others to retain sanctions, while publicly calling for their removal. Reid and other Democrats gave us polite hearings, but left us in no doubt that the Obama administration would not change its policy. Ironically, the most support we got was from the conservative Republican Senator Inhofe, who responded positively by drafting a new bill designed to repeal the Zimbabwe Democracy and Economic Recovery Act of 2001, which, however, never saw the light of day without Democratic support.

I arrived back into the teeth of a civil servants' strike which had severely disrupted the commencement of the 2010 school year. The strike, which was discussed by cabinet on 23 February, revealed an intriguing side to Mugabe's character. MDC-T minister of the Public Service, Eliphas Mukonoweshuro, presented a report recommending that "stern measures" be taken against the striking workers, including teachers, who formed the overwhelming majority of civil servants. Surprisingly, the ensuing debate had a non-partisan flavour with many MDC-T and ZANU PF supporting Mukonoweshuro's suggestion that legal action be taken to fire people. I found myself in a minority when I ventured that our "primary focus should be on negotiation not law". I asked what we proposed to do – were we going to "fire 90,000 teachers?" The only significant voices in my support came from Finance minister Biti and Industry and Commerce minister Ncube, both of whom were sceptical of what going to court could achieve. It was all going very badly. I was even criticised by Mines minister Obert Mpofu for having the temerity to meet union leaders in the midst of the strike. Everything changed when Mugabe spoke up, having heard the debate rage for about an hour. He didn't speak long but what he said abruptly ended the debate: "I don't like the legal route, we must negotiate," he said. The ZANU PF ministers calling for harsh action were silenced instantly, along with the few MDC-T ministers who had supported the call for harsh action. Although the strike spluttered on for a while longer, we did manage to get teachers back into classrooms. It was also the last sustained strike action during my tenure.

The afternoon following that cabinet meeting, an incident unfolded which well illustrates the schizophrenic nature of the GNU. Several months before I had entered into discussions with Zimbabwean Olympic swimming star Kirsty Coventry and the Australian embassy about the supply of several thousand small plastic "lapdesks" for rural schools. The conventional wooden desks in many schools were not reparable and we couldn't afford to replace them. The innovative "lapdesks", which were colourfully inscribed with the alphabet, numeric table and other teaching aids, provided a superb stop-gap. Coventry had lent her name to the exercise, which made the lapdesks instantly attractive to young children. The launch of the distribution exercise, which involved Coventry and the Australian ambassador John Courtney, had been planned weeks before. It was to be held on 24 February at Blackfordby Primary School just outside the municipal boundaries in Harare South constituency. Within minutes of my arrival back in my office from cabinet on 23 February 2010, I received a call from the ZANU PF MP for Harare South, Hubert Nyanhongo. Nyanhongo peremptorily informed me that he was unhappy with the chosen venue which, he said, should be changed to a school of his choosing. As politely as possible I told Nyanhongo that the choice of venue was the ministry's prerogative and that in any event it was too late to change the venue because fliers and other materials had already been produced, advertising Blackfordby School. Nyanhongo was most displeased and threatened that there "would be consequences". I was in no mood to be coerced so, having warned the permanent secretary, Dr Mahere, Coventry and Courtney, we proceeded with our plans for the next day. Blackfordby School, although close to Harare, has the air of a rural school, set as it is among maize and tobacco fields. We arrived the next morning through forests of maturing maize which opened up into the school grounds which had been festively decorated by the children for the grand occasion. The event started on time and developed into a typically joyous Zimbabwean school experience, with lusty renditions of the national anthem, songs and dances. The handover of the lapdesks had just been completed when we heard the sound of men, aggressively singing revolutionary songs, marching towards the school through the maize fields. Having warned the headmaster of the threat, we all braced ourselves for what was to follow. Sure enough a crowd of about 30 young men emerged from the maize field toyi-toying, but as they reached the open playing fields they stopped. Their singing quickly evaporated. All I can presume is that they saw the happy scene of young children, teachers and parents in front of them, which embarrassed them sufficiently to ignore the orders of their Honourable MP. They turned tail and disappeared into the maize again. On our way out later we passed them at a local beerhall. I made sure to give them a vigorous wave.

As the first anniversary of the GNU passed, cabinet had begun to find a rhythm. Although certain issues still raised temperatures, most meetings passed with constructive debate, if not much action. Almost every meeting started with Agriculture minister Made's report on crop and food assessments, which in turn gave me the opportunity to promote conservation agriculture whenever I could. On 13 April 2010, Made reported that there had been a dramatic decline in crop yields the previous season, with communal lands only achieving an average of 0.7 tonnes per hectare and even commercial farms achieving only 2.4 tonnes.

Although I was not a farmer, I was aware of "the ten tonne club" citation among commercial farmers and that conservation farming methods were achieving three-tonne yields on non-irrigated crops grown in communal areas. On this occasion I spoke again about the need for government to embrace conservation/zero-tillage farming methods and was interested when my comments received the support of Vice-President Mujuru. She told the meeting that some people in her constituency had adopted the techniques with astonishing results. In the same meeting I spoke about the growing menace of veld fires, deliberately started, that were destroying thousands of square kilometres of farmland every year. Even Mugabe joined in condemning the practice. But, as I recorded in my diary, "the debate just died, with no resolutions made!"[676] This became typical of cabinet; there were many fine debates, with fine statements of intent, but there it would end. We would simply move to another topic without any resolutions passed, and no actions required of the responsible minister.

At least cabinet started punctually and met unfailingly nearly every Tuesday. Sadly, the same could not be said for the council of ministers meetings set for Thursdays, which were frequently cancelled or didn't start on time. Whereas ministers made sure they attended cabinet, ministers from all parties started to treat council meetings casually, in the process diminishing council's gravitas. Given that council was such a critical component of the GPA, I didn't understand why the office of the prime minister was not fully exploiting the opportunities provided by this body. It seemed to me a year into the GNU that many other priorities were misplaced. The size of the prime minister's cavalcade was still being debated as an "outstanding issue". MDC ministers had taken delivery of Mercedes Benz vehicles, making them indistinguishable in the eyes of the electorate from their ZANU PF counterparts.

Around this time a further practice commenced which demonstrated how MDC ministers were being slowly assimilated by ZANU PF's political culture. One morning I arrived at Bulawayo airport for my flight to Harare and boarded the bus with the rest of the passengers to get from the terminal to the aircraft. I noticed a swanky new vehicle parked on the apron outside the terminal and saw that it followed our bus, arriving at the steps of the aircraft once we had all taken our seats in the aircraft. Out stepped MDC-T Deputy Prime Minister Khupe who then boarded the aircraft with two aides in tow. As we all buckled up, the flight attendant commenced her safety instructions by greeting the "Honourable Deputy Prime Minister Thokozani Khupe", repeating the prelude every time she addressed us for the remainder of the flight. These were long-standing ZANU PF practices which I thought were the antithesis of servant leadership. While this happened in the confines of an aircraft, in my mind it was emblematic of a deeper malaise – that of becoming comfortable with the trappings of office. In fairness to Khupe, she was not alone. The other deputy prime minister, the MDC-M's Mutambara, allowed similar fawning conduct. Indeed all of us MDC ministers, from both parties, must have appeared equally comfortable with the trappings of office.

When the MDC was formed in 1999 our slogan was "*Chinja maitiro, guqula izenzo*" ("change your deeds"). I feared in the eyes of the electorate it would appear as if the only things that were changing were the people in charge, not the deeds.

In late April 2010 tragedy struck the MDC which in turn was the catalyst of a major personal trial – the mauling of our then eight-year-old daughter Bethany by a lioness. Founder MDC member Renson Gasela, who had been tried for treason with Tsvangirai and Ncube in 2002/2003, was killed with two other MDC members when the vehicle in which he was travelling rammed into a front-end loader, which had been parked at night without warning lights on the Zvishavane to Gweru road. In anticipation of Gasela's funeral, which was due to take place in Gweru on Saturday, 1 May, Jenny and I, together with our children Scott and Bethany, decided to spend the previous night at Andy Conolly's Antelope Park game reserve on the outskirts of Gweru. Conolly's homestead at Antelope Park is surrounded by cages that house lions that are part of a breeding programme. While we were having breakfast with Conolly, before going to Gasela's funeral, one of his relatives (a young man in his mid twenties) offered to take Scott and Bethany on a game drive. Having warned Bethany the previous evening of the need to stay well clear of the lion cages and knowing that her elder brother Scott (then aged 16) was with her, we agreed. No sooner had they walked off, though, than I had an uncanny sense that something was wrong and so I got up from the breakfast table to follow them out. When I got to the parking area at the back of the house, I realised that Scott had not gone with Bethany after all. He told me that the young man had taken Bethany on a motorcycle, preventing him from being able to accompany her.

No sooner had I received this information than I heard a bloodcurdling scream coming from an area north of the homestead, blocked from my vision by buildings. Scott and I sprinted around about 150 metres to be confronted by the horrifying sight of Bethany pinned up against the fence of a lion enclosure with her right arm through the fence in the mouth of a massive nine-year-old lioness. Conolly's relative was vainly holding onto Bethany, shouting hysterically, while a second lioness was trying to grab my daughter's left leg through the fence. I moved in, placing my arms around Bethany and using my leg to pull her leg away from the clutches of the second lion, which had snagged her boot with a claw. Bethany's face was pressed against the fence, with her left arm engulfed by the lioness which, thankfully, had simply locked her jaws around her arm and wasn't chewing or pulling at it. In fact the lioness seemed at a loss as to what to do next; she looked unflinchingly at me with piercing golden yellow eyes as I shouted at her. I then tried to shove my hand through the fence to poke her eyes, but the gauge was too small and I couldn't get my hand through. Scott, who had been standing next to me, saw the helplessness of our situation and he ran back to the house to call Conolly, who arrived shortly afterwards, armed with a pistol. Instantly realising that there was no other way to get the lioness to release her grip, he shot through the fence at her lower abdomen. Thankfully, the lioness let go of Bethany's arm and ran away. Her final bite had severed Bethany's humerus and her right arm dangled limply through the fence. I gingerly pulled my child's shattered arm back through the fence, took her in my arms and ran back to the homestead, with blood pouring out onto my shirt. Bethany quietly whimpered that she never wanted to scratch a lion again.

After stabilising her in Gweru, we arranged to casevac Bethany to Harare, but there was one last hitch. The only airport we could use was Thornhill airbase, where the South Africans had destroyed most of Zimbabwe's air force back in 1982, and permission had to be obtained for a medical rescue service aircraft to land there. It seemed to take an eternity to get permission, but when it came through we drove to Thornhill, which was almost derelict. There was little sign of any air force activity there and not a single air force plane on the tarmac. The elephant grass surrounding the runway had not been cut, which almost brought all our lives to a premature end. As the twin Beechcraft King Air plane reached V2 and the co-pilot called "rotate", two huge grey herons flew out of the grass into the path of the aircraft. I was sitting between the pilots on the jump seat and we all instinctively ducked as the birds narrowly missed the wings and propellors.

Bethany received world-class medical attention at St Anne's Hospital in Harare over the next few weeks. She was stabilised within hours of her arrival by a surgical team that included a neurosurgeon who told us how fortunate she had been: the lion's final bite, which broke her humerus, had missed her brachial artery by a few millimetres; although it had severed her radial nerve, the covering sheath was intact. Although Bethany's right arm was partially paralysed, the neurosurgeon was confident that the nerve would grow back. Providentially, a top Zimbabwean orthopaedic surgeon who, because of the economic chaos prior to the GNU, had taken work in Britain, was in the process of relocating to Zimbabwe and flew into Harare the next day. In addition a paediatric anaesthetist also happened to be in Harare that week. Together, in a series of operations, they restored Bethany, who remained partially paralysed for a few months until one Sunday afternoon in August 2010 when we saw a faint flicker of movement in her hand, the first sign that the nerve was repairing itself. Bethany has since recovered fully save for a Harry Potter zig-zag of a scar on her right arm.

In time we were able to work out what had happened that fateful morning. After driving off on the motorcycle, the young man stopped near one of the lion cages and went across to scratch a lioness which was rubbing up against the side of a fence. He encouraged a hesitant Bethany to join him, which she did by scratching the lioness on her side. As quick as a flash the lioness whipped round and grabbed Bethany's index finger, which was protruding through the fence, in her teeth. Having a tooth-hold on the finger, the lioness then used her immense power to pull Bethany's arm in through the fence, first gouging a huge hole in her lower arm before taking the final bite that shattered the humerus. As I later said, the devil had his way for a few seconds when the lion bit, but then the Kingdom took over. I was shaken by the incident, but we were all comforted by the outpouring of sympathy across the political divide. In the first cabinet meeting I attended following the incident, Mugabe took me aside to ask after Bethany. He appeared genuinely concerned about her, which was rather ironic given that operatives under his jurisdiction had done their best to kill me in Bethany's presence seven years earlier.

CHAPTER 26

REACHING OUT
MAY 2010 TO AUGUST 2011

"A new patriotic consciousness has to be developed, not one based simply on the well-worn notion of the unity of Nigeria often touted by our corrupt leaders, but one based on an awareness of the responsibility of leaders to the led."

– CHINUA ACHEBE, *THERE WAS A COUNTRY*[677]

While I was still distracted by Bethany's hospitalisation, one positive development was happening. This was the acquittal of Roy Bennett by the High Court on 10 May 2010. Bennett had originally been charged with treason, but this was changed to "conspiring to acquire arms with a view to disrupting essential services". The trial, which lasted some six months, turned out to be a farce. Attorney General Tomana, who personally prosecuted the matter, failed to produce any tangible evidence against Bennett and on occasions went to extreme lengths in his efforts to link Bennett to a crime. Although Mugabe still flatly refused to swear in Bennett as deputy minister of Agriculture, his acquittal removed a key source of tension in the GNU. This more positive outlook governed our cabinet discussions the day after Bennett's acquittal, when we debated the country's finances and the need to get the Multi Donor Trust Fund (MDTF) up and running. Biti explained that although the MDTF had been established by the World Bank in June 2009, it was not functioning yet. One of the reasons for this was that the GNU was sending out mixed messages to the international community. In continuing to promote its Indigenisation Act ZANU PF was scaring potential investors off because of the act's provision that 51 per cent of all Zimbabwean businesses be owned by indigenous Zimbabweans. In addition, the windfall profits being made in the Chiadzwa and Marange diamond fields were not being adequately accounted for, nor was Treasury receiving the royalties it expected from them. Biti complained that Chiadzwa "would not get the negative attention it was if there was transparency, compliance with law and evidence that the proceeds were going towards Zimbabwe's roads, schools and hospitals".[678]

Biti, Ncube and I all spoke of the need to get our own house in order if we were to secure international support and direct foreign investment. I spoke about the February meeting Minister Matinenga and I had had with Senate majority leader Harry Reid in the US, who had started off our meeting by telling us there was no chance of the Zimbabwe Democracy and Economic Recovery Act (ZDERA) being amended, but changed his tune when Matinenga and I had argued that peace should be given a chance. Biti strongly supported my line by imploring ZANU PF Minister Kasukuwere, who was responsible for the Indigenisation Act, to repeal investment-hostile regulations; he also supported me in suggesting that the attorney general and police, responsible for the recent arrest of human rights activists such as WOZA's Jenni Williams, rather focus on criminals.

By mid 2011 the education sector was in much better fettle: teachers were back teaching, the textbook printing orders were under way and a broad consensus was building around a short- to medium-term development plan. This progress gave me the confidence to focus more time on my other responsibilities, namely Sport, Arts and Culture. In particular, I was still eager to get Zimbabwe Cricket's Test status back, but there had been very little progress since I had met the MCC in London in June 2009. I hoped that David Cameron's new Conservative government might be more amenable to giving the ECB the green light for a resumption of cricketing ties, but discussions with the British embassy revealed that more would have to be done.

Mugabe was a domestic hot potato in the UK, and his role as patron of Zimbabwe Cricket was a major obstacle. Both the Zimbabwe Cricket Board and former Test cricketer friends of mine advised that it would be prudent to first get Test nations' "A" teams to tour, as that would better acclimatise the crop of young Zimbabwean cricketers to the longer form of the game. Having kept in contact with Australian Prime Minister Kevin

Rudd since meeting him in 2008, and aware that he was sympathetic to our need to make the GPA work, I decided to direct my focus towards persuading the Australians to send their "A" team to tour. I also had word that the New Zealanders were more receptive than England. They had cancelled a scheduled tour to Zimbabwe in March 2010 on the grounds of "players' safety", invoking my wrath. Pointing to Nelson Mandela's support of the 1995 Rugby World Cup, which he had used to help stabilise a tense country in transition from apartheid, I argued that a tour would not only help us in our "quest to regain test status (and) bring much joy to the Zimbabwean cricketing public" but would also "help our peaceful transition to democracy".[679] My comments had resonated positively with the New Zealand cricketing public, opening the door for me to meet New Zealand Foreign and Sports minister Murray McCullay in Wellington on 14 June, followed by a meeting with New Zealand Cricket in Christchurch. Both McCullay and New Zealand Cricket's Justin Vaughan were sympathetic, resulting in an agreement that New Zealand would tour. There was an unexpected bonus from that trip when McCullay told me that New Zealand would contribute US$1 million to the Education Transition Fund as well.

From there I travelled to Melbourne and Canberra, where I met Cricket Australia's James Sutherland and the Australian Foreign minister Stephen Smith. Both needed little encouragement to support what we were trying to achieve and gave their full backing to a tour by Australia "A" at the earliest opportunity.

Soon after I returned home, the bad faith and duplicity of some people in the Zimbabwe Cricket Board was exposed. During a stop-over at Sydney airport on my flight back to Zimbabwe, I met former Australian Prime Minister John Howard, who at the time was campaigning for the presidency of the ICC. Although he had support from several Test nations, Zimbabwe held a crucial swing vote, without which he was unlikely to secure the post. Howard had been particularly outspoken against Mugabe in 2002 and had imposed a variety of sanctions against ZANU PF leaders, including travel bans against Zimbabwe Cricket's chairman, Peter Chingoka, and CEO, Ozias Bvute. Needing Zimbabwe's vote, Howard now asked for my support, which I agreed to give him. Aside from my respect for Howard, I thought this would provide a unique way to engender goodwill and bolster our argument for Zimbabwe's Test return – and even go a little way towards the general lifting of sanctions.

In an interview with the *Sydney Morning Herald*, when I was asked about antagonistic elements on the board, I said it would have to ask whether it was "in the business of making friends or in the business of alienating"[680] itself. It was with this in mind that I met with Mugabe on 22 June when I got home to Zimbabwe. Although the primary reason for the meeting was to encourage his approval of the new Zimbabwe Schools Examination Council (ZIMSEC) board I had nominated, I also raised Howard's nomination to the ICC and arrival in Zimbabwe that day, explaining how I thought our support would benefit Zimbabwe Cricket and the GNU. Mugabe's response intrigued me: "What was between me and John Howard is past – the decision must be made solely on what is in the best interests of Zimbabwe Cricket."[681]

As the meeting ended Mugabe enquired after Bethany. He wanted to know all the details and asked whether she had received adequate medical attention. In my diary that evening I recorded that it was a "curious meeting" in which Mugabe appeared "genuinely concerned for Bethany". The same entry records that while the rest of Mugabe's body appeared "fit and that of a younger man", "his eyes betrayed his real age"; they were "strained and tired".

I told Howard about Mugabe's response when I met him for dinner that evening at the Australian embassy. Howard described his meeting with Zimbabwe Cricket's Chingoka and Bvute, which had taken place soon after his arrival, as having been tense. Although they were polite, they had given him no assurances of support. Howard told them of his wish "to see Zimbabwe fully re-integrated into the world cricket family",[682] but they appeared unmoved. Far from seeing this as an opportunity to build bridges, it emerged that Chingoka and Bvute revelled in having Howard plead for their vote. This sentiment was reflected in ZANU PF's mouthpiece which described Howard in an editorial as a "reprehensible individual". "What goes around comes around" were the almost leering words used.[683]

When the ICC meeting convened to vote on Howard's nomination on 29 June, Chingoka played a deft hand. India, Sri Lanka, Bangladesh, Pakistan, South Africa and the West Indies signed a letter rejecting Howard's nomination. Behind the scenes, however, Zimbabwe Cricket "orchestrated the anti-Howard campaign, but did not sign the letter".[684] Without overtly flouting my wishes, the hardline elements in Zimbabwe Cricket got their revenge on Howard. Although the Australian and New

Zealand tours were unaffected by this duplicity, a unique opportunity to build political bridges was lost.

Although I was annoyed by these machinations, I felt compelled to do everything in my power to ensure that the GNU worked. I was grilled about this by Stephen Sackur on 22 July 2010 when I appeared on BBC's Hardtalk for a second time. Sackur pointed to ongoing land invasions, the arrests of people involved in the constitutional reform programme and the Indigenisation Act as evidence that ZANU PF were holding sway. His underlying premise was that Mugabe was cynically exploiting the GNU solely for his own ends. In response, while conceding that there were "hardliners in Government who (were) trying to break the agreement", I pointed out that there were "moderates who wanted the GNU"[685] to work. At the time I couldn't publicly name who I viewed as hardline or moderate, but having been in cabinet some eighteen months now it was crystal clear to me who fell into which camp within ZANU PF. Mnangagwa led the hardline group, which included Mines minster Mpofu and Indigenisation minister Kasukuwere. Vice-President Joice Mujuru led the moderate camp, which included Didymus Mutasa, Tourism minister Mzembi and virtually all the ZANU PF women cabinet ministers. In between there was a large amorphous mass of ministers who didn't appear to be hardliners but who kept their loyalties close to their chests. It was hard to see where Mugabe fitted in, as he tended to stay out of cabinet debates. On some issues, such as education, he was very supportive and expressed moderate views, but on other issues, such as land and indigenisation, he tended to side with the hardliners. "Moderate", of course, was a relative term – I meant a "ZANU PF moderate", not necessarily a "democratic moderate". Those falling into the moderate camp, aside from wanting the GNU to work, appeared to have renounced violence and were committed to seeing the constitutional reform process continue. None of this could be explained on Hardtalk but these sentiments underpinned what I said during the interview. In the same interview I called again for sanctions to be removed, arguing that their retention played into the hands of the hardliners who, ironically, were happy for them to be retained. Not only did sanctions provide an excuse for not fulfilling their side of the GPA, but they provided the perfect scapegoat for all manner of ills for which ZANU PF itself was responsible.

Soon after this I travelled to China wearing my minister of Arts and Culture hat. I viewed my invitation to China as another facet of the hardliner/moderate divide within cabinet. Surprisingly, the Chinese embassy went to great lengths to secure my agreement to travel. I wasn't sure why they were so keen to have me visit, but after a few days in Beijing their motivation became clearer. At every turn the officials accompanying me were at pains to describe China as a country in transition; although they didn't have a multiparty system, this was gradually being introduced, so they argued, at local government level. Although I had government minders accompany me throughout, all of them discussed flaws in the Chinese system and proudly showed me around cultural sites which evidenced a more tolerant past. I was flown all the way to Dunhuang to be shown the Mogao caves, also known as the Caves of a Thousand Buddhas, located at a religious and cultural crossroad on the ancient Silk Road. The caves contain some of the finest examples of Buddhist art spanning a period of a thousand years. Although angered that thousands of the Dunhuang manuscripts stored in the caves had been scattered throughout the world, the Chinese government officials accompanying me were nevertheless proud of the diversity of thought and religion evinced by this World Heritage Site. The trip concluded with a meeting with my Chinese counterpart, Minister Cai Wu, who generously handed me a government grant to be used in my absolute discretion in Zimbabwe. (The money was used to purchase musical instruments for the Zimbabwe Music Academy in Bulawayo.) I was left with the distinct impression that moderates within the Chinese leadership, similar to "ZANU PF moderates", supported the GNU and a peaceful manner of resolving the Zimbabwean crisis. The warmth of my reception belied fears I had that the Chinese were working against the GNU.

I flew from Beijing to attend Beyond Borders Scotland, an annual gathering of artists and politicians which seeks to promote international cultural exchange, dialogue and reconciliation. There could not have been a more vivid contrast than coming from the Gobi Desert to the land of my forefathers, the Scottish Borders. Mark Muller Stuart QC, one of the trustees of ZLDAF, and director of Beyond Borders Scotland, was keen to help me persuade the English, Scottish and Irish cricket teams to tour Zimbabwe. He drove me across Scotland to meet the Scottish cricket team and management in Ayr. They were in fact desperate to travel to Zimbabwe to fulfil an ICC obligation, but told me that they had been encouraged by the British Foreign Office not to.

From Scotland, I travelled to London where Andy Flower, still the English coach, set up a meeting for me with Hugh Robertson, the Conservative Sports minister, on the sidelines of the third Test between England and Pakistan at the Oval on 19 August. With Flower's support I explained to Robertson how important it was to support peaceful reform processes through sporting contacts. I likened it to the early days following Mandela's release when the West Indies had hosted an all-white South African team – there was no guarantee then that the process of reform would continue, but it was right for the international community to give it a chance. Robertson was sympathetic, but said there were deeper political issues at stake, putting any decision beyond his mandate. I was later advised that Prime Minister David Cameron had taken a personal interest in the issue: the Conservatives' stance would not change; the prospect of England touring Zimbabwe was a bridge too far.

The Irish, however, were a different kettle of fish. I received word that they were keen to tour but that their players needed some assurances regarding their safety, so I flew to Belfast to meet the players. It didn't take much to persuade them all to come; indeed the moment I explained that the British government was encouraging teams *not* to tour, their resolve to do the opposite hardened. Within a month of that meeting the Irish travelled to Zimbabwe to play three ODIs. I suspect that part of their enthusiasm was derived from the belief that Zimbabwe would be easy meat, but they were over optimistic; as grateful as I was that the Irish responded positively to my invitation, I was delighted when Zimbabwe won the series.

The MDC-M suffered a second massive blow at the end of August 2010 when its vice-president Gibson Sibanda died after a brave battle against cancer. Coming soon after Renson Gasela's death in April, Sibanda's death removed our most inspirational leader. His burial at his rural home in Filabusi on 29 August brought together almost the entire original MDC leadership. Tsvangirai spoke of his regret about comments he had made after the MDC split. "I am sorry, Gibson, for what we said at that moment, it was a moment of weakness and it was not worth it,"[686] Tsvangirai said emotionally. Sibanda had provided him with "stability and guidance" in his personal life and political career, calling him a "unifier", unlike any other. Tsvangirai's words resonated with my own feelings about Sibanda. Even my own appointment as minister of Education had come about because of Sibanda's selflessness; he was more senior than me in the party and should have been appointed to cabinet before me, but he was happy to subordinate his own interests to what he felt was the national interest. Instead, he was appointed to be minister of state for National Healing (a non-cabinet position) alongside ZANU PF's John Nkomo and MDC-T's Sekai Holland. In that role he had quietly but effectively repaired lines of communication between all the political protagonists.

On 8 September 2010, Tsvangirai and I spoke at the launch of the exercise to distribute some 13 million primary textbooks to over 5 000 schools throughout Zimbabwe. Following UNICEF's award of the publishing contract to Longman Zimbabwe at the beginning of the year, a vast amount of work had been done to facilitate the distribution of the books. Indeed the easiest aspect was to print the books. It was another challenge entirely to arrange to deliver the correct number of books to all of Zimbabwe's schools, 70 per cent of which were located in rural areas. UNICEF, with my agreement, had rented a massive warehouse on the outskirts of Harare, where it developed a computerised system to pack and distribute books. In the course of the year, using satellite technology, the ministry and UNICEF had identified the GPS locations of all our schools; combined with this was an exercise to determine the needs of every school. Surprisingly, these two exercises revealed that there were in fact several hundred more schools than were in the ministry's own records!

At the launch I spoke of some of the logistical challenges: "a total of 12,000 metric tonnes of school supplies (500 truckloads), 13,250,000 textbooks (would be) distributed across the country to the remotest parts of Zimbabwe within three months" which would result in "each child" receiving copies of all books in "the four core subjects in a 1:1 ratio".[687] It was a joyous occasion, only tempered by what I knew was brewing in cabinet against me. The previous day there had been a robust debate in cabinet about education. In the course of the discussion I noticed that Minister of Higher Education Mudenge (who sat to my immediate right) was surreptitiously reading a document entitled "Education – sanctioning the economy from within". Although I could only read snippets of the document, it appeared to focus on the textbook contract and complained about the foreword I had written to be inserted in every one of the 13 million textbooks. Although Mudenge didn't speak to the document that day, I was forewarned that something was afoot. I wasn't surprised that the foreword, which I had drafted soon after the contract was awarded to Longmans, would annoy ZANU PF:

"This textbook is a gift of Zimbabwe's friends in the international community which include Australia, Denmark, the EU, Finland, Germany, Japan, Netherlands, Norway, Sweden, the United Kingdom and the United States of America. Through the wonderful generosity of these countries and our ability to work together in the Education Transition Fund we have been able to produce several million textbooks like this one which are being distributed countrywide to all schools. This gift is a demonstration of the great love our friends have for Zimbabwe and her children. I hope that you will respect this spirit of generosity and love by looking after this book well. Please try to cover it and keep it out of the rain and dirt. Under no circumstances should this book ever be sold because it is a gift. My hope is that with this book in your hands and with the help of your teacher you will be excited to learn more and through that you will play a role in building Zimbabwe into the jewel of Africa."[688]

I had discussed the foreword with both Dzingai Mutumbuka and my permanent secretary, Dr Mahere, both of whom approved it before it was sent to UNICEF. It was designed by me as a simple message to children to look after the books, but also to make a point about which countries had made the exercise possible. I knew that it would be controversial because despite the general request I had put out to all embassies, ZANU PF's traditional friends had not responded. The revelation about the donors' identities drove a coach and horses through ZANU PF's propaganda line that Western sanctions were in place against the *people* of Zimbabwe. Although Dr Mahere had not appreciated the political impact of the foreword, the propagandists within ZANU PF understood instantly and were livid.

Girding my loins in anticipation of an attack, I waited to see what ZANU PF would do. I knew that because of the divisions within their own ranks, any attack would probably come from its hardline faction. In early October I personally experienced the general divisions within ZANU PF when I received an invitation from Minister of State in the President's Office Didymus Mutasa to open a new classroom block at Sherengi School in the Headlands district of his constituency. Although I had been warmly received by most of my Provincial Education directors, I had noticed that I received few invitations to visit schools from some, particularly those stationed in ZANU PF heartland areas like Mashonaland. There was no obligation on Mutasa to invite me; I interpreted it as olive branch and was not disappointed when I visited Sherengi School on 1 October. Mutasa spoke positively about the work I was doing, including the distribution of textbooks. The entire visit was deeply encouraging; as usual the children, teachers and parents were delightful. I was the only white face in a sea of black smiles. There was one constant depressing reminder of the challenges that still lay ahead, however. The road to the school went through former commercial farms. Being the beginning of summer, some of Zimbabwe's most productive agricultural lands in the district should have been prepared, ready for maize, tobacco and other crops. Instead there was little sign of activity. Headlands was one of the worst affected by ZANU PF's land programme and few commercial farmers were left in the district.

The first salvo of the attack on me was fired in cabinet on 19 October. I had given notice to the cabinet secretariat that, because I had to drive up from Bulawayo, rather than fly, I would be late. Instead of giving my apologies for being late, the secretariat removed my name plate, giving the impression to the rest of cabinet, including my immediate neighbour Mudenge, that I would not be coming at all. When I quietly slipped in at 10.30 am, taking a spare seat by the door on the northern side of the cabinet room instead of my usual seat on the western side, Mudenge, who hadn't seen me come in, was in full flight against me. He criticised the awarding of the textbook contract, making a variety of accusations, including that Longman Zimbabwe had little market share and that UNICEF was acting in cahoots with Longman internationally. He then sensationally suggested that there was an international pattern: UNICEF had granted Longman contracts in Iraq and Afghanistan, the inference being that this was part of a sinister regime change agenda. As he was warming to his subject, he said, "it is pity the Minister is not here", to which I retorted, "I am", which first shocked and then silenced him.

I responded by saying I was not surprised by the attack as I had been anticipating it for weeks. I then recounted the entire history of the tender, explaining the cartel, the windfall profit of some US$10 million which had been avoided and the fact that the contract had been adjudicated on in Copenhagen by UNICEF. The price of an average textbook had plummeted from an excess of $5 per copy to $0.70 cents. Mudenge, I said, was "economical about the truth" because Longman Zimbabwe in fact enjoyed 65 per cent of market share and all its books had been approved by the ministry for well over a decade.

The debate then opened up to others and at this point a number of ministers, including two ZANU PF ministers, slipped me notes, elaborating on what Mudenge had said prior to my arrival. One such note shocked me: it disclosed that Mudenge had referred to an internal memorandum of Permanent Secretary Mahere which I had not seen but which had got into Mudenge's hands. Another note encouraged me – a ZANU PF minister wrote, "Well done! You did it for our children and I sincerely appreciate that when you are playing soccer and you get tackled it means you are doing something positive!"[689] As the debate raged on it was not clear which way it would go. The knives were out, especially the inference that I was part of some regime change agenda. But it came to a halt in an instant. Mugabe, who had been listening quietly, asked me whether the books now being distributed had been approved by the ministry and used before. When I reiterated they had all been approved, and that some had been in use for over 20 years, Mugabe killed the debate by saying, "Our children have been using these books for years and need them now. This is an old issue and we need to move on." Mudenge and the other ZANU PF ministers who had supported him were left stranded and nothing more was said about the matter.

The second salvo was directed against me a few weeks later. On 29 October I gave the annual Lozikeyi Lecture at the Bulawayo National Art Gallery on the topic "Looking into the future: Art and the Law". The lecture series is in honour of Queen Lozikeyi, one of Lobengula's wives. It had been a traumatic year for the National Arts Gallery in Bulawayo because it had been the focus of a clash between ZANU PF interests and art. An exhibition by local artist Owen Maseko, entitled *Sibathontisele*, regarding the Gukurahundi, had opened a can of worms. Shortly after the exhibition opened, both Owen Maseko and the director of the gallery, Voti Thebe, were arrested. I intervened as minister for Arts and Culture and had managed to get both released. But subsequently the exhibition itself was banned by the Censorship Board, which fell under a ZANU PF-controlled ministry, and Owen Maseko was charged with bringing the name of the President into disrepute. One of his paintings graphically linked a caricature of Mugabe to the massacres.

In my speech, quoting Pablo Picasso and Irish poet WB Yeats respectively ("Art is a lie that makes us realise truth" and "Art is but a vision of reality"),[690] I argued that because art was not actual reality, it could portray reality in a moderated or graduated way – which in turn could help Zimbabweans "to grapple with our past and current failings and successes in a palatable manner".[691] Speaking of both Rhodesian and post-independence atrocities, such as Nyadzonia and Gukurahundi (the latter I described as a "politicide if not genocide") I said that art could become "that 'realisation of truth' and that 'vision of reality' which (could) enable us to get past the very first hurdle of acknowledging our past".[692]

My speech was an appeal for us to use art to reconcile, not an attempt to inflame emotions. Inevitably, the press isolated the dramatic sound-bites in my speech, in particular my comment about Gukurahundi, sparking a furious reaction from the Zimbabwe National Liberation War Veterans Association (ZNLWVA). On 4 November I received a letter from ZLVWA which started with the sentence "Minister Coltart you will never cease to amaze!!" Accusing me of being an unrepentant Selous Scout, it demanded an apology and a withdrawal of my statement "within seven days or else (I) should resign from (my) post as Minister".[693] The letter was followed by a series of vitriolic threats made against me in the press by Joseph Chinotimba. I responded by publishing the letter I had written in reply to ZNLWVA, which included the following statement:

> "As my speech (and many others I have given) makes clear, I strongly believe that racial discrimination and many other actions of the Rhodesian Front government were unjust and wrong. However, we now all have an obligation to reconcile and move forward in the best interests of our beloved nation and her future – which predominantly rests in all our children. As my speech makes clear, if we do not deal with the mistakes we have all made in the past in different ways, then our nation will be doomed to repeat them in future."[694]

My reply didn't satisfy Chinotimba and his comrades. If anything their baying for my resignation increased. Resolved that I needed to speak to them directly, I asked Deputy Prime Minister Mutambara to help arrange a meeting with the ZNLWVA executive, which happened on 18 November. Chinotimba started by recounting atrocities that had occurred during the war, and accusing me of selectively ignoring them and stirring up hostility. As I replied, I could see their glazed expressions; there was so much bitterness welling up within that they were initially deafened to me, the embodiment of battles they had fought over three decades before. I took my time, decrying the bitterness of war. I likened all the events of the past as poison sitting at the bottom of a well – while the country had moved forward, I said, as long as the violence of the past remained unresolved it would continue to poison us all. I argued that we needed a process to heal our nation. I told the veterans that, ironically, I had been criticised by whites for suggesting that we (as whites) had not confronted our own past and complicity in human rights abuses. As the meeting drew to a close, with the veterans all now listening, I suggested that Chinotimba and his colleagues should speak to ZIPRA veterans about the 1980s, because I thought they would find that the "wounds of violence in Matabeleland had not healed and there was a danger of mistaking a closed wound for healing".[695] The meeting ended on a remarkably cordial note. The threats against me ended and never resurfaced. At the time I was deeply struck by the destructive legacy of the war. Although I didn't mention it in the meeting, I was reminded of the words of English singer Paul Hardcastle's 1985 hit "19" (which itself was named because 19 was the average age of Vietnam veterans) which recounts that half of those veterans suffer from post-traumatic stress disorder. The song contains the searing lyric that hundreds of thousands of American men are still mentally fighting in Vietnam. It seemed to me that there were thousands of veterans on both sides of our conflict who were still so badly affected by the war that they couldn't see beyond their own bitterness. Thousands of men, from both sides of the conflict, were still suffering from PTSD with no medical help to overcome it.

Almost two years into the GNU many whites, thousands of them veterans themselves, especially those who were farmers, were angry about its inability to stop further land invasions and corruption. That November, I was asked to debate in our church the topic "Government of National Unity – the only viable option or just compromise and corruption?" A member of our church, a white farmer, debating the motion expressed the views of many when he said that we (in the GNU) were "unequally yoked", that we were governed by fear and had compromised on a range of matters. In response, I agreed that while there had been compromise, we needed to remember where we had been just two years before – in a nation facing total collapse. Objectively, I argued, there was less suffering: since the start of the GNU clinics and schools had reopened, water supplies and roads were being repaired, the economy had grown 8 per cent in 2010 and bank deposits were up to US$2 billion from a few hundred thousand when we started. I pointed to the "profound contradiction of ZANU PF propaganda which blamed all our woes on sanctions"[696] – sanctions were still in place. Despite sanctions, I said, the economy was surging ahead. I asked the audience to consider what the viable, non-violent options were in late 2008 and even then, in late 2010. I could see in the meeting many whites were so consumed by their own bitterness from the past that they could not hear what I was trying to say.

The sentiments expressed in that church meeting were reflected in wider society: many people remained unconvinced and a stream of hostile mail from some white people continued. In the delicate balancing act of keeping the GNU on track I empathised with those who had lost everything but wasn't surprised they didn't understand the depth of my concern. Another poem I wrote at the time summed up my private feelings. I called it "Land Reform":

Frantic cries to redress injustice
Shatter lives of black and white
Young men with bloodshot eyes
High on propaganda and weeds of hate
Inflamed by wicked Old Men
Are used to satisfy the greed
Of fat criminals masquerading
As politicians concerned about the poor

Fallow fields reveal the truth
Lone Maize stalks the land
Reminding of a time gone past
When food was grown for people
Outflanked by thorns
Bush returning, crowding out
Our future.

I made my second appearance at the Education World Forum (EWF) in London in January 2011, a gathering of Education ministers from throughout the world. On the sidelines of the meeting I met the British minister for International Development, Andrew Mitchell, to press for more British support for education. Mitchell, whom I had first met in 2009 when he was in opposition, was friendly and supportive but opened by saying that their focus was "on creating conditions for a free and fair election" and that "substantial resources for education would only flow thereafter".[697] I urged a change in focus, telling him that "it was little good just focusing on the election" as there needed to be "deliverables". Aside from the critical need to ensure that we didn't suffer a lost generation of children, it was also necessary to "persuade people that there could be a better life under a different, more progressive government". I pointed out that whereas the German government had donated some US$18 million to the ETF, the British had then contributed only £1 million which, although enormously helpful, did not tally with Britain's historical interest in Zimbabwe. Mitchell, who had started the meeting rather formally, relaxed, extended the time and concluded by assuring me that they would listen carefully to what I had said. He was true to his word. In the following few years while Mitchell remained in that office British support for the ETF grew dramatically, to such an extent that by 2012/2013 DFID almost single-handedly kept the Basic Education Assistance Model (BEAM – a safety net programme for vulnerable children) afloat.

My trip to the EWF coincided with the MDC-M's second congress which was held in Harare on the weekend of 8 and 9 January. Once again I did not contest for high office and was again elected, *in absentia*, as secretary for Legal Affairs. The congress, however, resulted in a change of president, with Welshman Ncube taking over from Arthur Mutambara. Advising that he would not contest the presidency, Mutambara praised the party for being the only one in Zimbabwe to have a transparent change of leadership. "Before the national council met (in December 2010), I said I was not standing for any position because I believe in leadership renewal and it is good for our party democracy,"[698] Mutambara said to a standing ovation. Watching from afar, I was proud of the party and Mutambara, but my optimism was misplaced.

Shortly after the congress a few disgruntled members instituted a court case challenging the congress's decisions, which Mutambara used to his benefit. In a statement issued on 7 February, Mutambara said that he would "not recognise Welshman Ncube as President" until the "High Court (made) its ruling",[699] fully knowing that a ZANU PF-dominated High Court was unlikely to hand down a judgment quickly. What drove Mutambara was a decision taken by the new national executive to redeploy Mutambara from the office of Deputy Prime Minister to an ordinary cabinet minister so that Ncube could take over as Deputy Prime Minister. Aside from the party's desire to have its new president, Welshman Ncube, in the key position of a principal, there was considerable disquiet among rank-and-file members about the role that Mutambara was playing as a principal. Some felt that he had been far too accommodating of ZANU PF, and that some of his rhetoric sounded more ZANU PF than MDC.

The Global Political Agreement[700] explicitly named Mugabe as President and Tsvangirai as Prime Minister, but the two deputy prime ministers and vice-presidents were not named and were nominated by their respective parties. Mutambara argued that because he "occupied an office of state" and had "committed himself to serve for the entire duration of the inclusive government" he would not stand down. As disingenuous as the argument was, nothing could be done about it without a court order or political will shown by both Mugabe and Tsvangirai to respect the clear intent of the GPA. Consistent with the tactic employed in a long line of politically related lawsuits since the courts were subverted in 2001, the case gathered dust in the High Court. It soon became apparent that neither Mugabe nor Tsvangirai wanted the more acerbic Ncube as a fellow principal. Although they had different motivations for obstructing Ncube's appointment, their combined opposition to him ensured that Mutambara remained Deputy Prime Minister. While I was not surprised that Mugabe was happy to sow division between the two MDC parties, I was disappointed by Tsvangirai's conduct. I thought he had squandered an opportunity to present a united front against ZANU PF.

The impasse regarding Mutambara coincided with a deepening of general tension within the GNU. It became apparent that hardliners within ZANU PF were anxious to have a new election, but what was holding them up was the delay in finalising the new constitution. The GPA set out a broad timeframe and process for constitutional reform which included public hearings, two "All Stakeholder Conferences", a debate in parliament and a referendum. I had by that time handed over my co-chairmanship of COPAC to Edward Mkosi because it was impossible to fulfil my ministerial obligations and be intimately involved in the time-consuming reform process. However, I had been brought onto the deadlock-breaking Constitutional Management Committee, which comprised the original negotiators from the three GPA parties – namely, Chinamasa, Nicholas Goche (from ZANU PF), Biti, Mangoma (MDC-T), Misihairabwi-Mushonga, and Mzila-Ndlovu (MDC-N)[701] – so knew of the many problems COPAC faced. Constitutional Affairs Minister Matinenga's report to cabinet on 22 February exposed some of the underlying tensions.

Although the first All Stakeholders conference had been held and thematic committees would finish their work by March, there were funding constraints holding up the entire process. Matinenga explained to cabinet that the earliest we could expect a referendum would be September, and even that forecast was optimistic. This news alarmed some people, including Mugabe, Mnangagwa and my neighbour, Foreign minister Mumbengegwi, who muttered next to me that the process was taking far too long. When Matinenga explained that the "public" would have to be invited to the second Stakeholder Conference, Mugabe retorted, "What public?" Mnangagwa questioned the length of time for certain activities, at one point stating that the 30 days allocated for drafting could "take a day". I disagreed with Mnangagwa, arguing that drafting should not be rushed. I argued that we all "needed to understand the consensus emerging from the thematic committees" and even once we had a consensus it was important to "consider precedents and best practice from other jurisdictions".[702] The meeting ended with some very unhappy ZANU PF hardliners whose faction was becoming more defined as every week passed.

Tension within cabinet exploded when MDC-T Energy minister Elton Mangoma was arrested and detained on 10 March on what I thought at the time were spurious charges. Mangoma had been doing a superb job of stabilising the energy sector and it was inconceivable in my mind that there could be any merit to the criminal abuse of office charge for which he was arrested. I thought this was yet another effort of the hardliners to break the GNU because of their concerns, regarding where things were headed.

The hardliners' anxieties and their push for fresh elections were driven by revolutions against autocratic rulers in North Africa. Jonathan Moyo had written on 27 February 2011 that with the uprisings in North Africa, "no doubt vigilance has become the order of the day all around". He went on to opine: "Only God knows why these hopeless copycats, whose death wish is to be arrested at the Harare Gardens and be charged with treason in accordance with the rule of law they love preaching about, honestly think they can do an Egypt or Libya in Zimbabwe."[703]

While Mangoma was still sitting in a filthy police cell, the ZBC, in a blaze of publicity, reported that a little known "Fallen Heroes of Zimbabwe Trust" had "exhumed 280 bodies from a disused mine in Mount Darwin providing evidence of massive human rights atrocities"[704] committed by the Smith government. The ZNLWVA noted that the "remains showed that the Rhodesian Government had committed genocide". For the following two weeks ZBC news bulletins led with the spectacle of hundreds of dismembered remains being lifted out of the mine shaft. At the site senior ZANU PF officials explained to villagers and reporters what the "discovery" meant. ZANU PF Indigenisation minister Kasukuwere said: "After taking our resources, they [i.e. whites] had the audacity to throw our people in the mine shafts. It's an insult. We need to understand that the white people are not here for charity."[705] It seemed that there were some people determined to make political capital out of the incident, rather than honour the dead. What further confused the matter was that it appeared as if there was still flesh on some of the remains, bringing into question whether the remains were in fact all from the pre-1980 period. Human rights organisations also questioned the haphazard manner in which the bodies were being exhumed, in the process destroying critical evidence regarding whose remains they were and who was responsible for their dumping.

The "finding" of bodies in this mine shaft was accompanied by a new wave of meetings being banned, heightened surveillance, fresh attacks on civic society, increased numbers of political arrests, and violence. On 15 March I received a request from the German ambassador, Albrecht Conze, that I visit him urgently. When I met him that evening at his residence he told me that they had received credible intelligence that I was under threat again. He wasn't sure what action would be taken against me but he urged me to be vigilant. Conze made contact again a few days later to say that their sources thought it would either be an arrest or possibly another assassination attempt.

As things turned out, neither occurred, although a year later another attempt on my life was made. I don't know whether that attempt, which happened on 5 May 2012, had any connection to Conze's warning. In any event, cabinet meetings for the next few weeks were marked by low attendance and "simmering tension".[706] This state of affairs continued until mid April, when Vice-President Mujuru spoke in a remarkably forceful manner about the Mount Darwin exhumations. Towards the end of cabinet, on 12 April Minister Matinenga raised the issue again. Mujuru candidly responded that the local chief, Chief Kandeya, was acting in a "funny manner" and making "funny demands". She said they had "always known about the bodies in the mine shaft" and that "the real motivation was from some unscrupulous miners who believed that the mine was rich in gold and who needed to get the bodies out the way".[707] There were also "poisonous gases which made it dangerous to mine and exhume"; in her view it was "better to leave and memorialise the remains". Mujuru's comments, alongside a ZAPU[708] court interdict barring further exhumations, ended all further debate on the Mount Darwin mine shaft issue. I was surprised by Mujuru's strident comments, which distinguished her as a moderating force, clearly squared against hardliners who wanted to exploit the issue.

In the midst of this political wrangling I pressed ahead with plans to improve the education sector, in particular the need to reform the curriculum. I had been astonished to learn soon after taking over the ministry that the curriculum had last been comprehensively reformed in 1986. In 1999 the Nziramasanga Commission, appointed by Mugabe, had pinpointed that while Zimbabwe provided children with an excellent academic education, their vocational education was deficient. One of the Nziramasanga Commission's main recommendations was that the curriculum be overhauled to ensure that there was a better balance between academic and vocational subjects. Both my senior ministry staff and NEAB agreed that curriculum reform was a major priority. The Finns, who have one of the best vocational education curricula in the world, had provided the ETF with a generous grant to press ahead. In late 2010 I learnt about a Zimbabwean academic, Professor Josiah Tlou, who was a world-renowned expert in curriculum reform based at a top American university, Virginia Tech. The problem I faced was a deep-rooted concern within some ZANU PF elements about what comprehensive curriculum reform might do to certain subjects, especially history. I had made it clear that politicians should not be involved in the curriculum reform process – that we should leave this to the educational experts in every field. The existing history syllabus was not created in that way because it was (and remains to this day) a key element of ZANU PF's propaganda, having been drafted in an overtly partisan manner. Reading it in isolation an unknowing person would assume that Joshua Nkomo and ZAPU had played a minor role in the liberation struggle. It was also shockingly racist; the role of white democrats, people such as Garfield Todd, was under-played and one was left with the impression that most white people were racists. Unsurprisingly, Gukurahundi and Murambatsvina were not dealt with at all. Knowing that history would be the most controversial subject, I stressed that objective academic historians should be involved. But this would never satisfy those who wanted the partisan syllabus to be retained. Another major problem I faced was that the Education Act gave responsibility for the curriculum to the permanent secretary, not the minister. Although in a democracy this would make sense – to ensure that the curriculum was in the hands of an educationalist, not a politician – it meant that I could not push the reform agenda without the support of my permanent secretary, Dr Mahere, who had already demonstrated unswerving loyalty to ZANU PF. Mahere appeared to be deeply suspicious of Professor Tlou, and by the end of the first quarter of 2011 had successfully blocked any progress on the curriculum. I felt exceedingly frustrated by the lack of progress, and so on 4 April I took the bull by the horns. After cabinet Mugabe agreed to meet me that afternoon to discuss the curriculum reform process. From cabinet I went back to my office where I told Mahere and Tlou that we would be meeting the President in half an hour about the curriculum. This was the first either of them knew about the matter. Tlou had already told me that he knew Mugabe from the 1960s and so when we all met the two of them immediately began reminiscing; they got on like a house on fire. I then explained to Mugabe the need for comprehensive curriculum reform, about which he needed little persuasion, that I believed Tlou was eminently suited for the job but that the process was going far too slowly for my liking. The matter was urgent now, I said. I told him frankly about the history syllabus problem, but said that if needs be history should be set apart so that political disputes over its content should not obstruct or delay the wider process of curriculum reform. Mugabe agreed with me wholeheartedly and said that he was anxious that the process proceed without further delay. At no point did I point a finger at Mahere, but he received a clear message – that the need for urgent curriculum reform should not be impeded by politics.

Despite the meeting with Mugabe I found that many of the other projects I had initiated, such as Academies, were crawling along. I was not getting the professional support I needed from within the ministry. I remained unsure whether it was deliberate obstruction or just sheer incompetence. The duplicity shown the previous year, when an internal memorandum regarding the textbook contract had been given to Minister Mudenge, had shaken my confidence in some of my senior staff, but I felt I had little option but to soldier on. Matters came to a head in cabinet on 19 July when Finance minister Biti rhetorically asked whether the ministry of Education's failure to draw down on a $20 million budgetary allocation for the rehabilitation of schools was the result of "gross negligence or deliberate sabotage".[709] Knowing it was a political hot potato, I declined to answer the question; I said I would speak to the principals direct.

After cabinet I met with Tsvangirai and Mutambara, before meeting with Mugabe, each one on one. I told each that my permanent secretary wasn't up to the task of running the biggest government ministry, which employed almost two thirds of all civil servants and had the largest budget. In my meeting with Mugabe I said, "Mr President, I know that you have always been committed to providing Zimbabwean children with the best education possible. Whatever our other differences may be, I respect that commitment and am not here on some partisan political mission. However, if you want this government to deliver a quality education you simply must appoint a person who is going to get the job done." Mugabe expressed surprise but promised to look into the matter. The next day the cabinet secretary, Dr Sibanda, approached me at a funeral and said, "I know there is a problem and we need to deal with it." I never discussed the matter with Mugabe again and when a few months went by and nothing had changed I thought that I had been ignored. But I was wrong – eventually, although it was almost a year later, Dr Mahere was replaced by Constance Chigwamba. The wheel turned slowly but at least it did turn.

A week after meeting with Mugabe I delivered the 2011 Acton Lecture on Freedom and Religion at the parliament of New South Wales in Sydney. The annual Acton Lecture provides a platform to discuss how religion interacts with a free society, so I addressed the application of biblical standards to Western foreign policy, in particular the need to forsake violence as a means to obtain or maintain power and the application of the parable of the talents to the question of aid. Pointing to the inability of nuclear powers to stem terrorism, I argued that "the

West's greatest long term security lies in doing what it can to remove the sting of grinding poverty and ignorance in the breeding grounds of terrorism". Raw military power was insufficient to deal with this modern threat; "fair trade policies and development assistance, particularly investment in education (was) vital to the stability and security that the West needs so desperately".[710] Having said that, I bemoaned that so much assistance had been wasted on "profligate and corrupt governments". If governments in developing states could not be trusted with spending money correctly, the assistance should be channelled through responsible organisations. Ideologically, I had always had an aversion to aid, but I recognised that on occasions it was necessary, particularly investment in education. The disparity between money spent on defence and education the world over was appalling and the West had "a moral duty to be better stewards of the enormous wealth it has".

The events which occurred around my first cabinet meeting on my return home from Australia marked a watershed in Zimbabwean politics. Shortly before leaving my Ministry of Education office to walk across to cabinet on the morning of 16 August, I received word that General Solomon Mujuru had died in a fire at his farm in Beatrice overnight. Harare is the rumour capital of the world, so I treated the information with caution, but the moment I arrived at cabinet I realised that something was up. Hardly anyone was present; Joice Mujuru, Tsvangirai, Mnangagwa, Sekeramayi, Biti and Ncube were all absent. Mutambara immediately confirmed that Mujuru had died in suspicious circumstances. Mugabe eventually arrived about half an hour late, looking grim. He told us that General Mujuru had died in a fire at his farm; his body had been burnt beyond recognition but there was no word yet regarding the cause of the fire. The news was met with shocked silence by everyone present. The only hardliner there, Minister Mpofu, broke the silence by suggesting that cabinet adjourn, which I thought Mugabe would agree to. I was surprised when Mugabe responded by saying that business should go on, which it did. When the meeting finished Mugabe flew out to attend a SADC meeting in Angola. Before leaving Harare International airport he stopped in at 1 Commando Barracks to inspect General Mujuru's body, which had been placed in a military morgue.

I was intrigued by Mugabe's apparently nonchalant response to General Mujuru's horrific death. Mujuru, formerly Rex Nhongo, had been pivotal in securing ZANLA guerrillas' support for Mugabe when he went into exile in Mozambique in April 1975. At the time ZANLA guerrillas were unaware that Ndabaningi Sithole had been deposed while in prison and replaced by Mugabe as leader of ZANU. While the Mgagao Declaration signed in October 1975 by 43 officers had condemned Sithole's leadership and described Mugabe's leadership as "outstanding",[711] it still only described Mugabe as "a person who can act as a middleman". It was only when Mugabe gave an interview to the BBC on 21 January 1976, which the detained leaders of the DARE, Tongogara, Kangai and Gumbo, heard and approved of, that they wrote to Mugabe congratulating him.[712] The same letter attached a "declaration formally pledging support to" Mugabe. But at that time Nhongo, the overall commander of the Zimbabwe People's Army, was the most senior ZANLA guerrilla at liberty, and it fell to him to persuade guerrillas to accept Mugabe as their leader. A further complication was that President Machel of Mozambique didn't trust Mugabe and banished him to the coastal town of Quelimane. Once again Nhongo played a key role in August 1976 when Mugabe was smuggled, without the Mozambican government's knowledge, to meet guerrillas at Chimoio.[713] Following Tongogara's death at the end of the war in 1979, Nhongo assumed command of ZANLA during the critical transition in 1980 and was appointed by Mugabe as commander of the ZNA when General Walls resigned. In short, Nhongo had played a pivotal role in Mugabe's rise to power, which left me wondering why Mugabe had not cancelled his plans to travel to Angola.

General Mujuru was buried at Heroes Acre on Saturday, 20 August with military pomp and ceremony. Heroes Acre is located in the midst of msasa-clad hills west of Harare. Its centrepiece is a North Korean-made statue of two guerrillas which overlooks a massive amphitheatre that can seat thousands. On that day the crowd, in excess of a hundred thousand, was a restive, highly charged sea that swept into the hills and surrounded the tents where cabinet ministers and other dignitaries were seated. Unlike so many other national events, no one that day had to be ordered to attend. The crowd had come of its own volition to pay its respects and the buzz it generated was a powerful demonstration of the esteem in which General Mujuru was held. Vice-President Joice Mujuru arrived wearing a grey Salvation Army uniform, itself highly symbolic. She was demure for the entire occasion, leaving Mugabe to take centre stage. I was struck by Mugabe's countenance. Although certainly not jovial, he didn't appear grim or even particularly sad; indeed he even cracked a few jokes during his oration, much of which sounded more like a political speech than a eulogy. At the time most of us who attended thought that Mujuru's death was simply tragic, but not nefarious. One exception, though, was Dumiso Dabengwa, who sat close to me: at one point in the ceremony he said to me, "I think there is more to this than meets the eye."

CHAPTER 27

TOWARDS A NEW CONSTITUTION – THE END OF THE BEGINNING AUGUST 2011 TO MARCH 2013

"It was the best of times, it was the worst of times, it was the age of wisdom, it was the age of foolishness, it was the epoch of belief, it was the epoch of incredulity, it was the season of Light, it was the season of Darkness, it was the spring of hope, it was the winter of despair, we had everything before us, we had nothing before us."
– CHARLES DICKENS, *A TALE OF TWO CITIES*

Although suspicions abounded in the aftermath of General Mujuru's funeral, without hard evidence of foul play there was little political upheaval, which meant I could maintain my focus on education. The primary school textbook production and distribution project had gone well, with massive savings, 13 million books delivered and a 1:1 pupil/textbook ratio achieved. Textbooks in a range of the smaller indigenous languages were now being produced for the first time ever. Despite these positive developments, I remained frustrated by my inability to get a range of new policies implemented. Convinced that schools needed less government interference I had been working on new education regulations which would devolve authority to school heads of both government and private schools. Since 1980 successive Education ministers had enacted a bewildering array of statutory instruments which centralised power in the ministry over all schools, including church-run mission schools. Many of these regulations were unavailable to schools, some were out of print, all buried in a confusing maze; I decided to consolidate and rationalise them, at the same time intending to grant more autonomy to heads and local school authorities. This exercise revealed where the real power in the GPA lay.

Although the Education Act gave me, as minister, wide powers to enact regulations, any proposed regulations had to go through the attorney general's office and the cabinet Committee on Legislation before being printed by the Government Printers, all of which were controlled by ZANU PF ministers. In addition, I needed my senior civil servants, particularly the permanent secretary, to organise and smooth the passage of legislation. Partly because I understood these obstacles and partly because I wanted to secure a broad consensus within the ministry, I arranged a workshop for senior officials on 25 August 2011 to discuss my proposals. Although they received broad support from most, the permanent secretary openly opposed them. Shortly afterwards an article appeared in the *Sunday News*, quoting an unnamed source who alleged I had "sought to revert to the old Rhodesian system where Government had no say whatsoever in what happened at (private) schools".[714] The same article alleged I had "attempted to smuggle a clause granting (private) schools total independence". In a subtle way the race card was being used to frustrate autonomy being granted to all schools. There are two broad categories of private schools in Zimbabwe, namely Trust schools, which are predominately administered by whites (but have majority black students) and Mission schools, which are run by churches and overwhelmingly black. My proposed regulations applied to *all* categories of schools, government and both categories of private schools. Despite this, someone was distorting the facts to give the impression that my focus was solely on Trust schools, and that I was somehow trying to consolidate white rule through these schools.

There was a further insidious turn of events a few days after the *Sunday News* story appeared, when Indigenisation minister Kasukuwere brought new proposed laws to cabinet on 7 September, which recommended the indigenisation of private schools and sports clubs, as well as "art, entertainment and culture". I expressed my shock in private to Kasukuwere about not having been consulted. It turned out that a meeting had been held on 22 August, attended by Kasukuwere and three other ZANU PF cabinet ministers – and my permanent secretary, Dr Mahere. I had not been notified of the meeting, nor briefed about it. Behind my back, Dr Mahere had told the meeting that the ministry would "give guidance and monitor private schools", directly contradicting my autonomy proposals. Even worse were proposals to wrest effective control of all schools and cultural associations, both flagrant breaches of existing constitutional rights which allowed minorities to run their own schools and foster their cultural traditions.[715] I pointed out to Kasukuwere that I had demonstrated good faith by consulting widely and by appointing former ZANU leader Herbert Chitepo's daughter, Dr Thokozile Chitepo, as chair of the National Arts Council, demonstrating that I had no hidden agenda. Kasukuwere was taken aback and, to give credit to him, immediately withdrew the proposals, pending further discussions with me. The proposals never resurfaced; subsequent discussions in cabinet revealed that there was little appetite to mess with private schools. Mugabe had been well taught by Jesuits and all ministers sent their own children to Trust schools. The incident was the final straw regarding my working relationship with Dr Mahere, however. After Cabinet I complained again to the cabinet secretary, Dr Sibanda, who promised me that proceedings to secure a replacement were well in hand.

God works in strange and mysterious ways – a fact I was reminded of just a few days after the proposal to control private schools was buried in cabinet. I received a letter from ZANU PF stalwart Victoria Chitepo, widow of Herbert and mother of Thokozile, complaining about the goings on at Daramombe Anglican Mission Secondary School. The Anglican church had been riven by its unlawful takeover at the hands of self-proclaimed Archbishop Kunonga, the man who had given the homily at our February 2009 ministerial swearing in ceremony. Kunonga, with the assistance of the police, had taken over Harare's Anglican Cathedral and most Anglican churches in Mashonaland, at the same time praising Mugabe's leadership and ZANU PF's land policies. Kunonga's faction turned its attention to other Anglican properties. I had received reports of interference at Anglican schools but, without the support of ministry officials, was powerless to act. Mrs Chitepo's letter, which I received on 17 September, reported that Kunonga supporters had "tied up the (Daramombe) Headmaster and flogged him severely in front of the whole school" and "ordered all teachers to leave because they didn't pay allegiance to Kunonga".[716] Mrs Chitepo was writing to me "as an ordinary member of the Anglican Church", requesting that I "intervene by taking necessary action urgently". In an instant, the partisan sting was taken out of the private schools debate; here was evidence how politics was bad for education, raised by a revered member of ZANU PF. Not only did it enable me to resolve the narrow Anglican church issue but my arm was incalculably strengthened in the wider debate to lessen political control over schools.

Despite these successes in restraining the predatory instincts of some people, other concerns remained. I feared that some white-run Trust schools might interpret the recent events as licence to transform their schools into islands of privilege which, aside from being wrong, would also ultimately play into the hands of those who wanted to control them. With these thoughts in mind, I issued warnings at two Trust school events in the ensuing weeks. In the first, at the ATS annual summer school, I asked all Trust schools to consider what they could do to support impoverished government schools in their vicinity. Then on 12 October at Bulawayo Girls College speech day, quoting Martin Luther King, I reminded the girls that "an individual has not started living until (she) can rise above the narrow confines of (her) individualistic concerns to the broader concerns of all humanity".[717] I said that "while all ethnic/racial/cultural groups had a tendency to gravitate towards their own, multi cultural societies have so much more vigour". If we were to transform Zimbabwe we needed "to concentrate on issues which we (had) in common rather than those which divided".

On 3 November 2011 an opportunity presented itself to convey a strong message that the transformation of Zimbabwe's education system was being done in a non-partisan fashion. Having successfully delivered 13 million textbooks to over 5 000 primary schools countrywide, we had sufficient resources to go ahead with production of secondary school textbooks. This was launched at an event in Harare attended by Vice-President John Nkomo and Prime Minister Morgan Tsvangirai. Aside from celebrating the exercise to distribute over 7 million textbooks to almost 3 000 secondary schools, I was able to report other lesser known successes, including the updating of the computerised education database (which had last been done in 2006), the GPS siting of all schools, the training of School Development Committees at 5 670 primary schools, and the printing of braille textbooks for blind pupils. I also spoke about outstanding challenges: the need to finalise the revision of the education regulations, curriculum review and the establishment of academies for talented, disadvantaged children. I concluded by diplomatically bemoaning the scant resources our own government had contributed towards Education, pointing out that the Zimbabwean government's commitment towards non-salary expenditure amounted to only US$2 per child that year. Although the ministry of Education in theory was allocated the largest budget, I was aware that minimal actual disbursements had been made by Treasury, especially in comparison to other ministries, a fact which infuriated me. By the end of September 2011, Education had only received 25 per cent of its budgetary allocation, an amount of US$14.8 million, against US$79 million received by the office of the President and cabinet, US$66 million received by Agriculture, US$61 million by Defence and US$51 million by Home Affairs. It was impolitic to mention these facts at the launch but I vented at cabinet on 29 November, describing the Education's ministry's minute allocation as an "absolute scandal" and our national priorities as "warped".

As irritated as I was about our own failure to invest in education, I recognised that it was part of an international malaise, something I spoke to when I addressed the Education World Forum in London on 11 January 2012. The previous November in Copenhagen, when I had secured Zimbabwe's admission to the Global Partnership for Education (GPE), the world's principal conduit for education-related development aid, I was made aware that the GPE's entire annual budget for 46 countries was only US$2 billion. While stressing that the main responsibility for funding Zimbabwe's education system rested on government, I argued that the international community needed to "move from rhetoric to action by making education a priority"; I compared the "billions spent on wars in Iraq and Afghanistan, trillions spent on the retention of nuclear weapons" to the paltry amounts spent on education. Repeating the theme of my 2011 Acton Lecture in Sydney, I suggested that "the best way to promote world peace is through educating the world's poorest children", but this needed a "radical review of the developed world's funding priorities".[718]

The first fortnight of February 2012 brought two poignant reminders of the true nature of our government partners. On 8 February, my old friend and veteran human rights activist Paul Chizuze disappeared. Chizuze, who had been the second paralegal ever trained by the Bulawayo Legal Projects Centre and, with Joel Silonda, had played a pivotal role in gathering evidence of Fifth Brigade atrocities in Tsholotsho in 1995, was last seen driving his white Nissan Hardbody vehicle, which was subsequently recovered abandoned in Beitbridge, near the South African border. The discovery of his vehicle led some elements to suggest that he had skipped the country, which didn't square with those of us who knew him well. Despite numerous appeals by churches and human rights organisations, Chizuze has never been seen again. There have never been any substantial leads regarding what happened; like Patrick Nabanyama, he simply disappeared without a trace.

Although none of us know who is responsible, ZANU PF benefited the most from his death. Like Nabanyama, Chizuze didn't have a high enough profile for his disappearance to attract international condemnation; and yet many grim secrets were buried with him. A much younger man than Silonda, Chizuze had remained active in human rights work; he was the person most intimately acquainted with the sites of numerous mass graves throughout Matabeleland which, if unveiled, would be extremely discomfiting for the architects of the Gukurahundi.

A few days after Chizuze disappeared, the inquest into General Mujuru's death concluded in Harare, after hearing from 39 witnesses, some of whom provided the court with troubling accounts. According to one of Mujuru's own security guards, Clemence Runhare, he had arrived at an outer security gate at his Ruzambo farm in the Beatrice district at about 8 pm on 15 August 2011.[719] After passing through an inner security gate manned by three policemen, Mujuru obtained keys from a female domestic worker, Rosemary Short, and turned in for the night. Later that evening Runhare heard "two gunshots, two hours before being alerted to the burning farmhouse".[720] The same gunshots were heard by Short, who disregarded them thinking they were the police shooting snakes. At 1.40 am on 16 August one of the police officers "noticed smoke coming out through the roof of the farmhouse".[721] The officers, aided by farm labourers, fought the blaze and discovered Mujuru's body at 3.45 am, "still burning in the mini lounge of the farmhouse". Mujuru's body was so hot that the police had to "continue pouring buckets of water on the body but the fire would not be extinguished". Another witness, forensic expert Birthwell Mutandiro, testified that there were indications that Mujuru had died "before the fire spread into the room where his remains were found".[722] Mutandiro told the court that "the carpet beneath the body exhibited less fire damage compared to other areas (indicating) that the body prevented the carpet from catching fire". There were several other anomalies: Mujuru had not parked his car in the usual place and had left groceries and medication in the car; the farmhouse had low windows without burglar bars which were easy to step out of; front door and car keys could not be found. If Mujuru had been able to move from his bedroom to the mini lounge to evade a fire, why hadn't he just stepped out of one of the low windows? Fire Brigade expert Clever Mafoti gave evidence that there were "two sources of fire – in the main bedroom and the mini lounge", which he said was "in most cases due to arson and rarely as a result of an electrical fault".[723] The inquest also revealed that Mujuru had fallen out with his police guards. After the fire was quelled, the police failed to "adequately and properly cordon off the farmhouse", making it "impossible for experts to properly examine the scene and investigate the cause of the fire".[724]

But perhaps the most troubling revelation concerned the post-mortem. After the discovery of Mujuru's body, it was taken to 1 Commando Barracks in Harare where a post-mortem was conducted by a Cuban doctor who could hardly speak English and didn't have a practising certificate issued by Zimbabwe's Medical and Dental Practitioners Council.[725] Aside from the fact that Zimbabwe has many experienced pathologists who could have been called to perform the post-mortem on such an important figure, it emerged that several routine procedures, such as taking an X-ray of the body and extracting blood, had not been followed. Mujuru's family, unhappy with the state's actions, called a South African pathologist, Dr Perumel, who "directed a lot of criticism" at the Cuban doctor. The Cuban doctor explained that he had not taken an X-ray because the body was "heavily charred" and gave the same excuse for not taking blood, saying that there was "no longer any blood in the body". The presiding magistrate, Walter Chikwanha, dismissed a suggestion by Mujuru's family lawyer that a second post-mortem be done on the basis that it would add no value because "there was no blood to extract, no organs and brain to examine".[726] Inexplicably, the inanimate, moisture-less carpet on which Mujuru's body lay was not fully burnt and yet, according to the Cuban doctor, the portion of Mujuru's body that had lain against it was charred, without a drop of blood left.

By the close of the inquest there were more unanswered questions than answers, a situation that was compounded by the report issued by Chikwanha a few weeks later in which he found that "no evidence at all was placed before the court to show that there was foul play in the death of" Mujuru. Chikwanha didn't dwell too much on the anomalies and brushed aside the criticism of the Cuban doctor, describing it as "textbook criticism". The closest he came to establishing foul play was his comment that "it was to some extent a strange fire indeed". Indeed, it was a strange fire – no explanation was given for how a fire of such intensity could char Mujuru's body to a cinder and yet not destroy the house. Photographs of the house taken after the fire show it intact, with its corrugated-iron roof still in place. The same photographs show dark black streaks on the walls, window panes not cracked, and fascia boards still intact after the blaze, pot plants right outside the windows not frizzled – all consistent with an accelerant, such as fuel, being used.

The Mujuru family itself was disturbed by the findings. Thakor Kewada, their lawyer, said the family wanted to exhume the general's body. "We are no better off than before the inquiry started," he told the BBC's *Focus on Africa* programme. "I don't think the verdict brings closure," he said. "The authorities should allow us to exhume the body and get the pathologist we wish to call to examine the body."[727] But in the equally strange political environment of Zimbabwe nothing further was done. There was never any further post-mortem. Speculation regarding how Mujuru had died, whether as a result of foul play and the motives of those behind any such foul play, continued. It would take another three years before any sense could be made of Mujuru's death.

Against the backdrop of the Mujuru saga the COPAC continued its inexorable, if rather slow progress. On 20 February the Management Committee met in an effort to thrash out an agreement regarding four remaining areas of dispute: land, the number of vice-presidents, the death penalty, and citizenship. While the Management Committee, which was the deadlock-breaking mechanism of COPAC, had been meeting more frequently, this particular meeting was critical. Broad agreement had been reached by COPAC on virtually everything else but these key sticking points. If we couldn't agree, then the principals would have to, but that was itself highly problematic because of the ongoing dispute between the MDC-N on the one hand and MDC-T and ZANU PF on the other, regarding Mutambara's position as a principal. In a lengthy meeting attended by Tendai Biti, Elton Mangoma, Douglas Mwonzora (all MDC-T), Patrick Chinamasa, Paul Mangwana (both ZANU PF), Priscilla Misihairabwi-Mushonga, Moses Mzila-Ndlovu and me (all MDC-N), we moved closer to final agreement on everything save for the land issue.

Chinamasa had dug his heels in, steadfastly opposing a joint MDC-T and MDC-N proposal that title be granted in future, which ensured that agreement could not be achieved. I was appalled by how much we (the two MDCs) had already conceded on the land issue: in particular there were two racially discriminatory clauses I found offensive, one guaranteeing that "indigenous" Zimbabweans would receive full compensation for the value of any land and improvements compulsorily acquired by government, whereas "non-indigenous" Zimbabweans would not. The other was a clause that stated that ongoing acquisitions could be done on a racially discriminatory basis in future.[728] While I fully understood the need to redress historical inequities, my feeling was that the new constitution should draw a line in the sand and move on. Many if not most white farmers had bought their farms after Independence, so I didn't see why they should receive less compensation solely because of the colour of their skin. In addition, for all practical purposes the reality on the ground was that virtually all white-owned farms had already been acquired, and so I couldn't see the justification for ongoing discriminatory practices to be allowed by the constitution in the future. A further sting was that the compensation clause allowed white foreigners, whose investment in land was protected by bilateral protection agreements, to be paid full compensation. I pointed out the irony in the meeting that if one was black, Italian or German, one would receive full compensation, but if one was a fifth-generation white Zimbabwean, one would not. While my MDC colleagues were sympathetic, in the face of ZANU PF intransigence, they felt little could be done. My only consolation was that "indigenous" was not defined in the draft constitution,[729] opening up possibilities in future to explore the meaning of the word. The only truly "indigenous" people in Zimbabwe are the San people; any attempt to include some of the Nguni people, such as Ndebeles, would assist a claim that whites be included, because both settled in Zimbabwe in the same century.

There was more consensus on the other three issues. ZANU PF wanted two vice-presidents, whereas both MDCs wanted to cut down on the size of government. This wasn't a deal breaker, however. Likewise on the death penalty there was much common ground. Virtually all of us wanted it removed but had to contend with a deep-rooted sentiment expressed by the majority of Zimbabweans for its retention. As a result, much of our discussion centred on how we could limit its application and this meeting saw agreement being reached that the death penalty only be imposed where a court found there were "aggravating" circumstances. A substantial gulf existed between the two MDCs and ZANU PF regarding citizenship, with the former wanting an absolute birth right and the latter wanting an absolute ban on dual citizenship. In the discussion, it was clear that ZANU PF feared the prospect of several million Zimbabweans in the diaspora being able to claim citizenship and vote. There emerged another racially based issue – ZANU PF were adamant that first generation Zimbabweans born to British parents should not have a birth right. I suggested that if that was their concern, then at the very least they should allow first generation Zimbabweans whose parents were citizens of any SADC country to have a birth right.[730] Although progress was made, it took several more months of haggling for a first draft to be produced.

The improving dialogue within COPAC appeared to rub off on cabinet at this time with all members, other than a few hardliners, relaxing. Joice Mujuru in particular became more convivial. At the commencement of cabinet on 28 February Information minister Webster Shamu suggested that the previous minutes, which had referred to "potable water", should read "portable water". Mujuru asked, "What does the Minister of Education say?", to which I replied, "Potable, Hon Vice President." The debate ended. Later in that meeting, when I spoke about the need to make our Central Bank "lean and efficient and run by people in whom the financial sector have confidence", Mujuru chimed in support, saying that we "needed policy statements which encourage and build confidence".

During the 13 March cabinet, Home Affairs minister Mohadi opined that "it (needed) to be *retaliated* that road blocks are necessary", to which Mugabe responded, "Retaliated or reiterated?", causing a wave of titters through the room. At the next meeting, on 20 March, Mugabe joked at the beginning: "Ahh, I see Mr Coltart is here so now we can start." Then on arrival at cabinet on 27 March, when I found that my usual seat had not been allocated and sat down in a spare seat next to Minister Kasukuwere, Mugabe asked why I was sitting there and not in my usual seat. I responded, "Mr President – it's because I have been indigenised."

For all the mirth in cabinet, sinister forces were still at work. Nothing had been done to me to fulfil the warning given to me by the German ambassador Albrecht Conze in March the previous year that some action was being planned against me, and to a certain extent I had let my guard down. In April 2012 I went on vacation to South Africa with

Jenny and Bethany. We drove down in my ministry-issue Toyota. The day before we were due to drive home, Jenny and I went shopping at Woodmead shopping centre in Johannesburg. When we drove out of the shopping centre I became aware of a faint clunking noise that appeared to be coming from the right front wheel. Concerned about this noise, especially as we had a long drive ahead of us the next day, I took the vehicle to a local Toyota dealership and asked them to inspect it. Having checked the suspension and wheels, but without tightening the wheel bolts, the mechanics cleared the vehicle. Next morning, on Saturday, 5 May, we set off early for home. I drove more slowly than I usually did because I could periodically still hear the offending noise. All appeared to be going fine until we approached a toll-gate outside Louis Trichardt, about 100 kilometres from the Zimbabwe border. As we came up a rise and turned a gentle right-hand bend the noise I had heard suddenly escalated, except that now it was coming from the front left-hand side of the vehicle. Fortunately, I had already started to decelerate in anticipation of the toll-gate and now I slowed down even more. Suddenly the front left-hand wheel broke loose and bounced away from the vehicle, causing the Toyota to drop down onto its axle and dig into the tarmac. I managed to control the vehicle and brought it to a rest on the side of the road. An inspection of the left wheel hub revealed that the nuts on two of the bolts had worked their way off, eventually causing the remaining four bolts to shear, and the entire wheel to come off. Once again Providence saved us. Had the wheel come off 500 metres before or after where it did, I would have been going much faster than I was. This was a very busy road and it would have been exceptionally difficult to control the vehicle. Just 40 kilometres further on we would have been driving through the Soutpansberg mountain range where the road has sheer sides dropping hundreds of metres. Providence dealt us another kind hand in that the very first vehicle that stopped to assist us was driven by a couple from Bulawayo, Jonathan and Karyn Vincent. They had an empty car and a tow hitch to take our trailer! Having got my vehicle off the road, we bundled everything into their car and set off for Bulawayo.

But the mystery of what might have caused the wheel to loosen remained. Our reliable mechanic, who had serviced the vehicle in Bulawayo before we left for South Africa, insisted that all the wheel bolts were tight when he'd discharged it. Nor had we had any flat tyre or need to change the left wheel. Toyota themselves insisted that it was impossible for wheel nuts to loosen of their own accord. The consensus, then, was that two of the nuts must have been loosened deliberately by someone with malicious intent. Toyota explained that if two nuts were slightly loosened they would eventually come off, destabilising the entire wheel. The matter was reported to cabinet but as there was no obvious culprit, no action was taken. I was left in no doubt, though, that a further attempt had been made to cause me harm. I stepped up my security again.

By mid 2012, and three years into the GNU, the education sector had been stabilised: all our schools were open, teachers were back teaching, we had not had any strike action for a year, and over 23 million core textbooks had been delivered to primary and secondary schools, achieving a 1:1 ratio, the best in Africa. UNICEF were especially pleased with the success of the textbook programme and the ETF was lauded internationally as being one of UNICEF's best collaborative efforts with governments worldwide. Behind these headlines were many unsung heroes and heroines. One of them was Sister Catherine Jackson, an indefatigable Catholic nun who had partially lost her sight in 1985 and was faced with the strong probability of total blindness. She obtained sponsorship from Rotary to go to Australia for twelve months to learn Braille and how to teach it. Having received a donation (written on the back of a hamburger box) to help the blind in Zimbabwe, she set about launching the Dorothy Duncan Braille Library and Transcription Service in Harare. Thankfully, her blindness was arrested and she retained the sight of one eye. Sister Catherine made contact with me soon after I became minister of Education and made a strong case to me and UNICEF that ETF money should be spent on rehabilitating the library's printing capacity. This resulted in a contract which saw the production and delivery of thousands of new Braille books, commencing in April 2012.

Another quiet force for good was Father Fidelis Mukonori, who also came to see me soon after I took office and thereafter worked with me to get minority language textbooks produced. Mukonori had been viewed by many Zimbabweans as a somewhat controversial character, given his close relationship with Mugabe. However, he played a significant role in putting me in touch with minority language groups and advocating on their behalf. I became even more willing to listen to him in February 2012 when he produced a book entitled *The Genesis of Violence in Zimbabwe*, which appealed to all people to shun violence which, he argued, had become an accepted part of Zimbabwean political culture.

Mukonori must take credit for first focusing my attention on the need for all children to be able to learn in their mother tongue, which resulted in primary textbooks being produced for the first time in Tonga, Nambya and Kalanga. In addition, by the time I left office plans were well advanced to produce textbooks in other languages such as Sotho, Venda and Shangaan. The development of the new "mother tongue" policy within the Education segment of my ministry in fact became the centrepiece of my policy within the Cultural segment too. Believing that language is the most important component of every culture, the teaching of all indigenous languages in Zimbabwe through to A level was my principal focus within the context of an almost non-existent budget for Culture.

There were also unsung heroes within the ministry itself. One person, Peter Muzawazi, deserves special mention because he did more than any other single person to arrest declining literacy levels during my tenure. In July 2010, the UNDP produced a statistical digest stating that Zimbabwe had the highest literacy rate in Africa,[731] which did not tally with information I was being given by NEAB and other educationalists in Zimbabwe; they were all reporting to me that our literacy levels were plummeting. I publicly questioned the UNDP figures because they had been based on school attendance statistics rather than actual literacy tests. I understood that because of Zimbabweans' passion for education, children attended school, but those schools had been without teachers and textbooks for a period. Accordingly, mere attendance, in my book, did not necessarily translate into literacy. I was condemned as unpatriotic for making these remarks in cabinet by some ZANU PF ministers (in fairness, in the same meeting Mugabe backed me, stating that he, too, was worried about declining literacy rates). But I never had any empirically based facts on which to base my fears until Muzawazi, who was then Provincial Education director for Manicaland province, did some of his own research. He conducted a literacy test of all Grade 5 pupils (10-year-olds) in all Manicaland schools and came up with the shocking result that on average they had Grade 2 literacy levels. Off his own bat, he then implemented PLAP (Progressive Learning Assessment Programme), which identified children whose education had suffered under the chaotic years between 2006 and 2008 and provided them with remedial teaching. He brought his findings and suggestions directly to me; after I had sung his praises in cabinet he was promoted to director of

Policy in the ministry and PLAP was extended countrywide. Since then PLAP has played a major role in redressing the harm caused to children prior to the GNU.

Despite these beacons of hope, by mid 2012 I still faced major obstacles in delivering a quality education for all Zimbabwean children. A serious concern related to the government safety net which was designed to pay the school fees of orphans and vulnerable children – the Basic Education Assistance Module (BEAM). Turf warfare between the ministry of Education and the ministry of Labour and Social Welfare (which administered BEAM) was preventing an honest review of its efficacy. The situation was compounded by the woeful underfunding of BEAM by Treasury. In mid 2012, a report revealed that some 300 000 vulnerable children were not attending school because of funding shortages. Although I had persuaded Britain's DFID to provide stop-gap funding for BEAM, I knew that this would not provide a long-term solution to the crisis. Try as I might, it was impossible to get a consensus between the two ministries, a situation not helped by some of my own senior administrators who simply were not up to the task. In addition, the all-important curriculum review process was crawling along at a snail's pace. Using my long-standing friendship with the Open Society president, Aryeh Neier, I had managed to secure a grant of US $3 million for the curriculum review process, so it wasn't money that was the issue.

Dr Mahere appeared to be determined that it would not go ahead under my tenure, however. He had revealed his hand in one meeting – making it quite clear he wasn't prepared to move the process along and that it could wait for the next government. Given that the Education Act gave the secretary absolute power regarding amendment of the curriculum, I was hamstrung. Likewise the Academies programme – to transform 20 or so schools into centres of excellence for talented disadvantaged children – faced similar opposition. Although I had secured a generous grant from the German government to fund a couple of pilot schools, every stalling tactic in the book was being used to prevent the project from getting off the ground. I had visited Academies in the United Kingdom and on 29 May 2012, when I was in New York learning about American Charter schools in Harlem, news came through that Mugabe was in fact listening to my concerns. My personal secretary emailed to say that a new permanent secretary, Constance Chigwamba, had been appointed by the President. Better late than never, Mugabe had finally acted on the request I had made a year before.

My curious and unpredictable relationship with Mugabe took a further twist on 13 July 2012 when I was the host minister at the commissioning of an e-learning project at the John Nkomo High School in Tsholotsho. My primary duty was to give introductory remarks prior to the official opening of the project by Mugabe himself. Knowing that I was going into the heart of Tsholotsho, the district where the Fifth Brigade had first been deployed in the Gukurahundi in January 1983, I re-read human rights reports to brush up on what had happened in that area. The John Nkomo High School is located at Mazabisa, some fifteen kilometres north west of Tsholotsho town. The Fifth Brigade went on a rampage, in early February 1983, around a ten-kilometre radius of Mazabisa: seven teachers were murdered and thrown into a pit latrine at Emkayeni, a few kilometres west of the school; on 7 February several homesteads in the vicinity were burnt down and five young men shot dead. Four days later, at Zibinkululu village, 200 Fifth Brigade soldiers engaged in mass beatings, shootings and the burning down of huts, resulting in six people being murdered. In May 1983, ten schoolgirls were raped at Emkayeni. And so it went on – that small community surrounding the high school had suffered cruelly. Some 25 people had been murdered, 350 people beaten and tens of homesteads razed to the ground[732] during the Gukurahundi, and it was going to be my task to introduce some of its architects to the same community, albeit 29 years later. I drove out early – the drive itself was remarkable, given that the road to Tsholotsho was unchanged since it was first built in the 1950s and remains one of the worst in Zimbabwe – and found Vice-President John Nkomo already there. He invited me into his vehicle and, while waiting for Mugabe's helicopter to arrive, we drove three kilometres south to a small primary school. Nkomo told me that the school had been established by veteran Methodist minister and nationalist politician, Thompson Samkange, in 1922 and it was where he had done Sub A in 1944. It was a pleasant interlude with a dying man (Nkomo was to pass away only a few months later) I had known since representing ZAPU politicians in the 1980s. Nkomo's relatives must have suffered during the Gukurahundi, too, and it gave me some comfort to know that he at least was reconciled to the day's conundrum.

From the school Nkomo and I drove to the clearing where Mugabe's helicopter landed. Mnangagwa and Army commander, General

Constantine Chiwenga, who had both arrived in another Air Force helicopter shortly before Mugabe's, lined up behind Nkomo and me to greet Mugabe as he disembarked. I am sure the intense irony of the situation was not lost on any of us. From the clearing we repaired to the school's staffroom where Mugabe was briefed on the ceremony before everyone else, save for Mugabe, cabinet Secretary Dr Sibanda and me, left to tour the school. Sibanda then excused himself, leaving Mugabe and me alone together. The irony deepened further. No sooner had Sibanda stepped outside than Mugabe volunteered that his father and his father's "second wife" (instantly correcting himself by saying "actually customarily my second mother") had come from a village only some ten kilometres from the school. He told me his father had left home in 1934. Having been trained as a carpenter and builder by the Jesuits at Kutama Mission, he abandoned his family and took a second wife in this district, leaving Mugabe's mother to fend for the family. I pondered on whether he realised the utter brutality which the Fifth Brigade had visited on this area, where presumably he had relatives. This brief awkward moment was interrupted when Sibanda returned to call us for the start of the proceedings.

First of all we inspected a new computer laboratory and then were ushered to our seats on the podium, which was surrounded by a large crowd that had gathered around the school's football ground. Aside from my two sons, who had joined me for the event, I was the only white person there. There was a festive, even joyous air: a variety of local poets spoke, rousing everyone into sustained applause; local musicians got young and old rocking, followed by scintillating traditional dances performed by the local San community. I was not required to introduce Mugabe, so confined my remarks to the e-learning project before Vice-President Joice Mujuru introduced Mugabe to the exuberant crowd, saying, with unintended irony, "this son of the soil has left indelible marks on our soil".

When Mugabe started his address he turned to me and said:

"David Coltart is from the white community. When we started the inclusive government, I wondered whether he would actually fit in. When the inclusive government was formed I thought it was going to be a challenge for him to be among so many black people. I said to myself it is a challenge on the part of a person like him to be amongst many blacks and to be looked down upon by others who would ask what he is doing working with a terrible dictator like Robert Mugabe. But Minister Coltart, though being a white man, has shown a lot of commitment towards working with ordinary Zimbabweans and we have worked together well. We all have the right to freedom of choice and it is that choice that made Mr Coltart to choose to be among us. Well, we may have differences of political outlook, but what matters is that at the end of the day we are all Zimbabweans."[733]

The remarks and in fact the entire event were bizarre, but left me believing that there may be hope for the country. There would have been hardly a single person in the crowd left unscathed by the Gukurahundi and yet all that appeared, superficially at least, to be forgiven. It strengthened my belief that the development of schools, roads and hospitals in Matabeleland was a crucial step towards meaningful reconciliation. Furthermore, for me personally, whereas a decade before Mugabe had told a crowd at Harare airport that there was no place for me in Zimbabwe other than prison, he now publicly acknowledged that we were all Zimbabweans, and I took this to heart.

A few weeks after the Tsholotsho event I travelled to the United Kingdom to lead the Zimbabwean delegation at the London 2012 Olympics. I am the first to admit that I landed with my bum in the butter. On arrival at Heathrow I was allocated a spanking new BMW driven by a British judge who had volunteered his services, and this set the tone for the next two weeks. All the ministers of Sport who attended the Games were treated like royalty, and I was no exception. When I was issued with my accreditation pass it had the word "ALL" inscribed on it in bold letters; on asking what that meant, I was told I could attend *any* event I chose to.

My first priority was to follow all our Zimbabwean athletes. We had a small but vibrant team in swimming, rowing and athletics, and I made sure to attend every event they participated in. But I also made full use of the "ALL" and attended nearly all the major swimming and athletic finals. It wasn't all play, however. I met with William Hague on the sidelines to discuss Zimbabwe, and on Sunday, 12 August I had a productive discussion with British Deputy Prime Minister Nick Clegg shortly before the closing ceremony. In that meeting I stressed how important it was to give peace a chance in Zimbabwe. While the GPA and the GNU themselves were flawed, we were making progress towards a new constitution, which needed to be supported. In fact the British government was by this time pouring money into the education sector, which I was grateful for. Aside from keeping BEAM afloat, shortly before I left for the Olympics I had launched a new US$26 million DFID grant towards educating vulnerable girls. I suggested to Clegg that the British needed to engage Mugabe himself to encourage the process of reform. I explained that notwithstanding all the terrible things that had befallen Zimbabwe, the GNU and the GPA process was the only peaceful way of taking the country forward.

My discussion with Clegg yielded immediate, albeit informal, results. On 29 August a British citizen arrived in Harare for discussions with me. His visit was an "unofficial, exploratory trip" to see whether there was any opportunity for dialogue. Although "very close to Nick Clegg", the initiative was personal and came on the back of his "long association with Africa and work with Oliver Tambo, Thabo Mbeki and the then South African authorities in secret dialogue between the two during the period 1985–1991".[734] I spoke to Tsvangirai and Ncube to see whether they would welcome such an initiative and, having received the green light from them both, met with Mugabe, on 11 September, who immediately showed interest in meeting.

The last quarter of 2012 produced a stalemate in the GNU and cabinet. This was due to a combination of factors, but the dominant underpinning one was that the final procedures to complete the draft constitution were taking place, focusing attention on elections which would follow. But there were problems within cabinet. Vice-President Nkomo and Minister Mudenge were sickly and rarely present. Tsvangirai, too, was absent a great deal, having recently got married and away on honeymoon. Finally, the tension between Mugabe and Ncube in particular was painfully obvious. While Mugabe would interact jovially with most cabinet ministers, he studiously avoided contact with Ncube. While the principals were still meeting, they met under the cloud of knowing that one of the three parties to the GPA was unhappy.

Although the economy had continued to grow, Biti routinely came to cabinet complaining that diamond mines were not paying Treasury what they ought. On 2 October he reported that Treasury had received no diamond revenue for September against a budget of US$50 million.

Shortly afterwards a detailed report was published entitled "Reap what you sow: Greed and Corruption in Zimbabwe's Marange Diamond Fields",[735] which alleged staggering levels of corruption. It noted, for example, that one company, Trebo (Obert spelt backwards) & Khays, linked to Mines minister Obert Mpofu, had taken a 99.5 per cent stake in the Zimbabwe Allied Banking Group (ZABG) in 2012 after injecting US\$22.5 million.[736] The "Reap what you sow" report had a special section on Mpofu, entitled "Rags to riches: the Obert Mpofu story", which detailed a vast array of assets Mpofu was alleged to have acquired, stating: "… he has become very rich since becoming Minister of Mines".[737]

At the time my take-home salary as a minister was US\$3 500 per month, so I knew how much my colleagues were earning. I had also been a senior partner of one of the country's biggest law firms for 30 years, which gave me some insight into what money people can earn through honest enterprise. Although Mpofu claimed that the money generated by Trebo & Khays was because he was "a shrewd businessman",[738] others were not convinced. Mpofu never threatened to sue the authors of the report for defamation, giving further credence to its contents. Although he didn't name Mpofu, Finance minister Biti said at the time that "there (was) no doubt that a small coterie of individuals is benefiting from Zimbabwe diamonds. Some of us who are benefiting are not afraid to flaunt our monies. We are buying all kinds of assets".[739] Moreover, there was increasing evidence of a parallel administration – diamond revenue was clearly going somewhere and the suspicion was that it was primarily going into a ZANU PF war chest in preparation for the election.

Our concerns about the looting of national resources came to a head in cabinet on 13 November, when Biti spoke about the state of the economy prior to the presentation of his budget speech. The GNU had greatly improved Zimbabwe's economy: whereas GDP had plunged – 18 per cent in 2008 – it had grown steadily since the advent of the GNU, and in 2012 was set to grow by 5.6 per cent. It had grown faster between 2009 and 2011, but fears of a violent and fraudulent election were driving business confidence down. Biti told us that while diamond exports had generated US\$563 million in the first nine months of the year, Treasury had only received some US\$43 million in taxes, despite government in theory owning half of the largest company, Mbada. Biti at one point said "looting is now on a scale last seen during the time of Cecil John Rhodes". It wasn't confined to diamond receipts – despite billions of dollars worth of merchandise being imported, duty receipts were a paltry US$200 million to the end of September, indicating massive fraud at our borders. Even the money coming into Treasury was being misspent; projected foreign travel by the office of the president and cabinet was projected to be US$39 million, a figure that particularly enraged me given that the Ministry of Education had only received up to that time US$8 million, a fraction of the US$66 million originally budgeted to run over 72 administrative districts and 8 500 schools.

After Biti finished, I spoke, bemoaning our warped priorities. I pointed out that Singapore and Finland, two of the world's best education systems, had made education a budgetary priority for over four decades, something we weren't doing. In a statement that greatly angered the hardliners in cabinet, I questioned why we had just spent US$98 million constructing a new National Defence College, questioning "how can we spend US$98 million on this when our schools are collapsing and we have triple seating at many schools?" Mnangagwa, who was sitting next to me, took umbrage immediately, saying to me privately, "Education needs to be innovative like Defence – the National Defence College is being funded through 20 per cent of diamond revenues from Anjin (a joint venture company between the Chinese and the military)."[740] I responded that Education had no business in diamond mining, nor should Defence.

Despite the rising tensions within cabinet, the tentative discussions between Mugabe and me to explore a settlement with the British matured into a meeting attended by Mugabe, Mutasa, the British broker and myself on 27 November. The broker stressed that his role was informal and secret. His first task was to establish whether there was a broad desire to talk. Mugabe responded by saying he had no quarrel with the British people, so he was always ready to talk. The broker then suggested that Mugabe appoint "a trusted person who could act as an intermediary". At this point I offered to leave the meeting because I believed my role was confined to setting up the contact. Mugabe stopped me. "No – don't leave," he said. "I want you to continue to be part of the process." With that I remained and at the conclusion of the meeting Mugabe said that "future communications should continue to go through" me. The broker then went alone to meet Tsvangirai, Ncube and Mujuru. There were a few more discussions between Mugabe and me on the subject but, as the election season dawned with 2013, interest waned and nothing concrete ever came of the discussions.

The schizophrenic nature of the GNU came into focus early in the new year when once more I clashed with Zimbabwe Cricket. Through 2012 there had been simmering tensions between myself and the ZC board. Things came to a head when I received a delegation of senior black and white players claiming they had not been paid. I summoned the chairman and CEO of ZC, seeking an explanation. This resulted in the players being paid but it soured our relationship. But ultimately what caused our relationship to deteriorate further was a general directive I had given the Sports and Recreation Commission Board in 2012. In mid 2012 I had issued a ministerial directive,[741] in consultation with the SRC board, that all international matches (for all disciplines) should be rotated around the country, instead of only being held in Harare (as was generally the case with most sporting disciplines). In late 2012, after consulting again with the SRC board and sportspeople, I issued a further directive to the SRC that henceforth all national selection panels should be comprised of people who had played their respective sport at senior international level. There had been a number of selection controversies during my tenure – in bowls, football and cricket – involving selectors who had never played their sports at the highest level. I hoped that this new policy would resolve this. After the new policy was announced by the SRC all sports associations implemented it except for ZC. Within days a series of statements were issued through the government-controlled media, alleging that somehow my directive was racist and solely directed at the convenor of cricket selectors, a black person who had never played provincial cricket, never mind international cricket. Jonathan Moyo waded in too, describing the directive as "racist, illegal and barbaric". Calculating that an election was coming, ZC itself announced that it would defy the directive. There were, of course, several retired black Test cricketers who could have been appointed as selectors but none of them was political enough for the ZC board's liking, so had never been appointed. Because the policy had been announced by the SRC it was not mine to enforce, but some of the board were skittish and reluctant to get embroiled in a political battle.

It was in this atmosphere that, on 5 February, I met with Mugabe after cabinet. The main purpose of this meeting was for us to discuss the tentative talks involving the British broker, but we also discussed the cricket dispute. I explained that there was more to it than met the eye. The ZC board had got into a terrible financial mess and it was now some US$15 million in the red. In addition, I had received reports of financial impropriety. Tsvangirai and Ncube had also been briefed and were supportive so it came as a relief to get similar support from Mugabe, who said, "Don't worry about the racism allegations; I appreciate you briefing me, now you must do whatever is necessary to restore viability to cricket."

The SRC was hamstrung because, although I had written to Mugabe the previous October asking him to approve a new board, I had heard nothing further. Without the President's authority the SRC couldn't enforce its policy directive. The next day Mugabe approved the new SRC board, which included some people, such as David Ellman-Brown (a former chairman of ZC), who Mugabe knew would hold ZC to account. Subsequently, on 17 March I met with the CEO of the International Cricket Council, David Richardson, in Dubai, who provided me with some of the missing pieces of the puzzle I needed to prove there had been improper dealings within ZC.

Although I passed on the information I had gleaned to the SRC board, they were not able to hold ZC to account prior to my loss of office in July 2013 and thereafter, without further political backing, no further action was taken. However, Wisden India finally broke the story in June 2014. Several senior ZC board members were also directors of a Zimbabwean bank, Metbank. The Wisden report alleged that "in December 2011, when ZC received a $6m loan from the ICC that was designed to retire some of their debt, it (was) left in a non-interest-bearing account with Metbank for almost five months. Metbank benefited from its ability to loan the money out to third parties, while ZC suffered because its debt to the bank rose by around $300,000".[742] Neither Metbank nor any of its directors named in the report sued Wisden, giving credence to the allegations levelled against them. In January/February 2013, none of this evidence had seen the light of day, which enabled the culprits to use accusations of racism against me to divert attention away from their misdeeds.

This skulduggery paled into insignificance at the time because of far more momentous events that were taking place, particularly the constitutional reform process which was nearing completion. On 12 February Constitutional Affairs minister Matinenga reported that COPAC had endorsed the final draft on 31 January, which had been followed by parliament formally tabling and approving a motion for its adoption on 5 February. Our cabinet discussion focused on the process that should be adopted in the run up to a referendum, which the GPA mandated. While the three parties to the GNU had agreed to the draft constitution, there were significant voices, such as that of the NCA, that were firmly against the proposed constitution being adopted. They had not on principle participated in the process, believing that it unfairly favoured the three GNU political parties, and they made it clear that they would campaign for a "no" vote. I argued that "there should be no controversy in the Referendum process and full access to all media should be granted to those who opposed the new constitution". MDC-T minister Nelson Chamisa raised a laugh when he suggested, tongue in cheek, that the symbol for the "yes" vote should be "a clenched fist [the ZANU PF salute] and open hand [MDC] … together". As incongruous as this lighthearted suggestion was, it did sum up the gravity of the achievement: three political parties with radically different policies had managed to reach agreement.

Personally, I was in two minds about the new draft constitution because although I recognised it as a remarkable achievement, in my opinion it remained deeply flawed. Firstly, it did "not adequately cater for the fact that man cannot be trusted with power".[743] One thing the American founding fathers understood well was that if men are given unfettered or excessive power they have a natural tendency to abuse it, and to counter this they built in all sorts of checks and balances. Although the constitution was an improvement on the Lancaster House document (for example, executive powers in appointing judges, declaring states of emergency and appointing provincial governors had either been greatly reduced or removed altogether), it still gave far too much power to the executive. Secondly, the new constitutional order was going to be very expensive for a country that was already unable adequately to fund basic social services. The new parliament would "be far too large and expensive" and while the devolution clauses were welcome, "the number of provinces and size of provincial governments were going to make the attainment of this goal very expensive". Thirdly, the clauses on land were "blatantly racist" and would "inhibit investment in future". The line I hoped for had not been drawn on land seizures to conclude the historical injustice. White people under the new constitution could "never have security in owning agricultural land in future because it allowed any agricultural land to be taken from them in future simply because they are white". Such a racist clause, I argued, had "no place in any democratic constitution and would deter foreign investors from investing in Zimbabwe's agricultural sector in future".

On the eve of the election I issued a statement calling for a "yes" vote despite my concerns. I wrote the following:

"At the end of the day, for all the obvious flaws in both the process and content, the draft offered to the Zimbabwean electorate is an improvement on what we have. In the absence of any viable non violent alternative I hope that despite these flaws the Zimbabwean public will vote yes tomorrow.

"I am aware that there are some people, who I respect from a variety of backgrounds, who are urging a no vote. While I understand the nature and gravity of their concerns and objections they must ask themselves what a no vote will result in. In my view it will play into the hands of hardliners who ironically did all they could to derail the process, because they fear the positive effect of the good features in this new constitution. A no vote will result in Zimbabwe retaining its present constitution with all its objectionable clauses, including the identical land provisions which are so racist. But that will also mean that there will be no devolution of power, no dual citizen rights, no rights regarding children and in general the retention of the current deficient Bill of Rights. It will also mean that the President can declare a State of Emergency without Parliament being able to do much about it, and to exercise power in a wide range of matters as is the case now. A no vote will also plunge Zimbabwe into another period of uncertainty and possible political conflict. It will mean that our experiment in ending our penchant for settling our political differences using violence has failed.

"One may ask what the 'Yes' is for – it is in essence a yes to breaking the cycle of violence which has afflicted our nation for so long – a yes to taking an important step forward towards our ultimate goal of turning Zimbabwe into a vibrant democracy. No sane person would ever argue that this is the end of the road. In many respects it is simply the end of the beginning.

"Accordingly my prayer is that all Zimbabweans will turn out tomorrow and vote 'Yes'."[744]

The Zimbabwean electorate responded to our collective call and voted overwhelmingly "yes". The official results stated that 94.49% of the electorate voted, with some 179 489 voting no and an overwhelming 3 079 966 voting yes. While I believed that the Zimbabwean public had demonstrated overwhelming support for the new constitution, I was deeply troubled by the results, which bore little relation to the numbers of people who actually turned out. It served the interests of ZANU PF hardliners, whose operatives controlled the process, to inflate the numbers of people who voted, particularly in some rural areas, because this would help them justify brazen fraud in the elections which were to follow.

CHAPTER 28

BACK TO THE FUTURE
MARCH 2013 TO DECEMBER 2014

"Tho' much is taken, much abides; and though
We are not now that strength which in old days
Moved earth and heaven; that which we are, we are;
One equal temper of heroic hearts,
Made weak by time and fate, but strong in will
To strive, to seek, to find, and not to yield."
— ALFRED LORD TENNYSON, "ULYSSES"

The coterie of ZANU PF hardliners who had never wanted the GNU in the first place, and who had been pushing for early elections since 2011, were delighted that the final obstacle blocking elections, namely, a new constitution, had been removed. Given the history of Zimbabwe's elections, the fear in both MDCs was that violence would rear its ugly head again. Shortly before the constitutional referendum, on the night of 23 February, the twelve-year-old son of an MDC-T activist, Christpowers Maisiri, died when the hut he was sleeping in was set on fire. His father immediately accused ZANU PF, saying, "I know who did this – my house has been burned nine times before."[745] The murder generated an emotional debate in cabinet the following Tuesday, when MDC-T Minister Jameson Timba spoke about the contradiction between ZANU PF's words and its actions. A month before Mugabe had concluded his eulogy at Vice-President John Nkomo's funeral with a stirring, if somewhat novel, call: "Peace begins with me, peace begins with you, peace begins with all of us." Timba questioned the genuineness of that cry, as did I when I contributed to the debate. I said how encouraged I had been to hear Mugabe make that appeal but feared we were now "sliding back into violence".

Cabinet resolved to await a report from the police but when this was presented a week later by Co-Minister of Home Affairs Mohadi it exacerbated tensions. Not only was the report laced with gratuitous political comments, but it also suggested that the fire was an accident, which contradicted other evidence that pointed to it being arson. I spoke about the "crisis of public confidence in the ZRP" and the "danger that the incident could blow out of all proportion". The debate got bogged down on how we could get an objective report compiled to get to the truth of the matter, and ultimately foundered on this issue. No prosecutions were ever brought.

The aftermath of this tragedy gave rise to two positive developments. The first was the exposure of ZANU PF's vulnerability to accusations of violence. Timba did an excellent job in briefing SADC heads of state about the incident, which greatly annoyed the hardliners in cabinet. SADC heads were not prepared to tolerate another violent election and a strident message to that effect was conveyed to ZANU PF. Even their hardliners realised that they would have to behave themselves and there were no major incidents of violence during the entire campaign which followed. Secondly, the debate revealed sharp differences within ZANU PF. At the conclusion of the debate on 5 March, Mujuru made an intensely poignant comment, stating how we needed "to handle this carefully because we all (needed) each other – remember that some of us understand the pain of these infernos".[746]

A week later, at cabinet on 12 March, Mujuru left us in no doubt where her sympathies lay when she said that we needed a "copy of the JOMIC[747] report which I understand contradicts the ZRP report". In saying this she placed herself firmly in the camp of those who were dissatisfied with the police report. As if to highlight the differences between hardliners and moderates, Mnangagwa chipped in with a remarkably cynical comment referring to the Kenyan elections, congratulating Raila Odinga "for accepting the result and not running around East Africa complaining about 19 people who had died". While primarily a dig at Tsvangirai, the difference between his attitude and Mujuru's was startling.

It soon became apparent that ZANU PF's principal weapon would not be violence, but rather its manipulation of the electoral process in general, and the registration of voters in particular. Anticipating this, both MDCs had argued for effective clauses in both the new constitution and proposed new electoral laws to ensure that all citizens would be allowed to register as citizens and voters. Chapter 3 of the new constitution was entirely devoted to enshrining citizens' rights, in particular birth rights, which had been denied in terms of the many amendments made by ZANU PF to the Lancaster House constitution. In addition, Section 67(3) specified the, perhaps self-evident, right of all citizens over eighteen to vote and stand for public office. As part of this belt-and-braces approach there was a specific transitional provision[748] which obliged the registrar general, under the supervision of the Zimbabwe Electoral Commission, to "conduct a special and intensive voter registration and voters' roll inspection exercise for at least 30 days after the publication day" of the new constitution. Finally, agreement was reached among the negotiators and the principals that the new Electoral Act would have a clause entitling all political parties to a "searchable and analysable electronic copy of the voters' roll". This provision overcame the Supreme Court ruling we had failed to obtain way back in 2001, which was critical if we were to be able to audit the voters' roll. So as far as the laws were concerned, we were satisfied that the necessary protections were in place. The major problem was that both the registrar general's office and the ZEC were controlled by ZANU PF sympathisers or operatives. That was exacerbated by the fact that the ministry of Home Affairs, which the RG's office fell under, was effectively controlled by ZANU PF. Although the ministry was jointly run by ZANU PF and MDC-T ministers, the latter's Minister Theresa Makone had circles run around her by her counterpart and subordinates.

Within weeks of the constitutional referendum, signs emerged that the voter registration and inspection exercise would be compromised, despite the constitutional and legal safeguards. On 23 February, Makone gave a report to cabinet regarding the RG's office which didn't inspire confidence in me. Among other things she said that "read only copies" of the electronic voters' roll would be made available, which would be useless. Minister Misihairabwi-Mushonga complained that the RG's office was still trying to enforce laws that had been overturned by the new constitution, such as insisting that people renounce "foreign citizenship" before being allowed to register. Having heard of similar stories in Bulawayo, I reminded the meeting of the new constitutional rights and pointed out that in South Africa voters could check a website to see whether they were on the voters' roll.

Chinamasa and other ZANU PF ministers voiced their opposition to placing the voters' roll on the web. This debate set the tone for a succession of debates, indeed battles, around the voter registration process in the ensuing weeks. In our meeting on 30 April we agreed that a searchable copy would be made available, but to my amazement when I read the minutes of that meeting prior to our next meeting there was no mention of that agreement! When I sought to correct the minutes when cabinet commenced on 7 May, a spirited attempt was made by some hardliners to draw back from our agreement. In this meeting, Minister Ncube spelt out how the entire process was being subverted: the voter registration process had commenced on 29 April but when the MDC-N requested details of where it was taking place we were denied that information. The entire operation was cloaked in secrecy and the MDC-N only got the information of registration centres on 2 May. The ZEC advertised voter registration centres on 4 May for places that had already been visited by registration teams! A further facet of ZANU PF's strategy was revealed when Mugabe, loudly supported by Mnangagwa, stated as the meeting drew to a conclusion: "Time is not on our side, we have to have an election by June 29," being the fifth anniversary of his controversial election as President in 2008. None of the MDCs' lawyers, Biti, Ncube and myself, took much notice at the time of Mugabe's comment because we were aware that the existing constitution had a provision – 58(1) – stating that an election must be held within "four months after" the dissolution of parliament, namely, before the end of October 2013. Indeed the new constitution had not even been made law yet. Immediately after cabinet most of us walked across to parliament to pass Constitutional Amendment Bill 20 which ushered in the new constitution. The new constitution would only be officially "published" in the *Gazette* on 22 May, which would then be the date when the intensive voter registration process should begin. That was the law but hardliners within ZANU PF had other ideas.

Unbeknown to many of us at cabinet that day was that a few days earlier, on 2 May, an urgent application had been filed in the Supreme Court by a previously relatively unknown person, one Jealously Mbizvo Mawarire, citing Mugabe, Tsvangirai, Mutambara, Ncube and the attorney general, seeking an order that the elections be held "no later than June 30 2013". When our legal teams received the court papers it seemed a farcical application because of the clear wording of Section 58 of the current constitution, which was still law because the new constitution had not been published; in any event the new constitution's provisions regarding the timing of elections were prospective and had no bearing on the matter. It was in this frame of mind that we all again debated the voter registration exercise in the following cabinet meeting on 14 May. The issue dominated cabinet and revealed again profound differences of opinion within ZANU PF. Most MDC ministers spent time ridiculing the existing registration process and the state of the voters' roll. Minister Timba had us all in stitches when he revealed that Ian Douglas Smith and long-since-dead former RF minister of Justice Desmond Lardner-Burke were still on the voters' roll in his constituency. Even Mujuru chipped in, telling us she had bought a voters' roll for her constituency, Mount Darwin North, and found that in her own village, whereas over 100 were eligible, only nine people were actually registered. I noted in my diary:

> "Fascinating debate. Mnangagwa quiet, Kasukuwere holding his head as if he has a headache, Mpofu staring at the ceiling looking bleak – they hate this debate because they fear the electorate – absolutely and equally fascinating that Mujuru is totally comfortable."[749]

My suggestion that we involve the 106 000 teachers under my jurisdiction to assist the voter registration exercise was met with a stony silence from the hardliners, who didn't like where the process was going. Things got worse for the hardliners as the registration debate continued to dominate cabinet during the next meeting, held on 21 May. Chinamasa, who had tried to argue that aspiring new citizens needed both parents born in SADC, was put right when reminded that the new constitution only required one parent. A broad consensus was emerging that the registration process was fundamentally flawed, with only Mpofu and Mnangagwa vainly insisting that everything was fine in their own constituencies. There was a further major problem looming for the hardliners. Government had agreed to host the UN World Tourism Organisation (UNWTO) conference in August, which would clash with the projected date of the election. I raised this "elephant in the room", pointing out that the special 30-day registration exercise mandated by the new constitution only started when the new constitution was published (which happened the next day) and would last until late June. The election process, which had to last a minimum of 42 days, would only begin then, taking the election well into August – an election by the end of June or even July was legally impossible. This statement caused Mnangagwa to snap. He turned to me, and said aggressively, wagging his finger at me, "You concentrate on education and let us concentrate on the electoral process."[750]

Mnangagwa actually had no cause to fear because the new Constitutional Court was about to do his bidding. Immediately upon publication of the new constitution on 22 May, Mugabe appointed a few more judges, without consulting Tsvangirai as he was obliged to do in terms of the GPA, to enable the new Constitutional Court to operate. With equal alacrity the Constitutional Court then heard argument on the Mawarire case on 24 May. Mugabe's counsel conveniently concurred with Mawarire's lawyer's interpretation of the old constitution, agreeing that the President was "already out of time in fixing and proclaiming dates for the harmonised general elections".[751] Mutambara didn't bother to oppose the matter but both Tsvangirai and Ncube's counsel argued that as parliament had not yet been dissolved, and only had to be dissolved on 29 June, the four-month period required by the existing Lancaster House constitution only ran from then. The wording of the relevant clause – Section 58 of the old constitution – was unequivocally clear and so we were deeply shocked, but not surprised, when Chief Justice Chidyausiku, supported by seven other judges, handed down a judgment in Mawarire and Mugabe's favour on 31 May. However, even Chidyausiku could not find ways around the need for a minimum 42-day election period and so ordered that the election be held by "not later than 31 July 2013". Only Deputy Chief Justice Malaba was bold enough to disagree, handing down a dissenting judgment which said in part:

"The applicant has turned the clear and unambiguous language of the provisions into a subject-matter of a question of interpretation which has unfortunately plunged the court into irreconcilable differences of opinion. I, however, refuse to have wool cast over the inner eye of my mind on this matter.

"The contention that the President is under a duty to issue a proclamation fixing the day or days of the election within a period of four months before the date of automatic dissolution of

Parliament is difficult to justify. It requires that the word "after" in s 58(1) be ignored or expunged and in its place read the word "before". On what event would the proclamation fixing the date or dates of the election be based on except itself?

"The fact is that there is nothing in s 58(1) of the former Constitution imposing on the President an obligation to fix a day or days of the election to coincide with the date of the end of the natural life of Parliament."[752]

In a stroke the hardliners' position had been won. The "rule of law" would have to be complied with. The Constitutional Court was the highest court so there was no appeal. Although we could go back to parliament to amend the law, Mugabe, Mnangagwa and Chinamasa were steadfastly against this. The fact that this would completely subvert the voter registration process didn't bother them; indeed this was the motivation behind it all along. Disingenuously, they argued that their hands were now tied by the Constitutional Court and that the election would have to be held by 31 July.

There was one final obstacle lying in the path of the hardliners. The election could not be run in the absence of a new Electoral Act which complied with the dictates of the new constitution, which itself had introduced radical changes, such as proportional representation. The existing Electoral Act did not cater for these changes, rendering an election impossible. The two MDCs still controlled a majority in parliament, which meant that ZANU PF could not steamroll any legislation without our consent. This knowledge enabled us to debate the ongoing fraught voter registration exercise with some peace of mind when cabinet convened on 11 June, despite the recent Constitutional Court judgment.

The intensive registration exercise, which had begun on 23 May, was becoming increasingly farcical in the context of the date set for the election by the Constitutional Court. I pointed out that in Ward 4 of my constituency the voter registration exercise was only due to start on 2 July 2, *after* the close of nomination courts on 1 July. This would effectively bar any prospective candidate from standing for election, who had to be on the voters' roll before the sitting of the nomination court, but who had not managed to register yet! Biti pointed to the ridiculous allocation of voter registration centres with one rural constituency of Mhondoro, with a population of some 100 000 people, having more registration centres than Harare and Bulawayo, with combined populations of 4 million! There was also extensive debate about the new Electoral law due to be presented to parliament, with many ministers from both ZANU PF and the MDC parties making suggestions regarding what should be included. No agreement was reached regarding the final terms of the Electoral law. For example, in some of her concluding remarks ZANU PF Minister Muchena objected to some of the proposed provisions relating to the proportional representation's threshold system. I asked Chinamasa a series of questions about the content of the new law, seeking clarification of what form it would take. Our clear understanding was that these suggestions would be further debated thoroughly in parliament to achieve a consensus before becoming law. At no time did Justice Minister Chinamasa advise us that anything other than a parliamentary debate would be employed to introduce the new law (such as Presidential Powers regulations), nor did he present a final version of a proposed Electoral law for approval incorporating all the points that had been discussed that day in cabinet.

The ZANU PF hardliners had one last trick up their sleeves. Two days after the cabinet meeting, Mugabe published the Presidential Powers (Temporary Measures) (Amendment of Electoral Act) Regulations,[753] amending vast swathes of the old Electoral Act without going through parliament. The regulations, clearly Chinamasa'a creation, sought to rely on the Mawarire judgment in stating that it was "inexpedient to await the passage through Parliament of an Act". Mendaciously, the regulations stated that "Cabinet approved the needed amendments to the Electoral Act at its meeting on 11th June 2013". While it was correct that we had agreed some amendments, we had not agreed a final version which all of us had expected would be done in parliament when an entirely new Electoral bill would be presented.

But in any event the use of the Presidential Powers Act was illegal. Aside from the fact that parliament was in session and able to pass a new act, Section 157 of the new constitution made it clear that "an Act of Parliament must provide for the conduct of elections", not regulations. In addition, the Presidential Powers Act itself stated that regulations could not be issued for any matter "which the Constitution requires to be provided for by an Act".[754]

This brazen deception and abuse of law caused an unprecedented furore and an intense confrontation between the GPA partners at an extraordinary meeting of SADC heads of state in Maputo on Sunday, 16 June. In that meeting Ncube and Biti laid bare ZANU PF's deceitful conduct before the heads of state of South Africa, DRC, Botswana, Lesotho, Mozambique and Namibia, causing serious embarrassment to Mugabe. Although the communiqué issued after the meeting diplomatically only mentioned that the "validity of the electoral regulations" was an issue, it "agreed on the need for the Government of Zimbabwe to engage the Constitutional Court to seek more time beyond (the) 31 July deadline". It also called on the three parties to "create a conducive environment for holding credible elections".

Unsurprisingly, the principal architect of the Presidential Powers Regulations, Chinamasa, was not present when cabinet reconvened on 18 June. We all took turns to lambaste Chinamasa because he, more than any of the others, had been deceptive. Biti was the most severe, stating at one point "Coltart was right to ask questions (the previous week) because we have now seen that the Minister of Justice was already planning to spring a surprise – there was no way they could have been drafted so quickly and they must have been drafted even before Cabinet sat without us knowing". As had happened in previous meetings, a succession of ministers detailed serious anomalies in the voter registration process. As we hammered away at these concerns, ZANU PF ministers gradually tired and excused themselves, leaving only Mujuru, Mzembi, Nhema and Murerwa, plus Mugabe himself, still there at the end. Mugabe, looking tired, said we would only be able to resolve the impasse at a special meeting he would call to be attended by principals and lawyers from the three parties. The next afternoon, Mugabe convened the promised meeting at State House which was attended by him, Mujuru, Tsvangirai, Ncube, Mutambara, Biti, Matinenga, Goche, Mohadi, Chinamasa, Mnangagwa, Cabinet Secretary Dr Sibanda, Director General of the CIO Bonyongwe, my law partner Josephat Tshuma, and me. Most of the meeting was devoted to Biti and me explaining why the use of Presidential Powers was illegal, which Chinamasa struggled to respond to. He explained to Mugabe that he felt as if he was appearing in court but had not been given an opportunity to prepare his heads of argument in reply. It was a pathetic reply because he would have known full well what our arguments were from cabinet, the SADC Heads of State meeting, and from the various public articles written about the matter. Nevertheless

Mugabe adjourned the meeting, mumbling that it may be reconvened or else the principals would agree on a course of action. Such was our lack of confidence in what Mugabe, Tsvangirai and Mutambara would achieve that Biti, Tshuma and I met straight after the State House meeting to finalise court papers to challenge Mugabe's use of Presidential Powers regulations.

It was finally resolved by the principals that Chinamasa be ordered to bring an application to the Constitutional Court, seeking an extension of the election date. When he did so, his application for a two-week extension was couched in deliberately weak terms: it stated that he was perfectly happy with the Constitutional Court's ruling but that SADC had directed an extension. In other words, the only reason he offered the Constitutional Court to change their earlier ruling was a non-binding foreign direction, which wouldn't have impressed any court worth its salt. Nowhere did Chinamasa advert to the fact that the constitution would be breached in several respects if the 31 July date was not changed.

Lawyers for Tsvangirai and Ncube had to take the unusual step of opposing Chinamasa's application so that they could argue why the whole process was illegal. At the same time three further urgent applications, including the one Biti, Tshuma and I had worked on, were filed in the Constitutional Court seeking extensions and an order setting aside Mugabe's Proclamation of the election and use of Presidential Powers Regulations. But we knew that the strength of our arguments would have little bearing on the outcome of these cases.

Our only remaining card was unity. At the conclusion of cabinet on 25 June, Biti came up to me and said, "Just as the Constitutional Court is ZANU PF's game changer, so a coalition can be our game changer", and never was a truer word spoken. In fact since February I had been talking to Biti and Mangoma about how a coalition could best be organised. On 19 February, Mangoma and I had met after cabinet; since then there had been a series of tentative discussions between the MDC-T and MDC-N negotiators but these appeared to be drifting. I felt strongly that unless we formed a coalition we would see a repeat of 2008 and so I was frustrated by the lack of progress through March, April and May. Eventually, in early June, with ZANU PF's helter-skelter determination to have early elections now glaringly obvious, the MDC-N national executive formally appointed Paul Themba Nyathi and Priscilla Misihairabwi-Mushonga to negotiate. Having kept Ncube in the loop regarding my informal discussions with Mangoma and Biti, I got his blessing to continue those discussions.

Tsvangirai and I are both avid golfers, so on 8 June I arranged to play golf with him in Bulawayo, which provided a relaxed environment to better understand what was blocking the negotiations. After the State House meeting on 19 June had demonstrated ZANU PF's intentions so vividly, I wrote to Mangoma and Biti, setting out what I thought were the key elements of a coalition agreement:

a. Composition of the presidium. Much of the focus has been on getting support for one Presidential candidate and while I agree that it is important to agree on a single candidate to stand against Mugabe, if that is the sole focus we won't get beyond first base. The electorate will need to see hard evidence that the coalition or electoral pact is real and the best method of doing that is by ensuring that both the agreed Presidential candidate and the vice Presidential nominees are on the stump together.

b. Agreement not to split the vote at parliamentary level. The ideal of course would be to ensure that only one candidate from the coalition will stand in each seat but our primary election processes have gone too far for that. I think at the very least we need to urgently look at those marginal seats which we lost to Zanu PF last time around and in those seats alone we need to agree on which party should contest the seat.

c. Agreement regarding the size of Cabinet, the posts in Cabinet and the posts which will be allocated to participating parties in the coalition or electoral pact in the event of victory.

d. Agreement regarding the broad policies which will be implemented by the coalition in its first year. There also needs to be agreement regarding the principles which will be employed to govern disputes within the coalition to ensure its continuity for at least a given period if not for the entire 5 years of Parliament.[755]

Although I and others kept talking, there was so much bad blood between Tsvangirai and Ncube that by nomination day on 28 June nothing had been agreed to. By then it was too late. The MDC-T focus was on getting us to agree on one presidential candidate, namely Tsvangirai, but for that to happen there needed to be broad grassroots support and agreement at parliamentary level. Both MDC-T and MDC-N intended fielding candidates throughout the country, ensuring that once again we would split the vote. When the public realised that there would be no coalition agreement my in-box started to fill with hate mail again. It served no constructive purpose to reveal details of my private efforts to broker a coalition, so I just bit my tongue. The worst aspect for me about the failure to agree a coalition was that both MDCs couldn't now do the obvious – withdraw from the election. The electoral process was so flawed, so illegal, that the only logical step was to withdraw, which would compel SADC to hold ZANU PF to account. But such was the distrust between the MDC-T and MDC-N that neither could withdraw for fear that the other would remain in the election, winning seats and giving the process credibility.

My own appearance at the nomination court was the smoothest ever. For the first time since 2000 my citizenship wasn't questioned and my papers to stand in the Bulawayo East House of Assembly seat were accepted without a fuss. The MDC-N had asked me to stand in the Lower House again because of constitutional changes to the Senate. Henceforth the Senate would be elected by means of proportional representation, based on votes cast in the House of Assembly ballot. The party's thinking was that it would get more votes if I stood on my own rather than appeared on a party list for the Senate. My old Khumalo Senatorial constituency had been abolished; the original constituency had two House seats, Bulawayo East and Central, within it, so it made sense to contest one of those seats.

Shortly before nomination day I had wondered whether it was worthwhile standing again. Although once again I had a superb campaign team, from the outset of the campaign I knew the odds would be stacked against me. Aside from the deeply frustrating divisions within the opposition, it was clear to me that ZANU PF hardliners had learnt the lessons of 2008 and no stone would be left unturned in subverting the electoral process. When I expressed these reservations to my campaign manager he was appalled and spent a good half hour persuading me to submit my papers, which I then did.

My only remaining faint hope was that the Constitutional Court would act professionally in handling the challenge of the constitutionality of Mugabe's use of Presidential Powers to introduce the new electoral laws. Unlike the lightning quick way in which the Mawarire case had been handled, the Constitutional Court had delayed in setting down a date for hearing until 4 July.

The final cabinet meeting of the GNU was held on 2 July. All the hardliners were back in attendance, all of them looking smug. Obert Mpofu was gushing in his praise of Chinamasa, but the majority of ZANU PF ministers appeared strangely subdued. I wrote in my diary: "I fear that Mujuru is isolated." The GNU was brought to an end with a homily from Mugabe who told us that we needed "to do our best to have a peaceful election, the most non violent election ever". He concluded with a directive: "Please do not spill blood." Everyone, including Mnangagwa, pounded the table vigorously before leaving the room. Two days later the Constitutional Court peremptorily dismissed all four electoral cases brought before it. None of us was surprised. The last hurdle in ZANU PF's way had been cleared by a supportive court.

There was a small glimmer of sanity on 5 July when the MDC-N and ZAPU announced that they had entered into an electoral pact. In the press conference both Ncube and Dabengwa said they were open to cooperation with other parties. Shortly after the press conference I got a call from Tsvangirai, who sounded shocked and wanted to know whether it was true. In confirming the news, I told Tsvangirai that both leaders had expressed a willingness to expand the pact. Tsvangirai responded angrily, alleging that Ncube had not responded to calls or invitations to meetings. All I could do was reiterate that I personally was committed to a broad coalition and would do all I could to facilitate dialogue. As the call ended my heart sank with the realisation that any remote hope of a coalition between the two MDCs had been extinguished.

Although the election was less than a month away, I felt I couldn't abrogate my responsibilities as minister of Education. Three countries' education systems had particularly captured my attention – those of Singapore, Finland and South Korea. All were small countries like Zimbabwe and all had consistently scored well in PISA[756] (an international assessment of the competencies of fifteen-year-olds in reading, mathematics and science). I had negotiated an agreement with the South Koreans to bring out science and maths teachers, subjects in which we still had serious shortages of skilled teachers. Well before it became apparent that the election would be in July I had accepted an invitation to travel to Busan, South Korea, to attend the World Forum of Education Ministers, which included an opportunity to cement the Korean teacher arrangement, something I felt needed to be honoured. As a result, during the first week of the campaign, when I should have been on the stump in Bulawayo, I was on the other side of the world. And there was one final important education matter I had to attend to on my return. For several months I had been involved in the formulation of a new Schools Improvement Grant programme with UNICEF and the ETF. The idea was to channel donor money direct to schools across the country to rehabilitate their infrastructure. It was rather complicated because many remote rural schools would have to open bank accounts and we had to ensure that the millions of dollars disbursed would be spent correctly. This required one final meeting in Harare after I got back from Korea.

The net result was that my campaign only began in earnest on 17 July, a fortnight from the election. Although my campaign team were confident and we had received word that my opponents were pessimistic, I remained concerned about our prospects. In an interview I gave on 17 July, I said: "I am under no illusions. This is going to be a tough battle. I appreciate that this seat was lost by the party that I am standing for in 2008."[757]

Although, unlike previous elections, there was no violence, the campaign in Bulawayo East was marked by high levels of apathy and underhand tactics. None of my opponents appeared to be campaigning at all. My two main opponents from ZANU PF and MDC-T appeared to place their hope in winning on the back of their respective presidential candidates' popularity. Inevitably, though, things did get nasty in the final week. It started with the leader of one of my campaign teams, Malthus Ncube, being arrested by police on an accusation levelled against him by a ZANU PF operative that he had torn the corner off a poster of a ZANU PF city council candidate. The evening of 24 July and the next morning were spent bailing him out on spurious charges which were eventually dropped. If that wasn't bad enough, three days later ZANU PF thugs tore down scores of my posters in broad daylight along the Bulawayo airport road. I received a report soon after the thugs had started and immediately telephoned the Member in Charge of the same station where Ncube had been locked up. Despite their systematically tearing down all my posters from the airport along a fifteen-kilometre stretch into town, nothing was done by the police to stop the thugs, never mind arrest them all. I reported the matter to SADC observers who personally witnessed the thuggery but they were powerless to do anything.

But there were much more serious things happening nationally. Despite repeated requests to the ZEC for a copy of the voters' roll, by 26 July we still had not received one, prompting me to issue a statement pointing out the breach of the Electoral Act. At that stage we had not even received a paper copy of the roll. Worse was to follow. On 29 July, two days before the election, the chair of the ZEC, Rita Makarau, disingenuously announced that due to "logistical challenges" the RG's office "may not be in a position to issue the electronic copies".[758] In the same report she stated that "hard copies of the voters' roll can now be obtained by candidates from the office of the RG".

In a letter of complaint which I addressed to the Head of the SADC Observer team in Bulawayo on 30 July, I pointed out that as at 2 pm that day, just hours before the election, we had "not managed to obtain even a hard copy (paper) version of the roll".[759] In the same letter I documented six serious breaches of the Constitution and Electoral laws. What was particularly galling was the breach of the new Section 21 (7) of the Electoral laws – which specifically obliged the ZEC to provide an electronic copy which allowed "its contents to be searched and analysed" so as to enable political parties to search easily for particular voters and audit the roll for duplications or other anomalies. This was something we had fought hard for since 2001 and was now just brazenly disregarded, using the mendacious excuse that their computers could not generate a copy. I questioned how it could possibly be easier to print voluminous paper copies running into thousands of pages, and yet impossible, in this modern computer age, to burn a single CD with the same information on it.

The surest sign that ZANU PF hardliners had the whole election sewn up came on the eve of the election in Harare. On Monday, 29 July Tsvangirai addressed one of the largest rallies ever held in Zimbabwe when well over 100 000 MDC-T supporters converged on open grounds to the west of Harare's city centre. Photographs show a red carpet of enthusiastic people as far as the eye could see. It was objectively estimated to have been the largest political rally since Mugabe returned to Zimbabwe in 1980 and, as one journalist wrote at the time, should have "sent shivers down the spine of the man currently occupying State House". Despite all the electoral fraud, when I heard about the rally I thought the same – was it possible that Zimbabweans would turn out in such numbers to overwhelm even the electoral fraud? However, the next day I could see that Mugabe was completely nonplussed. Addressing a press conference, flanked by Mnangagwa, he paradoxically appeared supremely confident. When asked what he would do if he lost, Mugabe said flippantly, "Well, there are only two outcomes. Win or lose, you can't be both. You either win or lose. If you lose, then you must surrender to those who have won. If you win then those who have lost must also surrender to you, this is it. We will do so, yeah, comply with the rules."

A *New York Times* journalist asked whether he would continue governing with the MDC and Mugabe was remarkably confident, saying: "I don't think we will have the same result. I think we will have an outright victory."[760]

Vice-President Mujuru was nowhere to be seen. Mnangagwa didn't comment but sat with a smug look on his face. The moment Mugabe said that the loser should "surrender" I knew he was supremely confident of victory because he would never have said that if he felt it was he who would be doing the surrendering. Juxtaposing his confident statement with Tsvangirai's massive rally the day before didn't make sense unless Mugabe was privy to plans afoot that would guarantee his victory.

Those plans became obvious soon after polling commenced on 31 July. I had decided to focus my attention on the eight polling stations located within a two-kilometre radius of the only military barracks in Bulawayo East constituency, and so I went there at dawn. In the run up to the election, the ZEC had almost trebled the number of polling stations around the barracks without any justification or consultation. In the 2008 election there had been a relatively low turnout at the three polling stations which then surrounded the barracks, but when I arrived at the polling station directly opposite the barracks there was already a long queue outside the station comprised of young men who, although not in uniform, all had close-cropped hair and were wearing new jeans. As I drove around the other stations close to the barracks during the day I saw similar scenes – lines of young men waiting, with military discipline, to vote. I was later to learn that over 30 per cent of all new voter registrations in the constituency were from the military and police. I was also to learn that these young men voted early and often. In the course of the day disturbing reports filtered in. Numerous buses were seen ferrying young men into the constituency from Imbizo barracks located some 20 kilometres from Bulawayo. Subsequent analysis showed that 42 per cent of the ZANU PF candidate's votes came from these eight polling stations – out of the total of 39 spread throughout the constituency. What was equally remarkable is that the ZANU PF candidate's votes increased by a staggering 246 per cent over those received in 2008. In three of the polling stations located near to the barracks at the Museum, Thomas Rudland School, and Paddonhurst, the votes cast for Mugabe were remarkably consistent: 220, 220 and 224 votes. The votes cast for Mugabe in all the eight polling stations located around the barracks, bar one, were significantly greater than anywhere else in the constituency. In the four stations closest to the barracks Mugabe received 994 votes, more than all the votes he'd received in the entire constituency in 2008.

But other tricks were at play. Shortly after 8 am my pastor, Kevin Thomson, phoned to say that when he had tried to vote his name wasn't on the voters' roll. When he hunted around he established that his name was in another ward, but *outside* my constituency. Even though he had lived in the same house for over 20 years, somebody had unilaterally moved him out of my constituency. Reports rolled in of a massive turn-away of voters, and by the end of the day 1 218 had been turned away. The vast majority were people like Thomson who had been on the roll for decades. Another interesting pattern emerged: the vast majority of those who were turned away came from areas that had been my strongholds in 2008, with few being turned away in polling stations around the barracks.

There were many other serious anomalies and breaches of the Electoral law which came to light in the course of the day.[761] Each voter was required to dip a finger in what was supposed to be indelible pink ink to show that they had voted. We tested the ink using normal soap and it came off after a few washes. An appropriate chemical would have taken it off instantly. Compounding that situation was that ultraviolet lights used to check for ink in all previous elections were suddenly absent. Without any explanation this vital check to prevent multiple voting had been removed by the ZEC. The plan was ludicrously brazen: we had been denied access to the voters' roll so that we could not check whether people had been registered on multiple occasions; the ink designed to prevent them from voting again came off easily, and in any event the absence of the ultraviolet lights made it near possible to check.

Even so the military and the ZANU PF hardliners were not taking any chances. Despite a clear prohibition in the Electoral laws,[762] policemen were involved in recording the numbers of people who voted all day and were present when the count started – all the while communicating results by radio to some central command.

By the close of the poll it was clear to me that the electoral process had been totally subverted with military precision and planning. The only remaining question was whether I would survive the purge. As results came in through the night two things became apparent: Mugabe's votes in the presidential election had increased by an astonishing amount – 393 per cent; and the race for the parliamentary seat between the MDC-T candidate and me was neck and neck. As the results for each polling station came in there would be either a roar or cries of despair in our election headquarters. By the early hours of the morning I was 200 votes ahead with results from only three stations left to come in. We then waited inexplicably a few hours before the final results came through in a flurry, revealing that I had lost by 19 votes. Some of my campaign team burst into tears, but I experienced a remarkable and inexplicable peace.

A grim picture emerged as results came in from across the country. There had been massive fraud countrywide and ridiculous results. Tendai Biti, who had won his seat with a thumping 8 000 votes' majority in 2008, narrowly won by some 300 votes. Other key members of cabinet, like MDC-T's Elton Mangoma, had lost their seats. Mugabe had dramatically "increased" his share of the vote from 43.2% in 2008 to 61.09%, with Tsvangirai's share dropping from 47.9% to 33.94%. ZANU PF had secured over two thirds of the House of Assembly seats, with 197 against the MDC-T's 70 and MDC-N's 2.

Strangely, my dominant emotion was relief. I had an overwhelming sense that after 30 years of struggle I had been saved the trauma of having to go back to a parliament dominated once again by ZANU PF. Although I had lost to an MDC-T candidate, not a ZANU PF candidate, the result was just what ZANU PF hardliners wanted – namely, me out of their hair. When I was asked whether I would, given the narrow margin, demand a recount against my MDC-T opponent, I recoiled. The prospect of winning the recount and then having to beat my head against a brick wall for five years was anathema. My sense was that the good Lord had given me a chance to recharge my batteries. Having fought the good fight, it was time for a rest.

Although I wasn't surprised by the results, the MDC-T appeared paralysed by them. ZANU PF's cunning strategy of eschewing violence worked. Unlike previous elections, there was no blood in the streets to embarrass foreign observers. Western observers had been banned from attending so we relied on African observers to cry foul about the breaches of the law, but nearly all of them turned a blind eye to that. Their mandate, given the awful June 2008 elections, was to ensure that there was no violence, which there wasn't. Only SADC and the Botswana government voiced any concerns. The latter's Foreign minister, Phandu Skelemani, stated that "various incidents and circumstances were revealed that call into question whether the entire electoral process, and thus its final result, can be recognised as having been fair, transparent and credible". But the AU weighed in with comments that the elections were "free, honest and credible", allowing Mugabe to be sworn in on 22 August 2013 without the continental embarrassment that had attended him in 2008.

The MDC-T was in such disarray that although a few legal actions were started, they soon collapsed in a heap. While I produced a detailed report in mid August, cataloguing all the constitutional breaches and other illegalities, none of the parties opposed to ZANU PF, and even well-funded civic organisations, was able to produce reports quickly exposing and proving how ZANU PF had subverted the entire electoral process. This failure gave ZANU PF a monopoly over its message, namely, that they had enjoyed a stunning reversal of fortune. They could claim that they were the darlings of the Zimbabwean electorate once more.

The ZANU PF hardliners who had secured the victory were rewarded when Mugabe announced his new cabinet on 10 September: Mnangagwa was appointed Justice minister, Chinamasa, Finance; and Jonathan Moyo's rehabilitation was completed with his return as Information minister. Although entitled in terms of the new constitution to appoint two vice-presidents, Mugabe merely extended Joice Mujuru's tenure. With hindsight it is clear that he was biding his time; he would wait another year before moving against her and others associated with her.

While the moribund opposition was left licking its wounds, business confidence plummeted. The first sign of this was the funnelling of close to US$1 billion from Zimbabwe's banking sector to off-shore accounts. "By the end of June 2013 $800 million left the country due to elections," BancABC chief operating officer Francis Dzanya told shareholders at the group's financial results presentation on 14 August.[763] The run on banks and decline in the stock market continued after the election, worsening liquidity conditions in the market, in turn causing GDP to fall precipitously. By the end of 2013 the IMF estimated that Zimbabwe's GDP rate had fallen from 10.5% in 2012 to 3% in 2013.[764] Compounding capital flight was a massive external debt, a national budget devoured by unsustainably large salary bills, declining infrastructure, an adverse balance of payments position and, because of dollarisation, no financial instruments to stimulate the economy. For those of us now sitting on the sidelines as observers, our mantra quickly became "you can rig an election but you can't rig an economy".

I started my enforced sabbatical from politics by catching up after a frenzied fourteen years in public office. My office and its accumulated papers needed tidying up, a long-promised tree-house was built for my daughter, the Petra Schools trust, which I chaired, needed attention, a borehole was sunk at home, mountain biking became more frequent, and writing began. In November an old friend, retired US ambassador to Kenya, Mark Bellamy, put my name forward for a World Bank education post. I was in two minds, not knowing whether it was right to leave Zimbabwe, albeit temporarily, at that critical juncture when the country seemed rudderless. As it turned out, my mind was made up for me. Without backing from one's government, it was well nigh impossible to get the position. Aside from Zimbabwe still being suspended from the World Bank, my chances of getting an endorsement from ZANU PF were limited. With the country in limbo, my own year ended on a high with a visit to Malawi to celebrate my elder son Douglas's marriage to a Malawian, Chloë McGrath. One of the thoughts I have tried to instil in my children has been to think of Southern Africa rather than Zimbabwe, because its successful future, I believe, is dependent on its integration. It was pleasing for me to see this principle being put into practice through this SADC marriage. The wedding itself was a celebration of hope in the future – three of my son's groomsmen were young black Zimbabweans, a scenario almost unthinkable in my generation because of racial segregation.

Soon after we returned to Zimbabwe in early January 2014, the first signs of trauma within both ZANU PF and MDC-T manifested themselves. The entire country was taken by surprise on 23 January when the government-controlled *Herald* newspaper released details of salaries paid to executives of the medical aid society which catered for civil servants, PSMAS. The story provided shocking details of the CEO's salary – a staggering US$230 000 per month.[765] Intriguingly, the CEO,

Cuthbert Dube, was a well-known ZANU PF acolyte and not the first or only member of the party to be involved in nefarious conduct. *The Herald* had always been quick to expose sin in the opposition but had studiously turned a blind eye to rampant corruption within the party. A guiding hand in the revelation was revealed a few days later when new Information minister Jonathan Moyo, speaking to the military's Joint Command, joined the fray, castigating "false, even corrupt salaries"[766] in the public sector.

Watching from the sidelines I waited with baited breath to see how far the net would be cast. In cabinet allegations of rampant corruption within the diamond sector had been made; if this exposé was a genuine attempt to clear up corruption, I expected revelations across the board, including institutions controlled by hardliners and the military. While there were a few further stories implicating people, none appeared to implicate those close to the hardline faction within ZANU PF. My suspicions were confirmed when Vice-President Mujuru claimed that the ongoing graft stories appearing in the government-controlled press were politically motivated, warning a ZANU PF Women's Conference that there were some who adopted the mindset "if you can't beat them, join them and fight from within".[767] Mujuru's comments resulted in an emergency ZANU PF politburo meeting being convened on 14 February as Mugabe tried to stem the widening gulf between the two factions. His efforts were in vain – in the following three months, government-controlled newspapers dished out a neverending stream of saucy revelations about people, all of whom appeared to be aligned to the Mujuru faction. When Nathan Shamuyarira, ZANU PF's first Information minister in the 1980s, died in early June 2014, Mugabe used both the wake and funeral to lash out against Moyo. At the former he complained that "our Minister of Information (was) wanting to put people one against another".[768] "We now have weevils in our midst. ZANU-PF has weevils within its ranks,"[769] Mugabe told thousands of mourners attending Shamuyarira's burial at Heroes Acre.

The first quarter of 2014 revealed that the main opposition party, the MDC-T, was in a similar state of disarray. It first came to the surface when MDC-T deputy treasurer and former cabinet minister Elton Mangoma wrote to Tsvangirai telling him "it is time you consider leaving the office of the president of the movement".[770] Mangoma's letter spoke of a "crisis of leadership ... and confidence in the party". The letter was leaked, resulting in Mangoma's assault by MDC-T youths outside the party headquarters, Harvest House. Biti condemned the assault and then associated himself with Mangoma's comments; in his capacity as secretary general, Biti convened a National Council meeting which voted to suspend Tsvangirai and several other senior leaders. The following was included in a statement released after the meeting on 26 April:

> "Over the years, the MDC has developed tendencies and a culture that has led to the deviation from its core values. That culture has included the following: the use of violence as a way of settling disputes, corruption, disrespect of the constitution, a culture of impunity, the existence of parallel structures including a Kitchen Cabinet and vigilante groups associated with the leader."[771]

I was left with a profound sense of déjà vu. The statement could have been written in December 2005 because it touched on many issues which were of equal concern then. It was followed by other events reminiscent of the 2005 split. There were further counter suspensions and expulsions from those still loyal to Tsvangirai, who challenged the constitutionality of Biti's National Council meeting. By mid 2014, the split was irrevocable and had seriously damaged Tsvangirai. In my opinion, Biti and Mangoma were the MDC-T's best cabinet ministers by some margin. In addition other former cabinet ministers, such as Lucia Matibenga, Sam Nkomo and Gorden Moyo, sided with Biti and Mangoma, along with several of the MDC-T's best MPs, forming what they called the MDC Renewal Team.

Watching helplessly from the sidelines, I took no satisfaction in seeing MDC-T fall apart. My own MDC-N party had been all but annihilated in the 2013 election, leaving the MDC-T with the primary responsibility in parliament of holding ZANU PF to account. I found it ironic when I was contracted by an international organisation in mid 2014 to assist in peace negotiations in another conflict-riven African country. My own nation was tearing itself apart and needed help, but there was little role I could play. In August 2014, I was asked to provide consultancy services to a South African company, Paarl Media, seeking to expand its educational textbook business into the rest of Africa. The company had noted the success of the ETF textbook programme and wanted to use some of the lessons learned to persuade the international community to invest more in educational textbooks throughout Africa. Once again it seemed ironic that I was being called to assist other countries when the Zimbabwean education system had started to deteriorate again. All I could do domestically was speak to political leaders about what I felt was needed, which I summed up under two heads.

First, I argued, we needed a national consensus among democrats regarding the policies Zimbabwe needed to reverse its accelerating decline. Second, we needed to identify what was at the core of our political rot, namely, personality-based, rather than principle-based political parties. With such a broad and increasing array of aspiring leaders, I felt that democratic parties should focus on a shadow cabinet, rather than a single leader, from which could emerge a candidate to challenge ZANU PF in the next elections. I expressed my views to the president of my own party, Welshman Ncube. I had similar discussions with Tendai Biti, Dumiso Dabengwa and Simba Makoni. Eventually, on 22 October 2014 Morgan Tsvangirai came to see me at home, when I was able to spell out these ideas and concerns. All were receptive, but with so much water having gone under the bridge, ongoing distrust and hurt made the task difficult.

The week before I met Tsvangirai the quirky nature of Zimbabwean politics was evident again. When Mugabe announced his new cabinet in September 2013 he replaced me with three new cabinet ministers, one for Education, one for the specific task of Curriculum Reform, and one for Sport, Arts and Culture, its minister being Andrew Langa. Thirteen months on, in October 2014, Mugabe met with Langa while in Matabeleland and asked whether I had been "invited to take a tour" of the sports facilities in Bulawayo being built and renovated for the African Union Region 5 Under-20 Youth Games. One of my last acts in cabinet had been to argue that Bulawayo should be the host city for the Games which involved several Southern African nations in nine sporting disciplines. I had faced considerable opposition in my bid as most of my senior civil servants and a number of heavyweight ZANU PF cabinet ministers had wanted them held in Harare. However, on 21 May 2013, Mugabe, Tsvangirai and Vice-President Mujuru had all backed me, resulting in the immediate collapse of opposition to the proposal to hold them in Bulawayo.

Prior to cabinet Mujuru had asked me to speak to her outside about the Games. Once I had explained the full benefit (which went beyond mere sport and involved the building of a Games village which would then be used for badly needed student accommodation at the local

National Science and Technology University), she told me I "should go ahead with what I thought best",[772] before warmly grasping and shaking both my hands. Likewise, Mugabe spoke strongly within cabinet of the need for Bulawayo to host the Games. With my loss of office I had played no further role in the preparations for the Games, which were scheduled to be held in December 2014, until Mugabe raised the issue with Langa.

Accordingly, I was surprised to get a call from Langa on 17 October 2014, asking me if I could come to an urgent meeting about the Games. When we met the following day at the site of one of the Games' venues, Bulawayo municipal swimming pool, Langa had summoned the government-controlled press. In a brief ceremony Langa told the press that I would "receive red carpet treatment" during the sixth African Union Sports Council Region 5 Under-20 Youth Games for my "unwavering stance to bring the Games to Bulawayo".[773] Langa went on to tell the press:

> "This tour was necessitated by President Mugabe when we went
> for the official lighting of the Games' torch at State House. He said
> I should invite Coltart to see and appreciate his efforts because it's
> him who convinced Cabinet to have the Games in Bulawayo. He
> received a lot of resistance from some members of Cabinet, but
> kept on pushing until the President gave him his support, too. As
> late as yesterday, President Mugabe, who was in Lupane, asked me
> if I had invited Coltart to a tour."[774]

True to his word Langa gave me red carpet treatment during the tour that day, and right through to when the Games were held in December. The entire episode amazed me. I was the only individual candidate who had released a detailed report after the July 2013 exposing ZANU PF electoral fraud and since then had continued to make fiercely critical remarks about government, and yet Mugabe still chose to acknowledge and honour the work I had done to bring the Games to Bulawayo. As Churchill once said of the Russians, I found Mugabe "a riddle wrapped in a mystery inside an enigma".[775]

The irony deepened further in the ensuing weeks when Langa found himself a victim of the split between the Mnangagwa and Mujuru factions within ZANU PF, which came to a head as the Games commenced. Up until October Mugabe himself had not publicly taken sides; the first sign of a change in that thinking came on the same day Mugabe met Langa at Lupane, 16 October, when Mugabe's wife Grace, addressing a rally in Bindura, used the metaphor of "baby dumping" to describe what should be done with those leading factionalism within ZANU PF. Grace Mugabe then embarked on a nationwide tour which saw a daily increase in the invective directed Mujuru's way, culminating in a meeting on 23 October when Grace Mugabe alleged that Mujuru wanted "to use money to topple Mugabe", accusing her of being "rotten … a thief".[776] Knowing that Mujuru controlled nine out of ten of ZANU PF's provincial structures, I watched to see who would win a war of words between Grace Mugabe and Mujuru. Grace Mugabe ratcheted up her invective through November, eventually feeling bold enough on 17 November to demand that Mujuru "must leave now". Hate speech began to be heard more frequently. Grace Mugabe and others, such as Information minister Moyo, started referring to Mujuru's faction members as "Gamatox", an agricultural poison. Mugabe kept his own counsel, in public at least, until 2 December, when he finally accused Mujuru of trying to "oust him from the helm of the party and government" before firing her and eight cabinet ministers, all moderates, whom he accused of being behind a plot to topple him from power. Langa held on by the skin of his teeth as minister of Sport, until September 2015 (when he, too, was fired from cabinet), but he was removed as ZANU PF chairman for Matabeleland South province in the shake-up, along with the rest of Mujuru loyalists. On 12 December 2014 Emmerson Mnangagwa was appointed Vice-President, confirming the ascendancy of his hardline faction over Mujuru's. In an effort to assuage concerns in Matabeleland and comply with the 1987 Unity agreement between ZAPU and ZANU PF, Mugabe appointed former ZIPRA commander in charge of logistics Phelekezela Mphoko as the other vice-president the same day. It had become clear, however, that the velvet glove over the iron fist had been removed.

As 2014 drew to a close, I wondered where these dramatic events left the nation. It had never been absolutely clear during my days in cabinet where Mugabe's loyalties lay. Even after he showed his hand in dismissing Mujuru, I wondered how much influence his wife had exerted over her frail husband. It seemed from the outside that a pact had been entered into between Grace Mugabe and Mnangagwa, born of mutual self-interest. Mnangagwa needed the Mugabe brand to boost his prospects; Grace Mugabe needed the protection of Mnangagwa and the military in a post-Robert Mugabe era. Whatever the case, any hope that moderates would prevail within ZANU PF was dashed. With the opposition more split than ever, Zimbabwe's prospects looked grim.

CHAPTER 29

ENDURANCE INSPIRED BY HOPE
2015 ... AND BEYOND

"Forgetting what is behind and straining toward what is ahead, I press on toward the goal."
— Paul writing to the Philippians 3:13–14

One of our family's favourite traditions is to celebrate Hogmanay at Shalom campsite in the Matopos with another family, the Cunninghams, who have Scottish roots too. It is always a joyous, if not somewhat manic, evening, dancing the Gay Gordons and Strip the Willow, interspersed with treasure hunts locating clues which have been secreted in the bush surrounding the campsite. A Cambridge-educated Scot, David Cunningham came out to Zimbabwe in the 1950s to marry a Zimbabwean, Janet Conolly, whose father established Shalom campsite on his Maleme Ranch in 1958. David and Janet did pioneering work with Scripture Union in the 1960s and '70s which, among other things, conducted multiracial children's camps, at a time when racial interaction was discouraged by the RF regime. Likewise, Shalom campsite was inter-denominational and had been open to all races from its inception. In recent years its popularity has grown, with up to 16 000 people using it annually, including many orphans' camps. I first attended a camp at Shalom as a Cub in 1968 and was responsible for keeping an eye on it when I was a policeman stationed at Kezi in the 1970s. After returning to Zimbabwe in 1983, Jenny and I became close friends with the Cunninghams, out of which developed the Hogmanay tradition, which our children love. When my mother died in 2009 the Cunninghams allowed her to be buried close to Shalom; and it was at Shalom where our eldest daughter Jessica chose to be married on New Year's Eve 2010. So it was entirely natural that we should celebrate Hogmanay at Shalom on New Year's Eve 2014, but this year we did so with heavy hearts, wondering whether it would be the last time.

Although Maleme ranch had suffered the depredations of ZANU PF's land policy, with two thirds having been taken over by ZANU PF supporters in 2012, the portion of land where Shalom was had been left untouched. In addition to Shalom, the Cunninghams had developed an agricultural training college, Ebenezer Training Centre, in the remaining north west corner of Maleme Ranch, which had also been left alone. Ebenezer had been established to train some 75 young unemployed people per year from neighbouring communal lands in the use of zero-tillage agricultural techniques and business administration. However, on 18 December 2014 the Cunninghams were advised that Shalom had been allocated to the local Kezi CIO head, one Rodney Mashingaidze, and Ebenezer to the local district administrator; both were attractive properties because of their abundant water and infrastructure. Backed by the local hardline provincial governor, Mashingaidze in particular aggressively pursued his new asset, telling the Cunninghams that farming needed to stop immediately and that "any resistance would be considered an act of war". At the same time the Cunninghams were told that "if anything was moved from the farm it would be considered theft" and that the new owners would need to take an "inventory of their new assets" i.e. the moveables at Shalom and Ebenezer. This sword of Damocles hung over our heads as we saw the New Year in.

Early in January 2015, the Cunninghams got a letter advising them to move off by 1 February, which Mashingaidze acted on by locking all the gates to Shalom and moving an employee onto the farm to ensure that his newly acquired assets were secure. Although Ebenezer was not occupied at the time, because the two operate as an integral unit, its existence was threatened along with the training courses for young farmers from the area. Mashingaidze's occupation caused an uproar in the local community. The local chief, Malaki Masuku, wrote to government to complain that the move would bring "poverty and misery to the people in the area I rule over",[777] concluding, "I say no to the take over ... if it is to be done let it be done under my protest". The chief's letter was followed by a series of protests conducted by poor local farmers. The government and Mashingaidze, thinking they could ride out the storm, ignored the protests, inflaming tensions even more. "We have realised the immense development of this community due to our relationship with the farm and we will not let all that go to one man, who does not even come from this district,"[778] said one villager, Morris Ndlovu.

Eventually, on 9 March 2015 twelve elderly men (the oldest aged 72) arrived at Shalom where, armed with knobkerries and axes, they ordered Mashingaidze's worker to gather up his belongings and then frog-marched him nine kilometres to the nearest local business centre at Natisa. Mashingaidze, in his position as head of intelligence in Kezi, was able to rally the police, who arrested all twelve men at Natisa. A large crowd, including elderly women, which had gathered at Natisa in support of the men, upon seeing the arrest of the twelve immediately demanded that they all be arrested too. "It is our Canaan and we will not allow Mashingaidze to take away our only source of livelihood,"[779] a local Natisa resident, Dindila Dube, protested. Realising that they had bitten off more than they could chew, the police declined the offer and headed off to Kezi with the twelve accused men. Undeterred, the remaining crowd hired taxis and followed the police vehicle the 20 kilometres south to Kezi police station, where they all handed themselves in, demanding to be arrested. Kezi police cells, which haven't changed since I was stationed there in 1976, were never designed for such a large crowd, which spilled out into the yard. The police didn't get much sleep that night as the villagers kept each other entertained the whole night by singing and praying raucously. The next morning they were taken to court, still singing, where a further surprise confronted the government. The public prosecutor, no doubt thinking that the amount would intimidate the local farmers into submission, proposed that they each pay "US$300 bail and never set foot again at Maleme ranch".[780] The large crowd of some 40 villagers, to a man, to a woman, announced that they would not pay bail and were happy to await the trial in prison, a prospect that appalled the authorities. All was saved when the presiding magistrate hastily ordered that they be released on free bail.

Seeing the determination of the villagers, government backed down. On Sunday, 15 March new Vice-President Phelekeza Mphoko arrived at the farm to announce that Mashingaidze's allocation of the farm had been reversed. The news was met with "wild celebrations". Local villagers celebrated their triumph "with some drinking themselves silly".[781] Shalom and Ebenezer were saved. Since then church camps and agricultural training courses have resumed. My prayers and those of Christians across the nation were answered. Although this was just one episode, and an exception to the norm, the Shalom incident restored my hope, for it demonstrated that where goodwill exists, our troubled past can be overcome. The villagers were unconcerned by the colour of the Cunninghams' skin; what mattered to them was the quality of their hearts.

As we celebrated in the south, sinister things were happening in the north. On 9 March 2015, human rights activist and journalist Itai Dzamara was abducted by several men at a barbershop in Harare. The previous October, Dzamara had delivered a petition to Mugabe's office demanding that he stand down and that fresh elections be called. Since then Dzamara's informal movement called "Occupy Africa Unity Square" had conducted a number of protests in central Harare which had got him arrested a few times. In an interview conducted just days before his disappearance Dzamara spoke of a "core team of protesters numbering about 70, that have been marching and blowing whistles in the city"[782] which had increased on occasions to 300 people staging sit-ins at Africa Unity square. At the time, the split and besieged opposition was so focused on its internal trauma that it was not speaking out. Only the pesky Dzamara was speaking out provocatively. Sadly, Dzamara has never been seen again. Like Edson Sithole (disappeared by Rhodesian operatives), Patrick Nabanyama and Paul Chizuze before him, Dzamara has vanished without a trace, with little effort being made by the police and CIO to investigate his whereabouts. It has served as a chilling reminder of the true nature of the ZANU PF regime.

While ZANU PF's political wrangling distracted the public, the economy continued its downward spiral in the first quarter of 2015. With growing shortages of cash and plummeting business confidence, reports flooded in of businesses closing in greater numbers than ever. On 13 April, Finance minister Chinamasa announced a raft of measures designed to reduce current expenditure in advance of a trip to the IMF's spring meeting in Washington. Chinamasa, flanked by Information minister Jonathan Moyo and Mugabe's spokesman George Charamba, stated that government was struggling to meet its monthly civil servant salary bill of US$260 million. To tackle the problem he announced that "Government (had) decided to suspend bonus payments for civil servants in 2015 and 2016"; "the situation (would) be reviewed in 2017 in the event that (they were) able to build enough capacity".[783] Supine apologists and economists were rolled out by the government-controlled press to compliment Chinamasa for the decision – saying that while it was a tough call, it was the right one – before he flew off to Washington, no doubt to assure the IMF that government spending was being tackled. All went awry the following Saturday, 18 April, when Mugabe delivered his Independence Day speech at the National Sports Stadium in Harare. As he neared the end of his address, Mugabe appeared to depart from his prepared text when he drove a coach and horses through Chinamasa's statement, saying, "I want to make it clear that the report which was in the newspapers that bonuses were being withdrawn is not Government policy."[784] Accusing Chinamasa of never "consulting on the matter", Mugabe said the policy was "disgusting" and would "never be implemented". Chinamasa meekly apologised from Washington, no doubt his credibility before the IMF wrecked. I released a statement predicting that Chinamasa would return "not only with egg on his face, but with empty pockets too". Of greater concern was the disconnect within government. It was inconceivable that Chinamasa had gone on a frolic of his own; he must have secured cabinet approval for such a major policy change, something borne out by the presence of both the Information minister and Mugabe's own spokesman. Mugabe had recently turned 91: this appeared to be an indication of his incapacity to govern.

The mounting chaos within ZANU PF was mirrored in the opposition. One positive after the 2005 MDC split had been that agreement was reached not to declare seats vacant in parliament which would in turn cause a string of by-elections. However, the bitterness between MDC-T and Biti's MDC Renewal Team was so bad that the same accommodation was not reached. In March, MDC-T wrote to the speaker of parliament, my former client Jacob Mudenda, advising that Biti and 20 other MPs and senators no longer represented the party and should be expelled. Mudenda and ZANU PF gleefully obliged, expelling the group of 21 on 17 March. Although Biti tried to challenge their expulsion in court, this inevitably failed. In a stroke Parliament suddenly lost a large block of its most competent MPs, including some of Zimbabwe's best legal brains, such as Biti and Arnold Tsunga. If ever there was a case of shooting oneself in the foot, this was it. Although Biti's group had fallen out with the MDC-T, the national interest demanded that they remain in parliament.

The loss of Biti and others in parliament was then compounded by further splits within the broader MDC. In November 2014, Biti's MDC Renewal Team and the MDC-N had signed an agreement to reunify, something I supported wholeheartedly, but the process started to flounder in the opening quarter of 2015. I was in Washington for meetings with the World Bank, Global Partnership for Education and USAID on the African textbook project when I heard that the talks had been suspended on 22 May. Fully engrossed in writing and the textbook consultancy, I had not been intimately involved in the discussions, so the news came as a surprise. According to the MDC-N the reason for the collapse was that the MDC Renewal Team had problems within their own ranks and had decided to "go to their own congress to resolve their leadership questions".[785] Within days former cabinet minister Mangoma addressed a press conference to announce that there were "irreconcilable differences"[786] within the MDC Renewal Team and that it, too, was headed for a split. Mangoma was suspended by the MDC Renewal Team shortly afterwards, causing Mangoma to form yet another party – the Renewal Democrats of Zimbabwe – on 3 June. It was not only confusing but deeply disappointing; the original MDC was now split into four different factions, all with similar policies, each led by competent people, but all drawing off the same support base. The final act in this internecine struggle came when the MDC-T resolved not to contest the 21 by-elections resulting from their expulsion of Biti's group.

Shortly after I got back from Washington on 10 June, the by-elections were held throughout the country. The other factions of the MDC had also resolved not to contest the by-elections, which resulted in a clean sweep for ZANU PF. Worst of all was that, for the first time since 2000, ZANU PF got a toe-hold in Bulawayo again, winning four seats. Although the by-elections were not a true test of public support, and were marked by low turnouts, democratic space had been lost. Just as I felt in 2005 that the controversial senate seats should be contested, to retain absolute political control of urban areas, so it seemed a mistake to hand control of certain Bulawayo constituencies to ZANU PF. The MDCs' collective self-flagellation had served ZANU PF well.

The mandarins within ZANU PF could take little comfort from the MDC's implosion because of the dire state of the economy. In mid July 2015 the World Bank lowered Zimbabwe's economic growth forecast to 1 per cent, down from an initial projection of 3.2 per cent. Citing falling commodity prices, lack of domestic liquidity and poor foreign direct inflows, economists warned of the country being caught in a trap of deflation. The catastrophic state of the economy was graphically illustrated in the immediate aftermath of a controversial Supreme Court judgment handed down on 16 July 2015, which ruled that employers could lawfully terminate employment contracts without offering employees severance packages. It resulted in carnage: within a few weeks some 22 000 employees were dismissed countrywide by firms grateful that they could reduce their workforces so cheaply. ZANU PF responded slowly to the judgment and although Mugabe and others condemned it, Mugabe didn't use the Presidential Powers legislation at his disposal to stop it. The failure to intervene caused suspicion that ZANU PF heavyweights, whose own businesses were collapsing, were secretly supportive of the Supreme Court decision.

There were other signs that government's predicament was worsening monthly. In late July, Chinamasa exposed just how desperate the situation was. He confirmed the declining growth rate and the large and growing domestic debt in government parastatals such as the railways and Air Zimbabwe. Revenue projections were down, forcing him to take some desperate measures, including a new law imposing import duty on a variety of essentials, including books, the latter in violation of Zimbabwe's obligations in terms of the UNESCO Florence Agreement. In September, the government-controlled press spoke of a massive civil servant audit which would result in thousands being taken off the payroll. Tragically, it appeared that teachers rather than soldiers would be laid off. Government pensions, which used to be paid on the 25th of the month, were steadily pushed out and the September pension was only paid on 13 October, the November pension was only paid a few days before Christmas. The civil service bonus, controversially promised by Mugabe in April, had still not been paid by the end of 2015.

On 7 September, one of the most significant political events occurred since the MDC was launched sixteen years before at Rufaro Stadium in September 1999, with the publication in newspapers by Joice Mujuru of a manifesto. Although the manifesto did not officially link her to a new political movement being organised by her former ZANU PF colleagues, called People First, it was a significant shot across ZANU PF's bows. The manifesto rejected many of ZANU PF's core policies such as indigenisation and a racially based land reform policy. Indeed it contained policies strikingly similar to core MDC policies, calling as it did for the repeal of draconian legislation such as AIPPA and POSA. The announcement was favourably received by many, raising hopes that a broad coalition could still be formed to unseat ZANU PF. Within days it was apparent that Mujuru's announcement had rattled ZANU PF and Mugabe himself. Four days after Mujuru's announcement Mugabe announced the appointment of fourteen new ministers to an already bloated cabinet. The new cabinet, comprised of 72 ministers for a country of 13 million people, appeared to be a consolidation of Mnangagwa's power base. After the reshuffle my old ministry, Education, Sport, Arts and Culture, was to be run by no less than four ministers. Despite the growing budget deficit and need to cut back on government's salary bill, Mugabe appeared desperate to keep as many within his tent as possible. The appointments were followed the next day by a chilling statement from Mugabe's spokesman, who wrote the following:

> "There are many things which ZANU PF has put into abeyance, waiting for this moment. She (Mujuru) has provided a trigger and it can only be fast forward. She is set to be fought on many fronts. ZANU PF is a vicious, unyielding auditor."[787]

Mugabe himself showed signed signs of panic when he attempted to open parliament on 15 September. Bizarrely, he read out the wrong speech. It was the same speech, a State of the Nation address, that he had read over a month before. It did not set out government's legislative agenda and Mugabe himself did not appear to recognise that anything was amiss. Unlike the UK, where the Queen reads out a speech prepared for her by the prime minister, this was in theory Mugabe's own speech, setting out his own agenda. Some of the MDC MPs realised that he was delivering the wrong speech but were too scared to point it out. When Mugabe had delivered his State of the Nation address in August he had been drowned out by opposition benches' heckling. Not wanting a repeat, some ZANU PF supporters sent threatening messages to several MPs' cell phones, including my LRF colleagues Jessie Majome and Innocent Gonese, just prior to the opening ceremony. The uniform message, which all came from a sender called "Death", read "Warning!! Immunity ends in Parliament. If you step outside you become an ordinary citizen. Do the wise thing and not disturb proceedings in Parliament." They did the wise thing and kept quiet.

Embarrassingly, Mugabe had to reconvene Parliament the next day so that the correct speech could be tabled. Mugabe perhaps revealed his state of mind in a lunch called to celebrate the opening of Parliament when he focused almost exclusively on Mujuru's challenge and warned of an impending clampdown. Waving his fist in the air, the 91-year-old Mugabe said Mujuru could not compete against him as his fist was stronger and had felled Ian Smith during the war. He also lashed out against the media, warning "if we begin to take control now – rigid controls – don't cry foul."[788] It was classic Mugabe rhetoric. As he ended he said: "If you are dynamic and accepted by the people, well and good. The people will vote for you, but no violence please." The use of the second person appeared to indicate that the prohibition against violence only applied to others.

The divisions within ZANU PF deepened in the last quarter of 2015. The apparent pact entered into between Mnangagwa and Grace Mugabe in 2014, in the midst of Mujuru's ouster, seemed under threat as 2015 closed. Although there had been press speculation for months about an alliance between a group of younger ZANU PF cabinet ministers and Grace Mugabe, against Mnangagwa, that speculation only became a reality in November when Grace Mugabe embarked on another series of carefully orchestrated meet-the-people rallies which marked her as a politician with similar status to Mugabe himself. Aside from flying to many of the rallies in the presidential helicopter, Grace Mugabe was referred to as "Your Excellency" by swooning ZANU PF cabinet ministers; both the method of travel and the title were previously the sole preserve of Robert Mugabe himself. At the same time the ZANU PF Women's League, chaired by Grace Mugabe, embarked on a sustained campaign to undermine key Mnangagwa allies, some of whom were suspended from the party.

Shortly before the ZANU PF conference held at Victoria Falls in early December 2015, the Women's League proposed a resolution to reintroduce a provision that one of ZANU PF's two vice-presidents would have to be a woman. A similar clause had been used to deny Mnangagwa's appointment as Vice-President in 2004 when Joice Mujuru had ascended to that office. Although this time it was not clearly aimed at him, in the context of the other attacks on his supporters it appeared to be designed to frustrate his ambitions again. The resolution was passed at the conference, generating intense speculation regarding which vice-president would have to make way for a woman, possibly for Grace

Mugabe herself. In addition Mugabe issued an unprecedented attack on some veterans at the conference, stating, "Some people brag to others, 'I am so and so, I went to war and you did not go' nonsense. Stop bragging with your war credentials. Some will ask you, 'Did you go alone?' or 'What did you do there?'" The statement appeared to bolster Grace Mugabe's aspirations for higher office; she was a child during the war and so has no veterans' credentials. Over the last few years Grace Mugabe's power has grown in inverse proportion to Mugabe's declining health. As he has become more dependent on her, so her influence within ZANU PF has increased. As 2015 ended ZANU PF, rather like the MDC, was more divided than ever, with three factions emerging from the original entity supporting Mujuru, Mnangagwa and Grace Mugabe. With the opposition still seriously divided and ZANU PF becoming increasingly incoherent, the beginning of 2016 sees Zimbabwe with an unprecedented and dangerous power vacuum.

November 11, 2015 marked the fiftieth anniversary of the RF's UDI. Aside from a few low-key remembrances held by former white Rhodesians outside Zimbabwe, the day passed without much comment within Zimbabwe. Fifty years of misrule and abuse of power have ravaged Zimbabwe, leaving its economy in a pitiful state and its political system in chaos. Zimbabweans have reaped a bitter harvest from that fateful day. After decades of struggle Zimbabwe's economy is worse off than it was in the mid 1960s and it has made painstakingly slow progress towards a new democratic order.

* * *

As the American Civil War drew to a close in March 1865, Abraham Lincoln, in his second inaugural address, made the following comment:

> *Fondly do we hope, fervently do we pray, that this mighty scourge of war may speedily pass away. Yet, if God wills that it continue until all the wealth piled by the bondsman's two hundred and fifty years of unrequited toil shall be sunk, and until every drop of blood drawn by lash shall be paid by another drawn with the sword, as was said three thousand years ago, so it must be said, "The judgments of the Lord are true and righteous altogether."*

I and many other Zimbabweans have prayed for decades for corrupt and brutal rule to end, but there does not seem any immediate prospect of that. As Lincoln wrestled with why God allowed a vicious war to drag on, I have battled with the question why a vicious regime has remained in power for so long. The answer may be found in Lincoln's musings. While colonialism and white rule brought hospitals, schools, roads and railways, it also disrupted an existing culture and humiliated generations of black people. That legacy caused a war which in turn poisoned our entire society. One treacherous legacy resulted in another.

Many of the policies introduced by ZANU PF in the last fifteen years have been utterly self-destructive. For example, the ruinous land policies have all but destroyed the most important segment of Zimbabwe's economy. That in turn has led to vastly reduced revenues to the fiscus which in turn has led to one of the jewels in Mugabe's crown – the education sector – being seriously undermined. If ever there was a case of a national cutting off of one's nose to spite one's face, Zimbabwe provides it writ large. Intelligent people within ZANU PF have all but destroyed their own legacy. One explanation for this must be the effect that Post-Traumatic Stress Syndrome has had on an entire generation of Zimbabweans.

The reality of that legacy was forcefully brought home to me when I met Zimbabwean war veterans in November 2010. Zimbabwe has experienced similar trauma, indeed even worse, in one respect, than post-Vietnam America. In Zimbabwe many of the protagonists are still in the same country the war was fought in; nothing has been done to heal the wounds of the 1970s or 1980s, which have been allowed to fester. We still have tens of thousands of men and women fighting the war. It doesn't justify the gross human rights abuses that have been committed since 1980, but it does explain some of them. Until we have some process to enable us all to come to terms with our past, our past will continue to haunt us and stunt our ability to develop. Furthermore, unscrupulous politicians will continue to exploit that past to consolidate their power.

A poisoned society is not the only dreadful legacy of Zimbabwe's civil war. Another is that war itself has become acceptable in Zimbabwe, both domestically and internationally. There has never been a serious debate within Zimbabwe that our civil war was avoidable. It is just a given that there were never any other alternatives. While it is mere speculation, and written with the benefit of hindsight, the fact remains that our war *was* avoidable. I have no doubt that had Todd remained in power, like De Klerk in South Africa, he would have done everything possible to avoid war. It is hard to imagine him detaining nationalist leaders rather than talking to them. Furthermore, the likes of Martin Luther King are not eulogised in Zimbabwe. It is almost sacrilegious to suggest that had nationalist leaders used non-violent methods, war might have been avoided, even in the face of RF oppression. Whether the RF could have been defeated by Gandhian methods is a moot point, but the tragedy is that that suggestion is not even up for debate. War is considered an acceptable means of resolving major national or international problems and that culture is reflected by our ready engagement in Gukurahundi, Mozambique and the DRC since independence. It is also demonstrated in our massive defence spending at the expense of education, health and housing.

I am not a pacifist – I recognise that some wars, such as World War II was, are unavoidable and necessary. The ongoing tragedy for Zimbabwe is that war is not viewed as a last resort, as an evil that should be avoided at all costs. Rather it remains on the tip of our tongues and its use is readily threatened. The second tragedy is that because war itself is lauded, its child, violence, has become an acceptable means of resolving domestic political problems. In fact, violence is so deeply rooted in our political culture that it has become our default tactic.

Political rhetoric in Zimbabwe is still dominated by threats of violence. Even today, with all the division and confusion within our political parties, the threat remains that Zimbabwe will plunge back into violence to determine who succeeds Mugabe. But perhaps the gravest tragedy is that because we have extolled war so much, we have become blinded to the reality that it rarely achieves its intended purposes. Nationalist forces fought the struggle to liberate Zimbabweans from oppression, which in turn was intended to deliver economic and social development for the vast majority of Zimbabweans.

While the war ended racial discrimination and secured some major social benefits, such as the expansion of education, the fact remains that Zimbabweans are still oppressed by a tiny, corrupt ruling elite and the average per capita income is lower now than it was when the war was first started half a century ago. Tied to the debate about whether our war was avoidable is the question about whether greater liberty and economic development might have been achieved had war been avoided. Tragically, this question itself is anathema to many; but until we learn that lesson about our past, Zimbabweans will not fully understand why our nation continues to flounder.

There is some ancient wisdom on this subject. Some 3 000 years ago the Prophet Isaiah wrote that the House of Jacob "day after day (sought God) out", seemed "eager to know (God's) ways", and asked God "for just decisions".[789] They were a religious people who grumbled that while they had fasted and humbled themselves, God "had not seen it". Isaiah responded by pointing out that their "fasting (ended) in quarrelling and strife" and warned "you cannot fast as you do today and expect your voice to be heard on high".[790] Isaiah explains that the remedy, if a nation wants God to listen, is to "loose the chains of injustice, untie the cords of the yoke, set the oppressed free, break every yoke, do away with the pointing finger and malicious talk, share food with the hungry, provide the poor wanderer with shelter, clothe the naked and not to turn away from your own flesh and blood".[791] If that is done Isaiah promises that "light will break forth like the dawn, healing will quickly appear, ancient ruins will be rebuilt" and a nation will "be like a well-watered garden".

Zimbabwe is like the House of Jacob in many respects. It is an intensely religious nation; millions of Zimbabweans attend church every weekend; our new constitution acknowledges "the supremacy of Almighty God, in whose hands our future lies" and implores "the guidance and support of Almighty God". Our parliamentary standing orders mandate the saying of a prayer at the commencement of business – a prayer which explicitly recognises Jesus Christ. Through the calamity of the last fifteen years, there have been all-night prayer vigils, "Judgement nights" and fasts. Zimbabwe abounds in wealthy prophets, some of whom attract tens of thousands to their services, who proclaim a health, wealth and prosperity gospel. Some prophesy that Zimbabwe will be awash in gold nuggets, oil and untold riches. And yet, still the economy collapses, many people are disillusioned, and others leave. Celebrated young Zimbabwean author NoViolet Bulawayo captures this sentiment, particularly felt by young Zimbabweans, when she wrote recently of "siblings, bleak-eyed with dreams unfulfilled, fathers forlorn and defeated".[792]

It seems as if the good Lord has turned His back on a benighted land. The same prophets and many others in the wider church do not speak about the yokes which still burden Zimbabweans. This has been a practice for decades. Very few white churches and Christian leaders spoke out against the evil of racial discrimination and atrocities committed by Rhodesian forces during the war; few churches spoke out against Gukurahundi and Murambatsvina; black churches have tended to turn a blind eye to wholesale theft of white-owned commercial farms. Herein lies the rub: can we expect a just God to respond to an outwardly religious nation whose "fasting ends in quarrelling and strife"?

Lest this be viewed as unreasonable religious dogma, it needs to be said that there are sound secular studies which establish a relationship between good governance and sustainable long-term development. Indian Nobel prize winner, Amartya Sen, an atheist, in his book *Development as Freedom* establishes a "causal connection between democracy and the nonoccurence of famine".[793] Pointing out that while there are droughts in democracies, the "penalty of famines" is so great in democracies that their rulers prevent any threatening famine. A free press, he argues, "is the best early warning system a country threatened by famines can have". Ironically Sen, writing in 1999, lauded Zimbabwe, along with Botswana, as a democracy, but it is hard to imagine that he would still do so now. Since 1999, Zimbabwe has turned from being a net exporter of food to a net importer. Since 1999, Zimbabweans have faced constant food shortages, if not famines, and hundreds of thousands have died through the deadly combination of lack of food, poverty, and AIDS. Millions more have sought economic or political exile outside Zimbabwe during the same period. The point is that there are serious current secular studies which support Isaiah's remedy written thousands of years ago.

It would take another book to describe the current yokes that burden Zimbabweans and how they should be lifted. But at the core of Zimbabwe's crisis of governance, in my opinion, is a phenomenon which has uniquely afflicted our nation since it became a modern nation state over a hundred years ago.

In 1997 I startled a group of judges I spoke to, including current Chief Justice Chidyausiku, at a meeting in Masvingo when I said, "Rhodes begat Smith and Smith begat Mugabe." Rhodes was once described as "a very Colossus, who stood astride a continent which was too small a pedestal for the imperial dimensions of the man";[794] he was given demigod status by white Rhodesians, who named the country after him. In many respects Smith assumed Rhodes's mantle. He enjoyed unquestioned reverence by the vast majority of white Rhodesians. Mugabe is undoubtedly in that mould as well. He is the very soul of ZANU PF and despite the devastation he has wrought on Zimbabwe, stands astride the African continent as a man who brought white minority rule to an end. The tragedy is that this hero worship has become deeply ingrained in Zimbabwean political culture. The word of an individual means more than the constitution, more than age-old wisdom. This culture may well outlive Mugabe. We remain a people constantly searching for the next messiah, be that person Tsvangirai, Mnangagwa or Mujuru. And for so long as personality means more than policy or principle, Zimbabweans will not see "light break forth like the dawn".

Having identified one key yoke, one crucial method in lifting that yoke must be mentioned. Many foreigners have wondered why Zimbabweans have not long since overthrown the ZANU PF regime. The reason for this is, I believe, because common Zimbabweans have learnt the lessons of war; having experienced two in their lifetimes, they have no desire to start another. Although politicians have threatened wars and destruction, those thoughts have never gained traction among the vast majority of Zimbabweans. Thank goodness Zimbabwe has no strategic interest and has avoided the devastation the world has witnessed in the last decade in Iraq, Syria and Libya. Through all these years of struggle, I remain more convinced than ever that only the pursuit of non-violence will result in national healing and the "reconstruction of ancient ruins". We do not want or need the interference of the West or, for that matter, other African states to complete our journey towards a more democratic order. But that does not give licence to the West, the Commonwealth and Africa to turn a blind eye to the yokes that still bind Zimbabwe. While the West spoke out about the attacks on white farmers, it has tended to ignore the much graver assaults on the human rights of black Zimbabweans. Most African leaders, no doubt blinded by the planks in their own eyes, have consistently ignored the serious human rights violations committed in the 36 years of ZANU PF rule. While Zimbabweans must remain steadfastly committed to using non-violent methods to achieve change, this must be supported by the West, the Commonwealth and Africa – indeed, all democracies throughout the world, who must hold whoever rules Zimbabwe to respect the letter and spirit of our own constitution.

Zimbabwe has the potential to become the jewel of Africa – a beacon of hope for the entire continent. Her people are her most valuable asset. Zimbabweans are hardworking, literate, determined and considerate. She is endowed with varied and spectacular countryside – from the Zambezi River and Victoria Falls in the west to majestic mountains in the east, interspersed with sweeping savannah plains, verdant forests, rich, well-watered farmlands. There are valuable minerals galore: for a relatively small country, she has remarkable wealth in her soil – diamonds, gold, platinum, to name but a few. Unlike so many former African colonies, successive white minority governments were determined to stay so the original infrastructure is superb; while our cities, roads, railways and dams are in a bad state of repair, they were well built. Our location is also an important asset. We are slap bang in the middle of Southern Africa and all the major communication routes go through us. In short, Zimbabwe is abundantly blessed with nearly everything required to develop a vibrant state. It lacks just one critical ingredient – democracy. If we instil and root democracy, the country will boom. Our nation has never experienced real democracy; although there was a period in the 1950s when the first tentative steps were made towards a more democratic order, most of our history is a litany of oppressive rule.

The vast majority of Zimbabweans long for freedom. This desire was illustrated in the massive vote in favour of the new constitution in 2013, which, although flawed, resulted in a document which marks an important step forward. While by no means perfect – as I have written, it contains some serious flaws – it provides a useful foundation upon which to build. My hope is not for wholesale amendments but, in time, for considered amendments which are debated and which enjoy broad support among an overwhelming majority of Zimbabweans.

Many years ago ZANU PF copied Frelimo's old battle cry "*a luta continua*" – "the struggle continues" – to which they added "until final victory". In the pursuit of democracy there is never a final victory because democracy is a process, not an event. Even countries that have had democratic constitutions for over a century experience the evolution, refinement and, on occasion, reversal of democracy. Zimbabwe, as a young emerging democracy, is no different. The struggle continues – yes, it does indeed.

ACKNOWLEDGEMENTS

This book has been a long time coming and would not have been completed without the encouragement of many people. My literary agent, Judy Moir, first spoke to me about writing a book in 2001. At that time Zimbabwe was on the world's front pages and a book about the country might have been an easier sell; but she never gave up on the project and has been a tower of strength in bringing the idea to a reality. Aryeh Neier, former President of the Open Society, also deserves special mention because he provided support back in 2006, which enabled me to get critical background information researched and the book started.

Seven frenetic years intervened before I was able to restart writing in 2013, once again with the encouragement of Judy and also of Mark Muller Stuart QC. Judy's indefatigable spirit secured Bridget Impey's and Jacana Media's agreement to publish, and ever since Bridget has been a constant and enthusiastic supporter. I could not have wished for a better publisher. Jacana Media's Nadia Goetham, Megan Mance and Neilwe Mashigo also merit special thanks – they were indefatigable in the final few weeks, burning the midnight oil to ensure that the book was published on time.

My good friend Dr Wolf Krug has played a critically important role. Not only has he had an unwavering belief in the need for the book, but he also secured the support of Janina Otto and her Jua Foundation. Without the generous grant made by the Jua Foundation the book might never have seen the light of day. Janina supported the project purely on the strength of Wolf's recommendation, for which I am grateful. My thanks are also extended to the Hanns Seidel Stiftung for their advance purchase of books from Jacana, which will be donated to educational institutions in Zimbabwe.

A variety of my friends deserve special mention for their amazing backing, especially in this last year of writing: Steve and Jane Beaty, Mark, Dirk and Lesley Goldwasser, Trevor Harris, Tim and Eloise Leher, Willy Pabst, Henry and Charley-Ann Rhoads, Sue and Jug Thornton, and Butch and Karen Wolff. Our long-standing employees Sindi Mabhena and John Tlou ensured that I had a peaceful and efficient writing environment; I appreciate their years of faithful and trustworthy service in the face of oppression. Before Sindi, the late and much loved Agnes Mukosera showed remarkable courage and fortitude in the protection and care of our children when we were all under threat.

No book worth its salt is solely the product of the author and this book is no exception. My dear friends Paul Themba Nyathi and Shari Eppel read the very rough first draft and provided important constructive criticism of it, which greatly enhanced the final product. I am deeply indebted to my fellow lawyer Catherine Oborne, who devoted two months of her time – not only did she give vital legal input, but she read each successive draft of the book and interrogated facts and my perspectives, resulting in a work which is better equipped to face the attacks that will inevitably come from certain quarters. Elinor Burkett gave me invaluable advice when I first started writing, giving me lessons and insights which I applied to the entire book. Roger Stringer played a critically important role in refining the book and correcting some of the earlier errors I made. Dr Stuart Doran read the chapters on the Gukurahundi and made some important historical corrections of fact. Jonathan Simpson prepared the map. Albert Nyathi gave his permission to use the unnamed poem on page 213. There are others who provided input but who cannot be named because they still live in Zimbabwe and feel vulnerable. Our precious children Jessica, Douglas and Scott Winston have provided exceptionally valuable comments; our youngest, Bethany, kept me sane, entertained and quietly gave me many hours of company in my study as I wrote. Possibly my best critic has been my beloved wife Jenny, who read the book as it evolved and played a huge role in moulding the spirit of the book. That said, of course I bear full responsibility for the book and any flaws in it are mine.

All of this input along the way culminated in the book being edited by a person who became one of its best champions – Alison Lowry. A book this large can be a publisher's nightmare and Alison's vigorous support, that the entire story be told, played a crucial role in the final product. Alison's incisive mind and attention to detail have significantly improved the book. But most importantly Alison's ability to loosen up portions of dense legalese (and partisan detail) has made the book far more readable. She also lifted my spirits considerably during the editing process by continually expressing her belief in what the book hopes to achieve.

But what underpins the entire book is the love and support I have received from Jenny and our children. Without Jenny's affection, compassion, faith, balance, resilience and determination, I would never have survived the trials we have experienced. Most wives would have thrown in the towel years ago but Jenny has remained my rock and been unwavering in her support and care. Our children have sustained us both. My greatest fear was that they would be scarred and pay a heavy price for our idealism; while it has not all been plain sailing for them, by God's grace they have been strengthened through all they have experienced. Indeed, we have been richly blessed by their love and sparkling senses of humour, which have brightened even the darkest of days and given us hope for the future.

David Coltart

Bulawayo
Zimbabwe
December 2015

ENDNOTES

1 *Chronicle*, 5 September 2002. Mugabe was returning home from an Earth Summit. He went on to say: "We have many puppets here in the MDC led by their leader. Even in Parliament they will listen to what their white master, Coltart, tells them to do. We said we don't want that kind of partnership."

2 Collett, Joan. *A Time to Plant*. Published by Joan Collett, 1990, p 5

3 The Xhosa are part of the South African Nguni migration which slowly moved south from the region around the Great Lakes in Central Africa, displacing the original Khoisan hunter-gatherers of southern Africa. Xhosa peoples were well established by the time of the Dutch arrival at the Cape in the mid-17th century, and occupied much of eastern South Africa from the Fish River to land inhabited by Zulu speakers south of the modern city of Durban.

4 James Collett used a pejorative word here which is deeply offensive and so has been left out.

5 Letter from James Collett to Captain Campbell, 26 December 1834, as recorded in *A Time to Plant*. I have included this quote and the one below to reflect Collett's mood and views at the time. I do not include them apologetically or sympathetically, but simply to record the history accurately. As in footnote 4, the ellipsis indicates the omission of an offensive noun.

6 James Collett, journal entry, 31 March 1835. In Collett, *A Time to Plant*

7 *Graham's Town Journal*, 11 August 1849. In Collett, *A Time to Plant*

8 James Collett, journal entry, 19 April 1854. In Collett, *A Time to Plant*

9 The Mfecane was a period of widespread chaos and warfare among black ethnic communities in southern Africa during the period between 1815 and about 1840.

10 Moffat was anxious to get supplies to Livingstone and Mzilikazi went to extraordinary lengths to get them to Livingstone, including sending a party of men to near Victoria Falls. MacKenzie, Rob. *David Livingstone – The truth behind the legend*. Christian Focus Publications, 2003, p 229

11 Ransford, Oliver. *Bulawayo: Historic battleground of Rhodesia*, AA Balkema, 1968, p 1

12 My father's memoirs, published privately in 1995

13 Welensky, Sir Roy. *Welensky's 4000 Days*. Collins, 1964, p 67

14 At the funeral of Lady Grace Todd in December 2001 then ZANU PF Minister of Education Dr Aeneas Chigwedere in his eulogy had this to say about the role she played: "I am a product of the Grace Todd scheme (which) remained intact with very minor cosmetic changes right up to 1980." Although I was present and heard the speech myself,

it is also reported in Judith Todd, *Through the Darkness*. Struik Publishers, 2007, pp 418–20.

15 Barber, James. *The Road to Rebellion*. Oxford University Press, 1967, p 17

16 Hochschild, Adam. *King Leopold's Ghost*, Pan Books, 2012. Hochschild's is the best book I have read which documents the grave human rights abuses perpetrated by Belgium during its rule over what is now known as the DRC.

17 Barber, ibid, p 39

18 The word "coloured" – to describe people of mixed race – is used pejoratively in Europe but not so in Zimbabwe. People of mixed race in Zimbabwe refer to themselves as "coloured".

19 Barber, ibid, p 56, quoting *The Examiner*, 5 November 1960

20 Barber, ibid, p 156

21 Nkomo, Joshua. *Nkomo – The Story of My Life*. Methuen, 1984, p 102

22 Nkomo, ibid, p 106

23 Barber, ibid, p 170

24 Some dispute that Mnangagwa trained under ZANU, with some still asserting that he in fact trained under ZAPU.

25 Martin, David and Johnson, Phyllis. *The Struggle for Zimbabwe*. Zimbabwe Publishing House, 1981, p 11

26 Southern Rhodesia Legislative Assembly *Hansard*, 12 February 1962, Col 35, cited op cit in Barber, p 171

27 Letter to *The Daily News* by Michael Makaya, cited in Barber, op cit, p 210

28 Barber, ibid, p 207

29 Southern Rhodesia Legislative Assembly *Hansard*, 16 March 1965, cols 808–9, 810 and 1021)

30 Southern Rhodesia Legislative Assembly Hansard, September 1964, cited in Barber, op cit, p 290

31 Ian Douglas Smith. *The Great Betrayal*. Blake, 1997, pp 104 and 109

32 Todd, op cit, p 11

33 Todd, ibid, p 176

34 Ken Flower. *Serving Secretly*. John Murray, 1987, p 105

35 ZANLA, the Zimbabwe African National Liberation Army, was the military wing of ZANU. ZIPRA, the Zimbabwe People's Revolutionary Army, was the military wing of ZAPU.

36 Flower, ibid, pp 104–7

37 Flower, p 59

38 Smith, op cit, p 129

39 The British had coined the six so-called NIBMAR principles ("no independence before majority rule"), the fifth of which stated that the British government would have to be satisfied that any basis for independence was acceptable to the people of Rhodesia as a whole. The others were:
    1. The principle and intention of majority rule, already enshrined in the 1961 constitution, would have to be maintained and agreed;
    2. Guarantees against retrogressive amendments to the constitution;
    3. Immediate improvement in the political status of blacks;
    4. Progress towards ending racial discrimination; and
    5. Regardless of race, there was to be no oppression of the majority by the minority or vice versa.

40 Flower, ibid, p 84

41 Flower, ibid, p 85

42 Peter Baxter. *Rhodesia – Last outpost of the British Empire 1890–1980*. Galago, 2010, p 362

43 "Take your goods and leave, Ferriera". Some claim that this is a xenophobic Afrikaans song directed against Portuguese immigrants to South Africa.

44 "Spear of the Nation"

45 Wankie National Park is now known as Hwange National Park.

46 Article by MK guerrilla Sandile Sijake in http://www.zimdiaspora.com/index. php?option=com_content&view=article&id=2625:we-trained-operated-with-zipra-anc-

guerrilla&catid=38:travel-tips&Itemid=18

47 Smith, op cit, p 140

48 Quoted in *Rhodesia* by Peter Baxter, op cit, p 358

49 Flower, op cit, p 110

50 Smith, op cit, p 135

51 Smith, ibid, p 135

52 Achebe, Chinua. *There was Another Country – A personal history of Biafra.* Penguin, 2012, p 231

53 Achebe, ibid, p 214

54 Moorcroft, Paul L. *A Short Thousand Years.* Galaxie Press, 1979, p 25

55 Ironically, Smith, op cit, concedes in his book that the *Fearless* terms threw the NIBMAR principles "out the window".

56 Smith, ibid, p 148

57 Flower, op cit, p 96

58 Flower, ibid, p 97

59 In American terminology: "White Anglo Saxon Protestant"

60 Gibbs, Peter and Rudd, Robin. *The Bulawayo Club 1895–1995.* 1970, Bulawayo Club, p 31

61 Smith, op cit, p 153

62 Smith, ibid

63 Flower, op cit, pp 99-100

64 Flower, ibid, p 101

65 Baxter, op cit, p 376

66 Bhebe, N and Ranger, T. *Soldiers in Zimbabwe's Liberation War.* University of Zimbabwe Publications, 1995, p 12

67 Flower, op cit, p 115. "Chimurenga" is the Shona word used to describe the first uprising against British colonial rule soon after Rhodesia was settled.

68 Smith, op cit, pp 160–1

69 Flower, op cit, p 159

70 Flower, ibid, p 147

71 Mhanda, Wilfred. *Dzino: Memories of a freedom fighter.* Weaver Press, 2011, p 135

72 Mhanda, ibid, Chapter 6

73 Smith, ibid, pp 176–7

74 Nkomo, ibid, p 155

75 Smith, ibid, p 180

76 Flower, op cit, p 128

77 Nkomo, op cit, p 157

78 Letter to my parents, 9 March 1976

79 Nkomo, op cit, p 158

80 Now called Chipinge

81 Now called Nyanga

82 *Sadza* and *isitshwala* are the chiShona and isiNdebele names for the traditional Zimbabwean staple of ground white maize.

83 Letter to my parents, 3 May 1976

84 Mhanda, op cit, p 86

85 Baxter, op cit, p 441

86 Flower, op cit, p 152

87 Baxter, op cit, p 441

88 Flower, op cit, p 151

89 Martin and Johnson, op cit, p 242

90 Flower, op cit, p 157

91 Smith, op cit, p 198

92 Ian Smith's address to the nation, 24 September 1976

93 Smith's address, ibid, 24 September 1976

94 Letter to my parents, 13 October 1976

95 Letter to my parents, 31 October 1976

96 Smith, David and Simpson, Colin with Ian Davies. *Mugabe*. Pioneer Head, 1981, p 95
97 Flower, ibid, p 174
98 University of South Africa
99 Smith, op cit, p 230
100 Flower, op cit, p 177
101 Flower, op cit, p 180
102 *Guti* means light showers of rain in chiShona.
103 Letter to my parents, 4 September 1977
104 Smith, op cit, p 238
105 Letter to my parents, 18 October 1977. Internal Affairs was a non-military government department which dealt with the affairs of black Rhodesians, primarily in rural areas.
106 Letter to my parents, 19 October 1977
107 "Coloured" people, people of mixed race, were not recruited into the BSAP and had to do service in their own segregated Rhodesian army battalions. The Bachman-Turner Overdrive song "You Ain't Seen Nothing Yet" was a hit in Rhodesia, as it was elsewhere in the world, in the mid 1970s.
108 Letter to my parents, 24 October 1977
109 *The Chronicle*, 13 January 1977
110 Quoted in Moorcraft, op cit, p 88
111 Letter to my parents, 10 May 1978
112 Letter to my parents, 19 August 2014
113 Nkomo later in his memoirs acknowledged his error: "I then made an error of a different kind. The BBC telephoned me for a comment. They asked me what weapon the plane had been brought down with. I could not say it was a SAM 7; it was a secret. To turn the question aside, I answered that we had brought it down by throwing stones, and as I said so I laughed a bit. I was not laughing at the deaths of all those civilians, but at the evasive answer. The laugh was remembered, rather than my regret at those unnecessary deaths." Nkomo, ibid, p 167
114 Letter to my parents, 6 September 1978
115 Letter to my parents, 3 October 1978
116 Caute, David. *Under the Skin*. Penguin, 1983, p 346
117 Letter to my parents, 16 February 1979
118 Letter to my parents, 11 August 1979
119 Letter to my parents, 26 August 1979
120 Murphy, Professor Phillip. *Monarchy and the End of Empire*. Oxford University Press, 2014
121 Baxter, op cit, p 484
122 Letter to my parents, 25 September 1979
123 Smith, op cit, p 314
124 Personal interview with Dumiso Dabengwa, 17 November 2014
125 *Moto Magazine*, 2002
126 David Caute, op cit, p 436
127 Story as told to me by Judith Todd, 25 September 2014
128 Dr Stuart Doran's book on Gukurahundi (not yet published)
129 ZANLA also held back weapons and men in Mozambique and deliberately concealed this. Mujuru only came clean on this in 1981, by which time ZIPRA had effectively been emasculated.
130 Letter to my parents, 18 July 1980
131 *The Cape Argus*, 25 August 1980
132 *Cape Times*, 26 August 1980
133 Stiff, Peter. *Cry Zimbabwe*. Galago, 2000, p 40
134 Stiff, ibid, p 41
135 *The Chronicle*, 12 August 1980
136 *Zimbabwe Defence Forces Magazine*, Vol 7, Number 1, published December 1991, p 33
137 Nkomo, op cit, p 220

138 Nkomo, op cit, p 220

139 Stiff, ibid, p 76

140 Stiff, ibid, p 86

141 *The Herald*, 20 August 1981

142 Johnson, Phyllis and Martin, David. *Destructive Engagement*, p 48, quoting *The Herald*

143 Letter to my parents, 24 February 1982

144 Letter to my parents, 24 February 1982

145 *Sunday Mail*, 7 February

146 Todd, *Through the Darkness*, op cit, p 57

147 Nkomo, op cit, p 226

148 CCJP and LRF. *Gukurahundi – a report into the disturbances in Matabeleland*. Hurst & Co, 2007, p 66

149 Letter to my parents, 28 March 1982

150 Woods, Kevin. *The Kevin Woods Story – In the shadows of Mugabe's Gallows*. 30 degrees South Publishers (Pty) Ltd, 2007, p 86

151 CCJP & LRF, ibid, p 67

152 *The Chronicle*, 4 October 1982

153 *Zimbabwe Defence Forces Magazine*, Vol 7, No 1, December 1991, p 33

154 CCJP & LRF, ibid, p 74

155 This was the date given in the *Zimbabwe Defence Forces Magazine*, Vol 7, ibid. Other sources suggest that the pass out parade was earlier, in June 1982.

156 In this book I use the word "Gukurahundi" to describe the military action perpetrated by the Fifth Brigade and CIO against the civilian populations of Matabeleland North and South provinces, primarily during 1983 and 1984, which was designed to crush ZAPU's structures and support base.

157 *Zimbabwe Defence Forces Magazine*, ibid, p 35

158 Detailed written report given to me by David Joubert; conversations with Alex Goosen

159 Alexander, J. *Dissident Perspectives on Zimbabwe's Civil War*. Oxford, 1996, p 12

160 Article by Dinizulu Mbikokayise Macaphulana. In *Zimbabwe Independent*, 9 September 2015

161 Catholic Commission for Justice and Peace & Legal Resources Foundation. *Gukurahundi*. Hurst & Co, 2007, p 80

162 Davis, Dr Johanna Franziska. *Mission Accomplished – Dr Davis' Life Work in Zimbabwe*. Published by St John's Mission, 2013, pp 61–3

163 Todd, Judith. *Through the Darkness*. Zebra Press, 2007, p 52. The book does not state that Mutambara was acting under orders when he raped Todd. This fact was revealed to me in an interview I conducted with Todd on 17 November 2014.

164 Webb, Low and Barry letter, dated 30 November 1983, addressed to the Chihambakwe Commission of Inquiry

165 Jeremiah 17:7–9

166 Nkomo, ibid, p 2

167 CCJP & LRF, statement from "Witness 2409 AG" referred to in *Gukurahundi*, op cit, p 77

168 Davis, ibid, p 63

169 *The Chronicle*, 5 March 1983. DDT is a well-known poison.

170 Article 7(1) of the Rome Statute of the International Criminal Court, 17 July 1998

171 Stiff, ibid, p 190

172 Letter to my parents, 20 March 1983

173 Auret, M. *From Liberator to Dictator*. David Philip Publishers, 2009, p 81

174 *The Chronicle*, 6 April 1983

175 *The Chronicle*, 9 April 1983

176 CCJPP & LRF, op cit, p 85

177 *The Chronicle*, 8 April 1983

178 *The Chronicle*, ibid, 18 April 1983

179 *The Chronicle*, 15 April 1983

180 Letter to my parents, 2 May 1983
181 Auret, ibid, p 94
182 Lawyers Committee for Human Rights. *Zimbabwe: Wages of War*, New York: Lawyers Committee for Human Rights, 1986, p 38
183 Notice issued by BLPA dated 15 March 1983
184 *The Chronicle*, 14 September 1983
185 The statements I recorded that day are now included in the CCJP archives of the Gukurahundi.
186 Article 7 of Treaty of Rome Statute which established the International Criminal Court
187 *The Chronicle*, 14 January 1984
188 At independence the new government changed the name of traditional rural areas from Tribal Trust Lands, used by the Rhodesian government, to Communal Lands.
189 CCJP & LRF, op cit, p 224
190 CCJP & LRF, op cit, Part II (which is an entire chapter devoted to what happened in Matabeleland South in the first half of 1984)
191 Auret, ibid, p 85
192 *Zimbabwe Lawyers for Human Rights and the Legal Resources Foundation v The President of the Republic of Zimbabwe and the Attorney General* Judgment, SC12/03
193 *Zimbabwe Defence Forces Magazine*, ibid, p 36
194 *ZIANA*, 2 July 2000
195 Yap, Katri Pohjolainen. *Uprooting the Weeds*. University of Amsterdam doctoral thesis, published in September 2001, p 229, recording an interview with Dyck in Harare on 1 March 1994
196 CCJP & LRF, ibid, p 94
197 *LA Times*, 30 September 2007
198 CCJP & LRF, ibid, p 96
199 Auret, ibid, p 86
200 *The Herald*, 19 September 1985 and *The Chronicle*, 23 August 1985
201 Report contained in a letter to me, May 1984
202 Lawyers Committee for Human Rights, op cit, p 116
203 *The Citizen*, 9 August 1984
204 Lawyers Committee for Human Rights, op cit, p 117 and also the *Washington Post*, 6 November 1984
205 Not his real name
206 *New York Times*, 3 March 1985
207 *The Times* (London), 23 March 1985
208 *The Nation*, 31 August 1985
209 *The Herald*, 19 June 1985
210 *The Herald*, 21 June 1985
211 Lawyers Committee for Human Rights, op cit, p 126
212 My letter to the chairman of ZANU PF Matabeleland South, 20 June 1985
213 Auret, op cit, p 89
214 Auret, op cit, p 89
215 Lawyers Committee for Human Rights, op cit, p 127. Also *The Times*, 10 July 1985
216 *The Times* (London), 16 July 1985
217 *The Chronicle*, 23 August 1985
218 Statement made by Ndlovu, dated 14 October 1985
219 A method of torture in which the soles of the feet are beaten
220 Letter dated 21 January 1986 to Governor Jacob F Mudenda, sent by the Catholic, Anglican and Presbyterian churches
221 Todd, op cit, p 164
222 Todd, op cit, p 173
223 NOVIB is the Dutch affiliate of the international Oxfam organisation.
224 *Hansard*, 29 July 1987, p 620
225 *The Chronicle*, 22 September 1987

226 Notes in my Welshman Mabhena file dated 1 October 1987

227 Statutory Instrument 279A of 1987

228 Scott, Bob. *Saving Zimbabwe*. Compassionate Justice Books, 2009, p 51

229 Scott, ibid, p 52

230 Scott, ibid, p 110

231 Woods, op cit, p 126

232 *The Chronicle*, 9 November 1988

233 Jackson, PP. *Shattered Dreams*. AuthorHouse, 2010, pp 52–3

234 Heads of Argument in *The State v Frank Mpofu and others*, dated 26 July 1989

235 Moyo, Jonathan N. *Voting for Democracy*. University of Zimbabwe Publications, 1992, p 31

236 *Manica Post*, 30 June 1989

237 The Latin translates roughly to "You should have the body"; there is a recourse in law whereby a person can report an unlawful detention or imprisonment before a court, usually through a prison official.

238 Tsvangirai, Morgan. *At the Deep End*. Penguin Books, 2011, p 131

239 Jonathan Moyo, ibid, p 40

240 Notice of reasons for detention in terms of Section 53(1) of the Emergency Powers (Maintenance of Law and Order) regulations 1983 served on Sidanile by ZRP Luveve dated 14 November 1985

241 Note of a discussion I had with Inspector Chamba, dated 1 October 1987

242 Jonathan Moyo, ibid, p 75

243 CCJP report dated 26 March 1990; Jonathan Moyo, ibid, pp 77 and 209; New zimbabwe. com article, 27 May 2013 http://www.newzimbabwe.com/news-11231-Kombayi+famil y+speaks+as+CIO+boss+honoured/news.aspx

244 Jonathan Moyo, ibid, p 145

245 Richard Saunders, *Southern Africa Report*, Vol 11, No 4, p 8 http://www.africafiles.org/ article.asp?ID=3876

246 Affidavit of Senior Assistant Commissioner Hilario Zireva, filed in the case of *Musa Sibanda v The Commisioner of the ZRP*, High Court, Harare, 544/89, dated 29 May 1989

247 The equivalent of about US$10 000

248 War Victims Compensation Act Number 22 of 1980

249 Constitution of Zimbabwe Amendment (Number 10) Act 15 of 1990

250 Dr Enock Dumbutshena's address at the opening of the BLPC library, Bulawayo, 3 December 1990

251 My speech to KPMG Peat Marwick Seminar, Holiday Inn, Bulawayo, 6 May 1991

252 My speech, ibid, 6 May 1991

253 Speech delivered at MacDonald Hall, 1 December 1991

254 *The Chronicle*, 2 December 1991

255 *The Herald*, Comment, 4 December 1991

256 *Sunday Times*, 31 May 1992

257 A Blueprint for Zimbabwe – The Forum for Democractic Reform Trust. Discussion paper, published June 1992, p 1

258 David Coltart, "Elimination and Terror: The Establishment of Independent Enquiries in Zimbabwe". Paper presented to the Amnesty International Conference on political killings and 'disappearances', 5 September 1992, p 2

259 *Horizon Magazine*, January 1993, p 9

260 Poem by Albert Nyathi, published in *Horizon Magazine*, January 1993, p 9

261 Speech at the University of Zimbabwe, 29 October 1992

262 Christopher Hope. *Brothers Under the Skin – Travels in Tyranny*. Macmillan, 2003, p 109

263 Speech to FDR Trust members in Harare, 27 January 1993

264 Forum Party of Zimbabwe *Policy Papers*, 27 and 28 March 1993, p 6

265 *Financial Gazette*, 1 April 1993, p 4

266 "CSC boss fired for links with Forum". In *Financial Gazette*, 22 April 1993

267 *Sunday News*, 25 April 1993

268 *Financial Gazette*, ibid, 1 April 993

269 Speech given in Bulawayo, 9 June 1993

270 Speech given at Barham Green, Bulawayo, 27 October 1993

271 *Eastern Province Herald*, 18 January 1994

272 *Eastern Province Herald*, ibid

273 *Eastern Province Herald*, ibid

274 Jeremiah 15:19–21

275 *Eastern Province Herald*, June 1994

276 *Daily Gazette*, 9 June 1994

277 Legal Resources Foundation, *The Ninth Annual Report of the LRF for the year ended June 30 1993*, p 22. The total figure in 1994 went up to 7 451 but the statistics were consolidated in that report so it is not possible to isolate the cases handled by the BLPC. However, the BLPC continued to handle the bulk of the cases.

278 Mrs Sibanda eventually received payment of Z\$35 000 from government on 8 November 1994, five years after bringing the case to BLPC.

279 Letter written to Michael Auret, dated 4 July 1994

280 The Amani Trust was a Zimbabwean non-profit non-governmental organisation dedicated to preventing organised violence and torture, to advocacy for the rights of victims and to rehabilitation of victims through community-based care. It was established in 1993 and had its headquarters in Harare. The organisation was closed after Justice Minister Patrick Chinamasa declared various NGOs illegal, including the Amani Trust.

281 The information contained in this paragraph was obtained in an interview conducted in Bulawayo on 25 March 2015 with a close relative of Malunga's who was present on the day he died and who asked to remain anonymous. The suspicions outlined are shared by many members of the Malunga family, including his surviving children.

282 Letter to my parents, 18 November 1994

283 *The Daily Gazette*, 29 September 1994

284 War Victims Compensation Act (Number 22 of 1980)

285 Press statement released by David Coltart as director of BLPC, dated 8 November 1994

286 *The Chronicle*, 9 November 1994

287 *The Chronicle*, 16 October 1994

288 Letter to President Robert Mugabe, dated 1 November 1994, parts of which were published in *The Daily Gazette*, 21 November 1994

289 *The Herald*, 1 March 1995

290 Letter to David Coltart by the Law Society of Zimbabwe dated 18 May 1995

291 Report of the tribunal concerning the enquiry into the conduct of Justice FC Blackie, 28 November 1995; see also *The Herald*, 20 March 1996

292 Makumbe, John and Compagnon, Daniel. *Behind the Smokescreen – The Politics of Zimbabwe's 1995 General Elections*. University of Zimbabwe Publications, 2000, p 321

293 CCJP & LRF. *Breaking the Silence – Building True Peace*, February 1997, p 12

294 Speech given at the 10th anniversary of the Legal Resources Foundation, Harare, 10 November 1995

295 Letter to David Coltart from Shari Eppel recounting her experiences in compiling the report, March 2015

296 According to Rhodesian government statistics, more than 20 000 were killed during the war. From December 1972 to December 1979, 1 361 members of the Rhodesian security forces were killed, along with 10 450 guerrillas who were killed in Rhodesia, and an unquantified number in Mozambique and Zambia, 468 white civilians, and 7 790 black civilians. There are no accurate records regarding how many refugees and guerrillas died outside Rhodesia. Most historians estimate that about 30 000 people died during the conflict. See JK Cilliers, *Counter Insurgency in Rhodesia*, Croom Helm, 1985, p 241; also Paul Moorcroft & Peter McLaughlin, op cit, Jonathan Ball, 2008, p 197

297 Ndlovu, Mary. *History of the LRF*, Ch 18 (not yet published). Confirmed in a conversation with Verity Mundy, 24 November 2015

298 Letter to David Coltart from Shari Eppel, ibid

299 John Sogolani in an opinion piece in the *Sunday Mail*, 29 September 1996

300 Letter from Auret to me dated 26 February 2015

301 *Sunday Mail*, 11 May 1997

302 *Sunday Mail*, ibid

303 *Sunday News*, 11 May 1997

304 Letter to the LRF by Bishop Mutume dated 11 July 1997

305 Raftopoulos, Brian. "*The Labour Movement and the Emergence of Opposition Politics in Zimbabwe*" in *Striking Back,* Weaver Press, 2000, p 7

306 *Zimbabwe Independent*, 17 May 1986

307 "Hitler" was his real name, Hunzvi insisted, given to him by his parents. *The Independent*, 5 June 2001

308 Hill, Geoff. *The Battle for Zimbabwe*. Zebra Press, 2003, p 96

309 Sadomba, Zvakanyorwa Wilbert. *War Veterans in Zimbabwe's Revolution*. Boydell & Brewer Ltd, p 121

310 When the package was announced the Z$ was trading at about Z$14: US$1. After "Black Friday", 14 November 1997, the Z$ fell to Z$26: US$1

311 Letter From Claire Short to Kumbirai Kangai, 5 November 1997

312 Hill, op cit, p 101

313 *The Chronicle*, 2 February 1998

314 NCA Agenda, Vol 1, No 1, NCA, in February 1998, p 3

315 A Blueprint for Zimbabwe – Forum for Democratic reform trust, June 1992, p 1

316 *Rattigan v The Chief Immigration Officer* 1994(2)ZLR 54 (Supreme Court)

317 *Salem v The Chief Immigration Officer* 1994(2) ZLR 287 (S)

318 Speech to Rotary Club of Bulawayo South, 5 August 1996

319 *Zimbabwe Independent*, 6 February 1998

320 ZIANA report by Matilda Moyo, dated 25 February 1998

321 *The Herald*, 27 April 1998; and my speech entitled "A Critique of the Public Order and Security Bill", dated 25 April 1998

322 Speech given to the Media Institute of Southern Africa, Bulawayo, 9 May 1998

323 Some organisations put the death toll much higher. One estimate put out by *Reuters* on 22 August 2008 put it at 5.4 million, including those who died of starvation and disease.

324 Stiff, Peter. *Cry Zimbabwe*. Galago, 2000, p 259

325 *Zimbabwe Independent*, 13 November 1998

326 *The Standard*, 31 January 1999

327 *Sunday Times*, 14 February 1999

328 Presidential address delivered by President Robert Mugabe on ZTV at 9.30 pm, Saturday, 6 February 1999

329 *Sunday Mirror*, 15 January 1999

330 *The Australian*, 9 February 1999

331 *The Chronicle*, 12 March 1999

332 Proclamation 6 of 1999 made in terms of the Commissions of Inquiry Act Chapter 10:07 Statutory Instrument 138A of 1999

333 *Zimbabwe Independent*, 2 July 1999

334 Tsvangirai, op cit, p 228

335 Tsvangirai, ibid, p 238

336 *The Chronicle*, 18 October 1999

337 Legal Resources Foundation statement regarding the draft constitution, 13 December 1999

338 Letter by chair of the Finance committee, Commissioner Eric Bloch, to Justice Chidyausiku, dated 29 November 1999

339 "The smoke and mirrors constitution". Article published in the *Zimbabwe Independent*, 3 December 1999

340 Section 186(1) of the draft constitution of Zimbabwe, published on 29 November 1999

341 Section 46 of Chapter III, ibid

342 Blair, David. *Degrees in Violence*. Continuum, 2002, p 53

343 I was subsequently, on 14 February 2000, appointed Legal Secretary of the MDC
344 *The Herald*, 19 February 2000
345 The word "coloured" is used in Zimbabwe to describe people of mixed race.
346 *The Chronicle*, 14 March 2000
347 Press conference statement made on 2 March 2000, recorded in David Blair's *Degrees of Violence*, op cit, p 75
348 ZBC, 2 March 2000
349 Blair, op cit, p 92
350 *The Herald*, 14 April 2000
351 Tsvangirai, op cit, p 299
352 Blair, op cit, p 106
353 Not his real name. Yates still fears retribution to this day.
354 Letter to me from Kathy Olds, 27 September 2015
355 ZTV, 18 April 2000
356 Speech given at Church of Ascension, Hillside, Bulawayo, 26 April 2000
357 BBC report, 11 May 2000
358 Zimbabwe Human Rights Forum report, 15 May 2000
359 Speech given by Nelson Mandela at the launch of the UNICEF Global Partnership, Johannesburg, 6 May 2000
360 Remarks made at a press conference at State House recorded by David Blair, *Degrees in Violence*, op cit, p 143
361 *Sunday News*, 28 May 2000
362 *The Farmer*, 20 June 2000
363 Speech in the Large City Hall, 14 June 2000
364 Nabanyama had been named as one of my polling agents and was a key member of my campaign team. He was also the man who had first introduced me in Nketa in March.
365 Evidence given by Mrs Patricia Nabanyama at the trial of Ephraim Moyo and five others, NC 19–26/2002, p 54
366 *The Dispatch*, 9 June 2000. The report documents the threat levelled against Nabanyama well before his final disappearance.
367 Letter written by Patrick Nabanyama, 19 June 2000
368 Zimbabwe Human Rights Forum report, issued on 27 June 2000, documenting all the human rights abuses perpetrated in Zimbabwe since 15 February 2000. The same report found that 90.7 per cent of those responsible were ZANU PF supporters.
369 "Mabhunu" is a pejorative Shona word used to describe white farmers particularly.
370 Speech at Bulawayo Centenary Park Amphitheatre, Wednesday, 21 June 2000
371 Commonwealth Observer Mission report 2000. Quoted in the International Bar Association Report, Section 8.5
372 Joint statement signed by chairman of District 11 of Zimbabwe War Veterans Association, Aleck Moyo, and David Coltart, 7 July 2000
373 *Hansard*, 18 July 2000
374 *Hansard*, Vol 27, No 1, p 3
375 Isaiah 58:6–9
376 *Hansard*, Vol 27, No 6, p 338
377 LRF Annual Report for the year ended 30 June 2001, pp 6 and 20
378 *Zimbabwe Independent*, 11 August 2000. See also *Hansard*, Vol 27, No 14, p 1271
379 *Hansard*, Vol 27, No 14, p 1314
380 *Hansard*, Vol 27, No 14, p 1330
381 *Hansard*, Vol 27, No 14, p 1332
382 *Sunday Mail*, 1 October 2000
383 *Daily News*, 3 October 2000
384 Not his real name. Makoni protected us for several years and displayed remarkable bravery throughout.
385 Our children came through this trauma remarkably unscathed. One incident illustrates that although surrounded by violence, they could still rise above it. In August 2000 Scott's

Grade 2 teacher noticed that the boys had come in late from the playground and when asked to explain why they were late was told that they were playing "farmers and war vets". Further interrogation revealed that the head of the "farmers" was Lumbidzani, a black Ndebele lad; Scott was leader of the "war vets".

386 Letter to Brian Latham by the director of Information, 21 February 1996
387 Supreme Court of Zimbabwe Judgment No SC99/2000 and Constitutional Application No 130/2000
388 *Zimbabwe Independent*, 6 October 2000
389 Statutory Instrument 255A of 2000, dated 4 October 2000
390 Clemency Order 1 of 2000, 6 October 2000
391 *Sunday News*, 15 October 12000
392 Section 29 of the old Lancaster House constitution set out the procedures and ground for impeachment.
393 Impeachment petition moved by Gibson Sibanda, dated 20 October 2000
394 *Hansard*, Vol 27, No 24, p 2469
395 *Hansard*, ibid, p 2470
396 *The Chronicle*, 1 December 2000
397 *Herald*, 26 October 2000
398 *Herald*, ibid, 26 October 2000
399 *Herald*, ibid
400 Statement issued by Mike and Auret and David Coltart, 1 November 2000
401 *The Zimbabwe Mirror*, 3 November 2000 and *The Financial Gazette*, 2 November 2000
402 *Zimbabwe News*, Vol 33, No 9, November 2000
403 *Zimbabwe News*, ibid, p 4
404 *The Financial* Gazette, 2 November 2000
405 Blair, op cit, p 201
406 Electoral Act (Modification) (No3) Notice 2000, Statutory Instrument 318 of 2000
407 *Daily News*, 14 December 2000
408 Speech to ZANU PF central committee by President Mugabe, 13 December 2000, quoted in Blair, op cit, p 203
409 Speech to ZANU PF congress, 14 December 2000, quoted in *Irish Times*, 15 December 2000
410 *The Herald*, 19 January 2000
411 *Movement for Democractic Change v Minister of Justice and others* ZLR 2001(1) 69 (S)
412 McNally's account given to the International Bar Association and recorded in Blair, op cit, p 215
413 *Hansard*, Vol 27, No 44, p 4466
414 *The Herald*, 23 February 2001
415 Blair, op cit, p 218
416 *The Herald*, 26 January 2000
417 *Africa Defence Journal*, Newsflash No 2, 28 January 2001
418 Quote from Nyarota contained in Hill, *The Battle for Zimbabwe*, op cit, p 130
419 *Financial Gazette*, 8 March 2001; *Zimbabwe Independent*, 9 March 2001; Letter to David Coltart from "CJ"
420 Speech to the Law Society of England and Wales, London, 13 March 2001
421 First report, Portfolio Committee on Justice, Legal and Parliamentary Affairs, 24 May 2001, p 13, paragraph 4.9
422 Portfolio Committee on Justice report, ibid
423 Bonhoeffer, Dietrich. *Letters and Papers from Prison*, Fontana, 1959
424 Wikipedia http://en.wikipedia.org/wiki/Edson_Zvobgo
425 Speech delivered at Bulawayo Presbyterian Church, 7 July 2001
426 Amos 5:15 and 24
427 *Sunday News*, 8 July 2001
428 *The Sunday Telegraph*, 12 August 2001
429 *The Herald*, 28 August 2001

430 *The Chronicle*, 31 August 2001

431 *The Daily News*, 14 June 2001

432 Section 52(1) of the Postal and Telecommunications Regulations of 2001 stated that radios operating at less than 10mW were exempt from licensing.

433 *The Chronicle*, 10 September 2001

434 *The Chronicle*, ibid, 10 September 2001

435 *The Chronicle*, 11 September 2001

436 *The Zimbabwe Independent*, 14 September 2001

437 *Tsvangirai v Manyonda* HC 8139/2000

438 *Hansard*, Vol 28 No 19, 27 September 2001, p 1436

439 Letter by Supreme Court Judge Simba Muchechetere to *The Herald*, dated 28 September 2001

440 Hill, op cit, p 250

441 *The Standard*, 18 November 2001

442 *The Standard*, ibid, 18 November 2001

443 *The Standard*, ibid, 18 November 2001

444 Police Diary Log of CID Law and Order Division for Western Commonage CR 151/2/11/01, produced at the subsequent trial

445 Police Diary Log entry 10 dated 14.00, 7 November 2001

446 Police Diary Log, ibid, entry 13

447 ZTV 8 pm news bulletin, Sunday, 11 November 2001

448 http://insiderzim.com/mpofu-in-coltart-elimination-plot/ 14 November 2001

449 CAAZ Notam A0188/01, 15.30, 15 November 2001

450 *The Observer*, 18 November 2001

451 Hill, op cit, p 251. See also Human Rights Watch report, November 2001

452 *The Chronicle*, 20 November 2001

453 *The Chronicle*, ibid, 20 November 2001

454 *The Chronicle*, ibid, 20 November 2001

455 *Hansard*, Vol 28, No 26, 20 November 2001, p 2110

456 *The Chronicle*, 21 November 2001

457 *Daily* News, 28 November 2001

458 *Simon Spooner v The State* HB 51/2001 Case number HCB 247/2001, p 14

459 *The State v Ephraim Moyo and 5 others* HC 19-26/2002. Transcript of proceedings, p 165

460 *The State v Moyo*, ibid, p 173

461 *The Times*, 6 March 2004

462 *The State v Sonny Masera and 5 others* HC 175-81/02 dated 5 Augus 2004, p 9

463 Document provided to me by Dumiso Dabengwa in February 2015, which is now in safe custody outside Zimbabwe. The document names the operatives, but because the allegations cannot be proved I have just used their initials.

464 SAPA report, 5 December 2001

465 *The Guardian*, 22 January 2002

466 *Hansard*, Vol 28, No 38, 8 January 2002, p 3462

467 *Hansard*, Vol 28,No 40, dated 10 January 2002, p 3833

468 Moyo, Jonathan N. *Voting for Democracy*. University of Zimbabwe Publications, 1992, op cit, p 31

469 *Murungu* is a pejorative term in the Shona language for a white man.

470 *Hansard*, Vol 28, No 41, 15 January 2002, p 3869

471 *Hansard*, Vol 28, No 41, ibid, p 3870

472 *Hansard*, Vol 28, No 46, 29 January 2002, p 4169

473 *Hansard*, Vol 28, No 48, 31 January 2002 p 4476

474 ZANU PF election manifesto, published in *The Chronicle*, 1 February 2002

475 MDC Justice Policy document, February 2002

476 Mpala died two years later. His assailants, three war veterans, were sentenced to four years' imprisonment in 2007. *The Standard*, 5 October 2007

477 Amnesty International statement UA40/02, 7 February 2002

478 Statement of Baleni Moyo, recorded on 2 April 2003
479 An open-backed vehicle
480 Jeanette Cross was released that afternoon and not charged, but the film in her camera was confiscated.
481 HC 11843/2001
482 HC 12092/2001
483 HC 12015/2001 and 11943/2001
484 SC 30/2002
485 SC 46/2002
486 Electoral Act (Modification) Notice 2002 (SI 41D of 2002), published on 5 March, three days before the election was due to commence
487 SC 76/2002
488 HC 2800/2002
489 Section 53(4) of the then Electoral Act
490 HC 2815/2002
491 Preliminary report 2002 Presidential Elections, published by the MDC Election Directorate, dated March 2002
492 Sisi Khampepe and Dikgang Moseneke, Judges of the High Court of South Africa, Report on the 2002 Presidential Elections of Zimbabwe 2002, published by the Mail & Guardian http://cdn.mg.co.za/content/documents/2014/11/14/reportonthe2002presidentialelectionsofzimbabwe.pdf
493 *Hansard*, Vol 28, No 49 7 May 2002, pp 4571–83
494 *The Scotsman*, 14 May 2002
495 *The New Yorker*, 3 June 2002, p 66
496 Statement of Vice-President Gibson Sibanda, 22 July 2002
497 *Hansard*, Vol 29, No 1, 23 July 2002, p 3
498 MDC statement regarding food distribution, 16 July 2002 prepared by David Coltart
499 *New York Times*, 7 August 2002, p A17
500 *The Chronicle*, 5 September 2002
501 Letter entitled "Mr President: Leave David Coltart alone" written by Siphosami Malunga. Published in the *Zimbabwe Independent*, 20 September 2002
502 *Morgan Tsvangirai v The Registrar General of Elections* HC 3493/2002, 10 July 2002
503 *Hansard*, Vol 29, No 14, pp 1135–50
504 Todd, Judith. *Through the Darkness: A life in Zimbabwe*, op cit, p 421
505 Letter written by David Coltart to Secretary General Kofi Annan, 12 November 2002
506 *Hansard*, Vol 29, No 19, 14 November 2002, p 1398
507 *Hansard*, Vol 29, No 20, 26 November 2002, pp 1547–50
508 Article by Alistair Sparks, 1 February 2013
509 Transitional Authority proposals dated 8 December 2002
510 Taken from my contemporaneous notes taken of the meeting and conveyed to South African veteran journalist Alastair Sparks, who wrote an article entitled "The Full Story of What is Going on in Zimbabwe", February 2003
511 Olonga, Henry. *Blood, Sweat and Treason*. Vision Sports Publishing, 2010, p 217
512 Olonga, ibid, p 229
513 A report on police brutality, 24 February to 25 March 2003: The Solidarity Peace Trust, p 12
514 The attempt was reported in the independent media and several diplomats also voiced concern to the Zimbabwean ministry of Foreign Affairs.
515 Not his real name
516 LDF report for the period 1 April to 31 January 2006. The report is dated 4 February 2006.
517 Not his real name
518 Executive Order 13288 of March 6 2003. Federal Register Volume 68, Number 46
519 Not her real name
520 Statement made by Mugabe at a rally in Nyamandlovu on 13 June 2003, reported in

"Playing with Fire", published by the Zimbabwe Institute, March 2004, p 3
521 Auret, op cit, p 170
522 *State v Tsvangirai and others* HH 119–2003, 8 August 2003
523 *Zimbabwe Independent*, 12 September 2003
524 *Mail & Guardian*, 28 November 2007
525 *News24* archives, 30 January 2009
526 Petitioner's Heads of Argument in Case number 3616/2002, filed on 13 October 2003, p viii
527 *The Guardian*, 6 March 2009 http://www.theguardian.com/world/2009/mar/06/zimbabwe-judge-stolen-land-mugabe
528 *Subverting Justice.* Solidarity Peace Trust report, March 2005, p 34
529 *The Guardian*, 14 November 2003
530 *Hansard*, Vol 30, No 21, 20 November 2003, p 1447
531 *Hansard*, Vol 30, No 24, 10 December 2003, p 1759
532 *Hansard*, Vol 30, No 24, 10 December 2003, p 1692
533 *The Harare Commonwealth Declaration – The association's fundamental values,* signed at the CHOGM meeting in Harare, 20 October 1991
534 Section 17 of the Privileges, Immunities and Powers of Parliament Act Chapter 2:08 imposed hefty penalties if an MP debated any matter in which he had a direct pecuniary interest.
535 *Hansard*, Vol 30, No 30, 21 January 2004, p 2368
536 *Hansard*, Vol 30, No 31, 22 January 2004 p 2465
537 *Hansard*, Vol 30, No 31, ibid, p 2467
538 *The Telegraph,* 27 February 2004
539 *This Day*, 9 March 2004
540 The Zimbabwe Institute. *Playing with Fire*, March 2004, pp 15 and 16
541 Letter written by Archbishop Desmond Tutu in support of the Zimbabwe Defence and Aid Fund, March 2004
542 Herbstein, Denis. *White Lies – Canon Collins and the Secret War against Apartheid.* James Curry Publishers, 2004, p 331
543 *White Lies*, ibid, pp 257–260
544 *Eastern Cape Herald*, 22 April 2004
545 *Hansard*, Vol 30, No 44, 18 May 2004, p 3298
546 Letter addressed to David Coltart by KM Chokuda, Clerk of the Privileges Committee, 29 July 2004
547 Zimbabwean slang for "new kids on the block" or "upstarts"
548 *The Sunday Mail*, 25 July 2004
549 *The Sunday Mail*, ibid, 25 July 2004
550 *Zimbabwe Independent*, 30 July 2004
551 *Zimbabwe Independent*, ibid, 30 July 2004
552 Tsvangirai, op cit, p 368
553 *Report of the MDC Commission of Inquiry into the disruption of the Harare Provincial Congress and the dispute between Hon Tapiwa Mashakada, on one hand, and Hons Learnmore Jongwe, Job Sikhala and Tafadzwa Musekiwa on the other hand*, MDC, 7 November 2001
554 Evidence given by Chirilele, MDC Commission of Inquiry into disturbances at MDC Headquarters, May 2005, p 8
555 *MDC Commission of Inquiry into disturbances at Party Headquarters*, MDC, May 2005, ibid, p 9
556 Bizos, George. *Odyssey to Freedom.* Random House, 2007, p 566
557 *Hansard*, Vol 31, No 14, 27 October 2004, pp 809–12
558 What Bennett didn't have time to list and detail was the excess of 120 documented cases of human rights abuses committed against himself, his family and workers.
559 *Hansard*, Vol 32, No 15, 28 October 2004, p 904
560 *Hansard*, ibid, p 951

561 "Tsholotsho Saga: The untold story". Opinion piece by Jonathan Moyo in the *Zimbabwe Independent*, 17 December 2004
562 According to the 2012 census, 99.7 per cent of Zimbabwe's population is black, with as few as 57 000 white, coloured and Asian people left in the country. There are two major ethnolinguistic categories, namely, Shona and Ndebele, comprising 70 per cent and 20 per cent respectively. Within the Shona linguistic group there are several sub-ethnic groups, including the Zezuru, Karanga and Manyica.
563 Moyo, "Tsholotsho Saga", ibid
564 Moyo, "Tsholotsho Saga", ibid
565 *No War in Zimbabwe – An account of the exodus of a nation's people*, Solidarity Peace Trust, November 2004, p 8
566 *Hansard*, Vol 31, No 20, 16 November 2004, p 1705
567 SADC Principles and Guidelines Governing Democratic Elections, adopted by the SADC Summit, Mauritius, August 2004
568 Solidarity Peace Trust. *Out for the Count: Democracy in Zimbabwe*, May 2005, p 11
569 *The Chronicle*, 17 February 2005
570 *The Mirror*, 18 February 2005
571 South African Citizenship Act 1995 (Act 88 of 1995)
572 Letter to Walton Jessop Attorneys by the DG Home Affairs
573 Opinion of J G Dickerson, 28 January 2005
574 *The Sunday Telegraph*, 20 March 2005
575 Quoted as stating this in March 2005 in *Out for the Count*, Solidarity Peace Trust, op cit
576 HC 10321/03 and HC 10237/04
577 LDF report for period 1 April 2003 to 31 January 2006
578 Notes made of the meeting by Shari Eppel, May 2005
579 *Hansard*, Vol 32, No 5, 23 June 2005, p 152
580 *Hansard*, ibid, p 133
581 *Hansard*, ibid, p 64
582 Tibaijuka, Anna Kajumulo. Report of the Fact-finding mission to Zimbabwe re Operation Murambatsvina, United Nations, 18 July 2005, p 7
583 Tibaijuka, ibid, p 39
584 Article 7 of the Rome Statute of the International Criminal Court
585 Statement drafted by David Coltart on 14 July 2005, tabled at the MDC national executive meeting held in Harare on 15 July 2005
586 *Hansard*, Vol 32, No 25, p 1926
587 Volume 1 of "What the People Said", Constitutional Commission Report, November 1999, p 561
588 Letter to an MDC national council member, 7 November 2005
589 Email from David Coltart to Innocent Chigonda, 9 December 2005
590 Letter to Geoff Nyarota, 11 January 2006
591 SW Radio Africa report, 20 December 2005
592 Letter to Geoff Nyarota, ibid, 11 January 2006
593 Inspection and Analysis of the Voting Residue Pertaining to the 2002 Presidential Elections. Report prepared by the MDC Legal department, February 2006, p 101
594 Embassy cable, dated 13 February 2006, recording the conversation
595 Embassy cable, ibid, 13 February 2006
596 Although the suffix MDC-T only came into use in March 2008, for sake of convenience and understanding I have used it, and MDC-M, with effect from February 2006 in this narrative. The official names used by the two parties in the March 2008 election were in fact MDC-T and MDC, which remain their respective official names.
597 Letter to Roy Bennett, 26 April 2006
598 One was Peta Thornycroft, a doyenne of the journalism fraternity in Southern Africa. The other journalist has requested anonymity.
599 David Coltart letter to Bulawayo South constituents, 23 May 2006
600 Statement issued by me on 15 June 2006

601 SW Radio Africa report, 3 July 2006

602 Wikileaks record of US embassy cable, dated 3 October 2006

603 Wikileaks, ibid, 3 October 2006

604 MDC-T commission of inquiry report into assault on Hon Stevenson and others, 11 September 2006, p 107, para 39.3

605 Tonderai Ndira is recorded as victim number 247 on an MDC-T Youth Assembly Roll of Honour http://mdc-youthassembly.blogspot.com/p/roll-of-honor.html

606 *The Telegraph*, 9 April 2006

607 BBC Hardtalk interview, 12 October 2006

608 Gwanda magistrate's court summons issued against Paul Themba Nyathi, 26 October 2006

609 Minutes prepared by David Coltart of the meeting held at Irene Country Club, 25 August 2006

610 See, for example, "ZANU PF knows how to play dirty" in *The Herald*, 23 September 2013

611 Minutes by David Coltart of the meeting held at The Grace hotel, Johannesburg, 26 November 2006

612 David Coltart statement issued as MDC shadow Justice minister, 19 February 2007

613 *Hansard*, Vol 33, No 23, 30 November 2006, p 929

614 Statement issued by David Coltart in Helsinki, 13 March 2007

615 Interview with Tony Jones of the Australian Broadcasting Corporation's Lateline programme, 13 March 2007

616 *The Chronicle*, 17 March 2007

617 MDC draft coalition agreement agreed to by the negotiating parties at Irene, 9 April 2007

618 *Hansard*, Vol 33, No 52, 13 June 2007

619 Statement issued by Obert Mpofu, 25 June 2007

620 *Zimbabwe Independent*, 30 January 2009

621 Gardner, Jerome. *Zimbabwe: Warm Heart Ugly Face*, 2010, p 84

622 Gardner, ibid, p 87

623 Gardner, ibid, p 91

624 Gardner, ibid, p 93

625 *Newsweek*, 3 September 2007

626 Robert Mugabe quoted in Solidarity Peace Trust report entitled "A difficult dialogue: Zimbabwe-South Africa economic relations since 2000", 23 October 2007. *The Chronicle*, 2 October 2007

627 *Hansard*, Vol 34, No 16, 30 October 2007

628 *Hansard*, Vol 34, No 23, 29 November 2007

629 Christmas letter to friends, December 2007

630 Gardner, ibid, p 109

631 Barclay, Philip. *Zimbabwe – Years of Hope and Despair*. Bloomsbury, 2010, p 37

632 Transitional Reunification draft agreement between the MDC formations prepared for endorsement of factions on 2 February 2008

633 King, Coretta Scott. *The Words of Martin Luther King*. Newmarket Press, 1987, p 74

634 Interviews with Tendai Biti, Welshman Ncube, Paul Themba Nyathi and Stella Allberry on 30 July 2015, who attended the respective meetings. Biti and Ncube have a different recollection regarding the split of parliamentary seats, but all are agreed that it was the Bulawayo contingent of the MDC-T who ultimately scuppered the agreement.

635 Tsvangirai, ibid, p 476

636 I have used the description MDC-M to describe the MDC party for sake of clarity, to distinguish it from the MDC-T. The name "MDC" is in fact the legal name of the party, which is currently led by Professor Welshman Ncube.

637 Letter by Roy Bennett to *The Cape Argus*, 17 February 2008

638 David Coltart letter to the *Cape Argus*, 1 March 2008

639 Statement recorded from MDC-M campaign worker, March 2008

640 A few seats were not contested because of candidates dying in the run up to the election.

641 *The Star*, 14 April 2008

642 "Mugabe's diabolical plot exposed". In the *Sunday Independent*, 20 April 2008

643 Solidarity Peace Trust, "Punishing Dissent, Silencing Citizens", 21 May 2008, p 57

644 "Punishing Dissent", ibid, p 57

645 MDC Youth Assembly Roll of Honour, which records some 322 members murdered, most of whom were killed during the 2008 run-off presidential election http://mdc-youthassembly.blogspot.com/p/roll-of-honor.html

646 Solidarity Peace Trust, ibid, p 28

647 Search warrant issued against Craig Edy, 27 May 2008

648 *The Chronicle*, 30 May 2008

649 SABC News, 28 April 2008

650 Speech delivered in the Swedish parliament, Stockholm, 9 June 2008

651 LDF report dated 31 January 2009

652 Tsvangirai, op cit, p 496

653 *Associated Press*, 22 June 2008

654 *Sunday Times*, 22 June 2008

655 SADC Election Observer Mission: Preliminary Statement, 27 June 2008

656 Preliminary Statement of the African Union Observer Mission, 29 June 2008

657 The Pan-African Parliament Election Observer Mission to the Presidential Run-Off and Parliamentary by-Elections in Zimbabwe: Interim Statement, 29 June 2008

658 *The Herald*, 27 June 2008

659 Parliament of Zimbabwe Standing Orders, Section 6

660 *Zimbabwe Independent*, 29 August 2008

661 Parliament of Zimbabwe Standing Orders 14 and 15 of Appendix B: outlaw the accepting of a bribe by a member to influence his conduct and offering a member a reward "in respect of the promotion of opposition to any matter".

662 *Jonathan Moyo and others v Zvoma, Clerk of Parliament and Lovemore Moyo* SC28/10, 10 March 2001 p 1

663 BBC News, 9 September 2008

664 Gardner, ibid, p 117

665 *Hansard*, Vol 18, No 10, 5 February 2009, p 258

666 *The Chronicle*, 24 February 2009

667 Press conference given by Bennett in 2010, quoted in http://www.freezimbabwe.com/resources.php

668 SADC Heads of Government communiqué issued at Pretoria, 27 January 2009

669 *The Herald*, 14 March 2009

670 Speech given at the launch of the ETF, Harare, 14 September 2009

671 ETF speech, ibid, 14 September 2009

672 Minutes of private meeting with Robert Mugabe, 20 October 2009

673 Statement of Morgan Tsvangirai, 28 October 2009

674 Tsvangirai statement, ibid, 28 October 2009

675 *Zimbabwe Independent*, 27 November 2009

676 Diary notes, 13 April 2010

677 Achebe, Chinua. *There Was a Country*, Penguin Books, 2012, p 253

678 Diary notes, 11 May 2010

679 *New Zealand Herald*, 24 March 2010

680 *Sydney Morning Herald*, 18 June 2010

681 Diary minute of 22 June 2010

682 *The Herald*, 24 June 2010

683 *The Herald*, editorial, 24 June 2010

684 *The Telegraph*, 30 June 2010

685 BBC Hardtalk interview with Stephen Sackur, 22 July 2010

686 SW Radio Africa, 30 August 2010

687 *The Herald*, 9 September 2010

688 Foreword by Senator David Coltart inserted in all UNICEF books, April 2010

689 Notes passed to me in cabinet, 19 October 2010
690 WB Yeats, "Ego Dominus Tuus"
691 Annual Lozikeyi Lecture, 29 October 2010
692 Lozikeyi Lecture, ibid
693 Letter to David Coltart by Cde Mpofu and Joseph Chinotimba of ZNLWVA, 4 November 2010
694 Excerpt from a letter I wrote to ZNLWVA, 5 November 2010, published in NewZimbabwe.com on 12 November 2010
695 Minutes of meeting held at Deputy Prime Minister Mutambara's office with ZNLWVA, 18 November 2010
696 Speech given at Whitestone Chapel, 7 November 2010
697 My minute of a meeting held with the Rt Hon Andrew Mitchell, London, 10 January 2011
698 *The Standard*, 9 January 2011
699 Statement issued by Arthur Mutambara, 7 February 2011
700 Section 20.1.6 of the GPA
701 Again for ease of reference, although the official, legal name of the party was MDC, I have called it the MDC-N – representing the party then under the presidency of Welshman Ncube.
702 David Coltart minutes of cabinet discussions, 22 February 2011
703 *Sunday Mail*, 27 February 2011
704 ZBC report, 13 March 2011
705 *Mail & Guardian*, 25 March 2011
706 My minute of the cabinet meeting held on 22 March 2011
707 My minute of the cabinet meeting held on 12 April 2011
708 The December 1987 Accord between ZANU PF and ZAPU had seen the dissolution of ZAPU. However, a number of former ZAPU leaders, including Dumiso Dabengwa, resuscitated ZAPU in November 2008 and since then it has become once again a fully fledged political party in Zimbabwe.
709 My minute of cabinet, 19 July 2011
710 Senator David Coltart. *The 2011 Acton Lecture*. Centre for Independent Studies, Sydney, 2001, p 8
711 Martin, David and Johnson, Phyllis. *The Struggle for Zimbabwe*. Zimbabwe Publishing House, 1981, p 202
712 Martin and Johnson, ibid, p 211
713 Mhanda, op cit, p 135
714 *Sunday News*, 4 September 2011
715 Section 20(3) of the Lancaster House Constitution allowed all people to "establish and maintain" their own schools. Sections 19, 20 and 21 allowed minorities freedom of conscience, expression and association.
716 Letter to me by Victoria Chitepo, dated 16 September 2011
717 Speech to Girls College, 12 October 2011
718 Speech given to ministers' plenary session of the the Education World Forum, London, 11 January 2012
719 Zimonline report, 20 January 2012
720 Zimonline report, ibid
721 Inquest report of Provincial Magistrate Walter Chikwanha, 14 March 2012
722 *Zimbabwe Independent*, 15 February 2012
723 *Zimbabwe Independent*, ibid, 15 February 2012
724 Inquest report, ibid
725 Inquest report, ibid
726 Inquest report, ibid
727 BBC's Focus on Africa programme, 16 March 2012
728 These agreements found their way into the new constitution as Sections 295 and 72(3)(c)
729 The word "indigenous" is not defined in Zimbabwe's new constitution, which became law in 2013. The only other place it is used in Zimbabwean law is in the Indigenisation

and Economic Empowerment Act, Chapter 14:33, which defines an "indigenous Zimbabwean" as "any person who, before the 18th April, 1980, was disadvantaged by unfair discrimination on the grounds of his or her race, and any descendant of such person". A succession of ZANU PF ministers have made it clear that whites are not viewed as "indigenous".

730 This suggestion eventually found its form in Section 43(2)(a) of the constitution, which allows first generation Zimbabweans, one of whose parents was a SADC citizen, to claim an absolute birth right. Without this provision I would not personally have obtained a constitutional birth right.

731 *The Nation*, 14 July 2010

732 *Breaking the Silence*, op cit, pp 97–9

733 *The Chronicle*, 14 July 2012; *Newsday*, 14 July 2012; and my own notes made at the ceremony

734 Letter to David Coltart by the broker, 22 August 2012. The man, whose name I am not at liberty to reveal, was at pains to explain that his trip had no official sanction from either Clegg or the British government, but was his personal initiative in response to concerns expressed by Clegg.

735 Partnership Africa Canada report, issued in November 2012

736 *The Herald*, 17 October 2012

737 Partnership Africa Canada report, ibid, p 25

738 *New* zimbabwe.com 17 June 2012 http://www.newzimbabwe.com/news-8269-Mpofu+ splashes+US$23m+on+local+bank/news.aspx

739 *New* zimbabwe.com, ibid

740 Mugabe confirmed the funding arrangements for the National Defence College on a few occasions. See, for example, *The Herald*, 6 September 2013 http://www.herald.co.zw/ ndc-response-to-national-security/

741 Section 23 of the SRC Act gave the minister the power to issue directives in the national interest.

742 Wisden India, 13 June 2014 http://www.wisdenindia.com/cricket-article/debt-leaves- zimbabwe-cricket-dire-straits/113875

743 Statement issued by David Coltart on the eve of the referendum, 16 March 2013

744 Statement, ibid

745 *The Telegraph*, 24 February 2013

746 My cabinet diary, 5 March 2013

747 The Joint Monitoring and Implementation Committee was established in terms of clause 22.1 of the GPA to "ensure full and proper implementation" of the agreement. It was comprised of four members of each of the three parties, namely, ZANU PF, MDC-T and MDC-N.

748 Sixth Schedule, Part 3, Section 6(3) of the constitution

749 Diary note, recorded in cabinet on 14 May 2013

750 Diary note, recorded in cabinet on 21 May 2013

751 *Jealously Mbizvo Mawarire v Robert Mugabe and others* Constitutional Application 146/2013 Judgment Number 1/13

752 Dissenting judgment of Malaba DCJ in *Mawarire v Mugabe*, ibid

753 Statutory Instrument 85 of 2013

754 Section 2(2)(c) of the Presidential Powers (Temporary Measures) Act Chapter 10:20

755 My letter to Elton Mangoma and Tendai Biti, 19 June 2013

756 Programme for International Student Assessment

757 *Newsday*, 18 July 2013

758 *The Herald*, 30 July 2013

759 Letter to Head of the SADC Observer Mission Hon Situ Musokotwane MP, 30 July 2013

760 Transcript of Mugabe's press conference, 30 July 2013 http://www.sankofasofa.com/ docs/feed/item/transcription-press-conference-zimbabwe-president-robert-mugabe- july-30-2013

761 Immediately after the election, on 10 August 2013 I prepared a detailed report on all the

anomalies – http://www.davidcoltart.com/2013/08/report-regarding-breaches-of-the-electoral-act-and-the-constitution-in-bulawayo-east-constituency/

762 Section 62(2) of the Electoral Act prohibited the police from being present during the counting process.

763 The Source, 15 August 2013 http://source.co.zw/2013/08/zimbabwe-loses-nearly-1billion-in-run-up-to-elections/

764 International Monetary Fund, "Statementat the Conclusion of an IMF Mission on Zimbabwe". Press release No 14/135, 27 March 2014; Ledriz, "The 2014 National Budget Statement"

765 The Herald, 23 January 2014

766 The Herald, 24 January 2014

767 Newsday, 11 February 2014

768 The Herald, 7 June 2014

769 Independent on Line, 7 June 2014

770 Letter by Elton Mangoma to Tsvangirai, 26 January 2014, published in http://nehandaradio.com/2014/01/26/mangomas-letter-to-oust-tsvangirai/

771 Statement released by MDC-T faction calling itself the Democratic Renewal Campaign Team, 26 April 2014

772 Cabinet diary notes, 21 May 2013

773 The Chronicle, 18 October 2014

774 The Chronicle, ibid, 18 October 2014

775 Winston Churchill radio broadcast, 1 October 1939

776 Newsday, 3 March 2015

777 Letter of Chief Malaki Nzula Masuku to the Chief Lands Officer, Kezi, 31 December 2014

778 Radio Dialogue interview, 26 February 2015 http://www.channelzim.net/home/16-featured/4275-villagers-vow-to-block-maleme-ranch-take-over

779 Southern Eye, 10 March 2015

780 The Chronicle, 11 March 2015

781 Radio VOP, 16 March 2015

782 Interview with Nehanda Radio, 13 February 2015

783 The Africa Report, 14 April 2015

784 The Standard, 19 April 2015

785 Newsday, 23 May 2015

786 New zimbabwe.com, 27 May 2015

787 Article written by Nathaniel Manheru in The Herald, 12 September 2015. Manheru is widely accepted as the nom de plume of George Charamba, Mugabe's spokesman.

788 Daily News, 16 September 2015

789 Isaiah 58:2

790 Isaiah, 58:4

791 Isaiah, 58:6–7

792 Bulawayo, NoViolet. We Need New Names, Chatto & Windus, 2013, p 243

793 Amartya Sen. Development as Freedom, Random House, 1999, p 180

794 Stead, WT. Review of Reviews, Vol 13, 1896

LIST OF ACRONYMS

AAG	Affirmative Action Group
AFZ	Air Force of Zimbabwe
AIPPA	Access to Information and Protection of Privacy Act
ANC	African National Congress (the SA organisation)
ANC	African National Council (Muzorewa's party)
ATS	Association of Trust Schools
BCM	Black Consciousness Movement
BEAM	Basic Education Assistance Model
BLAC	Bulawayo Legal Aid Clinic
BLPA	Bulawayo Legal Practitioners' Association
BLPC	Bulawayo Legal Projects Centre
CAP	Central Africa Party
CAZ	Conservative Alliance of Zimbabwe
CASALAF	Central and Southern African Legal Assistance Foundation
CBC	Christian Brothers College
CCJP	Catholic Commission for Justice and Peace
CDU	Christian Democratic Union
CFU	Commercial Farmers' Union
CHOGM	Commonwealth Heads of Government Meeting
CID	Criminal Investigation Department
CIO	Central Intelligence Organisation
COIN	Counter Insurgency Training

COMOPS	Combined Operations
COPAC	Constitution Parliamentary Select Committee
CVR	Central Vehicle Registry
DFID	Department for International Development
DP	Dominion Party
DRC	Democratic Republic of Congo
EAAF	Argentinian Forensic Anthropology Team
ECB	England and Wales Cricket Board
ECM	European Common Market
ESAP	Economic Structural Adjustment Programme
ETF	Education Transition Fund
EWF	Education World Forum
FDR	Forum for Democratic Reform
FP	Forum Party
FRELIMO	Mozambique Liberation Front
FROLIZI	Front for the Liberation of Zimbabwe
GMB	Grain Marketing Board
GNU	Government of National Unity
GPA	Global Political Agreement
GPE	Global Partnership for Education
ICC	International Cricket Council
ICC	International Criminal Court
ICTJ	International Center for Transitional Justice
IDAF	International Defence and Aid Fund
IMF	International Monetary Fund
IZG	Independent Zimbabwe Group
JOC	Joint Operations Command
KAS	Konrad-Adenauer-Stiftung
LDF	Legal Defence Fund
LI	Liberal International
LOMA	Law and Order (Maintenance) Act
MDC	Movement for Democratic Change
MDTF	Multi Donor Trust Fund
MK	Umkhonto we Sizwe
MNR	Mozambique National Resistance
MOU	Memorandum of Understanding
MPLA	People's Movement for the Liberation of the People of Angola

NCA	National Constitutional Assembly
NDP	National Democratic Party
NEAB	National Education Advisory Board
NIBMAR	No Independence Before Majority Rule
ZNLWVA	Zimbabwe National Liberation War Veterans Association
NRZ	National Railways of Zimbabwe
OAU	Organisation of African Unity
ODI	One Day International
OP	Observation Point
PATU	Police Anti-Terrorist Unit
PCC	People's Caretaker Council
PF	Patriotic Front
PGHQ	Police General Headquarters
PISA	Programme for International Student Assessment
PISI	Police Internal Security Intelligence
PLAP	Progressive Learning Assessment Programme
POSA	Public Order and Security Act
PSC	Public Service Commission
PSMAS	Premier Service Medical Aid Society
PTUZ	Progressive Teachers' Union of Zimbabwe
RAF	Royal Air Force
RBC	Rhodesian Broadcasting Corporation
RCD	Rally for Congolese Democracy
RF	Rhodesian Front
RP	Rhodesia Party
SALDEF	South African Legal Defence Fund
SB	Special Branch
SPP	Senior Public Prosecutor
SRC	Sports and Recreation Commission
SWA	South-West Africa
TTL	Tribal Trust Land
UDI	Unilateral Declaration of Independence
UANC	United African National Council
UFP	United Federal Party
UNWTO	UN World Tourism Organisation
ZABG	Zimbabwe Allied Banking Group
ZANLA	Zimbabwe African National Liberation Army

ZANU	Zimbabwe African National Union
ZAPU	Zimbabwe African People's Union
ZBC	Zimbabwe Broadcasting Corporation
ZBF	Zimbabwe Benefit Fund
ZCB	Zimbabwe Cricket Board
ZCTU	Zimbabwe Congress of Trade Unions
ZDERA	Zimbabwe Democracy and Recovery Act
ZDI	Zimbabwe Defence Industries
ZEC	Zimbabwe Electoral Commission
ZFM	Zimbabwe Freedom Movement
ZIMSEC	Zimbabwe Schools Examination Council
ZIMTA	Zimbabwe Teachers' Association
ZIPA	Zimbabwe People's Army
ZIPRA	Zimbabwe People's Revolutionary Army
ZISCO	Zimbabwe Iron and Steel Company
ZLDAF	Zimbabwe Legal Defence and Aid Fund
ZLHR	Zimbabwe Lawyers for Human Rights
ZNA	Zimbabwe National Army
ZRP	Zimbabwe Republic Police
ZUM	Zimbabwe Unity Movement

SELECT BIBLIOGRAPHY

Achebe, Chinua. *There Was a Country – A Personal History of Biafra*, Penguin Books, 2012

Alexander, Jocelyn, McGregor, JoAnn and Ranger, Terence. *Violence and Memory – One Hundred Years in the "Dark Forests" of Matabeleland*, Heinemann, 2000

Auret, Michael. *From Liberator to Dictator*, David Philip Publishers, 2009

Barber, James. *Rhodesia – The Road to Rebellion*, Oxford University Press, 1967

Barclay, Philip. *Zimbabwe – Years of Hope and Despair*, Bloomsbury, 2010

Baxter, Peter. *Rhodesia – Last Outpost of the British Empire*, Galago, 2010

Bizos, George. *Odyssey to Freedom*, Random House, 2007

Blair, David. *Degrees in Violence*, Continuum, 2002

Boraine, Alex. *A Life in Transition*, Struik, 2008

Bulawayo, NoViolet. *We Need New Names*, Chatto & Windus, 2013

Burrett, Rob. *Bulawayo at 120*, Khami Press, 2014

Carver, Richard. *Zimbabwe – A Break With the Past?*, The Africa Watch Committee, 1989

Catholic Commission for Justice and Peace & Legal Resources Foundation. *Gukurahundi*, Hurst & Co, 2007

Davis, Dr JF. *Mission Accomplished – Dr Davis' Life and Work in Zimbabwe*, St John's Mission, 2013

Gardner, Jerome. *Zimbabwe – Warm Heart Ugly Face*, Jerome Gardner, 2010

Garrow, David. *Bearing the Cross – Martin Luther King, JR, and the Southern Christian Leadership Conference*. Quill William Morrow, 1999

Godwin, Peter. *Mukiwa*, Picador, 1996

Goodwin, Doris Kearns. *Team of Rivals*, Penguin Books, 2009

Greenfield, JM. *Testimony of a Rhodesian Federal*, Books of Rhodesia, 1978

Herbstein, Denis. *White Lies*, James Currey Publishers, 2004

Hill, Geoff. *The Battle for Zimbabwe – The Final Countdown*, Zebra Press, 2003

Hochschild, Adam. *King Leopold's Ghost – A Story of Greed, Terror and Heroism in Colonial Africa*, Pan Books, 2012

Hope, Christopher. *Brothers Under the Skin*, Macmillan, 2003

King, Loretta Scott (selected by). *The Words of Martin Luther King Jr*, Newmarket Press, 1983

Lawyers Committee for Human Rights. *Zimbabwe – Wages of War*, Lawyers Committee for Human Rights, 1986

Makumbe, John M and Compagnon, Daniel. *Behind the Smokescreen – The Politics of Zimbabwe's 1995 General Elections*, University of Zimbabwe Publications, 2000

Martin, David and Johnson, Phyllis. *The Chitepo Assassination*, Zimbabwe Publishing House, 1985

Martin, David and Johnson, Phyllis. *The Struggle for Zimbabwe*, Zimbabwe Publishing House, 1981

Metaxas, Eric. *Bonhoeffer – Pastor, Martyr, Prophet, Spy*, Thomas Melson, 2010

Mhanda, Wilfred. *Dzino – Memories of a Freedom Fighter*, Weaver Press, 2011Moorcraft, Paul L. A Short Thousand Years, Galaxie Press, 1980

Moorcraft, Paul L and McLaughlin, Peter. *The Rhodesian War – A Military History*, Jonathan Ball, 2008

Moyo, Jonathan N. *Voting for Democracy*, University of Zimbabwe Publications, 1992

Msipa, Cephas. *In Pursuit of Freedom and Justice – A Memoir*. Weaver Press, 2015

Nkomo, Joshua. *Nkomo – The Story of My Life*, Methuen, 1984

Olonga, Henry. *Blood, Sweat and Treason*, Vision Sports Publishing, 2010

Raftopoulos, Brian and Mlambo, Alois (eds). *Becoming Zimbabwe – A History From the Pre-colonial Period to 2008*, Weaver Press, 2009

Ranger, Terence. *Bulawayo Burning – The Social History of a Southern African City 1893-1960*, James Currey, 2010

Ransford, Oliver. *Bulawayo – Historic Battleground of Rhodesia*, AA Balkema, 1968

Scott, Bob. *Saving Zimbabwe*, Compassionate Justice Books, 2009

Sen, Amartya. *Development as Freedom*, Anchor Books, 1999

Smith, David and Simpson, Colin. *Mugabe*, Pioneer Head, 1981

Smith, Ian Douglas. *The Great Betrayal*, Blake, 1997

Stiff, Peter. *Cry Zimbabwe*, Galago, 2000

Todd, Judith. *Through the Darkness*, Struik, 2007

Tredgold, Robert C. *The Rhodesia That Was My Life*, 1968

Tsvangirai, Morgan. *At The Deep End*, Penguin Books, 2011

Welensky, Sir Roy. *Welensky's 4000 Days*, Collins, 1964

Werner, Richard. *Tears of the Dead*, Edinburgh University Press, 1991

Woods, Kevin. *The Kevin Woods Story – In the Shadows of Mugabe's Gallows*, 30 Degrees South Publishers, 2007

Yap, Katri Pohjolianen. *Uprooting the Weeds – Power, Ethnicity and Violence in the Matabeleland Conflict 1980–1987*, University of Amsterdam, 2001

Zimbabwe Defence Forces Magazine Vol 7, No 1, Zimbabwe National Army, 1981

INDEX

The names of major political parties and major cities in Zimbabwe have not been included in this index.